Handbook for Research

—— in ——

Cooperative Education
and Internships

Handbook for Research
— in —
Cooperative Education
and Internships

Edited by

Patricia L. Linn
Adam Howard
Eric Miller
Antioch College

2004

LAWRENCE ERLBAUM ASSOCIATES, PUBLISHERS
Mahwah, New Jersey   London

Lawrence Erlbaum Associates, Inc., Publishers
10 Industrial Avenue
Mahwah, NJ 07430

Cover design by Kathryn Houghtaling Lacey

Library of Congress Cataloging-in-Publication Data

Handbook for research in cooperative education and internships / edited by
Patricia L. Linn, Adam Howard, Eric Miller.
p. cm.
Includes bibliographical references and index.
ISBN 0-8058-4120-2 (cloth : alk. paper)
ISBN 0-8058-4121-0 (pbk. : alk. paper)
1. Education, Cooperative—Research. 2. Internship programs—Research.
I. Linn, Patricia L. II. Howard, Adam. III. Miller, Eric, 1957–

LC1049.H36   2003
371.2'27'072—dc21   2003044783
                                                                CIP

Books published by Lawrence Erlbaum Associates are printed on acid-free
paper, and their bindings are chosen for strength and durability.

Printed in the United States of America
10 9 8 7 6 5 4 3 2 1

For J. D. Dawson

Contents

Preface   xi

Author Biographies   xv

Part I   Cooperative Education and Internships in Context

1   Cooperative Education and Internships at the Threshold   3
of the Twenty-First Century
Adam Howard

2   Theories About Learning and Development in Cooperative   11
Education and Internships
Patricia L. Linn

Part II   Beginning Phase of Research Projects

3   Getting Started and Achieving Buy-In: Co-op Education   31
Is Continuous, Contextualized Learning
Garnet Grosjean

4   Identifying Resources: Ethics in Cooperative Education   53
Frances Ricks

5   Researching in Cooperative Education: How a Practitioner   71
    Met the Challenge
    Chris Eames

Part III   Methods and Analysis

6   Combining Quantitative and Qualitative Data: A Lifespan Study   97
    of Cooperative Education
    Patricia L. Linn

7   Choosing a Research Instrument: Investigating the Benefits   115
    of Cooperative Education
    Geraldine Van Gyn

8   Analyzing Data With Statistics: Business Internship Effects   137
    on Postgraduate Employment
    Patricia Gochenauer and Anthony Winter

9   How to Measure Complex Learning Processes: The Nature   157
    of Learning in Cooperative Education
    Nancy Johnston, Nello Angerilli, and Natalia Gajdamaschko

10 Correlation Analysis in a Natural Experiment Design: Seeking   191
    the Opportune Grade Point Average Cutoff for Internships
    Michael L. Maynard

11 Issues in Case Study Methodology: Examining the Influences   207
    of Class Status on Cooperative Education Experiences
    Adam Howard and Tom Haugsby

Part IV   Dissemination, Use, and Application

12 Considering the Needs of Different Stakeholders: The Impact   229
    of Co-op Job Quality on Post-Graduation Earnings
    Neal Fogg and Mark Putnam

13 Program Evaluation in a Business Environment: An Employer's   251
    Journey With Cooperative Education
    Marilyn Mayo

14 Dissemination of Research to Reform Practice: Fishing 279
(and Lawyering) to Learn
Brook K. Baker

15 Writing for Publication: Preparation of the Research Report 301
Patricia M. Rowe

Part V   Overriding Considerations

16 Using Theory in Research I: Understanding the Learning 315
Experienced in Structured Internships in Construction
Engineering
Robert K. Tener

17 Using Theory in Research II: Atypical Cross-Cultural 337
Experiences That Lead to Growth
Eric Miller

18 Program Assessment I: A Focused Approach to Measuring 363
Learning Outcomes
Cheryl Cates and Brenda LeMaster

19 Program Assessment II: Cooperative Education Objectives 383
Nestled in ABET EC2000 Criterion 3: a-k
Gwen Lee-Thomas and Arleen Anderson

20 Ethical Issues in Experimental and Qualitative Research 403
Adam Howard

Part VI   Implications for Research and Practice

21 Implications for Research and Practice 421
Patricia L. Linn and Eric Miller

Author Index 439

Subject Index 447

Preface

Nearly 30 years ago, Asa Knowles and Associates edited a comprehensive handbook on cooperative education during the years of accelerated growth of cooperative education. Their work, *Handbook of Cooperative Education* (1971), met the fundamental need of the larger academic community of cooperative education by offering a practical guide for understanding "... its philosophy and objectives; the development and administration of its programs; its operating procedures; its relevance to special groups; and its academic, general, and financial administrative practices" (p. ix). Their work continues to be a useful resource for program development.

Although program development is still important, the field has reached a point of maturity when evaluation and assessment are the keys to establishing a more integrated position in higher education. Cooperative education and internships are at a point where research needs to become a top priority. *Handbook for Research in Cooperative Education and Internships* assembles outstanding recent research on work-based education and practical information about key research design issues.

The aim of this book is to help co-op and internship educators design, carry out, and disseminate quality research and evaluation studies. The handbook offers examples of current and leading-edge research and evaluation studies about work-based education, but with a practical twist: The chapter authors frame their study within a key research design issue. By combining descriptions of exemplary current research and evaluation studies with practical advise from top researchers in the field, our hope is that readers find this book to be a useful tool to design and carry out their own studies as well as a resource for what current research is discovering and affirming about the field itself. It is also our hope that experiential educators from other fields like study abroad and service-learning will find this book a resource in conducting research on experiential learning and teaching.

ORGANIZATION

This book is divided into four sections, three represent a particular stage of research and the fourth section addresses some of the overriding considerations when planning, conducting, and disseminating research.

In the first section, the authors address a number of issues relating to getting a project started. Grosjean (chap. 3) discusses some ways to generate ideas about research questions and how research questions develop and change during the course of a study. Eames (chap. 5) describes how practitioners can manage to fit research in their workload and the impact this additional responsibility has on their overall work life. In her study on ethics in internships and co-ops, Ricks (chap. 4) discusses some ways to identify funding and other necessary resources for conducting research. In these chapters, the authors offer helpful suggestions on how to start a research project.

The authors in the second section offer a variety of methodological examples and explain their process of deciding on particular methods for gathering data and their overall methodological approach. Through this discussion, the authors highlight the various strengths and weakness of qualitative and quantitative methods in conducting research on work-based education. Linn (chap. 6) discusses ways of combining qualitative and quantitative methods to design more comprehensive research projects and to explore research inquiry in multiple and diverse ways. Maynard (chap. 10) describes a research process used to make decisions about an internship program. Gochenauer and Winter (chap. 8) discuss ways of using data generated from institutional practices to investigate research questions. Howard and Haugsby (chap. 11) explore the possibilities of case construction and action research. Van Gyn (chap. 7) discusses what researchers need to consider in deciding what research instrument they use in their investigations. Johnston, Angerilli, and Gajdamaschko (chap. 9) describe one way of measuring complex learning processes in co-op. The authors in this section discuss some of the various ways of conducting research and the benefits and limitations of different methods.

In the third section the authors discuss a variety of approaches to disseminating research findings. Fogg and Putnam (chap. 12) describe how they made decisions about who needs to know about the findings of their research and how they developed different ways of presenting research findings according to the needs and interests of different groups of people. Baker (chap. 14) discusses the importance of disseminating research to reform practice. Mayo (chap. 13) describes an employer's process of evaluating a co-op program. Rowe (chap. 15) identifies ways to incorporate writing and presenting at conferences and meetings into the workload of practitioners. In this section, the authors stress the importance of disseminating research to improve practice.

Unlike the other three sections of this handbook, the fourth section does not focus on just one stage of the research process but instead addresses important questions and concerns that are relevant throughout the course of a research project. In this section the authors address three overriding issues: Tener (chap. 16) and Miller (chap. 17) discuss the use of theory in research; Cates and LeMaster (chap. 18) and Lee-Thomas and Anderson (chap. 19) address the role and relationship of program assessment to research; and Howard explores some of the ethical considerations in research.

Although the organization of the book generally follows the sequence of planning, conducting, and disseminating a research project, the chapters provide collectively a kind of map of various routes and destinations calling attention to points of interest and side trips of their research journey. Giving advice along the way, the authors take the reader with them on this journey.

Our goal is that this handbook will end up on the back of your desk, dog-eared and soiled from repeated use. If you have a particular question about a research issue, use the index and go to the chapter or chapters that discuss that issue. If you want to do research but are not sure how to start, begin with the first section, and move through the book in a more linear way. However you proceed, present or write your findings. We all have an obligation to add to the body of knowledge about learning and teaching in work-based education.

ACKNOWLEDGMENTS

This book has been an exiting journey for us, but it was not a journey that we took alone. We would like to thank our colleagues in the Center for Cooperative Education at Antioch College, who supported our vision and forgave our directing time and energy in this way for the past 2 years. Susan Eklund-Leen was Director of the Center during this period of time and never failed in her enthusiasm for the Handbook. Co-op students Staci Willits, Jonah Liebert, Steve Corfman, and Rachel Fischer served as Editorial Assistants, and we thank them for their meticulous work and patience when we needed time to figure our what the next step was. Thanks to Joel Pomerantz for his help with the figures in chapters 2 and 21.

The Pierson-Lovelace Foundation provided support for Pat Linn's research and covered some of the postage and supply costs for the book. The Antioch College Faculty Fund supported the costs of indexing the book.

Our first round of chapter reviews were done by other contributors to the Handbook, but we needed three outside reviews in this stage: Antioch colleagues Judith Schimpf and Cheryl Keen each reviewed a chapter; thank you for this help. James Wilson also reviewed a chapter, and we appreciated his feedback. Lawrence Erlbaum Associates (LEA) then selected three anonymous reviewers, and we thank them for their thoughtful comments, gentle suggestions, and words of support for the project. The Cooperative Education and Internship Association and the National Society for

Experiential Education offered moral support for the project and have offered to comarket the book as well. Finally, thanks to Naomi Silverman and her staff at LEA for their support of our project and their intelligent editorial guidance.

—Adam Howard, Pat Linn, and Eric Miller

REFERENCES

Knowles, A., & Associates. (1971). *Handbook of cooperative education*. San Francisco: Jossey-Bass.

Author Biographies

Patricia L. Linn is the J.D. Dawson Professor of Cooperative Education and Professor of Psychology at Antioch College. She is a developmental psychologist who advises students and works with employers in Antioch's Center for Cooperative Education. Dr. Linn is Project Director for an ongoing lifespan study of cooperative education there. She won the 2000 Ralph W. Tyler award for outstanding research in cooperative education from the Cooperative Education and Internship Association, and also chairs that group's Research Committee.

Adam Howard is an Assistant Professor of Education at Antioch College. Before coming to Antioch, he taught high school English and directed a nonprofit organization designed to prepare inner-city students for academically rigorous high school programs. Dr. Howard is a qualitative researcher and his research focuses on the influence of class status on academic achievement. He also has published articles and presented papers on service learning, cross-cultural experiential education, and the teaching and learning process of cooperative education. In 2000 he won the Rising Leader award from the National Society for Experiential Education.

Eric Miller is an Assistant Professor of Cooperative Education at Antioch College. He has a Master of Arts in English with a focus on writing and editing. Before coming to Antioch, he taught English as a second language at a vocational college in Tokyo, Japan. Prior to going to Japan he was a social worker in community mental health and worked with the Ohio Department of Mental Health in the development of community based support systems. Mr. Miller's research inquiries in cooperative education have been into the nature of cross-cultural experiential learning. He has presented on atypical cross-cultural experiential learning at several recent conferences.

Arleen Anderson is the Director of Cooperative Education and Internship Programs and Assistant Director of Career Services at Rose-Hulman Institute of Technology in Terre Haute Indiana. Anderson has presented at various conferences on career choices, resume building, interviewing techniques, and employee savvy.

Nello Angerilli is a former Director of Cooperative Education at Simon Fraser University (SFM) and now Executive Director, SFU International. Dr. Angerilli's interests in higher education emerge from more than 20 years of involvement as an instructor, professor, and manager in the higher education system of British Columbia and several developing countries abroad. His work has included the identification of the need to introduce skills and competencies in academic curricula through work-study in order to ensure that higher education is relevant to the world of work. Dr. Angerilli has authored or co-authored 26 peer reviewed research papers in national and international journals and more than 50 technical papers in addition to invitational papers delivered internationally.

Brook K. Baker is a law professor at Northeastern University School of Law where he directs the first-year Legal Practice Program. Professor Baker has written extensively about a theory of ecological learning, which he has presented to multiple audiences including legal clinicians, legal writing specialists, and most recently at a 2001 National Conference on Practice-Oriented Education held at Northeastern. Professor Baker has consulted extensively in South Africa where he has collaborated in the development of a more intensive skills pedagogy. Professor Baker is active in campaigns for increasing access to affordable medicines for people living with HIV/AIDS in Africa.

Cheryl Cates is an Associate Professor and the Associate Director for Pedagogic Development for the Division of Professional Practice at the University of Cincinnati. In 1999 she co-authored *Learning Outcomes, The Educational Value of Cooperative Education*. She has received research grants on the state (OCEA), regional (MCEA) and national (CEA) level. She has presented papers at the World Association for Cooperative Education, the Cooperative Education Association, and the Cooperative Education Division of the American Society of Engineering. She has a Master of Business Administration degree.

Chris Eames is a co-op placement coordinator and lecturer in Biological Sciences at the University of Waikato, New Zealand. He holds an MSc in biochemistry and microbiology. Chris is working toward a PhD in cooperative education at Waikato.

He has been a Council member of the NZ Association for Cooperative Education (NZACE) for 7 years.

Neal Fogg is Senior Research Analyst and Coordinator of Policy Studies in the Office of University Planning and Research at Northeastern University. Prior to that, he was Senior Research Associate at the Center for Labor Market Studies, an economic consulting firm housed at Northeastern. He received his PhD in Economics (Labor) from Northeastern University in 1996.

Natalia Gajdamaschko is a Research Scientist at the Center For Imaginative Education at Faculty of Education of Simon Fraser University. She is an educational psychologist trained in Moscow (Russia) and has extensive experience as a psychologist and educator in North America and overseas. Previously Dr. Gajdamaschko was a Visiting Fellow at the University of Georgia's Carl Vinson Institute of Government and Torrance Center for Creative Studies. She has written several papers about Q-methodology and its application in various educational fields.

Patricia M. Gochenauer is Director of Career Services at Shepherd College in Shepherdstown, West Virginia. She obtained a Master of Science in Counseling (concentration in Student Personnel) from Shippensburg University. While serving as graduate assistant for the Business Internship Program, she completed this internship research project as a graduation requirement.

Garnet Grosjean, PhD, is Research Coordinator of the Center for Policy Studies in Higher Education and Training at The University of British Columbia. He is also Academic Coordinator for the Doctor of Leadership and Policy Program, and Managing Editor of the academic journal *Policy Explorations*. His research interests include experiential education, learning, and work.

Tom Haugsby is Professor of Cooperative Education and Director of The Center for Cooperative Education at Antioch College. He also served as Director of Antioch's Adult Degree Completion Program and Associate Dean of Faculty. He has long been interested in the role of experiential learning and the development of civic intelligence and public involvement in policy-making. Drawing on his three terms on his local school board and state-wide committees associated with that office, he has recently consulted with smaller rural school boards on citizen involvement in passing levies, superintendent and principal evaluations and locally generated assessment processes and standards. Recently, with Adam Howard, he has become interested in the influence social class has on experiential learning.

Nancy Johnston is Director of Cooperative Education at Simon Fraser University, one of Canada's oldest, largest, and most diverse co-op programs. She is also founding member and current Chair of the Association for Cooperative Education's Research and Initiatives Committee for BC/Yukon and a 14-year veteran Co-op administrator. In 1997 she was awarded the Canadian Association for Cooperative Education's (CAFCE) Dr. Graham Branton Research Award in recognition of her outstanding contributions to the advancement of Cooperative Education through her thesis research on "The Nature of Learning in Cooperative Education."

Gwen Lee-Thomas, PhD is the Director of Assessment in the Office of Institutional Research, Planning and Assessment at Rose-Hulman Institute of Technology in Terre Haute, IN. She has conducted and presented at various workshops, national and regional conferences on program and classroom assessment. In addition, she is an adjunct faculty member at Indiana State University in the School of Education where she teaches Program Evaluation in the Counseling Department and holds graduate faculty status in the Educational Leadership, Administration and Foundations Department.

Brenda LeMaster is the Vice Provost for Institutional Effectiveness at the University of Cincinnati, and Professor of Professional Practice. She has 28 years of experience in cooperative education, including service as the Associate Director of the University of Cincinnati's Professional Practice Program. She is past Chair of the Cooperative Education Division of the American Society for Engineering Education, has served as a reader for Title VIII grants, and is a CED certified consultant-evaluator. She coordinated institution-wide reporting on the assessment of student learning for the regional accreditation self-study, and has served as a site visitor for two regional accreditation associations.

Michael L. Maynard, PhD, is Associate Professor of Advertising at Temple University. He is Director of Graduate Studies in the School of Communications and Theater, and Director of Advertising in the Department of Journalism. His areas of research include mass media analysis, the relationship between mass communication and culture as well as textual analyses of television and print advertising in Japan.

Marilyn Mayo is the manager of the IBM Cooperative Education and Internship programs. She is part of the IBM university recruiting and staffing organization in Human Resources, USA. She is responsible for the success of the IBM student employment programs and is focused on process improvements, hiring strategies and measurements. Marilyn has been involved with experiential programs for the past 7 years and has been with IBM more than 25 years. Marilyn is currently a board member of the Cooperative Education and Internship Association and an active member of the North Carolina Cooperative Education Association. She resides in Raleigh, NC with her husband, John.

Mark Putnam is Director of University Planning and Research at Northeastern University. Before joining Northeastern, he served in a series of senior administrative capacities at Connecticut College, including Vice President for Planning and Enrollment Management. He received his EdD in Higher Education Administration from Teachers College, Columbia University in 1994.

Frances Ricks, PhD, is the Associate Dean of Graduate Studies and a professor in the School of Child and Youth Care at the University of Victoria in Victoria, British Columbia. Her work and publications focus on ethics in Child and Youth Care, mentoring, community development, transformational-education, case management and practice, research evaluation, and working with families

Patricia M. Rowe is a Professor of Psychology at the University of Waterloo in Canada. Her research interests are in decision making in the employment interview, especially the decisions made about co-op students for work terms and in the effects of cooperative education on subsequent work behavior. She is currently the editor of the *Journal of Cooperative Education*.

Robert K. Tener, PhD, PE, is Consulting Executive in Civil Engineering and Director of Internships for construction engineering majors at Purdue University. With more than 30 years' industry experience, he is a registered professional engineer and the recipient of numerous awards and honors for professional, academic, and teaching achievements. A graduate of the U.S. Military Academy at West Point, his postgraduate degrees are in structural engineering from Iowa State University.

Geraldine H. Van Gyn, PhD, is a professor in the Faculty of Education at the University of Victoria in British Columbia, Canada and Director of the University of Victoria Learning and Teaching Center. Twice recipient of the Tyler Award for Distinguished Research in Cooperative Education, she has been involved in cooperative education practice and research since 1986.

Anthony S. Winter, DEd, is Associate Dean and Business Internship Director in the John L. Grove College of Business at Shippensburg University in Shippensburg, Pennsylvania.

Part I

Cooperative Education
and Internships in Context

1

Cooperative Education and Internships at the Threshold of the Twenty-First Century

Adam Howard
Antioch College

CHALLENGES FACING THE WORK FORCE AND HIGHER EDUCATION

Work-based education is at a critical juncture. Both the popular press and management texts claim that the notion of *career* as it has been historically known, where worker loyalty was repaid with a lifetime job with a single firm, is gone forever (Goleman, 1998; Lewis, 2000; Tulgan, 1995). Rather, young workers find they need skills to manage their *own* careers. Many are discovering that the traditional college setting of classrooms plus dorm life may not prepare them well to become successful workers in a competitive new environment. Students, colleges, and employers are all asking how young people can be prepared better for these challenges.

Employers feel that academic programs for the most part have not adequately provided students with the essential skills to be competent in the workplace (Foggin, 1992). They suggest colleges drastically change their way of preparing students for employment (Gardner & Korth, 1997; Muller, Porter, & Rehder, 1991). More specifically, in a study conducted by Business-Higher Education Forum (1997), business leaders agreed that recent graduates were deficient in communication skills, the ability to work in teams, flexibility, the ability to accept ambiguity comfortably, the ability to work with people from diverse backgrounds, understanding of globalization and its implications, and ethics training.

3

How can colleges and universities respond to these challenges to help students align their educational paths with their career plans and provide the kinds of skills that employers say they want? Cooperative education is an excellent educational model to introduce students to, and prepare them for, the rigors of the workplace. In 1906, Herman Schneider, a University of Cincinnati engineering professor and dean, founded cooperative education because he recognized that most students need and/or want to work while attending college. He observed that the jobs his students obtained were either menial or unrelated to their career goals. Through cooperative education, Schneider found a way to satisfy students' financial needs as well as provide them with meaningful experiences.

Although the concept of cooperative education originated nearly 100 years ago, cooperative education did not flourish until the 1960s when the federal government provided funding for new program development. Title VIII of the Higher Education Act of 1965 set aside funds for co-op programs and many colleges and universities used this money to establish their co-op programs. During this time, co-operative education experienced rapid and expansive growth. Where there had been approximately 60 co-op programs in 1956, by 1971 there were 225, and at the peak in 1986, there were 1,012. However, soon after co-op's peak, federal funding was gradually reduced and by 1996, it was discontinued. Since the decrease and eventual elimination of federal funding, colleges and universities throughout the country have shut down nearly 400 co-op programs, and countless other co-op programs have become marginalized in their institutions. Although the number of co-op programs have decreased, the number of students placed in cooperative education jobs—about 250,000 each year—has not decreased (Pettit, 1998).

Today, despite lack of federal support, co-op seems to be finding a second wind. Cooperative education is once again attracting the attention of colleges and universities eager to establish educational programs to better prepare students for employment. The primary reason for this interest is co-op prepares students to make a smooth and intentional transition from college to the workplace by providing them with opportunities to explore the world beyond the classroom. Students are placed in real-world contexts and required to make decisions, negotiate their different roles as students and workers, develop relationships with co-workers and supervisors, take on responsibilities, and work as members of teams. During co-op experiences, students are neither "just students" nor are they full-fledged employees, rather, they are both at the same time. Through the educational experiences gained from this dual role, students begin developing the necessary skills to transition from student to professional.

Cooperative education provides students with unique learning outcomes and learning processes that prepare them for the world beyond the confines of educational institutions. When students can build experiences in varied work environments as part of their undergraduate preparation, they learn to adapt to change, they build a set of marketable skills, and develop the self-confidence they need to manage their own careers. There is new evidence from Antioch research (Linn, 1999; Linn & Ferguson, 1999) that graduates of a cooperative education program attributed their success to this combination of work and study, even 50 years later.

THE NEED FOR RESEARCH

Although co-op educators know from their experience with students that the combination of work and study is a powerful learning model for undergraduates, co-op has not been fully integrated in higher education. For the most part, cooperative education's livelihood has relied on the fluctuation of federal and other forms of funding and on the good will of higher education administrators who understand the value of experiential learning. This unreliable dependency has not only marginalized the field of cooperative education but also has significantly contributed to the continued lack of relationship between the workforce and higher education. In order to establish a more integrated position in higher education, research needs to become a top priority in the field of cooperative education. As Weaver (1993) pointed out, "to be credible, cooperative education must be able to substantiate claims that cooperative education practice is good educational practice and be able to relate cooperative education practice to the theoretical framework of education" (p. 10).

The field of cooperative education and internships has not made consistent and systematic efforts to surface questions and then seek answers, as have other fields of study. Furthermore, the existing body of research in co-op and internships "has fallen short of the ideal of scientific inquiry to illuminate relationships, predict effects, explain findings in light of existing theory, or contribute to theory development" (Wilson, 1988, p. 83). Many experienced co-op professionals (e.g., Bartkus & Stull, 1997; Ricks, Cutt, Branton, Lokent, & Van Gyn, 1993) have highlighted the need for research in cooperative education in order to become more credible and prominent.

In addition to establishing legitimacy in higher education, co-op educators are under increased pressure, and have bigger incentives than in the past, to document the learning outcomes of students who participate in co-op. Today's climate in higher education focuses heavily on student learning outcomes. One source of this pressure is the accreditation process; accreditation agencies now insist that educators define learning outcomes, measure them, and revise programs based on the results. Just like educators in classroom programs, co-op educators must demonstrate that student learning outcomes are being met. As Cates and Jones (1999) pointed out, "… co-op is an educational program. It is imperative that co-op professionals demonstrate that co-op is educational and not simply concerned with employment" (p. 66). Not only do co-op educators need to document the learning in co-op but also design assessment efforts that contribute to the overall assessment goals of their institutions.

These assessment trends and cooperative education's current status and position in higher education suggest that educators working in co-op programs need tools to help them design and carry out research and evaluation studies. For years, co-op educators have predominantly relied on research models such as the *researcher-practitioner* model (Howard, 1986; Tinsley, Tinsley, Boone, & Shim-Li, 1993) or the *reflective practice* model (Schön, 1983; Van Gyn, 1996). Although these models provide co-op educators an opportunity to examine individual features of their programs and to reflect on their practices, these models can have a limited scope and may be overly simplistic. These research models have most commonly been used to compare students who co-oped with those who did not on single variable such as starting salary. In order for research to have a more prominent place in the field of cooperative education, co-op educators need a diverse range of more sophisticated models that attempt to describe and understand the complex cognitive, social, and career-building outcomes of alternating work and study and how these outcomes happen.

Co-op educators sometimes face an uphill battle in trying to justify our outside-the-classroom programs as having a legitimate place within the academy. For most educators, learning in the academy means learning inside the classroom: scholarly learning, not practical learning. Because we strive for academic legitimacy, we may also feel obligated to employ research methodologies with unquestioned legitimacy: experimental methods and quantitative analyses where results can be validated with statistical procedures. Although these methods are the best choice for some research questions, the method should not determine the research question, rather, the research question should guide the choice of a method. In this book the reader will find a wide variety of research methodologies being used in service of different types of research questions. Both quantitative and qualitative methods are used, alone and in combination, depending on the researchers' particular curiosities. We feel strongly that research and evaluation of co-op and internship programs should encompass as much methodological variety as in other types of research on learning and education. Employers face the similar need to justify their co-op and internship programs. They need to demonstrate that these programs are economically beneficial to their company and will help recruit talented new employees.

CONDUCTING RESEARCH

Researchers are confronted with a variety of questions during the research process. To engage in research is to engage in a questioning process filled with dilemmas along the way. Of course, some questions can be and should be answered before beginning a research project. By planning and thinking things out beforehand, researchers are more equipped to deal with the dilemmas they face during the course of a study. This book is divided into four sections that line up with the stages of conducting research. Here I summarize some of the questions that surface throughout the book for researchers to consider in their planning and thinking.

Part I: The Beginning Phase of a Research Project

Decisions are made throughout any research project, but the first important question is: What should I study? Although this question seems simple, determining what needs to be researched is often the most difficult part of the overall project. Frequently, people get bogged down with "getting it right" when they are formulating research questions instead of exploring ideas about potential research inquiry. As Bogdan and Biklen (1992) pointed out, "the exact decisions you make are not always crucial, but it is crucial that you make them" (p. 59). Although initial decisions about what to study are important to make, the research questions most often become more defined and even sometimes drastically change as the research project progresses.

Once researchers have determined what needs to be researched the questions then become: How do I find the time to conduct a research project? Where do I find the necessary resources to conduct research? Finding time and resources are other initial obstacles to overcome. Co-op and internship educators are in a difficult position. For the most part, they are not provided the time in their schedule to conduct research but have the pressure to assess their programs and document student learning outcomes. Because of this, educators in work-based programs are required to balance this contradictory tension in order to conduct research. During the initial phase, they also have to find the necessary funding and resources for conducting research. In order to do this, they have to locate sources of funding and then develop strategies to successfully secure these resources.

Part II: Methods and Analysis

Decisions about methodological options and strategies for any research inquiry depend on answers to several questions:

- Who is the information for and who will use the research findings?
- What information is needed?
- How is the information going to be used? What is the purpose of the evaluation begin done?
- When is the information needed?
- What resources are available to conduct the research project?
- Given answers to the above questions, what methods are appropriate?

Answers to these questions will guide educators about the kinds of data that will be most appropriate and useful in a particular research project. But as Cronbach (1982) reminded us, "There is no single best plan for an evaluation, not even for an inquiry into a particular program, at a particular time, with a particular budget" (p. 231).

In designing a research study, researchers must consider the strengths and weaknesses of qualitative and quantitative methods of collecting data. Qualitative methods allow both depth and detail because researchers are not constrained by predetermined categories of analysis. On the other hand, quantitative methods most often require the use of standardized measures in order to fit what is being studied into a limited number of predetermined categories to which numbers are assigned.

In terms of analysis, statistics are used to help understand the data collected in quantitative research investigations. Statistics allow researchers to describe the data and to make inferences, on the basis of sample data, about a population. In contrast, Rosaldo (1989) maintained that analysis in qualitative approach is about "making the familiar strange and the strange familiar" instead of surfacing the "brute timeless facts of nature" (p. 39). In qualitative approach, analysis involves working with the data, organizing the data, synthesizing the data, searching for patterns, finding what is important, and deciding what you will tell others.

Because qualitative and quantitative methods offer different strengths and weaknesses, researchers make decisions about what methods are appropriate for their research projects. Although there are fundamental differences between qualitative and quantitative methods, researchers can employ both these approaches in the same study in order to make full use of their data and explore their research question in a variety of ways.

Part III: Dissemination, Use, and Application

Disseminating research findings is a very important part of conducting research because one goal of research is to add to our knowledge base about cooperative education. In making decisions about dissemination researchers need to ask: Who needs to know about the study's findings? How do I share the information discovered from this research with others? In determining who needs to know about the research findings, it is helpful to revisit your initial decisions that led you to particular research questions. In doing so, you may further discover who would benefit from knowing about the discoveries of your research project. Individuals within your institution, policy makers, funding agencies, and other co-op educators are just some of the individuals and groups who benefit from research on cooperative education.

There are various forums for reporting research findings: national conferences and other professional meetings, publications outside and within the field of co-op, and meetings within your institution. Each forum requires different approaches and formats for disseminating research. Researchers make important decisions about these approaches and formats so that the information they are sharing is understood. They have to determine what is appropriate and most effective in sharing the findings of their research.

The most common format for disseminating research findings is to present at a meeting, get feedback, and then turn the findings into a written report. The conventional format of a research report is usually organized in the following way: statement of the problem, conceptual framework, research questions, methodology, data analysis, conclusions, and discussion. Qualitative studies do not report data but, instead, they report scenes—that is, accounts of researchers' engagements throughout the study with informants in their surroundings. There are multiple issues to consider in writing a report (e.g., style, audience, tone) and researchers are faced with a series of choices in producing research reports.

Part IV: Overriding Considerations

As researchers plan, conduct, and disseminate their research, they confront and must make decisions about various overriding issues that influence and, at times, can direct their overall research process. These overriding issues surface some difficult questions about the purpose and process of research such as: How do researchers combine their program assessment efforts with their research projects? What are some of the different goals and processes of assessment and research? In what ways should theory guide the research project? How do researchers work out ethical dilemmas? Researchers are frequently confronted with these types of questions about overriding issues throughout the entire research project.

Co-op and internship educators conduct assessment of their programs for various reasons, often times to meet both internal and external demands. The significance of assessment, however, develops from what educators reaffirm and discover about teaching and learning. Through this direct relationship with practice, well-administered assessment projects are important contributions to the body of research on co-op and internships because they provide educators information about not only individual programs but also best practices.

Researchers are faced with difficult decisions about what constitutes doing the right thing throughout the research process. Ethical dilemmas are not easily resolved and are paramount when planning, conducting, and evaluating research. The degree to which research is or is not ethical relies on the continuous efforts of researchers to protect participants' rights to privacy, dignity, and confidentiality, and to avoid subjecting them to harm. Ethical considerations should be at the forefront of researchers' efforts to expand the scope of research on cooperative education and internships in order to further protect those who participate in research.

These questions and others are discussed in the following chapters. Authors offer answers to an assortment of questions that they had to consider before starting a research project, during their study, and after they had gathered their data. Situating their studies in a discussion of research dilemmas, the following chapters not only offer theory and research about work-based education but also take the reader on various and diverse research journeys.

REFERENCES

Bartkus, K. R., & Stull, W. A. (1997). Some thoughts about research in cooperative education. *Journal of Cooperative Education, 32*(2), 7–16.

Bogdan, R., & Biklen, S. K. (1992). *Qualitative research for education: An introduction to theory and methods*. Boston: Allyn and Bacon.

Business-Higher Education Forum (1997). Spanning the chasm: Corporate and academic cooperation to improve work-force participation. *NSEE Quarterly, 23*(3), 6–9.

Cates, C., & Jones, P. (1999). *Learning outcomes: The educational value of cooperative education*. Columbia, MD: Cooperative Education Association.

Cronbach, L. J. (1982). *Designing evaluations of educational and social programs*. San Francisco: Jossey-Bass.

Foggin, J. H. (1992). Meeting customer needs. *Survey of Business, 28*, 6–9.

Gardner, P. D. (1997). It's 2010: Do you know who and where your students are? *Journal of Cooperative Education, 32*(2), 86–103.

Goleman, D. (1998). *Working with emotional intelligence*. New York: Bantam.

Howard, G. (1986). The scientist-practitioner in counseling psychology: Toward a deeper integration of theory, research, and practice. *The Counseling Psychologist, 14*(1), 61–105.

Lewis, M. (2000, March 5). The artist in the gray flannel pajamas. *The New York Times Magazine*, 45–48.

Linn, P. (1999). Learning that lasts a lifetime. *Liberal Education, 85*(3), 2–11.

Linn, P., & Ferguson, J. (1999). A lifespan study of cooperative education graduates: Quantitative aspects. *Journal of Cooperative Education, 34*(3), 30–41.

Muller, H. J., Porter, J. L., & Rehder, R. R. (1991). Reinventing the MBA the European way. *Business Horizons, 34*, 83–91.

Pettit, D. E. (1998). 1998 census of cooperative education executive summary. *Cooperative Education Experience*, 4–5.

Ricks, F., Cutt, J., Branton, G., Loken, M., Van Gyn, G. (1993). Reflections on the cooperative education literature. *Journal of Cooperative Education, 29*(1), 6–23.

Rosaldo, R. (1989). *Culture and truth: The remaking of social analysis*. Boston: Beacon Press.

Schön, D. A. (1983). *The reflective practitioner*. New York: Basic Books

Tinsley, E., Tinsley, H., Boone, S., & Shim-Li, C. (1993). Prediction of scientist-practitioner behavior using personality scores outlined during graduate school. *Journal of Counseling Psychology, 40*(4), 511–517.

Tulgan, B. (1995). *Managing generation X*. Santa Monica, CA: Merritt.

Van Gyn, G. H. (1996). Reflective practice: The needs of professions and the promise of cooperative education. *Journal of Cooperative Education, 31*(2–3), 103–131.

Weaver, K. A. (1993). Research and employer oriented learning objectives. *Journal of Cooperative Education, 28*(3), 7–11.

Wilson, J. W. (1988). Research in cooperative education. *Journal of Cooperative Education, 24*(2–3), 77–89.

2

Theories About Learning and Development in Cooperative Education and Internships

Patricia L. Linn
Antioch College

WHY STUDY LEARNING THEORIES?

As professionals interested in research on experiential learning, sooner or later we find ourselves searching for a theory to guide us in our work. That search might happen sooner if we want to start a research project by using theories to guide us in finding a question, developing an hypothesis, and choosing variables to study. That search might happen later if we have already collected information and are trying to assess or interpret those data.

Another motive for studying learning theories is to guide our practice in working with students to enhance their learning. The more we know about how learning happens and about development in late adolescence, the better we can support student learning.

There is at least one more motive for understanding learning theories: We seek theoretical justifications to support our belief that learning outside traditional classroom settings is "real learning." Such justifications are important because of biases in the academy that favor classroom learning over other forms. If learning theories support the idea that education can happen in a variety of contexts, then classroom faculty and academic administrators might be convinced to award academic credit and institutional resources for experiential learning programs.

Many authors in this Handbook referred to learning theories and the authors used those theories in a variety of ways. For example, Miller (chap. 17) used theories from three different intellectual traditions to understand a student's cross cultural experience. He borrows theory from cross-cultural experiential learning to frame his questions, looks to anthropology to suggest a methodology, and draws from African-American Studies and identity theories to help him interpret his data. Tener (chap. 16) read what other authors said about a published theory to discern how well-accepted it was and to find a theory focused on the learning process (rather than outcomes) to help him analyze his students' written reports and justify his program. I use theories in my project (chap. 6) to develop interview questions on the front end of the inquiry, to suggest concepts to search for in my interview transcripts after the data were collected, and to suggest interpretations of the findings. James Wilson, considered to be the father of cooperative education research (see e.g., Wilson & Lyons, 1961) challenged researchers 15 years ago to use and develop theory to guide our work in order to legitimize the field (Wilson, 1988). The central and varied uses of theory by most researchers in this volume is a good sign for the field of experiential learning research.

THIS CHAPTER'S PURPOSES

One purpose of this chapter is to review theories about learning and development in late adolescence, selected from the universe of all possible theories, and summarize them very briefly. The reader looking for more complete descriptions of the theories is referred to the theorists' original work, to a text by Cates and Jones (1999), or to particular chapters in this Handbook. In choosing certain theories to summarize over others, my own biases about theories I have found useful and my background as a developmental psychologist will be evident. Other writers might have focused on different realms of theory, for example the field of management has a rich set of theories that guide research and practice in that area.

The very proliferation of theory in the study of experiential learning that Wilson (1988) and others called for can also create a difficulty for the researcher: It is easy to become overwhelmed by the large number of theories that a search of the literature will reveal. Theory proliferation often happens when there is a growing interest in a young research area. Researchers tend to settle in after several decades to a handful of key theories that generate testable hypotheses (such theories are called *heuristic*) and theories that help us interpret our data (*hermeneutic* theories). In the meantime, however, it can be confusing when a researcher finds such a wide array of theories that it is difficult to know which one or ones to use.

How does one choose a particular theory or theories to focus on? Are all theories equally applicable for various levels of analysis of student learning outside the classroom? In this chapter I offer a framework for organizing some important theories. A framework is needed to allow us to consider theories in relation to each other, in order to make it easier to decide which theory might be most useful. Furthermore, if we can understand how theories work at different levels of analysis of our students' learning experiences, then we can situate our own research project (e.g., a study of a particular feature of a single co-op or internship experience) and consider that project in broader contexts. One type of broad context is to consider one's work in a developmental context (e.g., the context of 4 years of postsecondary education or the context of a lifetime of learning and work). Another type of broad context is to consider social contexts (e.g., class- or culture-bound ideas of schooling in general) not typically found in the literature on experiential education.

The consideration of broad developmental contexts is important because we work with students for a relatively short portion of their developmental journey, yet we hope our programs impact them in a lasting way. When we consider broad social contexts, we keep in mind that our students come from, and graduate into, a variety of class and cultural settings. Finally, when we remain open to ways individuals learn to survive and thrive in settings not normally considered formal schooling, we remain mindful of the wide variety of ways people learn to work and so capture the most complete picture of learning in the workplace.

INTRODUCING A FRAMEWORK

In order to explain the new organizational framework introduced in this chapter, the metaphor of a *camera lens* will be employed. Consider that our inquiries into student learning use various levels of *focus* on the student and the work she or he is doing. The most narrow focus is on a particular work experience, defined by time and space; an example is a single co-op work term or internship experience. This level of focus is represented in Fig. 2.1 as the innermost circle. It is the most commonly used focus of studies in this volume and in research journals that publish studies about experiential learning. Perhaps not coincidentally, it is also an area that encompasses a large array of relevant learning theories; only a few are described here.

If we take a step back, and broaden the focus, we now see through our camera's viewer a student's entire college experience and beyond. This middle level of focus is represented in Fig. 2.1 by the middle-sized circle. For most cooperative education programs, this level of focus encompasses multiple co-op work terms, and those work terms are located within the context of classroom study and life in a community, whether that community is a residential campus or, if our students commute, a hometown. For educators involved with internship programs, there may be a single work experience, but again that experience is embedded in broader school and life experiences. Note also that at this level we have encompassed more of the student's developmental journey: 2, 4, or more years' worth. I say 4 or more years because even though the period of time between matriculation and graduation is the extent of many educators' concerns, in the present model this middle level of focus may also be used to encompass life after college. Employers understand, perhaps more clearly than educators, that we should all be concerned about longitudinal effects of our programs as students move into work and social networks beyond graduation.

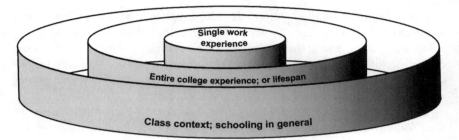

FIG. 2.1.   Levels of analysis of student work-based learning.

If the middle-most circle in Fig. 2.1 encompasses a lifespan developmental period, what does the outer-most circle describe? Here I intend the focus of our camera to extend beyond a consideration of an individual student's life, to a conceptually broader arena: schooling in general. Where do our educational programs fit within frameworks like the socio-economic class structure and non-Western notions about training for work? Some theorists have compared schools across class lines, or investigated education and training in non-Western cultures. The chapters in this volume represent international educational programs, but they are limited to programs within English-speaking Western cultures (the U.S., Canada, and New Zealand). What does one find if theories are considered with our camera lens set to an extreme depth of field? How might these theories help us understand our own programs in a new way?

FILLING IN THE FRAMEWORK

The Inner Ring

Let us begin with the inner-most circle in Fig. 2.1, the one focused on a particular work experience. Here there are many theories that might help generate research questions, hypotheses to test, and variables to measure, or that might be useful to interpret already-collected data. I briefly discuss theories about learning styles, self-efficacy and practical intelligence. Many other learning theories, for example ones that focus on multiple intelligences or learning taxonomies, could also fall within this level.

Perhaps David Kolb (1984) is cited most often in experiential education research as a theorist whose learning cycle helps researchers define their projects, interpret their data, or justify their programs. The reader looking for a full description of Kolb's theory should consult his book, chapter 16 (Tener) in this volume, or Cates and Jones (1999). Very briefly, Kolb argued that in any effective learning experience, four stages can be discerned: concrete experience, reflective observation, abstract conceptualization, and active experimentation. The learner engages in an experience, reflects on the experience from various perspectives, forms a personal theory or finds a grander theory to explain his or her observations, and uses the theory to guide future action, and so the cycle begins again. Kolb's (1999) Learning Style Inventory is a frequently used self-assessment of a learner's preference for one or more of the four phases of the cycle. Such preferences provide useful self-knowledge, however educators and employers are often encouraged to provide learning activities that challenge students to engage all four phases. The implication here is that a full understanding of a concept or skill will result if the learner moves through the whole cycle. Because completing a task in the workplace often requires students to move through all four phases (see, e.g., Tener, chap. 16, this volume) for examples from the field of construction engineering), it is not surprising that Kolb's theory is frequently invoked by researchers studying student learning from work.

Albert Bandura (1986) developed a theory on people's beliefs about how effective they are in the world. *Self-efficacy* is the term he used for the belief that one is capable of succeeding at challenging tasks. *Self-efficacy* refers to a sense of competence for new tasks that are similar to ones where success was achieved before, as distinct from the more global trait commonly called *self-confidence*. Bandura discovered that when you want to predict how well someone will perform on a certain task, a measure of self-efficacy will predict performance more accurately than a measure of ability.

Joyce Fletcher (1990) applied Bandura's (1986) theory to cooperative education. Her article is an excellent model if you want to take a theory not originally cast as a theory about experiential learning and deduce hypotheses from it that can be tested in experiential learning settings (if this theory is true, then my students will …). If you are interested in the concept of self-efficacy in terms of an outcome measure for your program, I recommend Fletcher's article because she suggested so many specific and testable hypotheses.

One of the few theories about learning that has research support from a study in a cooperative education setting is the theory of *practical intelligence* by Sternberg and Wagner (1986). This article includes a full description of their theory. Practical intelligence is what enables us to acquire practical skills: "knowing how" rather than "knowing that" as is often the focus of classroom learning. The low correlations[1] between IQ measures and job performance suggest that most competencies required in the workplace are not measured by standard tests of intelligence. Williams, Sternberg, Rashotte, and Wagner (1993) found differences in a measure of practical intelligence between a co-op group with as little as 5 months of cooperative education experience and a control group with no such experience. If you are interested in

---

[1]*Correlation* is a statistical term referring to the size and direction of the relationship between two measures. Correlations vary between −1.00 and +1.00. Correlations that are negative show that when one measure goes up, the other tends to go down. Positive correlations mean that the two measures both go up or down together. The correlations found between IQ and work performance are generally reported as about +.20, positive but close to .00, meaning that IQ and work performance are quite independent of each other. That is, knowing someone's IQ does not offer much information about how well they will perform at work.

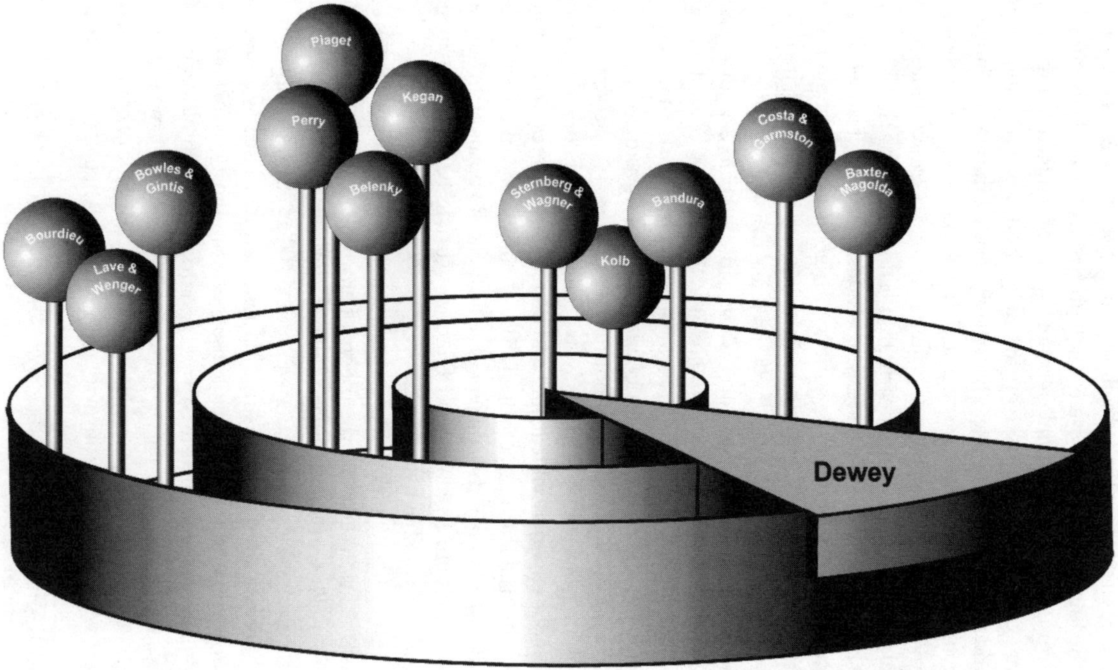

FIG. 2.2. Theorists located in the framework.

more ideas about the many ways a person can be considered intelligent, see also Gardner (1993).

Figure 2.2 shows Kolb, Bandura, and Sternberg and Wagner in the innermost circle because these theories are easily applied to a particular experiential learning situation. For example, a student's paper or the transcript of an interview used to credit a cooperative education or internship experience could be analyzed for evidence of one or more phases of Kolb's cycle, statements that reflect growing self-efficacy, or achievement in developing and using a new skill successfully. Or, hypotheses and measures to assess a program component could be developed using these theories as starting points. Chapters in this volume by Tener (chap. 16), Linn (chap. 6), and Miller (chap. 17) all use learning or developmental theories to help them understand particular work experiences. Ricks (chap. 4), Baker (chap. 14), and Fogg and Putnam (chap. 12) borrowed theory from philosophy, legal education, and economics, respectively, to suggest variables and interpret their data.

Note that the theories in the inner-most circle focus on different dimensions of human experience: phases of learning (Kolb), that aspect of the self-concept called *efficacy* (Bandura) and knowing how to do things (Sternberg and Wagner). It is important to differentiate among different dimensions of human experience in order to avoid confusing or lumping together behaviors or attitudes that are different. For example, self-confidence is a different aspect of the self-concept than is self-efficacy because the former is a global trait and the latter specific to feeling competent in particular situations similar to one's previous realm of experience. To be sure you are measuring the behavior or attitude you intend to measure (i.e., to ensure *content validity*), there is no shortcut to careful study of a theory you are considering for your project. The theorist's book or article is the primary source and therefore a good place to start. If the primary source makes too many assumptions about your background in psychology or research methods to make it understandable, look for other writers who have interpreted the theories. Some authors in this volume include in their annotated bibliographies these secondary sources (see, e.g., the Ignelzi, 2000, reference below or the frequent referencing of the Cates & Jones, 1999, text in several chapters).

The choice of which of the theories described previously, or others, to use might be based on hunches we make, drawing on our experiences as educators. For example, I thought that Bandura's (1986) theory of self-efficacy might be useful for my research because I could bring to mind many examples of students who described in co-op crediting conferences how they learned a professional skill or work style from watching mentors on the job (Bandura called this *vicarious learning*). I also knew students who were tentative or frightened of new challenges before they went on co-op but who returned from a work experience claiming that they felt competent to handle a certain range of new situations now that they had success in that arena (Bandura's *enactive mastery*). These hunches led me to include questions in my interview protocol about learning from mentors, and to interpret stories of co-op learning in terms of enactive mastery versus self-confidence.

The Middle Ring

Next we move to the middle-most circle, which represents a wider view, both developmentally and historically.[2] In Fig. 2.2 you see several theories, including Piaget, Perry, Belenky, Baxter Magolda, Kegan, and Costa and Garmston. Although the various theories located in the inner circle focused on different dimensions of human experience, the theories listed in this part of Fig. 2.2 are related to each other like branches from a central root. All these theories focus on that dimension of human functioning called *cognition*, a term from psychology that refers to thinking, learning, and memory.

The root of all of the learning theories in the middle-most circle is the work of theorist Jean Piaget. Piaget (1963, 1972) was interested in the origins of thought, a field called *epistemology*. Piaget's original theory covered infancy through adolescence but has been extended to considerations of adult intellectual development (see, e.g., Commons, Richards, & Armon, 1984). For our purposes here, Piaget's important contribution was to observe and record that humans are active processors of information around them, creating meaning in qualitatively different ways as they mature. We take in information and fit it into our existing mental frameworks (i.e., we *assimilate*) until our framework no longer fits, and then (often reluctantly) we change our framework (i.e., we *accommodate*; see Cates & Jones, 1999, for a fuller discussion of these last two concepts).

Piaget (1963) argued that the ways humans actively construct reality go through predictable changes in an invariant order with increasing maturity (i.e., *stages*), and that those stages are universal, regardless of cultural or environmental context. These two claims have been questioned by subsequent researchers, but Piaget's observations of humans as active processors had a revolutionary impact on psychology and education. This so-called "cognitive revolution" followed the era of behaviorism, and that cognitive root is still growing today (see Bruner, 1990, for a thoughtful exposition of this intellectual history). One important implication for educators and employers is that our students don't just know less than we do (as behaviorism would have predicted), rather they often construct their realities in very different ways than we do, and resist different constructions unless we take care to lead them from their framework to ours.

William Perry (1970) applied Piaget's theory to his work helping Harvard men in a context that might be called an *academic support center* today. Piaget used open-ended questions in his research to allow children to inform him of the meaning they made of their world. Perry followed this lead by asking his students: What stands out for you over this last year in college? From this one "big" question, Perry heard his students describe their failures and triumphs, and he took note of how the

---

[2]Remember that living through an historical era and developing increased maturity are factors that co-occur, and so must be considered together as we broaden the focus of our learning analysis beyond one work situation and try to understand the changes we see there.

content of the students' answers changed as they returned to talk to him across their 4 or more years of university. From these interviews, Perry developed a theory that describes intellectual and ethical development in late adolescence.

Many educators have found Perry's (1970) description of the qualitatively different ways his students constructed reality to be helpful in understanding their own students. It is not just that our students know less than we do, rather, they center on different dimensions of the learning environment than we might think they do. Employers will find this theory useful, too. We all have experienced the frustration of carefully teaching our reality to a student, yet that student continues to cling to his or her own perspective. Why don't they get it? It can be useful and reassuring to read that students change in predictable ways in their thinking about where knowledge comes from, how it is acquired, what role others play in their education, and how to make difficult decisions in ambiguous circumstances.

From here the trunk of the theoretical tree splits. Theorists Belenky, Baxter Magolda, Kegan, and Costa and Garmston all cite Perry in their work. They approach the same questions of where knowledge comes from and how we obtain it but from different perspectives based on their geography and their professional disciplines. Mary Belenky and her colleagues (Belenky, Clinchy, Goldberger, & Tarule, 1986) wanted to extend Perry's (1970) work to include both working-class women they knew in rural Vermont and women college students. They were surprised to find some different stages of intellectual development than Perry had found, hence the title of their book, *Women's Ways of Knowing*. For example, in working with rural undereducated women, Belenky and her colleagues found a stage they called *silence*. That is, some women felt completely dependent on authorities for knowledge and denied that they were knowers at all. None of Perry's privileged Harvard men had invoked such deprecating self-descriptions, even when they were failing a class. If you are studying women or students in general who have been economically or educationally deprived, and you are interested in cognitive influences of your program, I recommend this book.

Robert Kegan (1982, 1994; see also Ignelzi, 2000 for a helpful overview) used the term *meaning-making* to describe that active construction of reality that Piaget and Perry had observed before him. Kegan came from a therapeutic tradition, and often used stories told to him in clinical settings as data to support his theory. He also described qualitatively different stages but from a lifespan perspective. One reason his (1994) book is so popular is that he has studied adults as well as students and claimed that if we understood better how others make meaning differently than we do, we could avoid many conflicts with our children, our life partners, and our coworkers. Kegan's theory is helpful to educators and employers because he offered practical advice about how to encourage students to move forward in their way of constructing reality and encourages patience in those situations we have all had with students who "just don't get it." Those challenges to move to a new framework should be balanced with support because it is often difficult to give up one comfortable and familiar way of thinking about the world (e.g., "If I just read everything my professor [or boss] gives me, I'll gain knowledge.") and move toward a new way (e.g., "Truth depends on your perspective and authorities [professors or employers] often disagree about what is true.").

Baxter Magolda (1992, 2000, 2001) came from the student personnel field; her work embeds cognitive development during college within residential campus life. Unfortunately, she doesn't consider student work experiences during college in her research. The stages she described for intellectual change in late adolescence are somewhat different from Perry's (1970) and Kegan's (1994), and she found gender differences similar to Belenky et al. (1986). Here, again, we run into the risk of getting overwhelmed by several slightly different theories all describing cognitive development in late adolescence as stimulated by higher educational experiences, but Baxter Magolda (2000, especially chap. 7) offered a very useful overview that shows how these various theories are more alike than different. Again, these are stages of constructing reality, a very relevant concern in our attempts to understand how our students learn in the workplace.

In the first stage, there is the belief in a single truth that authorities have and pass along to others. Such knowledge is thought by the student to be universal and not influenced by context. Most college students have moved beyond this stage when they come to us, but they may retreat to it when challenged by a frightening new situation such a work placement in a setting very different from familiar ones. Gradually uncertainty and ambiguity creep in and disrupt this comfortable belief in a universal truth. For example, imagine a situation in which a classroom engineering professor and an employer disagree about how to perform a certain skill. Who is right? Students are forced to accommodate their framework to consider that what is "true" now appears to depends on one's situation and perspective.

Baxter Magolda (2000) and the other theorists in this section agree that many students then come to believe that everyone must have a right to his or her own opinion. Some students in this stage even resent having their papers graded or their work evaluated: Who is the professor (or employer) to score the student's work, since truth is so relative? In the absence of a framework for evaluating the relative worth of different opinions, subjectivity runs rampant.

Next comes what Baxter Magolda (2000) called the "Great Accommodation." Recall that Piaget (1963) used the term *accommodation* to refer to that process when one's framework for meaning-making has to change because there is too much information that will not fit in the old framework (i.e., that can no longer be *assimilated*). Accepting the world as a place full of uncertainty and ambiguity is an uncomfortable passage, and does not happen overnight. There are likely periods of retreat, to relying on experts for knowledge or to guide action. For example, co-op employer Doreen Ganley believes that students sometimes retreat by relying on teams to make decisions when they should be ready for independent thought (Linn & Ganley, 2002). The important self-understanding that emerges with the Great Accommodation is that students claim their own role as a knower and an authority. It is not that students stop listening to parents, educators, and employers who have more experience than they do but rather that students take what they find to be useful from others and combine that information with their own knowledge that stems from their research and lived experience.

Ignelzi (2000) offered some useful advice about how to determine at what stage our students are so that we can understand them better and guide them along this intellectual path. He asked his students what kind of support they think they will need in a particular endeavor. The students' answers to this question tend to reflect their stage of intellectual development. For example, do the students ask for direction to guide them in every step or ask for repeated feedback to determine whether they are doing the right thing? If so, it is unlikely that they have traversed the Great Accommodation. However, if they ask for some leeway to use their own good judgment and some patience to allow them to figure out how to be most effective, that is one indication that they have entered the stage of generative knowing.

Although theorists differ in what they call the stage that follows the Great Accommodation, they do have in common a description of an active knower who can generate their own perspective taking context into account and judging the merits of different views held by others (i.e., a *generative knower*; Baxter Magolda, 2000). Kegan (1994) called such students *self-authoring*. Self-authorship is one of several *metaskills* (superordinate skills above the level of specific work skills like writing business reports) that Hall (1996) and others have described as important for employability.

Many of the theorists we have covered in this section say that few undergraduates move beyond the Great Accommodation, but rather during their first postgraduate job they are challenged to become generative knowers. One hypothesis that begs testing is whether undergraduates who are employed in cooperative education or internship work settings move through the Great Accommodation and enter the stage of generative knowing by virtue of the cognitive challenges that work situations and independent living provide. Cognitive stage theory provides one explanation for studies that have shown co-op students at an advantage in the postgraduate workplace over students who have not participated in these programs (e.g., Gardner, 1992; Jarrell, 1974).

Finally, in terms of the middle circle of Fig. 2.2, I've included Costa and Garmston (1998), who are emeritus professors of education and codirectors of the Institute for Intelligent Behavior in California. They argued that there are many forces that encourage us to "think small" about educational outcomes: national and state educational goals, behaviorist theories that focus on minute skills, practical matters of how easy it is to measure more narrow outcomes, and what they call our "historical obsession with the disciplines as separate stores of knowledge to be acquired" (p. 14). They argued that a broader view of educational outcomes broadens the meanings that students derive from a curriculum and that this is important to create citizens of a democratic and global society. Although K–12 educators were the target audience for their paper, I think their scheme works for higher education settings as well.

Many new teachers focus only on *activities*: How will I fill the class time? As they gain confidence, the cumulative effects of these activities—the *content* knowledge that is gained—becomes the focus. Content next becomes a vehicle for what Costa and Garmston (1998) called *processes*, but we usually talk about them as skills: testing hypotheses or posing questions. As educators mature further, they begin to think on a systems level about outcomes. Colleagues discover a shared vision, transcend disciplinary boundaries, and consider outcomes as *dispositions* or habits of the mind. Some examples of dispositions the authors use include critical thinking, thinking about your own thinking, called *metacognition* (self-authoring is an example); creative thinking, moving, or making; and risk-taking (p. 12). Such habits are the keys to becoming lifelong learners. *States of mind* represent the broadest level of outcomes that Costa and Garmston (1998) considered. Here they include self-efficacy, flexibility (including adapting to change), craftsmanship, consciousness (self-monitoring), and, finally, interdependence. Most employers would agree that these states of mind define a successful worker.

One point to keep in mind as we move from the inner toward the outer circles in Fig. 2.2 is that any theory I placed in a particular circle could also be used at a broader level as well. Albert Einstein once said, "... new frameworks are like climbing a mountain—the larger view encompasses, rather than rejects the earlier more restricted view" (cited in Costa & Garmston, 1998).

The Outer Ring

Finally we have reached the outmost circle! Here we use the broadest depth of field that the camera (our metaphor for this framework of learning theories) will allow: questions of schooling in general. Jean Lave is a Professor of Education at U.C. Berkeley and is one theorist associated with *situated learning theory* (SLT). Lave studies learning, but she is rarely found near a school. Her interest has been in the math ability of unschooled young tailor apprentices in Liberia, or the math thinking used by a woman shopping for groceries and deciding how many apples to buy for her family (Lave, 1988).

Lave might say that a school, at least a traditional one with rows of chairs and a person defined as a *teacher* transmitting knowledge to other persons defined as *students*, is the least likely place for learning to happen. Traditional theories of learning focus on transmission of knowledge from professor to student and the later transfer of that knowledge in the real world. Knowledge is dichotomized: abstract versus concrete, theory versus practice. SLT theorists view such dichotomies as wrongheaded, rather, they see all learning as contextual, and the result of social participation (Lave, 1993; Lave & Wenger, 1991).

Social participation is key in SLT because learners are *newcomers* entering *communities of practice*. Those central to the community of practice are called *old timers*; they invite newcomers into roles as legitimate, although peripheral, participants in their community. Old timers strive to make the community of practice transparent to newcomers who move gradually toward center, welcoming in new newcomers as they themselves had been welcomed. Lave and Wegner (1991) called such settings *legitimate peripheral participation*. Legitimate as in relevant, real. Peripheral versus full participation, participation as in becoming an active member of a community of practice.

Apprenticeships in both Western and non-Western cultures have been the focus of several of Lave's studies, hence the relevance of her work to this volume on student learning in cooperative education and internships. By apprenticeship, she doesn't mean only the often exploitative historical form associated with feudal Europe. One chapter of Lave and Wenger (1991) is called "Midwives, Tailors, Quartermasters, Butchers, and Non-drinking Alcoholics." The chapter title demonstrates the wide range of practices in which she and her colleagues have found that learning takes place in similar ways: Newcomers and old-timers exist in relation to each other and the social situation in which they find themselves.

In SLT it is human social activity that yields learning. Here you can see why a traditional classroom might be seen as an odd set up for learning because social participation is usually minimized and its forms are tightly controlled. Lave and Wenger (1991) argued, "The notion of participation ... dissolves dichotomies between cerebral and embodied activity, between contemplation and involvement, between abstraction and experience: Person, actions, and the world are implicated in all thought, speech, knowing, and learning" (p. 52).

SLT could be a useful theory to explain the power of students' learning outside the classroom in service learning, internships, or cooperative education. Students become newcomers in communities of practicing social workers, teachers, engineers or business professionals. Employers serve as old-timers who offer sequentially more central participation, ideally just outside the newcomer's comfort zone.

To go one step further, consider broadening our application of SLT to general education classroom experiences (e.g., programs that ask students to take science, art, and humanities classes) and residential campus roles (e.g., moving from being a dorm resident to becoming a hall advisor). Now it becomes evident that colleges and universities have the potential to offer students the opportunity to move from periphery toward center many times over, as budding biologists, painters, writers, or (as a residence hall advisor) student services personnel. In this way SLT suggests that our students' learning experiences in the classroom, the workplace, and in the dorm are more alike than different: All these contexts bring students in as newcomers and move them into legitimate peripheral participation. I argue that our students learn how to enter a new community of practice by these repeated challenges in higher education contexts. This notion is similar to other metaskills named in the growing literature about what kinds of careers students in school today are likely to face after graduation (Costa & Garmston [1998] called this skill *flexibility*; Gardner [1998] and Hall [1996] called it *adaptability*). By looking outside of formal school settings and into underdeveloped cultures, Lave and her colleagues offer us a new perspective on the breadth of effects of our higher education programs on students' lives. In this volume, note the use of SLT by Grosjean (chap. 3), Eames (chap. 5), Linn (chap. 6) and Baker (chap. 14).

Finally, I want to describe briefly some theories that focus on schooling in terms of *social class*. Here we cross disciplinary boundaries from psychology and education into sociology. All of the theories, Lave included, that I've placed in the outermost circle cited Karl Marx (1906) as the source of the idea that workers have knowledge based on their practice as workers. This idea was radical because intellectual and manual labor were separated during the Industrial Revolution. In cottage industries thinking and doing had been accomplished by the same individual. With the advent of capitalism and the division of labor, intellectual work was valued and manual labor devalued. I argue that educators in cooperative education and internship programs face this same bias against manual labor when we struggle for legitimacy within the academy.

There are many sociological theories that attempt to explain how and why social class membership tends to be reproduced from generation to generation (see McLeod, 1995, chap. 2 for a readable overview[3]). These *social reproduction theories* often focus on schools because Western cultural ideology suggests that schools are the "great equalizers." Theorists like Bowles and Gintis (1976) and Bourdieu (1977) argued that schools do not offer a level playing field, they reproduce social inequality. Bowles and Gintis (1976) compared working-class and middle-class schools in terms of the degree of control of students versus encouragements to think independently and creatively. They found that by requiring students to conform without question to rules and obey all authorities, schools in working-class neighborhoods tend to promote dispositions required by blue-collar jobs like doing what you are told and being on time. Middle-class schools, in contrast, encouraged critical and creative thinking and nonconformity, dispositions required to be a successful manager or other professional. But why do some children within the same school fail while others succeed?

Bourdieu (1977) used the term *cultural capital* to refer to the cultural knowledge and ways of being in the world that parents pass on to children. Schools and teachers tend to value the cultural knowledge and activities of upper class parents. Parents who take their children to films, theater, and musical events, and who can afford to travel with their children pass along cultural as well as economic capital that promote school success. Lower class children without such cultural capital are bound to have less success in a school where their type of cultural knowledge is devalued. Note how Howard and Haugsby (chap. 11, this volume) used the notion of cultural capital to mediate conflicts when students and employers struggled across class lines to understand each other.

Cooperative education and internship programs, particularly ones in the context of liberal arts programs, face an intriguing dilemma as we struggle for legitimacy in the

---

[3]Thanks to Adam Howard for this reference and some ideas in this section of the chapter.

competitive higher education market. What role does work play in higher education settings that are traditionally focused on the intellectual? What right do co-op educators or internship coordinators have to grant academic credit? How do classroom faculty feel when students come to their classes with more current practice experience than they have themselves? When students have current practice experience, how do roles of teacher and learner shift? Do we lose anything important if we narrow our celebration of the broad learning encountered by students in the workplace to legitimize only that learning that tracks closely with classroom learning in the major? Should every student, regardless of social class and professional aspirations learn both how to think critically and to perform well in the workplace? Should high schools track students into college preparatory versus vocational training? What do we intend when we set GPA criteria for admission to our work programs, despite the low correlations between academic and workplace achievement? These questions and others become grist for the mill of experiential learning research when theories like those in the outermost circle in Fig. 2.2 are considered.

Dewey's Philosophy

The philosophy of John Dewey is both central to any discussion of experiential learning and so wide-ranging in its application that it is difficult locate it in the framework of theories offered here. I have situated Dewey's work to cross-cut the three rings in Fig. 2.2 in order to capture these contradictory dimensions of his work. Dewey was so prolific that it is also difficult to choose a citation. I recommend Archambault's (1964) collection of Dewey's selected writings on education. Archambault said in his preface that "It is commonplace that everyone talks about Dewey and no one reads him" (p. ix). His collection allows us to locate and read Dewey's original essays and chapters in their entirety, all focused on topics of interest to educators and written between 1895 and 1939.

Dewey's writings can help us guide a student when planning for and reflecting on a work-based learning experience to consider a wide range of intellectual interests that can be stimulated by a single experience (i.e., the inner circle of Fig. 2.1).

> Gardening, for example, need not be taught for the sake of preparing future gardeners, or as an agreeable way of passing time. It affords an avenue of approach to knowledge of the place farming and horticulture have had in the history of the race and which they occupy in present social organization. Carried on in an environment educationally controlled, they are means for making a study of the facts of growth, the chemistry of soil, the role of light, air and moisture. (Dewey, 1916, p. 235)

Dewey also offered as early as 1897, a philosophy that presages the focus on self-development offered by Perry, Kegan and others in the middle circle of Fig. 2.2:

> With the advent of democracy and modern industrial conditions, it is impossible to foretell definitely just what civilization will be twenty years from now. Hence it is

impossible to prepare the child for any precise set of conditions. To prepare him for the future life means to give him command of himself. (reprinted in Archambault, 1964, p. 429)

Now with the decline of the industrial age and the advent of a society based on knowledge, it is again difficult to foresee the futures our students will find for themselves. Learning about the self by risking new settings, new challenges and new demands may be the most effective learning that higher education can offer.

Finally, Dewey also insisted at the turn of the last century that "… it is the business of every one interested in education to insist upon the school as the primary and most effective interest of social progress and reform" (reprinted in Archambault, 1964, p. 438). He argued against traditional education because it assumes the learner is ignorant, the teacher wise, and that the division of knowledge into disciplines was artificial and confining (NSEE Foundations Document Committee, 1998). He also argued against the separation of vocational and intellectual training, insisting rather that such dualities are artificial and result from industrial capitalism. Because Dewey's theory speaks about individual learning experiences, development of students across time, and questions traditional schooling as an institution, Dewey's philosophy of education can be useful at any level of analysis of student work-based learning.

CONCLUSIONS

The framework provided in this chapter is intended to help the reader organize the many theories available to guide our research endeavors. The theoretical examples offered here are limited to those I've encountered in my own search for guidance for my research; many others could be profitably reviewed if time and space allowed. If you encounter other theories and wish to incorporate them into this model, consider the depth of field that the theory encompasses. Some kinds of learning happen in a relatively narrow band of space and time. If we could follow our students around in the workplace in real time (a plan they would do well to resist), we might observe them performing a skill they never performed before. How did they figure that out? Place any theories that might suggest a learning process or help us understand specific outcomes in the innermost circle.

My bias as a developmental psychologist is that we must move forward from one-shot studies to investigate how work placements fit in the context of a school term, a degree program, or even within a lifetime. The theories in the middle circle of the framework might help guide such endeavors; other theories that broaden the focus from one work experience to a longer time frame could be added here.

What about the outer ring? Must we simultaneously consider narrow moments of learning and broad ideas about the socioeconomics of schooling? Yes! Writers like Lave and Bourdieu keep us mindful of the important place our work takes in cultural reproduction, and such mindfulness is key to preparing students to meet the challenges of a global economy where the gap is widening between the rich and the poor. Those of us who work on the boundaries between school and work have a special responsibility to help young people to find a way to make a difference, not just to make a living.

REFERENCES

Archambault, R. D. (Ed.). (1964). *John Dewey on education: Selected writings*. New York: The Modern Library.

Bandura, A. (1986). *Social foundations of thought and action: A social cognitive theory*. Englewood Cliffs, NJ: Prentice Hall.

Baxter Magolda, M. B. (1992). *Knowing and reasoning in college: Gender-related patterns in students' intellectual development*. San Francisco: Jossey-Bass.

Baxter Magolda, M. B. (Ed.). (2000, Summer). Teaching to promote intellectual and personal maturity incorporating students' worldviews and identities into the learning process. *New Directions for Teaching and Learning, 82*, San Francisco, CA: Jossey-Bass.

Baxter Magolda, M. B. (2001). *Making their own way: Narratives for transforming higher education to promote self-development*. Sterling, VA: Stylus.

Belenky, M. F., Clinchy, B. M., Goldberger, N. R., & Tarule, J. M. (1986). *Women's ways of knowing: The development of self, voice and mind*. New York: Basic Books.

Bourdieu, P. (1977). *Outline of a theory of practice*. Cambridge, UK: Cambridge University Press.

Bowles, S., & Gintis, H. (1976). *Schooling in capitalist America*. New York: Basic Books.

Bruner, J. S. (1990). *Acts of meaning*. Cambridge, MA: Harvard University Press.

Cates, C., & Jones, P. (1999). *Learning outcomes: The educational value of cooperative education*. Columbia, MD: Cooperative Education Association.

Commons, M. L., Richards, F. A., & Armon, C. (Eds.). (1984). *Beyond formal operations: Late adolescent and adult cognitive development*. New York: Praeger.

Costa, A. L., & Garmston, R. J. (1998). Maturing outcomes. *Encounter: Education for Meaning and Social Justice, 11*, 10–18.

Dewey, J. (1916). *Democracy and education*. New York: MacMillan.

Fletcher, J. (1990). Self-esteem and cooperative education: A theoretical framework. *Journal of Cooperative Education, 27*, 41–55.

Gardner, H. (1993). *Multiple intelligences: The theory in practice*. New York: Basic Books.

Gardner, P. D. (1992). Starting salary outcomes of cooperative education graduates. *Journal of Cooperative Education, 27*, 16–26.

Gardner, P. D. (1998). Are college seniors prepared to work? In J. N. Gardner, G. Van der Veer, & Associates (Eds.), *The senior year experience: Facilitating integration, reflection, closure, and transition* (pp. 60–78). San Francisco: Jossey-Bass.

Hall, D. T. (1996). Protean careers of the 21st century. *Academy of Management Executive, 10*, 8–16.

Ignelzi, M. (2000, Summer). Meaning-making in the learning and teaching process. In M. B. Magolda (Ed.), Teaching to promote intellectual and personal maturity incorporating students' worldviews and identities into the learning process. *New Directions for Teaching and Learning, 82*, 5–15.

Jarrell, D. (1974). Co-ops and nonco-ops at NASA. *Journal of Cooperative Education, 10*, 51–54.

Kegan, R. (1982). *The evolving self: Problem and process in human development*. Cambridge, MA: Harvard University Press.

Kegan, R. (1994). *In over our heads: The mental demands of modern life.* Cambridge, MA: Harvard University Press.

Kolb, D. A. (1984). *Experiential learning: Experience as the source of learning and development.* Englewood Cliffs, NJ: Prentice Hall.

Kolb, D. A. (1999). *Learning style inventory.* Boston: Hay/McBer.

Lave, J. (1988). *Cognition in practice: Mind, mathematics, and culture in everyday life.* Cambridge, England: Cambridge University Press.

Lave, J. (1993). The practice of learning. In S. Chaiklin & J. Lave (Eds.), *Understanding practice: Perspectives on activity and context* (pp. 3–32). Cambridge, England: Cambridge University Press.

Lave, J., & Wegner, E. (1991). *Situated learning: Legitimate peripheral participation.* Cambridge, England: Cambridge University Press.

Linn, P. L., & Ganley, D. (2002, May 16). *We are all coaches: Do we understand our players?* Keynote presentation to the Ohio Cooperative Education Association, Canton, OH.

Marx, K. (1906). *Capital: A Critique of Political Economy.* (S. Moore & E. Aveling, Trans.). Edited by F. Engels. New York: Random House.

McLeod, J. (1995). *Ain't no makin' it.* Boulder, CO: Westview.

NSEE Foundations Document Committee. (1998). Foundations of experiential education, December, 1997. *NSEE Quarterly, 23*(3), 1; 18–22.

Perry, W. G., Jr. (1970). *Forms of intellectual and ethical development in the college years: A scheme.* Austin, TX: Holt, Rinehart, & Winston.

Piaget, J. (1963). *The origin of intelligence in children* (2nd ed.). New York: Norton.

Piaget, J. (1972). Intellectual evolution from adolescence to adulthood. *Human Development, 15,* 1–12.

Sternberg, R. J., & Wagner, R. K. (Eds.). (1986). *Practical intelligence: Nature and origins of competence in the everyday world.* New York: Cambridge University Press.

Williams, W. M., Sternberg, R. J., Rashotte, C. A., & Wagner, R. K. (1993). Assessing the value of cooperative education. *Journal of Cooperative Education, 28*(2), 32–55.

Wilson, J. W. (1988). Research in cooperative education. *Journal of Cooperative Education, 24*(2–3), 77–89.

Wilson, J. W., & Lyons, E. H. (1961). *Work-study college programs.* New York: Harper & Brothers.

Part II

Beginning Phase
of Research Projects

3

Getting Started and Achieving Buy-In: Co-op Education Is Continuous, Contextualized Learning

Garnet Grosjean
The University of British Columbia

Key questions addressed in this chapter:

☞ How does context affect learning in co-op?

☞ How does one negotiate buy-in to a study from all stakeholders?

☞ How does co-op affect students' perceptions of learning and work?

☞ How do students make meaning of the co-op process?

INTRODUCTION

Learning is something we do every day. It is not restricted to the classroom or training center, although these are the traditional sites of research on learning and we have come to know quite a lot about learning in these environments. In these formal settings, we have devised ways to test the amount of learning that takes place, and we have developed a range of strategies to help people learn better. Researchers have started thinking more broadly about what affects the way people learn. We began to look beyond the content of learning to the surroundings in which it occurred. Learning context began to take on a new meaning and importance once we realized that we do not learn in isolation. Our surroundings provide a variety of cues that contribute not only to *what* we learn, but also to *how* we learn.

31

This chapter is about the importance of context to the what and how of learning in co-op programs. It addresses how students come to make meaning from their experience of co-op. I present findings of a study of co-op students' perceptions of learning and work. These findings indicate that the social setting—classroom or workplace—is more than mere background; it is integral to the learning process. Co-op programs combine classroom and workplace learning, alternating students between each context. As a result, through reflection and praxis (reflection-in-action), students are able to engage in what I call *continuous contextualized learning*. As an analogy, think of the Möbius strip with its single edge and continuous looping (see Fig. 3.1). The single edge represents the continuous learning that takes place as co-op students alternate between the classroom and workplace contexts (represented by the two ends of the loop).

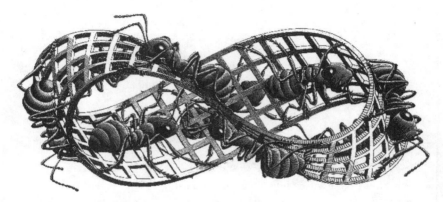

FIG. 3.1.   M. C. Escher's Möbius Strip II © 2003 Cordon Art B. V.-Baarn- Holland.

One goal of the chapter is to argue that the context in which a learning activity takes place is crucial to the way co-op students develop knowledge and skills. A second goal is to address the question of obtaining *buy-in* when conducting a research study. *Buy-in* means obtaining support and endorsement from individuals at all levels of the institution under consideration as a research site. Buy-in is a core requirement for a successful study, in that it is a precondition for access to key data and informants. To achieve buy-in, researchers must present projects in a way that resonates with those whose cooperation is required. Cooperation can not be mandated. Participants must perceive a benefit from taking part in the study.

I begin with a brief overview of the preparation required to undertake this study and outline my review of the literature on co-op education, learning, and context. I then describe the setting for the study, the programs and participants, and the research design. The findings I present in the final section detail how students interpret the continuous contextualized learning they experience in the co-op classroom and workplace.

PREPARING FOR MY RESEARCH STUDY

Once I decided on a topic for my research study, I needed to find out if any previous work had been done. One of the first steps in this process was to conduct a review of the research literature. There are three reasons to do a literature review before proceeding with a study: The literature indicates what research has been done in an area of interest; it also provides information on where gaps exist in current knowledge; and it provides a framework for, and establishes the importance of, a study.

In my case, I found it necessary to review a range of different types of literature before deciding where a study of contextualized learning in co-op could make a contribution.

Decision Point: Which literature should I review for my study?
- Because I was interested in studying learning in co-op education programs I began by reviewing the co-op literature.
- My initial review revealed that the majority of co-op research was confined to a small number of scholarly publications, a variety of reports and proceedings of co-op conferences, and a number of doctoral dissertations on various aspects of co-op education. I decided to concentrate on literature related to co-op's pedagogical role.
- Because I was interested in how learning happens in co-op programs, I sought out literature on learning. This area posed more of a challenge. The literature on learning is vast, and I had to keep narrowing my focus to avoid being overwhelmed by sheer volume. By restricting myself to literature that focused on the importance of context to learning, I was able to determine that my study would make a contribution in the area of workplace and classroom learning.

Co-op Education Literature

Co-op's strong practitioner orientation has produced several lines of enquiry that attempt to legitimate co-op as a pedagogically sound form of education. Studies on the impact of co-op participation on career development emphasize the importance of co-op on a student's career decisions and approach to finding a first job (Pittenger, 1993; Sharma, 1995). Studies on personal growth indicate that co-op experiences enhance students' self-confidence, values, and attitudes (Fletcher, 1990), whereas other research indicates an increase in student independence, social maturity and interpersonal skills (Fletcher, 1989; Rowe 1992; Williams, Sternberg, Rashotte, & Wagner, 1993).

Further strengthening the case for co-op, the literature asserts that co-op students get better jobs, get them faster, make more money and are, in general, well rounded and productive citizens (Petryszak & Toby, 1989; Somers, 1995; Wessels &

Pumphrey, 1995). Studies show that co-op graduates are more likely to obtain jobs related to their academic background (Brown, 1976) and that co-op students possess significantly more practical job knowledge than non-co-op students (Williams et al., 1993; Wilson, 1988). In general, co-op students display more tacit knowledge than their non-co-op counterparts, suggesting that they develop a stronger operational understanding of how and why the world of work operates as it does. Co-op's combination of classroom and workplace experience can have a demonstrable and measurable impact on co-op students in as little as 5 months (Williams et al., 1993).

Despite the importance attributed to co-op education in the literature and the positive views held about these programs by researchers, little systematic information has been collected on the experience of students as they engage with the different stages of the co-op process. Also missing from the literature are studies of the importance of context on the learning that occurs during the co-op process. In the following section, I briefly review the literature on the relation between learning and context.

Learning and Context Literature

Learning has been defined as "an active process of constructive sense-making" (Engeström, 1994, p. 9). In other words, learners construct a picture of the world and explanations of its different phenomena by "correlating and merging newly acquired material into their ongoing activity and earlier constructions" (p. 12). Although considerable research has been conducted on learning and motivation in a classroom context, less is known about learning in the workplace context. Our understanding of the skills and competencies that constitute good work performance remains limited. Likewise, we do not fully understand how skills and competencies are acquired. We do know, however, that learning is influenced by the particular context in which it occurs. But, what do we mean when we talk about context? A central and recurring theme in discussions of context is the idea of the meaning structures associated with time, place, person, and circumstance. In the classroom the context includes the curriculum, teachers and students, equipment and furnishings, and the educational institution's attitude toward education. The workplace context is a formal and professional—rather than social—setting. It includes the norms and values of the constitutive professions, equipment and machinery used for production, and a shared culture of understanding of how things are done in a particular workplace.

The context structures the learning that can occur in a particular situation because it specifies not only what can be learned and how it will be learned but also the meaning that society attributes to that learning. Think of it like this: A word in a sentence takes on specific meaning from the words that surround it and from the social context in which it is uttered. In the same way, the context that surrounds an individual in a learning situation, whether in the classroom or the workplace, gives that learning specific meanings. What we learn, and how we learn, depends on influences embedded in the context where the experience takes place.

When students encounter a new learning situation they compare contextual information with beliefs acquired earlier. *Meaningful* learning occurs when new knowledge merges with and transforms former knowledge, resulting in a higher quality of understanding. Contextualized learning leads to deep-level learning (Engeström, 1994; Marton, Hounsell, & Entwistle, 1997). Educational programs that rotate between the classroom and the workplace allow participants to accumulate learning experiences in both contexts. Through a process of praxis or reflection-in-action, students begin to supplement previous, incomplete perceptions with more complete understandings of how the world works (Grosjean, 1999b). These understandings are then internalized as knowledge. The ways that students compare internalized knowledge with external stimuli is an individualized process—a strategy for learning. Learning strategies are one way of classifying students' approaches to learning (Ausubel, Novak, & Hanesian, 1978; Marton & Säljö, 1976; Svensson, 1977).

Theories of situated learning focus on the relationship between learning and the social contexts where learning occurs (Lave & Wenger, 1991; Wenger 1998). Learning occurs generally through experiencing the activities and cultural norms of the discipline (Lave, 1991). Co-op students move from novice toward expert through coparticipation with members of the disciplinary community. Thus, coparticipation allows for learning through performance and engagement within a community of practice rather than solely through cognitive acquisition of knowledge—the dominant mode in the academic context (Brown, Collins, & Duguid, 1989; Lave & Wenger, 1991; Rogoff, 1990).

Research on situated learning highlights the need to provide students with a real-world context for education and training, in order to prepare them for the world of work. Situated learning theory (SLT) provides a theoretical base for educational programs, like co-op, that include a workplace or experiential learning component.

Experiential learning is a key factor in the current debate on the relevance of university education. The difficulty faced by conventional graduates, in comparison to co-op graduates, in securing meaningful employment immediately upon graduation calls into question the traditional separation between academic and vocational education, that is, between the world of learning and the world of work (Matson & Matson, 1995). A widening expectations gap separates what stakeholders want from universities and what universities provide in terms of the changing opportunity structures of the labor market. Suggestions that the marketplace values graduates with real-world experience increases the demand for an experientially relevant education attuned to the shifting demands of the new economy (Business-Higher Education Forum, 1997; Grosjean, 1998).

By the time I completed the literature review, I was able to identify specific gaps in current knowledge about learning in co-op education. For example, although co-op students are rotated between the classroom and the workplace, the literature pays little attention is to the impact of these different contexts on the way co-op students learn.

Having determined the problem I wished to address, I needed to consider the methods I would use to collect data. If I wished to conduct a study based on testing a theory, and analyzed with statistical procedures, then I would choose a quantitative method. On the other hand, if my intention was to construct a complex, holistic picture of a problem or phenomenon, then I would choose a qualitative method. A quantitative study would require the formation of hypotheses, and a random selection of participants. A qualitative study would rely on well-constructed research questions to guide the study, and a purposeful selection of participants. Before proceeding, I needed to decide whether to develop research questions or hypotheses to guide the study.

Decision Point: Do I formulate research questions or hypotheses?
- I had to decide whether I needed hypotheses or research questions. Hypotheses are useful in experimental or quasi-experimental studies where explanations of outcomes or predictions are sought. Research questions are better suited to qualitative studies that seek to interpret or understand participant experience.
- Because my study would focus on understanding and meaning-making, important information could be derived from the way students described their experiences, therefore, I required research questions to guide my study. These are the key questions listed in the box that begins the chapter.

In the remainder of this chapter, I integrate what we have discussed so far into a description of the study I conducted on contextualized learning in co-op. We begin with the setting for the study.

THE SETTING

In selecting a setting for my study, I considered the relative importance of a number of characteristics. These included accessibility and ease of entry to the site, range of programs and informants from which to choose, and the presence of a potentially rich mix of processes and constraining factors to investigate. After careful consideration, I selected Coast University (a pseudonym), as the setting for my study.

Coast University is a community of slightly more than 17,000 students, and 1,900 faculty and staff. It is located on approximately 350 acres overlooking the ocean, just 15 minutes from a major metropolitan center. The campus reflects the architectural style of the 1960s, predominantly low-rise concrete structures. In good weather, the main library and the fountain that dominate the east side of campus are central gathering places for students. In inclement weather, they tend to congregate in the Student Union Building and the various campus cafeterias. The area's natural beauty and hospitable climate makes the campus a popular destination for undergraduates; nearly three-fourths of Coast University's registered students relocate from outside the local metropolitan area.

Coast University is ranked one of Canada's leading comprehensive universities, with a tradition of excellence in the arts and sciences. It has a well-established reputation for innovative interdisciplinary research and strong professional schools. The university is noted, as well, for its pioneering work in distance education, and support for innovative teaching. One of Coast University's distinct attractions is its extensive co-op education programs. Co-op permeates the ethos of the university, which boasts one of the largest university cooperative education programs in Canada, with co-ops in 46 academic areas. Thus, Coast University was an ideal site for my study of co-op, but access was not guaranteed. It had to be negotiated.

Decision Point: How did I get administrators to buy in to the study?
University administrators are mutually competitive and acutely aware of the relative positioning of their institutions. To gain support for my study, I researched how Coast University contributed to the overall provincial system of higher education, and how its co-op programs were perceived by employers in the region. Armed with this information, I set about convincing administrators that it was in their best interests to allow me to conduct my study at Coast University. With its broad range of co-op programs, I suggested that Coast would be a superior location to my home university with its more limited range of co-op options. Because my interest in students' perceptions of learning and work coincided with the desire of administrators to enhance Coast's profile in the province, approval was granted.

I then approached the Director of Co-op with my proposal to conduct research on how co-op students make meaning out of their co-op experience. The proposal was well received and the Director's office supported the study throughout.

THE PROGRAMS AND PARTICIPANTS

After enlisting support of the university administration and the Co-op Director, I set about selecting a representative group of co-op programs and soliciting support from co-op staff.

Decision Point: How did I persuade co-op staff to buy-in as key informants?
The first step was to convene a meeting of co-op program managers and coordinators from the various departments of the university to request their assistance with the study. I previewed my ideas and goals with them and discussed

timing and data collection methods. Co-op staff were invited to suggest areas of investigation to include in the study. My purpose was to have them act not only as points of access and support, but also as valuable human resources to which I could repeatedly return as the study progressed. By establishing these relationships early on, I was able to limit the number of time-consuming cul-de-sacs encountered during data gathering. The coordinators became key informants and facilitators for my study, and as such played a valuable role in the research. For example, coordinators were instrumental in negotiations with faculty instructors to allow me to administer the student survey during regular class time.

From the broad range of programs offered at the University, I had to find a way to select those that would provide sufficient data to satisfy the parameters of the study. I developed four selection criteria. First, the stability of the program was assessed on the basis of the length of time it had been operating and the growth in work placements of students over the years. Second, I determined whether the program was voluntary or mandatory. Third, evidence was sought of a clearly defined labor market for students completing the program. Fourth, I considered whether the program adhered to the structure of disciplinary programs established by Becher (1989).

Briefly, Becher (1989) presented a rationale that suggests academic disciplines possess recognizable identities and particular cultural attributes. He pointed out that the professional language and literature of a disciplinary group play a key role in establishing its cultural identity. Therefore, each academic discipline defines and defends its own identity and intellectual territory with a variety of devices that exclude those lacking the same cultural attributes. Cultural attributes include the "traditions, customs, and practices, transmitted knowledge, beliefs, morals and rules of conduct, as well as their linguistic and symbolic forms of communication and the meanings they share" (p. 24). Becher devised a four-fold typology: hard/pure, hard/applied, soft/pure, and soft/applied as a way of classifying the knowledge domains that underpin academic disciplinary cultures. The natural sciences and mathematics are located in the hard/pure quadrant, whereas hard/applied contains the science-based professions. The soft/applied quadrant encompasses the social professions, and the soft/pure includes the humanities and social sciences.

Because of the diverse cultures and knowledge domains in academic disciplines I reason that the experience of co-op students in different programs would vary. Although not designed as a comparative study, I nonetheless sought to investigate a broad range of student experiences. I carefully reviewed the co-op programs to find one that fit each of Becher's categories. Figure 3.2 contains selection criteria and indicates how I classified the four co-op programs according to Becher's model.

Before a study can proceed, research methods must be selected. The description of the methodology and study design that follows provides insight into how my thinking developed during the planning of the study.

Hard Pure	Soft Pure
CHEMISTRY CO-OP *established 1977* *100 placements (96/97)* *voluntary co-op* *defined labor market*	**GEOGRAPHY CO-OP** *established 1978* *210 placements (96/97)* *voluntary co-op* *mixed labor market*
Hard Applied	Soft Applied
ENGINEERING CO-OP *established 1983* *591 placements (96/97)* *mandatory co-op* *defined labor market*	**BUSINESS CO-OP** *established 1990* *548 placements (96/97)* *mandatory co-op* *mixed labor market*

FIG. 3.2.   Co-op programs selected.

DESIGN OF THE STUDY

The research was approached as a case study (Merriam, 1988; Stake, 1995; Yin, 1994), using a combination of quantitative and qualitative methods. A survey allowed collection of information on a large number of co-op students, providing data that could be statistically manipulated to provide an overall picture of the types of students who participate in co-op and their general satisfaction with the program. Collecting this type of information is important as it allows for comparison with other co-op programs. But it sheds little light on the process of students' learning in co-op. To understand how co-op students make meaning of the process and how context affects learning I adopted an ethnographic approach that included participant observation and in-depth interviews.

As shown in Fig. 3.3 the case study contained four nested levels: (1) the university, (2) the co-op department, (3) the four individual co-op programs selected for the study, and (4) the co-op students. Participants selected for interviews represented these four constituencies. My sampling strategy was *purposeful sampling* following Patton (1990), or what LeCompte and Priessle (1993) referred to as *criterion-based selection*. Using this strategy, particular settings, persons, or events are selected deliberately in order to provide important information that might not be obtained from other sources. In other words, where required, I selected people whose comprehensive knowledge of, or involvement with, co-op education, could assist me in finding answers to my research questions. Participant interviews were tape-recorded and transcribed verbatim. Interview data was subsequently entered into a qualitative database and analyzed using Atlas.ti© software.[1]

---

[1]Researchers interested in computer-aided qualitative data analysis should consult Kelle (1995) or Weitzman and Miles (1995) for a review of qualitative software packages.

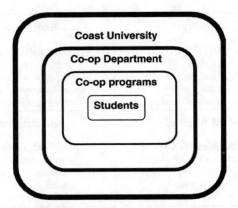

FIG. 3.3.   Nested case study.

Co-op policy was assessed using university documents and analysis of interviews with senior members of the administration ($n = 7$). These individuals provided information that helped me understand the context within which co-op education was delivered. I conducted informal and formal interviews with faculty ($n = 27$), the Director of Co-op ($n = 1$), and co-op coordinators ($n = 6$) to determine whether they shared an institutional perception of the role and function of co-op education, and its place in the university structure. This background information, combined with the results of in-depth interviews with co-op students ($n = 45$), allowed me to begin answering the question: How does the structure of co-op education impact students' understanding of learning and work? Analysis of in-depth interviews with co-op students also helped me understand the question: How do students make meaning of the co-op process?

Following a series of pilot-tests, the student survey was administered to classes of second-year, third-year, and fourth-year students in the four programs selected for the study. Because classes in disciplines with voluntary co-op programs also contained non-co-op students, a way had to be found to obtain information from the co-op students during the subsequent interview phase, although not overtly excluding the other students.

Decision Point: Selecting student participants for the study
The decision on how to select students for the study required careful deliberation. The survey and interview questions were designed to produce data I considered relevant to an understanding of the nature and process of co-op education. The study was not designed as a comparative study to test differences between programs or between co-op and non-co-op students. Students had to complete the survey, however, before they could volunteer to participate in the interview phase of the study. Because certain classes (those from

nonmandatory co-op programs) contained co-op and non-co-op students, a practical and logistical way of administering the survey was required. During a meeting with the co-op director and the coordinators from each program, it was decided that all students in the selected classes would complete the survey, but only co-op students would be interviewed.

Because the survey was to be administered during class time it required the support and assistance of not only co-op coordinators and faculty, but also the students who would participate in the study.

Decision Point: Achieving buy-in from students

To allow students an option of participating in the study, faculty announced ahead of time the date the in-class survey would take place. On the date in question, I gave a short pitch, asking students to help me find out more about their perceptions of learning and work. I asked them to complete the survey and, if they were interested, to volunteer for confidential interviews where they could describe their experience in greater detail. None of the students in the selected classes opted out of the survey, and approximately 34% of survey participants volunteered to be interviewed.

From this number I selected a purposeful sample of 45 students. After interviewing them, I sustained their interest in the study by maintaining e-mail contact. This also allowed me to solicit further information. Additionally, I asked students to check their interview transcripts for accuracy, providing further opportunities for reinforcement and discussion.

In total, the student survey was administered to 27 classes of second, third, and fourth year, students in Business, Chemistry, Engineering, and Geography. Of the 1,040 survey forms distributed, 1,012 were complete and usable, for an adjusted completion rate of 97.3%.

Even with careful planning, there comes a point in most studies where the unanticipated strikes; when, as Robert Burns (1785/1983) put it, "The best laid schemes o' mice and men gang aft agley." (pp. 268–269). As described later, faculty resistance threatened to derail the project. This called for a reconsideration of planning and renegotiation of the conditions of support to allow the study to progress.

Although faculty fully understand research issues, research on co-op itself may carry little interest for them. Because co-op is not considered an academic discipline, it is marginalized as an area of faculty research in many institutions. Also, some faculty are reluctant to grant access to their classes for the purpose of in-class observations. Others are concerned about strangers taking notes as they teach. This is especially the case during times when teaching evaluations are being conducted.

Faculty may also resist requests for interview because of time constraints. If a study is to succeed, faculty reluctance must be overcome.

Decision Point: Ensuring Faculty Buy-in

When I began the study, co-op coordinators acted as liaison for me with faculty, negotiating access for in-class observations and the survey. After each observation, I introduced myself to the instructor and requested an informal interview. This coordinator-led approach was reasonably successful for the first three classes I observed. When I arrived to observe the fourth class, however, the instructor did not wish me to observe his class, nor would he agree to an interview. This caught me by surprise, and put the future of the study in jeopardy.

I convened a meeting of the co-op coordinators and two supportive faculty members to find a way around this dilemma. We decided to combine in-class observation and the student survey into one visit, rather than two. This proved both efficient and effective during the remainder of the study. We also decided that, in each program, the co-op coordinators would introduce me to faculty ahead of time, allowing me to describe the study and have faculty buy into it. That way, when I subsequently arrived at a selected class, the instructor knew who I was and why I was there. I was able to conduct my observations and the instructor would turn the class over to me for the last 20 minutes, to allow me to administer the survey.

An unintended benefit of this arrangement was that I could engage instructors in conversation while the students completed the survey questionnaires. These initial classroom conversations inevitably led to offers to continue after the class was dismissed, or at a later scheduled time. This strategy alleviated the earlier problem of getting faculty to commit time for interviews and relying on co-op coordinators to approach faculty on my behalf. I could now schedule faculty interviews directly, and faculty were more relaxed and forthcoming in responding to questions. These interviews engaged faculty interest in my study, and a number followed up with me later, to find out how the study was progressing, and offer further assistance.

In the next section I present a selection of the findings of my study. I begin with a brief presentation of the quantitative results to provide an overview of the students enrolled in co-op programs. I then selectively use students' quotes to present qualitative results on learning and context.

SURVEY RESULTS

Of the 1,012 students surveyed, 73% ($n = 737$) were co-op students. Unless otherwise stated, the following results relate only to the co-op students in the sample. Of these, 64% were male and 36% female. Only one program—Engineering—shows a marked gender disparity, with considerably more males than females in the sample. One-fourth of the students (26%) are between 18 and 20 years of age; a further 36% are 21 to 22, and 24% are 23 to 24 years of age. A smaller number of students (14%) are 25 years or older. There was neither a marked difference between the ages of male and female students, nor in the distribution of ages across programs.

An approximation of co-op students' socioeconomic status can be inferred from parents' combined occupations. More than two thirds (69%) of respondents classified fathers' occupations into four broad categories: professional (38%), senior management (14%), craft and trades workers (9%), and technician (8%). The top four occupational classifications for mothers—accounting for 70% of the total—included: professional (34%), service and sales (14%), clerical (14%), and never employed (8%).

On average, more than one half of co-op students in the study had some form of paid work experience prior to entering university. Two thirds of Geography (66%) and Engineering students (65%), and one half of Business students (56%) worked between high school and university. Less than one half of Chemistry students (43%) had work experience when they enrolled in university. Few co-op students, however, had worked in areas related to their current field of study between high school and university. The prime motivators for undertaking employment were to make money for tuition and to gain work experience.

Students pursued co-op for a variety of individual reasons. Each initially approached higher education with a learning orientation, structured around academic, personal, vocational, or social reasons that ultimately motivated them to seek this type of education. These reasons were not made explicit in the survey data but become apparent through student interviews. Because this chapter focuses on the effects of context on learning, and thus process and meaning, the majority of findings reported in the remainder of the chapter are drawn from the qualitative results of the study.

Student Interviews: Learning and Context

Because co-op students alternate between the work term and the classroom, they draw on their experiences in both contexts to develop their perceptions of learning and work. The boundaries between the two contexts are permeable; we can not assign learning to one camp and work to another. However, certain activities can be more clearly presented if we maintain an analytic distinction, at least initially. For example, the workplace is where co-op students have an opportunity to develop skills and experience in the practical application of theories they may have only learned about in the classroom, while learning how to be a professional in their field. Meanwhile, the university combines academic preparation with work experience and professional training in an attempt to ensure the relevance of classroom education to real-world employment. In presenting the findings, I frame co-op students' experience in the academic context as learning *for* the workplace, and their experience on the co-op work-term as learning *in* the workplace.

Co-op students distinguish between learning from books and learning through hands-on application. What I call the *co-op effect* is the perception that learning takes place as a result of the activities of practical application in the workplace, rather than through the activities of the classroom. What goes on in the classroom, students suggest, is not learning but study, or the learning about a discipline. For co-op students, classroom learning does not take on meaning until there is an opportunity for practical application. This leads to student concerns about the potential for transferring classroom learning from one context to another, more practical one. Although they learn disciplinary skills in the academic context, these skills are usually transitional to workplace applications, not reflective of them. In other words, students consider disciplinary skills learned in the academic context as skills developed *for* the workplace and skills learned *in* the workplace as grounded in practice and, therefore, a way to strengthen understanding of the range of potential applications.

Learning in the Workplace Context.   To understand how co-op students develop skills and expertise in the workplace, we must first acknowledge that workplace cultures embed particular values. There is increasing evidence that learning, and motivation for learning, are mediated by activities embedded in a context that makes sense and matters to the learner (Billet, 1999; Engeström, 1994; Grosjean, 1996; Grosjean, 2003). Co-op students describe entering the workplace with little or no specific knowledge and gradually becoming more expert as they become familiar with, and actively use, the work setting. The specific social, symbolic, technical, and material resources available in the workplace enable co-op students to complete assigned tasks with increasing success (Grosjean, 2000; Scribner, 1984). Therefore, the environment is not just the context in which a problem is embedded but is an active component of problem solving.

Whereas approximately one fourth of students interviewed spoke of the importance of being able to practice in the workplace what they previously learned in class, more than one half spoke of the impact that learning in the workplace had on their academic performance. A third-year female engineering student described learning skills in one work term that "actually helped [her] in a subsequent work term." Her academic courses did not help her on the job, but "skills learned on the job helped her once she returned to the classroom" [CSP13].[2] This emphasis puts learning flows in reverse, with workplace learning providing students with a better understanding of their academic coursework.

---

[2]Alpha-numeric codes are used in this chapter to identify study participants. This ensures that participants' identity is not revealed.

You learn a lot more on the job because you can see how it ties in so many different ways to what you are learning. And that is better. In class we might learn a particular concept A, whereas in the work place we learned B, C, and D. But they tie into A! But we never knew that they tied in until we did it. So yeah, I think you learn more in the workplace. And, you come back with skills that you wouldn't have learned otherwise. [CSP31]

I think it's really good that you get paid to go and learn, and to go and do all this stuff, and really, you are still a student. And you don't really know what you're doing yet, but I found that things I learned on my work term were really helpful when I came back to university and started taking more courses. [CSP12]

A majority of students contend that learning skills in the milieu of workplace practice leads to a deeper understanding than can be obtained in the classroom.

When you do it from an application standpoint, you're curious as to "Hey, what happened here?" Because you don't know what's happening, you have to basically think about what was going on, and you learn a lot more in the workplace when you're doing the problem solving, than when someone in the classroom just tells you what's going to happen. [CSP26]

Going through almost any academic program without having to apply the knowledge, you don't really know what it pertains to. It doesn't matter what you learn, unless you use it. It has no bearing on your own personal life if you don't have to use that knowledge. [CSP31]

Co-op students assign higher importance to learning in the workplace than in the classroom. During the interviews, when asked "what does learning mean to you?," most students immediately began discussing what they had learned in the workplace, rather than the classroom. When pressed about learning through coursework, they largely restricted their responses to brief discussions about whether instructors were good or bad. Effort was required to get them to talk about their classroom learning. In contrast, they were enthusiastic about discussing workplace learning and about how the experience would help them in their future professions.

When co-op students arrive at a workplace to begin a work term, they enter a community of practice. Membership in a community of practice requires co-op students to undergo a process of enculturation into the professional environment. Learning and skill development take place during this process. It is through interactions in the workplace and participation in the activities that make up a profession that students begin to adopt the characteristics of its members, and start to develop a professional persona.

It comes down to the way you carry yourself more than anything. And that is something that I learned on the work terms. [CSP44]

It was incredible learning on my last work term, just working with them as a co-op student. We took part in everything. We were shown how to do stuff and learned on our own. We took part in all the group meetings, and it made us feel like real engineers. [CSP13]

In the workplace students are encouraged to think like a professional and to see their role as one of becoming a junior professional rather than a co-op student. Becoming a professional requires the development of effective interpersonal skills.

> In a professional type job, you interact with a lot of people and a lot of different personalities, and you have to learn how to deal with those personalities and how to get around that. It is something that you don't really get much of in school. [CSP15]

> Just being aware of what I should be learning and being aware of what things I want to take away from the whole process. I'm more conscious of what I'm doing when I'm in a workplace, because each one is different. A lot of different things, like being able to get along with other people, meeting deadlines, learning from other people, or just being in a place where you can learn from using the equipment, all of those things are inherent to the professional workplace. [CSP31]

In the workplace, as students are learning disciplinary skills, they are also learning to be members of a situated community (Lave & Wenger, 1991), while being disciplined as members of a profession (Foucault, 1977). In this way, co-op students learn not only content knowledge but also disciplinary norms, expectations, and standards in a particular area.

The learning that happens in the workplace seems to possess a durable, lasting quality. The activity involved in practical application in the workplace affects how students remember, and subsequently recall the procedure when required.

> When I learn something in the workplace I remember it. Once I have a chance to use it, it just makes sense. I could go back to the same job that I did four years ago and still remember how to do all the basics. I may be a bit rusty, but I will remember it, whereas if I was to go back and try to recite a formula I learned in first year, no way! [CSP31]

> There are a lot of times where we will look at a concept in one of my classes and I think I understand it at the time, but I can't remember it later. Whereas on my work term, if we work on that concept, and I can see how it applies, it sticks. I will remember that forever. [CSP45]

Students' descriptions of their activities in the workplace indicate that learning in the richly contextualized environment of the workplace is different for co-op students than the learning that happens in the academic context of the classroom. Students consider the environment of the workplace as more than just an alternative context for learning. To them it is a more dynamic and robust site of learning. On the other hand they see the learning in the classroom as disembedded from the context of professional practice.

Learning in the Academic Context.   Classrooms are sites where students learn standards of disciplinary practice while being disciplined into the role of university student (Biggs, 1987; Entwistle, 1996). That is not to say that disciplinary skills are not learned in the academic context. But despite attempts to simulate the professional context in the classroom, disciplinary practices and discourse learned there will not be those of the workplace. As student comments make evident, learning workplace procedures in the classroom does not seem real ("It's still just in a book. It's not really real," and "I just keep thinking it is school, it isn't real") and, therefore, the procedures aren't taken seriously. The academic context within which the students are taught certain disciplinary procedures is perceived to be distinctly different from the professional context to which co-op students aspire. Social roles and communicative practices are also perceived as distinctly different in academic and workplace settings.

Whether in the workplace or the classroom, learning and skill development are mediated by learning strategies. In the classroom, time and competitive pressures leads some students to adopt a learning strategy that addresses the immediate needs of reproducing facts on a test (surface-level learning) rather than fostering understanding (deep-level learning). Students perceive that the academic assessment and reward system in the classroom favor those with well-developed memorization skills, rather than well-developed understanding. It is easy for students to shift from a deep to a surface-level learning strategy to accommodate perceived assessment objectives, but this shift is often difficult in reverse (Engeström, 1994). Evidence indicates that some co-op students develop a compromise strategy or *strategic approach* by finding a middle ground (Grosjean, 1999a, 2001). In other words, in some courses students adopt a surface-level strategy because assessment is based on accurately reproduced facts, and in others students use a deep approach where assessment encourages the demonstration of understanding.

Ramsden and Entwistle (1981) indicated how perceptions of the methods of assessment used to evaluate progress in academic courses can influence students' attitudes and approaches to learning. When I asked students what was the primary objective of their coursework they invariably answered that the objective was to get good grades. Therefore, what appears important to students in the academic context is not necessarily the development of an in-depth understanding of the foundations of a discipline. Rather it is the accumulation of a sufficiently high GPA that can be parlayed into future co-op opportunities. Faculty members confirm that students with high GPAs find the co-op program somewhat easier, suggesting that what finally matters to both instructors and students is less the academic work undertaken in the classroom, than the grade assigned to the work.

Differences in the academic and workplace contexts can not easily be resolved. With a mandate to assist the professionalization of students by allowing them to benefit from the synergy of dual learning contexts, co-op education carries built-in conflicts between the workplace and the classroom. For example, in the classroom, co-op students demonstrate their learning of theoretical principles by appropriate reproduction on assignments such as tests; in the workplace, knowledge is demonstrated through proficient practice. Co-op, however, uses two sets of criteria for assessing student achievement and progress. One set is designed to assess understanding through reproduction of the principles of practice (academic grades); the other assesses understanding through demonstrated proficiency in practice (employer's evaluation). Although both methods of assessment are employed in co-op, only one carries academic credit.

Students in co-op programs at Coast University receive no academic credit for completion of work terms but must successfully complete a prescribed number of discipline-specific work terms in order to graduate with the co-op designation. Successful completion of work terms is judged by the quality of the student's work-term report and an employer evaluation. Academic credit, however, is reserved for those activities that take place in the classroom and can be assessed using traditional academic criteria. Although attempts are made to extend the academic context into the workplace through the development of learning objectives for work terms, the academy still rewards cognitive understanding over the development of procedural knowledge and practical skills. It seems at odds with itself and with the mainstream educational curriculum by using differing evaluation criteria.

Summary
- The context in which a learning activity takes place is crucial to the way co-op students develop knowledge and skills.
- The structured rotation between classroom and workplace enables co-op students to engage in continuous, contextualized learning.
- Obtaining support and endorsement (buy-in) for the study from individuals at all levels of the institution is a core requirement for a successful study.
- Co-op work terms produce a *co-op effect* that shapes students' perceptions of learning and work and profoundly impacts their experience of the co-op program.
- The power of the academic context, particularly through setting and assessment of academic progress, influences co-op students attitudes and approaches to learning.

ANNOTATED BIBLIOGRAPHY

Engeström, Y. (1994). *Training for change: New approach to instruction and learning in working life*. Geneva: International Labor Office. This highly readable book (which easily doubles as a training manual) provides insights into contextualized learning. It helped shape my thinking about the ways in which learning, and motivation for learning, are mediated by activities embedded in a context that makes sense to the learner. It also helped me understand how the structured alternation between classroom and workplace in co-op results in continuous contextualized learning.

Marton, F., Hounsell, D., & Entwistle, N., (1997). *The experience of learning.* Edinburgh: Scottish Academic Press. This is a book I refer to often. Unlike some other edited collections, this book has a strong focus—research on student learning in higher education. The 15 chapters report on a series of related studies of the way students learn in higher education. Each is written around a research focus developed by Ference Marton called *phenomenography*. Findings are drawn from the systematic presentation of extracts from interview transcripts and presented in such a way that the learners appear to be speaking directly to the reader about their experiences.

Wenger, E. (1998). *Communities of practice: Learning, meaning, and identity.* Cambridge: Cambridge University Press. Following an earlier collaboration with Jean Lave on *Situated Learning* (1991), Étienne Wenger has gone on to develop a social theory of learning in communities of practice. Learning is the engine of practice, he says, and practice is the history of that learning. The process of engaging in practice involves both acting and knowing. In other words, manual activity is not carried out in the absence of mental activity. This book was a valuable resource in shaping my thinking about the importance of the situations in which learning takes place.

Rogoff, B. (1990). *Apprenticeship in thinking: Cognitive development in social context.* New York: Oxford University Press. A comprehensive work on the situated nature of learning that I found useful. Although based on research of cognition in children, the concepts translate well to adult learning, particularly in relation to the development of knowledge as a product of the activity and situations in which it is produced. Barbara Rogoff pointed out the role of peer interaction in enhancing, motivating, and channeling the choice of activities in learning situations. The social roots of cognition are stressed, and the interaction between mind and behavior becomes key. Viewed in this way, the basic unit of analysis shifts from the individual to the active participation of people in socially constituted practices.

Sharma, L. A., Mannell, R. C., & Rowe, P. M. (1995). The relation between education-related work experiences and career expectations. *Journal of Cooperative Education, XXX* (3), 39–47. This work assisted my thinking about the importance and location of intrinsic and extrinsic rewards in the formation of career expectations and job outcomes of co-op participants. It points out the relevancy of the work experience component of co-op and how expectations for support and encouragement from the work organization impact students' career decisions.

Biggs, J. B. (1987). *Student approaches to learning and studying.* Melbourne: Australian Council for Educational Research. This work is part of a growing body of evidence that attests to the effect of context on learning in the university classroom. Biggs shows how a rigid system of rules and norms enforces power differentials in the classroom, leaving students with little opportunity to influence the development of, or make changes to, the curriculum. Denied options, many students simply strive for the academic grades that constitute the currency of the university.

REFERENCES

Ausubel, D. P., Novak, J. S., & Hanesian, H. (1978). *Educational psychology: A cognitive view.* New York, NY, USA: Holt, Rinehart, & Winston.

Becher, T. (1989). *Academic tribes and territories: Intellectual enquiry and the culture of disciplines.* Milton Keynes, England: SRHE/Open University Press.

Biggs, J. B. (1987). *Student approaches to learning and studying.* Melbourne: Australian Council for Educational Research.

Billett, S. (1999). Guided learning at work. In D. Boud & J. Garrick (Eds.), *Understanding learning at work* (pp. 151–164). London Routledge.

Brown, J. S., Collins, A., & Duguid, P. (1989). Situated cognition and culture of learning. *Educational Researcher, 18*(1), 32–42.

Brown, S. (1976). *Cooperative education and career education: A comparative study of alumni.* Boston: Northeastern University, Cooperative Education Research Center.

Burns, R. (1983). To a mouse. In A. W. Allison, H. Barrows, C. R. Blake, A. J. Carr, A. M. Eastman, & H. M. English, Jr. (Eds.), *The Norton anthology of poetry* (pp. 268–269). London: Norton. (Original work published in 1785)

Business-Higher Education Forum (1997). Spanning the chasm: Corporate and academic cooperation to improve work-force participation. *NSEE Quarterly, 23*(3), 6–9.

Engeström, Y. (1994). *Training for change: New approach to instruction and learning in working life.* Geneva, Switzerland: International Labor Office.

Entwistle, H. (1996). Ideologies in adult education. In A. C. Tuijnman (Ed.), *International encyclopedia of adult education and training* (2nd ed., pp. 182–187). Oxford: Pergamon.

Fletcher, J. K. (1989). Student outcomes: What do we know and how do we know it? *Journal of Cooperative Education, XXVI*(1), 26–38.

Fletcher, J. K. (1990). Self-esteem and cooperative education: A theoretical framework. *Journal of Cooperative Education, XXVI*(1), 46–54

Foucault, M. (1977). *Discipline & punish: The birth of the prison.* (A. Sheridan, Trans., 2nd ed.). New York: Random House.

Grosjean, G. (1996, June). *Generalized specialists–specialized generalists: Education and the changing workplace.* In Proceedings of the Combined Conference, Canadian Association for the Study of Adult Education/Canadian Association of Adult Education, University of Manitoba, Winnipeg, Manitoba, Canada, pp. 149–156.

Grosjean, G. (1998). Education and work in a market-driven economy: Policy implications. *Learning Quarterly, 2*(1), 21–25.

Grosjean, G. (1999a). *Higher education and the economy: Enhancing articulation through co-op education.* Paper presented at the "What Skills Matter in the Economy?" Conference, Vancouver, British Columbia.

Grosjean, G. (1999b). *Experiential learning: Who benefits—who loses?* Paper presented at the Canadian Association for the study of Adult Education Conference, Sherbrooke, Quebec.

Grosjean, G. (2000). *Experiential capital and the knowledge economy: Implications for policy and practice.* Paper presented at the Western Research Network on Education and Training, 4th Annual Conference "Policy and Practice in Education and Training." University of British Columbia, Vancouver, Canada.

Grosjean, G. (2001). *The social organisation of learning: Educational provision, process and outcomes.* Paper presented at the Western Research Network on Education and Training, 5th Annual Conference, University of British Columbia, Vancouver, Canada.

Grosjean, G. (2003). Alternating education and training: Students' conceptions of learning in co-op. In H. G. Schuetze & R. Sweet (Eds.), *Integrating school and workplace learning in Canada: Principles and practice of alternation education.* Montreal: McGill-Queens University Press, pp. 175–196.

Kelle, U. (Ed.). (1995). *Computer-aided qualitative data analysis: Theories, methods and practice.* London: Sage.

Lave, J. (1991). Situated learning in communities of practice. In L. B. Resnick, J. M. Leaven, & S. D. Teasley (Eds.), *Perspectives on socially shared cognition* (pp. 63–82). Washington DC: American Psychological Association.

Lave, J., & Wenger, E. (1991). *Situated learning: Legitimate peripheral participation.* Cambridge, England: Cambridge University Press.

LeCompte, M. D., & Preissle, J. (1993). *Ethnography and qualitative design in education research* (2nd ed.). San Diego, CA: Academic Press.

Marton, F., & Säljö, R. (1976). On qualitative differences in learning: I. Outcome and Process. *British Journal of Educational Psychology, 4,* 4–11.

Marton, F., Hounsell, D., & Entwistle, N. (Eds.). (1997). *The experience of learning.* (2nd ed.). Edinburgh, Scotland: Scottish Academic Press.

Matson, L. C., & Matson, R. (1995). Changing times in higher education: An empirical look at cooperative education and liberal arts faculty. *Journal of Cooperative Education, XXXI*(1), 13–24.

Merriam, S. B. (1988). *Case study research in education: A qualitative approach.* San Francisco: Jossey-Bass.

Patton, M. Q. (1990). *Qualitative evaluation and research methods* (2nd ed.). Newbury Park, CA: Sage.

Petryszak, N., & Toby, A. (1989). *A comparative analysis of cooperative education and non-cooperative education graduates of Simon Fraser University.* Vancouver, Canada: Simon Fraser University. Unpublished manuscript.

Pittenger, K. (1993). The role of cooperative education in the career growth of engineering students. *Journal of Cooperative Education, XXVIII*(3), 21–29.

Ramsden, P., & Entwistle, N. J. (1981). Effects of academic departments on students approaches to studying. *British Journal of Educational Psychology, 51,* 368–383.

Rogoff, B. (1990). *Apprenticeship in thinking: Cognitive development in social context.* New York: Oxford University Press.

Rowe, P. M. (1992). A comparison of cooperative education graduates with two cohorts of regular graduates: Fellow entrants and fellow graduates. *Journal of Cooperative Education, XXVII*(3), 7–15.

Scribner, S. (1984). Studying working intelligence. In B. R. & J. Lave (Ed.), *Everyday cognition: Its development in social context* (pp. 9–40). Cambridge, MA: Harvard University Press.

Sharma, L. A., Mannell, R. C., & Rowe, P. M. (1995). The relationship between education-related work experiences and career expectations. *Journal of Cooperative Education, XXX*(3), 39–47.

Somers, G. (1995). The post-graduate pecuniary benefits of co-op participation: A review of the literature. *Journal of Cooperative Education, XXXI*(1), 25–41.

Stake, R. E. (1995). *The art of the case study research.* Thousand Oaks, CA: Sage.

Svensson, L. (1977). On qualitative differences in learning: III. Study, skill, and learning. *British Journal of Educational Psychology, 47,* 233–243.

Weitzman, E. A., & Miles, M. B. (1995). Computer programs for qualitative data analysis. Thousand Oaks, CA: Sage.

Wenger, E. (1998). *Communities of practice: Learning, meaning, and identity.* Cambridge: Cambridge University Press.

Wessels, W., & Pumphrey, G. (1995). The effects of cooperative education on job search time, quality of job placement and advancement. *Journal of Cooperative Education, XXXI*(1), 42–52.

Williams, W. M., Sternberg, R. J., Rashotte, C. A., & Wagner, R. K. (1993). Assessing the value of cooperative education. *Journal of Cooperative Education, XXVIII*(2), 32–55.

Wilson, J. W. (1988). Research in cooperative education. *Journal of Cooperative Education, XXIV*(2–3), 77–89.

Yin, R. K. (1994). Case study research: Design and methods. Thousand Oaks, CA: Sage.

4

Identifying Resources:
Ethics in Cooperative Education[1]

Frances Ricks
University of Victoria

Key questions addressed in this chapter:

☛ How can collaboration create research resources?

☛ How can action research be an effective cost saving approach?

☛ How much money does it take?

INTRODUCTION

Usually when we think of taking on new initiatives, we wonder how much is it going to cost. Sometimes we conclude that it will be too expensive or we don't have the time. This is particularly true when contemplating a research project within the academy. Faculty and professional employees are expected to get money for research and this expectation is often embedded in an attitude that research that is not funded is probably not worth doing, never mind reading. This chapter posits that research that is not funded can be a legitimate learning organization strategy (Senge, 1999) useful for decision making and planning.

Over the past 5 years I initiated and completed three research projects as learning organization strategies to provide useful information for decision making and planning at the University of Victoria in Victoria, British Columbia. All three pro-

---

[1]This study was conducted at the University of Victoria and reported at the CEA National Conference in Washington D.C. The research collaborators included: Audrey McFarlane, Engineering, Anne Field, Human and Social Development graduate student, and Frances Ricks, School of Child and Youth Care.

53

jects used action research approaches resulting in decision making that altered programs or initiatives within the University.

In this chapter the planning and implementation steps of one of these initiatives, A Study in Ethics in Cooperative Education, is described, and areas where time and money can be saved are made explicit. The research project was initiated by a cooperative education coordinator and researcher who were concerned about the lack of ethics education for cooperative education students, faculty, staff, and work site supervisors. Key funding or resource questions are revealed in conversation boxes throughout the reporting of the study.

First, here is a word about action research as a cost saving strategy. Action research has been known as a useful research approach within organizations and communities that want to make informed change. It has been around since the early 1950s when professionals were experimenting with community-based services and has much in common with research practitioner inquiry, action science and community development (Anderson, Herr, & Nihlen, 1994; Kemmis & McTaggart, 1988; Reason, 1988). Its intellectual foundations are tied to Moreno (1956), Freire (1974), and the critical theory associated with Habermas (1979) and the Frankfurt school. The approach is often used in organizations and communities because of its practical and theoretical outcomes. It pursues inquiry in a way that provides conditions for taking action, promoting change and the formation of a sense of community.

Decision Point: Creating Partnerships in Action Research

M: How about doing a research project on ethics in cooperative education? Let's get some interested cooperative education people together and discuss our mutual concerns and how we might work together. You and I both know that we need to prepare students to deal with ethical situations in work placements.

G: Great idea. Where would we get the time and money?

M: Well, I don't think it would cost much if we agreed to work together and shared the work. I have a graduate student who would like the research experience and has an interest in the topic. How about the Cooperative Education Director, another coordinator, the graduate student and the two of us?

The action research approach ensures rigorous empirical and reflective research processes, engages people who have been traditionally called *subjects* as active participants in the research process, and results in practical outcomes related to the lives or work of the participants and their communities (Dick, 1996; Stringer, 1999). Most importantly, it allows for participation from the inside and has great potential for being cost saving. As members of the community participate from beginning to end, they contribute their expertise and time leaving little or nothing to be done by hired help.

Decision Point: Knowing What You Want to Know

M: My initial thinking was that we examine perceptions and experiences of ethical dilemmas within cooperative education programs in order to understand awareness of ethical dilemmas and strategies for handling them.

G: Yes. If we understood their perceptions and experiences of ethical dilemmas we could create an educational program that might be useful in our cooperative education orientation programs and training. I think students need to be prepared for dealing with ethical issues in their work placements.

M: Let's get some faculty members involved, perhaps faculty members who know about applied ethics. They may be interested in using the information for curriculum planning or as part of their own research.

In action research the researcher acts as a facilitator, taking the community partners through a process of identifying the research questions, what can be taken as evidence to answer those questions, how to collect the information, what the information means, and make recommendations for future practice (Patton, 1997). This process helps to ensure that the learning that takes place is used for decision making and planning. This strategy is in keeping with learning-organization theory (Senge, 1999) that posits that organizations are responsible for monitoring their own learning by conducting on-site research and using it for their own learning and planning. It is also in keeping with participatory research that not only saves money but brings the community together around a common goal of researching problems in order to cocreate change (Stringer, 1999).

This study on ethics in cooperative education is an action research initiative. Our intent was to create a rigorous and reflective research process at no or little cost except for donated time or goods in kind. The author acted as the facilitator for a university working committee. This committee met throughout the study in order to determine the research design and questions, the method for the collection of information, and how to code the information and make meaning of it. The information and recommendations were made available to departments within the university for their consideration, decisions and action. One example of how faculty used the study was to establish workshops on professional ethics within a professional school. The project cost a total of $2,000 for the graduate student, all other costs were taken care of through donated time or goods in kind. The sidebar comments presented within the research report demonstrate the action research process whereas the research report presents the research process and results. Our purpose is to show that action research projects not only offer a creative solution to addressing organizational issues, they also offer an inexpensive solution to conducting research when you do not think you have the time or money to do it alone.

A STUDY OF ETHICS IN COOPERATIVE EDUCATION

We live in a time in which the ability to know truth has been replaced by a gnawing suspicion that the truth may be nothing more than our beliefs about what is true (Rorty, 1989). We are moving away from absolutes, toward thinking and feeling that nothing is assured because everything is constructed (Blum, 1994). Political correctness, critical theories, tolerance, and inclusion of diversity are stretching us to reformulate right from wrong in ways that are more tolerant and inclusive. Although there are vestiges of absolutes in religions and bureaucracy, and points of view such as political correctness, we currently find ourselves struggling to determine what is our best choice given all the circumstances.

An important consequence of these changing times is that we can no longer rely absolutely on codes of ethics or standards of practice to guide us in determining right from wrong in our professional and work settings (Blum, 1994). Codes of ethics have historically been written as rulebooks. However, more recent codes are being written to guide the moral thinker in making ethical decisions. Ethical decisions are framed as those in which one chooses one principle over another (Demarco, 1997; Kidder, 1996; Lantz, 2000) in order to do the least harm or to do the most good. Recent examples of principle-driven codes in Canada include the Canadian Nursing Code of Ethics, and the Canadian Psychological Association Code of Ethics, to mention a few.

Although codes are now presented as guidelines, and standards of practice are presented as examples of "best practice," when professional associations receive complaints about professional misconduct, associations do act and sometimes they act harshly. Therefore, it is important that individuals are capable of making mindful professional and ethical decisions that result in best choices while recognizing that solutions are not as absolute as might have been previously thought.

TEACHING ETHICS

Often professions do not teach ethics in the classroom. For example, in a survey of Child and Youth Care programs in post secondary education institutions in Canada (Ricks & Garfat, 1998), only 12% of the programs required a course on ethics. More typically these professional schools teach ethics as a subcomponent of other courses (e.g., practice courses).

A review of the literature on teaching ethics across allied health professions revealed the prevalence of a case approach. Case approaches usually involve teaching codes of ethics and standards of practice and having the learner practice using these guidelines to resolve hypothetical situations. Notably there is no evidence that such teaching has any impact on practice (Baldick, 1980; Delany & Socell, 1982; Eberlein, 1987; Gawthrop, 1990; Granum & Erickson, 1976; Handelsman, 1986; McGovem, 1988; Morrison & Teta, 1979; Rhodes, 1986; Warwick, 1980). In our view, this traditional teaching strategy is outcome oriented rather than process oriented. In other words, the focus is on getting the learner to come up with the right answer rather than teaching metacognition processes that focus on attending to unraveling the complexities of ethical dilemmas.

Evidence suggests that process-teaching strategies influence cognitive processes that in turn, impact on practice (Blum, 1994; Elsdon, 1998; Garfat & Ricks, 1995; Granum & Erickson, 1976; Howard, 1986; Schon, 1983, 1987). In light of this evidence we suggest that new ways need to be created for teaching ethical practice and ethical decision making. Further, we suggest that cooperative education programs provide opportunities for teaching ethical decision making. Cooperative education is in a good position to teach ethical reasoning across different work sites and from different professional perspectives. Before taking this leap into uncharted waters however, it seems advisable to inquire about the current "ethical scene" in cooperative education programs.

Decision Point: Sharing the Work Saves Money

M: Why not survey all the partners in cooperative education? Ask the students, coordinators, work site supervisors and faculty what they experience as ethical dilemmas and how they handle them?

G: You and I could collaborate on the design and how to collect the data!.

M: I have friends in cooperative education around the Province who could help us get participants within their institution. I can find a graduate research student who could collect and collate the data and the committee could interpret the data. You and I could write it up and present it at the next co-operative education conference. This would be a commitment of our time and we could share the nominal expenses that might be involved.

G: I could get a group of students that are in an intern program. It might be interesting to see if students in professional schools are more aware of ethical situations and have a better sense of what to do especially if they have been introduced to ethics in their coursework. This may give us some ideas of what kinds of education and training might be beneficial to cooperative education students that are not in professional programs.

METHODOLOGY

This research surveyed cooperative education faculty, coordinators, students, and work site supervisors, and students in an intern program on their experiences of ethical dilemmas in postsecondary education. Ethical dilemmas were defined as situations where there are two or more choices in which conflicting values are embedded. The choices may be based on conflicts between defined rules or standards and personal values, personal and professional rules or standards, two sets of professional values or two sets of personal values. They are contextual situations in which individuals identify conflicting values and resolve the conflict for themselves through value clarification in this situation. Codes of ethics can not and do not attempt to anticipate and define all the values that might be in conflict; nor do they determine which value should take precedence in particular circumstances. Previous research has shown that practitioners sometimes feel that they are in an ethical dilemma when in fact they are experiencing a practice issue (Ricks, 1997). Practice issues can be solved by knowledge of professional guidelines such as antiharassment guidelines.

Rather than impose our definitions of ethical dilemmas on participants, we used their perceptions and experiences. We assumed that how ethical dilemmas were experienced offers evidence of participants' awareness of such dilemmas. It was anticipated that the frequency and nature of ethical dilemmas experienced within cooperative education and an intern program outside cooperative education would be informative for creating useful educational strategies for these programs.

Procedures

Once we received permission from the University of Victoria's Human Subjects Committee to proceed with the study, universities and colleges in British Columbia that offered cooperative education programs and an intern program at the University of Victoria were approached to participate in the study. An onsite person at each institution was asked to assist in the collection of the data. The cooperative education programs were asked to recruit 10 persons in each category: faculty, cooperative education coordinators, students, and work site supervisors. Only students were surveyed in the intern program to determine whether ethics teaching affected ethical dilemma awareness. Survey data was collected using a written questionnaire that provided anonymity for participants.

The graduate student entered the survey data onto a spreadsheet using an Excel package. The graduate student, the cooperative education coordinator, and the researcher read and coded the responses that were then interpreted and taken to the committee for corroboration and additional interpretation.

Decision Point: Sharing the Work Generates Money

M: Now that we have the questionnaires back, let's get Susan to input the data and bring us the collated data. We could take an initial stab at generating themes and have the committee confirm or identify other themes that represent the dilemmas, practice issues and the critical issues for teaching ethics in cooperative education.

G: I think that we could get matching money from the Dean of Graduate Studies since Susan is a graduate student. I would be willing to put a $1,000 toward that from my budget.

Participants

Table 4.1 presents demographic information on survey participants. Of the 103 participants in the study there were 13 faculty, 8 coordinators, 22 work site supervisors, 34 cooperative education students, and 26 intern students, representing two universities and two colleges. The majority of students ($n = 39$) were aged 18 to 25; the next largest group ($n = 17$) were 26 to 35 years of age, with the remainder ($n = 4$) older than 36 years. Twenty one faculty, coordinators, and work site supervisors were in the two lower age categories (18–25 and 36–45), and 22 were in the two higher age categories (46–55 and 56–65). All participants were either involved in cooperative education or in the intern program although two faculty and two work site supervisors reported no direct involvement in work terms or practicums with students. Nine students reported not being involved in work terms or practicum at the time of the survey.

TABLE 4.1

Demographics of Respondents

	Faculty (n = 13)	Coordinators (n = 8)	Work Site Supervisors (n = 22)	Co-op Students (n = 34)	Intern Students (n = 26)
Gender					
Males	9	3	11	14	4
Females	3	5	11	19	22
Did not Designate	1			1	
Ages					
18–25			1	20	19
26–35		3	4	11	6
36–45	2	3	8	2	1
46–55	4		6	1	
56–65	6	2	3		
Did not Designate	1				
Institution					
University	5	4		20	26
College	8	4		14	
Involved in co-op work term/ practicum					
Yes	11	8	20	29	22
No	2		2	5	4

FINDINGS

When participants were asked whether they experienced ethical dilemmas in their practice 58% ($n = 60$) indicated yes and the other 42% ($n = 43$) indicated no. The data suggest that faculty (61%) and coordinators (75%) experience ethical dilemmas more often than work site supervisors (27%) and cooperative education students (53%). Eighty-five percent of the intern students reported ethical dilemmas. This was notably higher than 53% of the cooperative education students.

It was not always apparent from the descriptions whether participants were experiencing a practice issue or an ethical dilemma. Table 4.2 reports our analysis of their descriptions in terms of definitions of ethical dilemmas versus practice issues as defined for our study. Practice issues represent issues that can be solved by knowing what to do as identified by industry or professional practice standards and guidelines. Although not knowing what to do may feel like a dilemma there is some knowledge and known standard of practice about what to do in order to resolve the practice issue. Ethical dilemmas, on the other hand, involve situations in which there are conflicting values. As a result, no matter which choice is made, one is faced with the dilemma of knowing that one must make a choice of one value over the other in order to resolve the conflict (Kidder, 1996).

Table 4.3 indicates the content or substantive issues of the reported incidents. Ethical dilemmas were expressed as value conflicts within personal relationships in the professional context (e.g., having to interview and hire or not hire a friend's son or daughter); employer practices and ethics (e.g., being instructed to over-report hours or on how to handle warranty); work place requirements and practices (e.g., going through an interview knowing there is a preferred candidate); interpersonal conflicts and difficulties (e.g., people complaining and back biting); student practices and ethics (e.g., whether to truthfully report your work history on an application); and noncompliance with policy (e.g., making exceptions to # hours per work site in order to get funding). Ethical concerns varied according to groups: faculty, coordinators, and work site supervisors primarily indicated concern over noncompliance to policies whereas students mostly expressed concerned about employer and workplace practices and ethics.

TABLE 4.2
Reported Ethical Dilemmas and Practice Issues

	Faculty ($n = 12$)	Coordinators ($n = 12$)	Work Site Supervisors ($n = 14$)	Co-op Students ($n = 35$)	Intern Students ($n = 32$)
Ethical dilemmas ($n = 47$, 45%)	7 (58%)	6 (50%)	5 (36%)	14 (40%)	15 (48%)
Practice issues ($n = 58$, 55%)	5 (42%)	6 (50%)	9 (64%)	21 (60%)	17 (52%)

TABLE 4.3
Respondents' Theme for Reported Ethical Dilemma and Practice Issues

Ethical Dilemma Themes	Faculty (n = 12)	Coordinators (n = 12)	Work Site Supervisors (n = 14)	Co-op Students (n = 35)	Intern Students (n = 32)
Personal relationship in professional context	3 (25%)		2 (14%)		
Employer practices and ethics issues	1 (8%)	4 (33%)	3 (21%)	17 (49%)	14 (44%)
Workplace requirements and practices	2 (17%)		1 (7%)	6 (17%)	4 (13%)
Interpersonal conflicts and difficulties		1 (8%)	2 (14%)	8 (23%	1 (7%)
Student practices and Ethics		1 (8%)	2 (14%)	4 (11%)	13 (41%)
Noncompliance to policy	6 (50%)	6 (50%)	4 (29%)		

The nature of making exceptions to policy varied depending on the position held within cooperative education contexts. For example, as stated by one faculty member:

> Some students request an exception to complete their program studies on a work term. However, unless the situation is the result of medical events or course scheduling or cancellation or other constraints brought on by the institution, the request is supposed to be denied. Other students need their course load adjusted across terms to complete an academic term. In some cases this meets the best interest of the student and their circumstances and is of little consequence to the institution.

Clearly the faculty member is in a no-win situation. If the student is accommodated the policy will be violated. If the policy is enforced, the student's interests are not looked after. This represents a value conflict of the best interest of the individual student versus being fair to other students who follow the policy.

In terms of work site issues students encountered the following kind of dilemmas:

1. I was working for a company whose idea of customer service and warranty differed from my own. I was the only technician in a computer store in charge of dealing with customers, repairing computers, and deciding if the work done fell under warranty or not. There was constant pressure to charge for work that was under warranty and to sell replacement components beyond the customer's needs. My resolution was that I would deal with the customers when

their bill was fair, and when it was not, refer it to my supervisor who would charge the customer and deal with their concerns regarding warranty.

2. My work site was removed from the company's place of business. In my first week, the senior person on site, a regular employee of the company, recorded a large amount of hours for himself and myself that neither of us had worked. When I pointed this out to the other employee I was told not to worry about it. I crossed out the hours given to me but was left with the dilemma of what to do about the other employee. I did nothing for the following reasons: (a) Crossing out my hours would hopefully draw attention to the day. I trusted someone would question why there was only one person on site those days and why someone was working on days they shouldn't be; (b) I could not prove this person didn't work those days; (c) Because of the individual's position and ties I sincerely believe he was testing my personal integrity; (d) I was afraid of making waves.

In the first case, the student thinks he is taking responsibility for doing the right thing. However, the student may be in violation of warranty policy when he knowingly refers warranty issues to his supervisor. He knows the supervisor will charge for work covered under warranty and might oversell the customer beyond the customer's need. The student has determined that he will do the right thing and will let someone else do the wrong thing. This example raises the issue of how not taking action represents an ethical stance. In the second situation the student has a clear idea of the conflicts for himself but is unwilling to tackle the situation directly. The student is hoping that his or her obtuse actions will result in some kind of inquiry and that justice will be done.

Decision Point: Saving Money by Collective Meaning Making

M: Wow, look at these differences of experiences in terms of reporting ethical dilemmas and practice issues. I can't believe work site supervisors say they are not experiencing ethical dilemmas but go on to report incidents that clearly involve value conflicts. What do you think that means?

G: I don't know. Let's get our group together and go over the data. I am particularly curious about what they think the teaching opportunities are implied by these perceptions of ethical dilemmas.

ANALYSIS OF TEACHING OPPORTUNITIES FOR COOPERATIVE EDUCATION

The committee derived what they learned from these incidents as well as what would inform the teaching of ethics within cooperative education. Committee members considered what the cooperative education participants needed to know in order to handle the ethical dilemmas or professional practice issues and identified

two learning needs: knowledge that relates to professional standards of good practice and knowledge and skills that relate to the process of unraveling the situation in
order to gain a new perspective and make the best choice under the circumstances.

Professional Standards

An examination of the ethical dilemmas and practice issues reported by co-operative education participants (see Table 4.3) was considered in terms of teaching professional standards and best practices. Practice issues surfaced around how to
accommodate exceptions to policy, what constitutes appropriate practice, and
management of interpersonal conflicts.

There can be two kinds of knowledge lacking in best practice issues. One might
not know what the best practice is or one might not know how to, or have the skills
required to, conduct the best practice. For example, accommodation of exception
to policy issues requires knowledge of work place policies and human-rights legisla-
tion and one simply needs to know what they are.

An example of accommodation of exceptions to policy may help to clarify the nature of missing knowledge:

> A student sought a refund after finding out there was no work placement for him. He
> had participated in the placement process and the co-op coordinator was reluctant
> to refund his fees. Finally the student went to the registrar and head of the depart-
> ment and was awarded the refund.

In this example, faculty, students, work site supervisors and coordinators need to
know the policies regarding policy exceptions for fee refunds as well as the procedures for appeal. It may be that individuals are unaware of the standards, codes, or
policies, or that appropriate standards, codes, or policies do not exist. Second to
knowing the refund policy, the student needs to be aware of her rights and have the
capacity and capability to challenge the cooperative education coordinator by going further with the challenge. Such a process is not for the faint of heart and requires diplomatic and negotiation skills.

Here are some examples of practice issues exemplifying a violation of best practice standards:

> A faculty member trains students to remediate environmental damage caused by an
> employer's normal work activities. The faculty does not confront the employer and
> has resolved that the damage is already being done. The faculty member argues that
> training students to remediate the damage is a positive initiative even when it does
> not contribute to making the "damage-causing activity" more acceptable.

> A student reported that a customer wanted a specific video card for the PC. The stu-
> dent ordered the part because he knew they did not have a part that would work in
> this case. The purchasing manager who wanted to upsell the customer to a currently

stocked item over ruled the student. The purchasing manager changed the order without the customer's consent. Upon the customers return the manager told the customer it would be weeks for the special card to arrive and would the customer like to purchase another card that would work with his application. The customer agreed but the card did not work. The card then had to be reordered. In the end it took 3 weeks for the customer to get this PC to work.

Cooperative education practitioners must be able to counsel students as to the required practice standards in their industry by being familiar with specific workplace standards. For example, in the first case the faculty member and coordinator were not modeling best practice. The faculty member and coordinator could have worked with the employer and students to explore solutions for the damage-causing activity. As a last resort the faculty member could have consulted with the cooperative education coordinator to determine whether this was an appropriate learning environment for cooperative education students.

In the second case a faculty member, work site supervisor, or cooperative education coordinator had the opportunity to assist the student to think through practices of upselling the customer. What are the industry standards regarding upselling and what options for challenging such practices exist within this and other organizations?

Some professional standard issues involved interpersonal conflicts. Those who reported interpersonal conflicts recognized the problem (i.e., harassment, favoritism, disagreements, and lack of civility); they simply reported not knowing how to deal with it.

> My co-worker had a disagreement with another co-worker. One worker was a cooperative education student, the other a summer student. They would not talk or resolve their problems. I worried that it would reflect a bad light on all of us as students. I recommended that the aggravated co-workers attempt to resolve the issues. He took my advice and after a bit of explaining the two reconciled. I was unsure what to do in the beginning and still think it was a gamble for me to attempt to reconcile the two. It should have been my cooperative education coordinator.

> As students we heard a great deal of gossiping and backstabbing in the workplace. I felt very uncomfortable. I thought it best to keep quiet when the gossiping was occurring. I considered telling the boss or someone above these people so that someone could deal with it. But I didn't know what to do.

> I (faculty member) was inappropriate with a female student by telling jokes, making sexual innuendo statements, spending more time with this student over others, and asking this student to do some extra work for me. My supervisor warned me in a fair way to revise my behavior. At first I took it as jealousy. Later I realized I did not know what was inappropriate and that my supervisor was helping me professionally.

These examples demonstrate that while sometimes people do not know what is appropriate, other times they do not know how to act in the situation. Entry level instruction in communication and negotiation skills could give cooperative education participants the tools to use when they are faced with interpersonal conflicts.

Moral and Ethical Reasoning

Many of the issues reported suggested a lack of moral and ethical reasoning skills. In reviewing the incidents the committee identified that cooperative education personnel had trouble sorting out three aspects of moral and ethical reasoning: sorting the personal from the professional conflict, balancing conflicting needs, or recognizing ethical dilemmas for what they are: conflict of values in practice.

Moral and ethical reasoning is a bit more complex in terms of teaching. Ethical problem solving requires a decision-making process and there are many ethical decision-making models (Bunn, 1984; Heller, Drenth, Koopman, & Rus, 1988; Garfat & Ricks, 1995; Mintzberg, Raisisnghanim, & Theoret, 1976; Simon, 1960; Tymchuck, 1986). Such models build a process around three components:

- Finding occasions for making decisions that require being able to identify ethical dilemmas and practice issues,
- Seeking possible courses of action, and
- Choosing among the courses of action.

Ethical decision-making models vary between three and eight steps depending on the model. The teaching of models offers the learner a process that structures the gathering and organization of information around the dilemma or practice issue. For example, note the following process (Ricks & Griffin, 1995):

1. Identify the ethical components of the decision-making situation (what are the issues and/or practice that you think is problematic?)
2. Identify the relevant principles and values in light of the different people involved.
3. List all of the consequences for everyone involved under the condition of giving each principle primacy.
4. Classify the consequences as positive or negative.
5. Choose the alternative that produces the least amount of avoidable harm.
6. Act.
7. Evaluate the action and the decision process.
8. Assume responsibility for the consequences of the decision. This includes the correction if the ethical issues are not resolved.

The steps organize and give focus to the reasoner's attention and therefore to the data that would be collected. Theoretically speaking, the steps help to ensure that all the factors that need to be considered are given attention and thoughtful consideration.

Regardless of the model used to assist the learner in going through a process of unraveling the dilemma or practice issue, certain skills are required, particularly metacognition skills. Metacognition skills (Ricks & Griffin, 1995) include those thinking skills that allow the moral reasoner to be more effective at each step. First is the skill of being able to look at the situation in as many ways as possible (divergent thinking). Second, is the skill of pulling the situation apart while considering many different categories of information at once (analytical skills). Third, critical thinking is being able to challenge assumptions, about the role and importance of context, explore alternatives, and engage in reflective skepticism. Finally the skill of integrative thinking means being able to pull everything together in a meaningful way that leads to action. These thinking skills would be useful in considering professional issues as well, and are known to be requisites in reflective practice (Schon, 1987, 1993).

Finally, one of the most important considerations is that even when people know what to do, sometimes they simply will not do it (Kidder, 1996). The risk is too high or the costs are too great at a personal level. As a result they are overcome by fear and immobilized. The personal fears may not intrude on making the best choice but may impede acting on the best choice. For example, fear can restrict thinking about all the options. Under the condition of fear we can be reductionistic and generate only two options (e.g., I can lose like this, or I can lose like that).

This is when self-awareness may be useful. Through self-awareness one can learn how to recognize fear and understand what is immobilizing us. Understanding fear often opens up new opportunities to tackle issues in a new way. For example, a person may come to realize that they do not speak up because they seek to avoid conflict. However, in work settings management depends on workers speaking up and working things through. Unless we train students to recognize what keeps them from acting they may wrongly conclude that they do not know how to handle the situation. What they need to understand is that they are unwilling to handle the situation. Only with this recognition of their avoidance of conflict is there potential for speaking up and working things through.

SUMMARY

In this study, cooperative education students, faculty, coordinators, and work site supervisors identified ethical issues in their respective work sites. Their dilemmas can be classified as practice issues (issues that can be solved with knowledge and best practice guidelines) and ethical issues (situations in which guidelines do not and can not exist because they are situations of value conflict and will vary from situation to situation). Furthermore, the dilemmas can be categorized into two broad groups: (1) professional standards issues such as accommodation of exceptions to policy, inappropriate practice and interpersonal conflicts; and (2) moral and ethical reasoning issues such as personal and professional conflict, balancing conflicting needs, and recognition of ethical dilemmas.

Although it is impossible to prevent all ethical dilemmas from occurring, education can and should be able to minimize their occurrence and provide the means of effectively handling them. Within the cooperative education setting the opportunity exists to provide students with the resources, skills and knowledge needed to appropriately handle most practice issues. The cooperative education setting can also provide students with methods for working through moral and ethical reasoning issues.

Decision Point: Working Together Creates Resources

M: Great looking report. All we needed was good ideas and willing participants. We brought together the expertise of university faculty and cooperative education coordinators to consider this topic, and now we can decide which recommendations to implement.

G: The more partners there were, the less there was for any of us to do. It did help to have someone to play a leadership role by calling people together, summarizing decisions, and determining who was going to do what. Treat it as a community project and it can and will get done!

M: I am surprised how any people have small pockets of money for funding (university presidents, vice presidents, deans, chairs and heads of departments, and others who had discretionary funding). It seemed easier to get a small amount of money than to go for the whole amount.

G: What amazes me is that it only takes as much money as you have! The rest can be goods in kind, including time and talents.

M: Money doesn't really matter because when we get involved in initiatives like this it is because they make a difference. Making a difference is more important than money!

ANNOTATED BIBLIOGRAPHY

Blum, L. A. (1994). *Moral perception and particularity.* New York: Cambridge University Press. This book offers a collection of essays that reflect the author's evolution in thinking on developing and demonstrating a psychologically informed approach to moral theory. The essays speak to the importance of moral perception, moral excellence, and moral psychology. Blum made explicit, through argument and example that a person can not be a moral exemplar without having concern for the broader community, understanding different notions of morality, and what it means to assess someone as morally excellent. The breadth of the essays provides a unified discourse on the complexity of applied ethics.

Kidder, R. M. (1996). *How good people make tough choices.* New York: Fireside, Simon & Schuster. Pulitzer Prize Winner Barbara Tuchman inspired this book. Tuchman observed that although people have always acted immorally, public immorality is now more obvious to the average citizen. In the author's zeal to understand this awareness, the author concluded from her journalistic research that ethical dilemmas are value conflicts where right versus right and where there is no formula that can turn out the "answer." She further surmised that as people practice resolving dilemmas they find "ethics to be less a goal than a pathway, less a destination than a trip, less an inoculation that a process" (p. 176). The author urged us to become ethically fit through practice, exercise, and being mindful about doing right.

McGin, C. (1999). *The mysterious flame*. New York: Basic Books, Perseus Book Group. In the author's own words, this book is about the "mystery of consciousness." Consciousness is an important topic not only because without it we do not exist, but because of the relationship of consciousness to all aspects of our lives, including ethics and morality. The author explained in simple terms that the human intellect is not capable of unraveling the mystery because consciousness of not part of the material world, yet paradoxically we rely on the brain to manifest our consciousness. He posited that we can believe in consciousness knowing that we can not understand but suggested that reality is more than what our intelligence can make up. The book is provocative and poses opportunity for the bold.

Stringer, E. (1999). *Action research*. Thousand Oaks, CA: Sage. Ernest Stringer's book on action research provides a wonderful frame on research as inquiry in practice. While the author offered an overview of the inherent values of action research (empowerment, democracy, liberation, and life enhancement) he used each chapter to define the steps to take for those who want to be involved in the process of giving voice to change. The book is in essence a manual that guides the reader on what to do and avoids overstating the righteous thinking that sometimes prevails in action research literature.

REFERENCES

Anderson, G., Herr, K., & Nihlen, A. (1994). *Studying your own school: An educator's guide to qualitative practitioner research*. Thousand Oaks, CA: Corwin.

Baldick, T. (1980). Ethical discrimination ability of intern psychologists: A function of training in ethics. *Professional Psychology, 11*, 276–282.

Bunn, D. (1984). *Applied decision analysis*. New York: McGraw-Hill.

Blum, L. (1994). *Moral perception and particularity*. New York: Press Syndicate of the University of Cambridge.

Dick, B. (1996). Action Research and Evaluation On-Line Electronic resources on Action Research. Accessed on Feb. 2003 from: http://www.scu.edu.au/schools/gcm/ar/areol/aerolhome.html

Delany, J. T., & Socell, D. (1982). Do company ethics training programs make a difference: An empirical analysis. *Journal of Business Ethics, 11*, 719–727.

Demarco, J. (1997). Coherence and applied ethics. *Journal of Applied Philosophy, 14*(3), 289–300.

Eberlein, L. (1987). Introducing ethics to beginning psychologists: A problem-solving approach. *Professional Psychology: Research and Practice, 18*(4), 353–359.

Elsdon, I. (1998). Educating toward awareness: Self-awareness in ethical decision-making for child and youth care workers. *Journal of Child and Youth Care, 12*(3), 55–68.

Friere, P. (1974). *Pedagogy of the oppressed*. New York: Seabury.

Garfat, T., & Ricks, F. (1995). Self-driven ethical decision making: A model for child and youth care. *Child Care Forum, 24*(6), 393–404.

Gawthrop, J. C. (1990). *Effects of the problem solving approach in teaching ethics*. Unpublished Master's thesis, University of Victoria, Victoria, British Columbia, Canada.

Granum, R., & Erickson, R. (1976) How a learning model can affect confidential decision making. *Counselor Education and Supervision, 15*(4), 276–284.

Habermas, J. (1979). *Communication and the evolution of society*. (T. McCarthy, Trans.). Boston: Beacon.

Handelsman, M. M. (1986). Ethics training at the master's level: A national survey. *Professional Psychology: Research and Practice, 17*(1), 24–26.

Heller, F., Drenth, P., Kooperman, P., & Rus, V. (1988). Decisions in organizations: A three country comparative country. *Community Mental Health Journal, 25*(1), 42–49.

Howard, G. S. (1986). The scientist-practitioner in counseling psychology: Toward a deeper integration of theory, research, and practice. *The Counseling Psychologist, 14*(1), 61–105.

Holter, I. M., & Schwartz-Barcott, D. (1993). Action research: What is it? How has it been used and how can it be used in nursing? *Journal of Advanced Nursing, 128,* 298–304.

Kemmis, S., & McTaggart, R. (1988). *The action research planner.* Geelong, Victoria, Australia: Deankin University Press.

Kidder, R. (1996). *How good people make tough choices.* New York: Simon & Schuster.

Lantz, G. (2000). Applied ethics: What kind of ethics and what kind of ethicist? *Journal of Applied Philosophy, 17*(1), 12–28.

Moreno, J. (1956). *Sociometry and the science of man.* New York: Beacon.

McGovem, T. (1988). Teaching the ethical principles of psychology. *Teaching of Psychology, 15*(1), 22–26.

Mintzberg, H., Raisisnghanim, D., & Theoret, A. (1976). The structure of "unstructured" decision processes. *Administrative Science Quarterly, 21,* 246–275.

Morrison, J., & Teta, D. (1979). Impact of a humanistic approach on students' attitudes, attribution and ethical conflict. *Psychological Reports, 45,* 863–866.

Patton, M. Q. (1997). *Utilization-focused evaluation: The new century test* (3rd ed.). Thousand Oaks, CA: Sage.

Reason, P. (1988). *Human inquiry in action: Developments in new paradigm research.* London: Sage.

Rhodes, M. (1986). Ethical dilemmas in social work practice. Boston: Routledge.

Ricks, F. (1997). Perspectives on ethics in child and youth care. *Child & Youth Care Forum, 26*(3), 187–203.

Ricks, F., & Garfat, T. (1994). Ethics education in child and youth care: A Canadian survey. *Journal of Child and Youth Care, 11*(4), 69–76.

Ricks, F., & Griffin, S. (1995). *Best choice: Ethical decision making in human services.* Course material prepared for the Ministry of Skills, Labor and Training, Government of British Columbia, Victoria, British Columbia, Canada.

Rorty, R. (1989) *Contingency, irony, and solidarity.* Cambridge, MA: Cambridge University Press.

Schon, D. A. (1983). *The reflective practitioner: How practitioners think in action.* New York: Basic Books.

Schon, D. A. (1987). *Educating the reflective practitioner: Toward a new design for teaching and learning in the profession.* The Jossey-Bass Higher Education Series. (ERIC Document Reproduction Service No. 295518.)

Senge, P. (1999). *The dance of change: The challenges to sustaining momentum in learning organization.* New York: Doubleday/Currency.

Simon, H. (1982). *Models of bounded rationality: Behavioral economics and business organization.* Cambridge, MA: Massachusetts Institute of Technology.

Stringer, E. (1999). *Action research.* Thousand Oaks, CA: Sage.

Tymchuk, A. J. (1986). Guidelines for ethical decision making. *Canadian Psychology, 27,* 36–43.

Warwick, D. P. (1980). *The teaching of ethics in the social sciences.* Hastings-on-Hudson, NY: The Hastings Center.

5

Researching in Cooperative Education: How a Practitioner Met the Challenge

Chris Eames
The University of Waikato

Key questions addressed in this chapter:

☞ How and why did I get into research in cooperative education?

☞ What steps did I take to conduct the research?

This is the story of my induction into the world of research in cooperative education, or work-integrated learning. Like many practitioners, I was involved in running a successful cooperative education (co-op) program. I had plenty of ideas and anecdotal evidence for what went right in our program, but I had some questions too, about why and how it worked. This chapter describes the steps I went through to begin my first research project in cooperative education, raises some of the issues to consider, and presents a short case study from my project.

The questions I had about co-op stemmed from my position as a biology lecturer and co-op professional at the University of Waikato in New Zealand. I had become aware from my involvement in both the classroom and the workplace that the practice of science was often not the same in these two places and that learning in each could therefore be different. This led to a curiosity about how a student underwent the transition between the two. This curiosity may well have remained just that if I had not been encouraged to enroll in a doctoral program.

The PhD program at the University of Waikato is a thesis-only degree that normally takes 3 years full-time or 5 to 6 years part-time. As I wasn't in a career or financial position to study full-time, I opted for the part-time route. This would enable

me to conduct research in co-op whilst continuing to practice in it. This dual practice–research role approach has distinct advantages and disadvantages, which I discuss at the end of the chapter.

Decision Point: How will you get your research done?
Once I had decided to do some research, I had to decide how it was to be
done. I could have done it myself, or with colleagues, as part of my work. But
as I was being encouraged and supported to do a PhD, it made sense to tackle
it this way as a part-time student. The demands of a full-time job meant that I
had to be very disciplined in allocating time to the research. I handled this issue by dedicating one clear day each week to the research and squeezing my
work into the other four.
Other ways to carry out the research include supervising a research student to
do the project, for which you need a pool of suitable students and to be able to
supervise them. Or hiring a researcher to carry out the project, for which you
need money (see Ricks, chap. 4, this volume).

With enrolment complete, the commitment made, and some ideas I wanted
to research, I needed to focus my study. I had been working as a co-op professional for 5 years and like many of my colleagues had experienced many of the
successes of co-op such as securing excellent placements for students; students
gaining more certainty about their career direction and more confidence in their
ability to work; retaining employers year after year through successful placements; collaborations between those employers and the university extending
beyond the cooperative education arena; and graduates getting great jobs, often
with their co-op employers. It was clear that our program was successful in its
operational aims.

What I didn't understand was some of the nitty-gritty of how the educative processes in the placements worked, and from my earlier reading and attendance at
co-op conferences, it appeared that neither did many others. Amongst the cooperative education fraternity, there seemed to be some good understanding of the "cooperative" aspect but less of the "education." I wanted to find out more about this
educative aspect.

DOING A LITERATURE REVIEW

The first step in the investigation involved reading what others had researched and
written about in the field. A key issue at this point was to decide on what to read.
The logical place to start was the cooperative education literature, based largely on
the *Journal of Cooperative Education*, and searches of electronic databases using cooperative education and variations of this term as keywords.

I focused specifically on learning in co-op. Much of the early writing was anecdotal in nature and lacked any systematic approach (Finn, 1997; Wilson, 1989). Bartkus and Stull (1997) noted that "most of the research completed over the past 30 years is probably best described as applied-descriptive and evaluative in scope. It has been largely pragmatic in nature without a strong theoretical underpinning" (p. 9). There were calls for greater application of theory to research in co-op (Ricks et al., 1990).

In particular there were calls for research into educational outcomes of co-op programs (Ryan, Toohey, & Hughes, 1996; Van Gyn, Cutt, Loken, & Ricks, 1997). Research that had been done earlier (e.g., Wilson, 1980–1981) looked at desired educational objectives from the perspective of the employer, institution, and student. Other studies looked at academic progress as a measure of learning (Van Gyn et al., 1997), and enhancement of career identity (Weston, 1986), enhancement of interpersonal skills (Morton, Dawson, & Laing, 1993), and the development of practical intelligence and tacit knowledge (Williams, Sternberg, Rashotte, & Wagner, 1992) as outcomes. The latter study by Williams et al. was one of very few that sought to examine the learning process as well as the outcomes.

My reading showed that there had been little researched about the differences in learning that students experience between school or university and the workplace in cooperative education programs. It was also clear that there was a great need for research that could tie educational outcomes and processes found in cooperative education programs to educational theory. This need was driven in part by the desire to legitimize cooperative education within the mainstream of education. What I needed now was to examine educational theory to see if there was an existing idea, or ideas, that might provide a useful framework for my study.

THE THEORETICAL BACKGROUND

As I was interested in learning, I turned my attention to theories of learning. Not surprisingly this is a topic that has attracted much interest over the years and therefore a proportionately large number of theoretical ideas to explain learning have been espoused. Suffice to say that I restricted myself to those that were germane to the integration of classroom learning with learning at work. Many of these have recently been reviewed in relation to cooperative education (Cates & Jones, 1999), and I briefly discuss some here.

Bandura's (1977) social learning theory suggests that co-op students may learn not only from their own actions but also vicariously through the actions of others. This would certainly be possible in a co-op work placement in which a student is exposed to role models and other people already in practice. Another of Bandura's (1982) ideas, that of self-efficacy, has been examined by Fletcher (1990) as a useful construct to explain cooperative education outcomes. Self-efficacy is the individual's belief in their own ability to carry out tasks. Fletcher argued that cooperative education programs could enhance a student's self-efficacy, and therefore perhaps lead them to believe they had made the transition from student to practitioner.

Howard Gardner's (1983, 1999) Theory of Multiple Intelligences sees the existence of a varied number of potentials within an individual that can be activated within certain cultural settings. Cates and Jones (1999) proposed that co-op programs provide a great variety of cultural settings that could develop and allow expression of more of these potentials or intelligences. If this were so, a student could better discover where his or her potentials lie. This may be particularly important for those students who have not succeeded well in the traditional classroom education system with its emphasis on linguistic and logical-mathematical intelligences.

Notions of learning from experience naturally ally themselves to cooperative education, containing as it does a segment of work experience. Both the early ideas of John Dewey (Heinemann & DeFalco, 1990), and David Kolb's (1984) Theory of Experiential Learning (Cates & Jones, 1999) have been claimed to provide solid background for learning in cooperative education programs. Kolb's theory suggests a learning cycle that incorporates concrete experiences followed by observation and reflection leading to the formation of abstract concepts and ideas that are then tested in new situations, leading to new experiences and so on.

Each of these four ideas: social learning, development of self-efficacy, multiple intelligences, and experiential learning hold promise for contributing to our understanding of learning in cooperative education programs, and I did not exclude any from consideration as I analyzed my data. Indeed it was highly likely that I would find evidence for parts or all of each and a combined theory might emerge from the data (Glaser & Strauss, 1967). However another set of ideas attracted me, which attempted to explain the process of learning as a transition from newcomer to old-timer within a social and cultural background. As I was interested in transition into what I suspected was a new culture for the student, these sociocultural theories seemed to be appropriate to my study.

Sociocultural views of learning have developed from the ideas of Lev Vygotsky (1978) and from the fields of cultural psychology, sociology and anthropology. Vygotsky's contribution lies in his notions of mediated action, mediation occurring through tools and signs such as language and use of equipment. This means that learning is gained through the use and sharing of these tools and signs.

Another tenet of these theories of learning is that learning is a situated, participatory activity (Lave, 1991; Rogoff, 1975). Lave defined *situated learning* as emphasizing "the inherently socially negotiated quality of meaning and the interested, concerned character of the thought and action of persons engaged in activity" and "that learning, thinking, and knowing are relations among people engaged in activity *in, with, and arising from the socially and culturally structured world*" (p. 67). That is, learning is embedded in a social situation, can not be dissociated from it, and can only be understood within the context in which it occurred. Rogoff (1995) viewed participatory appropriation as individuals changing "through their involvement in activity, in the process becoming prepared for subsequent involvement in related activities" (p. 142). In this way individuals become enculturated into and become legitimate members of a functioning community.

A final tenet of sociocultural views of learning is that knowledge is distributed across a community of practice. In this viewpoint, knowledge is neither transmitted nor internalized, but rather it is "jointly constructed (appropriated) in the sense that it is neither handed down ready-made nor constructed by individuals on their own" (Salomon & Perkins, 1998, p. 9). Knowledge is created through interactions between people and gets distributed amongst those interacting (Pea, 1997).

In summary the sociocultural view suggests that learning is mediated, situated and distributed across a particular social, cultural, and historical setting. This view seeks to explain the process by which a newcomer is enculturated into that setting by the old-timers within it. The view offers a potential framework for understanding what and how a student, as a novice worker, learns in the workplace, and it was this view that was examined closely through the data. The sociocultural view takes into account the historical and the cultural in learning about working in a particular discipline or career role. This view is also cognizant of the social contribution to learning. Finally the view is orientated toward construction of meaning that students develop in what it means to them to be a practitioner, as they view the "old-timers" to be in their workplaces.

Whilst the theory can not be the only driver of the research, it helps to focus attention on the data collection, and provides a framework to interpret the answers. However it always remains open to modification by the data.

Decision Point: Which theoretical framework may help to explain the phenomenon you are interested in?

Choosing a theoretical framework proved to be a challenging process. Many ideas about how people learn have been written about, and contributions have come from diverse fields such as anthropology, psychology, sociology, and management, as well as education. For me this meant learning whole new sets of jargon, and often finding different terms in various fields that mean the same thing. Coupled with the fact that cooperative education programs have multidimensional learning environments that lend themselves to different interpretations, this plethora of viewpoints presented both an opportunity and a problem for making sense of learning ideas with respect to placements. I chose sociocultural views as the framework for my study as they allowed an examination of the social and cultural contributions to learning at university and at the workplace.

DETERMINING THE RESEARCH QUESTIONS

My review of the literature had shown me that my ideas needed further research, and had given me a theoretical framework to investigate them. Now I needed some research questions to work toward. This was a key step in the project and one that would set the focus for the study (Bell, 1993).

My curiosity about learning differences between academia and the workplace led me to the following questions:

- What and how does a student perceive they learn on a co-op placement?
- Does a student's perceived learning on placement help them make the transition between the world of academia and the world of work?

These research questions would allow an exploration of learning to promote understanding of the process in a descriptive and interpretive manner, that would provide a different perspective to that gained through a positivistic, hypothesis-testing approach (Peshkin, 1993).

Decision Point: What will your research questions be?
Consider: Can the question be researched, how does it sit in the current body of knowledge, why do you want it answered? My experience in co-op and the reading that I had undertaken as part of my work had led me to believe early on that these questions were important. But the literature review was invaluable in helping me refine my ideas and place them in the context of current theoretical ideas. I knew the questions could be researched as I had had many anecdotal discussions around these issues over the years with my students. I hoped that the opportunity to do some focused study of these issues would help develop a better understanding of the role that work placements play in our students' education.

Once I had settled on my questions, I pinned them to the wall above my desk and there they have remained throughout the study, both as a focal point for direction and for decision making. I now faced the issues of how to do the study, that is the methodology and methods.

METHODOLOGY AND METHODS

My own previous education was in the science field, and I had been schooled in logical-positivism. This indicated a quantitative approach to my research questions, filled with statistical data collection under rigorously controlled and replicable conditions. An examination of my cooperative education program, with its variability in individuals' interests and placement experiences, led me to believe that such an approach was unlikely to give meaningful answers to my questions. An alternative was required (see Linn, chap. 6, this volume, for a discussion of appropriate uses of quantitative and qualitative approaches).

I knew what I wanted to research but didn't have the skills or experience to know how to go about it, a problem that had been previously identified as prevalent amongst the co-op community (Bartkus & Stull, 1997).

Decision Point: Who can help with your research?

I was lucky in that my university has a high quality Center for Science and Technology Education Research (CSTER). Staff in this center have backgrounds in both science and technology and education theory and methods of research. They could advise on alternative approaches to tackling my questions. I was also fortunate in that the group of co-op practitioners that I worked with had begun to develop a research culture, providing a stimulating and supportive environment for doing research and moving us away from the feeling that we were mere "placement jockeys" (Mosbacker, 1969).

To look at the learning process I had to ask how learning occurred, and because how has to be based somewhere, I also needed to ask what was being learned and who contributed to it.

My science background prescribed an objective assessment of learning in which I could attempt to test the students' understanding of practicing science and technology against a normative view. But it was the students who were becoming the practitioners, not me. And the variety of practice spanned pure and applied research, industrial quality control and resource monitoring. So it seemed important that it was the students who provided the data, that it was their perceptions of what was learnt, and how, and who from. I needed to be able to access their meanings of the experiences and interpret them. This led to the choice of an interpretive approach based on student perceptions of their world (Cohen, Manion, & Morrison, 2000). This also sat well with the notion of sociocultural learning, based as it is on participants' perceptions of the social and cultural environments in which they are placed. It would be a naturalistic inquiry (Lincoln & Guba, 1985) in which the subjects would be studied in their natural context.

Having decided on methodology (the overarching approach that would be used), it became easy to choose methods (the actual tools for collecting data), the choice also being consistent with the research questions (Patton, 1990). As I was interested in the perceptions of the students, the use of interviews would allow me to explore these. The semistructured interview, in which I had a set of topic questions to ask but that would still allow the student and I to be flexible in our conversation, would allow for open dialogue about the key issues of interest. It would also allow me to tailor the interview to the particular workplace and the student.

Participant observation, in which the researcher spends time in the setting alongside the subject, is often used in conjunction with interviewing in ethnographic studies (Adler & Adler, 1998). However I decided against using this method for two reasons: Firstly, I wasn't sure if this would contribute to my understanding of the students' perceptions of their learning, and secondly, there were procedural difficulties with gaining access to many of the work sites, often due to safety issues.

My research questions focused on transition and hence process, and therefore it made sense for the research to be transitional as well, in other words to be a longitudinal study. This would allow me to follow a cohort of students through their degrees and examine the learning that contributed to the transition along the way. The longitudinal process of the study opened the way for multiple interviews in which previous experiences and perceptions reported could be revisited. This would allow for changes to be explored and perform a type of triangulation function (i.e., using multiple sources of information to ensure greater validity and reliability in the data, Cohen et al., 2000).

Before beginning the interview-based longitudinal study, I wanted to get a feel for the how, what, and who factors in learning on placement so that I could focus my interview questions. So I conducted a survey of recent graduates of the program about their retrospective perceptions of their learning in the work placement. This survey included both open questions that gave me some qualitative data to interpret and closed questions that gave me quantitative data that could be statistically analyzed to obtain a broad picture of the key issues.

Decision Point: What type of research will you do?
Some options are ethnography, case studies, correlational research, experimentation, or action research. This decision was, and to some extent, still is one of the most difficult for me to have made. Having been so long grounded in scientific notions of logical-positivism, it was very hard for me to come to terms with the use of an interpretive methodology. Even now, although I feel comfortable working within this approach, I sometimes find myself drawn back toward the scientific viewpoint when considering my data. Using new methods did not prove as demanding, although conducting good interviews takes practice. Doing pilot interviews is essential to test your questions, and mock interviews with an experienced interviewer present to provide feedback on style are helpful.

THE RESEARCH SETTING

In order to investigate my research questions I needed some subjects. Having a position as a co-op coordinator meant I could embed my research in the cooperative education program that I worked in at the University of Waikato. This Bachelor of Science (Technology) degree program is offered in science and technology, has been in operation since 1974, and places approximately 170 students per year.

As the research was a naturalistic inquiry the context of my research setting must be described in some detail, so I have included a summary of the placement program here. It is a 4-year degree in contrast with the non-co-op 3-year BSc degree also offered at the University. A number of science majors are offered, such as physics, chemistry, biology, the earth sciences, computer science, and a variety of multidisciplinary programs, such as biochemistry, biotechnology, forestry and environmental science. Essentially the degree consists of a BSc with the addition of two management papers and a total of 12 months relevant paid work experience, comprising two work placements, 1 of 3 months duration at the end of the second year, and the other of 9 months duration at the end of the third year (Coll, 1996; see Fig. 5.1). Student placements are organized by co-op coordinators who are also faculty members (Coll & Eames, 2000). These placements are in a great variety of workplaces, and a difficulty I faced was how to make sense of this variety in my research.

In recent years, postsecondary education in New Zealand has undergone a number of changes that have impacted on students and the program. The introduction of substantial course fees, increased competitiveness amongst institutions for students and decreasing government funding in the sector have all combined to drive down student numbers and sharpen students' demands for a quality education. In addition there have been conflicting signals within the country regarding the status of a career in science and technology. On the one hand, government rhetoric has supported the need for science and technology graduates to boost our economy, whilst on the other hand, reducing funding to postsecondary institutions and public research organizations in these areas. It was within this contextual background that the research took place.

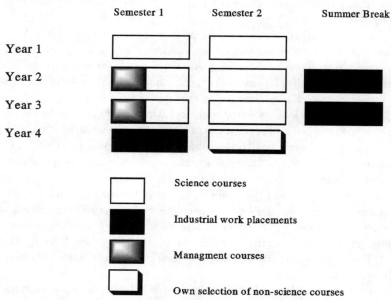

FIG. 5.1.   Structure of the BSc (Technology) degree (Coll & Eames, 2000).

THE RESEARCH DESIGN

I now had some research questions, some theoretical ideas to investigate, some techniques for doing the research, and a setting. Next I needed a plan for collecting data!

Decision Point: What sampling plan will you use?
In making this decision I considered issues such as sample size and any other characteristics of the sample that may have impacted on the data. The sample of graduates was limited to who was available. The sample of interviewees for the longitudinal study was large enough to allow for attrition over time but also to have fair representation from the population of students.

The first step was to carry out the graduate survey to gain some direction for the interviews. A questionnaire was posted out to 125 graduates who had completed placements within the BSc (Technology) program as part of their undergraduate degree. These 125 graduates were selected on the basis of our knowledge of their whereabouts and so retained some bias because of this.

The sample of 125 graduates had completed their last placement between 1989 and 1997, the sample being 29% of the graduate population over that period. Of the 125 surveys sent out, 95 were returned at a response rate of 77%, 77 (62%) being returned in the first instance and the remainder after a follow up letter. Respondents were approximately spread in their subject majors in proportion to the spread of majors in the population. Of respondents, 81% had completed their degree in the past 3 years.

As described earlier, students in the program generally carry out at least two placements, so graduates were asked to consider only their last placement in the program when answering the survey questions, as responses may have differed between their placements. This potential variation was a weakness of this method of data collection, which was addressed in the later longitudinal study.

Questions in the survey gathered background information about the placement, asked for open responses of perceptions of learning from a what, how and who perspective, examined some detail on learning of working knowledges (Simon, Dippo, & Schenke, 1991) such as theory, skills, language, and relationships, and sought views on assessment of the work placement.

Briefly, the outcomes of the graduate survey indicated that students felt they learnt specific theory and skills in the workplace, as well as more transferable skills. They felt they learnt by doing tasks and by interacting with supervisors and co-workers, and they saw their workmates as critical to their learning (Eames, 2001). These outcomes gave me some confirmation of direction for the next phase of the research.

I could now proceed with the longitudinal study. A cohort of students was selected from all second-year students in the BSc (Technology) program. Participation was invited in such a way that a balance was attempted across gender, across subject majors in proportion to the total population, and across a range of industry sectors.

Before beginning this phase of the study, I needed to acknowledge the ethical considerations of the project. Most importantly my role as placement coordinator to biology students meant that I had to exclude these from the project as I could be viewed as examiner by some of these students, which might have influenced what they would tell me about their learning. Secondly, I had to make my intentions very clear to the participants in the project, get their informed consent, and assure them of the confidentiality of our interviews. This involved the approval of an ethics proposal by the University's Human Ethics Committee and the provision of information to participants of what they would be involved in and how their data would be treated and stored. On at least a couple of occasions I was placed in an ethical dilemma when I became aware of issues in the placements, and I had to abstain from offering direct advice, and instead pointed the issue-raiser toward another source of help.

A group of 22 students agreed to participate in the study, 12 males and 10 females. Each participant has been interviewed individually on at least four occasions as specified in Table 5.1. The interviews investigated the learning experiences of the students in their science and technology workplaces and the integration of these experiences with their learning at university (see Appendix for an example of an interview protocol from Interview 2).

After the first set of interviews in the workplace (Interview 2) I became concerned that by conducting just one interview toward the end of the first placement, I was only tapping into what isolated elements students could remember over the preceding 3 months. I felt I needed more regular data to chart learning changes more closely. So I invited five students to have more regular interviewing during their second work placement. These students were interviewed four to five times during this placement.

All interviews were audiotaped, transcribed verbatim and the participants were given the opportunity to check and comment on the accuracy of the transcripts. Data analysis presented me with my next dilemma, and it is important that analyti-

TABLE 5.1

Schedule of Interviews

Interview 1	Before beginning first placement, at end of second year of study
Interview 2	Toward the end of the first placement in the workplace (placement duration 3 months)
Interview 3	After first placement, and before second placement, while in third year of study
Interview 4	During second and final placement in the workplace (placement duration ranged from 3 to 9 months)

cal techniques are considered carefully before collection of data. There are a number of strategies available for analysis of textual data (for discussion see Linn, chap. 6, this volume). I performed content analysis using simple and modifiable categories. As I was searching for meaning I needed to closely analyze not only the content of what the students had said to me, but also their meanings. I reduced the data (Miles & Huberman, 1984) down to a series of case studies, which I then analyzed in-depth. This data reduction involved searching the transcripts for quotes that would provide evidence for the students' perception of their learning. These quotes were compiled into case studies for each student and categories emerged for quotes of similar themes. Some of these categories were based around the theoretical framework whereas others emerged from the data. The categorization of quotes involved both within-case analysis and cross-case analysis. This was necessarily a big task but also one that meant that I became extremely close to the data. Coding of the quotes within the analysis that listed the participant, the interview number, and the page number of the transcript from where the quote originated, allowed me to keep track of the data.

Decision Point: How will you structure your data collection?
The data collection was the most interesting phase of the project. Interviewing the participants gave me an excellent chance to learn about their experiences. I found that I needed to be flexible and responsive to what they were saying, which caused me to change my questions at times during an interview, and to alter my interview schedule to get more concentrated information from some students.

How will you handle and analyze your data? I generated more than 100 transcripts during the course of the project. Although this is a large number, over the duration of the 5 years of the project, I found I was able to generally remember who had said what and when, and perhaps more importantly, recall the meaning the participants ascribed to their comments through timing, inflection, and tone of voice. Even today I can still "hear" them making particular comments. For me this made a fairly manual system of content analysis possible. For others using computer packages such as NUDIST has been invaluable.

To complete this chapter I now present one brief case study from my research so that it might be possible to see where my research decisions have led me. A pseudonym has been used for the participant. Excerpts provided here have been edited lightly for sense.

LEARNING TO RESEARCH: THE CASE OF BRIAN

Brian is a chemistry major and a high academic achiever, scoring in the A range for all his university courses. He is a New Zealand European and was 19 when he entered the program, entering university directly after his secondary schooling. His interest in science stemmed from his school days although he wasn't able to ascribe his interest to any one influence. Brian's choice of study was driven by his own interest and his view that science would get him a good job. His parents had not been scientists but had been supportive of what Brian wanted to do.

In the program, Brian had two 3-month chemistry work placements over the summers of 1998 and 1999 and 1999 and 2000. He worked in two different Crown Research Institutes (CRIs) in New Zealand. The CRIs are mainly government-funded and are individually focused on a particular segment of New Zealand science research (e.g., forestry, agriculture). Since their inauguration in 1992, they have been driven to a competitive funding model that has created a more applied focus to the research, and the imposition of business methods. This was the context within which Brian found himself and which he was able to contrast to the university setting.

Learning Differences Between University and the Workplace

Within an educational institution, as science educators we are often constrained by the lack of time and resources in our desire to expose our students to researching in science. Large class sizes and limited equipment often mean that undergraduates are seldom given the chance to do practical research. The laboratory exercises that they do are rather confined to demonstrating principles and particular techniques. The graduates come out of this training with an awareness of what tools are used in science research but little or no actual experience.

Toward the end of his first placement Brian recognized this difficulty in learning how to research in a university undergraduate program and the difference between his experiences there and in the workplace:

> At university it's structured, where you're being taught the theory in the lectures and tutorials, and then in the labs it's very controlled skills, they sort of feed you skills, a skill at a time as it were. (In the workplace) it's sort of bringing together all the relevant skills, teaching you how to use different machinery as it becomes necessary, and often you're making leaps forward from what you've learnt at university.

Brian emphasized here the controlled nature of learning skills at university, the feeding of skills, as opposed to the need-to-know environment that he encountered in the workplace, where the activity is situated in a context.

Research Practice

His second placement had a very applied focus and he was able to discern a difference between the type of research and researchers that he had previously been exposed to at university:

I'm talking about the sort of technological product development that you get in a sort of an institute, that there's emphasis, at least this group's emphasis toward developing products. In the university we get exposure to people's research interests and most of the people I'm in contact with have more sort of I suppose purist research interests and they're sort of more into pure research with a little bit of applied but I'm coming into contact here with quite a lot of applied material and I can therefore make the link between the chemistry theory and the technological practice.

Brian felt that the placement was showing him theory in action and giving him direct relevance to his studies. Earlier in the same interview he used the phrase "a sort of real world context which you could never get in a university" when discussing his experience of the workplace. This appears to indicate that Brian believes that the university is not able to teach him about the real world in the way that the workplace can. It also implies a cultural shift from the institution to the workplace, an environment in which the learning is different.

Brian also noted his discovery of the complexity of the nature of the scientific research process in his placement:

It's taught me that often the research can't be fully structured like right from the beginning with contingency factors having to be allowed for and often interesting sort of tangents might arise that are worth pursuing or can be pursued later. So it is sort of like a spider's web if you like of ideas and knowledge that have been generated.

It would be difficult to imagine how a student could come to this understanding without being immersed in a research situation. No amount of tuition and description could substitute for a personal discovery of the intricacies of the research process. Brian also learnt how to play in his research during his first placement.

I have found that it is quite common, at least in the group I am working in, to experiment quite loosely i.e. dabble, to try and see if different ideas will work before doing more structured analysis. Sometimes this trial and error process forms the basis for the experimentation and can throw up interesting results or new ideas that can be further investigated. This sort of work is helping to develop my investigative and experimental skills and is very interesting.

For the first time, Brian found himself in an environment where there were no clear endpoints, no well-known answers to laboratory experiments performed by years of student classes. The exposure during his degree to this way of working provided Brian with a chance to find out how he felt toward research before he committed himself to a career. It has the potential to be greatly disturbing and almost frightening as the comforting boundaries of classroom science are removed. In Brian's case it was a great stimulus as he remarked towards the end of his first placement:

These new experiences have given me a greater appreciation of the research/experimentation process in action first hand and have generated in me a sense of excitement and a great deal of enthusiasm and interest, as I am at the center of this research process.

These remarks point to Brian appropriating the manner of working of the people around him. Finding that "it was quite common to dabble" allowed him to develop new skills and ways of working that were commensurate with the community within which he found himself (Rogoff, 1995).

However, not all went smoothly for Brian, and the reality check was quite revealing for him. His placements taught him about the frustration of research:

> Research seldom goes smoothly and often there's a lot of frustration and things don't sort of go well or turn out the way you'd like. It was annoying. I guess it was slightly surprising. I guess I would have liked things to have gone a bit more smoothly because when you're at university, the little labs are quite structured and they've been done before so things tend to go quite smoothly because of that.

This disturbance in thinking has created a perceptual change for Brian about how research proceeds. Having previously been exposed only to laboratory work that proceeded as the class manual dictated, and "incorrect and unexplainable" results had been rationalized by the instructor in terms of operator error, this new experience did not fit with Brian's constructs of what happened during research experimentation. Interestingly, at the end of his second placement he had developed strategies to cope with the research not progressing as expected.

> When it doesn't go smoothly your plans tend to collapse a lot, or part of them do, and you sort of just got to wipe those away and re-form a set of new plans to take you on. I always find that you have to think about "What can I do next to further the research, keep the ball rolling", because its easy to get bogged down if things don't go right, trying to think of ways to get the ball rolling toward your goal.

Brian resolved these dilemmas in a number of ways, particularly in discussions with his supervisors at work.

> Things we thought would go right and didn't, we sit down and have a brainstorm, and think what can we do now to improve this and get a result, and then we think "aha we can do this" and we go off and pursue that, and that either falls down or works. We work together and talk to each other, but also sometimes you have to make the decision on your own.

Conceptions of a Researcher

Through these activities Brian was able to learn from the established practitioners—the "old-timers"—and to develop his own understanding of what a researcher is:

> I think a good researcher is a person who is flexible and is able to adopt new paths readily and quickly when they need to, but at the same time can work out how to most efficiently use that time within that environment of uncertainty. To try and judge which avenues of investigation will reveal the best results the quickest.

This combination of experience from working with practitioners and reflection became a dominant theme in Brian's discussion of what led him to understand what it was like to do science research. By the end of his second placement, with a total of 6 months research work experience behind him, Brian felt that he had matured somewhat as a researcher, and developed new skills and a new way of thinking:

> It's the ability to exercise judgment in research, to know what to pursue and what not to pursue, to know which techniques to use, which is a knowledge thing, to be able to do things systematically and methodically and at the same time to record everything very thoroughly, well I think that those sorts of factors, the factors in recording, the ability to contribute ideas about where the research is actually going, the knowledge that I've learnt about the general area, I mean all those things have increased, and my skill base, my techniques has increased.

This statement echoes Bandura's (1982) notion of self-efficacy, the development of self-belief about one's ability. After 6 months of work experience in research environments Brian was focusing on the importance of judgment, on the ability to make informed decisions about which research avenues to progress. He ascribed his learning of judgment to experience: "It's just experience, experience, experience, and the more the better." This emphasis on experience permeated many of our discussions, and it is hard to ignore the impact that Brian attributed to getting experience in his placements.

Brian also acknowledged that the opportunity to work alongside practicing professionals was an important contributor to the development of his research skills. He gave an example of learning from stories from his first placement:

> I suppose the anecdotal stories that your supervisors give you about what they've done in the past and the problems that they've encountered and that sort of thing, it helps you to sort of flesh out your idea of the research process and the way people do things.

The use of stories in a learning context to describe previously experienced situations that led to problem resolution was identified by Brian as a means of modeling a factor in the research process. He gave a second example in his second placement, in a different research organization: "Yeah, well working alongside them contributes to your knowledge and to your ability. You get ideas on ways of doing things from them, and so that helps you enormously you know." Brian was able to see the value of the transfer potential of the accumulated knowledge and skills of the practitioners around him to his learning of the practice of science research. This participatory appropriation of the distributed knowledge in the community was seen as a particularly valuable means of learning. As was noted earlier, such learning is difficult to achieve within an undergraduate degree in an educational institution.

Case Study Conclusion

Brian's case study revealed that he felt that he had learnt a lot about becoming a science researcher through his co-op work placements. Through being situated in the context of work, he had appropriated some of the culture of the community and through the experience he felt he had moved some way from being a student toward becoming a practitioner. Through his participation in the science research community, he came to understand that the direction of research changes as new data becomes available and problems are encountered. He experienced the excitement and the frustration of the research process and how knowledge and ideas are shared amongst the scientific community. He observed how the community could be divided into participants who have different roles.

Finally he began to come to understand what it means to work as a science researcher. He identified the characteristics of a good researcher and developed a perception of whether he could pursue a science research career. At the time of the writing, Brian has just completed his Masters degree in chemistry research, and is just about to embark on a PhD in the same area. It is impossible to say whether Brian would have taken this career route had he not undertaken the work placements that he has, but Brian is adamant that his work placements experiences gave him a much clearer idea of what to expect, enabling him to make a more informed decision.

At the time of writing, the remainder of the case studies in this research project are being finalized and are pointing toward conclusions similar to those found in Brian's case. In particular the strong contribution of the social aspect of the workplace to learning is evident. It is hoped that further reports on this work will be available in the literature soon.

What has been exciting about doing this project has been the chance to research in the area of my work—cooperative education. I realize that what I have done is but a small piece of research, yet the project has been of direct relevance and benefit to my understanding of my work and possibly it will make a contribution to others' understanding of theirs. I have gained skills that have given me access to the world of the researcher, and whilst I am still very much at the newcomer stage, this project has provided me with tools that I can use for further research into co-op. I encourage you to get into co-op research and make your own contribution so that we may all better understand the discipline of cooperative education.

Summary
- My research began with questions to be addressed. These emerged from personal experience and were refined by a review of published literature.
- My research needed a theoretical framework to provide structure. The framework helped inform the data collection and analysis.

- My research was carried out using an interpretive methodology and methods that were appropriate to answer the research questions (i.e. interviews and a survey).
- Research needs time and space. The decision to go part-time on a PhD was the only option for me, but I still needed to find the time to do the work. I have seen the demise of fellow students because this issue had not been clarified before beginning. For me as a part-timer, the longitudinal study has worked really well, giving me time to collect my data, process it, and let it sit and mull around between analysis sessions. The downside of being part-time is the fragments of time that are hard to knit together into continuous thought. Progress is sometimes agonizingly slow and you have to be very patient. Toward the end, I have been able to get two chunks of a couple of months to work solidly on the project and the difference in being able to concentrate on the work at hand for some days on end was enormous and probably essential to completion.
- Research needs a supportive environment. Building alliances with people with useful knowledge and skills is highly beneficial, even if done at a distance.

ANNOTATED BIBLIOGRAPHY

Bartkus, K. R., & Stull, W. A. (1997). Some thoughts about research in co-op. *Journal of Cooperative Education, 32*(2), 7–16. This article kicks off a research edition of the Journal and makes a strong call for the importance of research into co-op.

Bell, J. (1993). *Doing your research project*. Bristol, PA: Open University Press. This is an easy-to-read introduction to reasons for research and methods and analysis—a good place to start.

Cates, C., & Jones, P. (1999). *Learning outcomes: The educational value of cooperative education*. Columbia, MD: Cooperative Education Association. This is a very useful guide to learning outcomes, including material on learning theories, and other practical considerations for co-op programs.

Cohen, L., Manion, L., & Morrison, K. (2000). *Research methods in education* (5th ed.). London: Routledge-Farmer. This is a very accessible book concerning methodology and methods, including both quantitative and qualitative viewpoints.

Rogoff, B. (1995). Observing sociocultural activity on three planes: Participatory appropriation, guided participation and apprenticeship. In J. V. Wertsch, P. del Rio, & A. Alvarez (Eds.), *Sociocultural studies of mind*. Cambridge: Cambridge University Press. This is a good starting chapter for sociocultural ideas. Other chapters in the same book are also very interesting for co-op, but some are a little technical.

REFERENCES

Adler, P. A., & Adler, P. (1998). Observational techniques. In N. K. Denzin & Y. S. Lincoln (Eds.), *Collecting and interpreting qualitative materials* (pp. 377–392). Thousand Oaks, CA: Sage.

Bandura, A. (1977). *Social learning theory*. Englewood Cliffs, NJ: Prentice Hall.

Bandura, A. (1982). Self-efficacy: Mechanisms in human agency. *American Psychologist, 37*, 122–147.

Bartkus, K. R., & Stull, W. A. (1997). Some thoughts about research in co-op. *Journal of Cooperative Education, 32*(2), 7–16.

Bell, J. (1993). *Doing your research project.* Bristol, PA: Open University Press.

Cates, C., & Jones, P. (1999). *Learning outcomes: The educational value of cooperative education.* Columbia, MD: Cooperative Education Association.

Cohen, L., Manion, L., & Morrison, K. (2000). *Research methods in education* (5th ed.). London: Routledge-Farmer.

Coll, R. K. (1996). The BSc (Technology) degree: Responding to the challenges of the education marketplace. *Journal of Cooperative Education, 32*(1), 29–35.

Coll, R. K., & Eames, C. W. (2000). The role of the placement coordinator: An alternative model. *Asia-Pacific Journal of Cooperative Education, 1*(1), 9–14.

Eames, C. W. (2001). Learning in the workplace through cooperative education placements: Beginning a longitudinal qualitative study. *Journal of Cooperative Education, 35*(2–3), 76–83.

Finn, K. L. (1997). The spaces between: Toward a new paradigm for cooperative education. *Journal of Cooperative Education, 32*(2), 36–45.

Fletcher, J. K. (1990). Self-esteem and cooperative education: A theoretical framework. *Journal of Cooperative Education, 26*(3), 41–55.

Gardner, H. (1983). *Frames of mind: The theory of multiple intelligences.* New York: Basic Books.

Gardner, H. (1999). *Intelligence reframed: Multiple intelligences for the 21st century.* New York: Basic Books.

Glaser, B. G. & Strauss, A. L. (1967). *The discovery of grounded theory.* Chicago: Aldine.

Heinemann, H. N., & DeFalco, A. A. (1990). Dewey's pragmatism: A philosophical foundation for cooperative education. *Journal of Cooperative Education, 27*(1), 38–44.

Kolb, D. A. (1984). *Experiential learning: Experience as the source of learning and development.* Englewood Cliffs, NJ: Prentice Hall.

Lave, J. (1991). Situated learning in communities of practice. In L. B. Resnick, J. M. Levine, & S. D. Teasley (Eds.), *Shared cognition: Thinking as social practice, perspectives on socially shared cognition* (pp. 63–82). Washington, DC: American Psychological Association.

Lincoln, Y. S., & Guba, E. G. (1985). *Naturalistic inquiry.* Beverly Hills, CA: Sage.

Miles, M. B., & Huberman, A. M. (1984). *Qualitative data analysis—A sourcebook of new methods.* Beverley Hills, CA: Sage.

Morton, L. L., Dawson, P., & Laing, D. A. (1993). Interpersonal skill development through cooperative education. *Guidance and Counselling, 9*(2), 26–31.

Mosbacker, W. B. (1969). The role of the coordinator. *Journal of Cooperative Education, V*(2), 29–37.

Patton, M. Q. (1990). *Qualitative evaluation and research methods* (2nd ed.). Newbury Park, CA: Sage.

Pea, R. D. (1997). Practices of distributed intelligence and designs for education. In G. Salomon (Ed.), *Distributed cognitions: Psychological and educational considerations.* Cambridge: Cambridge University Press.

Peshkin, A. (1993). The goodness of qualitative research. *Educational Researcher, 22*(2), 24–30.

Ricks, F., Van Gyn, G., Branton, G., Cutt, J., Loken, M., & Ney, T. (1990). Theory and research in cooperative education: Practice implications. *Journal of Cooperative Education, 27*(1), 7–20.

Rogoff, B. (1995). Observing sociocultural activity on three planes: Participatory appropriation, guided participation and apprenticeship. In J. V. Wertsch, P. del Rio, & A. Alvarez (Eds.), *Sociocultural studies of mind* (pp. 139–164). Cambridge: Cambridge University Press.

Ryan, G., Toohey, S., & Hughes, C. (1996). The purpose, value and structure of the practicum in higher education: A literature review. *Higher Education, 31*, 355–377.

Salomon, G. & Perkins, D. N. (1998) Individual and social aspects of learning. *Review of Research in Education*, (Vol. 23, pp. 1–24). Itasca, IL: F.E. Peacock.

Simon, R. I., Dippo, D., & Schenke, A. (1991). *Learning work: A critical pedagogy of work education*. New York: Bergin & Garveys.

Van Gyn, G., Cutt, J., Loken, M., & Ricks, F. (1997). Investigating the educational benefits of cooperative education: A longitudinal study. *Journal of Cooperative Education, 32*(2), 70–85.

Vygotsky, L. S. (1978). *Mind in society*. Cambridge, MA: Harvard University Press.

Weston, W. D. (1986). Career identity and its relationship to participation in a cooperative education program. *Journal of Cooperative Education, 23*(1), 25–36.

Williams, W. M., Sternberg, R. J., Rashotte, C. A., & Wagner, R. K. (1992). Assessing the value of cooperative education. *Journal of Cooperative Education, 28*(2), 32–55.

Wilson, J. W. (1989). Assessing outcomes of cooperative education. *Journal of Cooperative Education, 25*(2), 38–45.

Wilson, R. L. (1980–1981). The national assessment of cooperative learning: A preliminary report. *Journal of Cooperative Education, 7*(3), 26–33.

Appendix
General Interview Protocol: Interview 2[1]

Interview 2

Name _____   Code _____

Date of Interview _____

1. Background
What is the official name of this organization?

What is your official position designation for this placement here?

Who is your work supervisor? How often do you see this person?

Who else do you work with? (What are their positions?)

How many months or weeks will you be working here roughly?

How many hours do you work a week?

What is your pay rate per hour?

2. The Workplace
Feelings for the Company and the Work

What has it been like working here?

What have you been doing?

How would you describe your role in this company?

How have you felt about this role—the work you have been doing?
    (Do you think your work is valuable?)

What value do you feel the work the company does has to society?

Have you done what you thought you were going to do? (Has any aspect of the
    work surprised you?)

Has the placement lived up to your expectations?

Have you felt motivated to do a good job here?

(If so) What motivates you to do a good job here?

How do you feel about how much you have been paid for what you do?

(In comparison to others here, or elsewhere?)

Has your pay rate influenced your thinking about a career in Science
    and Technology?

Induction and Belonging

What was like working here in the first few weeks?

Did you receive an induction or orientation?

---

[1]Not all questions were asked of each interviewee, and all individuals were asked specific follow-up questions from the first interview.

What did it involve? What did it cover?

Is there anything else you would liked to have known before you started working here?

How do you feel now about working here as compared to when you started?

Do you feel a part of this organization? Why or why not?

Culture and Purpose of the Organization

People talk about an organization having a particular culture or atmosphere, based around things like how hard people work, what they do at work, what they talk about.

Is there a particular culture or atmosphere here? How have you found this out?

Can you describe the purpose of this organization? (What is it here to do?)

What have you learnt about the type of work or industry (use specifics for each student) this organization is involved in from working here?

Has the placement helped you understand what it is like to be at work? How?

People at Work

What have the people been like? Have you got on with some or all of them? Why or why not?

(How have people at work reacted to you as a university student?)

Do your workmates think it's a good idea you are doing this placement as part of your degree? Why? (How do you know?)

Do you know how your workmates feel about working here?

Concerns and Mistakes

Have you any concerns about what you have been doing, or how the placement has gone?

Have you made any mistakes at work?

What happened?

Were there any repercussions?

What did you learn from it?

What do you do at work when you don't know or understand something?

Teamworking

Have you been working mainly individually or as a team member? (Mostly?) How do you feel about these ways of working?

3. Learning

Log Book

Have you been using your learning logbook? Is there anything there we could talk about?

Challenge and Opportunities
What have been the challenges for you (mental, physical, time management)?
Do you feel that you have had enough opportunities to learn here?

Conjunction With University Learning
What value has your university learning been to you in this work place?
Has it been relevant? (Have you been able to apply it?) (Has it been valuable to the company do you think?)
Are you learning in a different way to how you learnt at university? How?

Feedback and Assessment
Have you been getting feedback on how you are doing? How do you feel about the feedback you get? What forms does it take?
Do you feel they value the work you are doing here?
Do you feel you have had opportunities to contribute, comment, question?
How do you feel you should be assessed for your placement to be able to show your learning?

Working Knowledges
What theoretical knowledge have you learnt here?
How have you learnt this?
What skills have you learnt here?
How have you learnt them?
Are there particular ways of doing things around here? (e.g., work hours, breaks, techniques, asking for something, etc.). Are there any peculiar customs?
How have you learnt these things?
Is there any particular language (technical jargon, inhouse lingo, nicknames) used in this workplace?
How have you learnt it?
What have you learnt about getting on and working with people here (you to them and them to them)?
How have you learnt this?
How have you got with your supervisor workwise? Socially?
How have you got with your co-workers workwise? Socially?
What role has your university supervisor played in your placement so far?
What role has your placement coordinator played in your placement so far?
Has anyone else been helpful to your learning here? (How have they helped?)

Wrap-up
Is there anything else that you know now that you didn't before you started here?
How have you come to know it?

4. Science and Technology

Do you consider what you have been doing here as Science or Technology, or both? Why/why not?

What have you learnt about being a scientist/technologist in this placement?

What have you learnt about the process of doing science/technology in this placement?

5. Career Direction

What value do you place on your experience here? (Your learning).

Has working here influenced your thinking about your career and short term future?

Has working here helped you with your decision about what courses to take, and what career direction to follow?

How are you feeling now about going back to university?

Do you think you will be able to use at university things you have learnt here? How? What about longer term?

Part III

Methods and Analysis

6

Combining Quantitative and Qualitative Data: A Lifespan Study of Cooperative Education

Patricia L. Linn
Antioch College

Key questions addressed in this chapter:

☞ How do we decide what methodology to use?

☞ Will averages and other statistics capture the rich experiences our co-op students describe?

☞ Should my study employ one or multiple methods?

☞ How do the goals of experimental and qualitative studies differ?

☞ What are the benefits of collaborating with someone who brings a different perspective to the project?

In this chapter, I report on a study of graduates of Antioch College's liberal arts cooperative education program. The research design combines numbered data (the quantitative component of the study) with narrative data (the qualitative component). One goal of the chapter is to describe the study's findings to date; a second goal is to make explicit the decision points in combining quantitative and qualitative data.

I was trained as a research developmental psychologist. Such training in the 1970s focused on experimental or quasiexperimental designs, followed by the use of inferential statistics to assess the study outcomes. When I became a psychology professor at Antioch College, I carried on that tradition, teaching the same research methods and statistics I had learned to a new generation of psychologists.

Teaching at Antioch College, where all students alternate between terms of study on campus and terms of work at job sites across the country and abroad, led me to new questions about human development than those I had asked previously. I began to wonder about the development evident in my students when they returned from their cooperative education ("co-op") jobs. The students seemed to know themselves and the world in new ways after a term or two of alternating work and study. They even walked differently, and seemed to know more what they wanted from me as a teacher than before their co-op job. I found myself often doing double-takes when I realized that this was the same student I had taught only a term before.

Co-op educators, if they are trained in research design, are likely trained in experimental design. When asking questions about cooperative education or internships, they may struggle, as I did, with the difficulty of accommodating standard research designs to the questions they are asking. Experimental designs are useful to address questions about whether participation in co-op programs yields certain outcomes (e.g., higher starting salaries in the first job after graduation), when compared with students who do not co-op. In this example, the outcome (starting salaries) is known and assumed to be important and desired. A different research design, based on correlations, can be useful when *explanation* and *prediction* are the goals. For example, what student variables best explain an employer's evaluation of student job performance? Once explanatory variables are identified, predictions can be made about the employer evaluations other students are likely to receive, based on their data on the same explanatory variables. Again, the outcome (employer rating of job performance) is not questioned, but rather the variables that might predict it. These research questions are well-suited to standard research designs and numbered data. Indeed, many co-op educators and employers may feel that only such "scientific" and "objective" methods should be used to explain and justify our programs because the academy has traditionally valued such research methods over others.

Some questions about student outcomes may not be so easily addressed with standard research designs. My own question began to take this form: How does learning happen when students alternate between work and study? This question focuses attention on the process (vs. the outcomes) of learning, and the goal becomes understanding (vs. explanation or prediction). I suspected that such understanding would stem from the stories students were telling me about their experiences. I didn't want to exclude numbered data because summary statistics were also interesting to me, like the average number of different jobs taken or the range of employer ratings of job performance. However, the stories seemed to add a richness and level of detail in describing learning that the numbers could not capture. One basic tenet of research design is that the method chosen should suit the research question. In my case this guideline suggested that qualitative methods should be explored.

I searched the published literature but found few published studies on learning processes in cooperative education. I decided to design my own study. The steps to take to address my curiosity about workplace learning were not evident from my graduate research methods courses: How are interviews designed to collect learning stories? Can stories be data? Early on I found a useful handbook by Miles and Huberman (1994), who captured my concerns: "Words are fatter than numbers and usually have multiple meanings" (p. 56). How could I avoid being overwhelmed by the volume of text I wanted to collect? How do you analyze words? Does software exist to help make sense of textual data? This gap between my training and my needs as a researcher offered a positive professional development opportunity to teach myself interview methods, qualitative study design, and computer-aided qualitative data analysis. There are several approaches to qualitative research; this report describes one. Other approaches can be found in Denzin and Lincoln (1994), Glaser (1993), Miles and Huberman (1994), Patton (1990), and Wolcott (1994).

BACKGROUND LITERATURE

Fletcher (1990) divided research on cooperative education learning into two categories: studies of learning *outcomes* and studies of learning *processes*. I read some of the learning outcomes research. For example, Grantz and Thanos (1996) described influences on students' classroom learning from their internships, like recognizing multiple perspectives and taking responsibility for their learning. In terms of career development, cooperative education has been shown to enhance career identity (Weston, 1986), career planning (Mueller, 1992), employment opportunities (Eyler, 1995), and career decisions (Hackett, Croissant, & Schneider, 1992). Once students graduate and enter a career, their short-term career progress has been found to be positively influenced by prior participation in cooperative education, including the level of job responsibility they achieve (Gore, 1972), involvement in decision-making activities (Jarrell, 1974), and salary level (Gardner, 1992; Seidenberg, 1990). Psychological or personal outcomes positively related to co-op experience include students' short-term gains in social adjustment, attachment to their university, commitment to educational goals (Carrell & Rowe, 1993), autonomy, and the quality of their interpersonal relationships (Mueller, 1992).

Compared to the large number of studies on the outcomes of cooperative education learning, I could not find studies aimed at my questions about learning process. Just like other authors in this volume (Grosjean, chap. 3; Eames, chap. 5) who were interested in learning process, I looked for theories about learning that could guide me. Michelson (1996) argued that experiential forms of education must be built on a sound theoretical foundation so that we make intentional decisions about the teaching and learning process. There are various theoretical perspectives on experiential learning available for consideration (see chap. 2, this volume, for a review). I found Kolb's (1984) experiential learning theory, Bandura's (1986) theory of self-efficacy, the theory of practical intelligence by Sternberg and Wagner (1986), and situated learning theory (Lave & Wenger, 1991) all provided useful frameworks for interpreting data I collected for a lifespan study of Antioch graduates.

SETTING AND PROGRAM

Antioch College's cooperative education program was designed by Arthur Morgan and instituted in 1921. Morgan's (1920/1968) educational idea, which still guides Antioch's program today, is that work and study complement each other throughout a student's college career: "Until learning has tried itself out on life, it is not wisdom, but dreaming, or at best, opinion. Life never quite gets into books, and can never be mastered with books alone. It must be acquired also from contact with realities" (p. 179).

The graduates in this study received one credit for each week of work they completed successfully (i.e., their performance was rated as successful by their employers), and they were required to earn 90 co-op credits toward graduation over 5 years. Most students traveled cross-country to their co-op jobs, although some jobs were on-campus or with local employers. Credit was based on a co-op report written by the student and an employer evaluation; the report, evaluation and other materials were saved in Antioch's archive.

Decision Point: What kind of sample should I use?

I decided to study graduates who were at or near retirement so they could reflect on their long work and life histories. The archive has more complete records for some eras than others. I chose the 1946–1955 era. Some of my research questions seemed well-suited to choosing a *random sample* of graduates from the College's alumni/ae database and asking them to fill out a survey. For example, I wanted to know how many and what kinds of jobs or careers were typical of Antioch graduates. If the graduates were sampled randomly, I could generalize to the population of all graduates from this era (at least ones whose addresses were known by the college). The survey responses would give me the information I needed to pull a smaller, *purposeful sample* for the interviews. A purposeful sample does not have to be large because the goal is understanding individual human experience rather than drawing inferences to a population. A purposeful sample can be chosen to represent any dimension that is of particular interest, including extremes and median values. I decided to start with a random sample and developed a survey for them to fill out. I would analyze those data and use inferential statistics with them. I would then use variables from the survey like *gender, college major*, and *number of jobs taken across career* to choose a smaller, purposeful sample ($n = 32$) to interview in depth about their learning experiences. After preliminary analysis of the interviews, I selected just 15 graduates to fully analyze their interviews and various papers found in the archive and test some emerging interpretations of the graduates' experiences.

QUANTITATIVE METHODS

I selected a group of 120 graduates randomly from our alumni database of 1946–1955 graduates, oversampling women to allow a gender-balanced sample even though more than twice as many men than women graduated from Antioch in this era. Hoping for at least 40 positive responses, I was surprised when more than 60% ($n = 73$) of those contacted agreed to participate. Almost one half of the participants were women, and 69 of them were Euro-American. A *Work History Questionnaire* was then developed to find out what the typical career patterns were for our graduates from this era. The 14-page questionnaire asked for information about each job held since graduation and other relevant life events. We then pulled the respondents' co-op files from the archive and summarized their co-op job histories. The first round of analysis was to summarize in numbers these co-op histories drawn from the archive and career histories from the questionnaire and to relate the one set of numbers to the other. Some of the findings are described in the following; a full report of the quantitative findings can be found in Linn and Ferguson (1999).

QUANTITATIVE FINDINGS

First I describe the findings drawn from the archive. Co-op employers used a 12-point scale to rate students' work in five areas of performance: quality of work, quantity of work, level of responsibility taken, good judgment used, and cooperation with co-workers. On average the ratings were quite high: about 8.5 out of 12 for the first four performance areas and 9.2 for cooperation. However, there were low ratings given by employers to some students: 15 of the 73 had a mean rating (across the five areas of performance) below 6 for at least one job. This gets interesting later.

The greatest percentage of the sample (31%) were social science majors in college, with about 18% of the sample in each of education and sciences and math majors and the rest from business, engineering, humanities, and the arts. Table 6.1 describes the number and type of co-op jobs held by the sample. Notice that of the eight or so co-op jobs completed by these students only about 6 were major-related—this demonstrates Antioch's design for the co-op program to contribute to a student's general education as well as for building career skills and for career planning. We also compared some available demographic and co-op history variables for those who agreed to participate in the study and those who declined. The only variable that showed a significant group difference was number of co-op jobs held[1] with participants completing on average about one more co-op job than those who declined.

---

[1]$t(91) = 2.37$, $p < .05$. The *t*-test compares average scores between two groups and yields a value (2.37) based on the number of respondents (91) and a significance level (p) that suggests that the group difference in the number of co-op jobs taken would only be found less than 5/100 times by chance. Most social scientists agree that this is a reasonable chance of error to accept.

TABLE 6.1

Descriptive Statistics on Number and Type of Co-op Jobs Held by Sample ($n = 73$)

Variable	Mean	Standard Deviation	Range
Number of co-op jobs	8.4	2.1	4–15
Number of nonrepeating jobs	5.8	1.6	2–9
Number of jobs in cities new to them	3.6	1.5	1–9
Number of jobs related to major	6.2	2.3	0–11

What about the data provided on the *Work History Questionnaire?* The average age of the graduates at the time I contacted them was about 70 years (range 65–81 years), and 78% of them were retired from their primary occupation. About 32% of the sample had completed a master's degree, and another 14% had an advanced degree. The mean number of post-graduate jobs held was 6.5 (range 1–23). About 41% of the sample had been self-employed at some point during their careers. Also 41% (all were women) had taken time off (an average of 12 years) from working outside the home to care for children, but all the women had also worked outside the home.

When we looked for relationships between the co-op and career data set, one of the more intriguing findings involved those 15 students whose work performance had been rated as below average by their employers averaged across all five areas. We compared them with the other students who always performed well to see who earned graduate degrees after college. As shown in Table 6.2, most of the students with a low performance co-op went on to earn a graduate degree.[2] Of course we do not recommend poor performance on a co-op job if academic success is the goal;

TABLE 6.2

Low-Performance Co-ops by Graduate Degree

		Graduate	Degree
		Yes	No
Low-Performance Co-op	Yes	11	4
	No	22	36

$\chi^2 = 6, p \le .02$

---

[2]$\chi^2 (1) = 6, p = .02$. The Chi square test evaluates whether people fall into categories randomly or in a systematic pattern where the categories covary. In this case there is a strong tendency for the graduates who had a low performance co-op to also earn a graduate degree. The strength of the pattern is shown in the significance level of .02, which means that only 2/100 times would such a pattern occur by chance.

rather, we are intrigued by this finding because it seems to support Sternberg and Wagner's (1986) argument that work and school tap different kinds of intelligence.

In this first round analysis, correlations between co-op variables (e.g., number of co-op jobs held) and career variables (e.g., number of postgraduate jobs held) were nonsignificant. More complex patterns of co-op and career experiences were investigated next.

Pattern Analyses

The sample was broken down into four possible patterns of co-op/career job-taking to explore whether these subsets of respondents were differentiated on other study variables. The variables *number of different co-op jobs taken* and the *number of different postgraduate jobs taken* were first split at their medians (i.e., the middle-most score). For the *number of different postgraduate jobs taken* variable, we eliminated middle-level scores (scores of 5, $N = 9$) until the low and high groups differed significantly on the variable used to split them. The low and high groups differed significantly on the *number of different co-op jobs taken* variable without eliminating any scores. The two variables (now dichotomous) were then crossed, yielding four patterns of co-op/career job-taking: *low/low, low/high, high/low, and high/high*. For example, membership in the *low/high* group means the respondent experienced few different co-op job experiences, but went on to take a high number of different jobs across their careers. These four subsets of respondents were significantly different from each other on a number of variables. For example, as shown in Table 6.3, the groups differed significantly from expected patterns of self-employment.[3] Respondents with consistent patterns of job-taking across their lives (*low/low* and *high/high* patterns) were significantly more likely to be self-employed at some time than those with other patterns. We speculated that the students who tended to stay with one employer (the *low/low* group) accumulated enough capital to become self-employed. Others who moved frequently among different jobs (the *high/high* group) accumulated a type of human capital or what Bandura (1986) called *enactive mastery* experiences that gave them the confidence they needed to take the risk of becoming self-employed.

Self-Employment Types

Because self-employment during the career was a common experience in the sample and strongly predicted by other variables, it was explored further. Which graduates tended to become self-employed? Gender didn't predict self-employment: As

---

[3]$\chi^2 (3) = 11.9, p = .008$. The Chi square test evaluates whether people fall into categories randomly or in a systematic pattern where the categories covary. In this case there is a strong tendency for the graduates who fell in the categories of "consistent patterns of job-taking" to also fall in the "self-employed" category. The strength of the pattern is shown in the significance level of .008, which means that only 8/1000 times would such a pattern occur by chance.

TABLE 6.3

Observed (and Expected) Self-Employment of Graduates
in Four Co-op/Career Patterns

Co-op/Career Pattern[a]	Whether ever self-employed		
	Yes	No	Total
low/low	10 (7.0)	7 (10.0)	17
low/high	3 (7.8)	16 (11.2)	19
high/low	3 (5.3)	10 (7.7)	13
high/high	14 (9.9)	10 (14.1)	24
Total	30	43	73

Note. χ^2 (3) = 11.9, p = .008

[a]Patterns based on median splits of number of different jobs taken during co-op program and in postgraduate career.

many women as men were self-employed at least once during their careers. The self-employed were fairly evenly divided among college majors, with some tendency for more graduates than expected from the arts and humanities, as well as business majors, to become self-employed later on. We returned to the *Work History Questionnaires* and broke down self-employment further, based on definitions provided by Bird (1989). The 30 respondents who were self-employed were divided into two groups: those who worked alone as consultants or solo professionals (17 or 57%) and those who started their own businesses as entrepreneurs or shop owners (13 or 43%). These two types of self-employed workers were then compared in terms of other variable relationships. The types of self-employed workers fell unevenly across the co-op and career job-taking patterns, but there were not enough data to analyze the finding statistically. All the graduates who started businesses were equally divided between the two consistent patterns (*low/low* and *high/high*), and only consultants and solo professionals fell into the other two patterns. Again, the two consistent patterns may provide the financial and human capital to allow the creation of new businesses.

QUALITATIVE METHODS

Then I used what I knew about the careers of the 73 graduates to choose a subgroup of 32 to study further. In retrospect, a smaller interview pool could have been chosen and the data would have been more manageable. With the interviews, my goal shifted from generalizing from a sample to a population of Antioch College graduates to understanding: How did learning happen for these individuals? I chose a balanced number of men and women and graduates from a range of career types. The next steps were to interview them and to study their narrative co-op reports.

Decision Point: Using questionnaire data as a starting point for interview questions.

I wanted to develop an interview that revolved around a small number of open-ended questions, so that graduates had room to construct meaning of their experiences rather than my forcing their experiences into my own framework. However, the questionnaire data also piqued my curiosity about career patterns revealed there. For example, why had some respondents taken so many different career jobs whereas others had stuck with the same employer throughout their careers? I used what I knew about the respondents' college and career histories from the numbered data to generate probes, or follow-up questions, for the interview. For example, if a respondent had stayed with one employer until retirement, was this due to the absence of other opportunities, or were opportunities rejected in favor of staying put? If a respondent had taken a large number of different career jobs, moving frequently and trying out new kinds of work, were there adaptation skills they could identify, and where did those skills come from?

The interviews were completed over the phone, audiotaped, and then transcribed verbatim. The method yielded over 1,600 pages of text. Luckily there are software programs (I used QSR Nud*ist Vivo, 1999) designed to help researchers organize a large amount of text, code the ideas revealed there, think, and write about what is found.

Decision Point: Choosing a software package to allow computer-aided analysis of text.

There are many software packages available to help researchers organize, code, and retrieve textual data. Weitzman and Miles (1994) provided a reference for qualitative data analysis packages. Their book is user-friendly and very helpful. The authors not only provide full descriptions of 22 software packages and evaluate them on several common dimensions, but they also include a worksheet to help readers determine which package might best fit their study question and data. I found that the organization of the software descriptions into standard categories made it easy to compare across packages, and the worksheet led me to one or two packages to investigate further. I ordered trial versions of those packages and chose the one that fit my project and my preferences best.

QUALITATIVE FINDINGS

Early in the interview, before I revealed fully my particular interest in co-op learning, I asked the graduates to talk briefly about their classes at Antioch, their co-ops, and their experience of the participatory governance system that we call the *com-*

munity part of the program. Then I asked them to tell me what it was about Antioch, if anything, that had the biggest impact on them, letting them define for themselves what *biggest impact* meant. Their responses are shown in Table 6.4. Clearly the co-op program is perceived as the component with the biggest impact for this group of 32 graduates from the late 1940s and early 1950s. These data are a little difficult for us classroom faculty to accept because we would all like to think that our brilliant teaching will have the biggest impact on our students. Here is the power of experiential learning.

Decision Point: Summarizing qualitative data as numbers.

Some interview questions yield answers that can be summarized as numbers to help the reader understand how responses fall into a few categories. Respondents gave a variety of answers to the question, "What aspect of the Antioch program, if any, had the most impact on you?" But those answers seemed to fall into just four categories: co-op program, classroom program, campus community, and other. Turning text into numbers was useful to support the argument that cooperative education was perceived to have a strong impact in the lives of Antioch College graduates. Numbers that refer to categories represent a different level of measurement (*nominal* level) than numbers used to count age or jobs (*interval* level). The choice of which statistical analysis to use depends on the level of measurement; be sure to select a statistical analysis to match the level of measurement of your variables.

Our qualitative analyses of the co-op reports and interviews yielded a complex hierarchical-coding scheme that looks like the root structure of a large tree; it includes eight levels of code concepts, and the work is still in progress. These coded concepts include many types of work-related learning (e.g., skills like welding learned in a co-op job at a foundry). But many examples were also evident of what I

TABLE 6.4

Responses to Interview Question: What Had the Biggest Impact on You at Antioch?
(*n* = 32)

Answer	#	Summarized as
Co-op program	13	Co-op = 13
Intellectual atmosphere or particular coursework	5	Classroom = 5
Personal relationships or meeting diverse others	5	Community = 7
Race relations or harmony	2	
Built self-confidence	2	Other = 7
Too difficult to separate—whole package had impact	3	
Psychological counseling	1	
Political atmosphere	1	

call *5-to-9* learning because the learning happened between 5:00 p.m. and 9:00 a.m., or outside regular work hours. At their rooming houses, in bars, and invited to the boss' house for dinner, these students were immersed in learning that stemmed from living in new cities, away from home and campus life. There is only room here to sample a few of the excerpts from the co-op reports and interview transcripts. Dick Meisler, an Antioch graduate who was then a faculty colleague, helped me code and think about the co-op reports, but his training in philosophy also suggested a second approach.

Decision Point: To code or not to code?

My tendency when faced with mountains of textual data was to condense it into codes that stood for themes found to reoccur across individuals. My collaborator suggested that simultaneous with this coding process, we get together after having read through a graduate's entire file (admissions essays, first-year paper, co-op papers, employer evaluations, senior paper, Work History Questionnaire, interview transcripts) and spend several hours talking about that individual and their use of the Antioch program. Again, Miles and Huberman (1994) were useful in clarifying this second approach as *phenomenology*. Phenomenologists approach an interview transcript by keeping the context of the materials intact, reading through them repeatedly to try to understand the respondent's meaning. We evolved a combination approach: coding to discover common themes across the graduates and regularly spending the day with a graduate's entire file to attempt to fully understand his or her individual use of the program and to keep learning in its context.

Here is an example of a passage from a co-op report written in 1945 by a 21-year-old education major, co-oping at an alternative school in Illinois:

> For the first 2 weeks, I was in the courtyard in the morning, directing games with one of the other teachers. The games most commonly played were Pom Pom, Stone Tag, Red Rover, and Red Light. After the first few days I felt the need of introducing new games, and looked some up in the school library, which, incidentally, is an excellent one. I was amazed to see how readily the children responded to any new games presented to them, and how eager and attentive they were. I had previously seen children who rebelled against any new forms of play and would stick solely to the old familiar ones.

I coded this passage as an example of an *enactive mastery* experience, one of the sources of self-efficacy that Bandura (1986) identified. The student's preconceptions (about children accepting new games) were altered by a successful experience introducing new games. Note also her *problem finding* (she noticed the need for new activities) and her use of available resources (the school's library). This kind of work-related skill building is likely what Morgan and others had in mind when co-op programs were designed: The learning is planned and career-related.

Here is another quote from a co-op report—this one written in 1946 by a woman who was a political science major co-oping at the Research Institute of America in New York:

> One-hundred-eleventh Street [in New York City] is not a slum. From the outside it looks like a good section. Yet I feel now that I have a little more understanding of these conditions. Not only is it true that there is little time to clean house after work, but also no one likes to take a bath in a tub from which the cockroaches have to be swept, and with only two burners, it is hard to eat enough vegetables for a balanced diet. One finds oneself living on bread to a large degree. This is interesting to watch for a short period when one knows that one can go home again at the end and be just as before; only retaining a knowledge that things are different in another environment and knowing when one reads that federal housing projects are a waste since there is a class of people that ruin any place they get into, that it is rather the place that ruins the people.

This passage was coded as 5-to-9 learning, under a subcategory for learning that leads to new perspectives on *social injustice*. The learning happened because she was living in the inexpensive housing where student workers often find themselves. What is described is a dawning awareness of the influence of environment on physical and psychological well-being. She is both a participant ("one finds oneself living on bread ...") and an observer ("this is interesting to watch ...").

Finally, I want to offer some examples from the interviews completed 40 to 50 years after graduation. What stands out for graduates about their co-op learning as they look back from a point of retirement? Here we are finding evidence that *perceptual shifts* occur when multiple workplace experiences build on earlier ones. Take, for example, the following two excerpts, drawn from an interview with an engineer who graduated in 1952. In the first excerpt he is remembering his first co-op job where he worked with engineers who were doing ground-breaking work in human factors engineering:

> Every once in a while I'd go over to the [project test field] and they would use me for a guinea pig for various tests ... and the best thing about it was I had a lot of time in between tests, so I spent a lot of time in the library, reading the *Journal of Psychosomatic Medicine* and some of the other psychological books and things ... and it kind of encouraged me to make sure that when I did design things that they would be psychologically sound at least ... that was the thing we found in these aircraft instruments. Some of them just made absolutely no sense whatsoever. You know, they'd have some things where the "on" position of the switch would be up, and others the "on" position of the switch would be down ....

In this same interview, the graduate remembered a later co-op as a gas serviceman in Detroit:

> I think working for the gas company when I was servicing appliances, I would see a lot of dumb design features that I resolved to make sure when I was designing stuff that I

wouldn't design anything like [those appliances]. It's interesting to see how people use things that are designed by engineers who figure the people using them are going to be as smart as they are, and most of the people using the things that we design are not.

This graduate went on to tie an emerging awareness in his twenties of how to design things that people could use into a highly successful career in engineering design. His story led me to go back and sift through my interviews once again, to collect other such examples of perceptual shifts that result from multiple co-op experiences and seem important as graduates reflect back over their long careers. This finding felt like a step closer to our goal of describing processes of learning. We have also noticed some linguistic features of the textual data that seem to serve as markers of important workplace learning, like metaphors ("I was a sponge …"), conflicting adjectives ("a very small incident" but it "had a profound influence"), and deprecating comments used to frame learning stories ("this is probably unimportant but …"). These examples reflect thinking about thinking (psychologists call this *metacognition*).

The findings described here are drawn from the method of coding passages to reflect themes that repeat across the different graduates' materials. Dick Meisler's phenomenological approach led him to develop a format he called *storylines* to reflect his understanding of the full sweep of a graduate's life history as he or she entered Antioch, used the program to meet individual needs, graduated, and went on to an adult work life (Meisler & Linn, 2000). Here is an example of such a storyline, focused on an Antioch student who graduated in 1950.

When Louise tells her story in her college senior paper, she begins with a reminder that this is racist America and that she grew up in a segregated New York slum. But her main story is also about her family: her too-young unwed mother; her anxious and concerned grandmother, the dominant figure of her family, a woman who was ambitious, proud, and difficult; her remote uninvolved grandfather, who could pass for White, and did so, holding down a job that he could not have had if he were recognized as Black, even maintaining two residences to achieve the deception. Louise was raised by her grandmother for her first eleven years, during much of which her mother was not in the household. Then, when her mother remarried, Louise moved to her mother's apartment and joined a new nuclear family. Here Louise, by her own description, ruled the roost. She was valedictorian of her high-school class of 500. Louise wanted to go away to college, a desire that led to a family conflict over finances that resulted, she believes, in her mother's eventual divorce.

Louise went to a junior college for a year, and then to Antioch, helped by a loan from the family who employed her mother as a domestic and by funds from the college's Interracial Scholarship fund. In the 1940s, co-op educators had a problem placing African-American students, and Louise's co-op career is clearly a story of finding reasonably reliable, nonracist employers. She worked at a local industry that had been started by an Antioch graduate, and then worked as a recreation director for girls' cottages working for the Bureau of Juvenile Research in Ohio. Her most important job may have been working for the YMCA's Vocational Service Center in New York, which helped returning veterans plan for and begin their new careers. She returned to that job before she graduated. Louise then worked in an American Friends' race-relations project in DC and in a politically progressive work camp in Finland. The Finland placement gave her the opportunity to travel in Europe.

She spent a summer at home working while she considered dropping out of Antioch and transferring to another college. But she returned, and took a job down South in a rural-life school. She also had a social-work job in Pittsburgh. Louise arrived at Antioch frightened and intimidated. How could she compete with students who had so many advantages? The deck certainly was stacked against her. It wasn't easy, by her testimony, to be one of a very few African-American students on campus, even if the college was making good-faith efforts to integrate, even being a leader in the field. That was small comfort for a member of a very small minority, inevitably isolated in many ways on campus. Nevertheless, the narrative of each co-op job is one of growth and discovery. At this point, I don't know whether Louise was placed in social-change-oriented jobs because of her interests or because those employers were less likely to discriminate against Blacks. But without doubt, Louise increasingly identified with the social missions of the organizations she worked in, and her personal problems and concerns slowly move off center stage. That scared girl slowly, before our eyes, becomes a woman who is going to try to make the world a better place.

Louise married a man she met down south at the progressive rural school and lived in Chicago and moved to Seattle. She worked in community organizations and focused on public health. She was not too proud to do the difficult grass-roots work. Gradually, she rose in her organizations and assumed greater responsibilities. She became a community leader. Whenever she had the chance, she advocated for women and African Americans, and she often succeeded in moving toward the equalization of opportunities for them. Her early contact on co-op jobs with the Quaker ethos of the American Friends may have influenced her deeply. At very least it struck a chord in her, and her style of community work seems to have grown from it. She quotes the Quaker adage about work being love made real in the world, and she seems to have done a good job of living by it.

Going back and forth between these storylines (that encompass all the materials available to us as researchers) and the coded passages (removed from their context) has evolved into a strategy that is both satisfying and compelling. Satisfying in the sense that when a document in fully coded, it feels like progress is being made, but it is the fuller stories that span a graduate's life that draw us back to our most fundamental research question about how a college program can help a young person compose a life.

Finally, although the graduates politely answered my question about what part of the Antioch curriculum had the biggest impact on them, many graduates went on to argue that it was the program as a whole that impacted their development. These graduates saw their learning across various aspects of the curriculum as more alike than different. They learned how to learn, including adapting to the changes that inevitably occurred in their lives like divorce, getting fired, or moving to follow a spouse. Situated learning theory (Lave & Wenger, 1991) would predict that repeated entry into new communities of practice in liberal arts course requirements, in cooperative education jobs and through participation in the governance of the campus offered opportunities to move from periphery to center, and from newcomer to old-timer (see Linn, 2002, for a fuller discussion of situated learning theory and the residential liberal arts experience). Learning how to enter new communities of practice may be the most important way that co-op programs help graduates to succeed.

NEXT STEPS

We have now collected data from a mid-career group of graduates (graduation years 1976–1985). We are using the same methods as reported here with the new group and our questions will be essentially the same: How did learning happen and what seems important to the graduate about that learning now? From our work with the first cohort, we know more about various categories of learning to look for and which learning theories may serve us well as frameworks to understand the data. We can then compare the experiences of the two age cohorts to see which kinds of learning are consistently evident and which may be due to generational and career phase differences. Our work on this ongoing project about processes of co-op learning often feels like finding our way in the dark, however the combination of qualitative and quantitative methods seems to have the potential to capture both the commonalities across students' experiences and the unique quality of each student's co-op learning. I would be pleased to hear from any readers who would like to discuss these data or research issues in general.

Summary
- Co-op educators may not have training in quantitative or qualitative methods, but these methods can be self-taught.
- A combination of methods may work best to capture both average patterns of student experiences and the particular meanings students make of their individual experiences.
- Experimental and qualitative studies have different goals that lead to different choices about sampling.
- Numbered data can be used to suggest interview questions, and interview responses can be categorized numerically.
- Computer-aided qualitative data analysis software can help in the management of textual data.
- Collaborating with someone who offers a different perspective on how to approach the data can be very productive.

ANNOTATED BIBLIOGRAPHY

Fletcher, J. (1990). Self-esteem and cooperative education: A theoretical framework. *Journal of Cooperative Education, 27,* 41–55. Fletcher's article first helped me understand the distinction between outcome and process studies of co-op and so helped me to understand how my question differed from the questions usually asked in the co-op research literature. This is also a good example of using a theoretical framework (self-efficacy) to make predictions about co-op learning.

Miles, M. B., & Huberman, A. M. (1994). *Qualitative data analysis: An expanded sourcebook* (2nd ed.). Thousand Oaks, CA: Sage. This is a resource I turn to frequently as I move through the qualitative aspects of my research project. The first section helps one locate one's perspective among other qualitative approaches. Their approach then focuses on data displays: various ways of presenting summary data, making comparisons, and testing hypotheses. If you can't expect the audience of your project to read a long case study, their ideas about displays will be helpful.

Lave, J., & Wegner, E. (1991). *Situated learning: Legitimate peripheral participation.* Cambridge, England: Cambridge University Press. Don't be put off by the density of the Foreword, as the book itself is written in a straightforward style. This little book is useful on many levels: to bring to the table broad questions about schooling (not just educational programs); to understand how our classroom, co-op, and campus community programs are more alike than different; to provide a theoretical perspective on learning that fits cooperative education like a glove.

Wolcott, H. F. (1994). *Transforming qualitative data: Description, analysis and interpretation.* Thousand Oaks, CA: Sage. This author offers us a lifetime of experience working with textual data. What I found useful is his rubric for categorizing qualitative studies in terms of how much emphasis the researcher places on description, analysis, and interpretation. The book is then organized by those three activities, with examples from Wolcott's own work to demonstrate the varied emphases. His bias toward interpretation is obvious, and, together with Miles and Huberman (1994) helped me to understand why coding all my text did not yield conclusive answers but was one step toward the goal of interpretation. No computer program can accomplish the latter. Wolcott's justification of the use of single case studies was also enlightening. As someone who learned quantitative methods first, I was biased toward the belief that more is better; this is true of random, but not purposeful sampling.

Zaruba, K. E., Toma, J. D., & Stark, J. S. (1996). Criteria used for qualitative research in the refereeing process. *The Review of Higher Education, 19,* 435–460. This is a qualitative study that uses as data the comments made by reviewers about qualitative studies sent to them for review. Not only is the study a good example of a report of a qualitative study, but the data themselves guide the reader to understand the criteria reviewers use to judge a good qualitative study.

REFERENCES

Bandura, A. (1986). *Social foundations of thought and action: A social cognitive theory.* Englewood Cliffs, NJ: Prentice-Hall.

Bird, B. J. (1989). *Entrepreneurial behavior.* Glenview, IL: Foresman.

Carrell, S. E., & Rowe, P. M. (1993). Effects of cooperative education on student adaptation to university. *Journal of Cooperative Education, 29,* 33–40.

Denzin, N., & Lincoln, Y. S. (Eds.). (1994). *Handbook of qualitative research.* Thousand Oaks, CA: Sage.

Eyler, J. (1995). Graduates' assessment of the impact of a full-time college internship on their personal and professional lives. *College Student Journal, 29,* 186–194.

Fletcher, J. (1990). Self-esteem and cooperative education: A theoretical framework. *Journal of Cooperative Education, 27,* 41–55.

Gardner, P. D. (1992). Starting salary outcomes of cooperative education graduates. *Journal of Cooperative Education, 27,* 16–26.

Glaser, B. G. (1993). *Basics of grounded theory analysis*. Mills Valley, CA: Sociology Press.

Gore, G. (1972). New evidence of co-op system relevancy. *Journal of Cooperative Education, 8*, 7–14.

Grantz, R., & Thanos, M. (1996). Internships: Academic learning outcomes. *NSEE Quarterly, 22*(1), 10–11; 26.

Hackett, E. J., Croissant, J., & Schneider, B. (1992). Industry, academe, and the values of undergraduate engineers. *Research in Higher Education, 33*, 275–295.

Jarrell, D. (1974). Co-ops and nonco-ops at NASA. *Journal of Cooperative Education, 10*, 51–54.

Kolb, D. A. (1984). *Experiential learning: Experience as the source of learning and development*. Englewood Cliffs, NJ: Prentice-Hall.

Lave, J., & Wegner, E. (1991). *Situated learning: Legitimate peripheral participation*. Cambridge, England: Cambridge University Press.

Linn, P. L. (2002, March 18). Learning theory and the liberal arts. *LiberalArtsOnline*, [On-line] *2*(4). Available: http://www.liberalarts.wabash.edu/liberalartsonline

Linn, P. L., & Ferguson, J. (1999). A lifespan study of cooperative education graduates: Quantitative aspects. *Journal of Cooperative Education, 34*(3), 30–41.

Meisler, R., & Linn, P. L. (2000, June). *Varieties of growth and learning on co-op jobs*. Paper presented at the annual meeting of the Cooperative Education Association, Salt Lake City, Utah.

Michelson, E. (1996). Beyond Galileo's telescope: Situated knowledge and the assessment of experiential learning. *Adult Education Quarterly, 46*, 185–196.

Miles, M. B., & Huberman, A. M. (1994). *Qualitative data analysis: An expanded sourcebook* (2nd ed.). Thousand Oaks, CA: Sage.

Morgan, A. E. (1968). *Observations*. Yellow Springs, OH: Antioch Press. (Original work published 1920.)

Mueller, S. L. (1992). The effect of a cooperative education work experience on autonomy, sense of purpose, and mature interpersonal relationships. *Journal of Cooperative Education, 27*, 27–35.

Patton, M. Q. (1990). *Qualitative evaluation and research methods* (2nd ed.). Thousand Oaks, CA: Sage.

QSR Nud*ist Vivo [Computer software]. (1999). Thousand Oaks, CA: Sage.

Seidenberg, J. M. (1990). A "come-from-behind" victory for cooperative education. *Journal of Cooperative Education, 27*, 21–37.

Sternberg, R. J., & Wagner, R. K. (Eds.). (1986). *Practical intelligence: Nature and origins of competence in the everyday world*. New York: Cambridge University Press.

Weitzman, E., & Miles, M. B. (1994). *Computer programs for qualitative analysis*. Thousand Oaks, CA: Sage.

Weston, W. (1986). Career identity and its relationship to participation in a cooperative education program. *Journal of Cooperative Education, 23*, 25–36.

Wolcott, H. F. (1994). *Transforming qualitative data: Description, analysis and interpretation*. Thousand Oaks, CA: Sage.

7

Choosing a Research Instrument: Investigating the Benefits of Cooperative Education

Geraldine Van Gyn
University of Victoria

Key questions addressed in this chapter:

☞ **A. Issues of Measurement**

1. What are your intentions in collecting these data? What question do you want to answer?

2. Are you able to clearly define what it is that you want to measure?

3. Does your research question require that you collect objective, quantitative, and statistical data or does it require you to collect subjective, qualitative, or interpretative information?

☞ **B. Characteristics of the Instrument**

4. Are you trying to discriminate among events or individuals or should you be comparing your results to a standard?

5. Is there an instrument already available for your study or will you have to develop one?

6. If you have to administer this instrument to participants, is the instrument appropriate for the participants in your study?

7. For your purposes, does the instrument provide an appropriate measurement of your variable of interest?

8. Does the instrument produce constant and repeatable results, if that is what is required by your research question?

☞ C. Practical Concerns
   9. What resources are necessary to develop or procure and administer the instrument?
   10. What resources are necessary to analyze the data collected?

SETTING

The research described in this chapter was conducted from 1988 to 1991 at the University of Victoria (UVic) located in Victoria, British Columbia, Canada. The university had at the time of the study a student population of approximately 12,000 that included part-time and full-time undergraduate and graduate students. During this period the students at UVic were relatively homogeneous in profile, but there were a relatively small number of minority students, mainly from Pacific Rim countries. Cooperative education was practiced in 13 different programs across the faculties of Science, Social Sciences, Education, Engineering, Law, and Human and Social Development. These programs were administered from a central co-op office, but coordinators worked in specific program areas so the model for co-op was a decentralized one. Many new programs in co-op had begun in the early 1980s, and although there was general satisfaction by senior administration and government about co-op at UVic, there was also general concern by faculty members that the programs at UVic were becoming more vocational than intellectual. Cooperative education was often labeled *a training scheme*, or *job-driven*, and was frequently implicated in the perceived effort to vocationalize education in universities.

In these circumstances, an unlikely group of academics came together to understand and document the benefits of participation for students and the university in cooperative education, and in so doing, allay the fears of those in the academic ranks. The link among the chemistry professor who was the Director of Cooperative Education, the social psychologist, the faculty member from kinesiology, and the two economists was the shared belief that cooperative education was an effective educational strategy that needed to be recognized not only for its benefits to career development, but also for its potential to both create significant learning opportunities for students and contribute to their intellectual development. The motivation to substantiate such a notion was partly political, as the cooperative education program, a marginalized unit at UVic, needed more internal support.

THE RESEARCH

The Development Phase

The research question that spawned this research effort (Van Gyn, Cutt, Loken, & Ricks, 1997) was, "is there a difference between co-op students and regular students in the outcomes of their education?" Although there have been a number of studies conducted to address similar questions, notably Wilson and Lyons (1961), Smith (1965), and Lindenmeyer (1967), they were either descriptive in nature or had methodological flaws. Because these studies typically compared co-op to regular students at graduation only, none of these studies had used a research design that documented, in any reliable manner, changes due to the cooperative education program itself. Measurement of outcomes at the end of students' programs is problematical because differences between the co-op and regular groups of students could have been present from the beginning of their programs. Therefore any measured differences may have had nothing to do with their participation in a particular program. We were aware early on in our research planning that we had to use a *pretest and posttest* design. This design is one in which the researcher tests for a particular phenomenon (e.g., educational outcomes) prior to an intervention or treatment (e.g., learning in a university program) and then tests for the same phenomenon after the treatment (e.g., at the end of the program). The difference between the pretest score and the posttest score should reflect the impact of the treatment. The pretest and the posttest are the same test or versions of the same test given at different times. With this design you can measure changes due to treatments or interventions as well as compare the changes that may be the result of various treatments.

A second major problem with previous research was that educational benefits or outcomes were very poorly defined and usually the graduating grade point average (GPA) was used as a measure of educational gain. GPA is influenced by a number of factors in addition to the educational program and we did not regard it as a comprehensive or meaningful measure. We sought to use measures of educational outcomes that would encompass additional dimensions of learning that might result from students gaining both a university education and work experiences.

Decision Point: Do we choose a cross-sectional design or a longitudinal design?

Although not directly related to the choice of research instrument, we could not move forward on that issue until we were clear about what type of research design we would employ. In a *cross-sectional design*, information is collected from one or more samples at one point in time. For the purposes of our study, this would have meant measuring educational variables in a sample of students in the first year of their program, before the future co-ops experienced a work placement, and at the same time, measuring educational variables in a sample of students at the end of their fourth year, when co-ops have finished the majority of their work placements. This approach would have been more convenient in that we could have done it all at once. However, there was a down side to this convenience. We could not be assured that the differences we might see at fourth year were not particular to that sample and that those individuals would have the same characteristics as the students sampled in first year. A *longitudi-*

nal design requires that you test the same sample at various times. In our case, testing would have to take place during the sampled students' first year and then again during their fourth year. As a result the study would take much longer. However, we decided that the benefit of ensuring that changes were not due to differences in the samples but were likely due to the experiences they had during the intervening 3 years outweighed the inconvenience. Another consideration with a longitudinal design is the size of the sample or the number of participants. Because participants are tested over a long period of time, it is inevitable that some individuals will drop out of the study or drop out of the intervention. In our case, we had to think about the number of students who usually drop out of the university and factor that into our required number of participants. The sample tested in first year had to be large enough to ensure adequate numbers remaining in the study in the fourth year on which to base our conclusions. A longitudinal design is expensive to put into operation, but we decided that the rigor of the design would lead to improved credibility of our results. Credibility in our study was paramount. Following is a schematic of our study as it was conducted (*longitudinal*) and how it could have been conducted (*cross-sectional*).

TABLE 7.1

Longitudinal	Spring 1988: 1,000 co-ops and regular students in first year.	Spring 1991: 628 co-ops and regular students in fourth year.
Cross-Sectional	1,000 co-ops and regular students in first year. 1,000 co-ops and regular students in fourth year.	

As stated, one of the main criticisms leveled at previous research was the lack of assurance that the benefits identified in the graduating co-op samples were not a function of the sample itself but of the intervention. Perhaps it is the case that a typical student who chooses to do co-op is more motivated than the typical regular student and does better not because of the program itself but because of that character trait. Therefore, we not only needed to employ the pre–post test design, but we needed to figure out how we would ensure that the two samples, co-ops and regular students, in Year 1 of their programs were as much alike as possible on the variables that might influence eventual academic achievement.

> **Decision Point: How do we control for differences among students at the entry point (first year) so that differences that might be measured in fourth year are a result of the experiences of the intervening period and not of some difference that existed in first year between the co-ops and regular students?**

We were doing a type of experimental study (referred to as *ex post facto research*) in which the variable of interest or *independent variable* (participation or non-participation in co-op) could not be experimentally manipulated; that means that we could not place students randomly in co-op or regular program to ensure that there was no important difference between the two groups. Therefore, we had to use some mechanism to ensure that the groups were similar on critical variables that might affect their performance on any educational test (*the dependent variable*) that we might use for the pretest (before they entered second year and before any co-op experience) and posttest (after they had gone to university for 3 years and after their co-op experience). As our review of the educational literature indicated to us that there were numerous characteristics of students that could affect their academic achievement, we decided to take a two-tiered approach. At the first level, we recognized that most co-op programs screened applicants based on their GPA and that most of these programs required a minimum B for acceptance. GPA could certainly influence students' performance on an educational test. Therefore, we limited participation in the study to those students with a B average or higher in the academic term preceding the pretest. We then decided that prior to the posttest, we would match students on a variety of factors (pretest scores, age, gender, and prior work experience) and that we would examine the differences between the matched students on the posttest. The decision to ensure that any differences between the two groups were due to their educational experiences in the intervening years meant that more research assistance to do the matching was needed and we needed a sufficiently large pool of subjects in both the co-op and regular samples to ensure that we could form a reasonable number of matched pairs. As it turned out, of 582 students who completed the study, we were able to form 117 matched pairs. We could still compare the results of the co-op and regular students in the larger sample but the results of the matched pairs comparison were of most interest.

We initially intended to include in the study 1,000 co-op and regular students from the University of Victoria. However, we realized that there were some programs, notably engineering, that were mandatory cooperative education programs and therefore had no regular students in these programs at UVic. So we included students from the University of British Columbia, a large university in Vancouver, to complete our numbers.

We sought funding from the Social Sciences and Humanities Research Council of Canada for this 3-year study. The application process in itself was an extremely onerous task, but we knew that this type of longitudinal, large sample research was expensive and would require outside funding. A full-time research assistant was necessary to provide continued attention to the project as all members of the research team had their own particular research, teaching, and administrative workloads to fulfill. We estimated that the study would require approximately $150,000 (U.S.). Not many funding agencies grant this amount of money; in fact, our grant was supported through a special strategic initiative that encouraged research on the theme of "Education and Work in an Era of Change."

Our first application for funding was denied, but this is not atypical. Application to a funding agency in which the applications are peer reviewed is usually a highly competitive process and often one has to apply several times before receiving support. In our case, the adjudication committee's main concern was with our proposal for the assessment of the educational outcomes. In fact, we had not determined entirely how we would measure this very slippery construct. The adjudication committee recognized our dilemma and also saw sufficient merit in our proposal to grant a small amount of money to support the process of identifying or designing a good research instrument to measure the educational variables we had suggested were important. We were also encouraged to reapply in the next funding cycle.

It is the process of choosing this research instrument and the outcomes of its application that forms the basis of this chapter. There are numerous questions to be answered before choosing a research instrument, but the choice must be based on very careful analysis of the research question, the phenomenon to be measured, and the resources available to the researcher. Just to clarify the terminology used in this discussion, the research instrument is the tool you will use in your research for measurement purposes. This instrument can take many forms and, of course, the form depends on what you are measuring. It may be as simple as a recording sheet that indicates the frequency of occurrence of some event or may be as complex as a personality inventory or an in-depth interview protocol. The research instrument is just a tool that helps you to collect and record data (McMillan, 1996). The data may include numbers, words, and audio or video recordings but, once collected, must be subjected to some sort of analysis. The form of your data will limit how you can analyze it and subsequently determine the types of conclusions you can draw. So each step in the research process, from deciding on your question of interest, defining the variables of interest, structuring the process of the research, choosing the research instrument, collecting the data, analyzing the data, and then interpreting the data, is dependent on the steps that come before it.

Decision Point: What type of research instrument or measuring tool do we need for this study?

The literature informed us that there were various types of educational measures. Tests are instruments presented to each participant that contain a standard set of questions and are generally used for measuring cognitive and some noncognitive aspects of learning. Personality assessment measures are sometimes used to identify psychopathology or abnormal behavior but can also be used to measure traits related to learning and motivation such as cognitive style and locus of control. Inventories of attitude, values, and interest are also used in educational research to identify motivations, preferences, and goals. All of these instruments are categorized as *self-report* and have inherent problems related to participant motivation, honesty, and interest. However, many of these issues can be addressed in the design of the instrument and the way it is administered (McMillan, 1996). Observation and interview are the other types of educational measures. The main limitation with these direct data-gathering measures is that they usually involve collection of large amounts of data that must be distilled and managed in some way in order to prepare for analysis. Use of these types of measures can be very time consuming.

Given the various options and the intent of our study, we determined that a test of cognitive and some noncognitive aspects of learning was most appropriate to represent the educational outcomes of a university education. Inventories of attitude and values were of great interest but we agreed that the research question would be best answered by tapping into what students knew and what they could do.

Before we actually got to the stage of examining potential instruments or deciding on whether or not to design our own, we had to settle a number of issues in our approach to measurement. The first major problem we were confronted with was the identification and clear definition of the educational outcomes valued by postsecondary institutions. As these outcomes would be the *dependent variables* (i.e., the variables that we wanted to measure to determine the effects of the intervention) in our study, we had to ensure that they were valid representatives of student learning. For a more comprehensive treatment of the issue of measuring learning, refer to Johnston, Angerelli, and Gajdamaschko (chap. 9, this volume) and Cates and LeMaster (chap. 18, this volume). However, for the purposes of understanding how we chose an appropriate instrument for this research, our thinking about the process of measuring educational outcomes is described along with the conclusions we reached.

Decision Point: What should we include in our definition of educational outcomes?

This decision consumed a lot of time and energy and after all of us had read extensively and debated heatedly, we were no closer to a specific definition on which we could all agree. In the process, we wrote and had published a paper related to the educational outcomes of co-op (Branton et al., 1990). We finally decided that no matter how we defined educational outcomes it could be disputed or the claim could be made that it was not complete. Therefore, we chose to *operationally define* the term, which means that we chose working definitions of our *dependent variables* that describe measurable phenomena. The result is that when people read our work and we make reference to educational outcomes, they will know that we are referring to what we included in our *operational definition* of the term and nothing more.

A review of the literature indicated to us that knowledge, which included both general knowledge and strategic knowledge, was accepted as a standard outcome of formal education. However, there was a significant emphasis on metacognitive skills, which include knowing how to manage a task and to allocate time, processes for learning new information, and problem-solving skills. We also noted distinctions between knowledge that is represented by a symbol system (i.e., in writing) and knowledge that produces action (e.g., knowing how to design a web page.) In more simple terms, we recognized that we should be measuring not only what the students know but also their knowledge of how to apply knowledge in various contexts (cognitive skills), and how well they actually apply the knowledge to solving problems or making decisions.

In addition to the knowledge and cognitive skills of the learner, we came to understand that there was a domain, generally referred to as the affective domain, that we should also include in our educational outcomes. Specifically we agreed that we should include some way of measuring the values acquired by learners in their educational programs and how these values are expressed when making decisions or solving problems. So the domains we concluded must be represented in the test for educational outcomes were the cognitive domain (knowing), the procedural domain (doing), and the affective domain (valuing) to represent the variety of important outcomes of postsecondary education.

The literature on educational outcomes also informed us that seeking a general test of education across a variety of educational domains (e.g., humanities, social science, engineering, etc.) may be fruitless as the cognitive skills used in one domain (e.g., physics) may not be the same in another domain (e.g., sociology). A general test of learning may disadvantage one discipline-based group of students relative to another. Therefore any instrument that we needed to develop or adopt had to be sensitive to the various educational domains represented by the sample we would be testing.

Any measure of educational outcomes may be confounded by a myriad of other factors such as students' prior knowledge and experience, different levels of motivation, and differences in cognitive skills, to name just a few. A *confounding factor* is one that, in an experimental study, is neither accounted for nor controlled. Therefore any change in your variable of interest or dependent measure (in our study, performance on a test of educational outcomes) may be due to the intervention or treatment (in our study, 3 years in a university co-op or regular program) or may be due to some other uncontrolled factor (e.g., students' prior knowledge and experience). The task to determine a suitable research instrument was an extremely complex one and was the most difficult part of our research. We struggled with several issues regarding the measurement of education outcomes so that we would be very familiar with the criteria necessary to develop or to choose an appropriate instrument.

Decision Point: Should we collect objective, quantitative, and statistical data or must we collect subjective, qualitative, or interpretative information?

To put this dilemma in perspective, in designing a questionnaire, the researcher can choose questions requiring only a yes–no answer (closed-ended questions) or allow for whatever answer or description the respondent wanted to give (open-ended questions). The yes–no answers could be reduced to numerical frequencies. The open-ended answers would have to be coded or categorized in some descriptive manner. At the time we were developing this study, this question was not very important to us as we all assumed that objective measures of learning were appropriate to our goals. We also assumed that the study must have *generalizability* (our findings for our sample would be applicable to the population of university students from which the sample was drawn) and therefore must have a large sample. With our aim to test a large sample of students at two points in their academic program, numerical data were all we could handle. This was an appropriate decision because we were not as interested at that time in finding out what students learned in their university program as we were in measuring any differences between that learned by co-op and regular students.

The decision to collect quantitative data that can be reduced to numbers, or qualitative data, generally represented in words, should reflect the intent of your study. If you are interested in understanding the meaning of some experience or you wish to interpret some phenomenon, then numerical data is not very useful. In this instance, qualitative data gives you a richer picture of your variables of interest.

Decision Point: What about validity?

We thought that validity referred to the degree to which an instrument measures what it says it will measure (e.g., a ruler is a valid measurement tool of length). However, in our literature search on measuring educational outcomes, we found that measurement specialists in education and psychology determined that validity referred to the use of the test and not to just the test itself (Thorndike, 1997). They defined validity as "the appropriateness, meaningfulness, and usefulness of the specific inferences made from test scores" and stated that "the inferences regarding specific uses of a test are validated, not the test itself" (Standards for Educational and Psychological Testing, 1985, p. 9). To use our former example, a ruler may be a tool for measuring length, but the inference from the measurement may not be valid if the units are not precise enough for the task (e.g., the ruler measures in inches, and you are measuring the length of a microbe). Validity is also a matter of degree, not all or none, and that validity is specific to a purpose or use. No measure or test is valid in all circumstances (Linn & Gronlund, 1995). However, validity of an instrument must be established if the results of the research are to have any value. If we decided to develop our own test, we would have to conduct pilot studies to evaluate its degree of validity.

Decision Point: Because we have chosen a pretest and posttest design, we will have to apply the instrument twice. So how can we ensure that the instrument will produce repeatable results?

Reliability of an instrument is the extent to which the measurement is free from error, and error is measured by how consistent a person's score on the test will be from one testing session to another (McMillan, 1996). With the pretest–posttest design, we had to ensure that any change in performance on the test would be due to the treatment (i.e., the university program) and not a reliability error in the test. Lack of reliability can be attributed to many factors: (a) those associated with the test itself such as poor instructions and ambiguous wording, (b) those associated with the person taking the test, such as a change in motivation or anxiety level from one test to the next, and, (c) those related to the administration of the test such as a change in time of day for the test, change in environment, or a change in protocol from one test to the next. The reliability of an instrument can be measured by correlating the performance on a test given on one occasion to the performance on the same test on another occasion. Of course, this has to be repeated a number of times and then a correlation coefficient may be calculated. This is a statistic that can range between 0.00 and 0.99. If a correlation coefficient is less than 0.60, the reliability is inadequate for research purposes. We would have confidence in an instrument that had a reliability coefficient of 0.75 and above. Of course, we would have to choose a reliable instrument and we would have to ensure that the setting for administering the test would be similar in the pretest and posttest. We also decided that in order to ensure that the students were motivated in a similar fashion on both tests we should provide some incentive. However, the details of these decisions could only be made once we actually decided on which instrument we were going to use.

Decision Point: How do we ensure that the test we develop or choose is not biased with regard to race, sex, ethnic origin, geographic region, or other factors?

Good tests should produce similar scores and allow for the same probability of success for individual test takers of the same capability, regardless of their race, ethnic origin, geographic region, etcetera. As well, none of the test items should be offensive to anyone who takes the test.

There are processes in test development to minimize the effects of cultural or socioeconomic factors on individual test scores. These include an assessment of test items for offensive language or topics, an assessment of the dependency of the answers to the test items on cultural heritage, and application of statistical methods for detection of bias.

Decision Point: Is there an instrument already available for our study or should we develop our own?

Once we had become very familiar with all the criteria necessary for a good research instrument to measure educational outcomes, we decided that the requirements were much too complex for us to fulfill if we were to design our own instrument. We felt that we would need another year to design and pilot the instrument to ensure that it was both valid and reliable. Our resources and time were relatively limited, so we decided to look for a previously developed instrument that would meet our needs. Most well-designed tests have indicators of validity and reliability that have been established by those who constructed the test. We knew that it might be expensive to purchase an already-developed instrument but probably no more than the expense of developing our own instrument to test for educational outcomes.

The summary of all of our reading, discussions, and consultations suggested that we had to find a test that allowed for the collection of quantitative scores, had a high degree of reliability, was a valid indicator of the educational outcomes associated with participation in postsecondary education and was equally accessible to all participants in our study. Predictably, there were not a significant number of appropriate tests and most were limited by the fact that we were testing university students. The best instrument available for our purposes was developed by the American College Testing Program (ACT) and is referred to as the College Outcomes Measures Program test (COMP). Their literature stated that the COMP was designed "as a response to the growing need for materials and services to assist colleges and universities in efforts to improve general education and build support for their programs" (Steele, 1989, p. 1). Although not intended for the particular kind of research we were conducting, this test purported to "measure and evaluate the knowledge and skills (1) that undergraduates are expected to acquire as a result of engagement in university or college education programs, and, (2) that are important to effectively function in adult society" (p. 2). The COMP measures six outcome areas: three process areas and three content areas (see Table 7.2). It also was consistent with the theoretical model that we had proposed previously (Branton et al., 1990).

TABLE 7.2

The Interrelationships of the Process and Content Areas in the Objective Form of the College Outcomes Measures Program[1]

	Functioning Within Social Institutions	Using Science and Technology	Using Knowledge in the Liberal Arts
Communicating	About social institutions	About science and technology	About the arts
Solving Problems	Solving social problems	Solving scientific/ technological problems	Solving problems related to the arts
Clarifying Values	Clarifying social problems	Clarifying scientific/ technological values	Clarifying values related to the arts

[1]Adapted from Steele (1989).

The COMP met our criterion to include both knowledge and skills and it also addressed the cognitive, procedural, and values domains. Another feature of this test was that norms had been established for the test.

Decision Point: Was a norm-referenced test what we needed or should we be using a criterion-referenced test?

Tests can be categorized into two general groups: norm-referenced tests and criterion-referenced tests. These two tests are different in their intended purposes, the manner in which content is chosen, and the interpretation of the test results (Morris, Fitz-Gibbon, & Lindheim, 1987). Norm-referenced tests compare an individual test score to the scores of a well-defined reference group who have already taken the same test (Rudner, 1994). In the case of the COMP, freshman, sophomore, junior, and senior students in American postsecondary institutions were the reference group. This type of test would allow us to rank order the participants in our study and to determine if there was any significant difference between the scores of the co-op students and the regular students on the pretest and the posttest. Whereas norm-referenced tests determine the rank of students, criterion-referenced tests determine "... what test takers can do and what they know, not how they compare to others" (Anastasi, 1988, p. 102). Criterion-referenced tests report the performance of participants on a specified set of educational goals or outcomes in comparison to a predetermined performance level. In other words, it helps to determine how well students have learned the knowledge and skills that they are expected to have mastered (Bond, 1996).

After discussions with measurement specialists and personnel at ACT, we determined that it would be very difficult to determine performance standards for such a diverse disciplinary group and that a norm-referenced test was more appropriate for our study.

ACT provided us with extensive literature on the COMP that indicated that norms for the test had been established on a very large sample. This was impressive, as was the rigorous testing for reliability and validity. The reliability of this test has been measured by ACT at 0.98 for the total score and 0.97 to 0.98 for the six subscores. We were also reassured that considerable effort had been made to ensure that there were no biases against any ethnic or gender group.

Decision Point: Is the nature of the reference group of American college students similar enough to the Canadian university students in our study? We were not too concerned that the reference group may not be exactly the same as our sample because, as we argued, the main intent of the study was to examine differences between co-op and regular students in our sample. We did, however, do some investigation of standards in American and Canadian universities and found little that would indicate to us that the standards were different. We even spoke with personnel who were responsible for transfers between American and Canadian schools and were reassured that there was little difference.

The main drawback of the test was that it was 4½ hours in length. We were very concerned that students who would agree to commit that much time to a research study would be very difficult to find, unless we had a significant cash incentive. With 1,000 participants in our study, this was not an alternative. Fortunately, ACT also had produced a short-form proxy of the COMP called the *Objective Test* (OT). The major difference between the two tests was that the OT was answered in a multiple-choice format whereas the COMP consisted of open-ended questions. The time required to complete the OT was approximately 2 hours. Even that was predicted to be a problem in the recruitment of participants but it was certainly preferable to 4½ hours.

Because of the pre–post design, the OT was to be given to our participants twice. The difficulty of this was that students might learn from taking Test 1, which could produce higher scores on Test 2, although the tests were taken 3 years apart. One of the other benefits of choosing this commercially available test was that ACT personnel had developed different versions of the OT to address such issues. They were continually updating the tests to ensure that they were culturally appropriate and current. Our participants completed Form 8 of the OT for the pretest and then completed Form 10 for the posttest. These two forms, statistically equated by ACT, tested for the same learning outcomes but probed for these outcomes via different questions. Any change in test scores from Form 8 to Form 10 could be legitimately attributed to the students' experiences between tests and not from familiarity with the test itself.

> **Decision Point: The OT appeared to be what we needed for this study, but did we have the resources necessary to buy and administer the instrument, and pay for an analysis of the results?**
> We knew that this was going to be an expensive study and so our research proposal budget had to be adjusted accordingly. We were not sure if the granting agency would agree to the large sum necessary to use this instrument. The rationale that we used in the proposal indicated that the time required to develop such a resource, including research time to establish reliability and validity, would be prohibitive and that the costs of such a venture would most likely be greater than what we would have to pay for the use of the OT and for the analysis of the resulting data.
>
> From the perspective of the granting agency that we dealt with, a fundamental requirement in the strength of a grant was that we would be providing training in research methods for undergraduate and graduate students. Typically, students are very important in the development of instruments, pilot testing, data gathering, and data analysis. So one of the drawbacks in choosing the OT was not only the instrument already developed and reliability and validity standards established, but ACT was also responsible for data analysis. This reduced the opportunities for students to be involved in the research. Therefore when we wrote the grant proposal, we made sure there was substantial involvement of students in other aspects of the research.

The Implementation and Pretest Data-Analysis Phase

With a successful grant proposal, we were ready for implementation. Pretesting took place between October and February of 1988. One thousand participants were recruited and tested with the incentive of receiving $10 upon completion. In the final pretest analysis, 999 were used as one person became ill during the pretest. Almost all co-op students at our university took part, and this was only possible with the help and considerable effort of all co-op coordinators. Testing was conducted without incident, and we perceived that the students took their participation in the study very seriously. We received the pretest scores in April and experienced the first of several unexpected outcomes.

The vast majority of our participants had scored in the eightieth percentile or higher on the pretest OT, whereas, the norm established by ACT on students at a similar level in American institutions, was the fifty-seventh percentile. What this meant was that our participants, both co-op and regular students, had scored on average, higher than 80% of the members in the reference group. The actual average score for our large group of 999 students was 194.19, and for the matched pairs the average was

195.28. The mean total score for the reference groups cited by ACT (freshmen and sophomores at 4-year, degree-granting institutions) was 173.9 and 178.9 respectively. The same mean total score for graduating students from a 4-year program was 187.8. Because we had limited participation in our study to students with a B average or better, we had anticipated that the mean scores would be higher than the normative sample but did not anticipate that they would be so extremely high.

The term *ceiling* is used for the maximum score on a test or a limit on the performance of some task. For the OT the maximum score was 232. The ceiling effect refers to the limitation on improvements as the person taking the test approaches this theoretical upper bound. If students in our study were to produce the gains predicted by ACT that were based on the gains of the reference group, many of the students would produce a perfect score or very close to it. The real meaning for our study was a reduction in the opportunity for any effect to be reflected in the posttest scores. This would definitely limit our capability to discriminate between the participants in our study on the posttest. This was a harbinger of the difficulty that our research group would have in explaining our final results.

During the period between the pretest and the posttest, we engaged in a more detailed analysis of the data. Several results were very interesting with regard to the differences between co-op and regular students upon entry into their programs (Van Gyn, Branton, Cutt, Loken, & Ricks, 1994). Although we had limited participation in this study to students with at least a second-class standing (a B average or higher) for reasons previously indicated, the results showed that there were significantly more[1] co-op students with first-class standing (A average or higher) than regular students across all disciplines. In addition, co-op students on average scored significantly higher[2] (197.32) on the pretest than did the regular student (191.06). Interestingly, the main areas of difference in the scores on the OT were found in the two subscores related to Using Science and Technology and Problem Solving, and no difference was found in the other areas of Communication, Clarifying Values, Functioning in Social Institutions, or Using Knowledge in the Liberal Arts.

The other area in which we found an important difference was in the amount of paid work prior to admission to their current university program. Quite unexpectedly, we found that co-op students had significantly more work experience[3] than regular students in three of the four categories that were included. This was unexpected because previous research (Siedenberg, 1988) and, in keeping with conven-

---

[1] $F(1,997) = 14.86, p < .001$. The F test compares the average total scores for the two groups and the result (14.86) shows there was almost 15 times more variance between the groups as within them, based on the comparison of 997 values. The significance level (p) indicates that this result would happen 1 time in 1,000 by chance. So it is that probability (.001) that this finding is not true or correct.

[2] $F(997) = 11.32, p < .001$. This statistic is interpreted the same way as the previous one.

[3] Unrelated part-time work, $F = (1,997) = 11.93, p < .001$
Related part-time work, $F = (1,997) = 14.90, p < .001$
Related full-time work, $F = (1,997) = 5.14, p < .024$

tional wisdom, had suggested that the co-op students chose cooperative education programs because they did not have previous work experience and thought this was a good way to get it.

So our concerns about previous studies that did not control for differences between co-op and regular student samples before they began their programs were supported. The matched pairs strategy we had planned was necessary to control for the differences that were evident in the analysis of the pretest scores and GPA. In addition to the pre-entry variables of academic discipline, score on the pretest, gender, age, and time spent in university between the first and second test, we added the variable of amount of work experience prior to admission to a university program. However we could not do this matching until after the posttest, as we did not know if everyone would agree to take part in the posttest phase or if they all had stayed in their programs in the intervening years.

As it turned out, we were able to contact and sign up 582 of the original 1,000 students to participate in the posttest. The incentive had gone up considerably as students were now offered $25 to complete the second test. This incentive increase was thought to be necessary to ensure that the students were motivated and took the test seriously. Other precautions were taken to ensure that the posttest situation did not influence the students' performance. Testing was conducted in the same venues as the pretest, using the same instructions, and in most cases the same testers. Because of our care to recreate the pretest conditions, we were quite confident that any changes would be due to the intervening educational experiences and not any factors related to the test characteristics.

Final Analysis of Pretest and Posttest Scores and Findings

We received the analysis of the posttest in May 1991. The communication from ACT stated that:

> As you will note, posttest results for a sizable number of students were so much *lower* than their pretest results that their validity as an accurate measure of current levels of proficiency can be called into question. The probable cause of this problem is either lack of motivation or hostility/resistance to participant in the posttesting. Other institutions encountered this problem, but not for such a large proportion of their sample ... it is important that you to do your own followup [sic] interviews to explore student's explanations of their unexpectedly low performances. (Steele, personal communication, May 6, 1991)

The research team was totally mystified by this outcome and understandably concerned. The ceiling effect accounted for some of these results, but we did not find this a satisfactory explanation. Regression toward the mean was also anticipated but not to produce these kinds of results. *Regression toward the mean* is a statistical phenomenon that occurs when your sample does not represent the normal distribution of a population on a particular variable. If the scores are normally distributed and you put those scores on a graph they should form a bell shaped curve. As the reference mean was the fifty-seventh percentile but the mean student score of our sample was distributed around the eightieth percentile, graphing our scores produced a negatively skewed distribution (*skew* refers to a distribution's symmetry, in this case the distribution was asymmetrical, with a longer tail to the left). If we consider just the highest 10% pretest scorers, the likelihood of all these individuals being in the top 10% on the posttest is very low. If even just a few of the top pretest scorers fall below the top 10% on the posttest, their group's posttest mean will have to be closer to the population posttest mean than to their pretest mean. In other words, the mean of the sample appears to regress toward the mean of the population (in our case, the mean of the reference group) from pretest to posttest. Regression toward the mean is a group effect as very extreme scores in the pretest, if they are somewhat lower in the posttest, will significantly affect the mean of the whole group. This is a very interesting but tricky phenomenon that can be accounted for in a statistical manner but is not recognized in all instances by even the best researchers.

I have described a case in which the treatment has no effect on the posttest scores and the regression toward the mean makes it look like something happened, that is they did worse on the posttest, when in fact it was just an artifact of the statistics. If you consider a case such as ours in which one would presume that 3 years in a university program would result in improvements in the posttest, given that the test examined for the knowledge and skills that they had learned, the regression artifact could not account fully for the results. Although we mulled over the combination of a ceiling effect and regression toward the mean as two good reasons for the results, we really felt that there must be something else which caused the drop in scores of so many of our participants from the pretest to the posttest.

Decision Point: The results did not conform to what we had expected and we were not sure how to explain them. What now?

After 4 years or more of considerable work and financial investment, we were ready to throw up our hands and suggest that this phenomenon of education outcomes was too complex to study in this manner. However, we knew that there was an obligation to publish our results. Should we report the failure of our research to show any effect of a university education on the domains included in the OT or, as one of our more humorous colleagues suggested, show that our student became less educated after 3 years in the programs? We decided that our only route was to continue examining the data and the OT to see if we could learn anything more and help future researchers to avoid the problems we were encountering. There was some very interesting data collected in this study and we just had to rethink how we might work with it and prepare it for publication.

> The research process is an important one even if the results do not turn out as anticipated. The researcher has an ethical responsibility to publish research findings and to link them to previous research. If the research is done well, then the results are significant, in a literal sense, in whatever form they take and it then is the responsibility of the researcher to explain the outcomes in as clear and coherent fashion as possible.

As we had taken significant steps to ensure that motivation or hostility was not a factor, we did not agree with the ACT interpretation of the outcome. Interviews with students were an option but most students had left the university at this time so we would not have had a representative sample. Further follow up was prohibitively expensive.

After an extensive rereading of the materials provided by ACT and after many discussions with their researchers, we came across a statement in one of their publications on Form 10 of the OT that explained, "as the numbers of African-Americans and Hispanics enrolled in postsecondary institutions has increased substantially, Form 10 has been altered to include materials which would have cultural significance to these groups" (Steele, 1989, p. 13). Given that our sample of students in postsecondary institutions on the Canadian west coast included very few students with this cultural background, Form 10 was less culturally appropriate for this group than Form 8. Our students may have had more difficulty on Form 10 than the comparison American sample on which the norm was based, and in comparison to their experience on Form 8. An alternate explanation was that Form 8 was not culturally appropriate for the American students included in the norms and their scores were depressed because of this. At the time of this discovery, there was little that we could do to rectify the problem. At least we had another reason for the strange outcomes and this one, in combination with the ceiling effect and regression artifact, explained our results fairly well.

We returned to our original research question. Our hypothesis was that co-op students might receive enhanced educational benefits because of the integration of the university experience with the cooperative education work experiences in comparison to regular students whose university experiences and the work that they engaged in during summers and at other times was not integrated. When we examined the posttest scores of the matched pairs, these scores did support our original hypothesis, but they were not very persuasive. The co-op students did score significantly higher[4] on the posttest than did the matched regular students, and the difference was attributable to significantly higher[5] co-op scores in the domains of Functioning in Social Institutions and Problem Solving. Because the pretest scores of the matched pairs were not significantly different (195.44 for the co-ops and

---

[4] $F(1,232) = 5.44, p < .05$

[5] $F(1,232) = 5.38, p < .05$ and $F(1,232) = 4.16, p < .05$

195.11 for regular students) the difference between pretest and posttest scores was of less interest than the comparison of the scores from the posttest. So the drop in some scores or failure to increase in a significant fashion in others was still a concern but at least we were able to unlink that issue from the major question of our study. We thought it was significant that the two domains in which co-op students did better than regular students were not in the discipline-based domains of Using Science and Technology or Using the Knowledge of the Liberal Arts but rather Functioning in Social Institutions and Problem Solving. This finding supports the findings of Williams, Sternberg, Rashotte, and Wagner (1993) that co-ops have a demonstrable and measurable impact on the development of tacit knowledge. Tacit knowledge (Wagner & Sternberg, 1985; Sternberg & Wagner, 1992) is knowledge that enables us to operate in the everyday world and helps in the appropriate application of formal knowledge.

As much as we were disappointed in the methodological issues that tended to muddy the interpretation of the results, we were very satisfied that we had pursued our research question in a rigorous manner. We had also produced some very interesting results particularly about the students that enter co-op and how they differ from those who choose to enter regular programs.

SUMMARY

The main cause of the dilemma in our study was, we believe, differences in several critical characteristics between our sample and the sample within which ACT developed the OT norms. Of course, the obvious question is "would we use another instrument, given what we know now?" My sense is that because we were attempting, first and foremost, to document any measurable differences between the two student groups, and not necessarily the quality of the differences, this was the correct choice. We could not find a similar Canadian test that had been as carefully constructed. We simply underestimated the differences in cultural make-up between Canadian and American university students.

In hindsight (which of course is 20:20), our decision to follow a large sample quantitative research model in order to maximize the generalizability of our findings may not have been the right one. We now realize that to generalize to other countries, other geographical regions, or even other institutions may be a mistake because cultural context, which has many different facets, is such a significant factor. This conclusion is not only informed by the outcomes of our study but also by the postpositivistic thinking of those who do qualitative research. Linn (chap. 6, this volume) discusses the value of qualitative research in capturing the context that hindered us in our work and the value of understanding that context to help us understand cooperative education, or any other human phenomenon, we may be studying.

With reference to our work, although the OT made a thorough quantitative assessment of the educational outcomes in various domains, the use of a qualitative instrument may have yielded a much more rich and contextualized description of student learning that would have been impossible to generate via such instruments as the OT. An example of this type of alternative instrument is Kelly's (1958) Repertory Grid, originally developed for psychoanalysis but currently used very successfully for probing changes in individual understanding. This measurement tool reveals changes to the initial level of understanding of the individual participant and therefore is self-referenced. It is one that we are currently investigating for use in future research on cooperative education. Focus groups and in-depth interviews are also very important research tools to collect the variety of experiences and outcomes that accrue from an educational experience. When using such instruments, the researcher must be content to explore, in-depth, the learning experiences of a few individuals, perhaps no more than three or four, with the benefit of understanding them thoroughly and documenting the meaning of those experiences.

Quantitative and qualitative approaches, and the instruments appropriate for use with these approaches, are both legitimate for investigating phenomena related to cooperative education. The research question that you seek to answer, the intention for pursuing that question, and your own skills and resources will determine your choice of approaches and methods of measurement.

ANNOTATED BIBLIOGRAPHY

Goldman, B. A., & Mitchell, D. F. (1990). *Directory of unpublished experimental mental measurements* (Vol. 5). Dubuque, IA: Brown. This directory reviews behavioral and social science reference tools that were not marketed commercially at the time of publication of the directory. Tests included in the directory were obtained through an examination of 37 English language professional journals. The tests are grouped in 24 categories (e.g. achievement, motivational, perception), with Volume 5 adding an additional category not found in previous volumes (i.e., adjustment vocational). For each test the name, purpose, and source is given. In addition, at least four facts are given from the categories description (number of items, time required, and format), statistics, and related research.

Sweetland, R. C., & Keyser, D. J. (Eds.). (1986). *Tests—A comprehensive reference for assessments in psychology, education, and business* (2nd ed.). Kansas City, MO: Test Corporation of America. This is a reference book of assessment tools used in psychology, education, and business. Each test is described in detail in one section and may be cross-referenced in a second section. For each test the purpose and a description (number of items, format, variable measured, administration, foreign language availability, and special features) is given. Also, the name, author, time required, cost, scoring, and publisher information is provided. A quick scan key allows the reader to tell at a glance the target age group for the test, and whether the test is self-administered or requires an examiner.

Standards for educational and psychological Testing. (1985). Washington, DC: APA. This resource provides primary and conditional standards for reporting and evaluating tests. The standards include validity issues such as construct-related evidence, content-related evidence, criterion-related evidence, validity generalizations, and differential prediction. The standards also cover issues around reliability and errors of measurement.

RESOURCE LIST FOR RESEARCH INSTRUMENTS

Conoley, J. C., & Impara, J. C. (Eds.). (1995). *The twelfth mental measurements yearbook*. Lincoln, NE: Buros Institute of Mental Measurements.

Goldman, B. A., & Mitchell, D. F. (1990). *Directory of unpublished experimental mental measurements* (Vol. 5). Dubuque, IA: Brown.

Hammill, D. D., Brown, L., & Bryant, B. R. (1992). *A consumer's guide to tests in print* (2nd ed.). Austin, TX: PRO-ED.

Hersen, M., & Bellack, A. S. (Eds.). (1988). *Dictionary of behavioral assessment techniques*. New York: Pergammon.

Morris, L. L., Fitz-Gibbon, C. T., & Lindheim, E. (1987). *How to measure performance and use tests*. Newbury Park, CA: Sage.

Sweetland, R. C., & Keyser, D. J. (Eds.). (1986). *Tests—A comprehensive reference for assessments in psychology, education, and business* (2nd ed.). Kansas City, MO: Test Corporation of America.

Standards for educational and psychological testing. (1985). Washington, DC: APA.

REFERENCES

Anastasi, A. (1988). *Psychological testing*. New York: MacMillan.

Bond, L. A. (1996). Norm- and criterion-referenced testing. *Practical Assessment, Research & Evaluation, 5*(2). [On-line] Available: http://ericae.net/pare/getvn.asp?v=5&n=2

Branton, G., Van Gyn, G., Cutt, J., Loken, M., Ney, T., & Ricks, F. (1990). A model for assessing the learning benefits in co-operative education. *Journal of Cooperative Education, 26*(3), 30–40.

Kelly, G. (1958). Man's construction of his alternatives. In G. Lindzey (Ed.), *The assessment of human motives*. New York: Rinehart.

Lindenmeyer, R. S. (1967). A comparison of the academic progress of the cooperative and the four year student. *Journal of Cooperative Education, 3*(2), 8–18.

Linn, R. L., & Gronlund, N. E. (1995). *Measurement and assessment in teaching* (7th ed.). Upper Saddle River, NJ: Prentice-Hall.

McMillan, J. H. (1996). *Educational research: Fundamentals for the consumer* (2nd ed.). New York: HarperCollins.

Morris, L. L., Fitz-Gibbon, C. T., & Lindheim, E. (1987). *How to measure performance and use tests*. Thousand Oaks, CA: Sage.

Rudner, L. M. (1994). Questions to ask when evaluating tests. *Practical Assessment, Research and Evaluation, 4*(2). Available online: http://ericae.net/pare/getvn.asp?v=4&n=2

Siedenberg, J. M. (1988). Incorporating cooperative education into human capital theory: A solution to the student benefit dilemma. *Journal of Cooperative Education, 25*(1), 8–15.

Smith, H. (1965). The influence of participation in the cooperative program. *Journal of Cooperative Education, 3*(1), 7–20.

Standards for education and psychological testing. (1985). Washington, DC: APA.

Steele, J. M. (1989). *Review of COMP development: Instrument design and evaluation of the objective test for use in program evaluation*. Iowa City, IA: American College Testing Program.

Sternberg, R. J., & Wagner, R. K. (1992). Tacit knowledge: An unspoken key to managerial success. *Creativity and Innovation Management, 1*, 5–13.

Thorndike, R. M. (1997). *Measurement and evaluation in psychology and education* (6th ed.). Upper Saddle River, NJ: Prentice-Hall.

Van Gyn, G. H., Branton, G., Cutt, J., Loken, M., & Ricks, F. (1996). An investigation of some of the entry level characteristics between co-op and non co-op students. *Journal of Cooperative Education, 32*(1), 15–28.

Van Gyn, G. H., Cutt, J., Loken, M., & Ricks, F. (1997). Investigating the educational benefits of cooperative education. *Journal of Cooperative Education, 32*(2), 70–85.

Wagner, R. K., & Sternberg, R. J. (1985). Practical intelligence in real-world pursuits: The role of tacit knowledge. *Journal of Personality and Social Psychology, 48*, 436–458.

Williams, W. M., Sternberg, R., Rashotte, C. A., & Wagner, R. K. (1993). Assessing the value of cooperative education. *Journal of Cooperative Education, 28*(2), 32–55.

Wilson, J., & Lyons, E. (1961). *Work-Study college programs: Appraisal and report of the study of cooperative education.* New York: Harper & Brothers.

8

Analyzing Data With Statistics: Business Internship Effects on Postgraduate Employment

Patricia Gochenauer
Shepherd College

Anthony Winter
Shippensburg University

Key questions addressed in this chapter:

- ☞ How do we determine the selection (or construction) of a survey instrument?
- ☞ How can we simplify the data to make it more manageable and easier to analyze?
- ☞ How do we determine what statistical methods to use to analyze the data?
- ☞ What do we do when results are not statistically significant?
- ☞ How do we deal with limitations in research when participants self-report information?
- ☞ How do we handle statistically significant information that is not directly related to the original hypothesis?

Internships combine academic learning with supervised practical experience and serve as a link from the classroom to the workplace. They provide students with the opportunity to earn academic credit and professional work experience. At the same

137

time, internships allow students to graduate within a 4-year period because of the ability to earn academic credit for these experiences (Cates, 1999).

Over the last few years, many studies have been conducted on internships. Colleges and universities are increasingly becoming aware of the importance of internships as a component of academic programs. More and more, students are participating in some type of internship program (Filipczak, 1998). Eyler (1993) cited several studies, each showing that students appreciate the real-world challenges that internships provide. Furthermore, it is believed that internships contribute to career development by providing interns with the chance to explore different careers. Contacts made can be valuable for networking. Students are given the opportunity to explore different careers and gain valuable job search experience (Stanton, 1992). Due to our work with the Business Internship Program at Shippensburg University of Pennsylvania, we wanted to do further research on the program. We wanted to determine if length of time to obtain employment following graduation was shorter for interns versus noninterns and if starting salaries and job satisfaction were higher for interns compared to noninterns.

LITERATURE REVIEW

Researchers continue to study the impact of internships in terms of how they relate to education in the classroom, professional success, and satisfaction following graduation. This literature review examines and summarizes the significance of internships.

In 1985, only 1 out of 36 college graduates participated in some type of internship. In 1995, that number increased to one out of three graduates participating in an internship (Filipczak, 1998). Samer Hamadeh, co-author of the *Internship Bible* and president of Vault Reports, a publishing company in New York, conducted research showing that former interns contribute up to one third of the new employees hired right out of college (cited in Filipczak, 1998). Furthermore, Ryan and Krapels (1997) reported that the "number of internships available to students has grown by 37% over the past five years" (p. 126).

Student Learning

According to research cited in Eyler (1993), assessment of learning has mainly been limited to students' impressions. Students claim to learn more in the field than the classroom, and attempts to link internships with academic achievement have been mixed (Eyler, 1993). Despite mixed views, 95% of deans of schools accredited by the American Assembly of Collegiate Schools of Business (AACSB) who responded to a survey discussed in Alm (1996), believed internships complement academic programs and provide learning experiences that can not be gained elsewhere. However, the full benefit of internships is difficult to measure because internships occur off campus, removed from direct faculty supervision (Alm, 1996).

Job Satisfaction

According to Ryan and Cassidy (1996) students seldom report dissatisfaction with well-managed internships. When asked what they have learned from their internship experiences, students' responses related to outcomes that are not easily measured and do not clearly show up on exams or term papers, such as *growing, getting along, respecting differences,* and *new skills.* Internships also assist students in exploring their career interests. At the same time, internships increase the chance of students moving into careers within their own majors after graduation. Exposure to the workplace instills in students a sense of reality regarding career choice. There appears to be evidence of high job turnover and dissatisfaction among first-time, college-educated employees, which could be due to the lack of adjustment of graduates to the workplace (Gardner & Lambert, 1993). On the other hand, employees who have completed internships tend to demonstrate more realistic expectations and career goals (Casella & Brougham, 1995; Gardner & Lambert, 1993). Internships initiate learning opportunities that can improve job selection and provide low cost, hands-on job training to prospective employees. Furthermore, internships also benefit individuals by allowing them to determine if they fit the company and vice versa before making long-term commitments (Ryan & Krapels, 1997). All of these factors can contribute to job satisfaction in the workplace.

Starting Salary

Research has been conducted on salary expectations and starting salary ranges for business graduates, however, no research has been found comparing starting salaries of interns and noninterns upon graduation. For business majors, starting salaries tended to fall below the expectations of recent graduates. At the same time, the largest gains in salary were reported by liberal arts and business majors, the same individuals who had reported lower starting salaries than initially expected (Gardner & Lambert, 1993). "Graduates with degrees in business receive some of the highest entry-level salaries of all recent graduates—ranging from mid $30,000 to mid $40,000 for undergraduates" (Fields, 1996, p. 1). Business internships can be an excellent link to a student's first professional position, which may lead to more accurate expectations for starting salaries.

Job Placement Expectations

Results from Alexander Astin's annual Freshman Survey indicated that students perceive "items such as developing a network of contacts and locating a summer job or internship are practical, tangible, results-oriented activities that appear to be the best means of securing career-related employment" (McBride & Muffo, 1994, p. 28). Furthermore, according to research reviewed by Imel (1994), college graduates

with positive job-search outcomes began thinking about postgraduation employment during the first year of college. Students appear to be aware of the competitive
job market and hiring practices and are relying on internships to differentiate themselves from individuals who choose not to complete internships (Arnold & Cannon, 1998).

In the fall of 1988, Gardner and Lambert (1993) initiated a three-phase longitudinal study to determine pregraduation work expectations and workplace realities.
Approximately 2,000 seniors were randomly selected and invited to participate in
the study: 440 participants completed Phase I before graduation, and 150 participants remained at the completion of the final phase 18 months after beginning
work. The research found that salary expectations were fairly accurate, with the
greatest discrepancy in salary among those involved in business-related professions.
However, in Phase I respondents indicated they expected raises to be based on individual performance, when in reality, salaries increased quickly at the end of training
and probationary periods. Respondents also expected more frequent feedback from
their employers related to job performance. The lack of formal feedback appeared to
be of major significance to these individuals in their adjustment to professional employment. Gardner and Lambert recognized that "dissatisfaction with the job, the
inability to socialize into the organization, and office politics can all contribute to an
early exit from the organization" (p. 46).

Many employers are beginning to expand their internship programs, realizing
that interns may develop into full-time employees. This appears to be more efficient
and cost effective than hiring recent graduates without internship experience or
bringing in experienced individuals at higher starting salaries. According to the
Journal of Career Planning and Employment (1995), one college noticed a significant
increase in the number of employers that want to recruit interns. The *Journal of Career Planning and Employment* noted that many businesses are targeting up to 50% of
their hiring from internships. Several companies reported that internship programs
have decreased recruiting and training costs. The journal further mentioned that
recruiters recognize internships at other firms as valuable and up to 90% of interns
offered full-time positions accepted the offers. Many companies that recruit college
graduates will not even consider applicants who have not completed some type of
internship experience (Cates, 1999; Imel, 1994). Furthermore, strong internship
programs have been found to increase graduate placement, which can, in turn, increase the reputation and desirability of the university to prospective students
(Casella & Brougham, 1995).

According to Arnold and Cannon (1998), students without internship experience reported that participating in a full-time internship can be beneficial because
formal on-site training is provided, and it will lead to a full-time job. Students without this hands-on experience realize they are at a disadvantage when compared to
individuals with internship experience. Furthermore, individuals without internship experience may view internship opportunities as more important because of

the perceived difficulty of obtaining their first professional position following graduation. Gardner and Lambert (1993) stated:

> In his critical assessment of higher education, Alexander Astin asserted that 'students learn by becoming involved.' A first step, then, would be for us to inculcate students with a sense of reality by encouraging internships, cooperative education, and other career-related work experiences among students and faculty. These opportunities may not reveal all job aspects, but they would provide realistic previews of what work will be like. (p. 48)

CURRENT STUDY

Previous studies have examined student expectations of starting salaries following graduation from postsecondary institutions. However, information comparing intern and nonintern starting salaries appears to be lacking. One reason for conducting this study was to examine starting salaries to determine if they are higher for interns compared to noninterns. Furthermore, it appears that internships assist students in clarifying career goals and expectations, which could possibly lead to greater job satisfaction. Another reason for this study was to determine if job satisfaction tends to be higher for individuals who have completed internships compared to those who have not. Finally, although internships may increase job placement rates, there has been no study of length of time to obtain first-time professional employment when participating in internship experiences. This study also examined length of time to obtain employment following graduation to determine if it is greater for individuals who have not completed internships than students who participated in internships approved by the College of Business.

Setting and Program

This research focuses on internships within the College of Business at Shippensburg University of Pennsylvania. The institution enrolls approximately 6,200 undergraduates, with an approximate enrollment of 1,400 students in the College of Business. Since 1972, the College of Business has offered the Business Internship Program, which adds practical work experience to student classroom preparation. Each academic year, more than 100 students participate in approved internships. Eligibility to participate in business internships requires students to be a junior or senior and maintain a minimum grade point average of 2.0. To count for academic credit, the internship must be approved by the Director of the Business Internship Program and the department chair. In order to be approved, an internship must be directly related to the student's major and have professional duties and responsibilities. Students may earn from one to three credits per internship experience, which can be applied as free elective credit toward their degrees. Each student determines the number of credit hours he or she wishes to receive for each internship experience.

One credit internships require a minimum of 200 work hours, two credit internships require a minimum of 300 work hours, and three credit internships require a minimum of 400 work hours. Internship positions should be for pay with the exception of opportunities within nonprofit organizations. To obtain academic credit, students must meet the responsibilities and duties of the internship position as defined by the employer and approved by the Director of the Business Internship Program. In addition, they must maintain a daily log that briefly describes their tasks, responsibilities, and work-related experiences; submit a typewritten summary of the job to their faculty supervisor every month during the internship semester; prepare a summary report at the conclusion of the experience; and complete a final evaluation form.

METHODOLOGY

Participants and Survey Tool

The current study explored the effects of business internships on alumni job satisfaction, starting salary, and length of time following graduation to obtain professional employment. The participants for this study are College of Business alumni from Shippensburg University of Pennsylvania.

Decision Point: Once the decision has been made on what to assess, what survey tool should be used to conduct the assessment?

We wanted to ensure a decent return rate but didn't want to overwhelm students and alumni with multiple questionnaires and surveys to complete and return. The College of Business has been collecting data from alumni through the Business Graduate Survey for several years, with a 59.8% return rate for the 1998 graduating class. After reviewing this survey in detail, we discovered that it contained data related to the information we were seeking. Instead of going through additional time and expense to create and mail a separate survey, we decided to utilize the data from this survey to compile and analyze our results. Also, errors in sampling were avoided due to the fact that the entire population was asked to participate in this survey.

All College of Business alumni from the graduating class of 1998 at Shippensburg University of Pennsylvania were sent and asked to respond to a Business Graduate Survey (see Appendix). The survey was mailed to all 234 alumni, 101 female, 133 male. As an incentive, five respondents were selected randomly to receive a complimentary t-shirt. After three mailings, a total of 140 individuals (59.8%) had responded to the survey. Individuals were informed in writing that those interested could request a final copy of the results from the research.

Of the 140 respondents, 75 (53.6%) were male and 65 (46.4%) were female. All male respondents were White, United States citizens except for three: one Latino (noncitizen), one Asian American (citizen), and one Asian (noncitizen). All female respondents were White, United States citizens except for four: one Asian American (citizen), one African American (citizen), and two White (noncitizen). Respondents had completed business degrees in accounting (ACC), business information systems (BIS), economics (ECON), finance (FIN), human resource management (HRM), international management (IMGT), management (MGT), marketing (MKT), and office administration (OA). Out of the 140 respondents, 52 (37.1%) individuals had completed at least one internship for credit (between one to three credit hours) and 88 (62.9%) did not complete internships. Three individuals completed more than one internship experience for credit.

The survey used in this study requests self-reported data including starting salary, job satisfaction, and length of time to obtain employment after graduation.

Data Analysis

Information obtained from the surveys included major, starting salary, job satisfaction, length of time to obtain employment, how the first position was obtained, and whether the individual perceived internship or related work experience to be important. Before analyzing the surveys, additional information about each respondent was obtained from the university's mainframe. Additional data were collected in the following categories: social security number (only to ensure data was not duplicated), grade point average, whether or not individual completed an approved business internship for credit, gender, and ethnicity and citizenship status. Likert scales were used to assist in ranking job satisfaction, length of time to obtain employment, and value of internships (see Appendix). Also, to analyze starting salaries, the lowest salary in each salary range was used, with one exception. The figure $9,000 was used for the category "Less than $10,000."

Decision Point: In the survey, alumni were asked to submit a salary range. How will we get computable numbers from a range of numbers?
In order to obtain this data, we needed data with workable numbers (not ranges). To simplify this process, we used the bottom figure of each range of numbers.

Respondents were divided into two groups, those who completed internships and those who did not. Only those respondents who successfully completed one or more approved business internships for credit were categorized as having completed an internship.

Decision Point: How do we determine if information is statistically significant and worth further exploration?
We wanted to determine if there was a statistically significant difference between interns and noninterns in job satisfaction and length of time to obtain

employment. When analyzing categorical data, we initially used the chi square distribution to determine if the data varied randomly or showed a trend. The lower the probability (i.e., $p < .05$), the less likely the data is due to random variation and more likely shows a trend.

Chi square statistics were completed to determine if there were statistically significant differences between intern and nonintern respondents in the areas of job satisfaction, length of time to obtain employment following graduation, and perceived value of internships or work related experience.[1] After chi-square statistics were conducted and levels of significance were determined, mean percentages of grade point average, gender, and major were calculated to determine if they had any effect on the three outcome variables. In the area of perceived importance of internships or work-related experience, mean percentages were completed for each major in order to provide additional information.

Mean percentages were also calculated for intern versus nonintern respondents in various majors and lengths of time to obtain employment. First, respondents were separated according to college majors, and length of time to obtain employment following graduation was examined to determine if it was equal for respondents with internships or no internships. This was done to determine the number of individuals who obtained full-time positions during their senior year of college through their internship experiences. These percentages were not put into a statistical analysis; we only used them to "eyeball" the data to hunt for influence of major on these variables.

Decision Point: What statistical analysis should be used to analyze the results?
Linear regression could be used to look at each individual variable and its effect on salary. However, because we were comparing relationships of multiple variables, we decided to use a multiple regression analysis. We wanted to determine if the four independent variables can predict (have an effect on) the dependent variable (salary). In this case we selected $p < .05$ to determine if results were statistically significant. If $p < .05$, it means that there is less than a 5% probability that the estimated coefficient would be as large as it is, if the variables are unrelated. We made the criterion strict because we wanted to be really sure that our data aren't just being generated randomly.

Further examination of the data was conducted. A regression analysis was used to examine if salary was predicted by four independent variables: grade point average, gender, major, and whether or not individuals completed internships.

---

[1]The Chi Square test is used to determine if data varies randomly or shows a trend. For example, if the pattern shows a significance level of .05, it means there is only 5/100 times that the data occurs randomly; the other 95 times shows a trend.

Of the 140 returned surveys, only 134 were used in the analysis, due to incomplete information on the surveys. To analyze the information related to majors, individuals were separated into two categories: number-focused majors (accounting, business information systems, economics, and finance) and people-focused majors (international management, management, marketing, and human resource management). Number-focused majors require more skill with manipulating numbers and people-focused majors require more skill in human relationships.

Decision Point: How can the data be simplified?
Initially, the different majors were combined into two separate categories, based on the number-focused or people-focused nature of the major. This simplified the data, making it easier to analyze and also provided a method for comparing like majors. With regression analysis completed, it was easy to view the information and find any items with statistical significance. In this case, the regression analysis showed that females earned, on average, almost $4,000 less than males in their first full-time positions following graduation. After reviewing the results from the regression analysis, we were given a direction to head to further analyze male and female salaries.

RESULTS

The chi-square analysis of different levels of job satisfaction for intern and nonintern respondents was not significant χ^2 (1, $N = 135$) = 0.285, $p > .05$ (see Table 8.1).

The chi-square analysis that compared length of time to obtain employment following graduation for internship and non-internship students was statistically significant, χ^2 (1, $N = 138$) = 5.2, $p < .05$ (see Table 8.2). In comparing majors, respondents who completed internships generally obtained their first positions in less time than those who did not complete internships. Due to the low number of respondents within certain majors, raw data was calculated to provide information on percentages of respondents who completed internships and obtained their first position during their senior year. International management and office administration majors were not included due to the extremely low number of respondents. It ap-

TABLE 8.1
Internship Status and Job Satisfaction ($N = 135$)

		Job Satisfaction	
		Very Satisfied	Other
Internship	Yes	20	30
	No	38	47

Note. χ^2 (1) = 0.285, $p > .05$

TABLE 8.2
Internship Status and Length of Time to Obtain Employment (N = 138)

| | | When hired | |
		Senior Year	Later
Internship	Yes	33	20
	No	36	49

Note. X^2 (1) = 5.2, $p < .05$

pears that internships can lead to future employment. Eight accounting majors obtained their first positions through internship experiences, seven of who obtained these positions during their senior year. All three business information systems majors who obtained positions from their internships secured employment during their senior year. The same is true for finance and management majors. Two from each major obtained positions through their internships during their senior year of college. For marketing majors, out of the two individuals who obtained positions through their internships, one had secured this position during senior year of college. Three individuals who majored in human resource management or marketing claim that they obtained their positions through internships, however, there is no record of these individuals having completed approved internships for credit (see Table 8.3).

Decision Point: Some of the data analyzed did not result in statistical significance. Are these data still worth noting?

Although some of the data are not statistically significant, it is still worth mentioning negative findings in the research. The results may encourage further research by the same individual, or by other colleagues looking to explore that specific area in more detail in another research project.

Another area that was examined using the chi-square statistic was the respondents' perceptions of the importance of internships or work-related experience (see Table 8.4). Due to too few respondents within each major, the raw data were used to examine the perceived importance of internships or work-related experience for each major. The majority of respondents indicated that internships and work experience were *Very Important* or *Somewhat Important*. Even respondents who did not complete internships perceived them as being very important or somewhat important (see Table 8.5). Only 9 respondents out of 140 (6.4%) perceived internships and work experience as *Not Very Important*. More than one half (46 out of 88 or 52.3%) of the individuals who did not complete internships perceived work experience to be *Very Important*.

TABLE 8.3
Length of Time to Obtain Employment Following Graduation
Separated by Interns and Noninterns

		Months Following Graduation				
	Sr. Yr.	1–3	4–6	6+	Still Looking	# Obtained From Internship
Completed Approved Internship						
ACC (*n* = 17)	94.1%	—	5.9%	—	—	8
						(7 during senior year)
BIS (*n* = 7)	57.1%	28.6%	—	14.3%	—	3
						(3 during senior year)
ECON (*n* = 3)	50.0%	50.0%	—	—	—	—
FIN (*n* = 6)	50.0%	33.3%	—	—	—	2
						(2 during senior year)
HRM (*n* = 4)	25.0%	50.0%	25.0%	—	—	—
MGT (*n* = 5)	40.0%	—	20.0%	40.0%	—	2
						(2 during senior year)
MKT (*n* = 9)	44.4%	11.1%	44.4%	—	—	2
						(1 during senior year)
OA (*n* = 1)	100%	—	—	—	—	—
Did Not Complete Approved Internship						
ACC (*n* = 19)	36.8%	52.6%	5.3%	5.3%	—	—
BIS (*n* = 2)	50.0%	50.0%	—	—	—	—
ECON (*n* = 4)	25.0%	50.0%	25.0%	—	—	—
FIN (*n* = 16)	50.0%	37.5%	6.3%	—	6.3%	—
HRM (*n* = 8)	62.5%	12.5%	12.5%	12.5%	—	2
						(1 during senior year)[a]
IMGT (*n* = 1)	—	100%	—	—	—	—
MGT (*n* = 18)	33.3%	33.3%	16.7%	5.6%	—	—
MKT (*n* = 19)	42.1%	42.1%	10.5%	—	—	1
						(1 during senior year)[a]
OA (*n* = 1)	—	—	100%	—	—	—

Note. Percentages may not total 100% due to some respondents leaving question blank.

Number-Focused Majors: ACC = Accounting; BIS = Business Information Systems, ECON = Economics; FIN = Finance. People-Focused Majors: HRM = Human Resource Management; IMGT = International Management; MGT = Management;

MKT = Marketing; OA = Office Administration.

[a]Individuals reported obtaining position from internship, however, they did not complete an approved internship for credit.

TABLE 8.4

Internship Status and Perceived Importance of Internships and Work Related Experience (N = 137)

		Perceived Importance	
		Very Important	Other
Internship	Yes	42	9
	No	46	40

Note. X^2 (1) = 11.6, $p < .05$

TABLE 8.5

Perceived Importance of Internships and/or Work-related Experiences of Interns and Non-interns in Various Majors

	Level of Importance				
	Very	Somewhat	Not very	Do not know	Blank
	Completed Approved Internship				
ACC (n = 17)	82.4%	17.7%	—	—	—
BIS (n = 7)	85.7%	14.3%	—	—	—
ECON (n = 3)	33.3%	66.7%	—	—	—
FIN (n = 6)	100.0%	—	—	—	—
HRM (n = 4)	100.0%	—	—	—	—
MGT (n = 5)	60.0%	20.0%	—	—	20.0%
MKT (n = 9)	77.8%	22.2%	—	—	—
OA (n = 1)	100.0%	—	—	—	—
	Did Not Complete Approved Internship				
ACC (n = 19)	52.6%	36.8%	5.23%	5.3%	—
BIS (n = 2)	50.0%	—	50.0%	—	—
ECON (n = 4)	—	75.0%	25.0%	—	—
FIN (n = 16)	56.3%	25.0%	12.5%	6.3%	—
HRM (n = 8)	87.5%	12.3%	—	—	—
IMGT (n = 1)	—	—	—	100.0%	—
MGT (n = 18)	50.00%	33.3%	11.1%	—	5.6%
MKT (n = 19)	52.6%	26.3%	10.5%	5.3%	5.3%
OA (n = 1)	—	—	—	100.0%	—

Note. Number-Focused Majors: ACC = Accounting; BIS = Business Information Systems, ECON = Economics; FIN = Finance. People-Focused Majors: HRM = Human Resource Management; IMGT = International Management; MGT = Management; MKT = Marketing; OA = Office Administration.

> **Decision Point: What other results should be analyzed in conducting research?**
>
> Researchers should always be aware of the unexpected. When conducting research, it is important to review results that are not necessarily part of the initial hypothesis. In many cases, researchers stumble across unanticipated results. Although it was not part of the initial plan to compare starting salaries by gender, the results turned out to be statistically significant and worth noting. Additional research needs to be conducted to determine possible reasons for the large gap in starting salaries between men and women.

A regression analysis allowed us to ask which of several independent variables (GPA, gender, major, and internship status) predict salary level on the first position after college (see Table 8.6). Initially, majors were divided into number-focused (accounting, economics, finance, and business information systems) and people-focused (human resource management, international management, management, and marketing) categories. The only independent variable to yield significant results was gender ($t = -3.05$, $p < .01$). R Square in this case was 0.105 (see Table 8.7).[2] However, after obtaining these results, each major was examined individually with similar results. With all these items being comparable, findings indicated that

TABLE 8.6
Hierarchical Regression Analysis of Salary

Variable	Unstandardized Coefficients	Standard Error	T Stat	P-Value
Intercept	22.901	4.285		
GPA	2.767	1.502	1.843	0.068
Gender	-3.907[a]	1.280	-3.052*	0.003
Major	1.546	1.329	1.163	0.247
Internship (yes/no)	-0.739	1.342	-0.550	0.583

*$p < .01$.

[a]Indicates females earned, on average, $3907 less than males in first full time positions following graduation.

Note. The columns of the regression table show that a best-fitting regression line starts at about $22,900 salary (the "intercept" or "constant"). The coefficients associated with each variable are the slopes: You multiply them by the values of each predictor (GPA, gender, major), and add those numbers to the intercept to yield a predicted salary for each student. The t-statistic and associated p-value (statistical significance) indicate that "gender" is the only independent variable that significantly influences salary in this regression model.

---

[2]The R-Square value of 0.105 indicates that the variables in the estimated equation account for about 10% of the variation in salaries.

TABLE 8.7
Regression Statistics

Multiple R	0.324
R-Square	0.105
Adjusted R-Square	0.077
Standard Error	7.361

Note. Multiple R measures the association of Gender, GPA, Major, and Internships (yes–no) to salary. The higher the number, the better the fit. In this case, 0.32 indicates the strength of the association between the independent variables and the dependent variable.

R^2 measures the amount of salary variance accounted for by all the predictors. In this case, 0.105 (10.5%) of the variation in salary can be explained by the four independent variables GPA, Gender, Major, and Internship (yes–no).

R is the square root of the R-square value. R-Square adjusted is the R-Square value with degrees of freedom and the number of predictors taken into account. When the R-square is adjusted, it is a better predictor of the R-square in the whole population of students from which we've sampled.

The standard error of 7.36 is a measure of accuracy (i.e., the predictions based on the equation are accurate give or take 7.36) alternatively, 95% of the time, your predictions will be off by no more than 14.72 (or 2*7.36) either way.

female respondents earned approximately $4,000 less per year than male respondents ($p < .01$), regardless of whether they had completed an internship.

DISCUSSION

For the purpose of this study, one assumption was made. All respondents to the survey completed the same business core courses in the College of Business during their academic careers.

Decision Point: How do you allow for inaccuracies in self-reported results?
Quite frequently, individuals are asked to self-report information on survey forms. Unfortunately, this can lead to some inaccuracy. The best thing to do in this situation is be prepared. The survey instrument should contain clear and concise questions relevant to what you are attempting to assess. However, whenever respondents are reporting information of this nature, you need to mention self-reporting as a limitation in the research that is conducted.

Several limitations are present in this study. All respondents are self-reporting information including starting salary, job satisfaction, and length of time to obtain employment in the survey. This study was also limited to alumni from the 1998 graduating class in the College of Business from Shippensburg University of Pennsylvania. It is possible that differences in college majors and job market trends at the time may have impacted individuals' ability to obtain employment in major-related fields. Also, there is very little diversity among survey respondents. All respondents, except seven, are White and United States citizens. Additionally, the instrument has been utilized only by the College of Business at Shippensburg University of Pennsylvania. It has not been standardized beyond that specific population.

Another limitation involves determining those who completed internships. Information gathered was based solely on individuals who completed internships for credit that were approved by the College of Business. Some individuals may have completed unofficial internships or been employed in their career area while enrolled at the institution. Some respondents to the survey who did not complete internships approved by the College of Business may very well have participated in unofficial ones.

Implications

Judging from the results of this research and additional research mentioned in the literature review, individuals perceive internships as beneficial. However, specific results are difficult to measure. According to Ryan and Cassidy (1996) student responses regarding internships relate to items not easily measured or evident on exams and term papers. The same is true for the current research. A large number of respondents considered internships or work-related experience to be *Very Important* or *Somewhat Important*. Even individuals who did not complete internships perceived internships or work experience as being *Very Important* or *Somewhat Important*. However, from this research it is impossible to determine the factors that may have impacted individuals' perceptions about the value of internships or work-related experiences. Additional research should be conducted to determine why individuals rate internships or work experience as important when it comes to securing employment, even for those individuals who did not complete an internship for credit.

Due to these findings, it appears that internships provide valuable experiences to students, although results are difficult to measure. In light of this information, internship opportunities should be provided to students at this institution (and others), and students should be encouraged to take advantage of those opportunities. However, the College of Business should attempt to find ways to measure the outcomes of internships. Additional surveys that specifically relate to internships should be designed. In order to better measure the outcomes, an internship class for credit may be offered in conjunction with an internship. Assignments in this class may include projects that are being completed at the internship site, as well as papers or presentations on internship experiences. Offering more than pass–fail grades for the internship opportunities may provide an additional way to measure internship outcomes. By offering an internship class, students would be provided with the opportunity to relate classroom learning with internship experiences that are connected to the real world.

Although initial results showed no significance for job satisfaction and starting salary between interns and noninterns, additional research needs to be conducted. A larger sample size may prove beneficial in analyzing results. Perhaps those alumni who returned our survey are those with higher salaries or job satisfaction than those who didn't respond (i.e., the response rate impacted our results). Data from multiple years of surveys can be combined in order to increase the sample size. Another option would be to conduct a similar survey after a longer period following graduation has subsided (at least 5 years). The sample size is also lacking in diversity. Research needs to be conducted with more diverse samples to determine if different ethnicity affects any of the outcomes. Interviews with a small sample of participants may provide clues about more specific effects of diversity on the outcomes.

Finally, due to unexpected findings, further research on starting salaries for females versus males among business majors, as well as in other areas, needs to be conducted. Could gender bias by employers still be a factor? It has been well documented that there is still evidence of gender bias by employers. Lips (2003) cited several sources that indicate females continue to earn less than their male counterparts and rarely hold top executive positions. The College of Business at Shippensburg University of Pennsylvania has an obligation to investigate possible reasons for females earning approximately $4,000 less than males in their first professional positions after college and determine if any factors are influenced by their educational experiences at the institution. What is the ratio of male and female faculty teaching in the college of business? Is there a comparable number of female and male faculty? Is sexism still present inside, as well as outside, the classroom? When guests are invited to speak about their careers in the classroom and at business club meetings, are both male and female guests represented? Are female students encouraged to pursue the same careers as male students? Are female students taught to negotiate salary and will they pursue that during the hiring process? Finally, do females still view marriage and family as important and place higher value on those than higher paying careers? These may be possible reasons, but there may be different ones as well. These questions should be explored in an effort to determine the reasons for the large gap in starting salaries between men and women and then implement appropriate interventions.

Summary
- Selecting the right assessment instrument is important in any research project. The results should measure what they claim to measure. Also, you want to ensure adequate participation in the assessment. Overutilizing assessments and asking repeat information from participants on different assessments can discourage them from involvement in future research projects.
- In order to obtain manageable results, findings may have to be simplified or consolidated into workable categories.

- Common statistical methods used in comparing and analyzing research results include chi square distribution and regression analysis.
- Statistical significance is extremely important when conducting research. However, other information may also be noteworthy. Be detailed and specific when reporting research findings.
- Research projects can lead you in unexpected directions. Be ready to document and explore unanticipated findings.
- Realize there will be limitations to the research if participants are asked to self-report information. It is hoped that individuals will be honest and accurate in their reports, but this is not always the case; this still needs to be documented as a possible limitation.

ANNOTATED BIBLIOGRAPHY

Arnold, M. J., & Cannon, J. A. (1998, March–April). Student expectations of collegiate internship programs in business: A 10-year update. *Journal of Education for Business, 73*(4), 202–205. This resource was easy to read and contained informative research on internships. The article discusses the perceived importance of internships in obtaining full-time employment. Students are more and more using internships as a way to be more competitive in the job market after graduation.

Eyler, J. (1993, Fall). Comparing the impact of two internship experiences. *Journal of Cooperative Education, 29*(1), 41–52. This article examines two different internship programs and the impact of each on student learning. Research demonstrates how some internship programs have a major impact on student learning, where others may only have a minimal (if any) impact on enhancing student learning related to academic coursework.

Filipczak, B. (1998, April). The new interns. *Training, 35*(4), 46–48, 50. This article examines students' views of internships. Students are not only viewing internships as a way to make a few extra dollars. They want to learn and want to be challenged. They realize that collating and photocopying are not providing them with learning opportunities related to their majors, and they expect more.

Gardner, P. D., & Lambert, S. E. (1993 January). It's a hard, hard, hard, hard, hard, hard world. *Journal of Career Planning and Employment, 53*(2), 40–49. Gardner and Lambert completed research to measure student expectations and workplace realities. Data collected showed major differences between student expectations during their senior year and the reality of full-time employment 2 years after graduation. The article mentions that learning opportunities outside the classroom (i.e. internships, cooperative education opportunities, and other career-related experiences) may help to provide students with realistic expectations about the working world.

Ryan, M., & Cassidy, J. R. (1996, Summer). Internships and excellence. *Liberal Education, 82*(3), 16–23. This article discusses the importance of combining learning with hands on experiences. The article reviews components of different experiential education programs and discusses how these requirements may enhance student learning. Ryan and Cassidy pointed out that students can enhance what they are learning in experiential education opportunities as long as they take an active role in the process.

REFERENCES

Alm, C. T. (1996, November–December). Using student journals to improve the academic quality of internships. *Journal of Education for Business, 72*(2), 113–15.

Arnold, M. J., & Cannon, J. A. (1998, March–April). Student expectations of collegiate internship programs in business: A 10-year update. *Journal of Education for Business, 73*(4), 202–205.

Casella, D. A., & Brougham, C. E. (1995, August). What works: Student jobs open front doors to careers. *Journal of Career Planning and Employment, 55*(4), 24–27, 54–55.

Cates, M. L. (1999, October). Internship and co-op programs, a valuable combination for collegians. *Black Collegian, 30*(1), 84–87.

Eyler, J. (1993, Fall). Comparing the impact of two internship experiences. *Journal of Cooperative Education, 29*(1), 41–52.

Fields, C. D. (1996, December 12). Business schools and employment. *Black Issues in Higher Education, 13*(21), 16.

Filipczak, B. (1998, April). The new interns. *Training, 35*(4), 46–48, 50.

Gardner, P. D., & Lambert, S. E. (1993, January). It's a hard, hard, hard, hard, hard, hard world. *Journal of Career Planning and Employment, 53*(2), 40–49.

Imel, S. (1994). *Job search skills for the current economy.* Columbus, OH: ERIC Clearinghouse on Adult, Career, and Vocational Education. (ERIC Digest No. ED 376 274)

Journal of career planning and employment. (1995, November). *Reverberations from downsizings.* Author, 56(1), 6–8.

Lips, H. (2003). *A new psychology of women: Gender, culture, and ethnicity* (2nd ed.) New York: McGraw Hill.

McBride, J. L., Jr., & Muffo, J. A. (1994, March). Students assess their own career goals and service needs. *Journal of Career Planning and Employment, 54*(3), 26–63.

Ryan, M., & Cassidy, J. R. (1996, Summer). Internships and excellence. *Liberal Education, 82*(3), 16–23.

Ryan, C., & Krapels, R. H. (1997, December). Organizations and internships. *Business Communication Quarterly, 60*(4), 126–131.

Stanton, M. (1992, Summer). Internships: Learning by doing. *Occupational Outlook Quarterly, 36*(2), 30–33.

Appendix

1998 BUSINESS GRADUATE SURVEY

Name: _____
(Last Name, First Name, Maiden Name)

Home Phone: ( ) _____

Current Home Address:

_____

_____

Employer: _____

Job Title: _____

Work Phone: ( ) _____ Ext. _____

Work Address: _____

E-mail Address: _____

I am currently (check only most appropriate one):

☐ Employed full time in the business field prepared for as a major at SU
☐ Employed full time in a related business field
☐ Employed full time in a field unrelated to business
☐ Employed temporarily until desired position is available
☐ Employed part time
☐ Seeking employment
☐ Not seeking employment
☐ Self-employed related to major **or** ☐ related to other business area
☐ In military service
☐ Pursuing an advanced degree full time (If attending graduate school on a **full-time** or **part-time** basis, indicate university and major)

University _____ Major _____

DEGREE EARNED/MAJOR

_____

SALARY RANGE
☐ Less than $10,000
☐ $10-14,999
☐ $15-$19,999
☐ $20-$24,999
☐ $25-$29,999
☐ $30-$34,999
☐ $35-$39,999
☐ Over $40,000

SIZE OF EMPLOYER
BY NUMBER OF EMPLOYEES
☐ Less than 50
☐ 50 - 100
☐ 101 - 500
☐ 501 - 1,000
☐ 1,001 - 5,000
☐ 5,001 - 10,000
☐ 10,001 - 50,000
☐ More than 50,000

Are you employed in Pennsylvania? ☐ Yes ☐ No Indicate State/Country _____

Indicate your level of job satisfaction with your first full-time career position:
☐ Very Satisfied   ☐ Satisfied   ☐ Somewhat dissatisfied   ☐ Very dissatisfied

In seeking career employment, I limited my job search to:
☐ No specific geographic area   ☐ Specific geographic areas (Please specify) _____

I began seeking a full time career position:
☐ Before my senior year   ☐ 2nd semester my senior year
☐ 1st semester my senior year   ☐ After graduation

I secured my first full-time career position:
☐ During my senior year   ☐ 4-6 months after graduation   ☐ Still looking
☐ 1-3 months after graduation ☐ Beyond 6 months after graduation

When applying for career positions, I found that (check all that apply):
☐ There were a large number of openings in my field
☐ I had more difficulty than I expected finding a job in my field
☐ There were not many openings, thus I took a job in another field
☐ There were many openings, but I preferred to take a job in another field
☐ There were no openings in my field
☐ Openings in my field required a Master's degree
☐ My qualifications did not meet the job requirements
☐ I did not want a job in my field

After graduation I secured my first full-time career position through:
☐ Career Development Center (interviews, Catalyst, hot-line)
☐ Family or friends
☐ Employment agency
☐ An internship
☐ Faculty contacts
☐ Newspaper classifieds
☐ Job fairs
☐ Other (please specify) _____

Career Development Center: ☐ Very helpful   ☐ Somewhat helpful   ☐ Not helpful   ☐ Did not use

	Very Knowledgeable	Somewhat Knowledgeable	Not Knowledgeable	I Do Not Know
1. How knowledgeable were prospective employers about the institution?	☐	☐	☐	☐
2. How knowledgeable were prospective employers about the business program at the institution?	☐	☐	☐	☐
3. How knowledgeable were prospective employers about the AACSB accreditation of the business program at the institution?	☐	☐	☐	☐

	Very Important	Somewhat Important	Did Not Consider	I Do Not Know
4. If prospective employers were knowledgeable about the AACSB accreditation, how important did they consider this to be?	☐	☐	☐	☐

	High Quality	Average Quality	Low Quality	I Do Not Know
5. Do prospective employers consider the institution's College of Business program to be of	☐	☐	☐	☐

6. When seeking career employment, I found	Very Important	Somewhat Important	Not Very Important	I Do Not Know
A. Grade-point average to be	☐	☐	☐	☐
B. Computer skills to be	☐	☐	☐	☐
C. College internship/work experience in my desired career field to be	☐	☐	☐	☐
D. Work experience of any type to be	☐	☐	☐	☐
E. University extra-curricular activities to be	☐	☐	☐	☐
F. Leadership activities (university or community) to be	☐	☐	☐	☐
G. Business administration core courses to be	☐	☐	☐	☐
H. Course work in my major to be	☐	☐	☐	☐

Do you have any additional comments that you think might be helpful in recruiting prospective students for the College of Business?

_____

_____

_____

Please return to College of Business, Dean's Office,

Thank you for responding!

9

How to Measure
Complex Learning Processes:
The Nature of Learning
in Cooperative Education[1]

Nancy Johnston
Nello Angerilli
Natalia Gajdamaschko
Simon Fraser University

Key questions addressed in this chapter:

- What do key co-op stakeholders (students, practitioners, and administrators) think about co-op learning?

- How can we best measure stakeholder views regarding complex and subjective issues?

- Can we find a tool that truly reflects participants' views (some of which may be initially unknown to the investigators) versus one that measures their responses to investigators' predefined categories?

- What is Q methodology and how can it be used to help clarify complex issues?

- Are there world views regarding co-op and if yes, what are they?

[1]This study was supported by a grant from the Cooperative Education Association (CEA) and the Cooperative Education Division (CED) of the American Society of Engineering Education. The research was conducted through the Association for Cooperative Education—BC/Yukon's (ACE) Research and Initiatives Committee. ACE is the representative body of 23 post-secondary cooperative education institutions in British Columbia and the Yukon (Canada).

The research was based at Simon Fraser University (SFU), in Cooperative Education and involved participation from five other institutions' staff and students: University of British Columbia, B.C. Institute of Technology, Camosun College, Capilano College, and Douglas College. Initial pilot and field tests were conducted at SFU using SFU co-op students and practitioners from each of the six postsecondary institutions participating in the final data collection. These participants were from a variety of university and college programs including Arts, Sciences, Applied Sciences, as well as a small franchise of trade students and their co-op practitioner from a technical institute.

Demographic information collected from the participants included gender, number co-op terms completed, course of study, institution, and number years as co-op practitioner. Data were collected from a total of 120 participants: 92 students and 28 practitioners.

THE STARTING POINT:
QUESTIONS THAT GUIDED OUR INQUIRY

Much of the co-op research to date has looked at measuring various outcomes (including subsequent employability, wages, confidence, grades in school, satisfaction with educational program, etc.) particularly as they differ between co-op students and their non-co-op counterparts. Co-op has generally fared very well in these comparisons but why? How does the co-op experience contribute to these outcomes? As one co-op researcher has asked, "What is going on in the black box of co-op" (Ricks, Cutt, Branton, Loken, & van Gyn, 1993, p. 11)?

At Simon Fraser University we are very interested in understanding more about the nature of the learning that apparently contributes to the positive outcomes of cooperative education. For the past several years we have endeavored to rationalize better our practice in ways that reflect recent understandings of learning and transfer. What is learned through co-op, and how does this learning transfer from one context to another? How can we measure what one gains from a given co-op experience? How do Co-op practices mediate this learning, if at all? These questions remain unanswered, and largely unexplored, in co-op research. Until we better understand the co-op learning process, our practice as co-op educators will be limited, often driven by administrative objectives at the expense of learning. If we continue to ignore the pedagogical aspects of the co-op model we risk becoming nothing more than a job placement mechanism, with limited intentional and mediated educational value—nonessential to the goals and objectives of the institutions within which we reside.

But learning itself is very complex and theories abound on how students learn (Cates & Jones, 1999). Many of these theories involve the learner having concrete experiences, forming concepts, and applying these concepts in new situations. These require interactions between internal systems (cognitive and belief oriented) and external conditions (environmental and social), mediated by the learner's intellectual and motor skills, and their cognitive strategies. Kolb's (1984) experiential learning model may be one of the most relevant in terms of informing co-op learning. Within this model, the learning is continuous, with the learner experiencing, conceptualizing, and adapting as new situations arise. Here too, the learning is directed by the learner's needs and goals and mediated by periods of reflection and observation, in and on, their experiences. Clearly there is a very personal element to experiential learning—one that needs to be recognized whenever attempts to measure or define it are made.

Our challenge was to explore ways in which individual perspectives regarding the nature of co-op learning could be collectively captured and analyzed in order to be able to glean something about how co-op learning processes and outcomes are perceived by key stakeholders.

SOME BACKGROUND LITERATURE

Co-op as an educational model has been practiced since 1906 in North America and in the past 20 to 30 years its popularity has spread relatively rapidly and pervasively through most disciplines in the higher education system. Published research has largely focused on the effects of the co-op model on personal and career development aspects of students (e.g., Ricks et al., 1993). It is generally accepted that co-op programs have a substantial positive influence on graduate marketability, earning potential, academic achievement, job satisfaction and discipline relevance, and transition from school to work (Branton, et al., 1991b; HRDC, 1994; Petrysack & Toby, 1989; Porter, 1991). The general theme of much of this research is on the economic value of cooperative education as it relates to employability (Branton et al., 1991a). Further, repeated testimonials from business, industry, and co-op graduates confirm the role of cooperative education in developing skills relevant to employability in students. However, only a few studies (Johnston, 1996; Linn, 1999) have focused on the nature of the learning that occurs through these experiences or have examined the co-op curriculum, program, and pedagogy, particularly as it relates to students' academic programs and conceptualizations of learning in professional practice. As a result, the nature of learning in cooperative education is not well understood (Ricks et al., 1993).

> In empirical studies of cooperative education investigators have determined that "something happens" to students enrolled in a program called cooperative education. In these studies cooperative education is often undefined or inadequately defined, and how it works is not explained. This absence of operationalized concepts and operational models or frameworks for cooperative education means we are left with a half century of "black box" research. Typically this research examines students when they come out of the black box. (Ricks et al., 1993, p. 11)

Evers, Krmpotic, Rush, & Duncan-Robinson (1993) investigated the skill development process in a 3-year longitudinal study of Canadian university students and graduates. They investigated four base components of skill competence that included those of mobilizing innovation and change, managing people and tasks, communicating, and managing self. They also pursued information regarding where these skills were learned and compared co-op and regular students. They concluded that skills development appears to be linked to the changing experiences that these participants faced between school and work when they left the role of student for that of employee.

A *Review of Post Secondary Cooperative Education Funding in the Province of British Columbia* in 1992 stated that co-op is "creating a learning environment in which the (post secondary) curriculum is relevant to the real opportunity for placement in the working world" (Cooperative Education Fund Review Advisory Committee Report, 1992, p. 3). Specifically the report cited studies that show that co-op students perceived clarification of both educational and career goals (Wilson & Lyons, 1961), co-op graduates felt that they had received adequate career education during their academic careers (Brown, 1984), and co-op students were more confident of career choices, more motivated, and more satisfied both during and after work terms (Petrysack & Toby, 1989; Rowe, 1989; Weinstein, 1980). Several other studies linked experience in cooperative education with personal growth and change, particularly in the areas of self-esteem, confidence, autonomy, and interpersonal relationships (Cohen, 1978; Fletcher, 1989; Rowe, 1989; Wilson, 1974). Recent Canadian studies found improved job search, communication, and life-skills development as well as direct academic benefits including improved study skills, academic achievement, and student retention rates (Austin, 1988; Branton et al., 1991a).

Johnston (1996) investigated what and how co-op students learn in a study of university applied science co-op students pre, during, and post work term. Observations of the students working, and subsequent discussions of their experience with their supervisors and the investigator provides the events from which a conceptualization of co-op learning was developed. She described what was learned and how learning arose with specific attention to such processes as problem detection and recognition; problem framing and reframing; and problem solving through reflection in and on practice. Johnston (1996) demonstrated the importance of the changing concerns of co-op students as they move through the work term, the importance of student engagement in a community of practice, and the importance of learning by seeing, doing, and being shown.

More recently, a study by Linn (1999) at Antioch College, combined quantitative and qualitative methodologies to more deeply examine the learning processes (vs. outcomes) that were at play when students alternated between work and study over several generations of grads. Linn utilized the narratives that graduates related to her as sources of information regarding their own sense of their learning and complemented these with numbered data to provide a richer view of the learning that may be occurring.

D. K. Parks (http://www.kstamenov.com/dparks) has developed a tool for Predicting Learning Advancement through Cooperative Education (PLACE scale), designed to assess students' perceptions of their cooperative education learning experience. The PLACE scale records student responses to 34 statements created by the authors, based upon a four component model of cooperative education conceptualized by the authors. The four components of their model include:

- Career development
- Academic functions and achievement
- Work skills development
- Personal growth and development

This scale provides an interesting and useful addition to the ways by which we might measure co-op, though may be limited in fully reflecting student's perceptions due to the a priori meanings built into the scale items themselves.

In summary, although co-op education was specifically designed as a teaching model to educate students by complementing academic studies with related work experience, why and how it works has not been as clearly understood (Cates & Jones, 1999). By examining existing student learning theories and relating them to cooperative education, some insight into the complex and subjective process of co-op learning may result. The recent works of Johnston (1996) and Linn (1999) consider various theories regarding how co-op students may learn, and attempt to reflect students' perceptions of this complex issue, however there remains a need to develop a better understanding of the character of learning taking place in these work settings. In particular, there is a need to retain better the meanings that the learners give to the statements or scale items to which they respond. Only in this way will the findings truly reflect the subjects' perceptions of co-op learning versus the subjects' reactions to the researchers' perceptions of co-op learning—a quality (operant subjectivity) missing in more traditional methodology.

PURPOSE OF THE RESEARCH

Our principal purposes in this research were twofold: First we wanted to uncover the breadth and depth of opinions regarding the complex issue of learning through cooperative education and to explore any differences and similarities that might exist between stakeholder perspectives. In particular, we sought to understand more about student and practitioner perceptions of the theoretical underpinnings of co-op learning; what was learned, where and how this learning may be occurring, and to what extent it transferred across contexts.

Second, we sought to develop a way of assessing co-op learning that would, to the greatest extent possible, retain the respondents' perceptions, and reflect those perspectives unencumbered by any a priori meanings the researchers might ascribe. Co-op learners respond to similar experiences in different ways and construct different meanings from common experiences. It is then insufficient to measure only one construction of meaning, that of the researchers, when studying issues of significant complexity and subjectivity. Our research program, then, had two phases:

Phase I: research on existing approaches for measurement and assessment of experiential learning; and

Phase II: selection, development and application of Q-methodology for the measurement of attitudes, opinions, and perceptions of co-op students and practitioners. We report here on Phase II only.

METHODOLOGY: FINDING A METHODOLOGY WHICH BEST ANSWERS THE "MESSY" QUESTIONS

Decision Point: How can we measure such a complex issue?
Our first major decision point in this project revolved around the question of methodology. It was clear that there was great subjectivity and complexity in defining *co-op learning* (much less measuring it!). We sought to find a way that would best represent each participant's views and that might also allow for new perspectives to emerge that would inform our understanding of co-op and learning. We consulted with colleagues in the Faculty of Education and were put in touch with a visiting research scientist who had a background in educational psychology and recent research experiences in the science of subjectivity. She introduced us to a hybrid methodology called Q (Q Methodology).

We sought a methodological approach that did not define in advance any factors or groups of opinions about this complex issue, but rather one that would allow participants to inject their understandings of co-op and learning through their responses.

We were introduced to Q-Methodology (also known as Q or Q-method) as an example of a hybrid qualitative and quantitative methodology that differentiates itself from traditional r-methodology in that the results more truly reflect what respondents feel is important. In asking the rather subjective and complex questions around perceptions of learning, we sought a methodology that would allow respondents to create the main factors for analysis, rather than respond to perspectives or factors the researchers might present.

Q method makes it possible to correlate persons instead of tests or responses (Stephenson, 1978, 1980), thereby allowing the participants' perceptions to form the basis of the resultant factors. Rather than trying to define *independent variables* and testing them on a population of stakeholders, we "could analyze them instead from the point of view of the person who did the rating, because theirs are the actual operations at issue" (Stephenson, 1953, p. 40).

ABOUT Q METHOD

As research incorporating Q-methodology tends to be sequestered in a number of sub-disciplines not often associated with co-op education we provide a brief description of its strengths and operating procedures. For more in depth discussions you can refer to http://www.qmethod.org/

What is Q?

Fundamentally, Q methodology provides a foundation for the systematic study of subjectivity, and it is this central feature that recommends it to persons interested in qualitative aspects of human behavior. It has been used successfully to study various opinions on issues of public policy, public administration, privacy, leadership and learning, consumer attitudes, reader responses, etcetera. Q-Method presents a way of enhancing a traditional survey approach by ensuring a level of *operant subjectivity*—where the factors that emerge for interpretation are a result of the participants' responses vs. patterns of responses created by the participant responding to different variables with known characteristics and pre-established meanings (Brown, 2001). The researcher is then tasked with interpreting the world views generated by the respondent vs. interpreting the ways in which participants respond to the views presented by the researcher.

How Does Q work?

Most typically, a person is presented with a set of statements or images about some topic individually represented on cards or slips of paper. In our case, 55 statements regarding co-op and learning were presented to participants (see Appendix). They are asked to order them according to various levels of "agreement " and "disagreement" (these are often numbered from -3 for most strongly disagree through to $+3$ for most strongly agree). This physical ranking of the statements is referred to as *Q sorting*. The statements are matters of opinion only (not fact), and the fact that the Q sorter is ranking the statements from their own point of view is what brings subjectivity into the picture.

Respondents must have an opinion on all of the statements, and they are limited in terms of how many statements can be in any one of the rank orders. This forced sort condition only allows for a certain number of statements to be sorted into any of the 7 category options (-3 to $+3$). By specifying the number of sorting options the researcher influences the statistical distribution of the total items sorted (Denzine, 1998). In this case, we encouraged a normal distribution where sorts at the ends of the curve (-3 and $+3$) indicate the participants' strongest views, and those in the middle are more neutral. This forced sorting to fit a normal curve encourages deeper thought and elicits careful consideration of each statement with respect to relative rankings. Through this ranking process, participants give deeper meaning to the statements and it is this meaning that defines the emerging factors.

The rankings are then subject to factor analysis, and the resulting factors, inasmuch as they have arisen from individual subjectivities, indicate segments of subjectivity that exist. Because the interest of Q methodology is in the nature of the segments and the extent to which they are similar or dissimilar, the issue of large random samples, so fundamental to most social research, becomes relatively unimportant. In short, the focus is on eliciting a participant's deep personal perspectives while utilizing some of the most powerful statistical mechanics to help direct the researcher to uncover newly emerging views.

The next step involved ensuring that Q Method could be effectively administered and interpreted with respect to our questions regarding co-op learning.

Decision Point: Can we use Q effectively in this study as a way of measuring a complex phenomenon such as co-op learning?
An attractive and powerful feature of Q-sort methodology emerges from what is essentially a ranking process where the respondent can always see the relative rank order of their responses. This feature provides the opportunity for participants to continuously change their relative ranking of each response throughout the entire ranking procedure, which in general does not have a strict time limit imposed. Other rank-order statistical tools tend to increasingly limit the range of movement available to the respondent as the instrument is administered. Although it is often possible to change a response, in a noncritical survey most respondents are unlikely to do so once a choice has been made. The dynamic approach of Q allows for visual feedback and continuous adjustment of ranking through to the end of the procedure and in most instances requires continuous re-assessment and forced reranking of all responses. Thus, although the range of responses is limited by the statements presented, the opportunity to assign rank order remains the same throughout the test and is clearly visible, providing continuous feedback to the respondent and avoiding the 'channeling' effect of many rank-order surveys.

Therefore, because of its ability to better represent the highly subjective and complex responses regarding co-op learning, the fact that it offers investigators the ability to compare differences and similarities in opinions that might exist between stakeholders, and because of its flexibility in terms of administration and analysis (see more following), Q methodology was adopted for this research project.

Decision Point: How to administer Q?
Several of the administrators wondered about best or different ways of collecting data. At the time of the data collection for this project, individual sorts were the only options and the Q administrators for this research chose to administer the individual sorts to groups of 10 or more. Recently another option has been added that allows for virtual Q sorting. The latest innovation called

WebQ is a JavaScript application for Q-sorting questionnaire items online. In WebQ items are displayed in questionnaire format with radio buttons alongside each item for choosing ranking categories. Every time the user clicks the Update-function button, statements are reordered on screen into their momentarily selected category piles (piles of items are placed beneath each other).

When grouping and regrouping of items into their final rank-ordered categories is accomplished, the user is ready to click the Send button. Upon that, the data is pasted into a ready-to-send e-mail window, where the user can add some additional comments, and send the e-mail to the researcher's address.

A researcher's guide section describes how to set up WebQ for your own Q-sort project. See http://www.rz.unibw-muenchen.de/~p41bsmk/qmethod/

What is a Concourse?

In Q methodology, the scope of subjective commentary on a particular issue is referred to as a *concourse* (Stephenson, 1978), which in Latin means "a running together." In Q this refers to the array of ideas, attitudes, feelings, values, and perceptions that different individuals may associate with a topic, idea, process, or concept. This concourse is represented by a series of statements reflecting the breadth of opinions about the phenomenon being researched and these statements are sorted by the study participants according to their level of agreement or disagreement with each.

How Did We Create a Concourse on Co-op and Learning? (The Q Sample)

The concourse for co-op learning is potentially vast because stakeholders view co-op and learning in different ways as a result of being engaged in co-op in many different ways. We began by trying to capture the breadth and depth of opinions and views on co-op processes in order to create a sufficient but focused concourse. We aimed to integrate and reflect an array of co-op learning-associated opinions and research findings that would reflect an existing concourse. The researchers spoke with students and practitioners, conducted various literature reviews, and pilot tested an initial concourse of more than 100 statements. Based on the results of the pilot we eliminated statements that appeared to be redundant or ambiguous and added others to reflect elements of the concourse felt to be missing. We selected a sample of 55 statements that we believed represented the diversity of views and perceptions regarding learning in cooperative education. These statements were incorporated into a prototype instrument for further testing, which was subsequently ramped up to a field test with a small group of co-op student volunteers drawn from a number of different disciplines in a single institution. These students provided initial Q sort data for factor analysis as well as reported on any unclear, redundant or missing points of view in the concourse represented by the 55 statements.

The prototype was further refined on the basis of this pilot study and then introduced to a group of co-op practitioners from a number of co-op universities, colleges, institutes, and disciplines in British Columbia. The practitioners were provided with background knowledge regarding the goals and purpose of our study, the essential details of Q methodology necessary to understand the underlying process through which the tool works, specific instructions on how to administer Q, and practice as both administrators and participants. Data from this group, and subsequently the students of each of these practitioners, then formed the basis of our Q analysis and the results that we report here.

The Q-Sample

The Q sample of 55 statements was designed, on one hand, to be big enough to ensure representation of the range of perspectives and opinions in the concourse about co-op, and, on other hand, to be small enough to be practicable for the Q-sorting participants.

The 55 statements comprising the Q sample (Appendix A) were developed by the researchers to reflect the following aspects of co-op learning also selected by the researchers :

- What is learned (e.g., Statements 5, 9, 15, 19, 22, 27, 29);
- How this learning occurs (e.g., Statements 30, 32, 33, 35, 36, 37, 39, 41–45, 54, 55);
- Where the learning occurs (e.g., Statements 5–20);
- Whether and how the learning is linked to co-op practices (e.g., Statements 38, 46, 47, 48, 49);
- Transfer of co-op learning (e.g., Statements 2, 3, 28, 50, 51, 52, 54); and
- Whether and how co-op learning relates to existing models of experiential education (e.g., Statements 40–43).

THE P (PERSON) SAMPLE

The instrument was used with a total of 120 participants. Among them were university students (33), technical institute (trades programs) students (8), and college (independent, nondegree granting, mainly 2-year programs) students (51). Twenty-eight practitioners (co-op coordinators and managers) participated in total: 11 from universities, 16 from colleges, and one from a technical institute.

> **Decision Point: Why did we select 120 participants?**
> Given that Q method correlates persons versus responses, each participant's responses form the basis of the resulting factors. Inasmuch as a user of Q method is interested in the nature of the emergent factors and how they relate to each other versus how participants respond to predetermined factors, investigators are freed from the R-method, or traditional positivistic methodology, requirements of a large, random sample. We therefore allowed each Q administrator to select the sample size they wanted, and to include students and/or staff. In an effort to ensure multiple perspectives we selected the Q administrators from various program areas and institutions. This process resulted in 120 total participants in total.

RESULTS

PCQ Method software (www.pcqsoft.com/) was used to analyze the raw data. One outcome of Q analysis is a factor analysis[2] of the Q statements and an indication of how each respondent loads into each of the emergent clusters of Q statements. The statistically distinct clusters of statements which emerge from the factor analysis are known in Q as *factors*. They represent perspectives or worldviews on the research question. Although the process of factor analysis may determine that statistically different perspectives exist, it is then up to the researchers to look at which statements define those factors, how they relate to other factors, which of the participants loads into each factor, etcetera in order to try and determine what worldview each factor represents. This is an exciting part of the Q analysis as entirely unanticipated factors may emerge (or none at all!) and researchers must utilize their qualitative skills to interpret the outcomes. In order to help the researchers in their analysis, the PCQ analysis also provides information regarding:

- the distinguishing statements for each factor (those statements that most define the view represented by the factor that emerged)
- correlations between the sorts (how each of the views relates to the others)
- how the statements ranked within each factor, and
- statements sorted by their degree of consensus or disagreement amongst the factors.

---

[2]"Factor analysis in general is a method for classifying variables: in R (traditional) method, the variables are tests or traits; in this case, the variables are Q sorts. More accurately for our purposes, factor analysis is a method for determining how persons have classified themselves (although they are scarcely aware of having done so) since the process to be outlined shows the extent to which the Q sorts provided, fall into natural groupings by virtue of being similar or dissimilar to one another. If two people are like-minded on a topic, their Q sorts will be similar and they will both end up in the same factor. Hence, we do not classify them: they classify themselves on their own terms, which emerge as factors" (Brown, S., 1980 p. 208).

Decision Point: What other choices are available to assist with Q Sort analysis? Why did we choose PCQ?

SOFTWARE PACKAGES FOR THE ANALYSIS OF Q-SORT DATA

PCQ

PCQ3 by Mike Stricklin (mstrick@unlinfo.unl.edu) is a commercial factor-analysis program for Q-technique that runs under MS-DOS. A test copy can be downloaded from the (ftp://uwwvax.uww.edu/qarchive/) QArchive Ftp-Server. Specifically, PCQ allows one to easily enter data (Q-Sorts) the way they are collected (i.e., as piles of statement numbers). It computes intercorrelations among Q-Sorts, which are then factor analyzed. The PCQ analysis produces an extensive report with a variety of tables on factor loadings, statement factor scores, discriminating statements for each of the factors and as consensus statements across factors.

QUANAL

Like QMethod, Norman Van Tubergen's QUANAL is a FORTAN program, developed in the 1960s for mainframe platforms. It is rather complex and offers a great variety of features and options with respect to input-data structure, methods of analysis and the presentation of results. The current price is $400 for educational and nonprofit buyers. For further information contact Norm Van Tubergen at HUC129@UKCC.UKY.EDU

General Purpose Statistical Packages

Commercially available statistical packages like SPSS, though highly featured, user-friendly, flexible, etcetera, in many respects, do not provide optimal support for entering and factor-analyzing Q-sort data. Yet, they are indispensable for additional statistical procedures not available with QMethod software (e.g., analysis of variance). In practice, therefore, one often needs to use both, general and specialized statistical software, especially in cases of mixed Q- and R-designs.

For our purposes it made most sense to select the system that provided ample reports, was flexible, and was readily available at no cost. As we were not involved in a mixed Q- and R- design, the PCQ software was our choice for the data analysis phase.

For more information on Q studies see Q Study Archive at http://facstaff.uww.edu/cottlec/qarchive

Eight factors or clusters of perceptions regarding learning in coop education emerged from the Q analysis, as seen in Table 9.1. These factors represent groupings of perceptions, attitudes, and opinions regarding what is learned, in co-op, how it is learned and how co-op-based learning compares with campus-based learning. The factors are often said to represent world views about the subject, however any given respondent can "load" in more than one factor at statistically significant levels, and therefore hold more than one world view.

Decision Point: How do we interpret and label the emergent factors or "world views?"

This was one of the most interesting and challenging phases of the analysis. The authors wanted to ensure that each of our perspectives would be represented, independently derived from our own initial interpretations. We therefore agreed to review separately several key PCQ generated reports (e.g., the distinguishing statements for each factor, the factor matrix with defining sorts, the consensus and disagreement sorted statements). Each investigator then wrote up a brief overview of what they felt each factor represented. The researchers also looked at factor loading as a means of helping understand the various perspectives (e.g., how many practitioners vs. students, or university vs. college participants' views were represented in each factor at a statistically significant level).

Each individual's interpretations were then presented for discussion in a face-to-face meeting of the researchers. Interestingly, although we had ascribed slightly different motivations to each of the factors, many of our interpretations shared similar themes and perspectives. For Factor 2, the world view was fairly easily determined by the researchers based on clear distinguishing statements (about co-op practice) and the factor loading (heavily practitioner). For example, for this factor Nello's original report began with "this factor seems to focus more on the administration of co-op" and Nancy originally noted that "this factor seems most concerned with the administration, or elements, of co-op practice." Factor 2 ultimately became the "practitioner factor" and labeled as *Co-op Elements of Practice and Learning*.

TABLE 9.1

Summary of Factors, Defining Statements and Summary Commentary for a Q Analysis of Cooperative Education Learning Outcomes

Factor and Loading	Primary Defining Statement	Summary Commentary
• 1. Co-op is for Learning Technical Skills (dominant student factor) Loading: • 4 (14%) practitioners loaded here [3/4 from universities, 1 from college] • 40 students (43%) loaded here • 63% of technical institute students, 58% of university students and 31% of college students loaded in this factor	Work experience is the only real way to learn these work skills – you have to be part of the whole experience in order to really understand it.	Very positive regarding the value of work experience and its relationship with skill acquisition. Sees co-op as the best vehicle for learning discipline-specific technical skills and a better vehicle than school for learning other employability-related skills. Learning is seen to occur through repeated exposure and trial and error, with little perceived influence from co-op practices or processes (work reports, site visits, etc.).
• 2. Co-op Elements of Practice and Learning (dominant practitioner factor) Loading: • 61% (17/28) practitioners loaded in factor 2 • 22% of all students loaded in factor 2 (20/93)	Site visits to co-op students mid-way through their term provide a key opportunity for discussing the student's progress with respect to their learning objectives.	This practitioner-dominated factor seems to focus more on the administrative elements of co-op. As with the student loaded factor 1, it sees learning occurring mainly through repeated practice in real work situations but sees co-op elements, such as site visits, playing an important role in that learning. Factor 2 strongly disagrees "that co-op is a great job placement service."
• 3. Anti-Co-op: No Value Added View of Co-op Loadings: • 3 (11%) practitioners loaded here in the negative • 10 students loaded (11%), 3 (30%) in the negative so only 7% of all student respondents agreed with this worldview (and no practitioners did)	Students who work in related jobs throughout their schooling learn just as much as Co-op students do through their job placements.	This factor suggests that those attributes, largely positive, that we believe are associated with co-op are in fact more closely associated with the classroom side of school or a non-co-op work experience. Though there is recognition that some kinds of learning can occur on the job, it does not seem that the learning is either useful, or transferable to the classroom. School, or a related job, is where learning takes place and the co-op process does not add any substantial value.

• 4. Co-op Derives Classic Employability Outcomes

Loadings:
- 4 (14%) practitioners loaded [3 college and 1 university]
- 22 (24%) students loaded here [11 each (50%) from college and university, 0 from the institute]

Through Co-op, students learn to communicate effectively with others.

Significant work-related skills can be learned through co-op, including: team playing, communication, problem solving, and job-finding. This factor is very positive about the value of co-op to skill acquisition but does not highly rank the work report, or post co-op debriefings as contributing to the development of these employability skills. Co-op is viewed as a great way to learn these skills but how this occurs is not clear.

• 5. Co-op and Learning Models Focus

Loadings:
- 4 (14%) practitioners loaded here [3/4 from universities, 1 from college]
- 15 students (16%) loaded here [73% of all the students that loaded in this factor were college,12% were from universities]

Co-op students learn by engaging more and more fully in the workplace, slowly absorbing, and being absorbed by, the culture (cognitive, social, environmental, emotional) of their work community.

Respondents loading in this factor appear most interested in the learning aspects of co-op, seeing co-op beyond a series of employability outcomes and acknowledging situated learning theory as a possible underlying model for how co-op learning occurs. Useful transfer of information, attitudes, and skills occurs from school to work and between jobs but it is not clear that what is learned at work can be useful back in the school context.

• 6. Synergistic/Complementary Model
(School + Co-op = What is Needed for Employability Related Learning)

Loadings:
- 2 (7%) practitioners [1 each from college and universities]
- 7 students (8% of total)

Co-op students learn best through their own successes and failures at work as well as watching the successes and failures of others in the workplace.

This factor suggests that learning both at school and at work is important. Analysis and critical thinking are learned at school but some practical aspects of work can be learned by watching professionals. It seems that school is largely responsible for teaching process while work is better at providing content. The factor sees exposure to, and observation in, the workplace as key to learning, though specific co-op processes do not seem critical to assisting that learning.

(continued on next page)

171

TABLE 9.1 (continued)

Factor and Loading	Primary Defining Statement	Summary Commentary
• 7. **Co-op is for the Application of School-learned Skills to the Workplace** **Loadings:** • 2 practitioners (7%) – • 9 students (10% of all students) [0 university students; 25% of institute students and 14% of college students]	Co-op is the application of what is learned in school to a real work environment.	It seems that technical skills are not learned at work and the implication therefore is that they are learned in school. There is transfer of information between the classroom and work. Co-op is therefore seen as the place to apply the skills learned in school in the real world resulting in a better ability to market oneself upon graduation.
• 8. **Co-op Practitioner is Key Facilitator to the World of Work** **Loadings:** • 6 practitioners (21%) • 3 students (3%) [all from college representing 6% of total college students]	Through Co-op students learn what to expect in the world of work.	Co-op teaches about the world of work and it is not possible to learn this kind of material in school. Co-op is the place to apply theory to practice and learn about the "real world." Interestingly, this factor promotes co-op practitioners as being useful for a number of the essential functions of co-op—perhaps because a large percentage of practitioners loaded in this factor.

The eight factors that emerged from the PCQ analysis were then interpreted and identified by the researchers as:

Factor 1: Co-op is for learning technical skills (dominant student factor)
Factor 2: Co-op elements of practice and learning (dominant practitioner factor)
Factor 3: Anti-co-op: No value-added view of co-op
Factor 4: Co-op derives classic employability outcomes
Factor 5: Co-op and learning models focus
Factor 6: Synergistic/complementary model (school + co-op = what is needed for employability related learning)
Factor 7: Co-op is for the application of school-learned skills to the workplace
Factor 8: Co-op practitioner is key facilitator to the world of work.

Factor 1 became informally referred to by the researchers as the *student factor*. The pattern of association between respondents and factors (see Table 9.1) shows that 43% of all students significant statistically loaded in Factor 1 (40 students out of 93). At the same time only 14% of practitioners (4 out of 28) loaded in this factor, suggesting that it most represents students' perspectives on co-op learning, those being that co-op provides the environment for learning the technical or discipline-specific skills required in the workplace.

Factor 2, on the other hand, became known as the *practitioner factor*. The analysis results show that 17 out of 28 practitioners (61%) loaded at statistically significant levels into Factor 2, the factor that focuses most on aspects of co-op practice and their relation to learning. As only 20 out of 93 students (22%) loaded in this factor; this factor best represents the perceptions of a majority of practitioners in our study. Not surprisingly, it is distinguished by statements regarding elements of co-op practice such as site visits and work reports.

Factor 3, the anti-co-op factor, comprised only 7% of all student respondents. This is the only factor that represents a negative perspective regarding co-op and learning. No practitioners were positively associated with this factor. A few practitioners and students also loaded in this factor (at levels of statistical significance) in the *negative*, indicating their strong disagreement with those elements of the concourse they felt were anti-co-op. Together they created this negative perspective of co-op and learning, some in support of it, others in opposition.

Factor 4, the view that co-op learning results in the development of classic employability skills such as teamwork and communication, had 14% practitioner loading and 24% student loading, with equal representation from the college and university sectors but none from the technical institution. Although this factor has a modest practitioner loading, it is likely meaningful that almost one fourth of students were positively associated with his factor.

Factor 5 was the only factor that seemed to indicate an interest in various learning model-related statements. Although only 16% of students were associated with this factor, 73% were from colleges, 12% from universities and none from the technical institution. Of the 14% of practitioners associated with this factor, 75% were from universities. Perhaps this indicates a small but significant interest in better understanding co-op learning at a deeper level by some practitioners and students, particularly by college students and university practitioners.

Factor 6 loadings represented 7% of practitioners and 8% of students distributed relatively equally among institutions. This factor seemed to represent a view that both school-based learning and co-op learning were needed to best prepare students for the world of work.

Factor 7 consisted of 7% practitioner loadings (none from universities) and 10% of student loadings (also none from universities). This factor very much sees co-op as providing the opportunities to apply the skills learned in school to the workplace. It is perhaps not surprising, then, that those in this factor were exclusively from the college and technical institute sectors where the academic curriculum tends to be much more applied.

Factor 8, the practitioner as facilitator to the world of work factor, was created by 21% of practitioners, the second highest after Factor 2, and the smallest number of students (3%), all of whom were from colleges. This practitioner-dominant factor is the only one that positions the co-op coordinator as key to co-op learning. This factor also represents the view that co-op is the only way to learn what is needed for employability.

DISCUSSION

The emergent factors reveal the significant perceptions of the respondent co-op stakeholders regarding what is learned, how it is learned and where it is learned in addition to providing insight into the world views prevalent amongst this sample of co-op practitioners and students. Analysis of the statements that most define each on the factors provides further detail of the major and minor themes underlying each factor, and allows for comparing and contrasting stakeholder perceptions.

Factor 1: Co-op Is For Learning Technical Skills (Dominant Student Factor)

As noted, Factor 1 is the dominant student factor, largely representing a view that the worlds of school and work are very different with respect to learning. Factor 1 positions co-op as a critical way to learn the technical skills required in the workplace. Respondents strongly agreed with the statement that "work experience is the only real way to learn these work skills—you have to be a part of the whole experience in order to understand it" and sorted co-op positively versus school with respect to where they learn those skills.

At the same time, respondents who loaded into this factor at a level of statistical significance do not perceive a relation between "a grade received in a course and performance in the same subject areas in the workplace" (–3). In general they do not perceive school as the place to learn employability-related skills as they sorted in the negative those statements regarding school and the development of analytical and thinking skills, teamwork, big picture exposure, problem defining and solving, and knowledge regarding how one learns.

The respondents who comprise this factor believe that learning occurs through repeated practice in real situations (+2), experiencing their own success and failure (+3), and through experience and reflection (+1). They do not perceive that co-op practices other than their work provide a value-added experience though they acknowledge the workplace as key. They negatively sorted many co-op practices with respect to their learning including workshops (–1), site visits (–1), work reports (–2), and the role of the coordinator (–2).

Respondents associated with this factor appear to consider co-op as the best vehicle for learning discipline-specific technical skills and a better vehicle than school for other employability-related skills learning (although not the exclusive place to learn other employability-related skills). They believe that co-op learning occurs largely through repeated exposure and trial and error, and little of it appears to be significantly mediated by co-op practices or processes.

Factor 2: Co-op Elements of Practice and Learning (Dominant Practitioner Factor)

This factor seems most concerned with the administration, or elements, of co-op practice. More than in any other factor, site visits are seen as an important feature of co-op for learning and marketing purposes. Only respondents in this factor and Factor 8 (the other practitioner-loaded factor) sort site visits positively. Although respondents creating this factor value that something new is generally learned through co-op (they strongly disagree (–3) with the statement that "often nothing new is learned through co-op"), they do not believe that what is learned by students involves "getting a sense of what they don't know" (–2).

People loading into this factor strongly disagree that co-op is a great job placement service (–3) but it is unclear why—do they believe the jobs are not great, or the service is not, or that it is or should be much more than that? There is a lot of general agreement between this factor and Factor 1 (students) regarding how learning may occur. There is positive agreement by both factors regarding the value of learning by repeated practice in real work situations, through their own successes and failures, through experience and reflection, and from work supervisors.

Although this factor (2) and Factor 8 are heavily practitioner loaded, they differ in their views on what is learned and how it is learned. In particular they do not share perceptions regarding transfer of learning back to the classroom (the Factor 8 view supports Statement 2, which refers to transfer back to school, whereas Factor 2 participants rank this statement as neutral). They also differ on statements regarding the value of co-op with respect to obtaining and progressing in a job (Factor 2 participants sorted −1 for the related statement, and Factor 8 sorted it a +2). There are differing views as well regarding where and how co-op related learning occurs. Factor 2 rated the statements "co-op is a place for students to learn what makes them a good performer" at +2 and Factor 8 disagreed at −1. The factor 2 perspective is that co-op learning occurs through self-assessment and personal success and failure (+2), whereas the Factor 8 view is that self-assessment and personal success and failures do not play as important a role in that learning (ranking the related statements at −1).

Thus although Factor 8 practitioners share a more traditional view of co-op education as a vehicle for "the application of what is learned in school," this factor indicates a view that there may be other things emerging that are more complex than simply "applying school learning at work." However, Factor 2 respondents are somewhat unclear as to how these other learning issues (transfer of learning, new learning, etc.) may relate directly to their practice.

Factor 3: Anti-Co-op: No Value Added View of Co-op

This factor clearly represents the view that there is no special value to the co-op model with respect to learning most of the employability-related skills noted in the statements. This view suggests that those attributes, largely positive, typically associated with co-op education are in fact more closely associated with the classroom side of school. Moreover, this factor suggests that co-op does not add anything of particular value. Although there is recognition that some kinds of learning can occur on the job, participants loading in Factor 3 do not see a co-op experience as in any way being value-added. This is the only factor to agree strongly with Statement 50 that "as much can be learned in a related job as in a co-op job."

This group also views school as the primary place where learning occurs and positively sorts school as the place to learn to focus, prioritize, and respond to problems; as the place to develop teamwork and communication skills; and as the place to get a sense of the big picture. Respondents positively loading into Factor 3 are most likely to believe that co-op students may often learn nothing new through their co-op experiences, and are neutral even about co-op's role in career exploration. This group disagrees most strongly with Factor 2 (practitioner and administrative factor) on these issues. All in all, the anti-co-op view is that school is where learning takes place and co-op does not seem to add any special value.

This group is fairly small. Three percent of practitioners indicates disagreement with this negative world view of co-op. Although 10% of students loaded in this factor, only 7% of all student respondents clustered positively and share this view, the other 3% of students in this factor loaded negatively at statistically significant levels. Nevertheless, it is useful to be aware that this view exists among participants in cooperative education. Perhaps this reflects a larger group of students who do not believe in the co-op model or who have had particularly bad co-op experiences.

Factor 4: Classic Employability Outcomes

The Factor 4 perspective sees co-op as providing the classical employability outcomes such as communication skills, teamwork skills, problem solving, and job finding. It specifically views co-op as effective in giving students an opportunity to learn more about their career aspirations ($+2$) and how to get and progress in a job ($+2$). Co-op is largely viewed as a great place to acquire the employability skills that will be needed postgraduation ($+3$).

This factor speaks very positively about the value of co-op skill acquisition (job finding outcomes and various employability skills) although it is not clear the extent to which co-op processes assist in this skill acquisition. Respondents in this factor (who were mainly students) rated the value of the workshops as neutral (although this was the most positive sorting the workshops received); sorted at -2 the value of the work report as a learning tool; sorted as neutral the site visit as a learning experience; and ranked the value of debriefings after a work placement at -2. It seems this factor highly correlates co-op and employability outcomes but does not have a clear perspective regarding how or why this might be the case.

Factor 5: Co-op and Learning Models Focus

The study participants who loaded into this factor most strongly agreed with Statement 42 that "co-op students learn by engaging more and more fully in the workplace, slowly absorbing and being absorbed by the culture (cognitive, social, environmental, emotional) of their work community." This factor also defines itself by several other statements regarding how co-op learning may, or may not, occur. Respondents' perspectives that define this factor, recognize that co-op brings together a lot of complex elements including the cognitive and emotional aspects of culture and complex issues relating to transferability of skills.

Although there is great interest by respondents who load in this factor in how students learn, they did not sort traditional elements of co-op practice particularly highly (workshops at -2; work reports at -1; site visits, the role of the coordinator, and debriefing at 0 or neutral). This factor is also defined by the positive sorting of statements reflecting the notion of skill transfer at work ($+2$ on Statement 51; $+1$ on Statement 28; and $+1$ on Statement 27). There is less certainty, however, that effective transfer occurs from work back to the classroom (Statement 2 regarding bringing work skills back to school was sorted at 0). Perhaps this differentiation alludes to the general sense that near transfer (work to work) is nonproblematic but recognizes the challenges associated with the more distant transfer required between the worlds of school and work.

This factor also supports the notion that co-op students learn how much they don't know through their co-op experiences, again perhaps referring to the complex cultural systems they enter into in the workplace. Perhaps because of this reality expansion value of co-op, respondents in this factor see co-op as a good job placement service (+2). Although Factor 5 respondents share a view of co-op as a great job placement service with Factor 4 (+3), it is for very different reasons. The Factor 4 "employability outcomes" model views co-op as a way to gain useful skills for future employment, whereas the Factor 5 "learning" model views co-op as providing a great opportunity for students to learn through gradual participation and absorption into communities of work practice (a more process-oriented value). The value of various co-op practices in facilitating student learning in both factors is unclear at best.

Respondents loading in Factor 5 appear to favor the situated learning model to help explain some of the ways in which students may learn through their experiences. Interestingly, Factor 5 respondents do not believe that co-op students are more self-directed than other students, perhaps interpreting that the notion of self-direction might downplay the important role that others in a community of practice play with respect to one's learning.

The respondents loading in this factor appear a great deal more interested in the learning aspects of co-op than those in the other factors, and recognize the complexity therein. About equal percentages (~15%) of each of the student and practitioner participants loaded in this factor. The statements that define this factor, more than any other factor, relate to various models of learning and skills transfer (e.g. positively [+3] support situated learning, and are opposed to notions of reflection-in-practice [−2]—both statements reflect thinking about models of learning). This is a factor more interested in the cognitive- or process-oriented aspects of co-op learning than other factors and is the only world view that focuses more on co-op learning process than co-op outcomes.

Factor 6: Synergistic and Complementary Model (School + Co-op = What is Needed for Employability-Related Learning)

While acknowledging the important role of co-op, respondents loading in this factor also have a high regard for the role of their school learning with respect to their overall employability preparation. Each of these places has its special role in education. School is the place to learn theory, critical thinking, and analytical skills as well as how to focus on the right task and respond. Co-op is the place to apply theoretical knowledge in a very different setting (rated +2 statement that "co-op students learn the difference between a course in conflict management and an angry person yelling at you ..."). School cannot provide knowledge of the big picture in the way that co-op does nor is school the place where students learn "who to connect with when they graduate and are looking for career related work."

This factor sees the learning in co-op as very student mediated, strongly supporting (+3) the notion that co-op students learn best through their own successes and failures as well as by observing the successes and failures of others in the workplace. Respondents loading in this factor see the mechanism for co-op learning predominantly as exposure and observation (rating at a +3 Statement 36: "By watching other professionals, students learn a lot as part of a project team").

The world view expressed by the students and practitioners who created this factor is that the two types of education (co-op and traditional classroom) are necessary in order to learn what is needed for employability, citing different things being best learned in different places. This factor sees work experience as the only way to learn the so-called work-related skills or more discipline specific skills, but this is in and of itself is not enough. The Factor 6 perspective is that you also need school to develop the analytical and thinking skills to complement the technical and work-related skills in order to be an effective performer.

Factor 7: Co-op is for the Application of School-Learned Skills to Workplace

This factor represents the notion that co-op provides an avenue for the application of the theory learned in school to a real-world environment. It acknowledges the complementarity of school and co-op learning, as in Factor 6, but in a different way. This factor is the only one that clearly sees the role of school as teaching the relevant technical skills of a discipline and the role of co-op as providing for opportunities to apply those school-derived skills in the real world.

It could be simply stated that people loading heavily in this factor see school as teaching "A," co-op as providing an opportunity to practice "A," and industry needing a performer competent in "A." Respondents loading in Factor 6 (the previous complementary model factor) are more likely to see school as teaching "A," Co-op providing an opportunity to practice "A" and learn "B," and industry requiring a performer competent in ("A" + "B"). Perhaps it is not surprising that only college and institute students and practitioners loaded here as their curricula and educational goals more closely align with workplace specific and discipline specific employability skills than do universities.

This factor also supports the notion of skills transfer between school and work, having highly sorted the statement about "students bringing what they learned at work back to the classroom to make them better performers." In particular it is noted that what seems to be learned is "an ability to understand underlying key concepts" (+2). They are, however, not as sure that transfer from one work place to a new one will occur (rated neutral).

This group also sees school as a good place to learn to work as part of a team and communicate effectively, which may reflect a greater degree of cooperative learning in the college or institute system. Respondents loading in this factor also sorted positively the idea that students learn through their own failures and successes and by watching those of others in the workplace (+1). Regardless of what, where, or how they learn, this factor believes that co-op grads gain a better set of skills with which to sell themselves upon graduation.

Factor 8: Co-op Practitioner is Facilitator to the World of Work

This factor distinguishes itself in two ways: It proposes that co-op is the only way to learn and prepare for the world of work (not learnable in school) and that the co-op practitioner (coordinator) plays a positive role in facilitating this learning. This is the only factor in which respondents ranked the role of the coordinator in the positive (+1) with respect to learning (Statement 35). It also gave several co-op processes mixed reviews (e.g., site visits +2; work report –1, debriefings –2; workshops 0).

Respondents in this factor define *co-op* as the "application of theory to practice," reflecting elements of a very early, traditionally used definition of co-op. This factor sees the important outcomes of co-op as "students learning what to expect in the real world" and "co-op students learning how to get, and progress in a job." None of the distinguishing statements for this factor reflected issues around learning theory, process, or transfer. Again this may reflect a more simplistic view that sees co-op as a mechanism for enhancing employability with little or no attention paid to what new may be learned, how it is learned, or how it might be mobilized across contexts (e.g., from work back to school).

This factor, largely comprised of the subset of practitioners not loading into Factor 2, presents a view of students needing assistance in order to learn (sorted Statement #40 "co-op students learning best through experiences" at –1). They cite certain elements of co-op such as the site visit and the role of the co-ordinator as being important in facilitating this learning. They also see the site visit as a monitoring process to ensure the student is performing up to standard. This factor sees the world of work as a very different place and values the co-op experience for its ability to show students what to expect from the real world and the co-ordinator for ensuring standards and facilitating student learning. Within this context, they strongly disagree that co-op is a great "placement service."

CONCLUSIONS

The nature of learning in co-op is very complex. The views of co-op stakeholders on this topic are also very complex and highly subjective. The large majority of co-op research to date has not addressed this complex and subjective issue of learning, focusing rather on measuring sets of predefined outcomes such as number of months to secure a job post graduation, starting salaries, and student satisfaction.

This study sought to do two things:

1. Gain greater insight regarding the nature of co-op learning through the eyes of two key stakeholders: students and practitioners.
2. Explore and test a new methodology that would better allow stakeholders to express their personal perspective as well as provide researchers with the ability to compare and contrast the resultant data.

Our conclusions are presented in two sections reflecting these two purposes.

Conclusions Regarding Stakeholder Perspectives About Co-op Learning

Not surprisingly, the results indicate a fair amount of complexity regarding this issue. However, we were surprised by the emergence of so many different world views as evidenced by the emergence of eight statistically distinct factors. There does not seem to be a dominant discourse regarding co-op learning, but rather a concourse that reflects varied perspectives regarding both co-op outcomes and processes. Perhaps the large number of viewpoints is a reflection of both the complexity of the issue and the relatively limited discussion around this complex issue by co-op professionals. In the absence of any dominant, or well-researched, viewpoints both practitioners and students may have found themselves thinking about these statements for the first time. Their unconsolidated and developing views on the subject may be reflected in the number of factors that emerged.

As well, in British Columbia, co-op professionals have recently been exploring issues around co-op curriculum and its role in facilitating learning that has led to a much larger examination of current co-op practices. These discussions have pushed co-op professional perspectives in new, but still emerging directions and the "newness" of this discussion may also partially account for the breadth of opinions on the subject.

Perhaps the most disturbing, if not surprising, finding was the generally low value assessed to various co-op practices by all factors. Site visits, the role of the co-ordinator, work-term debriefings, and workshops were generally rated negatively or neutral with respect to their learning value. In particular the negative sorting of statements related to the value of the work report is one of the only consensus responses to emerge across all factors. As practitioners, it would appear that much work needs to be done to either improve the linkages between learning and elements of the co-op model, or improve the way in which we and our students understand those linkages, or both.

Another perhaps surprising finding concerned the fact that students and co-op coordinators, in general, do not share views on many elements of traditional co-op practice. Although the student-loaded factor and the practitioner-loaded factor both valued learning by repeated practice in real-world situations and through the success and failures of themselves and others, they differed on the value they ascribed to specific co-op practices with respect to mediating this learning. Predominately the student-loaded factor didn't value many co-op practices such as site visits, debriefings, work reports, etcetera, whereas the practitioner factors (2 and 8) generally sorted these practices higher (although not resoundingly so). The student factor also noted that "learning was assisted by work supervisors," whereas Factor 8 practitioners cited the co-op co-ordinator as an important facilitator. Both the stakeholders agree that the experience of trial and error is critical but students did not seem to highly value the role a co-ordinator might play in helping them reflect upon those experiences so as to help make that learning explicit and perhaps even more transferable. Again, it appears that the pedagogical underpinning s of co-op may not be clear to all students or practitioners and that some work could be done to help all co-op stakeholders come to better understand how co-op practice relates to co-op learning. It may also be the case that some co-op practice is not particularly pedagogically driven but perhaps rather more a result of administrative efficiencies or unquestioned habit. It is incumbent upon practitioners and managers of cooperative education to examine their key practices with respect to their role in learning if co-op is to be taken seriously as an educational model.

It is interesting to note that practitioners generally loaded into one of two factors: Factor 2, which focused on the elements of co-op practice and Factor 8, which focused on the practitioner. Factor 2 reflected some interest in how co-op learning might be occurring, whereas Factor 8 did not have any distinguishing statements regarding learning models or transfer. The two factors reflect very different practitioner orientations and may have implications on how the co-op model evolves within an educational context such as a university or college. As well, clear differences in world views seem to exist amongst participants from the various levels of postsecondary institutions and may speak to the need for the development of some distinctive ways in which we do business. For example, university co-op programs may wish to clearly define the dual role of co-op in both applying theory to real-world situations and developing new knowledge and skills. And co-op programs in the trades (institutes) may define their role as providing real-world opportunities to practice what has been learned in school. These two different roles then call for differences in how the desired outcomes are supported and measured.

The emergence of the anti-co-op factor was also a bit of a surprise in that throughout our research and pilot and field studies we had a great deal of difficulty finding a dissonant voice regarding the value of co-op. So although it is not surprising that this constituency exists, it emerged somewhat unexpectedly from the way in which participants responded to the various statements.

Finally, much more analysis of the data could be done to further explore questions and hypotheses that arose throughout our discussions and analysis. We became curious about what impact adding employer and faculty sorts to this data would have: Would the same factors remain? Would some collapse? Would new ones be created? We also wondered in what ways the degree of exposure of each respondent had influenced their sort. Would perspectives of co-op learning change over work terms? How about if we tested a group 2 years postgraduation? And what about the practitioners: Was there a difference between newcomers and old-timers? As with any research project we felt we had but skimmed the surface with our interpretations, and our initial findings raised as many questions as they informed. What is clear, however, is that the co-op learning concourse is rich with perspectives, each of which must be further explored in order to better understand this model of education and ultimately inform its evolution.

Conclusions Regarding the Q-Method in Co-op Research and Practice

The Q-method can be effectively applied to answer a variety of questions regarding cooperative education. Several questions regarding educational policy in co-op practice require examination and possible revision. Our study revealed more factors (points of view) on the nature of co-op processes than anticipated. Although the nature of learning in co-op is complex and it could be anticipated that there would be a diversity of views in the concourse, there was little in the research or existing concourse that would help us to predict the existence of the anti-co-op factor (Factor 3). Q thus allowed the detection of perspectives not previously found in the concourse.

Q-methodology also provides tremendous flexibility to the investigators with respect to research design. It allows for a mix of quantitative and qualitative analysis and is especially good for investigating patterns, processes, and change associated with issues of high complexity and subjectivity. In the case of this research we were able to hear the stakeholders by allowing their voices to emerge from the Q sorting process by way of the factor analysis. This allowed for new perspectives to come to light, which researchers may not have initially conceived of prior to the research itself and provided new ways of viewing this complex issue.

Another strength of Q is that because it correlates people across variables rather than factoring variables across people, each person can be treated as an experimental entity. This means that Q can be administered in a group or individual setting and rather than requiring a large randomly selected test group to respond to a smaller number of items, Q method allows for much smaller numbers of subjects to respond to a larger number of items. Although we were interested in including several of our colleagues across the province in this study, we did not have to do so in order to conduct a legitimate study and glean informative data. For example, the small pilot test we conducted with students allowed us to test the statements very easily and without the need to engage in a random sampling process, and readily provided very legitimate factors for analysis. By including the different stakeholder groups in the research, we did gather more pieces of information with which to help in our analysis (e.g., students, practitioners, and the three levels of postsecondary institutions) however very valid world views could have emerged from a less diversified stakeholder group of participants. A real administrative advantage was that we were able to engage any institution that wished to participate at whatever level they chose. In other words, there was no need to ensure equal representation or set minimal participation rates as each Q sort provided a valid contribution to the various world views that ultimately emerged.

The forced-sorting format selected by the investigators of this study also allows for the researchers to gain information about how each participant responds to a particular test item relative to another. Standard yes–no response formats indicate whether a particular statement is descriptive of the respondent (assuming independence between items). Q sort, on the other hand, is referred to as an *ipsitive* approach (Davis, 1987) meaning all items are interrelated and dependent on the participant's responses to previous items. This allows for another level of more contextualized feedback to be provided and for the potential emergence of new factors based on this deeper level of reflection and decision-making.

Finally, the cost of administering the actual sort and performing the initial factor analysis using Q was reasonable. The greatest time expenditures were associated with researching the concourse, development of the Q statements, and data entry. A 1-day training session was held for the other Q administrators and then all testing was completed in a single group sitting of approximately one hour per administrator. The data from each sitting was entered into the PCQ software available at no cost via the Internet, and subsequently a report was generated for further analysis and interpretation.

Q, like all statistical techniques, does require a certain amount of administrator knowledge in order to develop an appropriate concourse and to interpret the data generated by the PCQ method program. As researchers, we spent considerable time becoming familiar with Q method and benefitted from ongoing access to a peer-reviewed and published researcher familiar with the Q method who guided our analysis and interpretation. We consulted our Faculty of Education and were fortunate to have a visiting scholar who introduced us to Q and guided our research. This type of support may not always be available to all co-op researchers.

Further relevant applications of the Q method in co-op and other forms of higher education include:

- tracking attitudinal change across work terms;
- determining patterns regarding practice and various outcomes;
- comparing and contrasting stakeholder perspectives on other issues (e.g., students vs. employers vs. faculty views of a particular process or practice);
- elucidating modes of implementation; and
- justifying policy alternatives.

Summary
- Co-op learning is highly complex and subjective in nature, making it difficult to define and (therefore to) measure. Although outcomes define one aspect of this learning, process-oriented questions may require definition and measurement tools that better reflect this subjectivity and complexity.
- Q-method provides a new way to utilize both quantitative and qualitative analysis to help answer these highly subjective and complex questions. It also affords researchers significant flexibility in the research design.
- This Q study of co-op students and practitioners investigated co-op learning, processes, and outcomes with students and practitioners. Eight distinct world views or perspectives arose, indicating the complexity of the

issue and a relative lack of consensus regarding key co-op practices and their learning value.

ANNOTATED BIBLIOGRAPHY

Cates, C., & Jones, P. (1999). *Learning outcomes: The educational value of cooperative education.* Columbia, MD: Cooperative Education Association. In response to what some academicians have termed "the lack of a substantial body of research to document student learning from cooperative experiences," (Cates & Jones, 1999, p. 5) authors Cates and Jones compiled strategies and program examples for establishing learning outcomes, developing the pedagogy for learning, and implementing an assessment plan. The authors also presented various learning models and review principles of effective student learning. In so doing, Cates and Jones provided a useful framework for designing, delivering, positioning, and evaluating co-op programs that focus on the educational components of the model.

Denzine, G. M. (1998, April 3). The use of Q-methodology in student affairs research and practice. *Student Affairs Journal-Online* [Online], Available: http://sajo.org. The author described Q-methodology and discussed its potential usage in student affairs research and practice. He found one of the major benefits of the Q-study approach is the flexibility it offers the investigator in terms of research design. He suggested that Q-sort methodology is especially good for investigating patterns, processes, and change and thus is a very useful tool for studying many aspects of student affairs. The application of Q-methodology to student affairs provides the opportunity to combine quantitative and qualitative methodologies to explore practical questions.

Johnston, N. (1996). The nature of learning in co-op education. Unpublished masters thesis, Simon Fraser University. Burnaby, British Columbia, Canada. The author engaged in a qualitative study of three applied science cooperative education students to explore issues regarding both what is learned through their co-op work term and how it is learned. The data are analyzed and interpreted with respect to some of the recent literature on employability and learning in practical contexts, with particular reference to the works of Schön (1983, 1987) and Lave and Wenger (1991). General categories emerging from the analysis regarding learning outcomes and processes were presented as a series of learning events, or interpretations of the stories told by the students as they reflected upon their co-op placements.

Stephenson, W. (1953). *The study of behavior: Q-technique and its methodology.* Chicago: University of Chicago Press. This is the definitive book on Q-methodology by its creator. Born in England, William Stephenson earned PhDs in both psychology and physics. He taught experimental psychology at Oxford University and directed the Institute of Experimental Psychology, also at Oxford. In this book, he examined conceptual and theoretical approaches to problems of the study of subjectivity and behavior. He discussed methodological issues of Q-methodology and provided a detailed description of Q-technique that offers an approach to the understanding of the subjectivity of individual human beings. Although it is more than 50 years old, this book provides the single perspective regarding to how and why Q was developed and gives insight into its origins in both physical and social science.

REFERENCES

Austin, T. A. (1988, October). Academic benefits of cooperative education. Paper presented at the Canadian Association For Cooperative Education Conference. Toronto, Canada.

Branton, G., Cutt, J., Loken, M., Ney, T., Ricks, R., & Van Gyn, G. (1991a). *Educational bene-fits of cooperative education*. Paper presented at the 7th World Conference on Co-op Education, Hong Kong.

Branton, G., Cutt, J., Loken, M., Ney, T., Ricks, R., & Van Gyn, G. (1991b). *Developments in cooperative education research*. Paper presented at the Canadian Association for Cooperative Education Conference, Kananaskis, Alberta, Canada.

Brown, S. J. (1984). *The influence of cooperative education on first job after graduation*. Boston: Northeastern University.

Brown, S. R. (2001). The history and principles of Q methodology in psychology and the social sciences. *Q Archives Online* [online], Available: http://facstaff.uww.edu/cottlec/QArchives/Bps.htm

Brown, S. R. (1980). *Political subjectivity: Application of Q methodology in political science*. New Haven, CT: Yale University.

Cates, C., & Jones, P. (1999). *Learning outcomes: The educational value of cooperative education*. Columbia, MD: Cooperative Education Association.

Cohen, A. J. (1978). *Co-operative education—A national assessment: Final report*, (Vol. 1). MD: Applied Management Associates.

Cooperative education funding review advisory committee. (1992). *A review of post secondary cooperative education funding in British Columbia*. Victoria, British Columbia, Canada: Ministry of Advanced Education, Training and Technology.

Davis, R. (1987). Scale construction. *Journal of Counseling Psychology, 34*, 481–489.

Denzine, G. M. (1998, April 3). The use of Q-methodology in student affairs research and practice. *Student Affairs Journal-Online* [Online], Available: http://sajo.org

Evers, F., Krmpotic, J., Rush, J., Duncan-Robinson, J. (1993). *Making the match: Phase II: Final technical report*. Western Business School, University of Western Ontario and Department of Sociology and Anthropology, University of Guelph, Ontario, Canada.

Fletcher, J. K. (1989). Student outcomes: What do we know and how do we know it? *Journal of Cooperative Education, 26*(1), 26–38.

Human resources development Canada, program evaluations branch (HRDC). (1994). *Evaluation of the cooperative education option: Summary report*. Government of Canada, Ottawa, Ontario, Canada.

Johnston, N. (1996). *The nature of learning in co-op education*. Unpublished master's thesis, Simon Fraser University, Burnaby, British Columbia, Canada.

Kolb, D., Rubin, I., McIntyre, J. (1984). *Organizational psychology: An experiential approach to organizational behavior*. Englewood Cliffs, NJ: Prentice-Hall.

Lave, J., & Wenger, E. (1991). *Situated learning: Legitimate peripheral participation*. New York: Cambridge University Press.

Linn, P. L. (1999, Summer). Learning that lasts a lifetime. *Liberal Education*, 26–35.

Petrysack, N., & Toby, A. (1989). *A comparative analysis of cooperative education and non cooperative education graduates of Simon Fraser University*. Unpublished manuscript, Co-operative Education Program, Simon Fraser University, Burnaby, British Columbia, Canada.

Porter, M. E. (1991). *Canada at a crossroads: The reality of a new competitive environment*. A study prepared for the Business Council on National Issues and the Government of Canada. Ottawa, Ontario.

Ricks, F., Cutt, J., Branton, G., Loken, M., & Van Gyn, G. (1993). Reflections on the co-operative education literature. *Journal of Cooperative Education, 29*(1), 6–23.

Rowe, P. M. (1989). Entry differences between students in cooperative and regular programs. *Journal of Cooperative Education, 26*(1), 16–25.

Schön, D. (1983). *The reflective practitioner: How professionals think in action*. New York: Basic Books.

Schön, D. (1987). *Educating the reflective practitioner: Toward a new design for teaching and learning in the professions*. San Francisco: Jossey-Bass.

Stephenson, W. (1953). *The study of behavior: Q-technique and its methodology*. Chicago: University of Chicago Press.

Stephenson, W. (1978). Concourse theory of communication. *Communication, 3,* 21–40.

Weinstein, D. S. (1980). *Cooperative education strategies and student career development. Cooperative Association Research Monograph No 1*. Boston: Northeastern University.

Wilson, J. W. (1974). *Impact of cooperative education upon personal development and growth values*. Boston: Cooperative Education Research Center, Northeastern University.

Wilson, J. W., & Lyons, E. H. (1961). *Work-study college programs*. New York: Harper & Rowe.

Appendix:
Q Statements Regarding Co-op and Learning

1. Co-op is the application of what is learned in school to a real work environment.
2. Co-op is bringing what you learned at work back to the classroom to make you a better student.
3. On co-op, students learn that what makes them a good performer is knowing how and when to use some of the things they've learned in school to solve problems.
4. Co-op is a great job placement service.
5. Through co-op students learn to work as part of a team.
6. Through school students learn to work as part of a team.
7. Through co-op students learn to communicate effectively with others.
8. Through school student learn to communicate effectively with others.
9. Through co-op students learn to find and solve problems.
10. Through school students learn to find and solve problems.
11. Through co-op students learn to analyze and think critically.
12. Through school students learn to analyze and think critically.
13. Through co-op students learn the technical skills for their discipline.
14. Through school students learn the technical skills for their discipline.
15. Through co-op students learn to focus in on the right task, prioritize, and respond.
16. Through school students learn to focus in on the right task, prioritize, and respond.
17. Through co-op students learn to see the big picture and know how they fit in it.
18. Through school students learn to see the big picture and know how they fit in it.
19. Through co-op students learn more about how they learn and how to learn from a variety of experiences.
20. Through school students learn more about how they learn and how to learn from a variety of experiences.
21. Students often feel they don't learn anything new through their co-op placements.
22. Through co-op students learn how to get and progress in a job.
23. Through co-op students learn more about what they really want to do with their career.
24. Through co-op student learn what to expect in the world of work.
25. Through co-op students learn how much they don't know.
26. Through co-op students learn who to connect with when they graduate and are looking for career related work.
27. Co-op students learn that there is a big difference between a case study on conflict management and an angry client yelling at you in your office.
28. Really good co-op students can take what they've learned elsewhere and figure out how to make it work in their new work placement.
29. Co-op students learn to identify their employability related strengths and weaknesses and develop them.

30. Co-op students learn new skills from their work supervisors and colleagues relevant to succeeding in the workplace.
31. Co-op students need co-op in order to learn how to write resumes and cover letters and prepare for interviews.
32. Work experience is the only real way to learn these work skills—you have to be part of the whole experience to really understand it.
33. Co-op students learn by talking with the other co-op students and friends about things that are going on at work and finding out how they would approach it.
34. Co-op students are more self-directed than non-co-op students.
35. Students learn through their co-op coordinator who helps them work through issues and decisions.
36. By watching other professionals, students can learn a lot as part of a project team.
37. Co-op students learn by repeated practice in real world situations such as interviews, staff meetings, project teams, etcetera.
38. Co-op workshops effectively prepare students for the world of work.
39. Students learn best when they are encouraged to reflect on their experiences and think about their learning.
40. Co-op students learn best through their own successes and failures at work as well as watching the successes and failures of others in the workplace.
41. Co-op students learn by experiencing an event, reflecting upon it, forming some generalizations based upon those observations, and testing the implications of those concepts in new situations.
42. Co-op students learn by engaging more and more fully in the workplace, slowly absorbing, and being absorbed by, the culture (cognitive, social, environmental, emotional) of their work community.
43. Problem solving on a co-op term requires more than just applying a set of solutions to a given situation, it is an art that you practice that requires on the spot reflection.
44. With co-op, a graduate has a better set of tools with which to sell themselves, and with which to be successful after graduation.
45. One way co-op students learn is by completing self-assessments that allow them to identify their skills and areas needing improvement.
46. The work report is a useful learning tool for co-op.
47. Site visits to co-op students mid-way through their term provide a key opportunity for discussing the student's progress with respect to their learning objectives.
48. Site visits serve as an excellent opportunity to market the co-op program with the employer while ensuring that the student is performing up to standard.
49. Debriefing a completed work term with a group of co-op students provides some of the best learning students can get through co-op.
50. Students who work in related jobs throughout their schooling learn just as mush as co-op students do through their job placements.

51. Experience at McDonalds can be very useful when starting a new job as a hotel front desk clerk.

52. Students who have been out on co-op seem to pick up the key concepts back in the classroom a lot faster than before their co-op experience.

53. There is a strong relationship between the grade a student receives in a course and their performance on the job in the same subject area.

54. Outstanding co-op students are able to see how apparently new and different situations share some common elements with their past experiences, and then use this experience to their advantage.

55. Co-op students often need coaching to recognize how skills can transfer across two very different situations.

10

Correlation Analysis in a Natural Experiment Design: Seeking the Opportune Grade Point Average Cutoff for Internships

Michael L. Maynard
Temple University

Key questions addressed in this chapter:

- ☞ How do we design a study to test the validity of a point on an index (grade point average)?
- ☞ How do we decide what variable to test?
- ☞ What is a natural experiment?
- ☞ What is correlation analysis?
- ☞ How far can we manipulate the data to achieve the answer to our research question?

In this chapter, I report on a study that correlates student grade point averages (GPAs) with the grades they earned in their internship. The research design calls for collecting self-reported data (student GPAs at the start of their internship) and comparing these data with the student final grades. The specific goal of the study is to determine the critical point, as measured in grade point average, where one may predict with assurance that the student will earn an A for the internship. The overall goal then is to adjust the minimum 3.0 GPA requirement downward in order to allow more students to benefit from the internship experience.

When I assumed the position of Internship Director for the Department of Journalism, Public Relations and Advertising at Temple University, I was encouraged to rethink all aspects of the program in order to give the program more visibility and increase the number of students enrolled each semester in the internship program. The first task was achieved, in part, by posting dozens of "calls for interns" on the walls adjacent to my office. In a short time, the walls were virtually covered with these notices. Additionally, *opportunity books* (three-ring binders) featuring the calls for interns from sponsors were organized by industry and placed in the school library. Students could then select the respective binder on advertising, public relations, news writing, broadcast journalism, magazine, or photojournalism; sift through the various offers; and possibly choose one or two hosts to contact.

The second task, increasing the number of students enrolled in the internship program, was achieved simply through visiting classes, getting the word out, meeting with various majors within our college, and advising students of the importance of having an internship during their undergraduate years. At the same time, however, it occurred to me that the goal of allowing more undergraduates to benefit from an internship also could be realized if the bar set at restricting eligibility was lowered. The twin restrictions at our college were junior status and a minimum 3.0 cumulative GPA (with a 4.0 being the top GPA).

Decision Point: What variable should I test? Should I challenge the junior status requirement or the minimum 3.0 GPA?

Allowing sophomores and freshmen to sign up for internships would certainly increase the universe of potential students who would benefit from the experience. But curricular concerns, sequential core course requirements, and the adjustments college students must make in their initial years mitigated against such a move. Moreover, the existing school policy requires our students to have taken at least two courses in their respective majors (i.e., advertising, public relations, etc.) before being eligible for an internship. As it turns out, they normally will not have completed this step until after their sophomore year.

Doing preliminary research on the variability of the GPA cutoff point for different universities as well as for different corporations led me to conclude that this variable was worthy of study. The University of Missouri, Emerson, Ohio University, Bradley, LSU, and Penn State, for instance, all set the GPA eligibility cutoff point under the 3.0 GPA minimum standard (Table 10.1). Cross referencing this information with GPA cutoff points from the industry revealed that although the 3.0 GPA was standard, it was not by any means absolute (Bard & Elliot, 1988; Oldham & Hamadeh, 1996, 1997). According to Bard & Elliot (1988), for example, the grade point average requirement for corporate training programs ranged from a high of 3.5 to a low of 2.5. Grumman and Wang Labs, for instance, required a minimum 3.5 GPA, whereas Norfolk Southern and Taco Bell (just to mention two) required a minimum 2.5 GPA. Given that the industry plays a significant role in evaluating our graduates as candidates for hire, the industry's flexibility in setting GPA eligibility levels lower than 3.0 encouraged me to pursue this line of investigation. I concluded that I would test the advisability of our school's eligibility requirement of a minimum 3.0 GPA.

TABLE 10.1

University Communication Departments: Grade Point Average Requirement for Internship Application

Syracuse	3.0
Temple	3.0
University of Texas	3.0
Oklahoma	3.0
UC/Fullerton	3.0
Illinois	3.0
Northwestern	3.0
Florida University	3.0
Emerson	2.7
Missouri	2.75
Ohio University	2.75
Bradley University	2.5
LSU	2.5
Penn State	2.5

BACKGROUND LITERATURE

In searching the literature, I could find no other research addressing specifically the viability of the minimum 3.0 GPA eligibility standard for cooperative education programs and internships. Although grades are not the only predictor of one's success in activities outside of the classroom, I found commentary in general about grades and the grading. For example, Alexander (1995) wrote that especially for classes that teach skills, grades are frequently used as a gauge for predicting success. Gross (1981) concluded that as a rough grade point threshold, students holding a B average or higher generally qualify for experiential learning and internships. Translated into the standard 4.0 numbering system, a B average, of course, is exactly 3.0. At some universities allowances are made for the difficulty of sustaining a high grade point average across all courses so that the student may hold an overall 2.75 GPA, and yet must reach a minimum 3.0 GPA in the student's major field of study (Meeske, 1988). Commenting on the need for rigor in structuring internships,

Ciofalo (1988) noted that to ensure successful ongoing relationships with the professional community, faculty usually require evidence of students' successful performance in various combinations of junior or senior status, requisite course work, and grade point average.

On the face of it, limiting student eligibility for cooperative education programs and internships to the 3.0 and higher cutoff makes sense because the 3.0 GPA implies *above average* status. Faculty can feel confident that the *above average* student will gain from the experience without damaging the program's reputation among professionals and in the community at large.

The literature indicates that the off-campus learning experience adds value to the student's education, and, more concretely, to the student's resume (Bourland-Davis, Graham, & Fulmer, 1997). That is, having completed an internship during one's undergraduate years is a smart career move. Rowland (1994) found that increasingly, experience is the deciding factor in employment when the student enters the job market. Redeker (1992) noted that college students appear to be using internships to gain an edge in the employment competition. In fact, according to Guadino (1988), the most important factor in getting a job after graduation is having a good, structured work–learn experience such as an internship during one's college years. Internships and cooperative education programs across all majors are so popular, according to the American Council on Education (Tooley, 1997) "nine out of ten four-year colleges now offer some sort of structured work experience connected to a student's major or career interest" (p. 76).

Internship programs are offered in most university communications departments because it is widely believed that the field experience in a professional communications situation adds a real-world component to the students' education. Becker (1990) found nearly universal acceptance of the internship as part of journalism schools. Equally so, Keenan's (1992) survey of advertising programs and Meeske's (1988) study of broadcast journalism programs indicated that 98% and 99%, respectively, of the schools surveyed offered internships or some sort of cooperative education arrangement as part of the curriculum.

As a result of the rising perceived value of internships, faculty internship directors are encouraged to instruct students to take multiple internships (Basow & Byrne, 1993). Because the internship experience is becoming a prerequisite for a job (Johnson, 1995), communications departments are encouraged to make internships available to more students majoring in public relations, broadcast journalism, advertising, and news writing.

SETTING AND PROGRAM

Temple University's journalism, public relations, and advertising internship program is based on the standard established by the Accrediting Council for Education in Journalism and Mass Communication, which states that credit may be awarded for monitored and carefully supervised field experience in journalism and mass communications. The Council also stipulates that the maximum number of credits a student may earn for an internship—and count toward the degree—is three. This policy encourages students to add an internship to their course of study as an elective, but to limit their experience to just one internship.[1] Roughly one third of our students take the internship for credit during their course of study in our program.

To qualify for the internship course, the student must be a news writing, public relations, or advertising major and must have completed at least 60 credit hours. The student applicant is required to have completed at least two courses in the major and to have earned a cumulative GPA of at least 3.0. In seeking out an internship, the student is directed to a list of about 75 media-related companies, including radio stations, newspapers, advertising agencies, television stations, and so forth. Philadelphia provides a rich source of communications opportunities, and at least with regard to approved internships for credit, each semester there are more companies requesting interns than there are students who accept them.

The internship director approves internships on the basis of whether or not the field experience contributes to the student's education in public relations, news writing, broadcast journalism, advertising, or photojournalism. Specific requirements are a minimum of 150 hours at the internship site, a log of daily activities, two evaluations from the site supervisor (one at the mid-point of the semester and the other at the end), final project, and timely submission of materials. Students generally negotiate a schedule where throughout the fall or spring semester they put in from 15 to 20 hours a week at the internship site. Summer internships usually allow for more flexibility in both the selection of internship and the arrangement of work hours.

The school follows the standard letter-grading system. The director determines the letter grade based on timely submission of materials, two evaluations of the student's progress, and quality of the final project. During the period of the study only one faculty member served as director, thus controlling for variability in grading standards.

In addition to the formatted evaluation sheet that asks for information on specific criteria, the second evaluation to be completed at the end of the internship asks the host supervisor to write out answers to questions such as: What responsibilities did the intern handle best? What assignments gave the intern most difficulty? Often, the internship host supervisor elaborates in sufficient detail so that by reading between the lines the director gleans a candid view of the intern's performance.

The student's individual project also plays a significant part in determining the final grade. Quality of writing, organization, presentation, and content factor heavily in assigning the course grade. The topic for the project, with consultation with the internship director, is decided by the intern. For public relations interns, the final pro-

---

[1]The maximum number of credits for the internship that count for the degree is three. A student who wishes to take more than one internship and have each count toward the degree may elect to take the internship for one or two credits. Thus, it is possible to take three one-credit internships. (The minimum number of hours and other requirements are the same, however.)

ject may be a three-ring binder filled with press releases, pitch letters and other intern-generated products that will serve as the intern's professional portfolio.

Although Temple University shares a concern for runaway grade inflation, the consensus among department faculty involved with managing the internship program is that the grade distribution need not follow the bell curve. Our department essentially favors a policy of leniency in grading internships. The thinking is that the extra effort necessary both logistically and interpersonally for the student to successfully join the host company and to complete the off-site internship, mitigates against grading on a curve. The tendency has been, in fact, to give students the benefit of the doubt such that grading for the internship starts with an "A" and ratchets downward in half-grade increments only as evidence of failure is revealed.

Decision Point: What research design is appropriate in testing the validity of the 3.0 GPA requirement?

It was clear to me that a *natural experiment* was most appropriate. That is, the natural variation in the target variable (GPA) could be used to my advantage. To capture the natural variation in student grade point averages I simply needed to make one *intervention*. I needed to ignore the 3.0 GPA standard, and essentially allow any junior or senior student to take an internship. Doing so would allow the independent variable (GPA) to vary, such that the GPAs of students of junior or above status with GPAs below 3.0 would be included in the study. This sample essentially would be the *test group*. Those students who entered the program with a 3.0 GPA or above essentially would be the *control group*. The question my research design is structured to answer is: How well does the *test group* perform in relation to the *control group*? Or, do students whose grade point average is under 3.0 perform worse in the internship than students whose grade point average is 3.0 and above? The grade is the *measurement instrument*. The design controls for bias in that one faculty member grades all internships.

METHOD

A census of the grade point averages and internship grades of 132 students enrolled in the internship program over a 2½ year period was conducted. During this period, we were experimenting with a more open policy that relaxed the 3.0 grade point average requirement. It was a natural experiment study because it occurred in the natural environment (not a laboratory), and the experiment was the open policy of allowing students whose GPA was under 3.0 to enroll in the internship program. The self-reported GPA, as required on the Internship Permission Slip, was essentially ignored as an eligibility factor at the time the student signed up for an internship.

It should also be mentioned that one of the department's goals for the internship program at this time was to increase visibility among our majors. It was generally thought that our external resources (the Philadelphia internship sites) were underutilized. Moreover, prior to this study, per semester only 10 to 12 students were signing up for internships. To increase visibility, dozens of calls for interns were placed on the walls of the hallway outside the internship director's office. A "take-one" holder filled with three-fold brochures outlining the internship program was placed on the director's door. In general, a buzz was created and word spread among our majors that there were ample opportunities for internships, and that the rules for qualification were being relaxed. Clearly this change in policy generated more interest in the program. And more to the point, the policy encouraged students whose grade point average fell below 3.0 to enroll in the program.

Accordingly, nearly every student who wanted an internship was accepted and given guidance in securing one. Efforts were made in matching students' abilities with the expectations of the internship hosts. Not every student succeeded in finding an internship, however, because of scheduling conflicts, competition from other students seeking the same internship, or simply a change of plans.

Decision Point: How large should my sample be?

I decided to run the experiment until I had at least 100 units of analysis, defined here as students who completed the internship during the period of the *relaxed GPA standard*. Although the sample would be a *census* (all units of analysis accounted for), I sought to stratify the census by running the experiment until at least one half of the student interns entered the program with a GPA that was under 3.0.

During the period of the study, an average of 26 students enrolled each semester. If each semester yielded a balance of 13 students above and 13 below the standard, it would have taken four semesters to reach the target of 100, evenly split at 50 above and 50 below. But on average slightly less than one half of the students were in the below-standard group. So it took longer than four semesters to achieve my objective of having one half of the sample in the below 3.0 GPA group.

At the completion of five academic semesters plus two summer sessions that spanned 2½ years, and after all grades were assigned and reported, the self-reported grade point averages on the Internship Permission Slips were re-examined. All but 17 students declared their grade point average.

Decision Point: I needed to make sure my data were clean.

I needed to confirm that the self-reported GPAs were accurate. But the only source for my data was the students' self-reported GPA at the start of the internship. So unobtrusively, I checked the student files in the department.

To keep the experiment as natural as possible, I retained the standard permission form students were required to fill out in applying for the internship. On this form, a blank space was provided for the student's grade point average. As mentioned earlier, for the design of the study, their self-reported GPA was actually unnecessary. In fact, at the time of their signing up for the internship, their self-reported GPA was essentially ignored. In retrospect, a more rigorous design would have controlled for bias more completely by eliminating the reported GPA from the standard permission form altogether.

After checking official transcripts, of the 17 students who failed to state their grade point average at the time of applying for an internship, 16 held a GPA of under 3.0. The one student above 3.0, who had earned a 3.6 GPA, perhaps simply forgot to write it in. The corrected grade point averages were entered.

Decision Point: Because my focus for this research is on those students whose GPA is under 3.0, should I also double check every one of the reported GPAs above 3.0?
I decided to conduct a *spot check* for the GPA above 3.0 group. I did this for two reasons. First, I wanted to feel confident in the accuracy of the data I was collecting. It should be mentioned that the students in our communications school had been conditioned to the regulation that only those with a GPA above 3.0 would be accepted into the internship program. So by and large, even if some of the students miscalculated their grade point average, they knew they were abiding by the regulations because they were confident their GPA was at least more than 3.0. Second, I knew that the more precise items of data I collected, the more options I would have to work with the data later on. So although I did not know exactly how I might use the information concerning the grade point averages of the above-standard groups, at the time, I reasoned that it was best to capture these data, and to make sure the data were accurate. The spot check assured me that this group was, in fact, quite accurate in the reporting of their grade point average.

Spot checks were conducted to validate the accuracy of the reported grade point averages ranging from 3.0 and higher. Essentially all of the highest averages (3.3 and above) were valid, with some actually underestimating the number by a few hundredths of a point. Middle-range grade point averages (3.0 to 3.3) were also accurate. Given the focus of this research, every reported grade point average under 3.0 was double checked for accuracy. Incorrectly stated averages were replaced with the correct averages. For those left blank, the correct GPA was supplied.

Decision Point: I needed to turn the categorical letter grades into discrete variables for measurement.
This was necessary because in order to offer descriptive statistics, make calculations, and to compare (correlate) variables, I needed to work with numbers.

Thus I converted the nominal letter grades into discrete numbers, with values corresponding to the hierarchical structure of the A through F grading index from 12 to 1.

Grade point averages, themselves, are calculated on a numbering system that corresponds to the letter grade system. Qualitative measurement is nominal, essentially a classification system. The letter grade is both a nominal and an ordinal measurement. In addition to the letter grade's categorical reflection of mutually exclusive and exhaustive categories (e.g., "A" and not "B," and not "C"), the letter grade is ordinal in that it reflects a ranking in order of its value on the dimension of academic achievement.

Letter grades were transposed into numbers, with A equal to 12, A– equal to 11, B+ equal to 10 and so on down to F equal to 1. Students who failed to complete the internship were given an *I* for incomplete. Although our school policy allows for students to replace the incomplete with an appropriate letter grade upon making up the course, if this is not achieved within 12 months, the *I* becomes an "F."[2] Accordingly, the two incompletes for the internship still remaining on the transcript at the time of this study were coded as F, equal to 1.

After all data were verified, the 132 cases of grade point average and corresponding final internship grade were entered into the Statistical Package for Social Sciences (SPSS) software. Runs were then made for descriptive statistics[3] and bivariate correlation.[4]

FINDINGS

Table 10.2 shows the distribution of grades among the 132 cases. As suggested earlier, as a result of the liberal grading policy, most students earned an A for their internship (57%), with B+ being the next most frequently assigned grade (15.2%). The mean of 10.3 (B+) for internship grades reflects the tendency toward leniency in grading internships. The B+ also closely approximates the overall grade distribution for the department. Only 6 students earned an F for their internship, and this number represents only 4.5% of the total cases (Table 10.2).

With regard to a measurement of the relation between grade point average and internship grade, Table 10.3 shows positive correlation. For the entire sample a relatively high correlation ($r = 0.51$) was found, which means 26% of the variance be-

---

[2]This policy may no longer be in effect at the time of this writing.

[3]Descriptive statistics are calculated for each variable separately and include the arithmetic average or mean, and the degree to which scores spread around the mean, called the *standard deviation*, and the highest versus lowest score, or range.

[4]Bivariate correlation characterizes the relation between two variables. That is, it shows the degree to which two variables vary together (positive correlation) or vary inversely (negative correlation).

TABLE 10.2
Grade Distribution

Value		Frequency	Percent	Cumulative Percent
1.00	F	6	4.5	4.5
6.00	C	10	7.6	12.1
8.00	B-	4	3.0	15.2
9.00	B	11	8.3	23.5
10.00	B+	20	15.2	38.6
11.00	A-	5	3.8	42.4
12.00	A	76	57.6	100.0
Total		132	100.0	100.0

Note. Mean 10.3, Std dev 2.7

TABLE 10.3
Internship Grade by Grade Point Average: Correlation Coefficients

GPA Grouping	(N)	r	r^2
All cases	132	.51	.26
Under 3.0	54	.68	.46
3.3 and above	44	.12	.01
3.0 to 3.3	34	−.04	.00
2.7 to 3.0	34	.00	.00
Under 2.7	20	.47	.22

tween internship grades can be explained by grade point average.[5] The below 3.0 group revealed the strongest correlation ($r = 0.68$), which would explain 46% of the variance. This finding suggests that the cumulative grade point index serves as a reliable grade predictor when the grade point average is below 3.0. For the bottom group of those students whose cumulative grade point average fell below 2.7, a positive correlation was found ($r = 0.47$), explaining 22% of the variance.

No relation between internship grade and grade point average was found for the top group of 3.3 GPA and above ($r = 0.12$) or for the target group of 2.7 to 3.0 ($r = .00$).

---

[5]The value of the correlation can be squared to indicate the amount of variance (variability) of the dependent variable (internship grade), explained by the independent variable (GPA).

> **Decision Point: What descriptive measurement should I present in order to show how the four groups compare with each other?**
>
> I decided to present the comparative means and standard deviation in order to show how each group performed in relation to each other. This step helps to see more precisely (a) how the groups are sorted, (b) how much variation there is in each group, and (c) how much distance separates the groups.
>
> As mentioned earlier, we can describe the 2.7–3.0 group as the *test (or target) group*, and the above-3.0 group (in particular, the 3.0–3.3 group) as the *control group*. The study seeks to compare the means of these two specific groups because the more similar the means are, the more we can say these two groups are functionally the same, (i.e., students with grade point averages within the range of 2.7 and 3.3 may be thought of as one group). Effectively, then, the middle point of 3.0 may be eliminated as a dividing point.

Table 10.4 summaries the findings of where meaningful differences in grades for internships begin to appear. The middle group's (3.0–3.3) mean of 10.7 (standard deviation = 1.5) was found to closely match the target group's (2.7–3.0) mean of 10.8 (standard deviation = 1.7). The top group of 3.3 and above, with a mean of 11.3 (standard deviation = 2.0) and the bottom group of under 2.7, with a mean of 6.6 (standard deviation = 3.9) clearly separated out from the two middle groups (see Table 10.5).

> **Decision Point: How can I manipulate the data in order to show the sharpest contrast between the group of students who succeeded in the internship, and the group of students who did not?**
>
> I decided to collapse the 132 grades into a dichotomy: A and *Other*, which I coded as *yes* and *no* (Table 10.5). This manipulation of the data achieves two objectives: (1) it divides students into two clear cut groups—those who followed all instructions correctly, achieved the prescribed learning objectives, and obeyed their internship hosts so that the cumulative result is success versus those who did not; and (2) it highlights in sharpest relief for purposes of contrast the differences between the GPA groupings.

As might be expected, by collapsing the data into a yes–no, either–or dichotomy (Table 10.5), the top group of 3.3 and above shows an overwhelming tendency to earn an A (36 yes, 8 no). The 2.5 and below GPA group, alternatively, shows an overwhelming tendency not to earn an A (2 yes, 16 no). Most telling for this study, both the grade point average grouping of 3.0 to 3.3 (17 yes, 17 no) and the 2.7 group (8 yes, 6 no) show an even, and near even split.

TABLE 10.4
Comparisons of Means

	Mean	SD
Highest group, 3.3 and above		
GPA	3.550	.180
Grade	11.295	2.007
$n = 44$		
Middle group, 3.0 to 3.3		
GPA	3.064	.093
Grade	10.765	1.539
$n = 34$		
Target group, 2.7 to 3.0		
GPA	2.791	.068
Grade	10.853	1.726
$n = 34$		
Lowest group, under 2.7		
GPA	2.323	.260
Grade	6.600	3.858
$n = 20$		

TABLE 10.5
Internship Grades by GPA Converted to Pass/Not Pass

GPA	Pass		Not Pass		Total	
3.3 and above	36		8		44	
3.0 – 3.3	17		17		34	
2.9	0	]	3	]	3	]
2.8	13	(21)	4	(13)	17	(34)
2.7	8	]	6	]	14	]
2.6	0		2		2	
2.5 and below	2		16		18	
(Total)	76		56		132	

Note. 21/34 = 62% of 2.7 - 2.9 group passed, 17/34 = 50% of 3.0 - 3.3 group passed.

LIMITATIONS OF THE STUDY

The cumulative grade point average each student had earned at the start of the internship in this study was the result of many different professors' evaluations. The criteria established by the various professors for what constitutes the value of an A, a B, a C, and so forth are not identical. For some professors, a more rigid grading system strictly adhering to the bell curve limits the number of As given per class. For other professors, no limit is established for the number of As.

Yet, as mentioned earlier, the approach taken by my department was to start with the presumption of an A, and ratchet downward as the intern shows evidence of insufficiency in meeting the standards for the course. The differences in the underlying assumptions of these two variables—the cumulative grade point average, and the resultant grade earned for the internship in this study—are factors limiting the validity of this study.

A second limitation to the study is the variability in judgment of the internship hosts. In assigning the grade, in addition to evaluating the quality of the students' final project and in noting the timeliness of fulfillment of their assignments, I relied heavily on the feedback from the internship host. What constitutes the criteria for a successful internship in a television station is likely to vary from what constitutes the criteria for a successful internship at an advertising agency. Even the standards at two different television stations are likely to vary.

A third limitation is my active participation in the study as the person assigning the final grade.[6] Although the student's self-reported GPA at the initiation of the internship was essentially ignored, some level of subjective judgment was inevitably at play as I interviewed each candidate. That is, the student's demeanor, manner of speech, and overall general appearance (neat or untidy) may have influenced my expectations for that student in successfully completing the internship.

DISCUSSION

The study achieved what it set out to achieve. The research design pointed to a methodology that, step by step, progressed through successive stages whereby, at the conclusion of the study, we could point to a finding. We set out to challenge the validity of the minimum 3.0 GPA requirement for acceptance into the internship program.

In order to capture the appropriate data, which in this case meant we would have to have interns whose grade point average was under the 3.0 standard, we conducted a natural experiment in which we relaxed the 3.0 GPA qualification standard to take advantage of the natural variability in student grade point averages. It required five semesters to reach a large enough sample (a census in this case) where

---

[6]Because I am instrumental in this study, and am active in determining one of the variables, my study falls under the category of *educational action research*. That is, in addition to being the researcher, I am also a participant.

we would have a modest measure of statistical power and where roughly one half of the students taking the internship had grade point averages below 3.0. Also, if indeed the study variables are related, the larger the sample, the greater the chance of finding a significant result.

The heart of this study addresses the question of how well the outcome of the internship (the student's final grade) correlates to the predictive assumption (3.0 GPA) that students who have achieved at least a B average are most qualified for the internship experience. Thus we were correlating two variables: grade point average and grade for the course.

The findings of this correlation study confirmed our assumption that students who have performed exceptionally well in the classroom also do well in the field experiential learning of the workplace. Predictably, students in the highest grade point average range of 3.3 and above earned an A for their internship. Our correlation study also showed that those with a GPA between 3.0 and 3.3 had a 50% chance of earning an A.

Most significant, however, this correlation analysis found that students with at least a 2.7 GPA are also likely to succeed in the same relative proportions as students within the 3.0 to 3.3 range. That is, about 62% of the 2.7 to 3.0 GPA students got an A and 50% of the 3.0 to 3.3 GPA students did. In contrast, students with grade point averages falling below 2.7, particularly those with a GPA of 2.5 or below, are more likely to perform poorly.

The obvious application of this finding is to lower the internship eligibility grade point average requirement to 2.7. Doing so would benefit more students, without jeopardizing the integrity of the internship program. Looking only at recent enrollment figures for majors in the department, for example, the 23 juniors and 36 seniors whose grade point averages fall between 2.9 and 2.7 would become eligible for internships under a new 2.7 standard. With no discernible loss of quality—as evidenced by the correlation between grade point average and performance—setting a 2.7 GPA cutoff point would allow 59 additional students to benefit from the internship experience.

In terms of this individual study, the dividing line between students who are capable of successfully completing the internship and those who are not appears to be the 2.7 grade point average. A closer look at the site supervisors' evaluations of students who received lower grades for their internships (students whose GPA is 2.5 or lower) confirms Daugherty's (1998) findings that personal behavioral traits and maturity are related to internship performance. For example, one internship host wrote that the intern "needs to work on tardiness a bit." Attitude, as well, plays a role in determining the internship outcome. A television station internship host wrote this about an intern whose grade point average was lower than 2.5, "I often felt that she had better things to do than be here at the station." In response to what gave the intern the most trouble, another supervisor wrote, "he seemed to lack the desire to learn more about all of the agency functions."

Although it is possible for a student with a 2.5 or lower grade point average to earn an A for the internship, this correlation analysis in a natural experiment study shows that one may predict with a high level of confidence that such a student will not earn an A. The study suggests that, at least with regard to the internship program at Temple University, (a) grade point average is a meaningful index, (b) the higher the grade point average the better, to a point, and (c) there is empirically driven justification for lowering the GPA requirement to 2.7.

CONCLUSION

Based on this study of the internship program at Temple University, the traditional 3.0 grade point average standard for internship eligibility appears to be too restrictive. It artificially prohibits candidates who otherwise qualify and would benefit from the internship experience. In addition, the qualities and skills—including people skills—necessary for undergraduates to cultivate in order to succeed in life may be learned equally well in the field as in the classroom.

Yet lowering the standard to 2.5 creates the problem of sending out students who have yet to "get it together" and who, by failing to follow a basic work ethic such as showing up on time, completing work on deadline, or performing chores with minimal difficulty might reflect negatively on the university. When the gap between where the student stands in terms of emotional adjustment and what level of maturity is expected to complete the internship is too great, it is best for all concerned that the student not be approved for the internship.

In terms of what this study accomplishes, whereas specific findings may not be generalized to other universities, the process of examining the relation (correlation) between grade point average and performance is instructive. With increasing concern for accountability in education, faculty in charge of cooperative education and internships who are trying to assess the outcomes of their programs will find the correlation analysis outlined in this chapter an unobtrusive way of measuring the validity of established standards. As evidenced in this project, a correlation study can yield hard data useful in determining the ideal GPA cutoff point for student eligibility to cooperative education and internship programs.

Summary
- The advantage of a natural experiment is that it allows the researcher to take advantage of naturally occurring variations in a variable.
- Categorical data may be converted into numbered data for statistical measurement.
- Research may be designed to challenge the validity of an academic standard.
- Research findings may be applied to academic policies in order to better serve students.

REFERENCES

Alexander, J. P. (1995). *Internships in communication*. Ames, IA: Iowa State University.

Bard, R., & Elliot, S. K. (1988). *The national directory of corporate training programs* (2nd ed.). New York: Doubleday.

Basow, R. R., & Byrne, M. V. (1993). Internship expectations and learning goals. *Journalism Educator, 46*(3), 48–54.

Becker, L. (1990). Annual enrollment census: Comparisons and projections. *Journalism Educator, 46*(3), 58–67.

Bourland-Davis, P. G., Graham, B. L., & Fulmer, H. W. (1997). Defining a public relations internship through feedback from the field. *Journalism & Mass Communication Educator, 52*, 26–33.

Ciofalo, A. (1988). Evaluating internships effectively. *Journalism Educator, 43*(2), 66–70.

Daugherty, E. (1998, August). *A phenomenological study of the internship experience: Reflections from three perspectives*. Paper presented to the Internships and Careers Interest Group of the Association for Educators in Journalism and Mass Communication, Baltimore, MD.

Gross, L. S. (1981). *The internship experience*. Belmont, CA: Wadsworth.

Guadino, J. L. (1988). Grass roots and inter-disciplinarian: A study of advertising agency recruiters' perceptions of the values of undergraduate advertising education. In J. Leckenby (Ed.), *Proceedings of the 1988 Conference of the American Academy of Advertising*, (pp. 79–83) Austin, TX.

Johnson, M. (1995). *Internships' impact on student finances*. Paper presented to the Internship and Placement Division of the Association for Education in Journalism and Mass Communication, Washington, D.C.

Keenan, K. (1992). Advertising field experience and experiential learning. *Journalism Educator, 47*(1), 48–55.

Meeske, M. D. (1988). Update: Broadcast intern programs and practices. *Journalism Educator, 43*(2), 75–77.

Oldham, M., & Hamadeh, S. (1997). *America's top internships*. New York: Princeton Review Publishing.

Oldham, M., & Hamadeh, S. (1996). *Internship Bible*. New York: Random House.

Redeker, L. L. (1992, September). Internships provide invaluable job preparation. *Public Relations Journal*, 20–21.

Rowland, M. (1994, June 5). Getting before-the-job experience. *The New York Times*, 15.

Tooley, J. A. (1997, November 17). Working for credit: How to make the most out of a semester-long internship. *U.S. News & World Report*, 76–78.

11

Issues in Case Study Methodology: Examining the Influences of Class Status on Cooperative Education Experiences

Adam Howard
Tom Haugsby
Antioch College

Key questions addressed in this chapter:

- ☞ How do we construct case studies through action research?
- ☞ What are the processes of case construction?
- ☞ What contributions are made to our profession from closely observing and researching a small number of individuals, given the thousands of students involved in cooperative education and internships at post-secondary institutions throughout the world?

We think of education as a social and cultural phenomenon, inextricably intercon-nected with a society's economic, political, and social structures; beliefs; and con-cerns. Situated among these relationships, education is about life. As John Dewey put it, education, "is about the making of a world" (in Purpel, 1999, p. 72). Students, educators and other individuals who are involved in the efforts of educational insti-tutions engage in the creation, recreation, and the maintenance of our culture, soci-ety, and community. In this construction process, we all participate, in varying degrees, in the complex task of determining what type of world we want to make, what type of world we are making, and what type of world is it possible to make. Of course, educational institutions are not solely responsible for "the making of world." They hold a vital and central relationship with other institutions and groups to contribute to the overall process.

Our notions of education guide our practices and understandings of our work as co-op educators. Our responsibilities of preparing students before, placing and supervising students on, and evaluating students after their co-op experiences are correlated with our efforts to have students work toward what Paulo Freire (1970) called *conscientization* (i.e., critical awareness). Conscientization is the ability to understand, analyze, problematize, and affect the sociopolitical, economic, and cultural realities that shape our lives. Students asking difficult questions about their own cultural assumptions of the world and rethinking the relationships they have with others outside their cultural group cultivate a critical awareness. Our role in this process is to engage students in dialogue about their making of a world as they navigate their way through their co-op experiences.

The real-world experiences and out-of-classroom context of co-op naturally provide opportunities for students to work toward critical awareness. While on co-op, students are required to make decisions, negotiate their different roles as students and workers, develop relationships with co-workers and supervisors, take on responsibilities, and work as members of teams. Students also have opportunities to understand, examine, and question the work they do while on co-op in relation to the larger society. Dewey (1916) used the following example to illustrate this aspect of work-based learning:

> Gardening, for example, need not be taught either for the sake of preparing future gardeners, or as an agreeable way of passing time. It affords an avenue of approach to knowledge of the place farming and horticulture have had in the history of the race and which they occupy in present social organization. Carried on in an environment educationally controlled, they are means for making a study of the facts of growth, the chemistry of the soil, the role of light, and moisture, injurious and helpful animal life, etc. ... Instead of the subject matter belonging to a peculiar study ... it will then belong to life. (p. 200)

Through observation and experience, we recognize that this educational landscape for co-op and internships is often restricted by the logistical demands of placing students on jobs, developing new opportunities for students and maintaining existing employer relationships, and documenting student participation and performance. The educational importance of students developing critical awareness takes a backseat in this process. To address this issue, we began regularly meeting 3 years ago to discuss various issues relating to student learning and our teaching. The research reported in this chapter emerged from our conversations during these meetings.

During our dialogues about teaching and learning, the influences of students' social class on their co-op experiences became a reoccurring theme. What are the influences of a student's class status on his or her co-op experiences? When students cross class boundaries during co-op (e.g., a student from a working-class background co-oping in a professional setting) what challenges do students face? In what different and similar ways do affluent and poor students experience the out-of-classroom context of co-op? These questions surfaced during our discussion and later became the guiding questions of the present study. The case studies presented in this chapter examine the experiences of two students from different economic backgrounds who crossed class boundaries during co-op.

In the following sections, we elaborate on the process of constructing a case for purposes of improving practice as well as contributing to the broader field. We emphasize the use of interpretive methodology to construct cases (Geertz, 1973; Erickson, 1986). This approach allows researchers to probe how people, in specific social interactions, interpret and make sense of their everyday interactions. Because we constructed the cases through action research, we then provide an overview of action research and its relevance in improving practice. Finally, we offer the two cases and present the findings of the study.

CASE STUDY METHODOLOGY

Case Study Approach

Case studies have the advantage of incorporating multifaceted elements that reveal their interactivity. They are organic depictions of phenomena and their interrelatedness. They are dynamic. They recognize that meaning is of great importance and that meaning results from an analysis of the dynamics of the many parts of phenomena. More like ethnographies or historical research than experimental research, case studies rely on the human interpretations of witnesses and participants simultaneously to derive and suggest meaning. In a basic description, a case study is a detailed examination of one setting, or an individual, a single collection of documents, or a particular event (Merriam, 1988).

Barbara McClintock, a biologist, provided insight into the nature and value of case construction. As Stephen Gould (1987) noted, she was committed to "following the peculiarities of individuals, not the mass properties of millions" (p. 167) in order to trace their complex interactions with each other and their environment. In her own words, she believed that one must understand:

> how it (each plant) grows, understand its parts, understand when something is going wrong with it. [An organism] isn't just a piece of plastic, it's something that is constantly being affected by the environment, constantly showing attributes or disabilities in its growth.... No two plants are exactly alike ... I start with the seeding and I don't want to leave it. I don't feel I really know the story if I don't watch the plant all the way along. So I know every plant in the field. I know them intimately and I find it a great pleasure to know them. (cited in Gould, 1987, pp. 167–168)

McClintock followed the narrative thread of an individual with the intent of understanding a phenomenon. In doing so, she recognized the importance of theoretical definitions and empirical details (Dyson, 1997).

The singular defining feature of case studies is its boundedness (Geertz, 1973). As Dyson (1997) pointed out, "Some unit of integrity (a person, a group, a community) is both outlined and contained by the researcher, who is studying, not the case of itself, but a case of *something*, some phenomenon …" (p. 168). Case studies are interpretations. Someone or a team decides what facts and data are relevant for inclusion in the case study. The researcher is continuously making decisions about what is, or is not, relevant to the case study. The researcher is required to make decisions about fundamental definitions of what exactly is being recorded or bounded by case studies. In writing case studies of communities, Geertz (1973) addressed this process of decision-making by stating:

> The locus of study is not the object of study.… You can study different things in different places, and some things … you can best study in confined localities.… It is with the kind of material produced by … almost obsessively fine-comb field study … that the mega-concepts with which contemporary social science is afflicted—legitimacy, modernization, integration, conflict … meaning—can be given the sort of sensible actuality that makes it possible to think not only realistically and concretely *about* them, but, what is more important, creatively and imaginatively *with* them. (p. 23)

The aim of case study research is to understand some aspect of human experience and then contextualize that experience within the individual's everyday world.

What, then, is the role of case studies in the assortment of scholarly approaches to researching cooperative education and internships? What contributions are made to our profession from closely observing and researching a small number of individuals, given the thousands of students involved in cooperative education and internships at postsecondary institutions throughout the world? First, case studies surface and initiate larger discussions of important issues within our field. By capturing and recording a phenomenon practitioners are afforded opportunities to closely examine central issues that are often lost within the particulars. Second, case studies are characteristically easier to accomplish than more complex, multisite or multisubject studies while providing useful insight about important issues. Because of the limited scope and typically contained location, the case study approach makes research more feasible and practical. Finally, case studies contribute to the larger body of research on co-op and internships. Case studies provide a means for a wide range of topics to be addressed and researched. Case studies also facilitate a process of identifying what topics need further investigation.

Constructing Case Studies

Researchers are not ventriloquists (Geertz, 1988). They do not speak for others. They, instead, capture others' lived experiences through writing. As writers, their work is to make another's world accessible and understandable by respecting the particulars and locating the recurring themes of that world. They begin their process by formulating questions that guide their inquiry into another's world. For case study research, these questions do not need to be specific as with other qualitative methodologies but do need to provide the necessary direction for inquiry.

Once questions have been surfaced then the task for the researcher is to gather data, review and explore the data, and make decisions about the direction of the study. Through this process of becoming more familiar with another's world, the general questions begin to take more shape and become more specific. After gathering data, researchers write to give form to their clumps of categorized and organized data. Writing allows the researcher to link together thoughts that have been developing throughout the entire research process. Writing is about constructing a text. Through writing, researchers engage in an act of constructing (see Table 11.1).

Through the writing process of considering and reconsidering the taken-for-granted, cases have the potential to reveal "dimensions of ... experience that are ordinarily invisible," and to "hear aspects of it ordinarily lost in silence" (Greene, 1988, p. 19). This potential for seeing and hearing new dimensions of experience provides the necessary conditions for researchers to go beyond old assumptions and conceptual boundaries.

ACTION RESEARCH

Eleanor Duckworth (1987) maintained that teachers, those who engage learners in phenomena and work to understand the sense they are making, are in an ideal position to pursue research questions about teaching and learning. She further argued that the types of questions teachers ask about their students' learning experiences are similar to those researchers ask about the nature of learning. Action research methodology relies on the ideal position of the practitioner in searching for answers

TABLE 11.1
The Process of Constructing a Case Study

Step 1:	*Gather raw case data.* These data include all the information collected about a person or program that is the focus of inquiry.
Step 2:	*Find patterns and develop category systems.* The researcher makes sense of the data by systematically identifying patterns, themes, and categories of analysis that emerge from the data. The researcher revisits guiding questions of the inquiry in order to situate the findings.
Step 3:	*Write a case study narrative.* The case study is a descriptive account of a person or program that provides the necessary information for the reader to understand that person or program. The case study is constructed either chronologically or thematically and sometimes both. The descriptions of a case study are holistic, considering the focus of inquiry, and include various factors, dimensions, and categories woven together.

to research questions. In doing so, action research directly challenges traditional understandings of research that insist the researcher must maintain distance from that which is being researched.

As with other research approaches, action research needs to be a consciously initiated process that is implemented with a plan for gathering data and analysis. As Patterson and Shannon (1993) so poignantly pointed out "methods of inquiry need not be sophisticated, but they must be systematic" (p. 9). Lytle and Cochran-Smith (1994) further explained:

> Systematic refers primarily to ways of gathering and recording information, documenting experiences inside and outside of classrooms, and making some kind of written record. Systematic also refers to ordered ways of collecting, rethinking, and analyzing ... events for which there may be truly partial or unwritten records. Intentional signals that [action] research is an activity that is planned rather than spontaneous. (p. 1154)

The methodology for action research is normally not very complicated and is essentially a five-step process (see Table 11.2).

Through a systematic process, action research is often guided by professional curiosity and improvement. Action research thus is a discovery process. It is inquiry learning with the intent of accomplishing one or both of the purposes typically motivating action research—program development or practice improvement.

RESEARCH PROJECT

In *Teaching to Transgress*, bell hooks (1994) argued that, "Class is rarely talked about in the United States; nowhere is there a more intense silence about the reality of class differences than in educational settings" (p. 177). In another work, hooks (2000) observed that although the gap between the poor and affluent continues to widen, as a nation we continue to avoid talking about societal issues relating to social class. This absence of dialogue about social class not only functions to maintain class divisions in our society but also prevents us from developing a critical awareness of the relationships among the political, economic and social structures in our society.

As Jean Anyon (1988) pointed out, "One's occupation and income level contribute significantly to one's social class, but they do not define it" (p. 367). She noted that social class is defined by relationships: relationship with the labor market, relationship with economic and political structures, relationship with others, and relationship with educational institutions. Our lives and experiences are shaped through these relationships. Consequently, the experiences of the poor are very different than those of the affluent. Through these different experiences, Bordieu (1977, 1984) maintained that human understanding is a form of socialized knowledge conditioned in specific habitats, therefore, individuals' epistemologies—that is, the origin, nature, methods, and limits of human knowledge—re-

TABLE 11.2

Action Research Model

Step 1:	*Research Topic* This stage involves most commonly three operational activities: observation, discussion, and formulation. The research begins with research questions or issues instead of a research project. The task for the researcher is to determine what questions and issues need to be researched.
Step 2:	*Research Design* The first step is concerned with the "why?" and this step is driven by "how?" The research design is the researcher's plan of how to methodically proceed. The design outlines the parameters, the tools, and the general guide of how to proceed.
Step 3:	*Data Collection and Analysis* There are various techniques for gathering data for both qualitative and quantitative methods: interviews, questionnaires, student records, etc. The analysis must be systematic. This stage is where the conclusions begin to emerge.
Step 4:	*Findings and Conclusions* There are clear connections between the research questions posed and the conclusions of the research. In this phase, the researcher typically considers how the findings can be used to improve programs and/or practice.
Step 5:	*Communication and Dissemination* Research should not be private once it's completed. It is a sharing enterprise. The results can be communicated in many different ways and typically depends on the original purpose of the research.

flect their cultural histories and social class origins. According to this theory, students do not enter school or a co-op or internship site neutral, but instead their views of school, of one another, and of work are filtered through specific habits. Students enter an educational experience with a particular knowledge of the social world, and, to some extent, the meanings they attach to the events of educational experiences to fit their home views (Alvarado & Ferguson, 1983; Bordieu, 1977; Young, 1990). The task for education, therefore, is to account for these differences in students' lives and experiences while establishing their overall program. Social interactions within an educational context are important not only in developing views of education, but "also in socializing more generalized conceptualizations of self and of the nature of the world" (Brantlinger, 1993, p. 5).

For those of us committed to social justice and working towards a critical awareness, we are implicated in our society's erasure of social class. The realities of social class that are so pervasive in American society should be addressed in order to break down class divisions. The real-world experiences and out-of-classroom context of co-op and internships inherently provide opportunities for social class realities to be addressed. The connection between the educational institution and the workplace established through internships and co-ops provides unique opportunities for students to examine experiences and perspectives defined by social class within and outside educational institutions.

Although co-ops and internships naturally provide these educational moments, students need to be offered an educational context to articulate and analyze these experiences and perspectives. Kolb's (1984) experiential learning theory provides a model for co-op and internship educators to consider in facilitating this educational context. According to Kolb, the learning cycle involves four stages: Concrete Experience, Reflective Observation, Abstract Conceptualization, and Active Experimentation. The learner engages in an experience, reflects on the experience from various perspectives, forms concepts that integrate his or her observations with theories, and uses these theories to guide future action. This approach to learning allows co-op and internships educators to engage students in dialogue about a wide-range of issues relating to social class. This discourse plays an important role in surfacing a topic that has been virtually ignored.

In our literature review of the research on cooperative education and internships, we found no studies that examined the influence of a student's class status on his or her co-op or internship experiences. Moreover, theoretical frameworks focusing on social class issues are absent in the body of research. In the present study, we respond to the lack of research and theory on the influences of social class on students' internships and co-op experiences by examining students' experiences crossing class boundaries during co-op. What are the influences of a student's class status on his or her co-op experiences? When students cross class boundaries during co-op what challenges do they face? In what different and similar ways do affluent and poor students experience the out-of-classroom context of co-op? These questions guided our inquiry as we attempted to break the silence of the issues relating to social class.

Method and Analysis

For the purposes of this study, we purposefully selected two students who had a co-op experience in which they crossed class boundaries. Through a typical case sampling (Patton, 1990), we selected the two students from a group of our advisees who had similar experiences. At the time of selection, we were seeking the "typical" experience of crossing class boundaries during co-op. To address the experiences of both affluent and poor students, we also selected students who had different class backgrounds. We used Jean Anyon's (1988) definition of social class in categorizing the two students. From Anyon's perspective, family income is important but other factors such as the educational levels and the occupations of parents are as significant in determining a person's social class. In this chapter, we use only two categories of social class, which are poor and affluent. Although we recognize there are various degrees to social class (e.g., working-class poor, nonworking poor, middle class, etc.), we use only poor and affluent to represent the range of social class to avoid getting bogged down with categories in our discussion.

> **Decision Point: How do we select students in our research when we are looking for "typical" experiences?**
>
> Unlike most other research methodologies, action research provides a systematic framework for researching individuals who the researcher knows outside the confines of the study. This familiarity with those being researched made it difficult for us to initially select the two students. We wanted to select students who had a typical experience of crossing class boundaries. How do you select students based on this primary criterion? This required us to define *typical* and then rely on our own recollections of our advisees' co-op experiences to identify a group of students who had a *typical* experience in crossing class boundaries during co-op. Although our knowledge of our advisees' co-op experiences was a benefit during the overall research project, our level of familiarity seemed to get in the way of us selecting the two students. Why them and not others? Are we most familiar with their co-ops and our knowledge is the reason we are selecting the students instead of their co-op experiences being typical? These were two of the questions that initially concerned us. We eventually determined that this dichotomy of familiarity versus sampling requirements did not correspond with the fluid boundaries of action research. Action research benefits from the researcher's familiarity with those being researched. Our initial response to choosing participants didn't fully accept this tenet that guides action research.

In gathering data, we collected advisors' notes documenting the planning, the experience itself and evaluation phases of the students' co-ops, advisors' notes about their communication with the employers, job summaries written by the students, employers' evaluations, and the students' papers about their co-op experiences. These data provided the essential scope for us to construct cases not only from information provided by the students but also from the points of view of their co-op advisors and employers.

> **Decision Point: Using peer review to generate multiple and diverse interpretations of the cases.**
>
> When the cases had been constructed we wanted to receive feedback and gather interpretations from peer review. We see a great value in peer review because we believe it is a way of putting our work out there in the professional arena to be critiqued. We also wanted others to examine the cases. At the point of completing case construction, we were the only ones who had read,

discussed, and interpreted the cases. We were looking for a means to extend beyond our own interpretations. We decided to present the cases at the National Society for Experiential Education Conference. In a conference session, we facilitated a process of analytically looking at the cases. This session was helpful in determining the findings of the study.

The procedures of analysis began by inductively reviewing the data sets. Inductively reviewing is an analytical process of combing through the data to identify emerging themes. After we identified the themes, we used interpretive methodology to construct the two cases (Erickson, 1986; Geertz, 1973). This approach allows researchers to probe how people, in specific social interactions, interpret and make sense of their everyday interactions. The primary purpose of this approach is to understanding others' understandings. Once the cases had been constructed we presented them at a national conference to gather multiple and diverse interpretations of the cases from our peers. These interpretations are reflected in the findings reported in this chapter.

Case 1: Jennifer's Co-op as a Teacher

Jennifer (a pseudonym, as are all names in the two cases) is a fourth-year student at Antioch College. She grew up poor, and since the age of 13 when her parents died she has been essentially independent. From 13 to 18, she lived in numerous temporary homes because her extended family did not assume responsibility for her well-being after the death of her parents. She came to Antioch after attending two other colleges. She was not able to afford the tuition at these other institutions and had to drop out of college. After a year of not attending school, she applied to Antioch and the school offered her enough financial aid to re-enter college.

Decision Point: How do we construct the two cases collaboratively?
In collaborative research, there is continuous negotiation of roles and responsibilities in completing the research project. When we were at the point of actually constructing the cases we needed to decide how we were going to divide the responsibility of writing the cases. Because writing plays a central role in case construction we wanted to maintain our collaborative efforts in organizing and then constructing the two cases. We decided to write the first draft of the cases independently after we had collaborated on identifying the themes in the data. Each of us had the task of constructing a first draft of one of the cases. After we completed the first drafts, we then worked together on each case to complete the case construction process. Although part of our case construction was completed independently, the overall process was collaborative.

Jennifer's first and second co-ops were on campus in two different departments. For her third co-op, she worked at McLean School in San Francisco. McLean is a private day school with an affluent student enrollment. Most of the staff come from middle-class to upper middle-class backgrounds. McLean School has been an employer of Antioch co-op students for 16 years. For compensation, they provide a small stipend and a room for the co-op student on the second floor of the school. The co-op student is the only person living at the school. The school does not have the facilities for students to shower so the director, Michelle, gives students a pass to a local gym for the students to use their facilities.

During Jennifer's first week of employment, she found another gym near the school that offered the opportunity for students to work 1 hour a week for membership dues. Jennifer made arrangements with this gym to work for her membership dues. Because she was a member at this gym, Jennifer no longer needed the membership that the school provided. Jennifer then asked Michelle for the $400 that the school would have paid the other gym. Michelle explained that this $400 was allocated for students' gym membership dues and was not part of the stipend. Michelle told Jennifer that the school offers a gym membership—not additional money for their stipend. Jennifer did not accept this explanation and persisted in asking Michelle for the money. After 4 weeks of Jennifer pressuring Michelle for the money, Jennifer received the $400.

Several weeks later, Jennifer was about to prepare her lunch and discovered that two pieces of fruit and some vegetables she had bought were not in the school's refrigerator. Co-op students are provided the third shelf of the school's refrigerator to store their food. The refrigerator also stores food for students and staff. Michelle had talked with Jennifer several times because Jennifer was using more space than what was designated for her. Michelle even offered to bring in a cooler for her to store her extra food.

By mistake, one of the teachers had used Jennifer's food for student lunches. Once Jennifer discovered her missing food she became very angry and began shouting at some teachers. When the teacher who took the food realized she had made a mistake she agreed to replace Jennifer's food. Jennifer was still not satisfied because she believed that the teacher had taken the food intentionally because Michelle had previous conversations with her about the amount of space she was using in the refrigerator. After this incident, Michelle called the Antioch job supervisor and explained what happened. Michelle explained to the supervisor that Jennifer became upset about the missing food because she believed Jennifer had an eating disorder.

Case 2: Gabe's Co-op as a Fisherman

Gabe is a first-year student and a legacy at Antioch. His father died when he was relatively young and his Antioch graduate mother raised him in a tourist town with a large population of artists in Arizona. As a hobby, his mother owns a small store that sells artwork. Although his mother is independently wealthy, she runs this business to sell her artwork. During his first co-op Gabe worked with an alumnus who owned a drag fishing boat off the west coast of the United States. Interestingly, the boat owner, Mike, grew up in a river town in Ohio, and he developed his knowledge of and skills for fishing while on various co-op jobs.

Gabe described being out on the water for days at a time, far enough off shore to take many hours to reach the fishing beds they will work. The method of fishing involved dragging nets along the bottom of the ocean and then pulling them aboard with winches and cables run through booms that jut out on each side of the boat. The cables draw in the nets and fish are dumped onto the deck, sorted and those with market value were sent below to ice rooms. The fish and other creatures with no market value were to be speared with a gaff and pitched overboard. This was Gabe's job and he hated it. He didn't hate it because it was back-breaking, although it was that too. He hated it because it was so wasteful and seemed so immoral to kill fish that wouldn't be used.

Gabe tried to avoid using the gaff and instead knelt on the deck to sort by hand. Fish, being slippery and wiggling creatures, are hard to pick up. It was also significantly more physically difficult because the tossing of fish involved different and less efficient leverages and greater distances to travel unaided by the gaff's rod. It was also a much slower process. Slowing the process of sorting meant that marketable fish sat on the deck and sun longer than when the gaffing process is used, which can cause those fish to lose their best market qualities and, therefore, price.

Gabe wrote:

> It's a crew of five doing the deck work and captaining the boat. We are at sea for 7 to 10 days at a time. All aboard, except I, are experienced fishermen. The hateful and immoral job I do has no meaning to them apart from the exhaustion it causes and the promise of financial rewards. Their jobs are equally exhausting, and we share duties as needed. But, they have simply either made their peace with this wasteful process or it never had the meaning for them that it has for me. Actually, when I talked to Mike about it, and he helped me understand why it has to be this way in economic terms, I was somewhat less morally offended than I was depressed about what this industry does. The rest of the crew just thinks I'm nuts or stupidly strange. I even tried to avoid using the gaff (this barbed steel probe on the end of a pole) and to pick up the fish, octopus and other undesirables, by hand. This was impossible because Mike and the rest of the crew would kill me! Not really, but it pissed them off royally. Mike really laid into me one day when I first tried this technique. Joey grabbed the gaff and went wildly to work sorting the catch and told me to get my "ass" below decks. I was ashamed and detested.

Perhaps because of the tension between Gabe and the crew, they worked independently or with limited social interaction. Gabe recalled a frightening incident that took place on this same trip. The boat was not the captain's own boat. So, the boat was not as familiar to him as his own boat would have been. At some critical point it became obvious that something was going very wrong with one of the winches. The captain warned them that something was wrong and gave a command that Gabe either didn't hear completely or it had no exact meaning to him as it did to the more experienced fisherman. The fishermen sought cover or otherwise got out of the way. Gabe made a sort of move away from where he had been standing. In seconds one of the winches was torn free from the foundation and hurled to the deck. It weighs hundreds of pounds and when it crashed into the deck broke partially through the decking and splashed fish guts all over the place. It landed 2 to 3 feet from where Gabe stood.

Gabe was petrified with fear. He could easily have jumped to the exact spot where the winch laid. It was pure dumb luck that saved his life or limb. There was nervous laughter and expressions of concern for him by the crew followed by an assessment of the problem. It quickly became more technical than Gabe understood, or due to his sheer panic, he just wasn't analytical about much of anything. The incident was discussed and joked about all the way back to port. After this incident, Gabe wanted to quit his job.

Discussion

Crossing Class Boundaries.   Both cases reveal the taken-for-granted realities of particular class positions and the difficulties in redrawing the boundaries constructed by class. In Jennifer's case, the tension in crossing class boundaries mainly arose from the economic dimension of class. This dimension emerged when the terms of compensation established before Jennifer began work changed during her co-op. In Jennifer's understanding, she made the necessary alternative arrangements to receive the $400 intended to pay students' gym memberships on co-op. She felt like she needed that money and thought she had found a way to receive it. The employer had a different understanding. The money allocated for membership fees was only designated for the intended purpose of paying a student's gym membership. The employer understood Jennifer's alternative arrangements as Jennifer's underhanded attempt to get more money from the school. In this exchange, Jennifer looked at the particulars of the compensation package, whereas the employer focused on the overall agreements.

Their disagreement about the storage and unintentional consumption of Jennifer's food was another incidence where economic dimensions of class surfaced. Jennifer had a limited amount of money to buy food and became upset when she discovered her co-workers and students had consumed her food. In her perspective, she did not see this as an accident because it threatened her financial means to replace the food. She had a straightforward understanding: She had bought the food and it belonged to her. Someone taking what belonged to her, either intentionally or accidentally, did not respect how difficult it was for her to have the money to buy food. As evident in Jennifer's case, the employer had a different understanding. She also had a straightforward response to the missing food: The food was taken by accident and was going to be replaced. The employer interpreted Jennifer's response to this situation as being too concerned with food, not buying food but food itself. This interpretation led her to the conclusion that Jennifer had an eating disorder. Their different perspectives and conclusions about this incident demonstrate the difficulties arising from contrasting orientations to money that are constructed through class realities.

Although Gabe's case involved the economic dimension of class, his case most completely reveals the moral dimension of class. During his co-op, Gabe eventually recognized not only the dangers of his work but also what he considered the morally repugnant waste in the fishing industry. His responsibilities and duties while on this co-op directly contradicted his moral stance. In his perspective, the waste associated with the fishing processes of sorting the catch did not justify the economic benefits. His moral convictions prevented him from relating to other crewmembers and his supervisor in a way he needed to for his safety. He was unwilling to fully learn processes that went against his moral beliefs. As a consequence, he jeopardized his own well being as well as the safety of the crew. Gabe wanted to quit his job when he finally discovered he did not have the power to change his working conditions to more closely correspond with his moral beliefs.

As evident in Gabe's case, his supervisor, Mike, had a different understanding of Gabe's performance in and attitude toward his work. He had a straightforward response to Gabe: He needed to do the labor he was getting paid to perform. In Mike's perspective, Gabe needed to do his job and learn the necessary duties of his work in order to maintain efficient and safe boat operations. For Mike and the crewmembers, the economic benefits of particular fishing processes and practices needed to be at the forefront of their work. They had to catch a certain amount of fish to make a profit. For Mike, Gabe's unwillingness to learn and do what he needed to do implied a lack of work ethic rather than a moral stance.

In both cases, differences in class realities created tensions between the employer and the co-oping student. Bordieu's (1977) concept of habitus, which he defined as "a system of lasting, transposable dispositions which, integrating past experiences, functions at every moment as a matrix of perceptions, appreciations, and actions" (pp. 82–83), provides some understanding of this tension. One's habitus is composed of their attitudes, beliefs and experiences of those inhabiting one's social world. This assortment of internalized values shapes an individual's attitudes toward work, for example. The tensions and conflicts arise, therefore, when an individual's habitus does not correspond with another individual's habitus. In both Jennifer and Gabe's experiences, their attitudes of work, of social interaction, and of the world did not correspond with their employer's understandings. Their conflicts developed from a lack of effective communication about these different class realities. The dimensions of social class were not adequately addressed to close the gap between the taken-for-granted understandings that are constructed by particular class positions. By not addressing these surfaced dimensions of class, the students were not provided the educational context to work toward critical awareness. The educational context of crossing class boundaries inherently provides educational opportunities for students to "cross over into different zones of cultural diversity and form ... hybrid and hyphenated identities in order to rethink the relationship of self to society, of self to other, and to deepen the moral vision of the social order" (McLaren, 1995, p. 22). Through reflective practice, students address dimensions and issues of class realities in order to work towards a critical awareness.

Reflective Practice.   Reflection is the identification of what has been learned so that further experiences can be constructed within an experience-enriched understanding. The educational process of reflection provides a means for students to cumulatively link their variety of experiences to one another. The process also provides a means for students to reconsider their assumptions of the world and their actions. This reconsideration provides an educational opportunity to make sense of their experiences so that they develop new understandings. Van Manen (1990) explained, "making something of a text or of a lived experience by interpreting its meaning is more accurately a process of insightful invention, discovery or disclosure—grasping and formulating a thematic understanding is not a rule-bound process but a free act of 'seeing' meaning" (p. 79).

By coming to an understanding of the meaning in experiences students are able to construct stories. This surfacing of their stories allows students to develop a deeper and fuller meaning for the experience because the stories become a sort of a text for the students to figure out. These stories also allow them to revisit their experiences and to have readily available a thematic understanding. Thematic understanding is gathered knowledge of previous experience that is available for us in our future experiences. These stories most importantly allow students to revisit and reconsider the past in order to shape their current and future experiences. The reflection process provides students with an opportunity to establish the beginnings of an on-going relationship with their experience.

Within this reflection process, the role of the educator is to facilitate the students' progress toward thematic understanding. This role requires us to ask the questions that need to be asked in order for students to further their critical inquiry of their co-op experience. Asking the right questions to facilitate this process is difficult. As Freire (1989) in his book with Faundez noted, "our interest in asking questions ... cannot remain simply at a level of asking questions for their own sake. What is supremely important is whenever possible to link question and answer to actions which can be performed or repeated in the future" (p. 38). In this respect, we can accomplish the difficult task of asking important questions when we are mindful of the educational outcomes of the student's co-op experience. What do we think is important for students to learn from their experience of crossing class boundaries?

Asking students to consider questions about class issues affirms our pedagogical presence in the reflection process.

PEDAGOGICALLY APPROACHING REFLECTIVE PRACTICE

In the two cases, we discovered that most of Jennifer and Gabe's experiences while on co-op revolved around tasks. They had a job to do and their supervisors and co-workers relied on them fulfilling their work responsibilities. The students performed various tasks at their work sites but did not engage in a meaningful level of reflective practice. Jennifer and Gabe did not broadly and critically think about their experiences until after they had completed their co-ops during the evaluation stage of the overall co-op process, which was facilitated by their co-op advisors. We also discovered that reflection rarely occurs as a natural component of work experience but requires the facilitation of the co-op educator. Although opportunities for reflection turn up in the real work context, the co-op educator needs to guide students toward locating and understanding naturally occurring opportunities for reflection.

After constructing and analyzing the cases, we reflected on our pedagogical approaches to facilitating reflective practice. What questions did we have Jennifer and Gabe consider before their co-ops? How did we prepare the students for crossing class boundaries? What interactions did we have with the students during the co-op experience itself? What interactions did we have with the employers? What questions did we ask during the evaluation process to facilitate reflection? Were we successful in creating the necessary educational conditions during the evaluation stage for Gabe and Jennifer to take what they've learned from their experience of crossing class boundaries to future experiences? These were some of the questions we considered during our reflection.

We came to realize that we didn't fully facilitate a process for reflective practice. Our efforts to have Gabe and Jennifer reflect on their experiences initially surfaced during the evaluation stage. At Antioch, students are required to complete a paper or project that allows them to reflect on their experiences and to examine various components of a culture such as historical heritage, language, environment, and institutionalized structures. They submit their paper or project to their co-op advisor and have a crediting conference to discuss their co-op. During Gabe and Jennifer's crediting conferences, class issues were brought up during our discussions, and we facilitated a class analysis of their experiences. In this analysis, we asked them to consider how the realities of class differences influenced their co-op experiences, what challenges they faced as they crossed class boundaries, and what they learned about their own cultural selves in relation to others. Because we had not surfaced these class issues prior to the crediting conference our discussions were limited to only beginning to discuss the complexities inherent in class issues. We did, however, introduce a new way of understanding their experiences, which allowed both students to continue discussing class issues in subsequent meetings with us.

Since our analysis of these two cases, we have taken a different approach to the overall co-op process when students cross class boundaries during their work experiences. We ask students to consider class issues throughout their entire co-op process. During the planning stage of students' co-ops, we aim to have them available for new interpretations and understandings of the world. Van Manen (1991) explained that by planning and thinking things out beforehand we are available in a meaningful way to learn from challenging, difficult, and puzzling situations. A purpose of and what guides the planning stage is to have students begin working toward this availability. This process requires asking difficult questions to establish an awareness of self and self in relation to others. This process also provides students the opportunity to identify and think about their educational objectives for the experience. Once these questions and goals are surfaced a framework develops for students to approach their co-op experiences educationally. The planning stage then becomes an opportunity for students to begin their inquiry within a thoughtful and meaningful framework. During the experience, we further develop the educational framework constructed in the planning stage. As we communicate with students, we find moments to have discussions about their experiences that surface class issues. When problems arise, such as communication problems between the student and his or her supervisor, we continue to be mindful of class issues and approach the problems by addressing class differences. By being more aware of class issues while supervising students on their co-ops, we continually present students with critical questions about their experiences in order for them to develop a critical awareness. Planning, the experience itself, and evaluation collectively provide a means to establish an educational tone that affords opportunities for students to struggle for meaning and become critically conscious of self and self in relation to others as they cross class boundaries.

CONCLUSION

The educational landscape of opportunities for cooperative education and internships uniquely provides experiences for students that position them to examine important and difficult issues about culture. Through the act of crossing class boundaries, students are challenged to construct new meanings for their own class realities and for the relationships they have with people outside their particular social class group. They develop these understandings by confronting and then working through complex situations and questions. This course of development provides the necessary conditions for students to continue beyond their co-op and internship experiences to work toward a critical awareness.

Case construction methodology provides a process for practitioners and researchers to capture this course of student development during co-ops and internships. Through the process of constructing cases, practitioners and researchers have opportunities to reflect on the lived experiences of students and address a wider range of issues in our field. Through this reflection and expanded scope of research, topics such as the influences of social class on co-op experience emerge from the shadows to enrich the ongoing conversations about the nature of the teaching and learning in cooperative education and internships.

Summary
- Constructing case studies through action research is a simple process that provides opportunities to practitioners and researchers to reflect on their practice and research a wider range of issues in our field.
- Action research is often motivated by professional curiosity and improvement, and is a discovery process.
- The researcher does not necessarily need to maintain distance from that which is being researched. A research project can benefit from an insider's perspective of the researcher.
- Research needs to be a consciously initiated process that is implemented with a plan for gathering data and analysis. Methods of inquiry do not need to be complex but they do need to be systematic.

ANNOTATED BIBLIOGRAPHY

Duckworth, E. (1987). *"The having of wonderful ideas" and other essays on teaching and learning.* New York: Teachers College Press. Duckworth offered a theoretical framework for conducting research as a teacher. In the book, she discussed the value of the unique insider's perspective of the teacher and provides a model for using this understanding to conduct research. We used this book to better understand the dual role of researcher and educator in action research. In the framework she provides, we were able to be mindful of the fluid boundaries of action research and the value of the researcher's closeness to those being researched.

Flood, J., Heath, S. B., & Lapp, D. (Eds.). (1997). *Handbook of research on teaching literacy through the communicative and visual arts.* New York: Macmillan. This research handbook provides a collection of studies on teaching literacy and situates the research within discussions about various methodological issues. The handbook covers the various types of research methodologies, including both qualitative and quantitative approaches. We found the handbook helpful in learning more about case construction and in identifying the important issues to consider in case study research. There are several chapters on case study research and we used them as guides in our own case construction. We also relied on the book as a resource for exploring general topics of qualitative inquiry. The handbook is not weighted down by jargon and is accessible to beginning researchers. We found the chapter authors' various approaches to their research and the research issues they covered helpful in our exploration of the diverse and multiple dimensions of case construction.

hooks, b. (1994). *Teaching to transgress: Education as the practice of freedom.* New York: Routledge.
In this book, bell hooks challenged postsecondary educators to transgress traditional educational boundaries in order to establish a pedagogical approach that values the talents, strengths, weaknesses, and voices of students. hooks also called on educators to address

issues that are not talked about in college and university communities. She believes we need to have more constructive dialogue about the influences of class, race, gender, and culture on educational practices and routines. We found this book helpful in our efforts of exploring a topic through research that has not been addressed in our field. She provided an approach for researchers and educators to transgress boundaries in order to surface issues that are absent in professional dialogue.

REFERENCES

Alvarado, M., & Ferguson, B. (1983). The curriculum, media studies, and discursivity. *Screen, 24*, 8–21.

Anyon, J. (1988). Social class and the hidden curriculum of work. In J. R. Gress (Ed.), *Curriculum: An introduction to the field* (pp. 366–389). Berkeley, CA: McCutchan.

Bordieu, P. (1977). *Outline of a theory in practice.* Cambridge, UK: Cambridge University Press.

Bordieu, P. (1984). *Distinction: A social critique of the judgment of taste.* Cambridge, MA: Harvard University Press.

Brantlinger, E. (1993). *The politics of social class in secondary school: Views of affluent and impoverished youth.* New York: Teachers College Press.

Dewey, J. (1916). *Democracy and education.* Carbondale, IL: Southern Illinois University.

Duckworth, E. (1987). *"The having of wonderful ideas" and other essays on teaching and learning.* New York: Teachers College Press.

Dyson, A. (1997). Children out of bounds: The power of case studies in expanding visions of literacy development. In J. Flood, S. B. Heath, & D. Lapp (Eds.), *Handbook of research on teaching literacy through the communicative and visual arts* (pp. 167–180). New York: Macmillan.

Freire, P. (1970). *Pedagogy of the oppressed.* New York: Seabury Press.

Freire, P., & Faundez, A. (1989). *Learning to question: A pedagogy of liberation.* New York: Continuum.

Erickson, F. (1986). Qualitative methods in research on teaching. In M. C. Wittrock (Ed.), *Handbook of research on teaching* (pp. 119–161). New York: Macmillan.

Geertz, C. (1973). *The interpretation of cultures.* New York: Basic Books.

Geertz, C. (1988). *Works and lives: The anthropologist as author.* Stanford, CA: Stanford University Press.

Gould, S. (1987). *An urchin in the storm: Essays about books and ideas.* New York: W. W. Norton.

Greene, M. (1988). *The dialectic of freedom.* New York: Teachers College Press.

hooks, b. (1994). *Teaching to transgress: Education as the practice of freedom.* New York: Routledge.

hooks, b. (2000). *Where we stand: Class matters.* New York: Routledge.

Kolb, D. A. (1984). *Experiential learning: Experience as the source of learning and development.* Englewood Cliffs, NJ: Prentice-Hall.

Lytle, S. L., & Cochran-Smith, M. (1994). Teacher-research in English. In A. C. Purves (Ed.), *Encyclopedia of English studies and language arts* (pp. 1153–1155). New York: Scholastic.

McLaren, P. (1995). *Critical pedagogy and predatory culture.* New York: Routledge.

Merriam, S. B. (1988). *The case study research in education.* San Francisco, CA: Jossey-Bass.

Paterson, L., & Shannon, P. (1993). Reflection, inquiry, action. In L. Patterson, C. M. Santa, K. G. Short, & K. Smith (Eds.), *Teachers and researchers: Reflection and action* (pp. 7–11). Newark, DE: International Reading Association.

Patton, M. (1990). *Qualitative evaluation and research methods* (2nd ed.). Newbury Park, CA: Sage.

Purpel, D. (1999). *Moral outrage in education.* New York: Peter Lang Publishing.

Van Manen, M. (1990). *Researching lived experience: Human science for an action sensitive pedagogy.* Albany, NY: State University of New York Press.

Van Manen, M. (1991). *The tact of teaching: The meaning of pedagogical thoughtfulness*. Albany, NY: State University of New York Press.

Young, R. (1990). *A critical theory of education: Habermas and our children's future*. New York: Teacher's College Press.

Part IV

Dissemination, Use, and Application

12

Considering the Needs of Different Stakeholders: The Impact of Co-op Job Quality on Post-Graduation Earnings

Neal Fogg
Mark Putnam
Northeastern University

Key questions addressed in this chapter:

- How do the research needs of practitioners and administrators differ?
- What are the basic elements of a comprehensive research plan, and why is such a plan important?
- Are post-Baccalaureate earnings influenced by coop job quality?
- What are the keys to effective dissemination of research findings?

INTRODUCTION

Any practicing researcher will tell you that research can be an isolating endeavor. Although there is some collaboration and discussion, in the end it comes down to the rather lengthy process of sitting down, reading and researching, working the data, and writing. In the context of research in higher education, this is unfortunate because the process of producing good, applied, practical research requires the collaboration of agents throughout the college or university. Certainly, at a minimum, the findings of research need to be conveyed in a clear manner that is both simplified and at the same time respectful of the inherent complexity of the subject matter.

When asked to write a chapter for this volume, we interpreted the topic "considering the needs of different stakeholders" to mean the process of reducing complex research findings to terms that can be understood and used by the two primary consumers of the research. These two stakeholders, namely the practitioners and the administrators, have fundamentally different research needs. It is the job of the researcher to address these needs in a systematic and clear manner, providing rigorous research that can be understood by individuals who do not share research backgrounds.

Aside from the problems associated with dissemination of research findings, two sets of activities must be completed before the actual research can begin. First, one must build institutional groundwork and promote an atmosphere of receptivity by recognizing and addressing the diverse research needs of practitioners and administrators. Second, one must develop and articulate a comprehensive research design, a roadmap, that specifies which questions should be addressed, the purposes of the research, and the data sources and methodologies to be used. Until these activities have begun, there can be little meaningful and useful communication of findings to nontechnical audiences, be they practitioners or administrators.

Following some background remarks, our discussion outlines our experience in building the institutional groundwork and developing the research design at Northeastern University. Following that, we review some still very preliminary results on the first research question that we chose to tackle: the impact of co-op job quality on postgraduation earnings. We end with some thoughts on dissemination of research findings. Throughout the discussion, we return to the theme of this chapter: conveying research findings to non-technical audiences and to practitioners and administrators.

BACKGROUND

The post-WWII period has been an interesting one for those studying the outcomes associated with higher education. The economic environment has changed markedly, as has the shape and role of the postsecondary education system. In the labor market, the demand side has been fundamentally altered by changes in both the industrial job content of the economy and changes in job duties within industries. These trends have created a job market that now demands, and rewards, highly educated, highly trained, highly literate individuals (Katz & Murphy, 1992). On the supply side, the GI Bill, the baby-boom, the Vietnam war, the birth dearth and then baby-boom echo, and the entry of women *en masse* into the job market all had lasting and profound impacts on the ways in which we age, go to school, and progress through professional careers.

In the postsecondary education system, for the past 20 years the environment has been one of rising costs, and rising benefits. It is clear that the rising benefits have been more dominant, as evidenced by the rising college enrollment rates of recent high-school graduates in the face of higher tuition and stagnant family incomes (Harrington & Sum, 1988). The continued, vast expansion of higher education during the post-WWII period might be viewed by some as reflecting a societal shift in taste toward an educated citizenry, or as a result of wise public policy, but an economist might see it as another case where capital is flowing to areas of high economic return. Whatever the case, the boom in higher education and the high level of resources devoted to it are not likely to change any time soon.

Concurrent with the rising costs, students and parents in the market for higher education appear to be increasingly sophisticated consumers and investors. They demand not just quality instruction, but such things as housing, Internet connections, and recreation centers. They also demand a return on their investment. Institutions have of course adapted and we see more and more signs of marketing geared to desirable market niches, claims of uniqueness, and intensely competitive recruitment. Aided by sophisticated software and increased computing capacity and speed, the process and the system are more data driven.

These changes in the labor market and in higher education have raised the stakes for students, for parents, and for colleges and universities. Consequently, one sees the move toward assessment and accountability. Administrators want answers, funders want answers, and program operators want answers. Those on the front lines, the practitioners who deal with the clients, also want answers, but they tend to have a deeper appreciation of the complexity of the underlying questions. Moreover, they tend to be interested in a fundamentally different set of questions. For institutional researchers, this means two things. First, to be effective, we must move beyond simple descriptive analysis to more sophisticated inferential statistics, that is, from an ability to describe to an ability to understand and explain. And second, to be effective, we must be able to convey our findings to both practitioners and administrators.

Ability to effectively convey research findings to nontechnical audiences is not just an advantage. It is an imperative. Those who can convey effectively are guaranteed a say in the evaluation and ultimately the operations of higher education programs, which include cooperative education programs. Providing the answers to practitioners and administrators and at the same time respecting the needs of both is a central challenge to researchers in higher education.

LAYING THE INSTITUTIONAL GROUNDWORK BY ADDRESSING THE RESEARCH NEEDS OF PRACTITIONERS AND ADMINISTRATORS

Two primary stakeholders, whose priorities differ in important ways, drive the research agenda for cooperative education and internships. We view these as archetypes because each would openly acknowledge the importance of the research interests of the other. In fact, their research interests overlap. What makes each of the perspectives unique, however, is that they are driven by a fundamentally different set of questions informing the design of an institutional research agenda.

Practitioners, whether they are co-op coordinators or faculty or career service professionals supporting internship programs, tend to approach research as students of their own practice. In other words, their interest in research is driven by a desire to provide more efficient services, increase satisfaction levels among students and employers, and develop more effective programming for all concerned. The primary goal of the practitioner is to find ways of enriching the experience for the participants, thereby complementing the academic program. In this way practitioners are educators, and although they may not teach in a traditional classroom, laboratory, or studio setting, they are designing educational experiences that are a key ingredient to the student's overall learning process.

College and university administrators, particularly at the senior level, are motivated to engage in research for different reasons. Although they fully acknowledge the importance of research that leads to improvements in practice, they wrestle with decisions regarding resource allocation, institutional effectiveness, and accreditation standards, and want to determine if in fact the program produces measurable results. They are fundamentally looking for a return on investment that is not expressed in terms of a net profit but in verifiable results demonstrating that value is being added to the student experience. Such value translates into improved academic reputation, stronger applicant pools, and increased opportunities for fund raising. Ultimately they are seeking to build an institution that is perceived to be continually increasing its quality in relationship to its net price and, therefore, increasing in value.

For practitioners and administrators, the research agenda is intended to inform a process of assessment and evaluation. It is here that the differences between the two archetypes clearly emerge. In developing a research plan, the practitioner is utilizing assessment techniques in a formative context with the objective of improving the effectiveness of the programs. This differs from administrators who are interested in evaluating the efficacy of the programs in a summative manner, in which the objective is to determine if the investment made in the program is worthwhile. As a result, the underlying questions asked by each group vary significantly. The practitioner is primarily focused on student and employer satisfaction with the experience as well as the self-reported development of knowledge and skills, whereas the administrator is focused on demonstrated specific learning, employment, and earnings outcomes.

The tension often emerges when practitioners are asked by administrators to present data and research findings that demonstrate programmatic success. Given the difference in perspectives represented by these groups, the expectations for what the research presentation should include are significantly different. The practitioner may interpret programmatic success to be represented by increasing participation rates, student and employer satisfaction, and balanced budgets. This information enables administrators to assess whether the program is operationally sound but does not inform a discussion about whether the programs are of any strategic value in accomplishing the institution's goals.

Most campuses today have dedicated resources to support an internal research function, commonly referred to as an Office of Institutional Research. Although the exact titles and responsibilities may vary (i.e., Office of Institutional Studies, Office of Planning and Analysis, etc.) the primary mission of institutional research is to turn data into information in support of decision making (Middaugh, 1990; Peterson, 1999; Saupe, 1990). Accordingly, the differing research agendas of practitioners and administrators can be integrated in a three-way partnership in which the institutional research function bridges the gap between the practitioners and the administrators, enabling the three to collaborate on a well-designed research program. To be specific, institutional research typically has at its disposal extant data contained in the administrative systems of the institution, institution-wide survey data collected on an annual or periodic basis, and information regarding other institutions that is publicly available or can be obtained through consortia. Thus, data gathered by practitioners can be combined with and analyzed in the context of these other institutional data sources, providing a rich information resource for all concerned. Although some practitioners may have the knowledge and skills needed to engage in research at this more detailed level, it is unlikely that many would be willing or able to devote the necessary time and energy.

The three-way partnership can only be effective if the Office of Institutional Research can indeed bridge the gap between practitioners and administrators. Such a bridging requires an ability to convey research findings to both groups. Given the growing importance of experiential learning, the development and implementation of a comprehensive research design is also essential. The research design provides a roadmap, allowing practitioners and administrators to see the whole picture and to therefore place research findings into a larger context. Forging a partnership between practitioners, institutional researchers, and administrators to execute and disseminate the findings of the research provides a basis for program improvement, builds trust and confidence among the partners, and improves the quality of decision making for the institution.

A COMPREHENSIVE RESEARCH DESIGN

Given the complexity inherent in managing institutions of higher education, leaders are often in search of a rational basis for making decisions regarding institutional priorities, resource allocation, and personnel. The lack of a comprehensive research design for key programs provides no end of frustration in attempting to make difficult choices among a set of very positive alternatives in which there is no clear wrong answer. The only thing worse than telling institutional leaders that there are no data available to answer a set of specific policy questions is to give them partial answers derived from multiple research instruments, with data collected episodically, from different populations, with questions that are worded in slightly different ways. For many leaders the concern is not that they will do something wrong. Rather, the concern is that they will not do something right and thereby fail to maximize the potential for success.

A comprehensive research agenda can enable an institution to provide a consistent and predictable context for assessment, evaluation, and decision-making. Figure 12.1 illustrates a comprehensive model for research on a cooperative education program. The model rests on the availability of data sources, which must be collected in a consistent manner. *Co-op Data* refers to data gathered within that operational unit that describes characteristics of each student's co-op placement. The availability and access to these data depend in large part on the nature of the administrative systems utilized by the institution. For those that have a fully integrated campus-wide system, these data may be easily accessible and consistently maintained. For others, however, data specific to co-op such as employers, placements, salaries, terms or dates, and job classifications, may not be contained in the existing administrative system and may be maintained within an independent system utilized only within the operational unit. From a research standpoint, these data on co-op experiences are essential and should form the backbone of the data sets used for the analysis.

The data sets should also include relevant *Student Records*, which describe the demographic and academic characteristics of each student included in the study. Combining student record data with co-op data dramatically expands the scope of

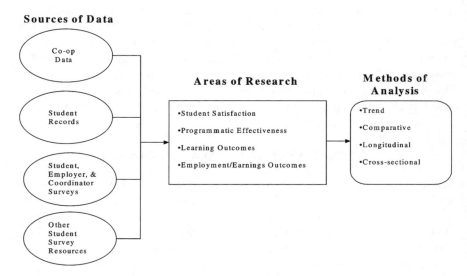

FIG. 12.1.   Research model for cooperative education.

possible research. Researchers then have the opportunity to include data elements that may be needed to control for certain effects, or data that may anticipate future research needs. For example, the hometown or state of origin for a student may be of marginal utility in the initial stages of a specific research agenda. However, an enrollment trend may emerge, a policy question may surface, or an opportunity for a new program may be proposed that would require a deeper analysis involving these variables. The point is that in building a comprehensive plan, some thought should be given to a potential scope of research that exceeds current needs and anticipates potential areas of inquiry.

In addition to the extant data available within the institution, *surveys* are typically utilized to gather information from participants regarding their evaluations of the program, satisfaction with the overall experience, and self-reported outcomes derived from participation. The data obtained from survey instruments can be incorporated into the data set in order to analyze the responses in a broader context. The key to integrating these various data sources is the presence of a unique identifier (e.g., social security number) that allows researchers to match student record data with responses offered on a survey. As a result, what we already know about students, including demographic information and academic profile and performance, can be analyzed with responses to satisfaction surveys, allowing us to draw connections between the co-op or internship program and the broader experience of the student. It then becomes possible to examine deeper questions that go beyond participation rates and satisfaction levels. For example, is student academic performance in college measurably affected by participation in a co-op or internship program, and does this impact remain after we control for student academic performance in high school? What is the profile of students who choose not to participate in a co-op or internship experience, and is there a higher level of attrition among these students?

In addition to ensuring that data sources are in place, *Areas of Research* should be identified as a collaborative exercise among practitioners, researchers, and administrators. In this example, the cooperative education research design highlights the combined interests expressed by all stakeholders in the research. This shared set of research questions creates a sense of common purpose for the effort and allows each group to express the importance they attach to the areas under study in relation to the role they play within the institution. Thus, the interests of all are affirmed and valued.

The *methods of analysis* establish the approaches that will be useful in maximizing the potential for producing useful findings. Many studies begin and end with the presentation of trends. In a simple *trend* analysis, one might find participation and satisfaction rates displayed over a 5- or 10-year period, leaving the reader to interpret the significance of the trends, if in fact any pattern can be detected. Presentations of this sort have the effect of turning practitioners and administrators into researchers, and it just may be the case that a flat line is viewed as sloping positively by practitioners and sloping negatively by administrators. This is not to demean trend analysis because its simplicity is often part of its power. But we would point out that the researcher's job does not end with trend analysis.

Comparative analysis goes a step further by presenting the data in comparison with other similar institutions or programs. A combined trend and comparative analysis can be even more helpful as one tracks a set of key indices over time in relationship to a set of comparators. These types of analyses are essentially descriptive and are certainly important as a foundation for research, but are limited in attempting to answer more complex policy questions.

A commitment to moving beyond this basic reporting and tracking stage opens the door to analyses that can answer key policy questions. Such analyses typically involve inferential statistics, which move beyond descriptive analysis in an attempt to explain patterns and behaviors. Moving to *longitudinal* and *cross-sectional* analysis allows the research to examine the experience of particular cohorts. In the case of longitudinal studies, a cohort is tracked for a defined period of time to determine how it changes as a consequence of experiences associated with a particular program or set of interventions. For a co-op program, the advantage of a longitudinal approach is that it permits the researcher to study the relation of co-op to outcomes such as retention and academic performance as the student progresses through his or her program of study. The cross-sectional analyses attempts to examine the experience of multiple cohorts as they reach certain points in time. For example, if the first co-op experience is normally scheduled for the fall term of the sophomore year, and we have tied that co-op experience to later outcomes (with longitudinal analysis), then we can use cross-sectional analysis to take a "snapshot" of each cohort as they pass through this stage. This could potentially improve planning and programs for each cohort as they age through the institution.

A variety of statistical and econometric techniques can be used to support each of these analytic approaches depending on the types of questions asked. Most commonly, we use some type of regression analysis. The strength of the regression equation is its ability to assess the independent impact of various characteristics or experiences on the outcome measure at hand. To illustrate our research efforts at Northeastern, we turn now to a regression analysis that assesses the impact of co-op job quality on the earnings of graduates 9 to 10 months after graduation.

Before concluding this section of our chapter, we emphasize that the development of a clear and comprehensive research plan helps practitioners and administrators to place research findings in context. The research plan, or roadmap, is designed to achieve the ultimate goal of effectively conveying research findings to the two audiences.

RESEARCH FINDINGS

Perhaps the most widely accepted empirical regularity in labor economics is the positive relation between educational attainment and earnings—the higher the education, the higher the earnings. The sources and magnitudes of the earnings premiums associated with various levels of attainment, interesting as they may be, need not concern us here. Perhaps the second most widely observed regularity is the positive relation between work experience and earnings, and this is more central to our purpose. As workers age, they gain work experience, become more productive, and earn more.

It is a fact of contemporary college life that students do not need co-op to gain work experience. Many students, indeed most of them, mix work and school during their educational careers (U.S. Bureau of the Census, 1995–2001). Summer jobs, internships, part-time jobs during school, work study jobs, co-op jobs, and jobs taken during interruptions in educational careers are all pathways through which students gain work experience. These days, most college graduates have quite a lot of work experience accumulated by the time they graduate. Because opportunities for gaining work experience are widely available, co-ops and internships need to provide more than just a job. (We are aware that readers with years of experience working with co-op programs, and we do not include ourselves in that group, would probably argue that co-op has always been more than just a job.)

To guide our research, we developed a chain of reasoning that proceeds along three steps. The first of these is an assertion or a working assumption, a claim that may or may not be proven empirically. The last two are also research questions but they have direct implications for the operations of co-op programs.

- Student outcomes (satisfaction, learning outcomes, postgraduation employment, and earnings) are directly linked to the quality of co-op jobs obtained;
- Therefore, we must identify the specific characteristics that make up a quality co-op job; and
- We must assess the extent to which and the reasons why some students do not obtain "quality" co-op jobs.

Decision Point: Which student outcome measure to tackle first?

There are many individuals in colleges and universities who are interested in examining the outcomes associated with co-op programs and internships. Some tend to focus on outcomes associated with learning and student development, others on satisfaction outcomes, and still others on employment and earnings outcomes after graduation.

Which of these outcomes should be addressed first? We chose post-graduation earnings, for a number of reasons. First, it is clearly important to students (and, by extension, administrators). Second, we have knowledge of an existing theoretical model and set of techniques and can therefore utilize that model. Finally, it can be done. We have all the data we need.

Once we have gained some experience analyzing post-graduation earnings, we can fairly easily extend the analysis to include other outcome measures.

Is all work experience the same, or are some jobs better than others? Do students in high-quality co-op jobs as undergraduates earn more after graduation than those in low-quality co-op jobs? Why would one think or expect that co-op job quality would influence earnings after graduation? We take as our framework a set of theoretical tools developed by labor economists in the 1950s and now known as the human capital school of economic thought (Becker, 1964). The human capital school posits that an individual's level of earnings is determined by their stock of human capital. Investments in human capital add to one's earnings by adding to one's stock of human capital. There are two main forms of human capital investments, namely education and work experience. Education increases knowledge via the classroom, whereas work experience increases knowledge, skills and abilities through a process of learning on-the-job.

But why should an individual's earnings be tied to their stock of human capital? The answer to this question centers on productivity. Workers with higher stocks of human capital are more productive, other things equal. This higher productivity, meaning they can produce more output per hour (and therefore more revenue for the firm), provides the incentive and necessity for the firm to increase the wage to retain (and attract) the higher productivity worker.

What does all of this have to do with co-ops and internships? Basically, we would argue that high-quality co-ops and internships are those that provide opportunities for students to develop their base of knowledge, their skills and abilities. In short, jobs that increase their stock of human capital. To co-op practitioners, this may all seem familiar, and that is because the cooperative education model is closely allied with the human capital school (Fogg & Harrington, 1999). It emphasizes the role of work-based learning in conjunction with classroom-based instruction as a means of developing the knowledge, skills, and abilities so highly demanded in the labor market today.

Empirically, can we show a relation between co-op job quality and earnings? In the earnings regressions discussed later, we expect to find a positive and statistically significant coefficient on the variable measuring the quality of the graduate's most recent co-op job. If our hypothesis is proven to be true, that is, if we find a positive and statistically significant coefficient, then we may infer that the high-quality co-op job was an investment in the human capital of the student, it added to their stock of human capital, and it increased their productivity. The higher productivity paved the way, and led to, the higher earnings.

Earnings regressions, or earnings functions, are probably the most widely used statistical tool in labor economics (Mincer, 1974). In an earnings function, the left-hand side, or dependent variable, is a measure of earnings. The right-hand side contains the independent or explanatory variables that are thought to influence earnings. Software programs process the data and produce an array of results. The most important regression results are the estimated coefficients on the explanatory variables and the t-statistics associated with these estimated coefficients. The t-statistics allow us to attach a level of significance to the coefficient. The level of significance indicates whether the estimated coefficient is significantly (in a statistical sense) different from zero.

If an estimated coefficient passes the test of statistical significance, then we interpret that coefficient as representing the *independent* (sometimes called *marginal* in a regression context) impact of the variable on earnings. What is meant by *independent*? It means the impact of the variable after controlling for the other factors that are included in the model. An example might be the relation between purchases of Jaguar automobiles, income, and education. A simple descriptive analysis of the data might reveal that highly educated people are more likely to buy Jaguars. However, in a regression equation we can control for both education and income and we may find that, after controlling for income, highly educated people are not more likely to buy Jaguars.

In our case, we have a variable measuring the quality of the graduate's most recent co-op job, and we would like to test the hypothesis that job quality has a significant (positive) effect on earnings after we control for other variables that are known to influence earnings. The survey instrument that we utilize contains an identification number that allows us to tie the survey back into the students' educational history at Northeastern. So we have the usual demographic information such as gender, race and ethnic origin, and age. We also have measures of academic performance such as high-school grade point average, cumulative grade point average as undergraduates, and degree major.

Inclusion of these variables on the right-hand side allows us to more accurately assess the independent impact of the quality of co-op job. For instance, one might see a simple relation between a graduate's quality rating of their most recent co-op job and their earnings. But it might just be the case that, say, pharmacy majors tend to rate their co-op jobs highly. In this case, it might be the pharmacy degree that is leading to the higher earnings, not the quality of the co-op job. By including two variables (or two sets of variables), one measuring co-op job quality and the other measuring major, we can assess the independent (or separate) impact of each.

What did we find with our data? In the spring of 2000 and the spring of 2001, we mailed surveys to students who had graduated with Bachelor's degrees in June of the previous year. We now have data for two classes, June 1999 and June 2000. For both classes, approximately 25% of the graduates responded to the mail survey. Phone follow-up of nonrespondents yielded an additional 15%, for an overall response rate of 40% for both classes. By the time our sample was restricted to full-time employed persons who had provided valid information on salary and the quality of their most recent co-op job, we had a total sample of 816 graduates.

The central methodological question in the study involves the definition and measurement of a variable to assess the quality of the co-op job because our hypothesis is that the quality of undergraduate co-op jobs has a positive impact of postgraduation earnings. In the spring of 2000, we added a series of questions to our graduate fol-low-up survey asking respondents to report the extent to which various skills were used on their most recent co-op jobs (thus our measure of job quality is a self-reported measure, i.e., we are not asking the co-op department or the employer to assess the quality of the job). Respondents were asked to report on 13 separate skills and job at-tributes, as follows:

- Your job was intellectually challenging.
- You used writing skills regularly.
- You used research skills regularly.
- You used state of the art technology regularly.
- You applied the knowledge learned in your major field of study regularly.
- You worked as part of a team of professionals.
- You were given a chance to do the things you do best.
- Your job required independent thought or action.
- Your job gave you the opportunity to interact with people.
- You got the feeling that the job itself was very significant or important in the broader scheme of things.
- You knew whether or not you were performing well or poorly on the job.
- Your supervisor was competent in doing her or his job.
- Your supervisor tried to enhance your learning on the job.

For our measure of quality, we used a simple summation of scores on these 13 in-dicators of quality. For each indicator, respondents checked a box ranging from 1 ("not at all true") to 4 ("very true"). Because there were 13 indicators of co-op job quality, our quality of co-op variable potentially ranged from 13 to 52. The median value for the measure was 43.5, the mean was 42.0, and the standard deviation was 7.1. The standard deviation suggests that roughly two thirds of the respondents rated their job between 35 and 49 (within one standard deviation of the mean), rep-resenting a wide variation in responses to the job-quality questions on the survey.

Our regression results are shown in Table 12.1. In any regression, the estimated impacts must be measured relative to a base group (also called a reference group). Most variables in the model are dichotomous or dummy variables that take on a value of 1 if the individual has the characteristic and 0 otherwise. In some cases, the base group represents those who did not have the characteristic. So, for instance, the base group for the coefficient on the variable for females is males, the base group for *foreign-born* is *not foreign-born*, and the base group for *enrolled* is *not enrolled*.

In other cases, there are sets of dummy variables and the base group is formed by leaving one group out of the equation. There are two main instances here. One is the estimated impact associated with race and ethnic origin. Respondents were classified into five race and ethnic groups, but only four dummy variables were com-puted and entered into the regression equation. The race group White was left out of the equation to be used as the reference group (the reader will notice that there is

TABLE 12.1
Regression Results Using Total Job Quality Index

	Effect on Earnings	Significance Level	Mean or Proportion With Characteristic
(Constant)	$29,203	0.000	10.539
Female	−4.1%	0.017	51.2%
Age	0.2%	0.558	23.4
Foreign Born	−1.1%	0.738	8.3%
African American	−5.6%	0.205	3.2%
Hispanic	−0.4%	0.927	2.8%
Asian, Pacific Islander	−2.3%	0.512	6.0%
Race Unknown	2.5%	0.312	16.1%
High School GPA	2.7%	0.143	3.03
Missing data for H.S. GPA	−2.7%	0.108	34.4%
QPA at Graduation	−0.2%	0.858	3.11
Enrolled in Grad School	−8.9%	0.007	5.5%
Art, Music	−22.1%	0.000	3.4%
Physical Science	−23.8%	0.000	5.3%
Communications	−18.8%	0.000	3.2%
Social Science	−9.8%	0.049	3.6%
Psychology	−26.7%	0.000	3.4%
Journalism	−20.4%	0.000	2.0%
Other Arts & Sciences	−24.8%	0.000	4.9%
Pharmacy	70.4%	0.000	4.5%
Physical Therapy	−0.7%	0.877	7.7%
Nursing	2.9%	0.565	4.7%
Other Health	−12.2%	0.007	4.5%
Accounting	−4.9%	0.348	3.2%
Finance	4.9%	0.323	4.4%
Marketing	0.4%	0.925	5.8%
Business MIS	23.2%	0.000	3.1%
Computer Science	42.4%	0.000	2.5%
Criminal Justice	−17.2%	0.000	11.2%
Chemical Engineering	18.0%	0.008	2.2%
Civil Engineering	−1.0%	0.848	3.9%
Mechanical/Industrial Engineering	22.0%	0.000	4.0%
Electrical/Computer Engineering	30.2%	0.000	3.1%
Engineering Technology	17.0%	0.004	3.3%

(continued on next page)

TABLE 12.1   (continued)

	Effect on Earnings	Significance Level	Mean or Proportion With Characteristic
Professional, Tech., Manag. Occup.	8.8%	0.001	87.9%
Job with Previous Employer	4.2%	0.023	31.7%
Degree was Required to Get Job	4.1%	0.037	71.1%
Job Closely Related to Major	−3.3%	0.073	64.5%
Co-op Job Quality Index	0.26%	0.024	42.0

Note. N = 816, Adjusted R-squared = .520

no variable for *White* in Table 12.1). In short, the coefficient associated with each of the four race and ethnic variables measures the earnings of that race or ethnic group relative to White respondents. The other instance in our case is the set of variables measuring major field of study. Our base group for this set of variables is *other business majors*. So when we report the independent impact of being an art or music major on earnings, the impact is relative to *other business* majors and not *all other majors except art and music.*

There are many interesting findings in the regression results apart from the estimated impact of co-op job quality. Females earned significantly less than males (4.1% less) and those enrolled in graduate school earned significantly less than those not enrolled (8.9% less). None of the variables representing the race or ethnic minorities were statistically significant, meaning that after controlling for the effects of all of the other variables included in the regression model, the post-graduation earnings of race and ethnic minorities were not any different from the earnings of their White counterparts. Age also had no impact on earnings. Finally, high-school grade point average and academic performance at Northeastern (as measured by cumulative QPA) had no significant impact on earnings 9 to 10 months after graduation.

There were wide variations in the impact of major field of study on postgraduation earnings, and we leave it to the reader to examine the estimated coefficients on the variables representing major field of study. The single largest negative coefficient was found on the variable representing psychology majors, who earned nearly 27% less than *other business* majors. The single largest positive coefficient was for pharmacy majors, who earned 70% more than *other business* majors.

Four other variables in the model represent job traits that previous research or theory has suggested have significant impacts on earnings (Harrington & Fogg, 1998). First, graduates who obtained jobs in professional, technical, managerial, or high-level sales occupations (known as college labor market occupations) earned approximately 9% more than those who did not obtain jobs in these occupational clusters. Second, individuals whose postgraduation jobs were with a previous co-op employer earned about 4% more than those whose jobs were not with a previous co-op employer. Third, graduates in jobs in which a college degree was required earned 4% more than those in jobs where a degree was not required. And fourth, graduates in jobs closely related to their undergraduate majors earned 3% less than those who were employed in jobs not closely related to their majors. This last finding was significant only at the 10% level of significance, which simply means that we can not be as confident (compared to the 5% level) that these impacts are different from zero.

Finally, we arrive at the results for the quality of co-op job variable. The regression results indicate that a one-point increase in the measure of co-op job quality led to a 0.26% increase in earnings. Alternatively, a one-standard deviation rise in the co-op job quality measure was associated with nearly a 2% rise in earnings. So, for example, individuals who rated their most recent co-op job at a 47 earned nearly 2% more than graduates who rated their job at 40. Our hypothesis is therefore supported—the quality of a student's most recent co-op job had a positive and statistically significant impact on earnings 9 to 10 months after graduation.

There are two final points to be made concerning the research as presented thus far. The first concerns validity of the research. We witnessed the positive coefficient on the quality of co-op job variable and attribute this to the quality of the co-op job. There may be other variables not included in the model that really deserve the credit. Put another way, those who rate their jobs highly may differ in systematic ways (not measured) from those who rate their jobs more poorly, and it may be these other systematic ways that are leading to the higher earnings. Insofar as omitted variables is a common problem in social science research, this is not really a problem, just an occupational hazard and something that a researcher should convey to his or her non-technical audiences.

The second point concerns the usefulness of the findings. As institutional researchers, we are often asked to examine issues and provide an analysis giving the university-wide picture. But the implications of research findings, and even the findings themselves, may differ by college, department, or even program. Although a lot can be learned from a university-wide analysis, to be of practical use the research in many cases must be refined, modified, or tailored to the level of the department.

We can say that it would be good to obtain high-quality jobs for our students because (as this research demonstrates) this would pay off in terms of higher postgraduation earnings. But to be more useful the practicing researcher will need to offer analysis and prescriptions at the departmental or even the program level. This is part of the research, digging deeper into what we mean by quality, that is really just beginning for us here at Northeastern. This is also the part that will require the most collaboration with the practitioners because just as they have little time to examine regression results and correlation matrices, we have little time to interact with students, employers, and academic faculty to find out what is really going on.

As a next logical step in our analysis, we have experimented with the quality of co-op measures in a number of ways in an effort to uncover the impact of particular aspects or skills on earnings. Findings in Table 12.2 are regression results from a model identical to the one presented previously except that the single quality of co-op variable has replaced by two quality-of-co-op variables. The first, labeled *mental* in the table, is a simple summation of scores from the following six indicators of co-op job quality:

- Your job was intellectually challenging.
- You used writing skills regularly.
- You used research skills regularly.
- You used state of the art technology regularly.
- You applied the knowledge learned in your major field of study regularly.
- Your job required independent thought or action.

The second, called *all other*, is a summation of scores on the other seven measures.

The regression results indicate that the utilization of mental skills on the most recent co-op job, if one accepts our definition of mental skills, paid off in terms of higher postgraduation earnings. The estimated percentage effect was .62%, meaning that a one-point rise in the index led to a .62% increase in earnings. The coefficient on the index measuring other job-quality attributes was not significantly different from zero, meaning that utilizing these other skills during the most recent co-op job did not lead to higher earnings after graduation.

Decision Point: How much is too much? (or, know when to say when).
The presentation of these findings has been simplified, and indeed it could have been considerably more complex. In the tables presented here, we have only three columns of numbers because we have left out the unstandardized coefficients, the standard errors, and the t-statistics (among other things). We have also left out information that might be of interest to academics or researchers trying to replicate our findings but only serve to confuse, distract, and alienate the nontechnical audience. For instance, marginal effects as displayed were computed from unstandardized regression coefficients, b, using the formula $e^b + 1$. Also, we have used the semilog form because it is well-known that the error term in this specification more closely approximates the classical assumption of normality. Finally, to lessen the influence of outliers we have excluded the ten observations with the highest difference (in absolute value) between actual and predicted log earnings.
Fascinating material, but bound to turn any nontechnical audience into a nonattentive audience. It is better to leave it out, and place it in an appendix.

Our point is perhaps best made by a reviewer of this chapter, who indicated in the margin of a draft, "Clarify—this adds little as it will be difficult for the reader to interpret." That is exactly our point. Keeping this material out of the text will enhance understanding of the important findings of the research.

TABLE 12.2
Regression Results Using Two Measures of Job Quality

	Effect on Earnings	Significance Level	Mean or Proportion With Characteristic
(Constant)	$29,524	0.000	10.539
Female	−3.9%	0.023	51.2%
Age	0.2%	0.535	23.4
Foreign Born	−0.9%	0.767	8.3%
African American	−5.3%	0.230	3.2%
Hispanic	−0.6%	0.899	2.8%
Asian, Pacific Islander	−2.2%	0.534	6.0%
Race Unknown	2.5%	0.316	16.1%
High School GPA	2.7%	0.141	3.03
Missing data for H.S. GPA	−2.8%	0.096	34.4%
QPA at Graduation	−0.3%	0.789	3.11
Enrolled in Grad School	−8.9%	0.007	5.5%
Art, Music	−21.7%	0.000	3.4%
Physical Science	−23.6%	0.000	5.3%
Communications	−18.5%	0.000	3.2%
Social Science	−9.0%	0.073	3.6%
Psychology	−26.2%	0.000	3.4%
Journalism	−20.5%	0.000	2.0%
Other Arts & Sciences	−24.4%	0.000	4.9%
Pharmacy	71.0%	0.000	4.5%
Physical Therapy	0.1%	0.976	7.7%
Nursing	3.4%	0.492	4.7%
Other Health	−11.9%	0.009	4.5%
Accounting	−5.0%	0.335	3.2%
Finance	5.2%	0.296	4.4%
Marketing	0.5%	0.903	5.8%
Business MIS	22.8%	0.000	3.1%
Computer Science	42.0%	0.000	2.5%
Criminal Justice	−17.0%	0.000	11.2%
Chemical Engineering	17.7%	0.009	2.2%
Civil Engineering	−0.8%	0.879	3.9%
Mechanical/Industrial Engineering	22.3%	0.000	4.0%
Electrical/Computer Engineering	30.3%	0.000	3.1%
Engineering Technology	16.9%	0.004	3.3%

(continued on next page)

TABLE 12.2   (*continued*)

	Effect on Earnings	Significance Level	Mean or Proportion With Characteristic
Professional, Tech., Manag. Occup.	8.6%	0.002	87.9%
Job with Previous Employer	4.4%	0.018	31.7%
Degree was Required to Get Job	4.0%	0.045	71.1%
Job Closely Related to Major	−3.3%	0.072	64.5%
Job Quality Index, Mental	0.62%	0.037	18.1
Job Quality Index, All Other	−0.05%	0.848	23.9

Note. $N = 816$, Adjusted R-squared $= .520$

KEYS TO EFFECTIVE DISSEMINATION OF RESEARCH FINDINGS

Effective dissemination of research findings is not accomplished simply because the report is well written, formatted properly, and distributed widely. Many would agree that our files are stuffed with reports that we have never fully utilized because the relevance of the research was never established. The success of dissemination is established in the design, by ensuring that from the outset we are not attempting to answer questions no one is asking. The following is a checklist of items to consider as the research project is being designed.

1. *Politics.* Research is not designed, implemented, or disseminated in a vacuum. The political environment surrounding the project should be assessed throughout. Care should be taken in getting the appropriate stakeholders to work together in a collaborative environment. The extent to which the institution as a whole acknowledges and owns the findings of the research will depend in large measure on the credibility and involvement of those who have sponsored the research and those who eventually endorse it.
2. *Participation.* Stakeholders involved in the research will vary widely in their ability to understand and contribute to the research project. For some the tracking and reporting of extant data is all they will need or be able to contribute. Others will bring sophisticated research backgrounds and will want to study the coefficients and other regression results. The task of the researcher is to make the process accessible to all.

3. *Precision.* Despite the varying levels of research expertise among the stakeholders, confidence is drawn from the degree of precision they see in the design and implementation. Setting a high standard for research methodology raises the bar on all types of reporting and research activities on campus. The rigor we introduce into the research agenda, however, should not be used to mystify but to instill a sense of confidence in solid research.

4. *Programmatic Relevance and Policy Implications.* Many institutional research studies have produced very interesting findings that in the end had little if any utility because they were esoteric and lost a direct connection to the programs and policy issues they were designed to inform. Researchers should keep the interests of the institution at the forefront and remind those directly involved in the project to avoid pursuing minutia and drifting away from the primary charge.

5. *Planning and Resource Allocation.* Although the potential impact of a study is difficult to predict, it is likely that in the end a comprehensive research design could produce results that will influence the institution's planning and budgeting decisions. The research can be especially helpful to decision makers if this is anticipated and the report is released in a timely fashion to inform the normal planning and budgeting cycles. A report that is released 2 weeks after the budget committee has completed its work for the year is unlikely to be much utility for some time, assuming that the study remains relevant until the next cycle.

SUMMARY AND CONCLUDING REMARKS

The environment in which institutional researchers operate has changed in a number of important ways. Most of the changes in the labor market, in the system of postsecondary education, and in the market for higher education have had the effect of increasing the need for sophisticated, relevant, and practical research.

For cooperative education programs, the main stakeholders in the research, practitioners and administrators, have different questions. Both sets of questions are complex and highly relevant. Moreover, the answers to each set of questions are important if we are to improve the product. Institutional researchers can play a role in bridging the gap between practitioners and administrators.

To be effective, institutional researchers must have the horsepower to develop and execute a comprehensive research agenda that moves beyond simple descriptive statistics to analyses that allow us to understand and explain behavior. Our research has shown that the quality of co-op jobs has a significant positive impact on earnings after graduation. This impact persists after controlling for a host of other factors that are known to influence earnings. In our view, we are not just claiming that job quality is important, we are proving it. But we need to dig deeper because not enough has emerged so far to influence, practically, the operations of the program.

Institutional researchers do need to have more than just a capacity for sophisticated research. They must also have the ability to convey the findings of the research to decision makers and persons who are in a position to use the information to alter or fine-tune programs and therefore enhance outcomes. This makes dissemination key, and gives rise to five considerations: politics, participation, precision, programmatic relevance and policy implications, and planning and resource allocation.

Summary
- The research needs of practitioners and administrators differ significantly. Practitioners tend to ask questions when the answers will shed light on improving the effectiveness of the program. Administrators are more concerned with questions related to resource allocation and institutional effectiveness. They need to know if the program produces a return that justifies the expenditure.
- A comprehensive research plan, important because it provides a roadmap to practitioners and administrators, contains elements that describe the data sources, the areas of research, and the methods of analysis.
- The earnings of Bachelor's degree recipients who were employed full-time 9 months after graduation are significantly influenced by co-op job quality as undergraduates.
- Effective dissemination of research findings requires that the researcher account for politics and allow for wide participation. The research must set a high standard of precision, be relevant for programs and policy, and produce results that can influence planning and resource allocation.

ANNOTATED BIBLIOGRAPHY

Birnbaum, R. (1988). *How colleges work: The cybernetics of academic organization and leadership*. San Francisco: Jossey-Bass. This classic text explores the organizational dynamics typical in institutions of higher education. The author examined a set of organizational typologies and notes the ways in which institutional leaders can better understand and interpret both the structural and political landscape.

Blaug, M. (Ed.). (1992). *The economic value of education: Studies in the economics of education*. Aldershot, Hants, England: Edward Elgar Publishing. This edited volume provides an excellent treatment of the varied impacts of education on the economy, on economic growth, and on the economic and social well-being of individuals.

Bolman, L. G., & Deal, T. E. (1997). *Reframing organizations: Artistry, choice, and leadership*. San Francisco: Jossey-Bass. The authors presented an approach for examining organizations by looking through different frames. These frames offer views of the organization that focus on the structural, symbolic, political, and human resource implications for decision making. The reader is encouraged to look at complex situations by adopting the unique views offered by the four frames.

Judy, R. W., & D'Amico, C. (1997). *Workforce 2020: Work and workers in the 21st century*, Indianapolis, IN: Hudson Institute. This sequel to the widely read *Workforce 2000* volume (also published by the Hudson Institute) presents a very readable review of changes in the workforce and in the workplace. It provides a useful context for the labor market in which college graduates operate.

REFERENCES

Becker, G. S. (1964). *Human capital: A theoretical and empirical analysis, with special reference to education*. New York: National Bureau of Economic Research.

Fogg, N. P., & Harrington, P. E. (1999, July). The influence of coop program participation on postgraduation earnings of Northeastern University graduates. Working Paper available from Northeastern University, Boston, MA.

Harrington, P., & Sum, A. (1988, September/October). Whatever happened to the college enrollment crisis? *Academe*, 17–22.

Harrington, P., & Fogg, N. P. (1998, March). *The contributions of cooperative education to the early labor market success of college graduates: Findings from a national survey*. Paper presented at the Cooperative Education Association Conference, Boston, MA.

Katz, L. F., & Murphy, K. M. (1992). Changes in relative wages, 1963–1987: Supply and demand factors. *Quarterly Journal of Economics*, 57(1), 35–78.

Middaugh, M. F. (1990). The nature and scope of institutional research. In J. B. Presley (Ed.). *Organizing effective institutional research offices, New Directions for Institutional Research* (pp. 35–48, no. 66) San Francisco: Jossey-Bass.

Mincer, J. (1974). *Schooling, experience, and earnings*. New York: Columbia University Press.

Peterson, M. W. (1999). The role of institutional research: From improvement to redesign. In M. W. Peterson (Ed.), *ASHE reader on planning and institutional research* (pp. 242–255). Needham Heights, MA: Pearson Custom Publishing.

Saupe, J. L. (1990). The functions of institutional research. In M. W. Peterson (Ed.) *ASHE reader on planning and institutional research* (pp. 211–223). Needham Heights, MA: Pearson Custom Publishing.

U.S. Bureau if the Census, Bureau of Labor Statistics (1995–2001). Current population Survey [machine-readable data file] / conducted by the Bureau of the Census for the Bureau of Labor Statistics. Washington, DC: Bureau of the Census.

13

Program Evaluation in a Business Environment: An Employer's Journey With Cooperative Education

Marilyn Mayo
IBM Corporation

Key questions addressed in this chapter:

- ☞ How do we re-energize the IBM Co-op/Intern program to provide a feeder candidate pool for regular hire?
- ☞ How do we measure success?
- ☞ How can we track the students and conversion progress?
- ☞ How do we improve the program to attract top talent?

INTRODUCTION AND BACKGROUND

International Business Machines Corporation (IBM) is a longtime supporter and participant in Cooperative Education and experiential education Programs. The purpose is to share with readers of this chapter the business application, dissemination, and use of cooperative education research in a business environment. This chapter provides information about the focus and actions taken within IBM in the United States as it transitioned to a more effective operational model and an approach to successful use of cooperative education and internships. The information provided demonstrates the value of co-op to our line management using data we have collected and program enhancements we have implemented.

BACKGROUND

In 1995 IBM consolidated recruiting and staffing functions throughout the United States into a centralized operation located in Raleigh, North Carolina. The consolidation was part of a major reengineering project within Human Resources to improve efficiencies and reduce costs. It also was directed toward becoming more competitive in recruiting new talent into the corporation as the company reentered the recruiting marketplace. The newly created team of staffing combined employees from the IBM Workforce Solutions organization who were located throughout the U.S. at major IBM sites and other IBM professionals into one staffing function with three unique groups: Experienced Professional Staffing, University Staffing, and Site Staffing. The Experienced Professional and University teams were relocated and joined as one staffing operation in Raleigh. The location was already the home of other consolidated human resource functions known as the IBM Human Resource Service Center.

As part of this action, University Staffing operations was created combining the efforts of the National Recruiting Organization field recruiting team and the University Staffing Representatives staff responsible for hiring of university students as new regular hires. It also resulted in the revitalization of the cooperative education and internship student employee program as a pipeline feeder pool for future university hires.

The new groups were dedicated to the identification, attraction, selection, and hiring of employees into IBM U.S. with the mission to provide recruiting and hiring services to all managers and divisions, with the exception of the Research Division. The Site Staffing functions, whose mission included the hiring of administrative and manufacturing personnel, remained located at 15 major site locations, and each site had responsibility for the needs of that location and regional geography.

In this chapter, the focus is on the evolution of the cooperative education and internship programs within IBM to position them within the company and externally as true feeder programs while accomplishing the objectives of providing an experiential opportunity through work assignments for students. I discuss some of the techniques, processes and tools developed over a 5-year period that have enabled IBM managers and IBM University Staffing to advance its student program to a new level of performance. A variety of metrics has been the gauge for providing our management team with progress reports and ultimately measurements of success. All of these actions have resulted in a stronger and more efficient recruiting effort, administration of the program, and more importantly, a process by which conversion of the students to regular hires is realized.

Areas to be discussed include: Development of measurements and matrixes, the Co-op ACT Session, reports, Student Satisfaction Survey, Project Conversion, the Master Co-op Database, and the Next Steps Assessment.

RENEWED FOCUS ON THE COOPERATIVE EDUCATION AND INTERNSHIP PROGRAM

The co-op program, as IBM refers to it, combines two types of student preprofessional hire programs: cooperative education and internships. IBM considers both of these experiential work programs as one. To qualify for our program, students are required to be enrolled full time at an accredited 4-, or 5-year college or university. Interns and co-ops and are placed in the same types of positions within the company. In most cases, the true cooperative education student usually works 6 months and returns for subsequent work assignments. The student intern usually works 3 months and only occasionally returns for an additional work term. Both programs are considered strategically critical to the identification and employment of future regular IBM employees and the overall success of the university hiring program.

Prior to the consolidation of staffing, student hiring was supported at the site locations. As managers created job requisitions and job descriptions, the staffing operation would recruit and identify candidates. Managers made the hiring decisions. Once students were hired, responsibility for these employees remained solely with the manager. Some managers made decisions to hire these students as regular employees; other managers considered student employees resources for temporary workload solutions.

Within the new University Staffing function, a small number of employees were identified to support the hiring requirements for student employees. This group of staffing representatives were responsible for all student hires across the country. They provided support for one fall-hiring season. IBM called its student programs, at that time, the preprofessional program. It combined cooperative education students who usually worked for 6-month assignments, and interns who worked only for the summer.

> **Decision Point: Should the hiring of co-ops and interns remain as a consolidated function in Raleigh University Staffing or should it return to the local environment within the Site Staffing operations?**
>
> A re-evaluation of support for the preprofessional program in fourth-quarter 1995, lead to the establishment of a program manager whose objective and goals were to redefine the program so that it provided a true pool of candidates for conversion to regular hire and to provide guidance in the areas of policy and practice for this staffing area. University Staffing and Site Staffing reexamined the decision to consolidate the preprofessional hiring function in one location. This model was understaffed and provided many challenges in attracting students to the multiple locations in IBM. In first-quarter 1996, the staffing leadership team concluded that hiring for the pre-professional program would be most effective if executed at the site location.

A staffing representative was identified at each of the 15 site locations with the responsibility of providing hiring assistance for the managers in that location or regional geography. In keeping with industry standards, the program nomenclature was adjusted and the program became identified as the IBM Cooperative Education and Internship program. No longer was it referred to as the preprofessional program.

The renewed team of Co-op/Intern Staffing Representatives (CIRs) and the Co-op and Intern program manager began sharing information and identifying areas for improvement. Continued responsibility for the program now shifted to the site teams who worked in collaboration with the co-op program manager. The overall work experience for these student employees was now on a course to be shared with the hiring managers and went beyond the tasks of the job. This was a major step toward the execution of a consistent program across the country.

MEASUREMENTS AND METRICS

Decision Point: How can we track on a national and site basis the students we employ? How can we measure success of the program and ultimately the conversion results?
Statistical data was needed to establish baseline knowledge about the size and the success of the current program. How many students were hired each year? How many were onboard nationally and at the site level at a point in time? How many students were converted from the co-op program to regular university hires? What are the current needs of the student program? What are the needs and desires of the students who come to work for IBM? What is the current mind set of IBM managers who hire student employees? What is the perspective of the IBM business units and divisions in regards to the student program? All of these questions and more needed to be answered and actions established based on the findings.

We began gathering data using two primary sources: the Resumix® tracking system and the corporate employee resource information system (CERIS). Both systems use a DB2™ database for information storage. Reports were created and examined, modified, and redesigned over time. Early reports contained information grouped by business unit divisions and location and contained specific information regarding the student: name, employee serial number, start date of assignment, projected end date of the assignment work location, manager name, and user-id. Separate reports contained data with school information, and degree and discipline information. Later reports evolved so as to provide indicators of success such as the divisional hiring targets for the current year, a divisional target for number of conversions needed to meet goals, the number of students onboard, a projected number of students needed in the program to meet conversion targets, and the number of offers and accepts yielded from the co-op and intern candidate pool.

It became clear that neither of these data sources could accurately provide all the data needed concerning these student employees. Resumix contained data needed during the preemployment phase; CERIS contained data once the student came onboard. Unlike other corporate hires, co-ops and interns have some unique attributes: They can be hired multiple times; they can work full time or part time; their graduation dates establish their eligibility for consideration for regular hire and these graduation dates change. Tracking these employees became a significant challenge. Yet, we were able to create monthly and annual reports that included data about the total number of students onboard, the number of students at each work location, which schools the students attend, the disciplines of study, and which divisions and managers hired students. Data challenges continued in the areas of identifying which students were eligible for conversion to regular hire and how many actually received offers for regular hire.

STUDENT PROGRAM IMPLEMENTATION

Simultaneous with the establishment of tracking processes was the examination of the quality of the program and the identification of student wants and needs. Sites began developing activities for the onboard students such as social gatherings like a luncheon barbecue and opportunities to learn about the business such as a technical speaker series. An internal web site was implemented exclusively targeted at the active student population. The web site contained general information applicable to all student employees, guidelines for the mentor program, a monthly newsletter, and links to specific information for the sites. The location information also provided specific details including a schedule of student activities hosted by that location's Co-op and Intern Recruiters. Over time, enhancements have been applied to the web site, and this is a tool, that will continue to receive focus.

A national Student Satisfaction Survey was implemented during fourth-quarter 1996 to begin measuring the effectiveness of the program from the perspective of the students. This survey was conducted biannually between December 1996 and December 2002. In 2001 the implementation scheduled was changed to annually and was conducted during July. July was chosen because the largest number of students are active employees during that month and have been employed long enough to have established an opinion of their work experience. Through the data collected with this instrument, staffing and business units are able to evaluate the effectiveness of the program and the attitudes of the student employees. The results of the survey are analyzed. Improvement plans are designed and many actions have been initiated as a direct result of student comments and suggestions. The questions included in the survey are shown in Appendix A. The results of the third-quarter 1999 Survey is presented in Fig. 13.1.

As more emphasis was placed on conversion of students to regular hires to help meet our staffing requirements, plans turned toward the organization of internal ca-

3Q 1999 CO-OP/INTERN SURVEY

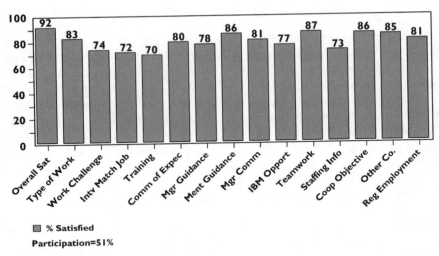

■ % Satisfied

Participation=51%

Fig. 13.1.   Student satisfaction survey.

reer fairs and providing students a chance to meet with hiring managers. An initiative named *Project Conversion* was established with the purpose of publicizing and executing plans to get offers for regular hire in the hands of students either before they returned to campus or soon thereafter. The elements of this initiative included: identification of the candidate pool to be students within one year of graduation, the identification of hiring requirements by IBM managers, and the matching of the two resulting in offers for employment. Project Conversion is a year-round activity but begins with the career fairs held at the large IBM sites in July when the largest number of students is onboard. Offers to co-ops and interns are tracked to ensure we optimize the candidate pool.

> **Decision Point: Having made progress in the organization of the student program, how do we elevate the program to receive more support from management and to immerse the program more fully into the IBM culture?**
> As staffing continued to identify areas to strengthen the program, it became clear that only with the full support of management and business units would we be successful in elevating the new elements of the student program into part of the IBM culture. Staffing leadership agreed in late 1998 to sponsor an ACT Session during the first quarter of 1999. Accelerate ... Change ... To-gether (ACT) is IBM's team-based problem solving methodology designed to

help address complex business issues while enabling change leadership and the advancement of a high-performance culture. It is a powerful tool for accelerating change across all IBM businesses and is based on the premise that if you clearly define the problem, bring together the right people and provide them with the right information, they will produce the right solution that addresses the business problem.

We reached the decision to use ACT for this business situation by asking these questions knowing that if the answer was "yes" to most of these, then the ACT methodology would be a good fit:

Is the business issue critical to IBM's success in the marketplace?

Is there at least one IBM executive who defines this as a critical issue to resolve, and who is committed to be personally involved in resolving it?

Will there be a significant return on investment (ROI) to IBM if the issue is resolved in the next 90 to 120 days? Can the issue be quantifiably measured?

Is the issue crossfunctional, crossorganizational or crossgeographic in nature?

Do working relationships between and among units need to be leveraged and improved to resolve this issue?

Could focused investment of resources over a 90 to 120 day period have a significantly positive impact on this issue?

Will a significant number of IBM stakeholders (i.e., customers, employees, business partners, etc.) receive meaningful benefits from the resolution of the business issue?

Is the degree of change required to resolve this issue significant (maybe even radical)?

The key characteristics of the ACT process are the focus on addressing real business issues, while demanding effective leadership behaviors, and demonstrating team-based skills, in a format that dramatically compresses cycle time for decisions and results in faster, better execution. In this case we used ACT to focus on reengineering or creating new processes, while empowering people to take actions through a collaborative effort among crossfunctional and multilevel participants who are brought together. ACT is a progression, which includes business consultation, ACT business meetings and change workshops.

THE CO-OP ACT SESSION

An ACT engagement is comprised of three phases:

Phase 1, The Scoping Phase, is where the preparation begins and where the foundation for success is built. During this stage the executive sponsor, the ACT lead consultant, the coordinator or project manager, and some key stakeholders come together to form a planning team. The planning team spends time thoroughly examining the problem in order to crisply define:

Which executive cares enough about resolving the issue to invest personal time as well as people and funding?

What is the business challenge and what are its major components?

What's at stake? How much can be gained if the issue is resolved? What are the implications if the issue isn't resolved?

Who are the key stakeholders who would benefit from the issue being resolved?

What executive support will be required to implement recommendations aimed at resolving the issue?

Have we tried to resolve the issue before? If so, why did we fail?

Who are the subject matter experts that will be required to develop solutions to the issue?

What are the logistical requirements to support the next phase of ACT, the ACT Business Meeting?

Phase 2, The ACT Business Meeting Phase, is a 3 to 5 day session where anywhere from 30 to 100 participants typically divided into 3 to 5 subteams work on parallel paths to resolve the major components of the business issue. At the end of the session, each team presents their top recommendations (i.e., the ones with the greatest impact that are do-able within 90 days) to a panel of decision makers who make on-the-spot decisions to either conceptually support or reject the team's suggestions. The decision panel is typically made up of the executive sponsor and any key stakeholder executives or managers whose support is anticipated to be critical to implementing changes aimed at the specific business issue. The approved recommendations are then carried forward and executed by the teams as part of the third phase of the ACT engagement.

Phase 3, The Execution Phase, is where the approved recommendations get combined into a single project plan, and execution is tracked through a series of formal 30-day checkpoint reviews with the executive sponsor, the ACT Lead Consultant, the ACT Coordinator and Project Manager, and key business meeting participants (team champions, decision makers, team experts, etc.). At the end of the 90 days, all Business Meeting participants are invited to participate in the 90 day celebration review with the executive sponsors. At this point, key improvements, benefits, and learnings are captured and the sustaining project elements should be integrated into the normal operations of the participating business units. The process of ACT is shown in Fig. 13.2.

University Staffing adopted the principles of ACT and applied these to the business issues associated with improving the Co-op and Internship Program. During the preparation phase, the challenge, goals, executive decision makers, and four teams were selected. The location and dates were established and consisted of a

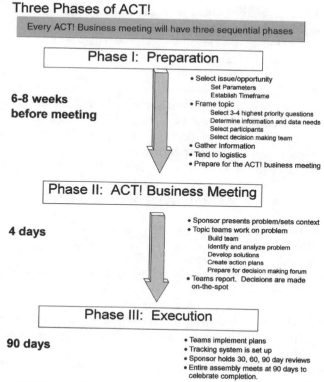

FIG. 13.2.   ACT Process Flow.

3-day business meeting. Roles and responsibilities were determined. The following section contains the results of the scoping phase:

Challenge: How do we reinvent our co-op and intern programs so they are clearly recognized inside and outside of IBM as best of class?

Goals:
- Improve conversion rate from Co-op and Intern to regular hire.
- Better facilitate exchange of global talent.
- Through student employment programs, advance IBM's image on campus as employer of choice for regular hire.
- Improve execution process from point of attraction to point of regular hire.

Decision makers:
- Vice President, Global Staffing
- Director, University Relations and Recruiting
- Controller, Human Resources

- General Manager, IBM Microelectronics Division
- Director, Global Employee Compensation
- Director of Human Resources, West Marketplace
- Vice President, Talent

Boundary Conditions (what's in—what's out):
- Recommendations must be within the approval ability of the decision makers.
- Recommendations must be implementable within 90 days.
- Recommendations should focus on improving IBM's image on campus and should link to the new image campaign.
- Increasing compensation is not the only answer.

TEAM 1: ATTRACTION AND SELECTION

Challenge: How do we attract and select the highest quality of students so they feel honored and privileged to begin a relationship with IBM?

Considerations:
- From where should we search for co-ops and interns? (Both traditional and alternative channels including international.)
- How can we provide opportunities for international coops?
- How do we expose students earlier in their university careers to IBM?
- How do we effectively incorporate the structured behavior-based interview into the IBM co-op selection process?
- How do we ensure the total engagement process communicates IBM's exclusivity and selectivity?
- How do we communicate to all IBM employees a new vision of co-ops and interns as a rich source of talent versus a short-term workforce solution?

Team 1 consisted of 11 members: 5 from human resources (1 from IBM Canada) and 6 from IBM business units including one executive. The major results of this team, which are illustrated in Fig. 13.3, placed focus on the campus recruiting of co-ops and interns. The success included a CD that contained the testimony of 10 students from across the U.S. A production company was hired to interview the students, prepare the footage, and ultimately create the CD. A total of 25,000 copies were ordered and distributed throughout the U.S. at various campus and recruiting events. Another outcome of this team was the design of the Campus Ambassador Program that utilizes former co-ops and interns as campus assistants for the National Recruiting Organization. For the schools identified by University Staffing, active co-ops and interns are invited to apply for the positions in June of each year. By August, a team of students is selected to represent IBM during each semester. This team, generally one student per school, provides IBM presence on campus with and without the extended recruiting team. They are equipped with IBM apparel and other recruiting collateral. They provide applicants and students with offers for em-

TEAM 1 Recommendations and Outcomes: Attraction and Selection

Create Image on Campus which attracts and excites co-ops and interns

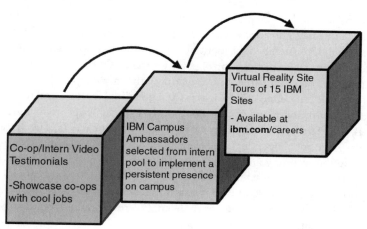

FIG. 13.3.   ACT Results Team 1.

ployment information about IBM. The other lasting contribution of this team was the creation of the IBM Virtual Tour. This picture tour of large IBM locations in the U.S. and Canada was developed by two interns hired for the summer. With the direction of a project manager, the Virtual Tour became a reality and permanent element on the IBM University recruiting web site. The ability for students to view some buildings and surrounding locations prior to moving to a new city for their work assignment was intended to familiarize them with IBM prior to their arrival.

TEAM 2: JOB QUALITY AND ASSIGNMENT

Challenge: How do we provide a rewarding job assignment experience to all our co-ops?

Considerations:

- How should we define job quality?
- How do we more effectively match skills, desires, and capabilities of applicants against job requirements?
- Do we need a tool kit to guide managers? If so, what should be in it?
- What role should mentoring play in enhancing the overall assignment experience?
- How do we foster recognition for work done by co-ops during assignment?
- How do we ensure the manager is ready to immediately engage co-ops into their assignments?

- How do you train, motivate, and monitor managers on the quality of job assignments?

Team 2 consisted of three employees from human resources and eight employees from business units including one executive. The major contributions of this team, as indicated in Fig 13.4, included the identification of the business unit technical resources program managers as the control point for the quality of co-op and intern positions; a better communication plan concerning the importance of the student program to provide a pipeline of candidates for regular hire; and several forms for use by both students and managers. Samples of these documents are included in Appendix B, The Attributes of a Quality Co-op Position; Appendix C, The Student Development Plan; and Appendix D, Student Feedback Form. It also defined a process to include the planning and projection of future co-op and intern positions, called requirements, during the regular talent planning cycle. This is the annual activity a division engages in to determine the skills and people needed to complete its business plan. The additional outcomes of Team 2 were centered around various pieces of communications and definition of roles.

TEAM 3: QUALITY OF THE EXPERIENCE

Challenge: How do we make sure that all aspects in addition to job assignment leave the students saying, "Wow, what a great experience"?

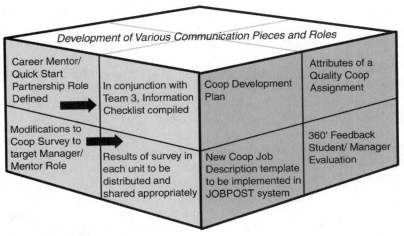

TEAM 2 Recommendations and Outcomes: Job Assignment Quality

Enhancements to the Quality of Coop/Intern Job Assignments

Development of Various Communication Pieces and Roles

| Career Mentor/ Quick Start Partnership Role Defined | In conjunction with Team 3, Information Checklist compiled | Coop Development Plan | Attributes of a Quality Coop Assignment |
| Modifications to Coop Survey to target Manager/ Mentor Role | Results of survey in each unit to be distributed and shared appropriately | New Coop Job Description template to be implemented in JOBPOST system | 360° Feedback Student/ Manager Evaluation |

FIG. 13.4.   ACT Results Team 2.

Considerations:
- What are the elements of a quality experience in addition to job content, and how do we implement them?
- How do we deploy a consistent hiring and orientation process?
- How can we provide an early, comprehensive view of IBM's culture, people, products, services, and opportunities?
- How do we facilitate the transition to work and the understanding of the IBM organization?
- How do we improve housing and transportation availability and acquisition?
- Would adding a community volunteer opportunity enhance the overall experience? If so, how should we structure it?

Team 3 consisted of six members from human resources and six from other business units. Their recommendations that were implemented, concerned improving the overall experience of the assignment. We called this the "WOW" experience. The goal was for each student to reflect on his/her time with IBM with a feeling of total appreciation of the experience. The specific outcomes included the implementation of a bimonthly newsletter on the Co-op and Intern intranet site; expansion of Summer Jam, an event developed by IBM Research that engages students and technical leaders in a brainstorming exercise, increased focus on housing options and relocation assistance for those students who need to move for their assignments; and a template, consisting of a menu of options, which will guide student activities in any location. The activities template focuses on three specific areas: educational, career, and social. In addition this team introduced the element of community service for students that provides them time during their work assignments to perform volunteer services. Figure 13.5 summarizes the contributions of this team.

TEAM 4: PLANNING AND EXECUTION

Challenge: How can Line organizations and Human Resources partner to improve the overall execution of the co-op program?
Considerations:
- How can we optimize a planning time table for business and staffing needs?
- How do we make the coop program more attractive to line managers?
- How do we improve line managers' ownership and accountability in the co-op and intern program?
- How can we ensure that every co-op and intern who should get a job offer receives one before they return to school?
- How can we ensure that the staffing support for co-op and intern program is appropriate for the organization being supported?

Team 4 members consisted of five members from human resources and five from business units. Their approved changes focus on planning and execution of pro-

TEAM 3 Recommendations and Outcomes:
Quality of the Work Experience

*Provide meaningful activities and resources to students to enhance
the quality of their overall experience*

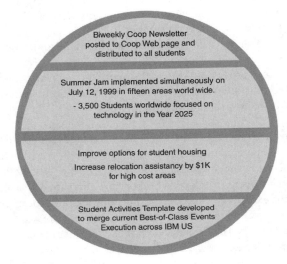

Biweekly Coop Newsletter
posted to Coop Web page and
distributed to all students

Summer Jam implemented simultaneously on
July 12, 1999 in fifteen areas world wide.

- 3,500 Students worldwide focused on
technology in the Year 2025

Improve options for student housing

Increase relocation assistancy by $1K
for high cost areas

Student Activities Template developed
to merge current Best-of-Class Events
Execution across IBM US

FIG. 13.5.   ACT Results Team 3.

cesses within the co-op operations department, including the establishment of a new position for a person to perform measurement tracking; development and use of checklists to help managers through the hire process; and the design and support of the Master Co-op Database. The database was discussed earlier in this chapter. See Fig. 13.6 which illustrates the key features of Team 4 outcomes.

The 3-day business meeting was held in February 1999 during which approximately 50 attendees participated. Day 1 consisted of introductions, overview of objectives and format, co-op and intern program details and questions (background), ACT Team assignments, and Team Working Sessions. Setting the environment and providing the participants with a snapshot of the current program was critical to engaging them into the process and to take the program forward. Samples used to demonstrate the current posture included the 1999 Student Satisfaction Survey, results of the IBM Team Talent student program benchmarking initiative and various reports from internal data.

Day 2 consisted entirely of Team Working Sessions. Day 3 consisted of one-half-day working session and the concluding event of presentations of recommendations to the decision makers. The recommendations that were approved by the decision makers are organized below by teams. The final chart, Fig. 13.7, summarizes most of the major changes and successes from the Co-op ACT Session.

TEAM 4 Recommendations and Outcomes:
Execution and Planning

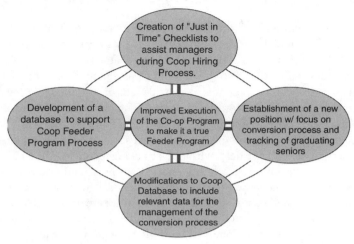

Creation of "Just in Time" Checklists to assist managers during Coop Hiring Process.

Development of a database to support Coop Feeder Program Process

Improved Execution of the Co-op Program to make it a true Feeder Program

Establishment of a new position w/ focus on conversion process and tracking of graduating seniors

Modifications to Coop Database to include relevant data for the management of the conversion process

FIG. 13.6.   ACT Results Team 4.

Overall Team Recommendation and Outcome:
Development of a Manager Toolkit Communication Package to consist of Documentation resulting from Co-op ACT

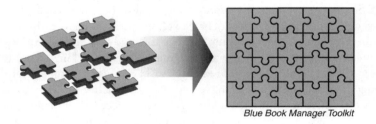

Blue Book Manager Toolkit

Components of the Manager Toolkit include:

- Attributes of a Great Coop Job Assignment
- Campus Ambassador Programs
- Student Development Plan
- Student Satisfaction Survey
- Activities Template
- Housing options improvements

- Mentor Program
- Summer Jam
- "Just in Time" Checklists
- Role of TRPMs
- National Newsletter, Web site Enhancements
- International Co-op Program

FIG. 13.7.   Summary of ACT Documentation.

IMPACT OF THE CO-OP ACT SESSION ON THE IBM COOPERATIVE EDUCATION AND INTERNSHIP PROGRAM

Three years have passed since the conclusion of the Co-op ACT session. The spirit still remains. Probably the most significant single result was the recommendation from Team 4 for the creation of the Co-op Master Database and the establishment of a new position within the Co-op Operations Department. This Lotus Notes database, which just reached its potential in Year 2001, meets the mark for providing detailed tracking capabilities for the program. The database is a repository of information from both of the original data sources used for measurement purposes, Resumix and CERIS, and combines the data to create an individual tracking record for each active student. The fields within the tracking record are then selected and organized so that specific pieces of information are presented at a glance. These data views are now customized to meet various needs. The national co-op operations team controls and administers the database. Data are organized and exported via spread sheets to form reports. Site co-op recruiters can view just the students located in their territories; the national recruiting organization can view students who attend the schools where they recruit; the divisional leadership team can view data specific to their business units and university staffing can view the Project Conversion candidate pool who are within 1 year of graduation and available for offers for regular hire. Additional functionality was imbedded to include creating e-mail distribution lists for the managers of the students; the capability to collect and store current student resumes through a resume builder tool; the distribution and collection of Student Performance Evaluations and the distribution and collection of the managers' Next Step Assessment. The Next Step Assessment (NSA) is an instrument used to identify the relationship between IBM and the student in respect to future hire. As students end their work assignments, their tracking record remains intact in the database but categorized as INACTIVE. When a student returns for subsequent work terms, the tracking record changes to active status during the hiring process. There are only a few additional needed pieces of information not currently available in this tool, but plans for future upgrades to the database will continue to enhance its utility and power.

Other areas identified from the Co-op ACT session live on. Recruiting on campus includes much greater focus on identification and attraction of cooperative education and internship students; the Virtual Tour is accessible from the IBM web site university page (http://www.ibm.com/careers) and will receive updates and enhancements; the International Student program, although small and controlled, continues to receive attention and improvements; the Campus Ambassador program is extremely successful as former co-ops and interns are selected each recruiting season to assist the National Recruiting Program managers with activities on campus. Ideas submitted through Team 2 are solidly imbedded in the IBM student program. Yearly talent planning includes the projection for the number of co-ops and interns needed during the impending recruiting season; the student development plan, student feedback form, information check lists, and attributes of a quality co-op assignment are regularly utilized. From Team 3, the Activities Template guides the Co-op and Intern Recruiters annually in their planning and execution of the events scheduled throughout the country throughout the year. The Manager's Toolkit is reviewed, revised, and distributed as needed; student housing continues to receive focus leading to the establishment of a dynamic web site containing site specific rental information, which is accessible to students after acceptance of the IBM job offer; the Co-op Connection Newsletter is published internally 15 times per year featuring articles about students and general informational topics.

Decision Point: Has the IBM Co-op and Internship Program become a high-performance culture and reached best of class?

Many indicators are available today that point to success. The ability to contain data via the Master Co-op Database truly elevated the overall performance of the operation. We clearly can identify who is eligible for an offer to convert to regular employment among students who literally come and go. Manager training sessions and consistent communications to both managers and students have improved the overall image of the program. But much more remains to be done.

CONTINUOUS IMPROVEMENTS

The IBM Cooperative Education and Internship program has many more attributes and practices than were included in this chapter. The Extreme Blue program is an example of innovative actions taken within the program to attract top talent.

EXTREME BLUE™: START SOMETHING BIG

A subset of the IBM Cooperative Education and Internship program was implemented in Summer 1999 when IBM launched the Extreme Blue summer internship experience at the IBM Lotus labs in Cambridge, Massachusetts. The program was spearheaded by John Patrick, Vice President, Internet Technology, under the leadership of Irving Wladawsky-Berger, Vice President, Technology and Strategy and the General Manager of the Internet Division at IBM. The Extreme Blue program is a big idea that started small, originally recruiting just 25 top computer science and engineering students to work as summer interns on significant development projects. The main goal for Extreme Blue was simple: expose a group of the finest students in their field to the best that IBM has to offer. It was originally targeted at attracting and retaining top college sophomores and juniors from leading computer science and engineering programs across the country. In the wake of the dot com boom, IBM identified that attracting top technical talent must be a top priority.

This first group of students joined IBM and helped IBM achieve some significant successes, including development of code that IBM integrated into the web site built for the Sydney Olympic Games. The program proves there is no better place to work by showing the students that they will have an immediate impact on the company, have access to world-class resources, work in an unbeatable professional environment, and be encouraged to continually further their education and improve technical vitality. IBM can build on this introduction into a long-term relationship. This improves IBM's ability to employ these individuals.

Since 1999, IBM has expanded its Extreme Blue recruiting efforts to attract both technical and MBA students. Crossfunctional teams strengthen IBM's ability to attract and retain top developers and entrepreneurs while incubating leading-edge technology projects. Although the dot com craze has faded, IBM recognizes that smart, talented individuals will always have interesting options in terms of employment, and IBM will not take their eye off the ball in the war for talent. By offering candidates a chance to conceive and develop the technology, business plan, and go-to-market strategy for an emerging technology project, the Extreme Blue program represents a unique opportunity for IBM to recruit top business and technical students who might otherwise not consider employment in IBM.

In 2002, almost 150 students joined the Extreme Blue program to tackle challenging development and business projects. These business and technical students worked together and created interdisciplinary teams: While the development interns wrote the code, the MBA worked on the business case and market analysis for the project assigned to the team. Extreme Blue program expanded to 11 IBM labs worldwide including Cambridge, Massachusetts; Austin, Texas; Almaden, California; Raleigh, North Carolina; Böblingen, Germany; Haifa Lab, Israel; Hursley Lab, England; Zurich, Switzerland; Uithoorn Lab, Netherlands; LaGaude, France; and Bejing, China.

NEXT STEPS

As the development and success of the Extreme Blue program indicates, the IBM Cooperative Education and Internship program will continue to make changes and improvements on its journey to best of class and to a higher performance level. Providing statistical data that validates the results since the implementation of the ACT session and other program improvements is not permissible due to the proprietary nature of IBM 's information. However, the results of the student satisfaction survey since its inception of 1996, have only indicated modest changes since 1998. The margin generally runs plus or minus two points in either direction in all categories except two. The areas that have shown significant improvement are Question 12, which asks about the information provided to the student by the staffing representative prior to hire, and Question 15 that asks if the student would consider IBM for regular, full-time employment. We believe changes in the prehire processes have contributed directly to an increase in satisfaction for Question 12. We can only speculate that the 15 to 17 point increase in the final question, that asks if the student will consider regular employment, is attributed to a better perception of the opportunities within the company.

In Spring 2002, IBM launched a U.S.-wide initiative that established new attributes of its student program. The name of the program was officially changed to Employment Pathways for Interns and Co-ops (EPIC). Along with the name change, which established a unique identity, were some program changes. One feature was a set of criteria for the selection of students. This criterion will be a guideline for line managers when considering students for work assignments. Also more emphasis was placed on choosing students from our investment schools. These are the colleges and universities that IBM deems best for our recruiting efforts and includes emphasis on diversity as well as academic standards. The final change was the centralization of the co-op/intern hiring process into the Raleigh, North Carolina University Staffing operation. The offer and hiring will now be completed for the full national program from a single office. The role of the staffing personnel residing in the site locations will include the execution of the activities for the students and continuing in the role of focal point for the students while active employees.

Time will tell if the centralized model is the best choice, but the pilot of this staffing change that took place for about 5 months, indicated favorable results and benefits. This centralization of co-op and intern hiring has allowed us to drive consistency into many parts of our student hiring process, which before operated differently. Consistent processes and tighter controls enable us to be in compliance with business controls and audit requirements. In addition, the centralization has forced all staffing representatives to become knowledgeable in both regular university and co-op hiring programs, giving us far greater flexibility to adjust internal resources in reaction to hiring programs. Separate from these benefits, we can leverage the new model to yield a stronger conversion outcome. The staffing representatives are more acquainted with the eligible students and work diligently with the management team to drive offers for regular hire.

Quantitative results are not yet available for the overall program evaluation. Since the transition to a national model, one student satisfaction survey has been completed (July 2002). The results demonstrated improvement in 8 out of 15 questions. Overall satisfaction remained consistent. The improved areas are:

Work challenge: +2%   Manager communications: +1%
Interview match job: +4%   Staffing information: +6%
Training: +2%   Compared to other companies: +6%
Manager Guidance: +1%   Would consider regular employment: +16%

The overall accept rate of co-op students converting to regular university hire has improved in 2002 to 88% from 84% in 2001. These results may be attributed to changes in practice, but could also be a by-product of the current economy and change in job market. There has been steady improvement in this accept rate over the past 3 years.

Reports and data will provide the indicators of success along with the opinions of the students, our success on campus and our ability to convert student employees to regular employment. The measurements and tools combined with successful conversion of these student employees to regular employees may indicate success, but the following student comments bring true meaning to the overall accomplishments.

STUDENT COMMENTS

The following comments are representative of student comments that indicate the value received by gaining knowledge through an internship or cooperative education assignment:

"The experience that I am having at IBM is one that you will never find in a college class room. I have access to so much information, get to use some of the latest e-commerce technology, and work with friendly and helpful co-workers. The best thing of all is that I am getting paid."

"The experience has been wonderful so far. The opportunity for hands on work and responsibility has been great."

"This is my third summer at IBM and the skills I have learned have prepared me for the transition from academic to work environment. In addition, the lessons I have learned are aligned with those taught to me in school."

"Working a 40-hour week was a large adjustment from my usual college routine life. It took me awhile to get to know my team members. Not because they lack social skills, but due to the nature of the project I am on. A government project whose extended deadline for go-live is August 10th. My team members were very busy and had a lot of stress. I learned a lot about how a corporate office works, how a matrixed organization as a corporation works and how to behave in the work place. I feel I have learned more socially than technically."

"I have really enjoyed my time here at IBM. It was indeed productive and I have had the opportunity to learn quite a lot and to see my work grow into a project of significance for my group (something that I can be proud of and that would carry on my coop legacy when I'm gone :-)). Having worked at several other corporations and reflecting on my summers there and comparing all of the above with my summer with IBM, I must say my time here as been memorable and it has indeed surpassed all my other experiences (for one, this was the first summer experience that my manager was able to keep me busy! And not just busy with meaningless work). With that said, I will definitely keep IBM in mind when I am deciding where my next summer internship and most importantly, my permanent placement, may be. Thank You."

Summary:
- IBM is and has been a long-time supporter of cooperative education and experiential training.
- The success of the IBM Cooperative Education and Internship program and subsequent conversion of these students to regular hire is critical to the success of the university hiring program.
- Management of information concerning the student programs provides key indicators of success.
- Using a formalized, facilitated action plan for implementing process improvements is a powerful change accelerator.
- Continuous focus on the needs of the business and the needs of the student employees will drive the program practices to higher levels of performance.

ANNOTATED BIBLIOGRAPHY

Scott, M. E. (1999). *Internship program best practices revisited: Undergraduate students benchmark quality and effectiveness: Report of findings.* West Hartford, CT: Scott Resource Group. This report presents the findings of a benchmark study by the Scott Resource group on behalf of a consortium of companies. This information could be useful to any employer who is interested in understanding current campus trends and mind sets of today's students about the job market.

Co-op Employer's Forum. (1991, January). *Features of a quality employer's co-op program.* Retrieved March 10, 2003, from Accreditation Council of Cooperative Education (ACCE) web site: http://www.co-opaccreditation.org/employer_quality.html

Hill, R. L. M. (1996). *Maximizing your co-op investment.* Retrieved March 10, 2003, from Accreditation Council of Cooperative Education (ACCE) web site: http://www.co-opaccreditation.org/employer_investment.html

These are two articles of special interest from the web site for the Accreditation Council of Cooperative Education. I recommend the Council's web site because it contains general descriptions of cooperative education components and therefore is a very useful guide for employers.

REFERENCES

IBM. DB2, and Extreme Blue are trademarks of International Business Machines Corporation in the United States, other countries or both.

Resumix® is a registered product of HotJobs Software.

IBM Chairman's Forum: Team talent—Student Programs Best Practices Survey Results, September 1998.

IBM Benchmarking Study, "Housing and Vacation Plans for Co-ops and Interns," April 12, 2001.

Appendix A:
Student Satisfaction Survey Questions

Questions 1–14 have the following 6 answer choices:
Very Satisfied
Satisfied
Neither Satisfied or Dissatisfied
Dissatisfied
Very Dissatisfied
Not Applicable

1. Overall, how satisfied are you with your work experience in IBM?
2. How satisfied are you with your job and the kind of work you do?
3. How satisfied are you with the challenge of the work assignment?
4. How satisfied are you with how well the job description provided during your interview with management actually matched your job responsibilities (telephone interview or campus interview)?
5. How satisfied are you with the amount of training provided?
6. How satisfied are you in knowing what is expected from you?
7. How satisfied are you with the guidance given by your mentor and manager?
8. How satisfied are you with the communication between you and your manager?
9. How satisfied are you with the resources made available to assist you in learning more about IBM?
10. How satisfied are you with the sharing of information/knowledge among your team/work group?
11. How satisfied are you with the information provided by your Human Resource Co-op/Intern Recruiter prior to your first day of employment (i.e. offer letter, directions, first-day start instructions, etc.)?
12. How satisfied are you with the co-op/intern program in achieving its purpose (i.e., expanding your classroom knowledge through practical work experience in a business environment)?
13. How satisfied are you with IBM's co-op/summer/intern program compared to other companies you have experienced?
14. Would you consider IBM for regular employment?
    Yes
    No

Please enter any general comments you have concerning the IBM Co-op, Summer Student and Intern programs.

Appendix B

ATTRIBUTES OF GREAT CO-OP JOB

Sense of Worth

- Job Makes Business/Technical Contribution
- Clear Expectations Defined
- Ownership to Accomplish Something
- Co-op Understands How Their Job Fits in Overall Project

Skills Development

- Assignment Tailored To Co-op Skills & Career Interest
- Career Mentorship
- Apply Skills During Work Experience
- Leave Job With Skills They Didn't Have At Job Start
- Presentations To Management
- Opportunity to Demonstrate Leadership

Contributing in a Team Environment

- Has The Tools To Perform Assignment Efficiently And Effectively
- Rapid Assimilation Into Project Team
- Opportunity To Learn Teaming Skills
- Feel Valued As Part of Team By Peers, Mentor & Manager

Job Experience Enrichment

- Interactions With Managers & Technical/Business Community
- Exposed To Multiple Parts Of The Business
- Opportunities To Be Creative, And/Or Work Outside The Box

Technical Co-op Networking

- Exchange Forums To Share Work Experiences
- "Poster Session" For Out-Of-Box Problem Solving
- Co-op Team To Address A Focused Business Problem

Developmental Feedback

- On-Going Interaction & Coaching By Mentor
- Bi-Directional Assessment With Management

- Career Development

Future Relationship

- Continued Employment Decision
- Outline Next Work Experience
- Campus Advocate

Appendix C

IBM Student Employee Development Plan

Instructions: Jointly determine with input from your student, the key developmental items/activities. How will those items be measured? What resources are needed to accomplish goals, and what is the time frame for completion?

Activity Specific activities that relate to job description	Responsibility Measurable activities that demonstrate understanding	Resources Needed Specific people/actions that will help complete activity	Time Frame Planned completion dates for activities	Results Actual results and accomplishments

Manager/Mentor's Name	Job Title	Employee's Name	Job Title
Manager/Mentor's Signature	Date	Employee's Signature	Date

Appendix D

STUDENT FEEDBACK—IBM Cooperative Education and Intern Program

Students, Managers and Mentors:

This form has been prepared to provide topics of discussion among students, mentors and managers. It is recommended that time be allocated at the end of the student work assignment to review and reflect on the overall experience.

Students, you should review these items in advance and be prepared to offer your candid opinions to your mentor and/or manager. This provides the leadership team the opportunity to receive an assessment of your work assignment. Using the scale below, place a rating in the box next to each item. This will help you express your feelings during your meeting with your manager and/or mentor. It is expected that some of the items for discussion may not have been part of every internship/co-op assignment. Choose "Not Applicable" for these points.

Evaluation Rating: 5 Strongly Agree
4 Agree
3 No Opinion
2 Disagree
1 Strongly Disagree
0 Not Applicable

I. The Internship/Co-op assignment provided me with:	Rating
opportunities to use academic skills	
opportunities to use work-related skills	
opportunities to perform progressively more challenging tasks/assignments	
variety of assignments	

II. During my Internship/Co-op assignment:	Rating
management's expectations were adequately explained to me	
work was checked for accuracy on a regular basis	
work was checked for completeness on a regular basis	
I had frequent discussions with my manager/mentor/team regarding my performance	
I received timely assistance from my manager/mentor/team leader with a particular problem or task	
I freely shared my ideas with management.	
I received adequate orientation to the organization and to my specific work environment	

I received formal training	
I received informal training	
I received relevant training	
I developed specialized knowledge/skills through practical experience	
I developed my oral presentation skills	
I developed my written presentation skills	

III. *The Internship/Co-op assignment provided me the opportunity to:*	*Rating*
develop specialized knowledge/skills	
develop and learn new problem solving techniques	
develop my analytical skills	
enhance my computer skills	
work with new software programs	
work with new hardware	
gain experience relating to people	
gain insights into the behavior of a large organization	
recognize ethical principles (who will say "no" to this?)	
practice ethical principles	

IV. *My internship experience:*	*Rating*
has helped me formulate my career objectives	
has helped me discover new areas of interest	
met my expectations.	

Overall evaluation of work assignment   _____   Outstanding
                                                                      Very Good
                                                                      Satisfactory
                                                                      Marginal
                                                                      Unsatisfactory

Briefly describe what was the GREATEST BENEFIT OF THIS WORK ASSIGN-MENT TO YOU? (personal development, skills/knowledge development)

WHAT ADVICE WOULD YOU GIVE TO A FUTURE COOP/INTERN WITH IBM?

Additional Comments:

14

Dissemination of Research to Reform Practice: Fishing (and Lawyering) to Learn

Brook K. Baker
Northeastern University

Key questions addressed in this chapter:

☞ How can real-life examples become a metaphor for learning?

☞ How do students evaluate their co-ops as learning experiences, and which variables impact on the quality of the learning experience?

☞ What theory or theories help explain our empirical findings, and how might that theory be framed to communicate convincingly with skeptical educators?

☞ Which audiences were we most interested in reaching, and what methods of dissemination were most appropriate for reaching those intended audiences?

☞ What specific pedagogical reforms were implicit in our findings, and in our theory of ecological learning for clinicians, co-op supervisors, and classroom teachers?

FINDING A METAPHOR: FISHING TO LEARN

Decision Point: How do you make theory come alive?
There is something inherently contradictory about articulating a new, lengthy, and abstract theory of ecological learning in language that does not

include real life examples from everyday life. The theory of ecological learning recognized that practice-based learning is ubiquitous and that it starts early in life. Thus, I wanted a metaphor that could join experience to abstraction. One of my early mentors told me that every successful piece of writing has to have a "hook." By word association, if for no other reason, I have found fishing-to-learn to be a useful metaphor for the ubiquitous process of ecological learning (Baker, 1999).

One of my earliest memories of fishing is casting for bass with my father and twin brother in the spring of 1954 on a big, artificial lake in Kentucky. I got to cast my new fishing lure, a green plug that looked a little bit like a fish, except it had all these hooks attached. There are lots of things that can go wrong when you are casting. Not only can you catch the hooks in trees, your own pants, and your brother's hat, but you can get the dreaded backlash. Getting a backlash was when I first discovered that fishing with us was not an unrelieved pleasure for my father. If the spool on your casting rod spins faster than the line is moving, chaos—like a pile of spaghetti—would appear in your casting reel. My inexpert fingers could not possibly unravel the mess, so Dad would patiently—and not so patiently—pull out the knots hoping that Gary didn't get a backlash on his next cast. My father tried to steady our boyish enthusiasm for heaving our plugs as fast and far as we could so that he too could fish. As his hand cradled mine, he put his thumb on top of mine to slow the speed of the spool, thus gentling my wild cast. The plug plopped into the water 3 feet from the sunken tree where the big one was waiting.

I don't fish much any more, but I do spend a lot of time on the beach watching other people fish, in particular my friend Red, who has learned next to the master, our friend Sully. When I first met Red, he was a beach husband who brought his young sons to the beach almost every day. Sully was an avid fisher, who had what I would call total commitment. He fished lakes and streams in the spring and fall; he fished through holes in frozen lakes in the winter; and he was the best surf caster on Plum Island all summer long. Sully would catch fish in multiple environments with varying equipment when everyone else was just drowning worms. Over time, Red became intrigued with Sully's ways and bought his first surf-casting pole. He set up shop along side Sully, watched how Sully tied his knots, baited his hook, and cast his line. He then fished hour after hour, day after day, week after week, with Sully on the weekend and vacations, but by himself the rest of the week. When fishing side by side, every now and then, Sully would give Red a little advice: "keep the tip up," or "want to try my new plug?" Over time, Sully showed Red everything, from where to put his sand spike to how to check his line for frays. But he did so within the rhythm of his own fishing.

Finally, after two seasons, I noticed that Red and Sully were fishing shoulder-to-shoulder, nearly equally accomplished. Sully usually cast a little farther and caught a couple more fish, but they now traded ideas, quietly, even by gesture. Red's transformation intrigued me so much that I asked him how he thought he learned to fish and more particularly how much Sully had "taught" him. At first Red looked puzzled, so I told him I was writing a law review article. Then, Red looked even more puzzled, but he grinned and shrugged his shoulders. "Watching, showing, trying, adapting … I don't know. I guess 80% was practice and 20% was Sully."

I'm not sure I've learned any life lessons from fishing (other than patience and don't run out of worms), but I do think that the way Red and I learned to fish by fishing is emblematic of the vast bulk of what I call ecological learning. We learned in the real world, in complex, interdependent, and changing environments (ecologies) where different contexts, conditions, and equipment required subtly different strategies and skills. We learned through the more expert guidance of accomplished fishing practitioners who welcomed us to their practice—not to interrupt their fishing but to join it. We were "instructed" not by long expositions on the theory of tides, fish, and bait but through trial and error where we watched our mentors assiduously and cast our hooks to the sea. Gradually, we could discern patterns in fishing, both from our own efforts and those of our guides. Those patterns became the lore of the beach, when a Northeaster brought in fish and when the blues were going to arrive. This fishing had authenticity and functionality—we would eat what we caught or return the fish for another day. In this sense, our fishing was valued—I still remember with pride my family eating the biggest bass any of us ever caught from that lucky cast long ago in Kentucky. These still exciting memories of fishing have become my metaphor for learning.

In this chapter, I describe an intellectual quest that initially pursued assessment and understanding of our long-standing co-op program at Northeastern University School of Law but that ultimately became a pedagogical crusade seeking broader reform in legal education (Givelber, Baker, McDevitt, & Miliano, 1995). Although multiple dilemmas arose during our research (e.g., how to analyze empirical data to extract its most salient lessons and how to synthesize myriad theoretical traditions, legal and nonlegal), this chapter focuses primarily on two interrelated conundrums: how to identify our key audiences and disseminate our findings to them and how to offer pedagogical reforms that were both meaningful for our own practice and that might have broader application in clinical legal education in particular and in legal education more broadly.

After describing the co-op program at Northeastern in the next section, in the third section I report a quantitative research project and theoretical investigation that attempted to make sense of what experience had taught us—namely that our co-op program was highly effective in structuring a complementary learning environment where students learned lawyering skills and values at the same time they learned how to manipulate legal doctrine in law school. Finally, in the fourth section I describe our efforts to disseminate our findings in a series of articles and our suggested reforms for legal education.

Our study began by analyzing students' Co-op Quality Questionnaires to establish whether our students found co-op to be a valuable learning experience and to uncover factors correlating positively or negatively with students' self-assessment of that learning. This empirical investigation soon became wedded to the intellectual task of trying to synthesize several theoretical traditions that directly or indirectly addressed practice-based learning. One body of familiar research was clinical scholarship written by law faculty who supervise students while providing direct representation to low-income clients. This literature described a contextualist (situated in an actual practice) and experiential (learning-by-doing) pedagogy that was highly dependent on high quality supervision, articulated theories of practice, and mandatory self-reflection (Barry, 1995; Hoffman, 1982, 1986; Kreiling, 1981; Report of the Committee on the Future of the In-House Clinic, [In-House Clinic Report], 1992; Shalleck, 1993–1994; Stark, Bauer, & Papillo, 1993; Tarr, 1990). That literature valued clinically supervised live-client clinics but disparaged less tightly supervised experiences of students working in externships with nonfaculty practitioners (American Bar Association Section of Legal Education and Admission to the Bar, 1992 [ABA MacCrate Report]; Laser, 1994; Motley, 1989; Rose, 1987; Stickgold, 1989) although there were a few defenders (Kotkin, 1989; Maher, 1990; Meltsner, Rowan, & Givelber, 1989). By implication, this literature was even more critical of full-time co-ops, where there was no role for a contemporaneous classroom component and where the student was left to learn solely under the tutelage of practitioners.

Nonetheless, we sensed that we had potential allies among legal clinicians who valued placing students in lawyering roles where they could be closely supervised while engaging in direct client representation. When reviewing the clinical literature, however, we discovered that it had adopted early theories of adult learning (Bloch, 1982) and learning cycles (Kotkin, 1989; Kreiling, 1981), and Schön's (1987) theory on reflective practicums (Laser, 1994), but that clinicians had not addressed more recent theories of situated and participatory learning (Courtney, 1992; Gardner, 1991; Lave, 1988; Lave & Wenger, 1991; Merriam & Caffarella, 1991; Rogoff, 1990); nor had it addressed an emerging field of contextualist cognitive science (Bruner, 1990; Gillespie, 1993; Light & Butterworth, 1993; Varela, Thompson, & Rosch, 1991). We reacted to educator-centric theories of learning latent in clinical scholarship and patent in the broader legal academy and wanted to challenge the accepted wisdom about how students learn in and through practice. To convince law professors in general, and clinicians in particular, that their school-centered assumptions were suspect, we knew we would have to expose them not only to a compelling empirical study but to a broader body of cross-disciplinary research and theory with which they were unfamiliar. Thus, our research dilemmas were three-fold: First, we had to design a high-quality study in which startling results had a compelling theoretical basis; second, we had to figure out how to identify and reach a broad and skeptical audience; and third, we had to figure out how to propose concrete practice-based reforms in legal education and clinical practice.

SETTING—COOPERATIVE LEGAL EDUCATION PROGRAM AT NORTHEASTERN UNIVERSITY SCHOOL OF LAW

If any law school were well positioned to do a study of practice-based learning and to compare it with school-based learning, Northeastern (NU), the nation's premiere public interest and only co-op law school, was that school. By 1991 when our research began, we had more than 20 years of experience as the most intensively practice-based law school in the country. Despite that long history, we had never undertaken a serious study of co-op. Accordingly, the then Dean Daniel Givelber and I, with the assistance of two social science researchers, started an investigation on both a theoretical and empirical basis. To understand the implications of our study, it is important to understand the nature of our program.

Upon successful completion of 9 months of academic studies that comprise a typical first year, students at NU School of Law are divided into two sections, alternating full-time work and academic quarters throughout the remaining 24 months of the second and third years. Students on co-op work for a variety of legal employers including large and small private firms, public defender and legal assistance organizations, federal and state judges and governmental agencies, corporate legal departments, consumer and special interest advocacy groups, and labor unions. Each student is encouraged to work in four different areas of law or types of legal employment in order to experience the diversity of opportunities, challenges, and satisfactions available to a practicing attorney. Students perform a variety of legal tasks, ranging from research and drafting of briefs and memoranda to assisting with trial preparation and representing clients under student practice rules. Each student's work performance is formally evaluated by a supervising attorney or attorneys, and the written evaluation becomes part of the student's permanent academic record (Alexander & Smith, 1988).

With very little direct law school oversight, but with some advanced preparation, administrative support, and law school debriefing, Northeastern's co-op program focuses supervisory and educational responsibility on the field supervisor and the student learner. This distinctive model of co-op supervision "contemplates an active interplay between the employer and the student with responsibility for supervision divided equally between them" (Alexander & Smith, 1988, p. 209). Students on co-op are encouraged to structure a supervisory relationship, to seek a variety of work in their interest areas, and to solicit guidance and feedback as needed, but the negotiation of these goals is left almost entirely to the student and the supervisor. The supervisor, in turn, should be available to give clear, appropriate assignments, including statements of key facts, client goals, and useful resources. In addition, the supervisor should clarify problems that arise and give expert guidance as needed.

Finally, the supervisor should give feedback, written and oral, to students about the adequacy of their performance.

Despite emphasizing student–supervisor interactions, the School of Law does not leave students completely on their own. The Co-op Office runs a first-year orientation program that includes a self-assessment workbook, a type-of-practice series, and an introduction to the supervisory process, feedback models, professional responsibility, and lawyering role issues. In addition, the first-year Legal Practice Program uses simulation pedagogy to teach basic competency in a range of real world skills. During co-op, there is no formal contact between the law school and the co-op supervisor or student except as initiated from the field. After such initiation, co-op professionals intervene to mediate problems and brainstorm solutions.

After a co-op ends, there are modest efforts to help students reflect on their work experiences and bring those experiences back to the classroom. When students return from their first co-op, they are required to attend a co-op residency program that asks a small group of students to debrief their experience, especially issues relating to supervision, the work performed, and the placement environment. Students are also required to complete a detailed Co-op Quality Questionnaire that evaluates the co-op as a learning experience. The vast bulk of student reflection and debriefing of co-op experiences, however, is undoubtedly ad hoc and informal—in the hallways, in social interactions with their classmates, and in upper level classrooms.

There are a number of distinctive features of the School of Law's co-op program that might affect students' practice-based learning. First, the institution is committed to the belief that students learn through work. Second, students work full-time, fully immersed in a practice setting, albeit only for 3 months at a time. Third, students have an opportunity to learn in four different lawyering contexts and to exercise a great deal of choice while doing so, not only with respect to type of practice, but the timing, sequence, and setting of their co-op experiences. Finally, our co-op program has been an excellent vehicle for promoting public interest work; 85% of our students satisfy our public interest requirement by performing at least one co-op in a public interest setting; thereafter, our graduates disproportionately enter public interest practice.

OUR STUDY: RESEARCH QUESTIONS, DATA, AND A NEW THEORY OF ECOLOGICAL LEARNING

Our Substantive Research Questions about the Impact of Cooperative Legal Education and Our Key Findings about Distinguishing Features of Good Versus Less Good Co-ops

In conducting our empirical study, we asked ourselves three big questions:

- First, what are the sources, and relative contributions, of practice-based versus school-based learning?

- Second, how do students rate co-op as an overall learning experience?
- Third, what factors correlate with a good versus less good learning experience?

We answered these questions in different ways drawing not only on our own data but on data provided by others.

Question 1: What Are the Relative Contributions of School-Based and Practice-Based Learning?

> **Decision Point: How to find data comparing what is learning in school versus on the job.**
>
> There was very little empirical research on relative sources of legal learning. We had no such data of our own and were reluctant to compose a new research instrument solely for this purpose. Fortunately, there were two previous empirical studies, although both required manipulation of existing data to weigh relative contributions of school-based and practice-based learning. One study was undertaken by Garth and Martin (1993) in their comprehensive survey of members of the Chicago and Missouri bars admitted within the past 5 years. There, respondents ranked the relative importance of 17 different legal skills for their actual day-to-day practice and also identified, from a list of 10 law school and nonlaw school sources, the sources that were most important in developing each identified skill. Although this study was limited by respondents' self-analysis of sources of learning, we decided to recalibrate the data to determine the relative weight of practice-based and school-based learning. Similarly, Zillman and Gregory (1986) had surveyed a large number of law graduates and law students in Utah asking whether they had clerked during law school and asking them to evaluate where, during law school, they had learned seven key legal skills.

Garth and Martin (1993) asked several hundred urban and rural respondents three questions about their sources of learning for important lawyering skills: (1) what was the "most important source of learning" for each skill;[1] (2) what skills did you learn "primarily in law school,"[2] and (3) what were the "three most important sources of learning" for each skill.[3] By tracking sources of learning and then totaling sources

---

[1]After adding up Garth and Martin's (1993) raw totals for each "most important source of learning" for each skill, we expressed that sum as a percentage of contribution to total learning of all the relevant skills. We then totaled school-based and practice-based learning.

[2]Another way of estimating the importance of school-based learning was to average data about skills "learned essentially through law school."

[3]Garth and Martin (1993) also asked their respondent to identify the "three most important sources of learning." After adding up the raw totals for each source of learning from Table 8 of their study, we expressed that sum as a percentage of contribution to total learning.

for all skills combined, we were able to reach a judgment about the relative importance of practice- and school-based learning. In sum, using Garth and Martin's
(1993) raw figures, we found in Tables 14.1, 14.2, and 14.3 that recent graduates estimated that practice-based sources of learning legal skills dramatically outweighed
school-based sources by a very significant margin (Givelber et al., 1995).

Garth and Martin's data confirmed earlier data from Zillman and Gregory (1986)
about the educational impact of law student employment during law school.[4] Zillman
and Gregory surveyed a large number of Utah graduates and their upper level student
body. Of the seven skills identified, law school was the primary source for only 22% of
the total learning whereas part-time legal work during school accounted for 34%.[5]

TABLE 14.1
Calculations Based on "Most Important Source" of Learning

Garth & Martin (1993)	Table 6 (Chicago Bar)	Table 7 (Missouri Bar)
#Repeat experience	30.8%	36.3%
#From colleagues	30.6%	18.4%
*General law school	21.7%	24.1%
#Law work during school	7.5%	5.1%
#Self-study	4.5%	9.1%
#Outside lawyers	1.0%	3.5%
*Simulations and clinics	1.4%	1.4%
*Moot court	.8%	.6%
*Law review	.6%	1.4%
#Continuing legal education	.4%	.5%

* Total law-school contribution	24.5%	27.5%
# Total practice-based contribution	75.5%	72.5%

TABLE 14.2
Calculations Based on Skills "Learned Essentially Through Law School"

	Chicago	Missouri
Law School	30%	33%
Nonlaw School	70%	67%

---

[4]The authors did not ask about the contribution of post-law school experience but rather about
the relative impact of practice-based and school-based learning during law school.

[5]As we did with the Garth and Martin (1993) data, we totaled the input of each source category
for all skills in Table 6 (p. 398) and stated the input for each source as a percentage of the total
learning.

TABLE 14.3

Calculations Based on "Three Most Important Sources of Learning"

School-Based Contribution		Practice-Based Contribution	
General law school	14.3%	Repeat experience	24.7%
Simulations and clinics	2.2%	From colleagues	23.7%
Moot court	1.4%	Law work during school	11.2%
Law review	1.2%	Self-study	7.3%
		Observing outside lawyers	7.0%
		Continuing legal education	1.7%
Total	19.1%	Total	81.9%

Question 2: How Do Students Rank Their NU Co-ops as Learning Experiences?

Decision Point: Could a questionnaire used to guide students' co-op choice reveal important data on co-op variables that impact learning? Early on in our research, we confronted the question of whether we wanted to design a new research instrument or whether we could rely on an existing source of data, the 10-page Co-op Quality Questionnaires that NU law students routinely fill out after each co-op. Unfortunately, the Co-op Quality Questionnaire had not been designed as a research instrument, but rather as a way for one generation of students to report to the next generation about the features of a co-op placement and about the student's subjective assessment of that particular placement. When deciding on where to apply for a co-op, students could review all of the Co-op Quality Questionnaires on file for a particular placement and decide whether the placement might appeal to them. Although the Questionnaire was not designed by a social scientist, lacked rigor in certain questions, and neglected what for us were important areas of potential inquiry, it did have the advantage that virtually all students filled them out and that they did so not for the purpose of advancing research but for the pragmatic purpose of informing peers.

We were also concerned that 10-point scale assessments of co-ops as learning experiences by students were relatively unstructured and subjective. However, we learned that there was almost no rigorous research on educational outcomes and that conducting double-blind outcome studies in legal education would verge on educational malpractice or institutional suicide. At the end of the day, given the vast wealth of information captured in the existing questionnaires, we decided to rely on data we coded from all questionnaires completed by the class of 1991.

The data for our analysis was derived from 532 questionnaires completed between 1989 and 1991 by 161 members of the Northeastern class graduating in 1991. The questionnaire required students to provide detailed demographic information and background descriptions of their law offices. Thereafter, students describe the work they performed, the match between their preparation and the work assigned, the quality and characteristics of the supervision they received, and their overall assessment of the co-op as a learning experience. Having confirmed the quantitative predominance of practice-based learning based on two previous studies, we now wanted to understand how students rated the quality of their co-op learning experiences.

In a nutshell, most students rated their co-ops extremely positively. According to our study (Givelber et al., 1995), when asked to evaluate their co-op as a learning experience on a scale of 1 to 10, more than one half (53.3%) ranked their experience as a 9 or 10, and 92% rated their experience as positively as 6 or higher. In terms of skills outcome, virtually all respondents (94.3%) reported that their skills had improved. Similarly, almost all of the students (96.9%) would recommend the job to others, three fourths (73.4%) without reservation. When rating the difficulty of their assignments, most students reported that the assigned work matched their ability, 85% reporting that the work assigned was always commensurate with their skills, whereas another 9.5% responding that this was sometimes, but not always, the case.[6] Finally, responding to a question about the adequacy of supervision, almost two thirds (64.2%) reported that the supervision they received was adequate. However, one out of five (21.6%) reported that the supervision was only *sometimes adequate*; the remaining 14.2% responded that the supervision was inadequate.

TABLE 14.4

Calculations Based on Primary Source of Learning, During Law School, for Seven Skills

Zillman & Gregory (1986)	
1. Clerkships (part-time work)	= 34%
2. Law School	= 22%
3. Cocurricular	= 13%
4. Clinical internship	= 3%
5. Nonlaw school sources	= 28%

---

[6]Most studies show that students learn best when asked to perform work within the outer limits of their general level of ability, within their "zone of proximal development." (Baker, 1994a, pp. 326–327; Rogoff, 1990). Of the 79 students who reported that the work was not commensurate with their abilities, 68 reported that the work was not sufficiently challenging. The 11 who reported that the work was too challenging cited both lack of subject matter expertise and lack of guidance.

Question 3: What Are the Determinants of a Good Co-op Learning Experience?

> **Decision Point: How do you reduce the number of variables to a manageable level for analysis?**
>
> The negative side of having a 10-page survey document is that we had potentially hundreds of variables to code and correlate. For example, should we investigate the location of the co-op or the presence of a single supervisor? Alternatively, because we didn't have a separate category on variety of work, how should we go about investigating whether being given a range of tasks was positively or negatively correlated with learning? To answer these questions, we had multiple team meetings during which we brainstormed factors in a co-op experience that might make a difference. Some were drawn from theoretical perspectives, but others arose from intuition and anecdotal evidence. By the end, out of dozens of items encoded from each questionnaire, we had identified 25 factors for our multiple-regression analysis falling roughly into three categories: personal demographics and characteristics of the placement, nature and quality of the work, and features of supervision. We then correlated these 25 factors against the students' Scale 1 to 10, quality-of-learning assessment.

To examine the impact of 25 different factors upon the students' evaluation of their co-op as a learning experience, we employed a multivariate regression analysis (Givelber et al., 1995).[7] Table 14.5 presents the data for the individual contribution of each variable to the total variance explained by our regression.[8]

Armed with our regression analysis, we found that only four factors out of 25 were statistically significant. Being kept busy and being able to get clarification on assignments were both equally and highly significant in the variance observed concerning students' self-assessment of their co-op a learning experience. Similarly, matching skills and assignments and honoring shared expectations also had statistically significant correlations. Interestingly, indeed surprisingly in terms of

---

[7]This is a statistical technique that allowed us to measure the degree of correlation between a given factor (e.g., amount of time idle) and the dependent variable (e.g., the ranking of the educational experience) controlling for the operation of all other factors. For example, using the data on time idle, the powerful relation between being bored and the co-op rank may lose its explanatory power once one controls for all the other variables. Multivariate analysis permits one to measure the relative influence of individual factors and the total explanatory power of all factors investigated.

[8]The larger numbers reported for the four "statistically significant factors" indicate their greater contribution to the overall regression. The "factors below statistical relevance" indicate were not significant according to standard assessment (t significance $> .05$). A variable that is reported as negative number (e.g., amount of time idle) is one whose presence has the effect of depressing the overall rank. At the bottom of Table 14.5, the figure known as R Square, represents the total contribution of all 25 variables to explaining the variance in educational rank. An R Square of 51.2 means that our 25 variables had remarkable explanatory power.

the clinical orthodoxy, adequate supervision—the next most influential fac-tor—was not quite statistically significant in explaining the value of the learning experience nor was in-court participation, another presumed favorite.

TABLE 14.5

Summary of Significance of Multiple Variables on Students' Assessment of Co-op as a Learning Experience in Declining Order of Significance

Statistically significant factors	(beta)
Amount of time spent idle	−.263**
Difficulty receiving clarification	−.263**
Work assigned commensurate with skills	−.155*
Supervisor honoring shared expectations	+.148*
Factors below statistical significance #	
Adequate supervision	+.140
In court participation	+.134
Lack of research guidelines	+.109
In court observation	+.104
Public interest	+.067
Judicial internship	+.065
Lack of clear client objectives	−.056
Written evaluation	−.056
Ethnicity	−.055
Salary amount	+.053
Union/corporate	+.039
Small firm	−.030
Gender	−.029
Age	+.029
Medium firm	−.029
Oral evaluation	−.023
Share mutual expectations with supervisor	+.019
Government office	+.019
Large firm	−.014
Lack of factual information	−.012
Legal aid/public defender	+.009
	R squared = .512

**t < .01,   *t < .05,   #t > .05

Synthesizing a Theory of Ecological Learning

> **Decision Point: Could we synthesize a new theory of "ecological" learning to explain our findings?**
>
> Although we had succeeded in conducting one of the first empirical studies of learning in legal education, we knew that our findings would be enhanced if we synthesized an explanatory theory. Once I undertook that theoretical synthesis, however, I had 140 pages, and it was still growing. We decided to summarize the new theory of ecological learning in our empirical article and that I would submit my more extended theoretical analyses in a series of separate articles (Baker, 1994a, 1994b, 1999). We did this for two reasons, first we wanted to emphasize the empirical findings that would have otherwise been buried in an avalanche of words and second because we anticipated that our findings might be pigeon-holed as school-specific and that we needed a full theoretical onslaught to loosen some of the prevailing assumptions that gripped legal education.

Drawing on a wide body of cognitive science and social practice theory, our article summarized a new theory of ecological learning, synthesizing five strands of investigation described further in the following: (1) contextualism, particularly cognitive contextualism; (2) experientialism and so-called learning cycles; (3) self-directed learning; (4) guided participation within the interpersonal dynamics of the workplace; and (5) the nature and replication of expertise (Givelber et al., 1995). We chose the central term *ecological* to evoke the complex interaction between human beings and the natural and social environments in which they find themselves—environmental interactions that are multifaceted, dynamic, and mutually interdependent. The net effect of this theory was the suggestion that students learn well in the real-world ecologies of co-op, externships, and even part-time work and that law schools should understand, value, and support this practice-based learning.

In an initial article, the theory of ecological learning focused first on environmental factors, the inevitable link between contextual constraints and cognitive response (Baker, 1994a; see Gillespie, 1993; Lave, 1988; Lave & Wenger, 1991; Light & Butterworth, 1993) and next on functional workplace activities and their legacies called learning (Baker, 1994a; see Dewey 1963; Jarvis, 1992). Thereafter, in a second paper, the theory moved both context and experience aside to personalize students' quest for autonomy (freedom of action), identity (a new sense of self as an adult worker), and self-realization (growth and competence) through work (Baker, 1994b, Bruner, 1990; Candy, 1991; Hart, 1992; Maslow, 1962; Merriam & Carfarella, 1991). Next, in a third paper, the quasiautonomous self was reconnected to the rich interpersonal ecology of the workplace where novices experience fluid forms of collaboration, role-modeling, supervision, and participatory guidance with their mentors and peers (Baker, 1999; Courtney, 1992; Lave & Wenger, 1991; Merriam & Caffarella, 1991;

Rogoff, 1990). The theory focused on the key relationship between a highly accomplished expert and a struggling novice to discern the nature of expertise and the circumstances of its replication (Baker, 1999; Blasi, 1995; Hoffman, 1992).

By the end of this extended explication, the composite theory of ecological learning proposed a contextualist and experientialist pedagogy that required placement in real world contexts and engagement in complex work assignments as the optimal, and perhaps only, way to learn domain-specific skills, dispositions, and values (Baker, 1994a). In such placements, students should be deeply involved in both repetitive and varied tasks that are challenging, yet matched to their existing skills. Even more importantly, the students' work should be valued internally by the student and externally by the social environment. Because students seek co-op experiences to explore a new sense of autonomy, competence, and identity, efforts should be made to decrease internal and external barriers to participation (Baker, 1994b). Students are supported in their quest for identity and competence through an interpersonal ecology where opportunities for role modeling and emulation, collaboration and mentoring, supervision and feedback, abound (Baker, 1999). In this interpersonal ecology, experts and peers provide multiple forms of guidance and support, both from their mutual participation in shared work projects and from direct and indirect forms of feedback that help calibrate the student's performance (Baker, 1999). In the ecology of expert–novice interactions, the most important moment of collaborative guidance is in-action, during performance, when the novice is and most engaged and most receptive to input (Baker, 1999).

In the end, the theory of ecological learning (extending well beyond its more modest empirical findings) challenged prevailing assumptions about the centrality of school-based theory and educator-centered reflection, proposing instead the primacy of subconscious processes, intuited patterns, and practice exemplars in the resolution of the authentic dilemmas of a practice domain (Baker, 1994a, 1999). To support novices' growing contextual competence and the evolution of their cognitive resources, workplace allies should participate in mutual work and use guidance-in-action as the most effective catalyst for replicating expertise (Baker, 1999). We capped our theory of ecological learning with the proposition that apprentice-like opportunities during school—at Northeastern, co-op—provide near optimal circumstances for developing situation skills, performance competencies and genuine understandings (Givelber et al., 1995).

DISSEMINATION AND REFORM

Selecting an Intended Audience

Decision Point: Where should we place our article and who was our intended audience?

At the end of our study, we realized that the placement of our empirical article and the placement of my more theoretical investigations would be critically

important. As far as we knew, there was only one law review distributed to all
law professors nationwide, the Journal of Legal Education, one of the few
peer-reviewed law reviews, most of which are student edited. Although submitting to the Journal of Legal Education temporarily precluded us from submitting elsewhere, and thus narrowed our prospects for publication, we
decided to go for the widest possible audience of legal educators. With respect
to the more theoretical articles, I decided to publish the first in a general law
review and the second in a law journal targeting clinical teachers.

As described previously, I completed my theoretical exegesis of cognitive contextualism, experiential learning, and a more modest role for theory and reflection
first. Because a recent report (ABA MacCrate Report, 1992) had questioned the
value of student employment and externships at the same time it valorized the traditional classroom and in-house clinics, I decided to frame my article as a critique
of this report. Thereafter, I submitted it to more than 100 general law reviews and
gratefully accepted an offer from a journal of good standing (Baker, 1994a).

When submitting our empirical article, we knew that the Journal of Legal
Education had the widest circulation among legal educators and that it was
particularly interested in reporting empirical research. Moreover, we knew
that law school regulators were in the middle of a process of tightening accreditation standards for law school externship programs, generally requiring
stricter oversight by legal educators. Although these regulations would not ad-
versely affect our co-op program at Northeastern because students did not get
academic credit for their co-ops, we decided to frame the conclusion of our article in terms of the debate about more stringent regulation. Because our findings suggested that the importance of educators and supervisors in
practice-based learning was exaggerated and that the most important features
of learning on the job were the quality of the work and regard shown for the
student and his or her performance, we questioned the regulatory stranglehold
that the American Bar Association and the Association of American Law
School were imposing (Givelber et al., 1995).

For my second long theoretical article on participatory and social sources of
learning (Baker, 1999), I decided to seek publication in the Clinical Law Review,
another peer-reviewed journal routinely read by legal clinicians. In drafting the
article, I took care to describe prevailing theories of clinical supervision (Baker,
1999). Pursuant to the prescriptions of clinic-based educators, proper supervision
in the workplace required clearly delineated educational goals, relatively
nondirective case supervision, and extensive critical feedback and reflection concerning performance after-the-fact (Barry, 1995; Hoffman, 1982, 1986; Report of
the Committee on the Future of the In-House Clinic, 1992; Kreiling, 1981;
Oglivy, 1996; Shalleck, 1993–1994; Stark et al., 1993). I summarized the clinical
model in Table 14.6. Under this idealized standard, most real-life supervision

TABLE 14.6
Current Clinical Model

Student Role	Clinical Pedagogy	Supervisor-Based Sources of Learning
1. Direct representation of live client with primary case responsibility.	1. Have a clear educational agenda.	1. Role modeling
	2. Be non-directive with respect to performance.	2. Top-down collaboration
2. Relatively self-reliant with respect to performance.	3. Help construct theories of lawyering.	3. Mentoring
		4. Case supervision and feedback.
3. Relatively dependent with respect to learning.	4. Engage in constructive conversation.	5. Guided self-reflection.
	5. Provide after-the-fact feedback.	
	6. Facilitate reflection and critique.	

Note. From (p. 26), by B. K. Baker, 1999.

paled by comparison. In the end, I challenged these assumptions, calling for a more participatory and practice-intensive pedagogy.

Recommendations for Educational Reform

Decision Point: How should we present our findings, theory, and recommendations so as to impact legal education?

In some ways, the findings of our empirical study were relatively mundane (Givelber et al., 1995). We showed that law students believe that they learn well from full-time co-ops in law offices, courthouses, and government agencies, and confirmed earlier studies that practice-based learning is remarkably robust. The data made sense in terms of a concurrently developed theory of ecological learning that drew heavily on investigations of contextualist cognition, situated learning, guided participation, and identity formation. It made sense that students were concerned with the work that they were doing, with being valued on the job, and with being considered a productive member of a team. Being kept busy, getting clarification on assignments, being given work within one's abilities, and honoring promises, all demonstrate respect for the student's emerging competence. Although our findings debunked theories that overtouted the necessities of supervision and although they confirmed the students' assessment of the value of learning on the job, the empirical findings alone did not readily support a broader and deeper range of specific reforms for legal education in general and clinical education in particular. Thus, in Baker (1999), I decided to expound a more detailed set of concrete recommendations for pedagogical reform.

Reforms for Co-op and Clinical Programs

The most radical implications of the theory of ecological learning might have been to relocate most of students' law school learning to real-world practice and to clinical programs where students perform useful tasks under expert guidance.

> Because of the contextual authenticity of well-staged and truly valued performances on the job, because of the quality of novice–expert interactions, and because of other wide-ranging supports in the workplace, the typical practice setting provides a truly meaningful opportunity for a novice to learn … skills through a process of enculturation. (Givelber et al., 1995, p. 27–28; see Baker, 1999; Gardner, 1991; Rogoff, 1990).

Here, the constraints and opportunities of context are most real. Here, the authenticity of purpose, the functionality of tasks, the determinacy of routine, and the fluidity and interactivity of social exchange combine to compose a field of action where students must do their utmost to solve problems collaboratively with others.

However, despite my enthusiasms, I understood that apprenticeships and co-op would not supplant university-based legal education. Thus, I offered several suggestions about how co-op and clinical supervisors might intensify students' immersion in the world of practice and how educators might prepare students for practice. Tables 14.7 and 14.8 report my suggested reforms.

Reforms for Classroom Teaching

In addition to recommending changes to clinical legal education, I have also proposed reforms for classroom teachers, particularly through conferences with clinical and legal writing faculty, namely that we create "virtual realities" in our classrooms (Baker, 1997). At present, the situational context of most classrooms is impoverished. Students do not sense that they are in true performative roles, solving real situational dilemmas because they are not exposed to people with realistic problems expressing real human concerns. Thus, we need greater realism in structuring tasks and in creating a simulated setting.

In creating a virtual reality, educators should not simply assign students a generic role in a generic workplace working for a generic client, patient, or customer. Instructors must try instead to make the practice setting real by describing a workforce, an ultimate consumer, and a particular set of institutional arrangements. Because real problems in the swampland of practice feature indeterminacy, classroom assignments should avoid the "closed-universe" syndrome where both facts

TABLE 14.7

Implications of a Theory of Ecological Learning for Clinicians' Practice

1. Encourage students to join a practice not to enter a proving ground. The standard of solo representation and of self-reliance is not necessarily conducive to learning.

2. Be alert to barriers to participation: internal, interpersonal, and institutional. If the value of practice-based education rests primarily on intense commitment to one's own participation, then self-doubt, passivity, and withdrawal must be challenged as must hierarchy and other systems of exclusion.

3. "Less talk, more action." In general, when given a choice between assigning more work or engaging in more "education" talk, choose work. Because students feel valued when they are given important work to do, it is important to keep students busy. In general, full time placements and high credit-hour programs are preferable to part-time and low credit-hour programs.

4. Create multiple opportunities for side-to-side collaboration. If it is true that interaction with peers is crucial to social learning, then clinicians should provide many opportunities for collaboration with peers, including "team assignments," formal "grand rounds," and other more informal means of peer discussion and feedback.

5. Create a coparticipatory alliance with students. Clinicians should be perceived by students as fully engaged in practice: as being as much at-risk as students are and as being senior colleagues. Although there is no ideal type of case for clinical practice, there may well be advantages to work on more complex cases where the supervisor and student share tasks and collaborate in total representation of a client.

6. Put your own performance on the line. Both for purposes of role modeling and to create occasions to explore and thematize exemplars of practice, clinicians should expose students to their own performances both indirectly and directly.

7. Contextualize performance. As experts with years of experience, clinicians are sensitive to contextual variables in a way that students are not. Accordingly, clinicians should point out landmarks and hidden features that structure the problem space (e.g., bureaucratic conventions, ethical dilemmas, and the like).

8. Be task-focused. If students' sense of engagement and opportunities for acculturation are largely dependent on opportunities for successful completion of lawyering tasks, then assign work in their zone of proximal development (doable but hard), provide easy avenues of clarification, and be attentive to the sequence of assignments.

9. Don't be shy, give advice and plenty of it. Rather than be nondirective at the time of performance, clinicians should offer multiple and pluralistic forms of guidance, support, and advice when it is most important—when the student is in the throes of a dilemma. In particular, clinicians should offer their expert heuristics as a challenge to students' more naïve strategies.

10. Broaden and deepen students' exposures. Developing expertise requires intensive participation in particular lawyering contexts, but it also requires broad exposure to the wider dimensions of practice. Accordingly, it may be particularly valuable for students to have several opportunities for clinical placements and/or for legal work during law school.

11. Create explicit bridges for the transfer of skills. Given the situational "glue" of students' practice experience and given the general difficulty in transferring skills and strategies from one context to another, clinicians should remain alert for opportunities to connect students' experiences and to articulate heuristics which might help solve analogous dilemmas in practice.

Note. From (p. 179), by B. K. Baker, 1999.

TABLE 14.8
Implications of a Theory of Ecological Learning for Students' Participation

1. Encourage students to participate in practice wholeheartedly. Students can not afford to be timid in their commitment to their practice opportunities. They must be motivated to participate enthusiastically and energetically.

2. Encourage students to be alert to internal and external barriers to participation. Self-doubt, passivity, and withdrawal must be recognized and overcome. Similarly, interpersonal dynamics and institutional patterns that frustrate students' attempts to participate robustly in the practice setting should be resisted and confronted.

3. Encourage students to seek assignments. Students feel valued when they have important work to do and are kept busy. Students should take initiative in seeking work opportunities, particularly opportunities that challenge them and broaden their exposure.

4. Encourage students to seek clarification. Students must become comfortable seeking clarification on their tasks, rather than spending too much time spinning their wheels. It's o.k. not to know how to do something; it's not o.k. to avoid seeking guidance.

5. Encourage students to seek opportunities for side-to-side collaboration. Because interaction with peers is crucial to social learning, students should seek opportunities for collaboration with peers as well as with senior practitioners.

6. Encourage students to seek opportunities to observe expert performances. To increase students' opportunities for emulation and exploration of vicarious practice experiences, students should try to observe the expert performances of senior colleagues.

7. Encourage students to question authority. Because there are significant dangers of acculturation to substandard forms of practice, of habituation to unethical conduct, and of unquestioning acceptance of oppressive legal culture, then students should be encouraged to adopt a critical stance and to remain vigilant during their practice-based experiences. In addition to questioning authority and standard procedures at work, students should have opportunities to discuss these issues at school with peers and with faculty.

Note. From (p. 60), by B. K. Baker, 1999.

and principles are known and static. Because students must create unique strategies suited to each project, students should feel a system of realistic opportunities and constraints. Contextualizing learning in virtual realities permits the development of situation assessment skills, which in turn permit the adaptation and deployment of performance skills.

Even if we do our best to contextualize our student's assignments, there is the related concern of whether to build skills and knowledge slowly and incrementally or whether to rely on complexity to draw forth competent performance. Surprisingly, integration through multiplicity and complexity is cognitively easier and more efficient than integration through isolation and simplification (Iran-Nejad, 1990). Given a certain baseline of predicate skills, people learn in an authentically rich context with multiple environmental messages better and more efficiently than in a simple, single-task, one-step-at-a-time controlled environment (Baker, 1994).

Summary

- The use of extended metaphors can enliven scholarship and make it more accessible to broader audiences.
- When engaged in a large-scale research project, particularly one whose theoretical propositions challenge the status quo, it is useful to consider breaking the research into a series of articles, and particularly to use one article to highlight empirical findings.
- As in any rhetorical context, it is important to consider audience and purpose both in framing and writing one's scholarship and in selecting forums for publication.
- When presenting cross-disciplinary research that relates to an existing body of literature in your field, it is important to summarize and compare the literatures in some depth, especially when one is proposing reform.
- When proposing reform, it is important to seek publication in journals widely read by your intended audience.
- When proposing reform, it is important to be as concrete as possible with your recommendations.

ANNOTATED BIBLIOGRAPHY

Garth, B., & Martin, P. (1993). Law schools and the construction of competence. *Journal of Legal Education, 43*, 469–510. Garth and Martin's study is one of the few high quality studies of sources of learning in legal education. Although it relied largely on self-reporting by respondents, it helped us understand the power of such reporting and it also confirmed our estimation that practice-based learning is the predominate mode of acquiring legal skills.

Gillespie, D. (1993). *The mind's we: Contextualism in cognitive psychology*. Carbondale: Southern Illinois University Press. Gillespie opened me to a new branch of contextualist cognitive psychology that more specifically focused on environmental and social context. It combined the emerging science of the mind with culture and the world at large.

Lave, J. (1988). *Cognition in practice: Mind, mathematics and culture in everyday life*. New York: Cambridge University Press. Lave has continued to make major contributions to theories of situated learning, but this early work was eye-opening to me because it demonstrated concretely how people can accomplish intellectual tasks concretely in practice that they fail in school.

Rogoff, B. (1990). *Apprenticeship in thinking: Cognitive development in social context*. New York: Oxford University Press. Rogoff developed theories of social learning, drawing on Russian antecedents that emphasized the importance of participation in a practice and guidance from knowledgeable peers and mentors. She helped us understand how knowledge is distributed in a workplace.

Hoffman, R. (Ed.). (1992). *The psychology of expertise: Cognitive research and empirical AI*. New York: Springer-Verlag. This was my first sustained introduction to an emerging body of literature on experts and novices. Because we were focusing on the interactions of experts and novices in the workplace, this research was crucial to our understanding.

REFERENCES

Alexander, A., & Smith, J. (1988). A practical guide to cooperative supervision for law students and legal employers. *Law Office, Economics, & Management, 29,* 207–227.

American Bar Association Section of Legal Education and Admission to the Bar. (1992). *Report of the task force on law schools and the profession: Narrowing the gap, legal education and professional development—An educational continuum.* American Bar Association, 750 North Lake Shore Drive, Chicago, IL 60611.

Baker, B. (1994a). Beyond MacCrate: The role of context, experience, theory, and reflection in ecological learning. *Arizona Law Review, 36,* 287–356.

Baker, B. (1994b). *"Self"-directed learning post-modernized: The role of autonomy, self, and self-realization in law student work experience.* Unpublished manuscript.

Baker, B. (1997). *A theory of ecological learning and its implications for research, analysis and writing programs.* Unpublished manuscript.

Baker, B. (1999). Learning to fish, fishing to learn: Guided participation in the interpersonal ecology of practice. *Clinical Law Review, 6,* 1–84.

Barry, M. (1995). Clinical supervision: Walking that fine line. *Clinical Law Review, 2,* 137–166.

Blasi, G. (1995). What lawyers know: Lawyering expertise, cognitive science, and the functions of theory. *Journal Legal Education, 45,* 313–397.

Bloch, F. (1982). The andragogical basis of clinical legal education. *Vanderbilt Law Review, 35,* 321–353.

Bruner, J. (1990). *Acts of meaning.* Cambridge, MA: Harvard University Press.

Candy, P. (1991). *Self-direction for lifelong learning: A comprehensive guide to theory and practice.* San Francisco: Jossey-Bass.

Courtney, S. (1992). *Why adults learn: Towards a theory of participation in adult education.* New York: Routledge.

Dewey, J. (1963). *Experience and education.* New York: Collier Books.

Gardner, H. (1991). *The unschooled mind: How children learn and think and how schools should teach.* New York: BasicBooks.

Garth, B., & Martin, P. (1993). Law schools and the construction of competence. *Journal of Legal Education, 43,* 469–510.

Gillespie, D. (1993). *The mind's we: Contextualism in cognitive psychology.* Carbondale: Southern Illinois University Press.

Givelber, J., Baker, B., McDevitt, J., & Miliano, R. (1995). Learning through work: An empirical study of legal internship. *Journal of Legal Education, 45,* 1–48.

Hart, M. (1992). *Working and educating for life: Feminist and international perspectives on adult education.* New York: Routledge.

Hoffman, P. (1982). Clinical course design and the supervisory process. *1982 Arizona State Law Journal,* 277–311.

Hoffman, P. (1986). The stages of the clinical supervisory relationship. *Antioch Law Journal, 4,* 301–312.

Hoffman, R. (Ed.). (1992). *The psychology of expertise: Cognitive research and empirical AI.* New York: Springer-Verlag.

Iran-Nejad, A. (1990). Active and dynamic self-regulation of learning processes. *Review of Educational Research, 60,* 573–578.

Jarvis, P. (1992). *Paradoxes of learning: On becoming an individual in society.* San Francisco: Jossey-Bass.

Kotkin, M. (1989). Reconsidering role assumption in clinical legal education. *New Mexico Law Review, 19,* 185–202.

Kreiling, K. (1981). Clinical education and lawyers' competency: The process of learning to learn through properly structured clinical supervision. *Maryland Law Review, 40,* 284–337.

Laser, G. (1994). Significant curricular developments: The MacCrate report and beyond. *Clinical Law Review*, *1*, 425–442.

Lave, J. (1988). *Cognition in practice: Mind, mathematics and culture in everyday life*. New York: Cambridge University Press.

Lave, J., & Wenger, E. (1991). *Situated learning: Legitimate peripheral participation*. New York: Cambridge University Press.

Light, P., & Butterworth, G. (Eds.). (1993). *Cognition and context: Ways of learning and knowing*. Hillsdale, NJ: Lawrence Erlbaum Associates.

Maher, S. (1990). The praise of folly: A defense of practice supervision in clinical legal education. *Nebraska Law Review*, *69*, 537–663.

Maslow, A. (1962). *Toward a psychology of being*. Princeton, NJ: Van Nostrand.

Meltsner, M., Rowan, J., & Givelber, D. (1989). The bike tour leader's dilemma: Talking About supervision. *Vermont Law Review*, *13*, 399–444.

Merriam, S., & Caffarella, R. (1991). *Learning in adulthood: A comprehensive guide*. San Francisco: Jossey-Bass.

Motley, J. (1989). Self-directed learning and the out-of-house placement. *New Mexico Law Review*, *19*, 211–229.

Oglivy, J. (1996). The use of journals in legal education: A tool for reflection. *Clinical Law Review*, *3*, 55–107.

Report of the Committee on the Future of the In-House Clinic (1992). *Journal Legal Education*, *42*, 508–574.

Rogoff, B. (1990). *Apprenticeship in thinking: Cognitive development in social context*. New York: Oxford University Press.

Rose, H. (1987). Legal externships: Can they be valuable clinical experiences for law students. *Nova Law Review*, *12*, 95–113.

Schön, D. (1987). *Educating the reflective practitioner*. San Francisco: Jossey-Bass.

Shalleck, A. (1993–1994). Clinical contexts: Theory and practice in law and supervision. *New York University Review of Law and Social Change*, *21*, 109–182.

Stark, J., Bauer, J., & Papillo, J. (1993). Directiveness in clinical supervision. *Boston University Public Interest Law Journal*, *3*, 35–94.

Stickgold, M. (1989). Exploring invisible curriculum: Clinical fieldwork in American law schools. *New Mexico Law Review*, *19*, 287–327.

Tarr, N. (1990). The skill of evaluation as an explicit goal of clinical training. *Pacific Law Journal*, *21*, 967–994.

Varela, F., Thompson, E., & Rosch, E. (1991). *The embodied mind: Cognitive science and human experience*. Cambridge, MA: MIT Press.

Zillman, D., & Gregory, V. (1986). Law student employment and legal education. *Journal of Legal Education*, *36*, 390–402.

15

Writing for Publication: Preparation of the Research Report

Patricia M. Rowe
University of Waterloo

Key questions addressed in this chapter:

☞ How do I decide whether my research is publishable?

☞ What are the parts of an article?

☞ What is APA style?

☞ What happens after I submit my article?

Imagine a chef who dreams up a new recipe, tries out various ingredients, perfects the proportions of herbs and spices, but refuses to serve the final dish to friends, guests, or customers. With such a chef we might never have tasted the delights of Oysters Rockefeller, or Coq au Vin, or perhaps even apple pie. Suppose an architect designed a new house, had it built, but never permitted anyone to see the plans or view even the exterior of the house. Would we remember Frank Lloyd Wright today if none of his houses were ever photographed, visited, or the plans shared with the world? Or think of the tales of artists who have destroyed their own works or writers who have burned their manuscripts. How many of those works were truly trash, and how many would have been viewed as masterpieces? Yet research that is not reported to others is like such recipes or house designs or works of art and literature: It benefits only the researcher, and might just as well never have been done as far as the rest of the world is concerned.

Having said this is not to deny that communicating one's work is difficult for many of us. The fun part is doing the research, the hard part is writing it up! Communication of research may take many forms, from an in-house report to one's own institution, to oral or poster presentations at conferences such as the annual conference of the Cooperative Education and Internship Association, to written articles for scientific journals such as the *Journal of Cooperative Education*. This latter form of communication is most important because it is *archival*; that is, journals are the repository of previous studies, reviews of the literature, and theories in the discipline, and are available to the researcher now and in the years to come. Only by accumulating knowledge in this way and building on the past do we advance our understanding, in our case, of work-integrated education. Whether one is preparing a talk for a conference or writing a paper for a journal, however, the processes involved and the content and organization of the material are similar. This chapter deals with some of the issues involved in preparing manuscripts for publication, a description of the parts of a research report, and a discussion of the publication process with reference to the *Journal of Cooperative Education*.

THE QUALITY OF THE RESEARCH

The first step is to decide whether the research is worthy of publication. Determining the quality of one's own research follows the same process that reviewers use in assessing manuscripts: Is the research significant to the field? Was the research design sound? Was there an adequate and appropriate sample? Was the statistical analysis meaningful? Did the results support the hypotheses? I would advise prospective authors in cooperative education, however, not to be too harsh about their own work. It is better to write a paper and have reviewers reject it than to put aside potentially worthwhile studies; moreover, the comments of reviewers are often very useful in future research and writing. A more important reason for not being overly cautious in submitting a manuscript is that research in cooperative education is still at an early stage of maturity, with little accumulated research on the variables affecting learning, on the outcomes of different forms of work-integrated education, or on the relatively few theories that have been advanced to explain the effects obtained.

ETHICAL CONSIDERATIONS IN PUBLICATION

Having decided that your research is worthy of publication you must now consider the ethics of publication. Here I am drawing upon the ethical code for psychologists, which was developed for that discipline but is applicable in other disciplines studying human behavior. One part of that code states that the published research must be original, or if previously published, the original publication must be acknowledged. In others words, an article or substantial parts of it must not have been published elsewhere without acknowledgment. You should also be aware that authors are normally required to assign copyright for the article to the publisher. Publication of the work in another journal, book, or other media, would constitute copyright violation. This policy does not preclude publication as an abstract or in a periodical with limited circulation or within an institution, but does prohibit publication in any form that is for public sale.

A second ethical consideration is that of authorship: *only* those, and *all* of those, who have contributed substantively to the research are accorded authorship status. Authors would normally include those who contributed in a substantial fashion to formulating the hypotheses, planning and conducting the statistical analyses, interpreting the results, or writing a significant portion of the results. The order of authors would usually be in the order of their contribution to the work. A student whose thesis formed the basis for the paper would usually be listed as the first or principal author. Lesser contributions to the project, such as collecting the data or recruiting of participants, should be acknowledged in the author's note.

ARTICLE FORMAT

Most psychological journals as well as journals in related disciplines follow the guidelines published by the American Psychological Association (APA). The most recent *Publication Manual of the American Psychological Association* (APA, 2001) is the fifth edition. The *Journal of Cooperative Education* publishes articles in APA format; authors are encouraged to follow the manual in the preparation of their manuscripts. Although this chapter provides some brief examples of APA format, and this *Handbook* follows the guidelines in the manual, you should obtain a copy and make use of it as you write up your study.

STYLE

Each individual has their own unique writing style, be it flowery, tedious, elegant, poetic, dull, spare, or boring. In drafting a research report, however, we must strive for clarity, precision, and a smooth and orderly expression of ideas. The goal is to develop a style that is clear and well-organized but still allows individuality of expression. The use of headings helps the reader understand the organization of the article, and the importance of its various parts. Chapter 3 of the manual (APA, 2001) provides advice on developing such a style, examples of common grammatical errors and incorrect sentence structure, guidelines to reduce bias in language, and how to organize your paper with headings. Other sources of information on writing style are the classic works by Fowler (1965) and Strunk and White (1979).

PARTS OF AN ARTICLE

Title Page

The title page contains the title, the names of the authors, and their institutional affiliation. The title of the article seems to be very straight forward, but, in fact, it is very important and sometimes difficult to write. It should be descriptive, but reasonably brief; attract the reader's attention, but not be frivolous; and be accurate for indexing or for use in references by others. The preferred form of author's name is first name, middle initial, and last name, to make it less likely that you will be mistaken for other authors. The institutional affiliation is the name of the institution where the research was conducted; if you have changed institutions since completing the study, your current address will appear in an author's note.

Abstract

The abstract is a brief summary of the research, and should contain the purpose, and a description of the methodology, important results, and conclusions. The *Journal of Cooperative Education* limits authors to 100 words or less, because of space constraints.

Introduction

The introduction to the article presents the problem to be examined in the study and how it is to be tackled. Because the introduction is identified by its position in the paper there is no need to label it as such. The rest of the introduction reviews the relevant literature, develops the problem, and states the purpose of the research. Your hypotheses or research questions, including the rationale for each one, should be stated here.

Method

This section provides a detailed account of how the research was conducted and permits the reader to evaluate the suitability of your methods and the validity of your results. It is conventionally divided into three labeled sections (participants, materials or apparatus, and procedure). In the participant subsection the characteristics of the sample are described, including specifics on age and gender, and any other variables that are relevant to the study. Published scales or questionnaires (referenced so that others may procure them) and specially created instruments (with information as to how to obtain them) are described in the materials subsection. The procedures subsection summarizes each step of the conduct of the research with enough information that a reader could replicate the research.

Results

The purpose of this section is to inform the reader of the findings of your study. First describe the main results and then report the data in sufficient detail to justify the conclusions to be drawn. This requires you to provide statistical confirmation of the observed effects. More information on how to present statistics and how much information should be included can be found in the APA *Publication Manual*.

Tables and figures are a useful way to present some of your results, and may enhance the readability of your report. Avoid using a table to present information that can be easily given in a sentence or two of the text. Each table and figure should be on a separate page and presented at the very end of the article. The text should refer to each table and figure, but it is not necessary to indicate in the text where the table or figure should appear. Tables should be double-spaced, and the standard font size should be used, even if they run over more than one page. The fact that you can squeeze a table onto one page by reducing font size, spacing, and margins does not mean the printer can readily place your table in the article. For example, if the character count, including spaces, of the widest entry row in a table is greater than 100 the table will not fit across the width of the *Journal of Cooperative Education*.

Discussion

The final section of the text of the article is the discussion, where you evaluate and interpret your results. Give a clear statement of the extent to which the findings support your original hypothesis, and the relation of your results to the previous literature. The implications of your research to theory as well as for practitioners in cooperative education should be mentioned. This section may be finished with a few statements about the conclusions that can be drawn from your study.

References

A listing of all references mentioned in the text must be listed in the reference section, and conversely, all references listed in this section must have been cited in the text. Reference formats should follow the style of the American Psychological Association. Examples of citations in the text and entries in the reference list appear in the appendixes at the end of this chapter.

Author Note

Following the reference section and on a separate page, information about the author or authors is presented. The author note identifies the institutional affiliation of each author, an e-mail address and a mailing address to which correspondence about the article may be sent, and acknowledgment of any financial support for the research. It also provides an opportunity to thank others for contributions or assistance in the conduct of the work. The author note is also the appropriate place for disclosure of such information as the fact that the research had been reported at a conference or was based upon material published elsewhere.

SELECTING THE APPROPRIATE PUBLICATION

There are a number of journals that may be possible places to publish studies in cooperative education, including journals in education, especially higher education, psychology, sociology, college placement, or even the specific discipline (e.g., engineering, nursing, or business) in which your study was conducted. The choice of journal should be based on which journal is likely to reach the readers who will find the information most useful. Large research projects (Wilson & Lyons, 1961) or collections of articles (Ryder, Wilson, & Associates, 1987) may be published separately as monographs.

The *Journal of Cooperative Education* is the only peer-reviewed journal devoted exclusively to work-integrated education and draws articles and readers from around the world. It publishes three kinds of articles: *research articles*, in which the author presents an account of an empirical study of some problem germane to work-integrated education; *essays*, in which the author presents a discussion, review, or analysis of some issue pertinent to work integrated education; and *descriptive articles*, in which the author describes an innovative program practice or procedure, a unique program, or an assessment of a local program. Guidelines for authors appear in every issue of the *Journal*.

MANUSCRIPT PREPARATION

Most journals prefer to produce the typeset version of your article directly from your word-processing disk, and thus the preparation of your manuscript should be done with that goal in mind. Manuscripts should be typed using a serif typeface (either Times New Roman or Courier) for text and tables, and a sans serif typeface should be used in figures. The font size should be 12 points. The functions of the word-processing program may be used to produce italics or bold typeface, as well as special characters such as Greek letters or accented letters. Double space between all lines in the manuscript, including footnotes, quotations, references, and all parts of tables. Margins should be 1 in. at the top, bottom, left and right sides of every page. Use flush left style of line length, not justified lines. Number all pages and provide a brief header above or to the left of the page number. Indent the first line of every paragraph, preferably using the default setting of the tab key.

THE PUBLICATION PROCESS

Because most readers of this *Handbook* will consider publication in the *Journal of Cooperative Education*, the publication process for that journal will be described. The sequence of activities and responsibilities of the people involved are, however, very similar to those followed by all professional journals. Prospective authors should consult the most recent issue of the *Journal* to obtain current requirements for manuscript submission and the address of the current editor. Sending the wrong number of copies of your manuscript to the wrong person could result in a serious delay in reviewing your article.

Very soon after the manuscript has been received a letter of acknowledgment, typically by e-mail, is sent to the corresponding author. If the topic of your article is deemed appropriate for the journal, the editor will send it out to review. All reviews are blind; that is, the identity of the author is concealed from reviewers. Two reviewers, at least one of whom is a member of the editorial board, review all articles submitted to *Journal of Cooperative Education*. The reviewers make their recommendations to the editor who has final authority for what is published. Allow at least 2 to 3 months, and often much more, for this step. Reviewers are busy people, sometimes a bit slow to complete the review, and the editor, too, may be in the midst of working on another journal issue when the reviews are returned.

There are four possible outcomes of the review process:

- *Accept.* The paper is accepted conditional on only minor revisions being made to the manuscript. Once the paper has been returned to the editor it will join the "in press" queue.
- *Accept with revisions.* The reviewers and editor request fairly substantial revisions, which, if made to the satisfaction of the editor, will result in the paper being published.
- *Revise and resubmit.* In the case of this decision the reviewers and the editor see merit in the manuscript and think that the paper may eventually warrant publication. If the author makes the revisions recommended in the comments, there is no commitment to publish but the manuscript will be sent for review, often to one or more of the same reviewers.
- *Reject.* Rejection of your paper indicates that the reviewers and the editor are not interested in publishing your paper. That is not to say that another journal may make a more favorable decision, but before submitting it to another journal you should review the comments carefully. Frequently, those comments may give suggestions for further analysis or indicate that they could not follow the description of your research; making those changes before submitting it elsewhere may improve your chances of acceptance.

Do not be disheartened by rejection or by the comments made by the reviewers. Many papers are rejected by most journals, not necessarily because they do not meet the standards for publication, but because there are too many good papers and there is only space to publish the very best ones. The *Journal of Cooperative Education* tries very hard to publish all research that contributes to our knowledge of cooperative education, and to help authors improve their manuscripts so that they may be published. If your paper is rejected, however, you should consider submitting it to another appropriate journal.

If your paper is accepted by *Journal of Cooperative Education* the next step is a review by the consulting editor and the editor to ensure correct spelling and grammar, consistency with current usage in the journal, and conformity to APA guidelines. As a result of these reviews there may be queries to the author for information on omitted references, page numbers for quotations, spelling of names, and other minor matters.

The paper is then prepared for publication. When the paper is typeset, the page proofs are sent by the editor to the author for final review. These proofs look very much as the article will appear in the journal. The author must review every detail of the article to make sure that there are no typographical or other errors. Authors are asked to return the page proofs promptly with any corrections. A few months later a copy of the issue containing the article will be sent to the author.

CONCLUSION

This chapter outlines some of the basic steps in preparing an article for publication. The intent is to be helpful, not to intimidate. Careful preparation of an article is, however, likely to increase the probability that it will be accepted and that readers will find the article informative and useful. Similarly, preparing material to be given in a poster or an oral presentation at a conference will benefit from some of this information.

Writing up an account of one's research is not an easy task, but many of us in cooperative education expect our students to write reports of their work experiences. Surely it is not asking too much that we, ourselves, should share with others the knowledge gained from conducting a research project.

Summary
- Research that is not communicated to others is a waste of time and energy, and benefits only the researcher.
- In preparing an article for publication, guidelines must be followed. In the case of cooperative education, the guidelines of the *American Psychological Association* are typically adopted.
- This chapter describes the parts of an article, the process of preparing it for publication, and the publication process of the *Journal of Cooperative Education*.

ANNOTATED BIBLIOGRAPHY

American Psychological Association. (2001). *Publication Manual of the American Psychological Association* (5th ed.). Washington, DC: Author. The first edition of this manual was published in 1952, and has been revised several times in the years since. Throughout the past 50 years it has become the manual of choice for writers not only in psychology, but also in other behavioral and social sciences. It includes advice on organizing material for the manuscript, suggestions for writing clearly, information on preparing tables and figures, as well as providing guidelines for what has become known as APA style. It is an invaluable resource for writing and presenting research clearly and effectively.

Fowler, H. W. (1965). *A dictionary of modern English usage* (2nd ed.). New York: Oxford University Press.

Strunk, W., Jr., & White, E. B. (1979). *The elements of style* (3rd ed.). New York: Macmillan.

These two books are classics in offering advice for improving one's writing style. Fowler's book is a dictionary of English usage and contains much useful information on grammar, spelling, and punctuation in addition to style.

REFERENCES

American Psychological Association. (2001). *Publication Manual of the American Psychological Association* (5th ed.). Washington, DC: Author.

Fowler, H. W. (1965). *A dictionary of modern English usage* (2nd ed.). New York: Oxford University Press.

Ryder, K. G., Wilson, J. W., & Associates. (1987). *Cooperative education in a new era*. San Francisco: Jossey-Bass.

Strunk, W., Jr., & White, E. B. (1979). *The elements of style* (3rd ed.). New York: Macmillan.

Wilson, J. W., & Lyons, E. H. (1961). *Work-study college programs*. New York: Harper.

Appendix A

EXAMPLES OF REFERENCE CITATIONS IN TEXT

One Work by One Author

Smith (1998) reviewed
One experiment (Jones, 2000) was conducted

One Work by Two Authors

Smith and Jones (1997) reported, or a study (Smith & Jones, 1997) found
- Always use both names every time the reference occurs.
- Use an ampersand if the names are enclosed in parentheses.

One Work by Two to Five Authors

Brown, Smith, and Evans (1995) examined, or it has been shown (Brown, Smith, & Evans, 1995)
- Use as first citation in text.

Brown et al. (1995) examined, or it has been shown (Brown et al. 1995)
- Use as first citation in subsequent paragraphs.
- Omit the year in subsequent citations within a paragraph.

One Work by Six or More Authors

Evans et al. (1999)
- Cite only the surname of the first author followed by et al. and the year for all citations.

Groups as Authors

If the name is long or readily identifiable, you may abbreviate it in subsequent citations, otherwise write it out in full:

Cooperative Education Association [CEA], (1993)
- Subsequently, write (CEA, 1993).

University of Waterloo (1995)
- Always written in full (University of Waterloo, 1995).

Works With No Author

- Use a short title, or the full title if it is short, for the parenthetical citation: ("Training the Workforce for the Future," 1989)
- If designated as "anonymous," cite it as such: (Anonymous, 1991)

Classical Works

Rousseau (1979 version)

Thoreau (1854/1976)

- If the date of publication is inapplicable for some old works, cite the year of the translation used, preceded by "trans.," or the year of the version used, followed by "version." If you know the original date of publication, it should be included in the citation.

Personal Communication

Letters, memos, e-mail messages, telephone conversations and the like are examples of personal communication. They should be cited only in the text and not included in the reference list. The text should appear as: (N. Nicholson, personal communication, November 10, 1989).

Appendix B

REFERENCE LIST

The general form references in the reference list is as follows:

Periodical

Author, A. A., Author, B. B., & Author, C. C. (2001). Title of the article. *Title of the Periodical, xx,* xxx–xxx.

Book

Author, A. A. (2001). *Title of work.* Location: Publisher.

Book Chapter

Author, B. B., & Author, C. C. (2000). Title of chapter. In A. Editor, B. Editor, & C. Editor (Eds.), *Title of book* (pp. xx–xx). Location: Publisher.

Some Principles for Arranging Entries in a Reference List

- Entries should be arranged in alphabetical order by the surname of the first author.
- Several works by the same author as the sole author should be arranged by the year of publication.
- One-author publications precede multiple-author entries.
- Multiple-author references with the same first author are arranged alphabetically by the surname of the second author, and so on.
- References by the same authors in the same order are arranged by year of publication.
- References by the same author or authors in the same order, published in the same year, should be arranged alphabetically by the first significant word in their titles. Lowercase letters (a, b, c, and so on) are placed immediately after the year within the parentheses, for example, Smith, P. J. (1998a).
- Works by different authors with the same surname are arranged alphabetically by the first initial.
- References with no authors are organized by the first significant word in their titles. If a work is signed "Anonymous," the entry is alphabetized as if Anonymous were a real name.

Part V

Overriding Considerations

16

Using Theory in Research I: Understanding the Learning Experience in Structured Internships in Construction Engineering

Robert K. Tener
Purdue University

Key questions addressed in this chapter:

- ☞ Does the knowledge gained by students through authentic involvement in construction internships constitute significant and uniquely valuable learning, not attainable in the academic setting?

- ☞ How can experiential learning theory be applied to better understand the actual learning observed in an undergraduate construction internship program?

- ☞ Can a simple, viable method be devised for guiding student interns to write about their learning experiences in straightforward and revealing ways, to enable discerning the learning modes they employed?

- ☞ How can these issues be researched in an unfunded, unsupported study?

INTRODUCTION

The purpose of the study reported in this chapter was to apply an established experiential learning theory to the learning observed in a contemporary, structured, internship program in order to explain, in ways not done before: how construction interns learn.

315

The underlying strategic motive for the research was to provide a logical basis for advocating more and better internship programs in undergraduate construction education programs. The author believes that (a) the experiential learning gained by students through authentic involvement in construction internships constitutes significant and uniquely valuable learning, and (b) much of the learning which is gained during these internships cannot be attained in any other way, especially not in the classroom. By demonstrating to engineering educators that well-structured construction internships are indispensable in undergraduate education we may provide motivation, to the benefit of future graduates, for more high quality internship programs among the U.S. universities whose graduates enter the practice of construction engineering and management.

The analysis and conclusions in this study may well be applicable to experiential learning in other engineering disciplines besides construction engineering. However, some characteristics of the working environments and the performance demands typically experienced by engineers in the construction workplace are fairly unique to that field. The author believes that the results of this study should be applied only to similar work environments until further research may demonstrate broader applicability.

An optimum "living laboratory" for this study exists. Student interns in the three-summer, mandatory internship program integral to the BS degree in Construction Engineering and Management at Purdue University undergo well-directed, well-reported learning experiences. Students' responses to questions designed to reveal their learning modes, eventually reported from 170 structured work periods over 2 years, could provide a valuable data source for analysis.

Decision Point: Shall we make the commitment to undertake this study?
In the face of uncertainties about how to develop a viable research strategy; whether funding support could be obtained; how much data and analysis would be needed to support eventual conclusions; and even whether useful conclusions might be reached, the author affirmatively decided to proceed with the study. Three fundamental conditions drove this determination. First, the author's curiosity about how construction interns really learn would not abate, and the internal desire to learn about this was quite compelling. Second, the strategic motive—to provide a logical basis for advocating more and better internship programs in undergraduate construction education programs—likewise compelled the search for ways to understand and communicate the nature and value of experiential learning in construction internships. Third, recognizing the value of our living laboratory—the structured, Purdue construction internship program, a ready source of information with an inherent, close degree of program control—was vital to the commitment to initiate this study.

From 1995 to 1998 the author, after beginning his work as Director of Internships in Purdue University's undergraduate construction engineering program, grew increasingly impressed with the unique and robust value of quality co-op and internship experience to graduates who enter professional practice in construction. Especially in the construction industry, the knowledge and abilities expected of a graduate during their early career can be remarkably enhanced through experiential learning from authentic involvement during their undergraduate experience. Graduates with quality co-op and internship experience in construction exhibit indispensable knowledge and skills which their construction employers demand. Yet only some 10% of U.S. construction education schools have field internship programs (Weber, 1998).

To provide a foundation for advocating more and better co-op and internship programs in undergraduate construction engineering programs, it seemed essential to find a way of describing the internship experience as a valid educational process. It was believed valuable to be able to demonstrate to engineering educators everywhere that well-structured construction internships provide true and indispensable learning and, in fact, ought to be an integral part of undergraduate construction education.

This motive moved the author to focus on a basic question: How do construction interns learn? The goal became one of proving that the learning experienced during quality construction internships can be interpreted and understood in terms of established learning theory. An initial search of the literature revealed little relevant previous research on experiential learning in construction environments, and encouraged the idea of a focused study of how interns learn using an existing, well-structured construction internship program as a living laboratory.

SETTING

The Purdue Construction Engineering and Management Internship Program

Purdue University's Bachelor of Science in Construction Engineering and Management (BSCEM) is an engineering degree accredited by the Accreditation Board for Engineering and Technology (ABET) and designed to prepare graduates for professional careers in the large, diverse U.S. construction industry. As a requirement for the degree since its origin in 1976, students must complete three 12-week internship periods, employed by a sponsor construction firm. Work periods are full-time, paid employment. Students qualify for entry into the CEM program following completion of the two-semester Freshman Engineering program. Admittance is by a comprehensive application and interview, through which the faculty gains assurance of the students' potential to succeed based on academic, aptitude, and attitude traits. Student interns work on-site, which may be at a major construction project underway or in company offices. Internship sponsor firms in the program are some 60 to 75 midsized to large, regional and national, professional construction contractors selected by Purdue on the basis of the quality of the construction experience and intern mentoring which they offer. Placement of interns with sponsor firms is arranged and closely controlled by the Internship Director, a faculty member who is an industry veteran. Firms enter into a written memorandum of agreement with the university for each student intern they sponsor. Overall, this program is well characterized as a partnership between the construction industry and the university (Tener, 1996).

Each CEM student intern completes his or her three work periods with the same sponsor firm, with occasional exceptions. Student work locations and job assignments are determined by each sponsor firm, with the concurrence of the Director of Internships for the initial summer work period. The firm's supervisor or mentor provides a written evaluation of the intern's performance to the university following each work period. Typically, students are assigned responsible work tasks on major construction projects, living away from home. At the conclusion of each work period, students write a report covering their experience during the period. The CEM Internship Director reviews each report to discern and evaluate both student and sponsor firm performance, and the reports are also provided to each student's faculty advisor.

Administratively, CEM interns register for each zero-credit internship work period and pay a registration fee. Intern wages are paid by the sponsor firm according to an intern wage scale, which is established by the BSCEM Industry Advisory Committee and adjusted annually, indexed to starting salaries of civil-engineering graduates nationally. The quality of each internship work experience is closely monitored by the Internship Director through visits to job sites (generally seeing about one half of the 140 interns each summer) and through feedback from the students' and the sponsor firms' evaluation reports as well as personal conversations with many of the interns. Active oversight of the program by the BSCEM Industry Advisory Committee, a group of 18 senior construction executives, provides the faculty with broad direction, guidance, and stewardship for the program on behalf of the construction industry.

Since the 1976 inception of the BSCEM program, the term "internship" has formally defined the students' work experience. *Internship* has a wide variety of meanings and connotations among university educators. In Purdue's BSCEM program and for this study, the conditions of the student experience and the faculty involvement are similar to those in well-coordinated co-op programs for engineering students. The value of the learning received and the extent of the university's focus on program outcomes may be considered more typical of programs termed *co-op* than of customarily perceived *internship* programs.

Specifically, the defining characteristics of these internships are:

- each student must successfully complete three full-time, 12-week internship work periods with a major U.S. construction firm as a requirement for the BS degree;
- students are selectively admitted to the program based on academic, attitude, and aptitude potentials determined through a comprehensive interview during their second semester in engineering. Admission is also contingent upon the Internship Director securing a sponsor firm for each student, which has been successfully accomplished in recent years;
- sponsor firms are qualified for the program based on the quality of construction experience and intern mentoring which they offer, entering into a written, three-year agreement with the university for each student placed;
- each student is matched to a sponsor firm by the faculty's Internship Director, who strives for the best attainable match of the student's potential and desires with the firm's goals and needs;
- a recommended, general sequence of internship work experiences, developed jointly by the faculty and construction industry advisors and aligned generally with the educational objectives of the degree program, is published by Purdue and generally respected by sponsor firms;
- student intern experiential learning and the academic program of study are synergistic; interns and graduates typically appreciate the crossover of learning from field to classroom and vice versa (as verified by surveys of graduating seniors, BSCEM alumni, and their employers);
- the university and the sponsor firms share the goal of high quality intern experience; learning outcomes are closely monitored by the university, and actions to improve the interns' learning experiences are a hallmark of the program; and
- among the routine documentation are sponsor firms' written evaluations of interns' work for each period, and student internship reports written in response to the Director of Internships' instructions and evaluated by him

The Conditions for the Study

Each summer 120 to 140 Purdue CEM interns report to their 3-month internship work periods with 60 to 70 major construction firms in 20 to 25 states. (Although occasional fall or spring intern work periods are scheduled, these are infrequent.) Their specific work assignments vary widely, but all can be characterized as authentic involvement. (The term *authentic involvement* applies to activities that expose the student to real, on-going, live situations with completely open-ended outcomes [although the faculty may influence the selection of situations, and set performance criteria to assure that certain learning objectives are met]. Authentic involvement includes a client [here, an employer] who has a real need to obtain a solution that has not yet been determined (Harrisberger, Heydinger, Seeley, & Talburtt, 1976). Construction interns experience learning situations in construction engineering and management very much like the situations and assignments they will experience after graduation. Student interns and their supervisor or mentors generally are highly motivated to achieve a high quality learning experience from the work period. During the second and third summers, interns are usually given increasingly responsible tasks that draw on their previous summer's experience and often on knowledge from fall and spring academic course work. Work environments vary, but generally, over the three internship periods, students spend considerable time engaged in field activities on-site with major construction projects. Work experiences also include significant office time on tasks directly involving construction engineering and management processes.

Students know that they will be required to submit a two-to-three-page report to the Internship Director summarizing their internship experience. Format and content for the summer internship reports is broadly prescribed in a midsummer letter to each intern, and typically students submit rather open-ended, expository essay-type reports. A separate document, the Student Internship Evaluation Form, is submitted by each student and used by the internship director (and to an extent by the sponsor firms) to evaluate the administrative and logistical elements of the internship period.

Before 1997, the summer internship reports had not been used for the purpose of understanding the learning experience undergone by construction interns. However, in reading what students chose to write about in hundreds of reports, the author was struck by how frequently their reflective observations revealed innate appreciation for the value of the learning they had experienced. It became apparent that the CEM internship program constitutes a living laboratory, which could be utilized for studying experiential learning in construction, with a significant degree of control available to the university faculty.

STARTING POINTS FOR THE RESEARCH

Decision Point: How should we begin? How can we develop a logical research strategy, devise an effective research plan, and develop a starting point?
Given the broad objective to understand and describe how construction interns learn, the challenge to develop a research strategy, and particularly to determine a starting point, arose. The author spent months scanning literature about co-op and intern programs and theories of experiential learning. These initial steps revealed no previous research comparable to our focus. During this literature search, there emerged the framing of the query: What if we could show, using information in student intern reports, how their actual learning conformed with an established experiential learning theory? It seemed meritorious, in order to be able to prove to engineering educators elsewhere that good construction internships are in fact real learning and

> therefore constitute an educational process, to develop a theoretically valid
> explanation for how this observed experiential learning takes place.

The strategy that emerged had two fundamental thrusts: Devise ways to use student reports to characterize how they were learning, and identify an established theory of experiential learning that could explain the learning gained as described in the student reports.

Decision Point: How shall we gain funding support for the work, or should we proceed without external support?
At about this time, the dilemma arose as to gaining support for the desired research. Two modest searches for external funding were unsuccessful. Although optimistic about the potential for obtaining funding support in the future, the author determined to proceed with neither external support nor faculty release time. Unfunded graduate student independent research studies (mini-theses) done by master's degree candidates in construction engineering were to prove suitable for this initial research effort.

In 1999 Michael Winstead, a graduate student in the Purdue CEM program, became intrigued with the objectives and the potential of the research strategy being developed. His exemplary, four-credit-hour mini-thesis (Winstead, 1999) launched the project and provided a substantial basis for identifying the viable experiential learning theory that could describe "how construction interns learn."

IDENTIFYING APPLICABLE THEORY AND RELATING IT TO CONSTRUCTION INTERNSHIPS

The Search

Various definitions and theories of experiential learning in higher education were examined, beginning with Bloom's taxonomy for the cognitive domain and considering as well the pioneering principles of John Dewey, Jean Piaget's theories of how intelligence is shaped by experience, Kurt Lewin's classic work in group dynamics, and William Perry's work illustrating how college students respond to their education. Valuable guidance during the search was found in the excellent book, *Teaching Engineering* (Wankat & Oreovicz, 1993).

It soon became clear that, among the models that address experiential learning, the most widely recognized theory is that of David Kolb. Kolb's (1984) underlying principle was that "knowledge results from the combination of grasping experience and transforming it." In his model, learning flows from concrete experience, to observation and reflection, then to the formation of abstract concepts and generalizations, to testing implications of new concepts in new situations.

In his seminal book, Kolb (1984) elaborated on the characteristics of experiential learning:

- Learning is best conceived as a process, not in terms of outcomes;
- Learning is a continuous process grounded in experience;
- The process of learning requires the resolution of conflicts between dialectically opposed modes of adaptation to the world;
- Learning is an holistic process of adaptation to the world;
- Learning involves transactions between the person and the environment; and
- Learning is the process of creating knowledge.

Kolb's summary statement, by which he offers a working definition of learning is, "Learning is the process whereby knowledge is created through the transformation of experience" (p. 38).

At the heart of Kolb's model "is a simple description of how experience is translated into concepts that can be used to guide the choice of new experiences" (Atkinson & Murrell, 1988, p. 374). Kolb (1984) described learning as a four-step cycle based on the orthogonal relationship of two continua of cognitive growth and learning: the concrete-abstract continuum and the reflective-active continuum (see Fig. 16.1). The concrete-abstract continuum, which represents how individuals gather (grasp) information from their environment, ranges from a preference for involvement with particular and palpable events to a preference for detached analysis. The reflective-active continuum, which represents how individuals process (transform) the information they gather, extends from learners who take a more observational role in learning to those who prefer active participation. Individuals must continually choose, along the respective continua, how they will gather and process information to resolve the problems and conflicts presented by any learning situation (Atkinson & Murrell, 1988).

According to Kolb (1984), experiential learning proceeds through these four modes, which require four different types of abilities. The *concrete experience* (CE) mode requires individuals to immerse themselves in the immediacy of the moment, relying on their intuitive and affective responses to the situation. For example, an intern reported that he was impressed to learn how complex the roles of the general contractor were, by "being completely immersed in the day-to-day details of the job." Conversely, *abstract conceptualization* (AC) calls for logical thinking and rational evaluation to create ideas that integrate their observations into logically sound theories. To illustrate, an intern reported that, upon observing how a new concrete pavement was marred and stained by the effects of construction operations after its placement, he conceived of possible alternative means of preventing the problem by protecting it with plywood, by altering the sequence of operations, or by phasing the concrete pours. *Reflective observation* (RO) demands a tentative, impartial perspec-

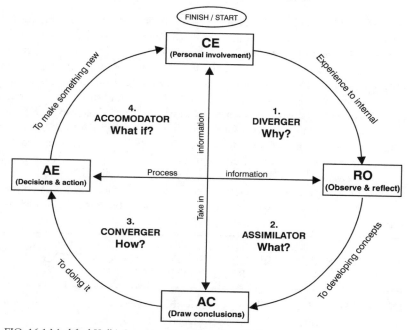

FIG. 16.1 Modified Kolb's Learning Cycle, based on Kolb (1984) and Wankat and Oreovicz (1993).

tive toward a learning situation—a willingness to patiently consider many alternatives. An intern evidenced RO as she reported that the most important learning from her internship was, "I need to take charge of my own learning," having realized this when she looked back and was disappointed in what she had not done or learned over the summer. *Active experimentation* (AE) stresses action, participation, and risk taking in learning, with an emphasis on pragmatically testing previously generated concepts. This learning mode was experienced by the intern who reported, "My most valuable learning was how to communicate with contractors on the phone. I did a lot of that and finally became good at it."

Decision Point: Why choose Kolb's model as the most relevant theory for this study?

The characteristics and the stature of Kolb's model of experiential learning are both relevant to the purposes and the setting of this study. This conclusion stemmed fundamentally from the fact that Kolb "takes an essentially structuralist approach to explaining [the] transformative process" of experiential learning (Hopkins, 1993). The theory is process based as opposed to, for instance, a psychological or phenomenological approach. The characteristics of Kolb's theory matched well our need to explain in straightforward terms how construction interns learn, given our well-defined set of learners undergoing authentic involvement in relatively similarly aligned internship experiences. Additionally, the structuralist and process-based nature of Kolb's model suited well our strategic intention to articulate, in logic and terminology that engineering educators would relate well to, the outcomes of internships as real learning. The broadly cited respect for Kolb's work was a convincing factor. "Kolb's learning cycle is useful for conceptualizing how people learn" (Wankat & Oreovicz, 1993, p. 293), and is widely applied in professional and human resource development according to Hopkins (Hopkins, 1993). Others have expanded on Kolb's model or used it to explain their theories. It was decided that Kolb's work comprises an established, experiential learning theory, highly applicable to construction internships.

THE SIMPLE DEVICE: DISCOVERING A METHOD AND APPLYING IT

Decision Point: How could we employ the interns' written reports as a means of discovering how they were learning?
During the early phases of this study it was expected that the students' written summer reports could somehow be employed to reveal information of value about how construction interns learn. But finding a viable means for guiding the students to record, straightforwardly and effectively, their observations about their learning was elusive. It was desired that, for this initial research effort, the students' observations be recorded in relatively simple ways, integral to the normal summer report requirements, without resorting to laborious or excessively detailed new formats. A separate survey questionnaire was decidedly not appropriate for this initial study. As described later, the author discovered and used a *simple device* (author's semantics), comprising two basic questions to which interns responded in their summer reports. Deciding to employ this simple device was a key breakthrough and thereafter, organization and execution of the work was straightforward.

The author's work as Internship Director includes field visits to construction interns at their summer work locations throughout the country. In 1999, while en route to the first intern job site (in California), the thought occurred that, if student interns were asked face-to-face what they were learning, the students' impromptu responses might be revealing. Rather instinctively, the phrase came to mind, "What is the *most important thing* you've learned here?" followed by, "*How* did you learn that?" Perhaps fortuitously, the very first test case using this conversation (described in the Appendix) was astonishingly successful. The first-year construction intern chose to respond spontaneously, yet thoughtfully and reflectively. His response indicated both his CE and his RO regarding a fundamental activity (communications among people on the job site). The efficacy of the simple device—the two questions—was immediately validated, and was further reinforced through the author's use of it in conversations with interns during many subsequent job site visits.

COLLECTING THE DATA

The Internship Director included the simple device questions in the written instructions to the summer interns for their summer reports during 1999 and 2000. About 3 weeks before the end of their summer work period, the interns received the instructions for their written reports, which were subsequently submitted on campus early in the fall semester. Students wrote responses to "what is the most important thing you learned this summer?" and "how did you learn that?" From the 198 student reports analyzed, 170 provided student responses adequate to reveal that their learning modes could be described in terms of Kolb's model for experiential learning.

The author and a research assistant spent time together to gain understanding and agreement about the meanings of Kolb's four learning modes in the context of construction interns' typical work environments and activities. The research assistant then studied each of the construction intern reports, focusing on the students' most valuable learning responses (Smaglik, 2000). The written descriptions of what and how students learned were compared with the four modes of Kolb's model of experiential learning, CE, RO, AC, and AE. In many cases students displayed several learning modes in their narrative. It was decided for this initial analysis to try to identify, based on the interns' descriptions, the learning ability that was most prominently utilized in each case. It may be possible to use these reports for a more refined, future analysis beyond the intent of the initial research effort.

An example illustrates the way that learning abilities were discerned. In an internship report, a student stated that her most valuable learning over the summer was the details of a concrete placement operation. She stated that she learned this information while hypothesizing an improved method for concrete delivery. As one of her tasks, the intern was assigned to a concrete placement operation. She constantly watched and absorbed the details of the operation (CE). After the initial stint of placing concrete, the intern reflected on the procedures that she observed in the placement operation. At this point she believed she observed a flaw in the concrete delivery process (RO). Having identified this flaw, the intern later tried to think of how to improve moving the concrete from the truck to the placement site, imagining several possible better ways (AC). The next day on the job, the intern tried out a new system, and observed its effectiveness (AE).

In learning about concrete placement processes, this intern has moved through the four stages of Kolb's model. Based on the intern's description of how she learned throughout the process, it was judged that the most prominent learning seemed to take place while the student was contemplating alternative new methods for concrete delivery. This experience was therefore classified as abstract conceptualization (Smaglik, 2000).

Excerpts from selected student reports with the learning modes identified are presented in the Appendix, and the numerical results of the learning mode analysis are in Table 16.1.

ANALYSIS OF THE DATA

Quantitative Data Analysis

As the data in Table 16.1 show, active experimentation was the most frequently encountered mode of learning (42% of cases), according to students reporting their most valuable learning experience in construction internships. Typically, students who adapted through this mode learned either a technical skill or something about themselves. For students whose most valuable learning experience was through reflective observation (33% of cases), either communication skills or something about their own identity were most typically learned. When concrete experience was reported (19% of cases), students typically learned a communication skill, with some instances of technical skills. Abstract conceptualization accounted for only 6% of the total number of experiences, each case involving the learning of a technical skill.

Additional Insights

Beyond the utility of these quantitative data, the student reports provided rewarding insights into the respective modes of adaptation to various, typical intern experiences in the construction workplace. By visualizing the experience that prompted the students' expository "what and how I learned," the reader can gain a clear and realistic appreciation for the learning mode that was employed. For example, adaptation through concrete experience typically occurs during a prebid conference or a job site meeting. By attending one of these activities, the intern has a rich opportunity to absorb the details of the experience, such as grasping exemplary or ineffec-

TABLE 16.1
Construction Student Intern Learning Modes

Learning Mode	1999 Reports	2000 Reports	Total	Percentage
Active experimentation	29	42	71	42%
Reflective observation	17	39	56	33%
Concrete experience	16	17	33	19%
Abstract conceptualization	5	5	10	6%
Total	67	103	170	100

tive oral communications, or absorbing the essence of personal interaction among professionals when emotionally debating over important issues.

Reflective observation typically takes place following an intern's telephone conversation with a subcontractor. After such telephone calls, interns often contemplate their end of the conversation and the effect that their communication had on the subcontractor. This reflection likewise often takes place after any number of intern activities, such as a meeting with a superior, a job coordination meeting, or a discussion with the architect about design details.

In adapting through abstract conceptualization, the intern may hypothesize about future opportunities to take certain action and about potential outcomes. Previously grasped experiences and observations are integrated into thinking about a new plan of action that the intern might put into play at a future time. For example, the intern may have been helping masons lay brick during a previous task, following which the intern may conceive of a plan for moving brick from storage to placement in a more efficient manner.

Adaptation through active experimentation occurs when the intern carries out ideas and plans previously developed. In the brick placement situation just described, the intern may have the opportunity, and make the choice, to put into play the improvement procedure that was conceived through abstract conceptualization.

Decision Point: Had we arrived at a valid basis for interpreting the nature of the learning modes, based on Kolb's model?

Upon analysis of 170 written reports by construction interns who had experienced a broad variety of work settings and learning situations, it was decided that we had a valid basis for concluding how interns learn. Interpreting, through Kolb's model, the interns' narrative descriptions of how they learned important things was sufficiently consistent and straightforward as to create good confidence that Kolb's four learning modes aptly described the actual experiential learning that had taken place.

The depth of understanding that one gains through study of construction intern responses can provide a powerful conviction that the experiential learning they describe is of a very real, uniquely valuable, and not otherwise attainable, nature and quality. A complete report of this study with further explanation of the analysis of student intern reports was published by Tener, Winstead, and Smaglik (2001).

From this data analysis, it was concluded that: (1) The "simple device" inquiry is an effective technique for generating information which, for initial levels of understanding and at a useful level of credibility, displays the nature of learning experienced in structured internships in construction; and (2) The learning experienced in these internships can be effectively interpreted and explained by Kolb's model of experiential learning.

Extending the Analysis

Some tentative inferences were developed as to learning styles that appear to be favored in a construction internship environment. Although the simple device questions to which students responded in this study were not intended to generate information about their learning styles, invoking Kolb's model provided some potentially useful indications.

As seen in Fig. 16.1, each quadrant of Kolb's model represents a learning style. Each quadrant is bounded by two learning modes. In the case of the accommodative style, concrete experience and active experimentation comprise the boundaries. Likewise, each of the other three styles (quadrants) have a closer relation to two particular learning modes. Then by grouping the learning mode data drawn from student reports (Table 16.1) pair-wise, it was believed that some preference for the respective quadrants of the model—learning styles—may be suggested, even if hypothetically.

Table 16.2 displays for each learning style the relative prevalence of the respective modes for the 170 student experiences. The sum of concrete experience plus active experimentation—bounding the accommodative learning style—has the highest score. One might presume from this that the accommodative learning style may be the most frequently encountered learning style in typical construction internship experiences.

To the author this makes sense. Taking a broad, subjective view of construction environments, accommodators would seem to be a style highly compatible with the kinds of tasks and learning situations encountered across a wide set of internship work settings. Likewise, the assimilative learning style would seem have the least relevance of the four styles for experiential learning in typical construction settings. It is interesting to contrast this realization with the observation that in engineering science courses in the university setting, the assimilator style is most relevant and the accommodator least relevant, as reported by P. C. Wankat (personal communication, September 20, 2001).

These tentative observations about learning styles certainly lack necessary rigor. For example, the learning mode data in Table 16.2 was not based on the same stu-

TABLE 16.2

Learning Styles Inferred from Learning Modes for Construction Interns

	Learning Mode				
Learning Style	Concrete Experience	Reflective Observation	Abstract Conceptualization	Active Experimentation	Total "Score"
Accommodative	19			42	61
Divergent	19	33			52
Convergent			6	42	48
Assimilative		33	6		39

dent having used the two modes. Further data sorting and analysis may provide a more effective probe of the idea of discerning learning style preferences for construction engineering and management interns.

A RELEVANT ANCILLARY ISSUE: SELF-EFFICACY DEVELOPMENT IN CONSTRUCTION INTERNSHIPS

A particularly significant benefit from construction internship experience is the development of the student's sense of self-efficacy. This fact is well understood by undergraduate interns, by program graduates, and by educators who are acquainted with construction internship outcomes. According to Bandura, *self-efficacy* may be thought of as people's judgments about their capabilities to carry out actions required of them to attain expected kinds of performances (Bandura, 1986). Superficially, self-efficacy may seem similar to self-confidence or self-esteem, which are simply people's opinions of themselves. Self-efficacy, however, influences human behavior in work environments more deeply than does self-esteem. Self-efficacy "plays a powerful role in determining the choices people make, the effort that they will expend, how long they will persevere in the face of challenge, and the degree of anxiety or confidence they will bring to the task at hand" (Emory University, 2000). The concept of self-efficacy provides an explanation as to why personal behavior can vary widely between persons of similar skill level attempting similar tasks. Construction internships almost universally enable students to develop their sense of self-efficacy in valuable ways.

The purposes of this study did not at the outset explicitly include research into self-efficacy development in internships, and the student reports in this study were not analyzed scientifically to assess self-efficacy development outcomes. Nonetheless, it was subjectively evident from scanning the student reports that almost every construction student intern gained significantly in this aspect. With further study of the student reports, it may be possible to support important conclusions about the nature of self-efficacy development during construction internships. It is the author's conviction that developing self-efficacy beliefs is a particularly valuable outcome of effective construction internships. If a method for documenting this outcome could be devised, then engineering educators could capitalize on this kind of learning as a bona fide educational process that could be integrated into program objectives. The Appendix includes several extracts from intern reports that reveal their having developed valuable new self-efficacy beliefs.

The point here is that important ancillary information, worthy of future, focused research, was discovered somewhat serendipitously in the process of an initial, broad study to apply experiential learning theory to observed learning during internships. Researchers can take satisfaction, even joy, in the prospects for such outcomes of their work.

SUMMARY AND CONCLUSIONS

Regarding Study Purposes

The general purpose of this study was to examine the nature of the learning that takes place during construction internships, and to describe it in terms of established learning theory. Its specific focus was to show that student learning from effective construction internships can be aptly described and interpreted by Kolb's model for experiential learning. Conclusions reached in regard to these purposes were:

1. It is possible, through the simple device of written student responses to two concise questions, to determine the learning modes, as defined by Kolb's model, demonstrated by students in effective construction internships.
2. For the conditions of this study, a majority (75%) of undergraduate construction interns reported prominent learning by the active experimentation (42%) or the reflective observation (33%) modes. Concrete experience (19%) and abstract conceptualization (6%) were less frequently encountered.
3. Significant insights into the particular learning modes displayed, and a deeper understanding of the ways that various intern experiences were actually translated into knowledge, was gained by studying the interns' written responses to the two simple device questions.
4. It may be inferred that the accommodative learning style may be the most frequently encountered learning style in typical construction internship experiences; this highly tentative hypothesis deserves more study.

Regarding the Underlying Strategic Motive for the Research

The underlying motive for this research was to provide a logical basis for advocating more and better internship programs in undergraduate construction education programs. If experiential learning gained by students through authentic involvement in construction internships does in fact create significant and uniquely valuable knowledge, then one must be able to understand this learning in terms of established learning theory.

The results of this study provided credible evidence for engineering educators that well-structured construction internships constitute real learning in terms of established learning theory. A basis now exists to test the assertion that such internships are indispensable in undergraduate construction education. We have begun a process that can provide motivation, to the benefit of future graduates, for more high quality internship programs among the U.S. universities whose graduates enter the practice of construction engineering and management.

Limitations of the study

Applicability of the conclusions reached here should be limited to effective construction internships, as described by their characteristics in the aforementioned *Setting* section. Nonetheless, the author believes that the conclusions and the implications of this study have significant potential value for advancing the understanding, and describing the educational value, of other experiential learning programs. Co-ops and internships that offer authentic involvement in many other engineering fields undoubtedly provide learning outcomes that can be understood in ways similar to those reported here.

Some important features of Kolb's model have not been invoked in this study. Particularly, no analysis was done to relate the grasping and transforming aspects of Kolb's learning theory to the observed student intern learning. For that reason, no substantive conclusions were reached as to learning styles.

RECOMMENDATIONS FOR FURTHER RESEARCH

The author envisions an exciting array of opportunities for further research, suggested by the work begun with this study. Some questions that arise, answers to which will be valuable to many engineering educators, are:

1. Is the knowledge gained during quality, authentic involvement co-ops and internships in construction unique to these types of learning experiences? To what extent is this learning unattainable in other environments, especially in academic settings? To what extent does this learning occur during co-ops and internships in other engineering disciplines?
2. To what extent do the learning modes and styles experienced by undergraduate interns match those needed for success in the early careers into which they graduate? Knowing this could sustain the argument that learning how to learn in internships comprises real knowledge, gained through an educational process deserving to be integrated into undergraduate engineering program objectives.
3. How do the grasping and transforming aspects of Kolb's learning theory describe experiential learning observed in student internships?
4. How do a student's learning modes progress as the student advances through second and third internship work periods? Are there ways of designing a sequence of internship assignments and tasks so as to maximize learning in preferred modes? What value might there be in designing a set of internship experiences that would challenge students to learn in non-preferred modes?
5. What preferred learning styles are most evident in successful construction engineers and managers in professional practice? Could knowing this help to guide entering freshmen to select their career field wisely?

6. In what ways can internships be made more effective for developing self-efficacy beliefs in undergraduate engineers?
7. To what extent, and how, can university experience with successful construction internship programs be used to advance other experiential learning programs?

The author is certain that continued exploration of the nature of learning from effective engineering co-ops and internships will reveal deeper and more convincing appreciation of their irreplaceable educational value.

ANNOTATED BIBLIOGRAPHY

Kolb, D. A. (1984). *Experiential learning: experience as the source of learning and development*. Englewood-Cliffs, NJ: Prentice-Hall. Kolb has developed "a comprehensive, systematic statement of the theory of experiential learning [in the form of a] structural model which forms the basis for a typology of individual learning styles and corresponding structures of knowledge" (flyleaf). This advanced text demands concentrated effort in order to comprehend and apply Kolb's model, with its depth, breadth, and universality. Yet its applicability is so general and illuminating that the reader can, by returning to study Kolb iteratively, continue to develop new insights about the nature of experiential learning.

Wankat, P. C., & Oreovicz, F. S. (1993). *Teaching engineering*. New York: McGraw-Hill (Available at www.ecn.purdue.edu/ChE/News/Publications). This beautifully written text was developed expressly to help new engineering faculty become good teachers. The three chapters on psychological types; models of cognitive development, and theories of learning are a valuable introductory source for educators in any area, including co-op and intern program educators.

REFERENCES

Atkinson, G., Jr., & Murrell, P. H. (1988). Kolb's experiential learning theory: A metamodel for career exploration. *Journal of Counseling and Development, 66*, 374–376.

Bandura, A. (1986). *Social foundations of thought and action: A social cognitive theory*. Englewood Cliffs, NJ: Prentice Hall.

Emory University (2000). *Overview of self-efficacy* [On-line]. Available: *www.emory.Edu/EDUCATION/mfp/eff.html*

Harrisberger, L., Heydinger, R., Seeley, J., & Talburtt, M. (1976). *Experiential learning in engineering education*. American Society for Engineering Education, Project Report, Washington, DC.

Hopkins, R. (1993). David Kolb's experiential learning machine. *Journal of Phenomenological Psychology, 1*, 46–62.

Kolb, D. A. (1984). *Experiential learning: experience as the source of learning and development*. Englewood-Cliffs, NJ: Prentice-Hall.

Smaglik, E. J. (2000). *Experiential learning in construction internships*. Independent research study. Purdue University Division of Construction Engineering and Management, West Lafayette, IN.

Tener, R. K. (1996). Industry-university partnerships for construction engineering education. *Journal of Professional Issues in Engineering Education and Practice, 4*, 156–162.

Tener, R. K., Winstead, M. S., & Smaglik, E. J. (2001). *Experiential learning from internships in construction engineering.* Paper presented at the American Society of Engineering Education Annual Conference, Session 1315, Washington, DC.

Wankat, P. C., & Oreovicz, F. S. (1993). *Teaching engineering.* New York: McGraw-Hill.

Weber, S. (1998). *Field internships for construction students: A survey.* Paper presented at the 1998 Associated Schools of Construction Conference, 61–78, Portland, ME.

Winstead, M. T. (1999). *Experiential education and construction internships: Learning how to learn.* Independent research study. Purdue University Division of Construction Engineering and Management, West Lafayette, IN.

Appendix: Excerpts from Student Reports

THE BARTLETT ANECDOTE

This excerpt from a job site conversation is relevant because it was the first time the author employed the "simple device" questions because the intern's response was both stunningly insightful and also illustrative of adaptive learning modes and because it served to prove, instantly, the utility of the simple device. The intern was in the fifth week of his first construction internship, working in the field on a major construction job, the building of a large, new suites-hotel facility. Our conversation at the conclusion of the job site visit:

Q: What is the most important thing you've learned so far this summer?
A: (After long pause and reflection): That would have to be the importance of good communications among all the people on the job site.
Q: How did you learn that?
A: Well, I was working on the concrete forming crew and we formed up that 15-foot high end wall over there. Our foreman has trouble communicating with the workers, and getting them to understand him, and we made some mistakes in the forms the first time. We placed the concrete, but it had to be all torn out and done over again. I thought that was a good lesson in the importance of good communications. But I've also watched our superintendent. At our job site meetings he has the knack of getting everyone to understand what he expects, and why everything is to be done his way. I want to be able to communicate in that way.

FROM WRITTEN INTERN REPORTS

The following excerpts, selected from student intern reports used in this study, reveal particularly clear or interesting student comments concerning the substance of their learning, and the learning mode employed.

REVEALING CONCRETE EXPERIENCE

My most valuable thing I learned is what it takes to make a project come together. I had never really knew how a bid process worked until I saw it firsthand ... I learned this by working with the others around me as well as trying to observe what everyone else did to make things run more smoothly. (B. J., 1999)

The most valuable thing I learned during this internship period was what it really took to completely manage a project ... I learned this by being completely immersed in the day to day operations of the job.... (M. R., 2000)

The most valuable thing that I learned this past summer was how the general contractor fits into the whole project … I learned this by going to the weekly job site meetings with the owner and design professionals and also seeing some of the interaction between the superintendent and the subcontractors. (M. M., 2000)

The most valuable thing I have learned during this internship period was communication skills … I learned this by just watching others interact. You can't really be taught this, other than just observing others. (C. L., 2000)

REVEALING REFLECTIVE OBSERVATION

The most valuable thing that I learned was not realized when on the job but while looking back and evaluating my experience. I found the most important thing is that I need to take charge of my own learning … I came to this realization when looking back and seeing what I was disappointed that I did not learn or do. (J. H., 2000)

The two most important things I learned this summer were (to) expect the unexpected and when it comes to estimating you can never be too thorough, or too anal. You have to be flexible and since I am a perfectionist, I wanted everything to be exactly as I planned. Well, I learned the hard way … It was a very stressful lesson … but I know that I will be able to reflect on this summer…. (M. V., 2000)

One important lesson I learned is it is essential to be a well rounded person to be successful. Knowing all the information covered in my engineering classes is not sufficient to be successful in my career. As I worked with various people this summer it became apparent the more you know, the greater potential you have for success. (T. K., 2000)

I realized this summer that as much fun as being in a city like San Francisco and being able to make good money, I desperately wanted to return to Purdue. I now know that when I graduate I want to be close to my friends and family…. (A. N., 2000)

REVEALING ABSTRACT CONCEPTUALIZATION

Throughout this internship, I learned one extremely valuable thing: The plans may be printed in black and white, but when it comes time to build them, there are many shades of gray that come into the picture. This was brought to my attention many times throughout the internship, but one time exemplifies this learning experience.

In the $17 million middle school, there is a lot of stained and scored concrete. It sounds simple on the plans. You pour the slab, score it, and then stain it. Where is the problem? The problem is since this is exposed concrete, and heavy equipment, such as lifts, will be running across it, it would be next to impossible to prevent any chipping, cracking, or gouging from occurring. You could put plywood over the concrete after you stain and score it to protect the concrete. Problem solved. Not exactly, what happens when rocks work their way under the plywood and then chip the concrete? You could hold down the concrete a couple of inches, come back and top it off, then stain and score it. If that is the case how do you set the structural steel to the correct elevation on the emdebs [sic]? What exactly do you do? These are just a few of the possible solutions to the particular problem. As you can see there are indeed problems introduced into the picture that plans do not account for. (R. K., 2000)

REVEALING ACTIVE EXPERIMENTATION

The most important thing I learned this summer is the fact that one has to compare the specifications to the take off sheet to make sure that all items are covered and nothing is forgotten. I learned the importance of this through (repetition) and made it a habit. (S. H., 1999)

The most valuable thing I learned this internship period was how to run a job site. I learned this because I was lucky enough that my superintendent went on vacation for a week. I ran the entire site by myself with a little help from the office … I did everything that a real superintendent would have done. (B. T., 2000)

The primary thing I feel most proud to have learned was not that I was learning to estimate and learn more about the project management side, rather it was how I was learning to do these tasks, as a full time employee would. (B. R., 2000)

… communication was the key learning for the summer. I was able to observe how my superiors dealt with individuals to accomplish their goals. I was able to take what I saw through them and then apply it to my own dealings with co-workers and the subcontractors I had to work with. (C. M., 1999)

REVEALING SELF-EFFICACY DEVELOPMENT

… over the past twelve weeks … I was able to apply skills (learned in my construction classes) and knowledge to my daily duties. Although at times some tasks were challenging and involved higher levels of responsibility, I was able to successfully accomplish everything that was assigned to me. (J. A., 1999)

The most valuable thing I learned this internship period was how to run a job site. I learned this because I was lucky enough that my superintendent went on vacation for a week. I ran the entire site by myself with a little help from the office … I did everything that a real superintendent would have done. (B. T., 2000)

The most valuable thing I learned this internship period would definitely have to be how to manage/run a project and deal with people. I was able to learn all of these things by actually being 'thrown' on the job without much prepping or knowledge of the project. I was able to learn by a hands-on approach as opposed to a theoretical approach. (J. C., 2000)

17

Using Theory in Research II: Atypical Cross-Cultural Experiences That Lead to Growth

Eric Miller
Antioch College

Key questions addressed in this chapter:

- How might we combine theories from several disciplines in a single study?
- How can a single case study using just one research subject best communicate meaningful information?
- What are the issues and challenges in making research in cooperative education relevant to other disciplines?
- Do cross-cultural literature and college requirements assume majority status of the students participating in cross-cultural programs?

In this chapter, I present a qualitative case study on the experience of one liberal arts co-op student at Antioch College. The study transgresses theoretical boundaries between experiential learning, cross-cultural experiential learning, and identity theory from an African-American studies perspective. The interpretation of the data from this study will say nothing directly about the employability of this student, the role of faculty or employers, or program assessment. It does, however, explore the meanings he took from his co-op experience and will help us better understand how he and perhaps others experience life in the American cultural landscape.

FIRST SOME BACKGROUND

I came to Antioch College in the summer of 1998 to work as a member of the faculty in the Center for Cooperative Education. I was assigned the international co-ops and began almost immediately to engage with my colleagues around questions regarding cross-cultural experiential learning. At the time, my knowledge of cross-cultural learning came, for the most part, from my personal experience as a learner living, working, and traveling in other countries as well as my experiences living in America. The discussion within the department arose from the fact that in 1993, Antioch College instituted a requirement for all students to complete a planned and evaluated cross-cultural experience. Approximately 80% of our students earn their cross-cultural credit through a co-op experience, the rest complete a cross-cultural study term.

It was within this context that I received a co-op paper containing the following paragraph:

> I can't exactly explain the amount to which I have changed after working and living in a queer community in San Francisco. San Francisco was my first ... exposure to an environment in which queer people owned and operated cultural, social and money earning institutions. All levels of society in a small part of San Francisco are continuously created and maintained for the use and benefit of queer people (not necessarily all queer people ... but ... some queer people).

This paragraph resonated with me in a way I did not expect; it provoked memories of my first visit to Jamaica at the age of 9. I am African American. I was born and grew up in America, but all of my grandparents immigrated to the U.S. from Jamaica and other parts of the West Indies. As a child, I was aware that our household culture was different from those of our neighbors. I realized that our family culture differed more from my friends' family cultures than theirs did from each others'. During my first visit to Jamaica, I saw myself reflected more clearly in the faces and culture of the people around me for the first time and wondered if I was feeling what my friends back in New Jersey felt when they saw themselves reflected clearly in each other. I recognized my student's experience of his first immersion in the queer culture of San Francisco as of a kind with my Jamaican experience.

After reading my student's paper, we met to have his crediting conference, the final debriefing session before credit is awarded for the co-op. In addition to credit for the co-op experience, he was also seeking cross-cultural credit. The official policy for the administration of the cross-cultural experience requirement states that the experience will take place in "an environment where learning is accomplished through active interaction with a different culture either within the U.S. or abroad" (Antioch College, 2000, p. 25). The student was a Euro-American gay male, and I think I surprised him when I was open to recognizing it as a special and specific type of cross-cultural experience, and agreed with him that he had satisfied the requirement. I even had a term for this type of experience: I called it a *going home experience*.

Although I awarded him credit for cross-cultural experience, my curiosity was piqued. Was I being overly creative in my interpretation of the criteria for awarding credit? Did the experience meet the intended objectives of the cross-cultural requirement? Were there other students having similar experiences? What were the deeper meanings embedded within these types of experience? I decided to explore.

Decision Point: What theoretical frameworks should I use?

There seemed to be too many points of reference for the questions I was asking. The phenomenon in question is being experienced within the context of a cooperative education program, but it was not limited to co-op. The theories applied to experiential education might be helpful in providing background, (e.g. Bandura's, 1986, self-efficacy theory), but the design and structure of co-op programs or intended outcomes did not seem likely to provide interesting or relevant information. The related field of intercultural experiential learning might provide more applicable theories for examining the experience. How would practitioners of intercultural experiential education view the argument that this experience is a cross-cultural experience? How would they examine it? What evidence would they look for to support or refute the claim? Also, there are basic underlying cultural questions that seemed best suited to examination and interpretation from an anthropological perspective. From a cultural perspective, who were the students before the experiences? How might these experiences have changed them as cultural beings? What were the cultural meanings inherent in the experiences? This experience is the experience of a minority within a minority. How would the identity theorists from the various minorities studies disciplines view and interpret the experience? Would this be the place to look for better understanding of the deeper meaning for the individual as well as for society? I decided to use them all. Cooperative education provides the setting for the experience. Intercultural experiential learning theory provided the means to problematize the original questions. The method of inquiry is one born of anthropology, and, identity theory from a minority studies perspective provides a context for a broader interpretation of the meanings of the experience.

THE CASE STUDY

The question that provided the impetus for the study was basic and straightforward. Could one reasonably argue that a first experience within a community with which one had a close identification be construed as cross-cultural? A search of the literature in cooperative education and cross-cultural experiential education turned up nothing directly addressing the question. I was unable to find anything in the literature surrounding the various perspectives on identity that similarly problematized the question. However, there are quite a number of accounts in fiction and memoirs of individuals' experiences of first time entry into communities with which they have a strong identification (e.g. Harris, 1992; Naipaul, 1964). Questions about the nature of this experience were ultimately the questions I hoped to explore through this study: What is the phenomenology of this experience? What is it like to go home to a culture that you've never been to before? What are the meanings to be drawn from it?

As I was interested in understanding the meaning that students and others might draw from these experiences, I decided early on that the study would be qualitative. I was interested in seeing whether or not this type of experience might be, if not common, one that could be found readily and how it might vary from one student to another. However, I didn't see how the study could easily employ an experimental method. Finding a large enough sample for a quantitative study was but one of the many barriers to that direction. (See Linn's [chap. 6, this volume] discussion on how choice of research method should suit the research question.)

The Sample

In this chapter I offer a sample of one. Henry Wolcott (1994) advised lone qualitative researchers to pursue one case study in depth (see Howard & Haugsby, chap. 11, this volume for a discussion on case studies). Wolcott suggested the final determination as to the sample size should be made on the basis of the problem being addressed. In this study, I felt that I needed to be able to follow my nose to explore the experiences as the student described them. I needed the room to first discern then substitute complex pictures for the simple ones, as Clifford Geertz (1973) put it, "while striving somehow to retain the persuasive clarity that went with the simple ones" (p. 33). Adding even one more student would only fog the picture.

I did not, however, begin with only one subject. My original subject, the one who raised the question in the first place, declined to be in the study. (He did, however, give permission for me to quote his co-op paper.) To find a student who had an experience that might fit the criteria was actually fairly easy. I asked my colleagues if they knew of any students who had co-oped in communities with which they felt they had a strong ancestral, cultural, or other identification but had never had the experience of living in those communities before the co-op. I very quickly had three students who fit the bill. A gay African-American student of mine had just handed in a co-op paper that suggested that his co-op in East Oakland, California was just such an experience. A colleague recommended I speak with a student of his, who is Japanese, but who grew up in the U.S. from about the age of 4 and was planning to go back to Japan for the first time to co-op. And, another colleague recommended I speak with a lesbian student of hers who had co-oped in San Francisco working as a research assistant with a drag king and sex educator.

I interviewed them all, as well as some students who had not yet had an experience of this nature and other nonstudents who could give background perspectives on the questions. In this chapter, I present my student, whom I will call Charlie. The data includes extensive interviews and material from his co-op paper. I have interviewed him three times totaling approximately 6 hours including a final interview. The final interview was done after I had given him the heavily edited transcript from the original interviews to check for accuracy and to add any missed data.

Decision Point: How will this be understood by the co-op community?
I have used professional association conferences as forums to test the viability of my idea. I presented the basic idea for this chapter, in varying forms, at four conferences: three times as actual conference presentations and once as a contribution to the discussion in a workshop on cross-cultural experiential learning. The first time I publicly mentioned the idea in a workshop discussion was at a Cooperative Education Association conference in Washington, D.C. (CEA). One or two heads turned to look in my direction and start nodding vigorously in affirmation. These were people who had this experience themselves and who encouraged me to investigate and document it. When asked by the presenter, about two thirds of the participants responded that they had lived abroad at sometime, and more than one half had advised students in cross-cultural settings. I was encouraged when some of the people of this audience almost immediately understood what I was talking about, and at least some seemed to agree that it might be understood as a cross-cultural experience.

Instrument

I designed an interview protocol with several goals in mind. I wanted first to learn how the student perceived his early experiences of culture. What was the culture of his family? What was the culture outside his home in the community around him? How did he feel in that community? Next, the basic problematizing question of the study was at root a simple yes or no question. Is this a cross-cultural experience? Qualitative studies don't ask or answer yes–no questions. However, the school policy issue required me to learn at minimum whether or not it is a reasonable question to ask. I decided to use concepts from the field of intercultural experiential learning to problematize the examination of the experience. Finally, I wanted to know what this experience meant. What did the student make of it? How did the student's understandings of and relationships to African-American culture and the dominant American culture change? I developed a protocol that allowed for a very free flowing interview but provided a structure that navigated the areas of inquiry.

The questions regarding the student's early experience were intended to obtain the personal life story of the student, asking the student to describe the cultural setting of his childhood and adolescence (Marable, 2000; van Manen, 1990; Wolcott, 1994). They provided a view of how the student perceived the cultural contexts of his life.

To examine the cross-cultural aspects of the experience I developed questions using ideas from Storti (1990) and Paige (1993), two prominent intercultural experiential learning theorists. My strategy was to use their assumptions of what elements are likely to be present in the experience of entering another culture for the first time and lay them as a template over this somewhat different experience to see how much the two might parallel each other.

Paige (1993) hypothesized that certain factors tend to intensify intercultural experience. He presented 10 factors that might be present in cross-cultural experience and hypothesized that the more influence they had the more psychologically intense the experience would be. The factors were:

- cultural difference between the sojourner and the host culture
- ethnocentrism
- language
- cultural immersion
- cultural isolation
- prior intercultural experience
- expectations
- visibility and invisibility
- status
- power and control

From these 10 factors I borrowed and incorporated into the protocol five: cultural difference, language, expectations, visibility–invisibility, and status. I decided not to use the other hypotheses for a variety of reasons. For example, finding a way to determine the level of *ethnocentrism* in a student would require a separate instrument, and *power and control* are present in some of the other hypotheses such as language, visibility–invisibility and status.

Storti (1990) asserted that the adjustments we make within our selves to other cultures are of two basic types. In making a *Type I* adjustment we have to adjust or get used to behavior on the part of the local people which annoys, confuses, or otherwise unsettles us. *Type II* adjustments require us to adjust our own behavior so that it does not annoy, confuse, or otherwise unsettle the local people (p. 15). I formulated questions for the protocol to determine whether or not Storti's Type I and Type II adjustments were present in this kind of experience.

The final concern arose from the question of practice with regard to the College policy for awarding cross-cultural credit. The stated objectives of the experiences are:

> The cross-cultural experience should help the student to form a clearer understanding and appreciation of both common characteristics of another culture's people and social institutions as well as their complexity and diversity. It should allow the student to experience the power of culture as a determinant of behavior, beliefs, and interactions of a people with their environment. Through fulfilling this requirement a

student should develop a sense of cultural humility and an appreciation of the sources and values of one's own culture. (Antioch College Center for Cooperative Education, 1998, p. 14)

I wasn't sure how to determine how a student's understandings, appreciation, and humility might have clarified and developed. I decided to look for it by asking a general question about how their perceptions of the two cultures had changed from the experience.

Decision Point: How would this be understood within the discipline of intercultural education?

I made my first formal presentation of this idea in a conference of the *Journal for Curriculum Theorizing*. The conference theme was culture and gender and roughly one third of the conference participants were involved in intercultural or cross-cultural education. Generally the ideas were well received and there was a lively discussion and general support for the notion that this might represent a particular kind of cross-cultural experience. However, it also became clear that some would perceive the argument as an essentialist notion that ethnicity and culture are inherent within individuals regardless of the extent of their isolation from the communities that engender them.

What follows is the presentation of the case study. It is for the most part in Charlie's own words, however I have heavily edited his words in three ways. First, for readability, I have removed most of Charlie's personal colloquial style keeping only what is required to preserve an impression of his personality in print. Second, I have organized the data to fit a logical progression. And last and most problematic, it was necessary to eliminate much of the data that was either redundant or not immediately relevant to the research questions, such as data that related to other subsequent co-ops. Further meaning might have been extracted from these data, however I found it more effective to reduce the amount of data and increase the analysis and interpretation to gain as much depth as possible.

The data are presented in three sections which are based on Wolcott's (1994) suggestion of three ways to "do something" with descriptive data. The sections are *description, analysis,* and *interpretation*. They are not by any means mutually exclusive, but do serve the useful purpose of shifting the emphasis and organizing the data in ways that allow us to ask different questions at different times. As Wolcott suggested, *description* is useful in presenting the setting and telling the story of who people are and what happened. The *analysis* essentially presents the findings in plain terms providing a systematic description of interrelationships and basic answers to questions about how things work. *Interpretation* addresses questions of meanings and contexts. In the analysis and interpretation sections, I introduce perspectives from African-American studies. This approach to creating new understanding is well within the traditions of African-American studies (Marable, 2000). In the interpretation section, I have relied heavily, but not exclusively, upon a collection of essays by African and African American scholars presented in a book edited by Marable (2000), *Dispatches From the Ebony Tower.*

DESCRIPTION

Cultural Origins

Where Charlie is From.   We moved to *the town* when I was seven, and I was in second grade. Before that, we lived outside of Carlisle, PA, which is probably just about 15 miles away. I can't remember there being any other Black kids in the elementary school system in either town.

I was the only Black person in my high school graduating class, but throughout my years there, there tended to be two or three other Black people in my class. We were not close friends but friends. Like I'd say hi to them in the hallway and occasionally talk to them after school or something like that.

Charlie was born and grew up in a small town outside of Carlisle, Pennsylvania. The 1990 and 2000 U.S. Census figures confirm Charlie's perception of the town being "about 99% White." The 1990 census in fact reports only two African-American people living in the town of 1,925 inhabitants, possibly missing two of Charlie's family members (The Pennsylvania State Data Center [PaSDC], 2001).

Contrast.   When I would go to a White person's house it would always feel incredibly different. One of the major factors in that was that I was raised Jehovah's Witness. We didn't celebrate holidays; we didn't believe in saluting the flag; we didn't go to a church; we didn't celebrate birthdays or any of that stuff. But, those were some of the main things going on in White people's houses. So, there were all those issues that really separated me from the White kids in the school. Plus my skin color, which I mean I was always seen as different because of that.

Also, my father worked on a Navy base, and my mother worked in York City as a social worker for a while. But the parents of a lot of people who I went to school with were farmers or operated small businesses in town. A lot of people who lived there were original to the county, so that was another big area of difference. I always felt different from that growing up in this place where a lot of the people just stayed in that one region and never left. It's kind of that Dutch-German descent thing going on. People used to laugh when I told them where I come from.

Misplaced.   My father's side was from Alabama, but we only went to see them but once when we went down for a funeral when I was in third grade. We were down there for about a week, but I don't remember all that much about it.

But, what we *would* do was, in the summers we would always go to northwest Ohio to a small town of about 250 people. My mother's side of the family lived there. She was born there. It's a tiny little town that's about a third Black, probably more than a third White and I'm not sure but about 20% Latino.

It's interesting that Charlie's perception of the town was that it was about one-third African American. The 2000 Census data show that it was actually only about 10% African-American and about 10% Latino and other minorities. Coming from a town where his was the only African-American family, it must have felt to him that there was a real and significant population of people of color in this small village.

Disconnect.   I did feel like there was something wrong. I didn't feel like I was connected in the way I should have been. I felt like there was a big difference in the way that I was raised and how my family was living and that of other people. Growing up, I had this idea that Black culture was in the rural and urban south and in northern and western cities. I thought okay that's not where I come from. When I would go to Northwest Ohio, that always felt different too because it was a rural area. So, my whole attachment to Black culture was coming out of this area in the rural north where we weren't even supposed to be.

Charlie was experiencing a profound cultural isolation. He could not find a reflection of himself in any of his surroundings or in popular sources of information. Compounding this was the fact that the limited cultural connection he had through family was not validated in mass-media images of African-American culture.

Trying to Connect.   "There was a show on cable called MTV Raps, and I would just listen to that. Like there was a period in my life, when I was in high school, when I would only listen to music that I knew had a black artist."

I asked, "Was that a way to feel connected?"

He answered, "Yeah at the time, I think that's what I thought. You know, that was the motivation."

Negative Contact.   Charlie went to a magnet high school for one half of his senior year. One half the kids were from the central neighborhoods of the city of Harrisburg, which is more than 60% Black and Hispanic (PaSDC, 2001).

There was always a big riff there because you had all the kids from Harrisburg hanging out over there and all the kids from the suburbs over here. It was hard for me because everyone knew I wasn't from the city schools. Being Black it was one of those weird situations where it was hard to fit in with either camp. I never developed friendships with the kids from the city. There was some hostility from the Harrisburg students and from the suburban students too. It wasn't aggressive though.

The Co-op Setting

Charlie's co-op in East Oakland was his third co-op. His first co-op was in New York at an organization that provides services for homeless people. In New York, he lived in a very diverse neighborhood that he characterized as being about one half Black, but the work environment was in a predominantly White neighborhood. His second co-op was with a community organizing group in Austin, Texas that facilitates an alliance of groups working to meet the needs of people who lack opportunities and resources. While there, he lived in a predominantly Latino neighborhood in a house owned and used by the organization as housing for its interns and other employees.

In Charlie's co-op paper, for the co-op we are examining here, he outlined his thinking about the kind of experience he would like to have:

> Back at my last co-op in the spring, I remember thinking of what I was looking for in my next job. I wanted to work at a place that was run by people of color and that worked more directly with the issues I cared about. A place that had a winning record when it came to their campaign [sic]. I wanted this because Whites ran all the places I've worked for in the past but their missions were for the most part about "helping people of color" [his emphasis]. It was important for me to know that people of color could "help" themselves and run our own organizations. Flipping through an internship book, I came upon a job that fit the description … and I knew I had found my next co-op.

The organization he found "is a racial justice organization dedicated to building a social justice movement led by people of color. The Center for Third World Organizing (CTWO) is a 20-year-old training and resource center that promotes and sustains direct action organizing in communities of color in the United States" (CTWO, 2000).

Decision Point: How will this be understood within African-American studies?

From the inception of the project, I realized I would not be able to do justice to the data without developing some understanding from the perspective of African-American identity theory and African-American studies in general. When the opportunity to present a paper at a regional conference of Black studies was announced, I asked a colleague, Assistant Professor of African and African-American Studies, Jahwara Giddings, if he would be interested in copresenting with me and providing a critique of my arguments. He was and through the process of preparing the presentation and long discussions before and after the conference, I began to distinguish areas within the field that would be relevant to my analysis and interpretation of the data. Additionally, the response to the presentation at the conference was very encouraging and gave me the confidence to proceed to place my analysis and interpretation within the African-American studies perspective.

ANALYSIS

How the Experience Unfolded

In this section we continue to look at Charlie's experience from his perspective but will analyze and categorize it from the perspective of the original research questions as well as from an African-American studies perspective. For the sake of clarity the analysis flows around the telling of the story.

At this point, I should also say that I venture very carefully and with humility into the field of African-American studies. It is not my discipline. I am simply drawing from it to help me better understand some of the meanings of this experience. I take some solace from the encouragement I have received when I shared these ideas with scholars in the discipline as well as what I have found in the literature to be a wide acceptance of the possibilities of learning at the edges of disciplines. To quote just one source, Manning Marable (2000) said, "Much of the most innovative and creative scholarship is produced at the borders, the intellectual spaces between old disciplines. The life of the mind in a university should never be fixed" (p. 256).

Expectations

Charlie recalled being in his mother's hometown in northwest Ohio and telling his family that he was going to Oakland, for his next co-op.

> *Oakland.*   I think it's hard to separate what I was thinking before I left from what other people were telling me and my reactions to that. They asked, "So what crazy place are you going to now?"
>
> I said, "Oakland California."
>
> They said, "What? You're going where? There are gangs!"
>
> We were in that tiny town where a third of the town is Black. My own family is Black, but for them, a *city*, you know what I mean. You don't go to a city, especially like Oakland a place that has such a reputation. So, they were telling me it was going to be a really dangerous thing.
>
> I think my reaction to that was "Oh, no it won't. It won't be like that at all." I expected that there would be crime, but I didn't expect it would be much more than anywhere else.
>
> One of the main reasons I was so excited to go to Oakland was because I had heard about how progressive and radical this Black community had been in terms of the Black Panthers and fighting against police brutality. So, I thought this must be a pretty active place. I just remember being really excited.
>
> I think I felt that in terms of the Black community I probably wouldn't fit in well. My whole exposure, prior to this, to a predominantly Black city comes from my experi-

ence in Harrisburg, when I was a senior in high school. My experience there was terrible, so I thought this will probably be like that. But, I also thought well it couldn't be. I was still excited to go. And, then when I got there and it was great fortunately.

I asked, "How was it, great?"

Well, because of my experience in Harrisburg, I had this expectation that people wouldn't be particularly nice to me. But instead, when I got there, whenever I'd go for a walk every single Black man that ever passed would nod and say "hi." East Oakland was like this really really nice place. It seemed like I had never been anyplace where you could just walk down the street and everybody would just says, "Hi," you know, "How you doing?" It was just like "Whoa!" I couldn't believe it.

I felt like I had let that reputation get into me. This expectation that everything would be mean. So, I felt that the experience of Oakland, the *reality*, was so different from Oakland the myth [my emphasis].

The community was great. I want to go back to Oakland someday.

The liberating quality at this point in his experience is palpable. Paige (1993) hypothesized that "the more unrealistic the sojourner's expectations of the host culture, the greater will be the psychological intensity of the experience" (p. 10). In his discussion about this hypothesis, he focused on the potential psychological letdown sojourners might feel if they enter a culture with unrealistically high expectations of their abilities to function in the culture. Minority students going to cultures with which they have no experience but do have an identity connection are likely to enter with high negative expectations based on internalized oppression received from a lifetime of bombardment from the media of the dominant culture (Hutchinson, 1997). Charlie, at this point in his studies, could dispel some of those negative images intellectually, but not emotionally. This was made more difficult by his previous, and only, experience with Black urban culture in high school. Paige did not discuss high negative expectations, but his hypothesis is confirmed by the high psychological intensity of the positive reaction Charlie had on arrival in Oakland. It was a "really really nice place."

The Co-op.   I didn't really know what community organizing was before I got out there. I thought it might be something like what I had already done, but it was different from anything that I had ever done before. Also, I didn't know what the organization was all about, I knew it was a people of color organization, but I didn't really know what it was when I went. It's amazing it addresses race, class, gender and sexuality all of them. That was really cool, and to see the staff and how they attract new people in Oakland.

Charlie's job was to assist in bringing residents of East Oakland into the political process. This was achieved in a variety of ways, but one of his primary responsibilities was to go out into the community and knock on doors and talk with residents about their concerns and about how they could get involved. He also did research on police violence, which was used in public meetings on the issue.

The Organization.   About 40% of the staff was Black. Then there was one from the Philippines and one from India, and my direct supervisor was everything. It's really interesting in organizations like this one. There are a lot of people who are very inter-mixed with all kinds of different races. It's so interesting. I don't know what it is about organizations that are just for people of color, but they tend to have people who are Indian and Jamaican and Black and everything. They tend to migrate toward these kinds of organizations.

In his book, *Race Matters*, Cornell West (1994) championed the notion of "a co-alition strategy that solicits genuine solidarity with those deeply committed to anti-racist struggle" (p. 44). This employer and its coalition were an excellent example of this idea in action.

Storti's Type I Adjustments

Storti called the adjustment one makes to things in the host culture that unsettle us Type I adjustments. His focus is mostly on the overt behavior of the people of the host culture. In our interview, I expanded the notion to include consideration of the environmental conditions. I have found from my own experience that often the reality of living in another culture is very much influenced by the environment such as architecture, pollution or differences in accessibility of goods and services.

Awakenings.   Where I was staying in East Oakland there were not many stores. When I first got there, I took a walk trying to find a place to eat. I only found a barred up pizza place where you have to buzz to get into the restaurant. It's because it's a lower income neighborhood and it's not gentrified yet. The flip side of not being gentrified is that you also don't get services. That was a really revealing experience for me because I came from a town where you just drive to the store.

In all the places I had lived before, access to a grocery store wasn't an issue. In West Oakland they didn't have a grocery store, and they had to have a demonstration to try to get one.

For me the problem was, okay, where do I get groceries, because a lot of people get their groceries in these little liquor stores. The feeling for me was that those are tiny little spaces where prices were jacked up. So, it's like, jeez, you know? I think that was one of the big things for me awakening to the fact that not all cities are 24 hours like a lot of places. I couldn't believe they had to battle to get a grocery store.

This is further evidence that this experience has some of the same elements of cross-cultural experience. The simple inconvenience of having to shop in the high-priced, low-choice stores of the area is not at all unlike the experience sojourners living in other countries have in adjusting to the local particularities of obtaining daily necessities. The additional element that indicates a cross-cultural condition and meaning comes from the fact that only people from the outside, such as Charlie, are shocked by this state of affairs. The situation differs from other cross-cultural situations in that the people on the inside are quite aware of the perceptions and conditions imposed from the outside and that they are contending with and attempting to combat. Charlie has understood from this experience that the "people who run these businesses, who come in from the outside and put up all their bars, do this because of their perceptions of the neighborhood." The outsiders are from a different cultural orientation. They are from the dominant culture or other foreign cultures and are imposing their reality and perceptions on this smaller disenfranchised culture. Y. Jones (1997) studied another midsized city and documented the systematic creation of a perception of a community from the outside. Louisville's "white controlled visual and print media construct [the image of] the African American communities in their midst, depicting blacks as criminals, victims of criminal behavior, rehabilitated criminals, and unfit mothers producing more of the same" (p. 133).

Being Included.   Charlie is a very politically aware student. He didn't experience many negative instances of Storti's Type I reactions provoked by the behavior of the people of Oakland whom he encountered through his work. Following is a description of one of the few he identified as such.

> I also had to deal with the fact that there were so many different races and ethnic groups in East Oakland. Sometimes I would go into a home and I'd be talking to ... say an African-American person who would say something about a Thai or Chinese person and go off into some prejudiced comment. When I was in Asian or Latino households, I'm sure they never said anything against a Black person because I am black. But, in a Black household I think some people felt they could say that. I would just cringe and hold my tongue, because I'm door knocking in this person's house trying to get them to come to an event.

I asked if there were things that people said that were offensive or unsettling in other ways? He replied, "I don't think so, not that I remember. No. They tend to be pretty nice people."

In the beginning of his experience of living in Oakland, being included was exhilarating full of pleasant Type I responses. Here at this stage he is beginning to feel the responsibility of being a member of the community and wondering how he should address some of the problems he found within it. Being included in a way that he did not want to be included was disturbing, especially since his purpose for being in the homes of people was to fight oppression. Cornell West's (1994) plea for a more inclusive coalition is often challenged even at the grassroots level.

Type II Adjustments and Visibility–Invisibility

Storti's notion of how we make adjustments in our behavior in order to avoid unsettling members of the host community overlap to some extent with Paige's (1993) ideas on visibility and invisibility. Some examples of aspects of our identities that at times may not be visible are religion, ancestry, and sexual orientation to name just a few. We often choose which aspects of our identities we will make visible depending on our commitment to them (White & Burke, 1987) or our perceptions of how they will be accepted by those around us. I focused for the most part on one invisible aspect of Charlie's identity. As I mentioned earlier, Charlie is gay. Charlie was accustomed to experiencing his gayness in the context of predominantly White communities, both at college and in his hometown while growing up. Being *out* and being *outed*, negotiating, and learning other people's perceptions of his sexuality provided another source of liberation for Charlie and adds an interesting layer to the meanings we might draw from his experience.

> ***Being Out.***   To most people, at the office, I was out. I was out to the staff, but I wasn't out to the members. I don't know. It's always a weird thing. At work there were workshops where we talked about ourselves and I was out, you know what I mean? When I was staying in the organization's house in Oakland, my roommate was a Hawaiian gay activist. So, when he came up to the main office and the project office he would talk about it a lot.

Initially Charlie had concerns that his sexual orientation, if it were to become known to the grassroots members, would provoke them to exclude him.

> ***Not Wanting to be Excluded.***   "I think I was always conscious of how people were going to perceive me. How are they going to perceive my voice, my mannerisms, things like that, because you're door knocking. I think I had a lot of sexuality concerns going into people's homes. Like how would I deal with that if that ever came to the forefront?"

> ***More About Being Out.***   The following exchange illustrates how Charlie's homosexuality provokes a Type II response in a fellow trainee. The process of *coming out* to this colleague and later being outed by him to total strangers reveals to Charlie that this part of his identity has different meanings in this community. Asking him if he had any problems being out while he was in East Oakland elicited this response:

> Yes! Yeah, I forgot! Oh, you're bringing back bad memories. [Laugh]

> So, I'm at my training. One night four of us from the training went for a walk and when we got back home to the house in East Oakland, I just said good night and went to bed.

> Fast forward to a week later. The training is over, and I'm in San Francisco, for the weekend. I was walking down the street and I see one of the guys from the training.

His name is Beanie. He was hardly ever at the training, but he was with us that night that we went for the walk.

So, we started hanging out and I ended up spending the night at his apartment. The next morning, out of the blue, Beanie says "Why didn't you go to bed with that White girl at the training?"

I said, "What? What are you talking about?"

He said, "Oh you know the White girl. Like I don't understand why you didn't sleep with her."

He said, she had come to his room and asked him "What's up with Charlie? Why didn't he do anything?" He told her "Oh, it's just because he doesn't like White girls."

I said, "What? Like, why did you tell her that?"

He said, "Well, I didn't want her to think that you were gay or anything."

I thought, "OH, jeez." You know? Now, I'm in this person's apartment, and I had spent the night. I was like "Oh, is it a good idea to come out to him?" So, I thought, "well maybe I'll say something so that he will gradually understand." I didn't know what to say, so I just blurted out, "Well you know? I have slept with men. Like I do like men."

He was like, "What? You're gay?"

I thought, "Oh, I shouldn't ... I should let him into this gradually." So, I said, "Well, I don't like most men."

But, then he just said, "OH, I don't understand how you could." So, we talked about it and I just laid it down that, "well I'm gay that's just that."

He just said, "Well you're still my buddy. I still respect you, but you know it's just crazy that you would be like that."

He was worse than a lot of people in Oakland, because he grew up in San Francisco.

This passage is packed with meaning. Beanie and the "White girl" had an expectation of sexual behavior that Charlie didn't have, understand, or detect at the time of the incident. Beanie had an expectation of Charlie's bias against White people that Charlie, at least in this context, did not have. Beanie preferred that explanation to the possibility that Charlie was gay. Beanie in fact assumed that Charlie would not want to be perceived as gay and would share Beanie's homophobia. Charlie was inexperienced in "coming out" in this new cultural context and may have missed cues and was unable to give the appropriate cues or language to more comfortably negotiate the situation. Two of the most meaningful aspects in the recounting of this episode come at the end. Beanie accepts Charlie despite his aversion to his homosexual identity, and Charlie understands that the force behind Beanie's aversion comes out of negative perceptions Beanie has developed from his experience in San Francisco.

A possible explanation of Beanie's quick acceptance of Charlie's homosexuality might come, at least in part, from the broadness of Blackness. In his article, *Why Blacks are Committed to Blackness*, Jones (1997) contended that this acceptance is rooted in the African-American acceptance of the "one drop rule," which necessarily implies a more inclusive community:

> It is because blackness has been adopted by so many persons of African descent around the globe that it is more broad than ethnicity.... Blackness is ... a normative and behavioral system, a way of looking at the world reflecting, deciding on how one ought to behave, and then acting accordingly.... Blackness is rooted in the one drop rule, in the absence of ethnicity among African Americans, and in the slave experience. (p. 50)

> Ironically, the African-American community includes descendants of all racial groups, demanding of them only that they identify themselves as black and commit themselves to the struggle for racial justice as blacks. (p. 70)

Beanie knew that Charlie was committed to his Black identity and to the struggle for racial justice and for Beanie that quickly outweighed issues of Charlie's sexual identity.

Charlie's Analysis.   For his part, Charlie applied a political analysis to be able to understand and accept Beanie's prejudice.

> This is kind of a gross generalization, but from my experience, Black people who are low income in San Francisco tend to be more homophobic than Black people in Oakland, because the dynamics in San Francisco are that of a Gay-led city. Gays are a *powerful* force politically [Charlie's emphasis]. The Gays who are powerful politically tend to be White and upper income. So, if you're lower income, you're being pushed out of San Francisco especially in districts like the Tenderloin and the Mission, and you're generally being pushed out by White Gay people. So, it's a whole different dynamic in San Francisco that tends to make Black people a lot more homophobic for economic reasons. Gays are a big part of the gentrification in San Francisco in a way that they're not in Oakland.

Acceptance.   Not long after that, I went for a walk with Beanie and there was another member of the public walking down the street and he turns to this guy and says "Hey my buddy here, he's gay. Don't you think that's wrong?"

> I hadn't been in Oakland that long. And, I feel like if you just turn to some random person in Harrisburg or New York and you're going to ask them that, I don't want to be around you. I'm like "Oh my god what's going on?"

> And, the guy just said, "Well you know if you're gay then you can't have children. So, that's wrong." But, he just said, "Whatever. You know it's your life." So, Beanie was really frustrated. He felt horrible.

Charlie had grown up experiencing his gayness as being yet another thing, in addition to his Blackness, that excluded him from his surrounding community. In Oakland, he was aware that homophobia was present, but he was beginning to find that perhaps it didn't automatically exclude him as he felt it had in communities of the dominant culture.

Language

I looked for evidence of language barriers and language acquisition issues. Paige hypothesized that "the less language ability the sojourner possesses, the greater will be the psychological intensity of the experience" (p. 7). In traditional intercultural experiential learning, language is usually a central factor in the quality of the experience. In examining Charlie's experience, I did not expect to find significant language issues, however in the African-American community how people talk can at times become a very important factor in how people perceive and respond to each other. I inquired as to whether or not he had noticed a language barrier?

> Definitely, with people in Oakland I might say something, "Oh, blah, blah blah," and people would be like, "What?" You know what I mean? They could never understand what I was saying.

> Oh Jeez! And sometimes *they* would say stuff and I would be like, "What?" I think that happened more when I would do youth presentations in high schools. But, with a lot of our members who were adults it didn't seem to be that much of a problem.

> Also, I wondered if I would speak like they speak when I left, but it didn't happen.

At this stage, Charlie did not consciously view this experience as cross-cultural, yet here he talks about an unfulfilled expectation of acquiring linguistic characteristics of the host community. He is looking for a type of transformation, which is not occurring. Following is another example of his attempts at changing his outward persona and being made aware of how he is different.

Body Language: Africanity Versus Afrocentricity.   When I brought up the question of language, interestingly enough, Charlie brought up body language.

> Oh it was crazy! Like in terms of just walking! Sometimes we would be in San Francisco in Beanie's neighborhood. He had a group of friends that we would always run into on the street and he would want to introduce me to everybody he knew.

> I would just be walking like this with my hands up like this.

> He wanted to introduce me to everybody, but he'd be like, "You can't walk like that."

> And I'd be like, "What do you mean?"

> And he'd go, "I can't introduce you to all these people when you're walking like that."

> "What do you mean? I can't walk like this? This is how I walk."

And he'd be like, "No, I'll show you how you have to walk."

And I was like, "Okay, I'll try."

And then I did it and he was like, "Oh, no. That's not it."

And I was like, "Well I can't do it. I just can't do that so … "

He had all these big problems with the way I walked, but I was just like, "That's just the way I walk."

I was all wrong. Dress … clothing … I mean the clothing and the walking and my speech was all off. Couldn't get any of it right. [laughing]

It is difficult to describe how Charlie walks because in fact there is little that is distinct or remarkable about it. How he walks is important because Beanie and his friends were decidedly of the African-American West Coast *gangsta* culture of the late 1990s. In his book, *Am I Black Enough for You?*, Todd Boyd (1997) observed that in addition to being a culture that springs from and is largely defined by rap music, gangsta culture is highly informed by the visual imagery of its lyrics. Rap is the cultural forum and ascendant means of expression for the young Black males of his generation. Charlie walks with short strides that revealed little influence of the rap rhythms or the gangsta culture of the place. Charlie, although phenotypically clearly African-American, was visually incongruous. He "couldn't get any of it right."

At this point in his development, Charlie is well on his way to achieving an Afrocentric understanding of the world, but he lacks Africanity. Molefi K. Asante (2000) defined *Africanity* as "the modality of African lifestyle" and further asserted that "Africanity is not Afrocentricity" (p. 202). In this sense Africanity would include many of the diverse African-American lifestyles including gangsta culture. *Afrocentricity* is a highly problematic term within the discourse on African-American identity. Here I use *Afrocentricity* in the narrow sense, and in a sense that I think most would agree is included in its meaning: a perspective that places people of African descent at the center of their analysis and understanding of the world (Asante, 2000; Ransby, 2000). Asante argued that "there are many people who have Africanity but are not Afrocentric" (p. 202). Charlie is Afrocentric but does not have much Africanity. He has spent so little time in African-American communities, even small communities within larger White communities. How could he possibly have developed an Africanity recognizable by Beanie and his friends on the streets of San Francisco? Yet, his ability to laugh about not being able to get any of it right indicates that he is getting comfortable with the fact of who he is within the heterogeneity of African-American communities.

Perceived Cultural Difference

I used Storti's (1990) ideas about Type I adjustments to explore Paige's hypothesis regarding cultural difference and realized that in addressing it in this way Charlie was only able to identify minor differences. The hypothesis being that "[t]he greater the degree of cultural difference between the sojourner's own culture and the target culture, the greater the degree of psychological intensity" (1993). The hypothesis stated in this manner requires us to know things that are very difficult to know. What is Charlie's cultural place, both geographically as well as existentially? How is that place or those places different from the culture of East Oakland? One of the minor differences Charlie noticed was that within the African-American community in East Oakland, there was a difference in the importance people there placed on age compared to the value he usually placed on it.

> *Elders.*   When I door knocked in the African-American neighborhoods, people always let me in, but I think they always preferred to talk to someone older. My sense of it was that I was pretty young. When I went door knocking even if I would get some one my age they would always go to get their parents. When I went with another member who was older, even if I was the one talking, they would gravitate to the older member.

Status

I was very interested to know how Charlie felt about how his status might have changed when he was living in East Oakland. Paige (1993) hypothesized that "[s]ojourners who do not feel they are getting the respect they deserve or, conversely, who feel they are receiving undeserved recognition will find the experience more psychologically intense" (p. 11). Also, I ran across a quote of V. S. Naipaul in Storti's book that influenced me to look for a downward shift in status. In his book, *An Area of Darkness*, Naipaul (1964) spoke of a kind of let down he experienced when he went to India for the first time:

> I was one of the crowd. In Trinidad to be an Indian was to be distinctive; in Egypt it was more so. Now in Bombay I entered a shop or a restaurant and awaited a special quality of response. And there was nothing. It was like being denied part of my reality. I was faceless. I might sink without a trace into the Indian crowd … Recognition of my difference was necessary to me. I felt the need to impose myself, and didn't know how. (p. 46)

It may seem counterintuitive to look in this direction, but African Americans who live and work in predominantly White institutions and communities are often the recipients of unwanted expert status on all-things Black. As much as we may dislike that status, we come to expect it. I was curious to know if, like Naipaul, Charlie missed that status. When I addressed the question head on I got little, partly due to the fact that the organization he worked for trained their workers to not be experts but to look for experts and leaders in the community. Thus, his role as an employee was to support others and he felt he was doing well when he was able to do so. However, there is ample evidence in the previous passages that Charlie was, for the most part, functioning as a social novice while he was in Oakland and that he was comfortable in that status.

INTERPRETATION AND CONCLUSIONS

The Antioch Questions

Antioch's cross-cultural experience requirement has two stated objectives. The first objective is that "the experience should help the student form a clearer understanding and appreciation of the common characteristics of another culture, and its complexity and diversity." The second objective is that by fulfilling this requirement a student should develop a "sense of cultural humility" and an "appreciation of the sources and values of their own culture" (Antioch College Catalog, 2000, p. 25). What does that mean for Charlie?

From His Co-op Paper.   Living in Oakland was probably one of the best aspects of the co-op. Across the country it seems to be a sin to be a person of color especially a Black male. White women clutch their purses and cross the street at the sight of us, White men get a disdainful look on their faces when they see us. The extreme hatred White society has for Black people is evident in the media and in day-to-day interactions. In the Black community internalized racism all too often affects us. Making us not trust ourselves and ostracize those in our community who look, act, or behave differently from mainstream norms. This is not true in Oakland. I found Oakland to be a place of unity where people of color especially Blacks feel empowered and are proud of themselves their culture and history in Oakland. A feeling of respect for people to live and be as they are was in the air. This was a powerful experience for me and added to my sense of self-esteem in who I am.

"Was This a Cross-Cultural Experience?"   I think when people look at cross-cultural stuff sometimes they think, "Well there is a culture that the person comes from and that they're rooted in. There is a place, outside more than just the family and the community where they've always been in the majority and now they're going to go somewhere different. But, for people like me it doesn't work that way. Like in no way do I feel like my hometown is my home. It's where I grew up for most of my life, but I never felt comfortable there."

"How Would You Compare How You Feel in Your Hometown Now to How You Felt in Oakland?"   I think, I always feel some hostility coming from people in my hometown. Like when I'm just walking down the street nobody will say anything. They won't call me a name, but in my experience they're thinking it. You know what I mean? They might nod at you, but it's just different there's no warmth there. I find it to be very racist.

Like with sexuality issues in my hometown. It's very straight, very homophobic. In Oakland a lot of the people are homophobic too, but their attitude is, "if that's what you're going to do then whatever." They'll disagree with it, but they still respect you as a person. In my hometown that isn't so.

I guess I've grown to see that it's more and more a place I don't want to be. I'd rather be in a place like Oakland. I just always felt different there, and I don't want to be there now even more so. When I get out of school, I want to go to Brooklyn. That's the plan.

Charlie always felt different in his hometown. He was always a foreigner and an outsider. In Oakland he got a taste of what it might be like to be an insider, a person who could see himself reflected more completely in others around him.

Cross-cultural experiences are usually defined and thought of as excursions outside of the comfort zones of the individual. They are expected to be exciting, exhilarating, and transformative but also less comfortable than staying at home. Charlie's experience was more comfortable, yet possibly it's also cross-cultural. Why do we have a cross-cultural requirement? Antioch's stated objectives exemplify a standard for expected outcomes of cross-cultural experience. We want our students to have an increased cultural sensitivity and humility when communicating across cultures, but perhaps these goals assume a White majority status and privilege, high self-esteem, and low humility. Charlie's tapping into the sources and values of his own culture instead has increased his self-esteem and possibly decreased his humility putting him on a more equal footing with the rest of the world, dominant and minority cultures alike.

Perhaps minority students coming from an experience like Charlie's can meet the objective, by *going home* rather than going abroad. Perhaps what they need is to elevate their self-esteem rather than their humility, which is tried, tested and demanded on a daily basis.

Understandings

African-American Cultural Diversity.   You have on one hand white culture telling us what African American culture is supposed to be and it's so different from what might actually be going on. And, you also have to deal with Black people saying that you're not Black enough.

So, you have these two really powerful things, but for me being here at Antioch I'm going around to the South, Georgia, the Sea Islands, Oakland and other places, and I'm just realizing that Black people are really varied and that culture is really varied. But, in this country they say that Black culture is like this, and for me growing up I really thought it was a really narrow thing. I got an image in my mind of what it was supposed to be and how I wasn't fitting into that. Then I see this whole heterogeneity thing and how it can be a lot of different things.

Charlie is coming to realize that he has not had *the* Black experience but *a* Black experience. "Like all other racial/ethnic groups, African Americans are a heterogeneous population. However, the media, social and biological scientists, and the majority population study and interact with blacks as if they are a homogeneous group that can be reduced to a single variable, race" (Hutchinson, 1997, p. 139). The Afrocentrist scholar Maulana Karenga (2000) put it this way, "there is no substitute for centering oneself in one's own culture and speaking one's own cultural truth" (p. 166). Charlie was not able to achieve a convincing Africanity, but he most definitely has achieved an African-American perspective on himself and the American cultural landscape. He has found his psychological, historical, economic, social, and moral location within the African-American community (Asante, 2000, p. 202). He has found his voice and has begun to speak his own cultural truth.

White and Burke (1987), found that the more committed an African American is to his or her African-American identity, the higher their self-esteem. And in a review of the literature on identity formation, Burt and Halpin (1998) concluded that, "[h]ow congruently African Americans are able to consolidate and make sense of their external and internal environments determines how effectively they will function, not only within the African American community, but also within society as a whole" (p. 14).

Charlie's experience would indicate that the idea that it was cross-cultural is a reasonable one to consider. He had to make adjustments, of the Type I variety, to his routines of daily life. He provoked some Type II responses in some members of the community. He learned how some aspects of his identity are perceived differently in this new community. He had expectations of acquiring certain cultural traits, although that did not occur in any significant ways. Although it was not an issue for him he did experience a change in his status from expert to novice. His understanding and appreciation of the diversity of American cultures has grown and his appreciation of his own cultural location has increased concomitantly.

Being a person involved in experiential education I always return to the ideas of John Dewey (1938) as a touch stone to reassure myself that there is some logic to my arguments. More than 60 years ago Dewey said:

> A primary responsibility of educators is that they not only be aware of the general principle of the shaping of actual experience by environing conditions, but that they also recognize in the concrete what surroundings are conducive to having experiences that lead to growth. Above all, they should know how to utilize the surroundings, physical and social, that exist so as to extract from them all that they have to contribute to building up experiences that are worth while. (p. 40)

Cornell West (2000) made the complementary statement to Dewey's appeal:

> I think ultimately it's a question of moral, political and ideological maturity. That is to say, all of us are born of circumstances not of our own choosing, therefore find ourselves shaped by a variety of different communities with their own parochialisms. We tend to focus on that which most immediately affects us, and as one lives one's life one can make these connections if one is able to exercise ... an imagination that's

able to empathize and sympathize with the suffering of others. To expand one's empathetic imagination requires not just courage but maturity, and by maturity all I mean is an acknowledgment of just how complex the world is, and acknowledgment of the fundamental need one has to grow. (p. 277)

Charlie's experience was indeed worthwhile and led to important growth and development. He learned that he has a place within the heterogeneous African-American culture and by extension the larger American cultural landscape. This understanding gives him traction or agency. Through this co-op experience he has begun to understand "just how complex the world is."

Summary
- Single-subject case studies can surface deep meaning in experiential learning.
- Theories from different disciplines can be combined within a single study to structure the study at various stages of its implementation.
- The theories from other disciplines can provide useful insights, understanding, and challenges for practice within cooperative education.
- Presenting your study ideas in a variety of settings and inviting critique can help shape your research in ways that may make it relevant to a variety of audiences.
- Some policies do not serve minority students as they are intended.

ANNOTATED BIBLIOGRAPHY

Marable, M. (Ed.). *Dispatches from the ebony tower: Intellectuals confront the African American experience*. New York: Columbia University Press. This is a recent collection of essays from many of the leading scholars in the field of African-American studies giving a reasonably wide perspective on current thinking within the field. It provided an excellent entrée into a broad field.

ERIC database (ERIC Document Reproduction Service [EDRS]) on-line at https://edrs.com/ ERIC Document Reproduction Service (EDRS), is the document delivery component of the Educational Resources Information Center (ERIC). Eric is the largest database in the world of articles about education. It is an source of published and unpublished articles and was where I located a review of the literature of African-American identity formation.

Johnson, A. G. (1995) *The Blackwell dictionary of sociology: A user's guide to sociological language*. Malden, MA: Blackwell. This dictionary gives long narrative definitions of terminology used in sociology, anthropology, and generally in the social sciences. It is intended for the use of students, but is a good resource for any new comer to reading and writing in the field.

REFERENCES

Antioch College. (2000). *Antioch College catalog*. Yellow Springs, OH: Author.

Antioch College Center for Cooperative Education. (1998). *Survival handbook.* Yellow Springs, OH: Author.

Asante, M. K. (2000). Afrocentricity, race, and reason. In M. Marable (Ed.), *Dispatches from the ebony tower: Intellectuals confront the African American experience* (pp. 195–203). New York: Columbia University Press.

Bandura, A. (1986). *Social foundations of thought and action: A social cognitive theory.* Englewood Cliffs, NJ: Prentice-Hall.

Boyd, T. (1997). *Am I black enough for you? Popular culture from the 'hood and beyond.* Bloomington, IN: Indiana University Press,

Burt, J. M., & Halpin, G. (1998). *African American identity development: A review of the literature.* New Orleans, LA: Mid-South Educational Research association. (ERIC database (ERIC Document Reproduction)

Center for Third World Organizing. (2001, September 20). About Us. Retrieved October 8, 2001, http://www.ctwo.org/about_us.html

Dewey, J. (1938). *Experience & education.* New York: Touchstone.

Geertz, C. (1973). *The interpretation of cultures; selected essays,* New York: Basic Books.

Harris, E. L. (1992). *Native stranger: A Black American's journey into the heart of Africa,* New York: Simon & Schuster.

Hutchinson, J. F. (1997). Creating a racial identity. In J. F. Hutchinson (Ed.), *Cultural portrayals of African Americans: Creating an ethnic/racial identity* (pp. 139–150). Westport, CN: Bergin & Garvey

Jones, R. S. (1997). Why Blacks are committed to Blackness. In J. F. Hutchinson (Ed.), *Cultural portrayals of African Americans: Creating an ethnic/racial identity* (pp. 49–73). Westport, CN: Bergin & Garvey.

Jones, Y. V. (1997). African-American cultural nationalism. In J. F. Hutchinson (Ed.), *Cultural portrayals of African Americans: Creating an ethnic/racial identity* (pp. 113–137). Westport, CN: Bergin & Garvey.

Karenga, M. (2000). Black studies: A critical reassessment. In M. Marable (Ed.), *Dispatches from the ebony tower: Intellectuals confront the African American experience,* (pp. 162–170). New York: Columbia University Press.

Marable, M. (Ed.). (2000). *Dispatches from the ebony tower: Intellectuals confront the African American experience* (pp. 1–28; 243–264). New York: Columbia University Press.

Naipaul, V. S. (1964). *An area of darkness.* New York: Macmillan.

Paige, R. M. (1993). On the nature of intercultural experiences and intercultural education. In R. M. Paige (Ed.), *Education for the intercultural experience* (pp. 1–19). Yarmouth, ME: Intercultural Press.

Pennsylvania State Data Center. (2001). *The municipal demographic profile, 2000 census: Summary of race and Hispanic or Latino origin.* On-line. Available: http://pasdc.hbg.psu.edu/pasdc/mcd_profiles/c133/m040/stfl_profile.html

Ransby, B. (2000). Afrocentrism, cultural nationalism, and the problem with esentialis definitions of race, gender, and sexuality. In M. Marable (Ed.), *Dispatches from the ebony tower: Intellectuals confront the African American experience,* (pp. 216–223). New York: Columbia University Press.

Storti, C. (1990). *The art of crossing cultures.* Yarmouth, ME: Intercultural Press.

van Manen, M. (1990). *Researching lived experience: Human science for an action sensitive pedagogy.* New York: State University of New York Press.

West, C. (1993). *Race matters.* Boston: Beacon Press.

White, C. L., & Burke, P. J. (1987). Ethnic role identity among Black and White college students: An interactionist approach. *Sociological Perspectives, 30*(3), 310–331.

Wolcott, H. F. (1994). *Transforming qualitative data: Description, analysis, and interpretation.* Thousand Oaks, CA: Sage.

18

Program Assessment I:
A Focused Approach to Measuring
Learning Outcomes

Cheryl Cates
Brenda LeMaster
University of Cincinnati

Key questions addressed in this chapter:

- Can we identify common learning outcomes we believe all students achieve regardless of discipline?
- What are some examples of these common learning outcomes?
- How do we move from a conceptual outcome to a clearly defined outcome measure?

In this chapter, we report on a pilot study conducted at the University of Cincinnati as the first step in a comprehensive and ongoing assessment program. One goal of the chapter is to describe the pilot study and its findings, while another goal is to describe the planning process used in the development of the assessment program itself.

BACKGROUND INFORMATION

The Division of Professional Practice at the University of Cincinnati is the centralized unit for the administration of all programs of cooperative education on our main campus. There are 16 full-time, tenure-track faculty members and two part-time adjunct faculty members in the Division who work with approximately

363

3,000 co-op students annually. These faculty are responsible for programs of cooperative education in five colleges: University College; Arts & Sciences; Business Administration; Design, Art, Architecture, & Planning (mandatory co-op program), and Engineering (mandatory co-op program). The program is full-time, alternating quarters of study and co-op in both 2- and 4-year models. Students in both the mandatory and optional co-op programs must complete a minimum of four quarters of co-op experience (although the majority of students complete six co-op quarters), complete an evaluation of their experience, and whatever assignment their Professional Practice advisor requires (including logs, journals, focused assignments, etc.). Although these students do not receive academic credit for participation in co-op, their participation is noted on their transcript, and completion of a minimum of four quarters of co-op experience is required for graduation. Students are required to remain with an employer for a minimum of two quarters, but may request an exception to this rule.

As tenured faculty whose academic specialty is cooperative education, we have long been engaged in activities to define, document and assess learning that results from the cooperative model. The assessment movement in higher education, along with the call for greater accountability in higher education has driven many discussions of pedagogy on campuses and in academic units across this country. This was true for the Division of Professional Practice. However, until the early 1990s we had no clearly stated divisional plan for formalizing our work. The opportunity to participate in the University of Cincinnati's (UC) Project to Improve and Reward Teaching (PIRT) provided us with an institutionally driven focus on teaching and the ability to formally explore ways to articulate the learning derived from cooperative experiences. As a result of the Division's participation in PIRT, a 5-year educational strategic plan was created, which focused on building assessment strategies that would allow us to measure individual student learning and evaluate program effectiveness.

As educators, the tensions between educating for a discipline and preparing students for the workplace are on-going. At UC that tension is evident in the fact that the overwhelming majority of cooperative education students are in professional programs. But, as accrediting bodies (regional as well as specialized and professional) begin to require more evidence of student learning in competencies beyond individual disciplines (critical thinking, civic engagement, teamwork), the important role of cooperative education and other work-based learning models is becoming more apparent. Documenting and assessing these learning outcomes remain a challenge in the academy. Palomba and Banta (1999) noted this challenge:

> Whether or not educators have been successful in helping students prepare for the workplace remains a subject of much debate. Philip D. Gardner's recent review of research evidence identifies a consistent theme: "College students show strength in their content or academic skill base but lack competencies to handle successfully the principal complex issues of work: interpersonal communication, teamwork, ap-

plied problem solving, time management, setting priorities, and taking initiative." (pp. 211–212)

The primary goals of our plan were simple: to focus student attention on specific areas of learning; to create a universally utilized set of instruments that include a defined student project to be completed while on the cooperative assignment; and to include multiple assessments that capture perspectives from the student, the employer, and the faculty member. Our hope was that these instruments, or learning modules would allow us to document and assess learning outcomes.

THE PLANNING PROCESS

The University of Cincinnati Division of Professional Practice embarked upon its program of assessment in 1994 with its involvement in a university-wide initiative to improve and reward teaching. As the first step in the division's project, we decided to brainstorm the question, "What did we want to accomplish with this project?" A group was formed to represent the various viewpoints that are critical to the successful operation of the division. In addition to the chairs of the PIRT project, we included the Director and Associate Director; the chair of the curriculum committee; the chair of the reappointment, promotion, and tenure committee; and the chair of the faculty policy advisory committee. This group formed our initial PIRT steering committee that led the division toward the creation of a comprehensive Educational Strategic Plan. Major components in this Plan were the articulation of specific learning outcomes that students would achieve as a result of participation in cooperative education experiences and an assessment plan to document and improve student learning.

Decision Point: What do we plan to assess?

As the first step in the process of determining specific learning outcomes, we began with a faculty retreat focused on learning outcomes. This retreat was designed to open a dialog on what we each saw as the learning outcomes of cooperative education and to look for common outcomes that all students achieve regardless of discipline. With this input, the steering committee was able to isolate four instructional goals that we have for all students regardless of discipline. Our instructional goals became:

- instruct and direct students in the integration of theory learned in the classroom and laboratory with professional applications and experiences used on practice assignments;
- increase students' technical knowledge and skills through discipline-related professional practice employment;
- increase students' understanding of organizational behavior and structures; and

- strengthen students' awareness, knowledge and development of the professional and interpersonal skills and behavior needed to be effective in the workplace.

Like many co-op professionals, our backgrounds are varied and more closely aligned with our own disciplines than with one another. So one of the first things we did to prepare for this undertaking was to take advantage of the many on-campus workshops that were offered to improve teaching and enhance student learning. This gave us a common reference point and some important training in educational theory. Although not every faculty member in the division attended every training session, there were enough faculty members that had a common understanding to enable us to provide some leadership and direction in the formation of an educational strategic plan.

Decision Point: How do we insure that we have all faculty members actively involved and supportive of this Educational Strategic Plan?
Because we saw this as a significant qualitative advancement in the way we do business, it was important to make sure that all faculty members were invested in the project. We managed this by a series of faculty meetings and retreats on the front end of the project, encouraging faculty members to attend workshops that were being offered on campus regarding teaching and learning, and then asking that each faculty member to join at least one of the work groups that would be working throughout the 5-year period. We did not have just one group that created a plan for the approval of the greater faculty. Instead we had a "relay-race" of committees and every faculty member was on at least one leg of the relay. This insured that the entire faculty participated in the formation of the plan and developed a sense of ownership of the plan. Figure 18.1 shows this committee structure.

This challenge faced by Professional Practice faculty in this process is the one addressed by Alexander Astin (2002) when he discussed the difference between conceptual outcomes and outcome measures.

Because they reflect the desired aims and objectives of the educational program, outcome measures are inevitably value based. The very act of choosing to assess certain outcomes rather than others clearly requires us to make value judgments. In this connection, it is important to distinguish between the value statement—a verbal description of some future condition or state of affairs that is considered desirable or important (e.g., competence in critical thinking)—and the actual measure selected to represent that outcome. The former might be referred to as the conceptual outcome; the latter as the outcome measure. The task in developing an appropriate outcome measure is thus to operationalize the conceptual outcome in some way (e.g., to develop a test of competence in critical thinking). (p. 38)

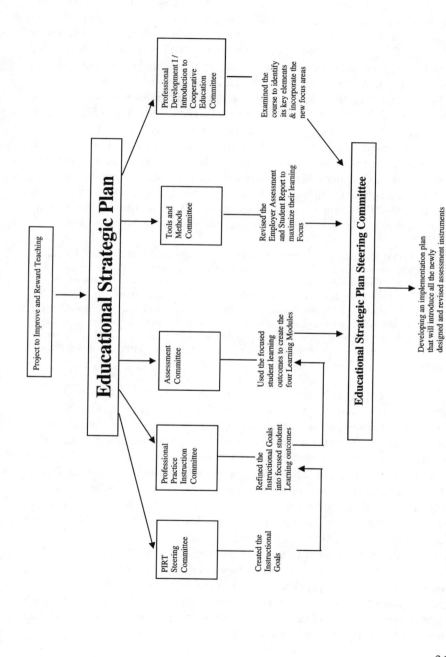

FIG. 18.1.   Process Flow Chart.

367

Because the faculty of the Division of Professional Practice were actively looking for ways to improve the curriculum of our cooperative education program, it was very necessary for us to follow the complicated process we did. When faculty evaluate or change curriculum, it is a process that requires developing a shared vision, or as Astin (2002) put it, a shared set of values, about what the curriculum is designed to do. Building an assessment and evaluation model required the faculty to revisit their values, and reaffirm curriculum. Building instruments to measure outcomes could not begin until there was a shared view of the program curriculum. Because there were 16 division faculty members, working with students in five different Colleges, and 35 different majors, these discussions took time.

With the instructional goals in place, the Division's participation in the UC sponsored PIRT project became a lesser priority than moving forward with the Division's Educational Strategic Plan. Faculty leadership in the project moved from the PIRT steering committee to the Professional Practice Instruction Committee. This committee took the instructional goals and refined them into student learning outcomes. This group developed the following educational purpose statement:

> Professional Practice Instruction optimizes the learning experience for the students who are enrolled in the Cooperative Education Program at the University of Cincinnati. This ongoing monitored instruction facilitates and focuses the process of integrating theory and practice through guided learning experiences and the development and application of students' observation, reflection, and evaluation skills. This teaching method, which is built on a foundation that was developed at the University of Cincinnati in 1906, leads to the realization of established Professional Practice learning outcomes acquired from discipline-related co-op work experiences.

Known internally as "The Cincinnati Plan: A Cooperative Education Curriculum for the 21st Century," and described by Dunn (1999, pp. 31–42), this document refined the original instructional goals into focused learning outcomes. As an interim step, each instructional goal was followed by a specific pedagogy that described how faculty in the Division of Professional Practice would achieve these instructional goals. This gave a more solid framework to help faculty achieve these instructional goals but the focus was still on faculty as teachers rather than students as learners. The next step was to shift the focus from teacher to learner by creating a set of student learning outcomes. This put the focus where we wanted it to be, but still this focus was broader than could be easily measured in an ongoing program of assessment. With the broader student learning outcomes in mind, the committee developed a set of focused-learning outcomes that took all previous work into consideration. For each of the focused-learning outcomes there was a corresponding set of statements that each began "co-op students will be able to …." These statements became the building blocks for our entire assessment program.

Decision Point: How can you go from a broad goal to a narrow focus?
Perhaps one of the more difficult tasks that faced our faculty was trying to shift the focus from our instructional goals, which were very broad and easily applied to all co-op students regardless of discipline, to a narrow and measurable focused learning outcome. Recognizing that we could not loose the universal applicability that was paramount in the instructional goal, our task was to come up with a set of statements "co-op students will be able to ..." that would apply to all students and yet be measurable. Through a series of meetings the committee was able to take a broad instructional goal such as "increase students' understanding of organizational behavior and structure" and operationalize it into specific outcomes, beginning with "co-op students will be able to":
- describe the culture of their workplace,
- articulate how the culture is reflected in the day-to-day activities of the organization, and
- analyze how the organization's culture impacts productivity.

As described earlier, our relay race continued with a third committee that turned the statements from the Professional Practice Instruction Committee into Learning Modules with focused learning outcomes. This committee, called the Assessment Committee, developed student projects around each of the focused learning outcomes and a three-pronged assessment program that includes the student, the employer, and the faculty. Initially the committee stayed true to its name and tried to focus exclusively on assessment. Quickly we discovered that the second committee had not given us a product and without it we would be incapable of assessment. Therefore, the Assessment Committee decided to create a student project that incorporated the focused-learning outcomes and developed our assessment instruments as a measurement of student performance on the project. The Assessment Committee, in Astin's (2002) words, operationalized the conceptual outcomes through the development of the focused-learning modules. These modules became the instrument to measure student outcomes.

Decision Point: In the context of cooperative education, is a focused student project a valid methodology for assessing learning?
The Assessment Committee determined that the Learning Modules provided a way to focus student learning on a specific objective. However, this concept had to be accepted by the entire faculty. And, before we could present the idea to the faculty, we had to draft a sample project for one of the learning modules. (An example of one of the learning modules follows). This sample would be a model for all learning modules we intended to develop. This part of the process took many months, and when presented, the faculty

received the idea positively. Once that buy-in was received, the Assessment Committee was able to fine-tune the format of the learning modules and work to develop the projects for each of the four Instructional Learning Goals.

We kept several things in mind as we created each of the learning module projects. We felt strongly that whatever we asked the students to do it could not be so overwhelming that it might infringe upon the work that the employer had for them that quarter. Rather than a completing a lengthy project we asked students to focus on a single issue or topic throughout the quarter. This required that the student project be something that they would become aware of at the beginning of the quarter but not be responsible for completing until the end of the quarter. Another thing we kept in mind was the important role of employers in both the student's learning and in the assessment of that learning. We felt that all co-op students should sit down with their employers at the beginning of the work term and mutually set expectations. The introduction of a focused student project could facilitate that meeting, involve employers early on in an introductory conversation about the focus area, and provide employers with a more solid foundation upon which to assess the student's learning (Cates & Jones, 1999, p. 49). Throughout the development of the learning modules and the student projects we utilized Primary Trait Analysis (PTA) as a method to focus on the learning we wanted to take place, and as a way to assess that learning. Walvoord and Anderson (1998) provided us with a variety of very good examples of how to use effective grading as a learning tool. They stated that "effective grading practices begin when the teacher says to herself, by the end of the course, I want my students to be able to ..." (p. 18). Although their book, *Effective Grading*, addresses classroom learning and classroom techniques, it was particularly helpful and much of the advice was transferable to a work-based learning environment. Our identification of a broad instructional goal, operationalized in several specific learning objectives, explored over the course of one work term, was our way of answering the question they pose.

Another objective we had for this project and subsequent assessments was to create a simple pretest and posttest. Because one of our goals was to document that students learn through co-op we thought finding some way to measure the value added by the cooperative experience was an important aspect of our assessment program. We also determined that we could collect some data by two assessment questions to be answered by both the student and the employer. Both the employer and the student were asked to assess their own and their student's understanding of these aspects of organizational culture at the beginning of the work quarter using a five-point Likert scale. At the end of the quarter they were asked to assess their own and their student's present understanding of these aspects of organizational culture using the same five-point scale.

> **Decision Point: Can a series of questions answered at one time serve as a pretest and posttest?**
>
> Because one of our most important objectives was to document student learning through their co-op experiences, we needed a before-and-after measurement. But we also wanted a simple project and simple assessment. We determined that by building into the process itself, a meeting and discussion on the topic area between employer and student at the beginning of the quarter we would be able to get a sense of the knowledge before. We also built into the process a meeting and assessment at the end of the quarter, which would quantify the student's learning at the end of the quarter. We decided that by asking both employer and student to reflect back to that earlier meeting and quantify their knowledge during the final assessment we would achieve a simple quantification of their "before" knowledge that we needed to make this project both manageable and effective in documenting learning before completion of the project and after. In addition, we asked students to attribute to where the majority of their learning in the area of focus originated, either co-op or classroom. We felt that asking students to think about this would help to emphasize to them the valuable role that cooperative experiences play in their overall learning and would help to highlight the transferability of learning from one environment to another. By making more explicit to students themselves, the skills, abilities and knowledge they possess, and by asking students to be aware of how what they have learned in the classroom transfers to the work assignment, and how what they have learned in the work assignment can be utilized in the classroom, students are more aware of the transferability of learning.

EXAMPLE OF LEARNING MODULE

Learning Goal: Increase Students' Understanding of Organizational Behavior and Structure

The Student Project Process

1. Meet with your supervisor at the beginning of the quarter. Explain the project that you will be working on this term. Solicit his or her help in identifying a mission statement for your organization.
2. Throughout the term and with the mission statement in mind, jot down notes for yourself regarding the daily activities that you are observing as it relates to the mission statement.
3. At the end of the term, complete the student project by answering the following questions:

The Student Project.

- Identify an official statement(s) relevant to organizational culture. This could be a mission statement, business statement or design philosophy, a statement of corporate goals or objectives, value statement, etc. Please attach examples of the official statement to this report. In your own words, describe your organization's culture based upon the attached statement(s).
- In the space below, cite example(s) of how day-to-day activities reflect the organization's stated culture. Do your examples support the official statement or contradict it? You could base your analysis on your own observations, discussions with colleagues about their perceptions, daily memos and other correspondence, the interactions that takes place between colleagues as they perform responsibilities, etc.
- Based upon your understanding of the example(s) which you identified above, explain how the culture that you observed impacts, positively or negatively, the productivity of the organization.

4. At the end of the term, complete the Student Assessment Form yourself and ask your employer to complete the Employer Assessment Form that relate to this project.

5. When you return to campus, submit the completed Student Project, Student Assessment Form and Employer Assessment Form.

Decision Point: Do we put students in the position of discussing their perceptions with their direct supervisor?

One of the issues we discussed at length is that of student interaction with supervisors in the completion and assessment of their student project. We felt that it was important that students had some interaction with their employers as those individuals are most qualified to guide students in forming correct assumptions. We also were aware of the fact that to provide an honest and valid analysis of their company might cause some students discomfort and put them in a position of criticizing their direct supervisor. Although we discussed the option of forcing students to develop the political skills to handle that conversation by requiring it as a part of the project, in the end we decided on another option. In the instructions provided to students we instruct them to discuss the project with their employer which may not necessarily be their direct supervisor. This allows students to chose the person within the company that they feel most comfortable in discussing their analysis. We also decided not to insert in the instructions or the project a requirement that students show their completed project to their employer. Employers are asked to provide an assessment of the students understanding of the issues but students could also demonstrate their understanding verbally without showing the written project and thereby provide employers with the necessary information needed to provide an assessment of their understanding of the subject.

Student and Employer Assessment of Learning

The Student Assessment and Employer Assessment were identical in the questions asked and five-point Likert scale used.

1. Assess your/the student's ability to describe the organizational culture in your workplace.
2. Assess your/the student's ability to articulate how the organizational culture is reflected in the day-to-day activities of your workplace.
3. Assess your/the student's ability to analyze how the organizational culture of your workplace impacts productivity.
4. Assess your/the student's understanding of these aspects of organizational culture at the beginning of the work quarter.
5. Assess your/the student's present understanding of these aspects of organizational culture.

Students were asked two additional questions in an attempt to quantify where they believed the primary source of their learning was and to determine if they would be able to use the knowledge gained through the project in other environments. Students were asked:

6. I believe that my current level of understanding of organizational culture [in general] can be primarily attributed to my experience from:

   - _____ % co-op assignment
   - _____ % classroom instruction
   - _____ % other
   - _____ 100%

7. As a result of this project, do you believe you can apply your knowledge of organizational culture to another work environment?

   - _____ YES
   - _____ NO

Faculty Assessment

The final assessment within this learning module was the Faculty Assessment. This assessment tool focused primarily on the student project itself because faculty members would not have been present at either of the meetings and discussions between employer and student. This assessment asked faculty members to:

- Assess the student's effectiveness in identifying an official statement(s) from the organization and in describing the organizational culture of his/her workplace.
- Assess the student's effectiveness in analyzing, from the cited example(s), how the organizational culture is reflected in day-to-day activities of his/her workplace.
- Assess the student's effectiveness in analyzing how the organizational culture of his/her workplace impacts productivity.
- Provide an overall evaluation of the project using the traditional A–F scale.

> **Decision Point: Is a Likert-scale the best option or should we develop a more complex primary trait analysis?**
> One of the challenges in any assessment project is developing the measurement scale. We believed that a simple *Excellent to Poor* scale would be sufficient but with that we must accept that one person's definition of what's excellent might not be the same as another person's. One of the best ways to compensate for these variances in terminology would be to develop a highly definitive grading scale again using the primary trait methodology. A compromise was reached that asked students and employers to utilize the Excellent to Poor scale, whereas a more detailed primary trait analysis based instrument was developed for the faculty assessment of the student project. This method would provide for a more uniform assessment across disciplines and compensate for faculty grading tendencies.

THE PILOT STUDY

With each of the portions of the Organizational Culture Learning Module in place, we decided that it was time to run a pilot study on the module. With research funding from the Cooperative Education Association at our disposal, we began the pilot study in the spring of 1999. Our timeline was:

- Completion of the Organizational Culture Learning Module: March 1999
- Distribution of the Module during Spring Quarter, 1999
- Students completed the Module during Summer Quarter, 1999
- Results gathered by faculty researchers during Fall Quarter, 1999
- Data analyzed during Winter Quarter, 2000
- Presentation created during Spring Quarter, 2000
- Results presented to the Cooperative Education Association, June 2000

> **Decision Point: What would be our methodology for the distribution and collection of the Learning Modules?**
> Because the use of Learning Modules was a new concept to our students, we determined that we needed to present the modules to students on an individ-

ual basis. Students must meet with their faculty adviser during each academic quarter, and these individual meetings would provide the perfect vehicle to distribute the modules and answer student questions and concerns. As each of these students returned to campus after their cooperative experience, they were required to submit the completed learning module along with the normally required student report. The quarter system provided the calendar requirements that would drive the completion of the pilot study.

Decision Point: How to determine the sample for the pilot administration?
The members of the Assessment Committee that created the Organizational Culture Learning Module were also the researchers for the pilot project. We would use our students that were working as section I co-op students in the summer of 1999 as our population. This would provide us with a mix of students from several disciplines including architecture, graphic design, industrial engineering, materials engineering, mechanical engineering, industrial management, and operations management. This sample included students from each of the three large co-op colleges of Engineering; Business; and Design, Architecture, Art, and Planning. This mix also provided us with students from optional as well as mandatory co-op programs. Our students were instructed to complete the module during their upcoming co-op work assignment and bring it back to campus for submission during their fall academic term. This is the methodology agreed upon by the four researchers during the planning process for the pilot study. But as happens when faculty members begin interacting on an individual basis with their students, some variations in faculty style showed themselves in the results of the pilot study. This glitch provided one of the more important findings of our study and greatly affected our decisions on implementation of the Learning Modules on a university-wide basis.

Three of the faculty members/researchers distributed the Organizational Culture Learning Module to their students during individual advising sessions. Within this group the response rate (determined by the completed projects turned in by students in their required meetings with faculty) ranged from a low of 50% to a high of 75%. The fourth faculty member found it too difficult to fit the additional task of distributing the Learning Module during an individual instructional session that was already quite filled. This faculty member decided that he would instead mail the Organizational Culture Learning Module to his students during the summer quarter with instructions for completion. This methodology elicited a 12% response rate. We learned that students definitely responded more favorably to the individual attention paid by the three faculty member/researchers during that individual session.

Yet even within that similar distribution methodology, some variations were evident in student response rate. One faculty member/researcher in explaining the Learning Module to her students further explained that it was part of a pilot study and research project. Another faculty member explained the project then told his students that this was their assignment for the summer quarter to replace the assignment from their previous quarter. Students who believed they were helping in a research project had the lowest response of 50%, whereas students who believed they were doing their homework had the highest response of 75%. From this we learned that the faculty member's attitude and instructions do have a significant effect on the student's attitude toward doing the project.

Decision Point: What do we do with modules that are not completed according to the instructions?

Although students were given explicit instructions both verbally but more importantly in writing as they read through the project, not all students followed those instructions. This left us with a dilemma: what do we do with the Learning Modules that were not properly completed? We discussed whether these were valid or invalid and decided that they were actually an important comparison group and should be included in our final analysis. We decided that it was important to look at whether students who did not follow instructions reported the same level of learning as those that did follow instructions. We also quickly discovered that the instruction that was not followed was that of involving the employer in a more direct way in their learning. This important distinction—employer involvement—was not part of our original research intent, yet it was too significant a finding to be left out of our analysis.

With the modules collected, we discovered another happy accident had occurred in the completion of this pilot study. Students were instructed to meet with their employer, involve their employer in the project in a minimal way, and get their employers to do an assessment of the student's learning before returning to campus. We discovered, however, that some students completed the project and student assessment without involving their employers. Although this was not in the design of the learning module itself, this glitch provided us with some of the most significant data we discovered from the pilot study. Through this happy accident of students not following instructions, we now had two groups to compare to one another: a group that did have employer involvement and a group that did not have employer involvement. In total we had 178 completed Organizational Culture Learning Modules. Of that 131 (74%) were completed per the original instructions and with their employer's involvement and 47 (26%) were completed without any employer involvement.

Decision Point: What should you do when you find mold on a petri dish?
Alexander Fleming faced that dilemma in 1928. He was trying to find a chemical that could stop bacterial infection, and in the disarray of his laboratory some petri dishes had started to grow mold. Rather than tossing them aside he decided to look closely at the dishes and discovered that in one of the dishes all around the mold the staph bacteria had been killed. The mold was from the Penicillium family, and Dr. Fleming had discovered something that would revolutionize medicine. Rather than seeing a failure caused by poor laboratory conditions, Dr. Fleming saw an opportunity to let the inevitable glitches of research work to his advantage. With our project, as with any research project, things will happen that the researcher did not intend. Use these unintended variances in procedures to ask questions about your research itself or particular practices that you have used. Very often it is the accidental discoveries that hold the most promise. The beauty of research is that it is never finished. One person's completed research project is another person's point of origin. In fact Alexander Fleming worked with his mold but couldn't refine it. In 1938 a team of researchers from Oxford University happened across Fleming's paper on penicillin and took it one step further by injecting it in live mice. They went on to try it on a few human subjects and saw amazing results. By now it was 1941 and the war effort required more penicillin than the Oxford team could produce. Those researchers flew to the United States to talk to chemical manufacturers. By the time the war ended, U.S. companies were making 650 billion units of penicillin each month.

Prior to examining the data collected in the pilot administration of the Organizational Culture Learning Module, we conducted focus groups of students and employers to collect their perceptions of the project. We were able to fine-tune the modules as a result of these discussions.

SOME INTERESTING FINDINGS

Looking at the data we determined that there were three areas of comparison that provided the most interesting results. The first area of comparison was to look at the results by the number of co-op quarters completed, regardless of discipline. The results were analyzed by students with one or two co-op quarters completed, or three or four co-op quarters completed, or five or more co-op quarters completed. One of the things we believed going into this study was that students will have their greatest learning about organizational behavior and structure during their initial co-op work assignments. Whereas a more seasoned student may still be learning about organizations, the initial assignments are typically a student's first exposure to the professional environment and, therefore, the most productive in terms of learning about that environment. We also decided to subdivide the responses into two categories, those completed with employer involvement and those completed without any employer involvement.

For students in their first two quarters of co-op experience, 93% of the students who had their employer's involvement reported an increase in their learning versus 50% of students without employer involvement. For students in their third or fourth co-op work term, 72% of students with their employer's involvement reported an increase in learning versus 53% of students without employer involvement. Finally, for students with five or more co-op work terms completed 62% of students who had employer involvement reported an increase in their learning versus 60% of students without employer involvement. The more inexperienced students reported the highest level of learning, particularly if they had the help of their employers. Students who had over a year's worth of co-op experience reported a more moderate level of learning with or without employer involvement. These findings supported two of our hypotheses: first that students learned more about organization culture in their first co-op work terms, and second, that the involvement of the employer is an important component in student learning.

Would faculty also perceive that student learning was stronger in the initial quarters and with employer involvement? For students with one or two co-op work terms completed, the average faculty grade for projects completed with employer involvement was 4.4 out of 5.0 versus 2.9 out of 5.0 for projects completed without employer involvement. For students with three or four co-op work quarters completed the average faculty grade for projects completed with employer involvement was 4.5 out of 5.0 versus 3.1 out of 5.0 for projects completed without employer involvement. For students with five or more co-op quarters completed the average faculty grade for projects completed with employer involvement was 4.6 out of 5.0 versus 2.7 out of 5.0 for projects completed without employer involvement. These findings seemed to support the student's perceptions. Both faculty and students gave higher marks to those projects completed with employer involvement. Faculty also consistently ranked the projects higher as students gained more co-op work experience. This finding supported our original belief that students will continue to learn about organizational culture.

Decision Point: How does student attitude toward the project impact learning?

As mentioned before, the students were given instructions to include their employers. If they chose to ignore those instructions, did that also mean that their attitude toward the entire project was somehow less than it should have been? Was this perhaps a more significant factor than employer involvement? Because the pilot study was not set up originally to measure student's attitude toward the project we could not determine if this factor was significant. We decided to look at what we could—employer involvement. Although we could not determine if the student's attitude was a factor, we did learn from

> this experience and determined that with a full-scale implementation we must be diligent about shaping students' attitudes on the front end.

A second analysis of the data showed that students perceived they had acquired the majority of their knowledge and understanding of organizational culture from their co-op work experiences. Students attributed the majority of their learning about organizational culture ranging from a low of 73% for industrial and operations management students to a high of 86% for materials engineering students. In fact, regardless of discipline area, students felt that their knowledge of organizational culture was coming from cooperative education.

Decision Point: What do you do about a particular subset of data that is significantly smaller than the rest?

In this pilot study we had a significant proportion of our sample from mandatory programs in Engineering and Design, Architecture, Art, and Planning. Although those colleges do represent the majority of co-op students (80%) at the University of Cincinnati, they represented 97% of the data collected. Although the response rates were approximately the same across the disciplines, there simply were not enough students in the two optional disciplines working in the summer of 1999. In the earlier analysis that did not subdivide by college, we chose to use the business students' responses. There were 111 Organizational Culture Learning Modules collected from students in the College of Engineering, 62 from students in the College of Design, Architecture, Art, and Planning and five from students in the College of Business. For this final manipulation, we chose to focus on only those colleges that had enough responses to be valid.

A third examination of the data was conducted by college regardless of the number of co-op quarters completed and subdivided into those with employer involvement and those without employer involvement. For this particular analysis, we used the two mandatory co-op colleges, the College of Design, Architecture, Art, and Planning and the College of Engineering. We determined that the number of responses from the College of Business Administration (five total responses) was too small to be valid, therefore, we chose not to include those responses in this particular analysis. Seventy-eight percent of engineering co-op students that had employer involvement in the completion of the learning module reported an increase in their learning compared to 44% of students without employer involvement. Within the College of Design, Architecture, Art, & Planning, 88% of students with employer involvement reported an increase in their learning related to the target area as compared to 67% of students without employer involvement Engineering students with employer involvement attributed 75% of their knowledge to co-op whereas students without employer involvement attributed 85% of their knowledge to co-op. Students from the College of Design, Architecture, Art, and Planning who had employer involvement attributed 79% of their learning to co-op whereas those without employer involvement attributed 71% of their learning to co-op.

In conclusion, we learned through our pilot study that by focusing student attention on a specific area of learning and introducing a targeted activity, student learning could be documented in that area. We learned how to use multiple measures of assessment to document student learning. We determined that employer involvement is important because students perceive that they learn more with employer involvement, and faculty evaluated student performance more positively in student projects with employer involvement. We discovered that the percentages of knowledge that students attributed to co-op and classroom are consistent regardless of discipline. We determined that instructions should be simplified and that student orientation to the modules is critical. We also earned that the co-op faculty member's behavior would impact student performance. As the University of Cincinnati moves forward with its assessment program, the knowledge gained from this pilot study has been, and will continue to be a valuable resource. Perhaps most importantly, we learned that we can by clearly defining our program goals, articulating learning outcomes, developing instruments to collect data on learning, analyzing the data we collected, and making changes to our process and projects, we have put in place an assessment program that is focused on documenting student learning through cooperative education. We have a long way to go, but we think we have found a way to get there.

Summary
- The Educational Strategic Plan at the University of Cincinnati has resulted in:
  - A comprehensive review of our curriculum
  - A renewed sense of shared values
  - Articulation of instructional goals deriving from our values
  - The development of learning outcome measures
  - An assessment process that will allow both the assessment of individual student performance and program effectiveness
- Through our pilot study we validated the use of a focused student project and multiple measures of assessment as a methodology for assessing student learning through co-op.
- We learned through our pilot study that by focusing student attention on a specific area of learning and introducing a targeted activity student learning could be documented in that area.
- Through a series of modified pretest and posttest questions asked of both students and employers we were able to document an increase in student learning through co-op.

- Variations in faculty style among the faculty members/researchers resulted in a variety of response rates and helped us make important decisions regarding implementation of the learning modules.
- Glitches in our research project actually provided some of our most important findings.

REFERENCES

Astin, A. (2002). *Assessment for excellence: The philosophy and practice of assessment and evaluation in higher education*. Westport, CT: Oryx Press.

Cates, C., & Jones, P. (1999). *Learning outcomes: The educational value of cooperative education*. Columbia, MD: Cooperative Education Association.

Dunn, M. (1999). Reframing cooperative education curriculum for the twenty-first century: The process, the plan, and the product. *Journal of Cooperative Education, 34*.

Palomba, C., & Banta, T. (1999). *Assessment essentials*. San Francisco: Jossey-Bass.

Walvoord, B., & Anderson, V. (1998). *Effective grading: A tool for learning and assessment*. San Francisco: Jossey-Bass.

19

Program Assessment II:
Cooperative Education Objectives
Nestled in ABET EC2000
Criterion 3: a-k

Gwen Lee-Thomas, PhD
Arleen Anderson
Rose-Hulman Institute of Technology

Key questions addressed in this chapter:

☞ Of the data that have been gathered already, how do we decide what to analyze?

☞ How can we analyze the data that have been collected in a manner that will garner the support of faculty for the co-op program?

☞ Can the data gathered be presented in a way that provides enough evidence to garner faculty support?

☞ What are the effective strategies for reporting the information to faculty?

☞ Is there inherent information within the data gathered that can inform decision-making for program improvement?

INTRODUCTION

A few years ago, the coordinator of the cooperative education and internship programs approached me about identifying ways to get more engineering faculty support. Because students view the professors as the experts in their educational experience, the coordinator felt that if the faculty encouraged students to take advantage of the co-op experience then more students would heed faculty advice. My initial response was to develop a comprehensive assessment plan that would gather data from several perspectives and cover all relevant facets of the program. The coordinator's response was "I have data. Why don't you come over, take a look, and see if what I have is what we need." Of course, in my experience, the data are usually somewhat decent at best and just totally useless at worst, but I agreed to take a look.

To my surprise, not only were the data good, the data had been gathered in an appropriate environment and were comprehensive with both qualitative[1] and quantitative[2] data from students and employers. More impressively, the data were nestled in the Accreditation Board for Engineering and Technology (ABET) Education Criterion (EC2000) 3: a–k.[3] When I asked the coordinator how she had come to gather these data in this manner, she said the evaluative instruments were garnered from professionals from the Cooperative Education Division of the American Society of Engineering Educators, whose members share instruments rather than reinvent the wheel. This set us on the path to looking at how the assessment of secondary data in cooperative education programs can be applied to the ABET EC2000 Criterion 3: a–k. In addition, how can the dissemination of these analyzed data be presented to faculty to foster greater support for the cooperative education program?

---

[1]Quantitative data refer to empirical or numerical data.

[2]Qualitative data usually refers to non-numerical data such as essay, open-ended, or oral discussions.

[3]ABET Criterion 3: a–k. Program Outcomes and Assessment
Engineering programs must demonstrate that their graduates have:
(a) An ability to apply knowledge of mathematics, science, and engineering.
(b) An ability to design and conduct experiments, as well as to analyze and interpret data.
(c) An ability to design a system, component, or process to meet desired needs.
(d) An ability to function on multidisciplinary teams.
(e) An ability to identify, formulate, and solve engineering problems.
(f) An understanding of professional and ethical responsibility.
(g) An ability to communicate effectively.
(h) The broad education necessary to understand the impact of engineering solutions in a global and societal context.
(i) A recognition of the need for, and an ability to engage in life-long learning.
(j) A knowledge of contemporary issues.
(k) An ability to use the techniques, skills, and modern engineering tools necessary for engineering practice.
Each program must have an assessment process with documented results. Evidence must be given that the results are applied to the further development and improvement of the program. The assessment process must demonstrate that the outcomes important to the mission of the institution and the objectives of the program, including those listed above, are being measured. Evidence that may be used includes, but is not limited to the following: student portfolios, including design projects; nationally-normed subject content examinations; alumni surveys that document professional accomplishments and career development activities; employer surveys; and placement data of graduates.

Setting

Rose-Hulman Institute of Technology is a 4-year residential, private college offering degrees in engineering, mathematics, and science that was established in 1874. The student body is made up of geographically diverse students from the state of Indiana, various states across the U.S. and international students. Rose-Hulman offers bachelor degrees in engineering, math, and science, master degrees in engineering and engineering management, with 15 humanities and social science minors and 4 certificate and interdisciplinary programs.

The students are also primarily traditional 18 to 25 year olds with an average SAT composite score of 1,310. Prior to enrolling, most Rose-Hulman students have taken mathematics and science advanced-placement courses, developed a familiarity with computers and various forms of technology, and are confident that they are enrolled in the major and school of their choice with little intent to change. Students tend to graduate within 4 years, participate in campus sports and organizational activities, and very few students work off campus.

For the past 4 years (1999–2000, 2000–2001, 2001–2002, and 2002–2003) Rose-Hulman has been ranked by US News & World Report as the best undergraduate engineering college where the highest degree awarded is a bachelor's or master's. The Cooperative Education Program at Rose-Hulman began in 1997 with a grant that had the co-op experience as a component for strengthening ties between Rose-Hulman students and business and industry. The program is an optional, alternating one, with about 10% of the students participating. Rose-Hulman is on a quarter system, and the program allows students to work at their co-op jobs a minimum of two quarters and a maximum of three quarters, consecutively.

The purpose of the Rose-Hulman Cooperative Education (co-op) program is to provide the student with an opportunity to gain hands-on, discipline-specific experience that complements and supplements classroom theoretical instruction. Students are encouraged to establish objectives specifying significant and appropriate learning that is expected to result from the co-op work experience. A successful experience is determined by the outcomes of the experience, not just for the experience alone. Categories of learning objectives included: (a) Knowledge Acquisition, (b) Intellectual and Functional Skill Development, (c) Problem-Solving, and (d) Clarified Values. To measure the effectiveness of the co-op experience for Rose-Hulman students, the office of Career Services collects data on co-op students using four different instruments (a) Inventory of Abilities: Self Analysis Profile, (b) Co-op Student Evaluation, (c) Employer Cooperative Education Evaluation Form, and (d) Student Essays.

In addition, the co-op director provides the students with three 75-minute workshops over a 3 week period. The first workshop consists of an overview of the co-op program, presentations by representatives from various areas of the Institute to help students understand how to keep abreast of "remaining a student" (i.e., registrar, housing, financial aid, etc.), and a panel discussion composed of three past co-op students who give 3-minute presentations on their personal co-op experiences then answer questions from the student audience. The second workshop occurs approximately 1 week after the first and offers interviewing skills and resume building techniques. The third workshop, which occurs the following week, has a guest speaker from a business that hires co-op students from Rose-Hulman. The guest speaker talks with the students on the "do's and don'ts" of being a full-time employee.

The Problem

There were two overarching dilemmas that were experienced when assessing the co-op program. First, competencies that engineering institutions have little to no difficulty in measuring are the hard technical skills that are traditional to an engineering program. However, when the ABET developed Engineering Criterion for the 21st century (EC2000) in 1995, there were skills the accrediting agency believed an engineer should demonstrate beyond the technical skills. These skills became known as *soft skills*, and there was a great deal of concern as to whether or not these soft skills could be measured. The soft skills included, but were not limited to, communication skills; interpersonal and social skills necessary to function on a multidisciplinary team; understanding of professional and ethical responsibility; and a recognition of the need for and an ability to engage in life-long learning. Engineering departments were expected to measure all of these skills.

Historically, the performance measures for a good engineer were based on the hard technical skills, so an even greater concern among engineering departments was whether or not these soft skills were their responsibility. These skills should be evident in a good engineer, but surely nontechnical departments should prepare engineers with nontechnical skills. Measuring soft skills as they relate to engineering education can become time-consuming and cumbersome; therefore, accurate measuring and comprehensive assessment are crucial. Because the co-op program can provide opportunities for students to acquire and demonstrate soft skills, assessing the students' co-op experiences was very beneficial for several departments when data were provided for accreditation. The dilemma posed at this point was that engineering faculty did not necessarily see assessing soft skills as an engineering issue and therefore using this approach to garner support would not work without reframing the purpose of the data beyond accreditation purposes.

The second dilemma was that although there was this good data gathered in an appropriate environment,[4] how the data would be used to provide informa-

---

[4]When determining what are *good data* in an appropriate atmosphere, it is important to be acutely aware of what you really want to know and the timing of when the instrument is completed in light of the experience. The co-op program coordinator wanted to know how competent students believed they were as a professional engineer and the source of acquiring professional engineering skills. Therefore, competency type instruments were used. In addition, the co-op coordinator wanted to know what employers believed were the competencies of the students—resulting in an instrument for employers to complete. An appropriate environment, in this sense, was referred to a non threatening atmosphere (completing the instruments wherever the student and employer wanted to be at the time) and after the student had completed the co-op experience.

tion for departments had to be determined by developing an effective assessment strategy.

Understanding the Basics of Assessment

Although the co-op coordinator already had obtained data for analysis, it is imperative that an effective assessment strategy is developed prior to gathering data.

Decision Point: What are the basic steps in an effective assessment strategy?

There are basically five questions that should be answered before starting any assessment process. These include: (1) What do we want to know?; (2) Why do we want to know it?; (3) Where can we find the information?; (4) How will we gather it?; and (5) What will we do with the information? Initially these questions appear relatively easy to answer, however, it often takes time to answer these questions in ways that will yield measurable outcomes. For my work, measurable outcomes refer to the development of competencies or proficiencies students are expected to demonstrate as a result of the co-op experience.

Gloria Rogers and Jean Sando (1996) published a step-by-step guide on developing an assessment plan that would be a helpful resource. The assessment guide is very thorough in providing basic information in developing goals, objectives, and performance criteria. Because organizations can determine the working definition of a goal, an objective, and a performance criteria that fit within what works best for their organization, it is important to note that the definitions used by Rogers and Sando can take on different meanings with different organizations. However, the working knowledge of each step is considered fundamental for effective assessment. In addition, because the assessment process itself can become cyclical as data are gathered and groups are identified, it is important to remember to remain flexible. It is just as important to remember that the initial goals, objectives, and performance criteria may need modification as the assessment work progresses.

Once the five basic assessment questions are answered in ways that can link measurable outcomes to the goals and objectives, analysis of the data must be done in a way that can inform the intended audience.

After analyzing the data, the results must be examined to determine implications of the findings. This includes assigning merit, worth, or value to the results thereby linking the results to the objectives. For example, if student presentation skills were found to be low when measured prior to the co-op experience and 90% of the students received high marks on oral presentations completed during a co-op experience, it can be inferred that the co-op experience helps improve oral communication skills.

Finally, what assessment practitioners refer to as *closing the loop* involves determining whether or not changes to the program, objectives, or goals should be made as a result of the findings. In most cases, there are no right or wrong answers; however, there should always be clearly identifiable links between the findings and the objectives before any consideration for changes are made.

Triangulation

Information on The Center for Multilingual and Multicultural Education in the School of Graduate Studies at George Mason University (2001) website, suggested that triangulation is "overlapping different types of evidence can help assure that your judgments are based on the strengths of all of your assessments rather than one tool's limitations." For the most part, assessment practitioners refer to the triangulation method as using a minimum of three different sources of information recognizing the overlapping evidence that will occur when the data are gathered. The three different sources can include three different instruments used for one or more groups, or gathering data from three different groups using one or more instruments. Of course, the more combinations of instruments and groups you use the more complex the process. It is then extremely important that the process remain as simple as possible, gathering needed information, only. With this working definition, the multiple data instruments used in the co-op program with overlapping types of evidence from students and employers posed a complexity issue that required careful analysis to maintain the integrity and credibility of the findings.

Decision Point: How would the various instruments work with the triangulation method?
In this case, there were two groups that were identified as sources of data with one to three different instruments per group. In addition, there was information gathered from different perspectives for different reasons. Specifically, there were two instruments that provided quantitative data from the students' perspective, one instrument that provided quantitative data from the employers' perspective, qualitative data from student essays, and employer and student interviews by the co-op coordinator conducted within the work environment. More importantly, the various instruments used to gather data from the student group covered the same measurable outcomes and therefore resulted in overlapping information that had to be examined, carefully.

METHOD

Our Office of Institutional Research, Planning and Assessment compiled all available data from Career Services for data analysis on students who co-oped during the 1997–1998 and 1998–1999 fall, winter, spring, and summer quarters. Data from each instrument were aggregated and analyzed in total as well as by major. Student files that contained data on any of the instruments covered in the next section were selected for the analysis. (All students did not have all instruments nor did all instruments have all questions answered, therefore the number of responses varied for each instrument.) As a result, there were approximately 36 out of 81 student files from which data were gathered representing 44% of the co-op students. The data were analyzed and reported for each of the instruments and aggregated with all majors and classes. Students from four departments (mechanical engineering [25], chemical engineering [9], electrical engineering [1], and civil engineering [1] were represented in the analysis).

Decision Point: To have or not to have a sample size and control groups?
Although there are quite a few similarities between research and assessment there are distinct differences that determined how and from whom the data are gathered. In research, it is necessary to ask a question (usually in the null) that tests a hypothesis. For example, there is no significant difference between the starting salaries of co-op students and non-co-op students. The hypothesis testing often requires a control or matched comparison group to determine if there are any significant differences between the two groups. The difference with assessment work is that questions on effectiveness in assessment are not designed as a hypothesis to be tested. Therefore the process by which the data are gathered and analyzed is not always based on the comparisons of two groups. The purpose of applying these data in cooperative education program was to determine how effective the co-op program was for the students who participated. Not to compare participants with nonparticipants. From this perspective, there was no need for a control or matched comparison group.

Instruments Used in Co-op Assessment

Instruments that were used to gather data for the co-op program were obtained from several different sources. The co-op director has a vast network across the country with co-op coordinators in different colleges and universities of different sizes, missions, and Carnegie classifications, and instruments were collected from this network. Each instrument was modified for the purpose of the co-op program at our institution, and more specifically, for the field of engineering. Data from the following instruments were analyzed.

Co-op Student Evaluation.   The purpose of the Co-op Student Evaluation was to obtain general information on the student and the company. Additionally, there was a questionnaire with a rating scale designed to obtain student responses on several items regarding the co-op experience as well as the students' perception of the assistance received from the Career Services Office. The questionnaire contained a 5-point Likert scale with options ranging from poor to excellent represented by numbers 1 to 5. There were also several open-ended questions, however, only the scaled questions were analyzed from this evaluation form.

Inventory of Abilities: Self-Analysis Profile.   This instrument was subdivided into three parts A, B, and C. Part A identified ten abilities that the student was expected to have as a result of the co-op experience. The student then rated their competence on each of these abilities from 1 to 10, with 1 representing very limited and 10 representing highly competent. Part B contained two open-ended questions that requested information on the students' opportunity to work with other engineering students from other schools. Part C of this instrument listed 10 ability items that were the same as those in Part A of the instrument. The student was asked to identify what percentage of their classroom experience versus extra-curricular activities contributed to their perceived competence in the 10 areas (most faculty and staff at the Institute refer to the co-op program as co-curricular activities; however, this instrument referred to the co-op program as an extra-curricular activity). This report contains quantitative data from parts A and C only.

Employer Cooperative Education Evaluation Form.   This form was completed by the students' employer and submitted to Career Services. The form included 10 ability items that were categorized as typifying work performance. This instrument consisted of a 6-point Likert scale from 5 to 1 with 5 being outstanding and 1 being unacceptable. The sixth point was N/A (not applicable).

Decision Point: Of the data gathered, what should we analyze?
To provide the most comprehensive view of the students abilities as a result of the co-op experience it was necessary to acquire the following: (a) the students view of how competent they were in their abilities, (b) from where did they believe these abilities were acquired (classroom or elsewhere), and (c) how did employers rate the students on these abilities. Because the instruments containing these data were quantitative it was helpful to have student essays that provided more insight into the numbers acquired from the analyses on the instruments. The essays provided more in depth understanding of why students responded in certain ways on the various instruments.

Student Essays.   Each co-op student was requested to submit a final report for each co-op tour. The purpose of the report was to have the student evaluate the educational content and quality of the co-op assignment. The report was to include a thoughtful analysis of what the student learned that would be presented as a job report or evaluation. The report was also expected to contain the students' objectives and their evaluation of how well the experience met them.

To adequately analyze the multiple data that had been gathered over a 2-year period, we first mapped each cooperative education objective to the corresponding EC2000 Criterion 3: a–k. (see Table 19.1) Once these items were mapped appropriately, we then used the triangulation method for determining what data would be used—instrument and source—student or employer. The data analyses included two quantitative measures. There were two components of the students' self-analysis profile instrument (Part A and Part C), and the employers' evaluation forms. The third set of data consisted of student essays describing their co-op experience.

TABLE 19.1.

**The Mapping of ABET EC2000 Criterion 3 a-k
and Cooperative Education Program Goals.**

EC2000 Criterion 3: a–k	*Cooperative Education Abilities*
Ability to design and conduct experiments, as well as analyze and interpret data.	
Ability to design a system, component or process to meet desired needs.	
Ability to function on multidisciplinary teams.	Interpersonal skills and teamwork: Ability to work on multidisciplinary teams.
Ability to identify, formulate and solve engineering problems.	Job knowledge: Ability to identify, formulate and solve engineering problems.
An understanding of professional and ethical responsibility	Judgment: An understanding of professional and ethical responsibility (judgment, dependability)
Ability to communicate effectively (interpersonally, formal presentations, and technical writing).	Communication: Formal presentations and Technical writing.
A broad education necessary to understand the impact of engineering solutions in a global and societal context.	
A recognition of the need for, and the ability to engage in life-long learning.	Personal Commitment
A knowledge of contemporary issues (in your discipline).	
An ability to use the techniques, skills and modern engineering tools necessary for engineering practice.	Technical Ability: Ability to use modern engineering and computing techniques, skills and tools.
	Appearance: Appropriate to the environment.
	Academic preparedness: Academic preparation for this position and assignment.

In an attempt to use the triangulation method, the two components of the self-analysis from the students served as one source, the surveys from employers served as a second source, and the essays served as a third source. As with triangulation, the sources of data from the students involved overlapping evidence of the objectives of the program as well as EC2000. (see Fig. 19.1).

Analysis Methodology

To analyze the data we decided to report student responses in percentages because there were no groups to establish as a comparison for the co-op students. A comparison group would have required matching a group of students who was similar to those who chose to co-op. Comparing these *matched* students would have required their completion of the assessment instruments. Without a control group or matched comparison group statistical analysis between groups were irrelevant—for obvious reasons. Same group statistics were not necessary because percentages would suffice for what the client wanted to know.

Decision Point: What statistical methods are necessary for this analysis?
In many cases, using instruments that require responses based on rankings (i.e., most important to least important); Likert scales (i.e., strongly disagree to strongly agree); and dichotomous responses (i.e., yes or no, true or false) can have results displayed in percentages. However, if you have two or more groups by which scores can be compared, there are more sophisticated methods. These include descriptive analysis such as frequencies, chi-square, multiple regression, mean comparisons via Independent T-Tests or Analysis of Variance (ANOVAs). It is important to remember that although sophisticated methods of analysis exist and answer more complex questions, if there

---

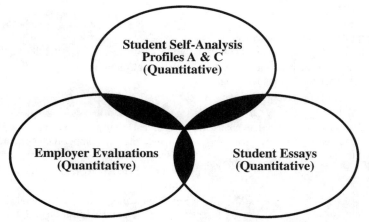

FIG. 19.1.   Triangulation Method of Assessment of Cooperative Education Program.

are no statistical experts available, percentages can be informative for simpler questions such as how many students agreed that their communication skills were improved as a result of participating in the co-op program.

FINDINGS

Self-Analysis: Part A

Part A of the Self-Analysis Profile consisted of 10 abilities the student was expected to have as a result of the co-op experience. (We did not decide on a rubric that determined how well a student was expected to demonstrate these abilities.) With this instrument, students rated their competence on each of these abilities on a scale from 1 to 10, with 1 representing very limited and 10 representing highly competent. All ratings were based on the students' perception of their level of competence after each co-op tour.

After analyzing the data from this instrument, findings revealed that 28% of the students rated their level of competence as an 8 on one item only. The rest of the items were rated between 5 (average) and 10 (highly competent) in clusters of 25%. (see Table 19.3).

It was interesting to note that although the students' ratings of their competence were on the higher end (8 to 10), the responses were not overwhelmingly clustered on this end of the continuum. Even more interesting was that 39% of the students rated all competency levels as *not applicable*. These results should prompt the question "why would 14 out of 36 students rate their engineering-related competencies as not applicable?"

Self-Analysis: Part C

Part C of the Self-Analysis Profile instrument listed the same 10 ability items that were listed in Part A. On this instrument, instead of rating their competence level, the student was asked to identify what percentage of their perceived competence in the 10 areas was due to their classroom experience as opposed to experiences in other areas such as extra-curricular activities or the co-op—identified as *other*.

What the data revealed was that student classroom experiences provided a balance to their *other* overall educational experience. There were quite a few competencies and abilities the students indicated they had received from the classroom experience as well as *other* experiences. The analyses even provided insight into what percentage of the experiences the students believed they received from *other* experiences and what percentage of the competencies were received from the classroom. After students identified what percentage of an experience came from the classroom versus other experiences, it was helpful to report the responses by breaking down 100% of an experience into increments. Categories were 0% to

TABLE 19.2
Self-Analysis, Part A

N = 36 Ability	Highly Competent				Average				Very Limited		
	10	9	8	7	6	5	4	3	2	1	N/A
(1) Ability to design and conduct experiments, as well as to analyze and interpret data.	3%	6%	28%	22%	0%	3%	0%	0%	0%	0%	39%
(2) Ability to design a system, component or process to meet desired needs.	3%	3%	14%	11%	25%	6%	0%	0%	0%	0%	39%
(3) Ability to function on a multidisciplinary team.	11%	22%	17%	11%	0%	0%	0%	0%	0%	0%	39%
(4) Ability to identify, formulate and solve engineering problems.	3%	17%	11%	22%	8%	0%	0%	0%	0%	0%	39%
(5) An understanding of professional and ethical responsibility.	22%	25%	8%	0%	6%	0%	0%	0%	0%	0%	39%
(6) Ability to communicate effectively											
a. on an interpersonal level;	14%	17%	19%	3%	3%	6%	0%	0%	0%	0%	39%
b. in formal presentations;	3%	8%	19%	17%	8%	3%	3%	0%	0%	0%	39%
c. in technical writing.	3%	11%	25%	6%	8%	6%	3%	0%	0%	0%	39%
(7) A broad education necessary to understand the impact of engineering solutions in a global and societal context.	8%	19%	11%	11%	8%	0%	3%	0%	0%	0%	39%
(8) A recognition of the need for, and the ability to engage in life-long learning.	25%	8%	17%	8%	0%	3%	0%	0%	0%	0%	39%
(9) A knowledge of contemporary issues (in your discipline).	3%	8%	8%	17%	14%	6%	3%	0%	3%	0%	39%
(10) An ability to use the techniques, skills and modern engineering necessary for engineering practice.	3%	6%	22%	14%	14%	3%	0%	0%	0%	0%	39%

TABLE 19.3
Results of Student Ratings on Part A of Self-Analysis

Ability	Rating (10 = Highly Competent to 6 = Average Competence)				
	10	9	8	7	6
Ability to engage in life-long learning	25%				
Understanding ethical responsibility		25%			
Technical Writing			25%		
Ability to design according to customer needs					25%

29%, 30% to 50%, 55% to 75%, and 80% to 100%. Then the percentage of students who identified the source of their competence was placed in a category. For example, 38% of the students indicated that 30% to 50% of their competence in the ability to design and conduct experiments as well as to analyze and interpret data came from other experiences. The highest percentage of students in the highest category (80%–100%) was with the ability to communicate effectively on an interpersonal level. Slightly less than half, (48%) of the students indicated that 80% to 100% of their ability came from classroom experiences.

Although these numbers provided some insight, we were not able to pinpoint if the other experiences were co-op experiences. This led us to understanding that the instruments should be more specific in asking what we really wanted to know.

In addition to these things, if you loosely couple the *other* experience to the classroom experience then you can see the connections between what both students and employers indicated in their evaluations of the students. Employers indicated that the students were even better prepared than the students themselves indicated in their self-analysis profiles in the areas of job knowledge, technical ability, and academic preparedness.

Essay Results

As part of the co-op experience agreement, the Co-op Office required students to submit an essay of their co-op experience. This essay was to be written based on whether or not the student believed that he or she reached their goals and met their objectives established at the onset of their co-op experience. The essay was also expected to include a thoughtful analysis of what the student learned that would be presented as a job report or evaluation. There were 17 essays submitted and analyzed.

TABLE 19.4
Self-Analysis Profile, Part C

Ability	0–29%		30–50%		55–75%		80–100%	
N = 21	Other Exp.	Class Exp.	Other Exp.	Class Exp.	Other Exp.	Class Exp.	Other Exp.	Class Exp.
(1) Ability to design and conduct experiments, as well as to analyze and interpret data.	5%	29%	38%	57%	29%	10%	29%	5%
(2) Ability to design a system, component or process to meet desired needs.	14%	24%	48%	38%	14%	29%	24%	10%
(3) Ability to function on a multidisciplinary team.	29%	19%	43%	29%	14%	29%	14%	24%
(4) Ability to identify, formulate and solve engineering problems.	5%	19%	38%	71%	38%	5%	19%	5%
(5) An understanding of professional and ethical responsibility.	24%	14%	52%	33%	5%	29%	19%	24%
(6) Ability to communicate effectively								
a. on an interpersonal level;	48%	14%	38%	19%	0%	19%	14%	48%
b. in formal presentations;	5%	48%	14%	38%	38%	10%	43%	5%
c. in technical writing.	5%	48%	29%	33%	24%	14%	43%	5%
(7) A broad education necessary to understand the impact of engineering solutions in a global and societal context.	14%	14%	62%	48%	10%	24%	14%	14%
(8) A recognition of the need for, and the ability to engage in life-long learning.	24%	10%	62%	43%	5%	24%	10%	24%
(9) A knowledge of contemporary issues (in your discipline)	29%	5%	52%	57%	14%	10%	5%	29%
(10) An ability to use the techniques, skills and modern engineering necessary for engineering practice.	10%	29%	38%	33%	24%	29%	29%	10%

The analysis of the student essays included identifying and coding common themes that appeared throughout the essays. Once coded, the comments were clustered together to formulate the number of comments that related to a particular area of the ABET criteria.

Although the essays were required so that the co-op coordinator could identify the objectives the students had established for themselves and whether or not those objectives were met in the co-op experience, many students did not identify their objectives clearly. The majority of the respondents basically indicated that they had learned a great deal from their co-op experience. What they learned ranged from developing an understanding of office politics to redesigning a current process to maximize efficiency. These quotes are specific to "recognition of the need for, and ability to engage in life-long learning."

Teamwork and Life-Long Learning:

"I was able to observe how people and personalities work together and how politics in a company can affect everything from the morale of the workers to the product itself." **(Mechanical Engineering/Economics)**

"I need to work on time management and putting more detail into my work. I also need to work on getting to know the politics of the work place and learning more about the company itself." **(Mechanical Engineering/Economics)**

Approximately 29% of the students conveyed that much of their classroom preparation contributed to their success in their ability to do well on their co-op assignments, and 18% indicated that their knowledge of how engineering, science, and math is applied in the real-world improved. Although Part C of the Self-Analysis Profile identified *other* experiences, the student comments cited specific classroom experiences as opposed to other extracurricular activities that were not necessarily tied to a specific ability.

The classes that helped me out the most were Engineering Statistics and my previous mathematics classes. I used a lot of different formulas to aid in calculations for various projects. I learned how the things in the classroom apply in the real world and although I didn't use everything, I was able to better understand the concepts taught in the classroom. **(Mechanical Engineering/Economics)**

More specifically, when the essays were compared to ABET EC2000 Criterion 3: a–k, several indices appeared. Forty-one percent indicated that their ability to communicate was enhanced by their co-op experience.

Improved my communication skills for both everyday business and engineering communication and formal written or oral communication. I also learned how to work effectively with a team or individuals with different personality types. **(Mechanical Engineering)**

As for life-long learning, 70% of the students identified some form of continuous learning or ability to learn something on their own, and 24% of the students identified experiences that contributed to their ability to use the techniques, skills, and modern engineering tools necessary for engineering practice.

> [My co-op experience] has given me an opportunity to work with different projects, structure my time, deal with the stress of life, work with groups, and prepare for the real world. The ability to adapt to software, measure correctly, and use common sense along with creativity and the qualities that make a good engineer. **(Mechanical Engineering)**

DISSEMINATION

After analyzing the data, the analyses were reported to the engineering departments in three forms. The first form was overall analysis of all co-op students in an engineering program. The second form included all students in an engineering program excluding the students from that particular department. The third analysis was presented for those students in that particular department only. These three methods of dissemination allowed the engineering departments to have an idea of their students' perception of their competency level in the ability to apply both technical and nontechnical skills, how other engineering students perceived their competency level with these abilities, and how all students perceived their competency level with these abilities.

Decision Point: What is the best way to report unrequested findings to Engineering Departments?

Developing reports for engineers in academia required the consideration of three concepts that are inherent to engineering. First, engineering is a technical field that is predicated on problem solving. Consistent with this approach, presenting the findings as a solution to measuring soft skills appeared appropriate. Second, the problem-solving process includes viewing the problems and the possibilities of solutions from different perspectives. Therefore, it was important to present the findings from three different viewpoints. Finally, because of the various ways problems are solved across engineering disciplines, the findings were presented in different formats such as texts, tables, charts, and graphs.

Although all departments did not use these data for their ABET reporting due to the small number of students participating or because other assessment measures were already available in their departments, the data analyses provided a more objective assessment of their students' soft skills as they related to ABET EC2000 Criterion 3: a–k and laid the groundwork for future data collection tracking and analysis.

LESSONS LEARNED

There were two lessons from the assessment of the cooperative education program as it relates to ABET EC2000 Criterion 3: a–k. The first lesson was that the triangulation method traditionally used in assessment can sometimes present a challenge if the data-gathering strategies are not mapped prior to the collection of the data. Although the multiple data sources were extremely useful (instruments as well as responses from students and employers), a comprehensive assessment strategy was acquired by using the triangulation model. This model along with being aware of what questions were to be answered allowed us to select what data would be part of the analysis. The second lesson was that we need to find a way to encourage faculty to use assessment data of co-op programs as a way of informing the curriculum rather than for ABET purposes only as well as encouraging more participation among their students. The disseminated data were used by some of the departments and appeared in their ABET reports. Now that the departments see how the co-op program helps develop and assess soft skills, there may be less apprehension with encouraging more students to participate in the co-op program. Encouraging students in this area helps not only develop some of the soft skills that can enhance professionalism as an engineer, but it also helps students demonstrate these skills in an authentic setting—the work place.

In the final analysis, promoting cooperative education programs in an engineering environment provides several challenges. However, all of these challenges can be met with effective dissemination of assessed data that are provided in ways that are informative and relevant.

Summary
- An effective assessment effort begins with answering the five basic assessment questions.
- When choosing what data to analyze, use the concept of triangulation as a blueprint.
- In addition to triangulation, comprehensiveness must be considered—gathering data from different sources in different ways.
- If possible, analysis should be both quantitative and qualitative. Quantitative data usually helps you understand what occurred, whereas qualitative data usually helps you understand why it occurred.
- Findings should be presented in ways that are conducive to the perspective of the intended audience.
- Be sure to select those findings that can be presented as solutions to the identified problems. Additional observations can be presented as add-ons if they appear relevant to the overall purpose of the program.

This assessment experience with the co-op program highlights the fact that faculty are in a position to receive information on soft skills without intruding on their technical skill-based pedagogy by encouraging participation in the co-op program. As well, the coordinator realized that there needed to be a more focused assessment for employers because it was still not clear to what component of academic preparedness the employer was referring when the students were rated *excellent*. Therefore this assessment effort also encouraged the coordinator to look more specifically at what was needed from the employer. Comprehensive assessment of the co-op program allowed for data gathering from students and employers to be analyzed in a way that facilitated dissemination of purposeful information for continuous improvement.

ANNOTATED BIBLIOGRAPHY

Boulmetis, J., & Dutwin, P. (2000). *The ABCs of evaluation: Timeless techniques for program and project managers*. San Francisco: Jossey-Bass. Written for any program type or setting, *The ABCs of Evaluation* shows how to select participants for the evaluation and how to deal with multiple goals and objectives, including those of the organization, the staff, and the client. Authors Boulmetis and Dutwin described different evaluation models, illustrated the circumstances under which each model can be used, and offered tips on identifying data sources and collecting the data itself. They also provided a sample report that focuses on the needs of program stakeholders. Throughout the book, there are charts, graphs, models, and lists to help organize, extend, and facilitate the understanding of each evaluation concept.

Center for Multilingual/Multicultural Education in the Graduate School of Education at George Mason University. (2001, September). [Online]. Available: http://gse.gmu.edu/ ell-ld/ELL-LDtriangulation.shtml Assessment can be used to more than just to measure your students. It can be used as a part of instruction. Authentic assessments are different from evaluation—the latter is more a form of judgment after the fact. Authentic assessment involves looking at how students construct information as they are learning and how they apply that information during classroom activities.

Lee-Thomas, G. (April 2001). *Diagnostic vs. prognostic assessment: Getting to the good stuff*. Presentation conducted at meeting of Best Assessment Processes IV: A Working Symposium, Terre Haute, IN. This is a powerpoint presentation presented to better help faculty, staff, and administrations better understand that the there are more informative assessment processes that can provide the *why* certain phenomena occur associated with teach-and-learning classroom dynamics. Diagnostic assessment is the use of certain data-gathering techniques that identify the condition or the *what* in an occurrence that may inform continuous improvement practices. Prognostic assessment is the use of multiple processes that complementarily provide insight into the *why* of an occurrence to more adequately predict future occurrence and in turn inform continuous improvement practices.

Rogers, G., & Sando, J. (1996). *Stepping ahead: As assessment plan development guide*. Terre Haute, IN: Rose-Hulman Institute of Technology. This document defines an eight-step process that can be used to develop an assessment plan. Following the description and definition of each step, an example from the NSF-funded Foundation Coalition's goal-development process is given. At the end of the Guide, an exercise is included, which can be used to lead a group through an exercise to develop an assessment plan. Although this document focuses on activities and performance related to student-learning outcomes, the sequence for developing an assessment plan can be applied to other institutional goals as well.

REFERENCES

Boulmetis, J., & Dutwin, P. (2000). The ABCs of evaluation: Timeless techniques for program and project managers. San Francisco, CA: Jossey-Bass.

Center for Multilingual/Multicultural Education in the School of Graduate Studies at George Mason University. (2001, September).

Engineering Accreditation Commission of the Accreditation Board for Engineering and Technology. (2000). *Engineering criteria 2000* (3rd ed.). Baltimore, MD: Accreditation Board for Engineering and Technology.

Lee-Thomas, G. (2001). Diagnostic vs. prognostic assessment: Getting to the good stuff. Symposium presented at the meeting of the *Best Assessment Processes IV: A Working Symposium*, Terre Haute, IN.

Lee-Thomas, G., & Anderson, A. (2000). Assessing cooperative education through the lines of ABET outcomes. *American Society of Engineering Education annual Conference Proceedings*, St. Louis, MO.

Rogers, G., & Sando, J. (1996). *Stepping ahead: An assessment plan development guide*. Rose-Hulman Institute of Technology. Terre Haute, IN.

US News and World Report College Rankings: http://www.usnews.com/usnews/edu/college/rankings/brief/engineering/nophd/topprogs_nophd_brief.php

20

Ethical Issues in Experimental and Qualitative Research

Adam Howard
Antioch College

Key questions addressed in this chapter:

☛ What are some of the ethical dilemmas that surface when planning, conducting, and evaluating research?

☛ What are some of the ethical principles that researchers need to be aware of?

☛ How do researchers make sure they are doing the right thing?

☛ What ethical obligations do researchers have to participants?

What does it mean to do the right thing?

In the 1960s, Stanley Milgram (1963, 1964, 1965), a Yale University professor and researcher, conducted a series of experiments to study the phenomenon of obedience to an authority figure. To find participants, he placed an ad in the local New Haven newspaper offering to pay $4.50 to men to participate in a scientific study of memory and learning being conducted at the University. The participants reported to Milgram's laboratory where they met a scientist dressed in a lab coat and another participant in the study, a middle-aged man named Mr. Wallace. Mr. Wallace was actually a coexperimenter. The participants did not know this and thought he was just another participant in the experiment.

At the beginning of the experiment, the scientist explained that the study would examine the effects of punishment on learning. During the experiment, one person would be the "teacher," who would administer the punishment, and the other person would be the "learner." Mr. Wallace and the participant then drew slips of paper to determine who would be the teacher and who would be the learner. The drawing was rigged and Mr. Wallace was always the learner.

The scientist strapped Mr. Wallace into an "electric chair" apparatus and attached electrodes to his wrists. The scientist explained that the straps were to prevent excessive movement while the learner was being shocked. He placed the participant, the teacher, in front of a sophisticated-looking shock machine in an adjacent room. The shock machine had 30 levers. The scientist told the participant that electric shocks would be delivered to Mr. Wallace when these levers were pressed. The first lever was labeled *15 volts*, the second *30 volts*, and so on, up to *450 volts*. The levers were also labeled *Slight Shock*, *Moderate Shock*, and so on, up to *Danger: Severe Shock*, followed by red X's above 400 volts. The scientist explained to the learner that, "Although the shocks can be extremely painful, they cause no permanent tissue damage" (Milgram, 1963, p. 373).

Mr. Wallace was instructed to learn a series of word pairs and then was given a test to determine if he could identify which words went together. Every time Mr. Wallace made a mistake, the teacher was to deliver a shock as punishment. Mr. Wallace was to receive a 15-volt shock after the first mistake, a 30-volt shock after the second mistake, and so on. Each time Mr. Wallace made a mistake, he supposedly received a greater shock. The teacher also was instructed to announce the voltage level before administering the shock. In reality, Mr. Wallace never received any shocks, but the participants in the study didn't know this. During the experiment, Mr. Wallace made mistake after mistake. When the participants "shocked" Mr. Wallace with about 120 volts, he began screaming in pain. When the 300-volt shock was administered, Mr. Wallace began pounding on the wall of the room, which was heard by the participant. After the 315-volt shock there were no responses given by the learner. The scientist told the learner to continue administering shocks when Mr. Wallace didn't respond to the questions after 5 to 10 seconds. The pain that Mr. Wallace seemed to be experiencing visibly upset the real participants. When the participants asked to quit the experiment, the scientist told them that they could quit but urged them to continue, using a series of verbal prods that stressed the importance of them continuing the experiment. If the participant refused to obey the scientist after the fourth prod, the experiment was terminated.

Milgram's study purportedly was an experiment on memory and learning, but he really was interested in learning more about obedience by seeing whether the participants would continue to obey the experimenter by administering higher levels of shock to the learner. His findings were important and generated new understandings about obedience. Approximately 65% of the participants continued to deliver shocks all the way up to 450 volts. These results challenged many of our beliefs about our ability to resist authority. The results of Milgram's study have implications for understanding obedience in real-life situations, such as Nazi Germany (Miller,

1986). But what about the ethics of the Milgram study? Did Milgram do the right thing in conducting his research?

MAJOR ETHICAL ISSUES IN RESEARCH

Physical and Psychological Harm

Across disciplines, researchers strongly agree that no harm should come to any person as a result of participating in research. Although there is widespread agreement, there have been some research studies that either inadvertently or knowingly caused subjects to experience physical and/or psychological harm. Probably the most well-known example of participants subjected to conditions that caused them physical harm was the infamous U.S. government-sponsored Tuskegee Experiment, when from 1932 to 1972 nearly 400 African-American men who were poor sharecroppers were denied treatment for syphilis. As reported by the *New York Times*, the Tuskegee Syphilis Study was revealed as "the longest nontherapeutic experiment on human beings in medical history" (Heller, 1972, p. 1). This experiment, of course, represents an extreme example of the possibilities for physical harm as a result of participating in a research study. Procedures that caused physical harm to participants have been rare but nonetheless have been and continue to be used in experiments. Procedures that conceivably cause some physical harm to participants require that great care be taken to make them ethically acceptable.

More common than physical stress is psychological stress (Cozby, 1997). The Milgram study obviously subjected participants to psychological stress by employing particular procedures that the researcher felt necessary to study obedience. As a means to address the participants' psychological stress they experienced during the experiment, Milgram followed the experiment with a debriefing session. This debriefing was Milgram's attempt to ethically address the psychological stress participants experienced during the experiment. It's certainly debatable whether debriefing participants after subjecting them to psychological stress is enough to be considered ethical. Some researchers believe it is necessary to subject participants to stressful conditions for the purposes of their study. In doing so, they position themselves to grapple with difficult ethical issues. In most studies, researchers can ethically address psychological stress by making sure participants are informed of the risks, a topic discussed later on.

Although the body of research on cooperative education and internships shows no evidence that researchers have designed studies in which participants are subjected to physical harm or psychological stress these ethical considerations may surface as the scope of research on co-op and internships broadens. As researchers develop new questions about co-op and internships and employ different procedures to investigate these questions, additional ethical considerations about protecting participants inherently emerge.

Deception

The Milgram experiment also illustrates the use of deception. Participants believed they were taking part in a study about memory and learning, when in reality they took part in a study on obedience. The procedures used in the Milgram experiment lacked what is called *informed consent*. The participants were not given an accurate description of the purpose of the study and the risks involved before they consented to participate in the experiment. Milgram found it necessary to use deception to create what he believed were the necessary conditions for studying how people respond to authority when asked to accomplish particular tasks—tasks we generally believe we would not perform. The often-cited justification for deceiving participants is that prior knowledge of the purpose of the study would contaminate the results. Deception is used to help ensure that the participants behave naturally so that researchers get a better picture of real behavior. Deception is commonly used when participants are likely to alter their behavior to please the experimenter or desire to be socially acceptable.

Herbert Kelman (1967) pointed out several problems with the use of deception. He noted:

> In our other interhuman relationships, most of us would never think of doing the kinds of things we do to our subjects—exposing others to lies and tricks, deliberately misleading them about the purposes of the interaction or withholding pertinent information, making promises or giving assurances that we intend to disregard. We would view such behavior as a violation of the respect to which all fellow humans are entitled and of the whole basis of our relationship with them. Yet we seem to forget that the experimenter–subject relationship ... is a real interhuman relationship, in which we have responsibility toward the subject as another human being whose dignity we must preserve. (as cited in Cozby, 1997, p. 32)

Kelman argued that deception is unethical. Some researchers argue that debriefing is an effective way of reducing the negative effects of deception in experiments (Smith, 1983; Smith & Richardson, 1983). Nonetheless, it is controversial whether the justifications for deception outweigh the potential unethical consequences (Rubin, 1985).

Cozby (1997) offered alternatives to deception by using role-playing and simulation techniques. To role-play, the experimenter describes a situation to participants and then asks them how they would respond to the situation. Another approach is to ask participants to predict how real participants would behave in particular situations. Role-playing, however, is not commonly considered to be a satisfactory alternative to deception (Freedman, 1969; Miller, 1972). The main problem is that simply reading a description and asking participants to respond does not involve them very deeply in that which is being studied. The participants are not a part of a real situation. Another problem with role-playing is that the results of the experiment are always questionable. Are we sure that people are able to accurately predict their own behavior or the behavior of others? For example, in the Milgram experiment, how many people would have predicted that they would be completely obedient?

A slight variation of role-playing is a simulation study, which simulates a real-world situation. Simulation studies do involve participants more in the situations of the experiment. Through role-playing in the simulated real-world situations, researchers can observe a wide range of human behavior such as processes of negotiation, problems solving, and so on.

Informed Consent

Ideally, researchers should provide participants with full informed consent. Informed consent means that research participants are informed about the purposes of the study, the risks involved with the procedures, and their rights to refuse or terminate participation in the study at any time. In other words, researchers provide participants with all information that might influence their decision to participate in the study. As an example, I provide the letter that I used during my dissertation study to seek informed consent from participants in the Appendix.

Deception, as used in Milgram's study for example, denies participants informed consent. Informed consent in Milgram's study means they would have been told that obedience was being studied. They would have been told that they could withdraw from the experiment and, most likely, the verbal prods Milgram used would have been worded differently. The participants would also have been told that they would be required to inflict painful shock on another person.

For some research projects, it is not always possible to provide participants with full informed consent. Research demonstrates that providing informed consent may in fact bias the responses of participants. For example, a study by Dill, Gilden, Hill, and Hanslka (1982) demonstrates that informed consent procedures do increase perceptions of control in stress experiments and consequently can affect the findings of the research. Another problem with informed consent for some research studies is that it may bias the sample. In Milgram's experiment, if participants had been told they would be asked to inflict painful shocks to the other person, some might have declined to participate in the study. Therefore, his findings could only be generalized to those *types* of people who agreed to participate.

Although informed consent may affect the findings of research, full informed consent is absolutely necessary when there are major risks associated with participation. Participants have the right to know these risks before making a decision whether to participate in a research study. There are good reasons to withhold informed consent. As an alternative, researchers most commonly provide a general description of the topic of the study and explain to participants that they can withdraw from the study without negative consequences at any time. As Cozby (1997) pointed out, participants usually do not expect full disclosure about the study prior to participation, as required in order to provide full informed consent.

Privacy and Confidentiality

Co-op and internship practitioners generally have an abundant of information accessible to study a wide range of research questions. Employer evaluations of students, students' papers about their experiences, and practitioners' notes about their meetings with students are just some of the data available for investigation. Although these documents and other information about students (e.g., GPA, personal information, etc.) are sources for rich data, researchers must take care to protect the privacy and rights of individuals. Students should be provided the opportunity to make free choices about whether to participate in a study or not. Participation in a research study is not limited to physical involvement but also includes offering information about oneself. Accordingly, researchers have an ethical obligation to obtain informed consent of individuals when using their information for research purposes. By securing informed consent, researchers protect individuals' rights of privacy.

Making sure those being researched have agreed to participate in a study is only the researcher's initial effort to protect individuals' rights of privacy during research. Researchers should protect participants' rights of privacy throughout the entire course of a study. The usual method of fulfilling this ongoing ethical obligation is to conceal the identity of participants. As Williams (1996) noted, "there is a longstanding practice among qualitative researchers to protect the identity and privacy of research participants" while gathering data and disseminating the results of research (p. 41). Most commonly, researchers do not identify participants or sites. Researchers use pseudonyms instead to replace the names of individuals and locations. This practice of participant anonymity is not unique to qualitative research but also typically used in other research approaches.

For qualitative research, the protection of anonymity is so fundamental that, as Marycarol Hopkins (1993) noted, researchers "do not even have to explain that [they] have used pseudonyms" (p. 124). But this practice of preserving participant anonymity often presents difficult ethical dilemmas for researchers. While protecting participants' rights of privacy by disguising their names and associations, this approach at the same time prevents participants from receiving recognition for their important contributions to the research. This strategy eliminates any opportunity for the participants to receive acknowledgment or praise. For example, a researcher is conducting a study at an institution that offers a praise-worthy co-op program. Through the course of the study, the researcher gathers a good amount of data, documenting the valuable learning outcomes achieved by participating in their co-op program. Naturally, the institution would benefit in various ways from the researcher's public acknowledgment of their excellence. But would the researcher compromise the participants' rights of privacy by publicly acknowledging the institution? In perplexing ethical dilemmas like the one in this example, the researcher is faced with the challenge of figuring out what is the right thing to do. Although full participant anonymity is not always possible or appropriate, the researcher has an ethical obligation to respect and protect participants' rights of privacy.

Representation

Researchers are called to protect the rights, safety, and sensitivities of their informants. This ethical code has been repeatedly compromised, however, when the results of research are disseminated (Cassell, 1978; Williams, 1996). As Williams (1996) pointed out, there are numerous examples when participants read what researchers wrote about their experiences and perceptions, and then felt hurt, embarrassed, angry, or deceived. These types of reactions from participants raise questions about objectivity, truth, and modes of representation. Are we able to speak for others without violating their realities? What does it mean to speak for others?

Representing the beliefs and behaviors of informants in qualitative research often requires difficult, but important, ethical decisions. In fact, Denzin and Lincoln (1994) suggested that "how best to describe and interpret the experiences" of others poses a crisis for qualitative researchers, a "crisis of representation" (p. 577). This is especially true when the researcher reports what Thomas Newkirk (1996) called *bad news*, findings that have the potential to hurt, embarrass, or anger participants. As Newkirk argued, researchers have an ethical obligation to make sure participants during the initial agreement fully understand that the researcher may surface difficult issues, problems and questions during the course of the study. "If this mention of possible 'bad news' is disturbing or alarming to [participants]," Newkirk (1996) stated, "they should be encouraged *not* to participate—that, after all, is the primary intent of the informed consent agreement" (p. 13). Although this may not completely solve the problems with reporting bad news to participants, the initial agreements are important in establishing a foundation for later discussions. During the study, the researcher then should raise issues as they occur and not wait until the participants read the findings to discover the problems and issues that the researcher surfaced. This is an important ethical consideration for researchers in their efforts to accurately describe participants' experiences and perceptions, while respecting their feelings about how they are represented.

Another ethical consideration for researchers is to examine their cultural positions in relation to those who participate in their research. As Chiseri-Strater (1996) pointed out, "researchers are positioned by age, gender, race, class, nationality, institutional affiliation, historical-personal circumstances, and intellectual predisposition" (p. 115). Researchers have a responsibility to be aware of the influences of their positions in representing participants' understandings and experiences, and how these influences are revealed and concealed during their research. This is a responsibility not only of qualitative researchers but also of those who conduct experimental studies. The researcher's decisions about instruments, procedures, and so forth need to take into account fully what cultural influences potentially may be imbedded in the various ways we search for answers to research questions.

Researcher's Roles

Because college students are adults, most of us believe that they are able to make free choices about whether to participate in a research study or not. But their decision to participate in a study may be constrained if the student has another type of relationship with the researcher. This situation most commonly develops when researchers solicit students from their own institutions to participate in studies. Participants, for example, may also be students in the researcher's classes or the researcher's advisees. In situations in which researchers have roles with participants outside the confines of their studies, they need to be conscious of the influence and power they have in their various roles. What power do researchers have? How does this power need to be addressed to protect the rights of participants? These are the types of questions researchers should address when negotiating their multiple roles with participants.

In addition to being mindful of and negotiating their multiple roles with participants, researchers also need to fulfill various obligations and responsibilities to those who participate in their research. Researchers normally make implicit contracts with participants during the course of a study. For example, if researchers promise to send a summary of the results to participants then they should do so. These promises are little details, but they are important in maintaining trust between participants and researchers.

Researchers also may have other roles that present ethical dilemmas for them to address. For example, Ulichny (1996) studied an urban high school's initiative to create a multicultural program for their African-American and Hispanic students. In her ethnographic study, Ulichny examined the reactions of students and staff to a multicultural program that was implemented in the high school as part of a larger school-wide restructuring initiative. The local university worked with the high school in developing and facilitating this restructuring effort. In addition to her role as a researcher, Ulichny was also the university-based facilitator and documenter of the multicultural program. Her dual role of program facilitator and researcher placed her in a position of determining the successes and failures of a program she facilitated. Because she naturally had an invested interest in the program, she had to address the ethical dilemmas that surfaced from her dual role in order to fulfill her responsibilities as a researcher.

Co-op and internship practitioners are usually required to wear different hats such as job supervisors, placement coordinators, faculty members, advisors, and so on. In conducting research, practitioners need to be aware of the influence and power of these various roles in upholding the rights of participants and fulfilling the responsibilities of a researcher. This requires finding the middle ground among roles and addressing the ethical dilemmas that naturally develop from this negotiation.

Fraud

The studies of Sir Cyril Burt (e.g., Burt, 1909, 1937, 1946, 1955) were instrumental in establishing how intelligence has been understood in the field of educational psychology for most of the past century. In his studies, he argued that intelligence is innate and that differences among social classes are largely products of heredity. For years, as Gould (1996) pointed out, "The combination of hereditarian bias with a reification of intelligence as a single, measurable entity defined Burt's unyielding position" (p. 304). In his series of studies, Burt reported that IQ scores of identical twins reared apart and raised in different socioeconomic environments were highly similar. The data of his research were used to support his argument that genetic influences on IQ are extremely important. He originally sampled less than 20 pairs of twins, but over the years this sample increased to more than 50 pairs. This sample was larger than any of the previous attempts to study twins reared apart.

However, Leon Kamin (1974) first noted that, although Burt increased his sample of twins over the years, the average correlation between pairs for IQ remained unchanged to the third decimal place. This unchanged correlation is virtually a mathematical impossibility. This observation led to the discovery that Burt's two collaborators, Margaret Howard and J. Conway, either had not in fact worked with him or had simply been fabricated. It was eventually discovered that Burt had fabricated his data to make the case for his belief that intelligence is innate.

Burt's studies are extreme examples of fraud. Cozby (1997) noted, "Fraud is not a major problem in science because researchers know that others will read their reports and conduct further studies, including replications" (p. 48). Although fraud is fortunately not a major problem, there are enough examples (see Gould, 1996) for us to consider the impact these examples have on our trust in reported research findings. We must trust that the reported results of research are accurate; otherwise, the entire purpose of research as means to generate knowledge is jeopardized.

Why, then, do researchers sometimes commit fraud? The main reason is that researchers at times find themselves under extreme pressures to produce impressive results. This reason, however, is not an adequate explanation because many researchers maintain high ethical standards under extreme pressures. Another reason is that researchers who feel a need to produce fraudulent data want their research findings to support their own beliefs. Again, this is not a sufficient explanation. There are no adequate justifications for fraud. Researchers have an ethical obligation to report their research accurately in order to uphold the taken-for-granted legitimacy of the knowledge gained from scientific investigation.

ETHICAL PRINCIPLES IN CONDUCTING RESEARCH

Various professional groups have created codes of ethics for research. As Cassell and Jacobs (1987) pointed out, "A code is concerned with aspirations as well as avoidances, it represents our desire and attempt to respect the rights of others, fulfill obligations, avoid harm and augment benefits to those we interact with" (p. 2). Research codes of ethics, in general, focus on individual rights to privacy, dignity, and confidentiality, and avoidance of harm (Punch, 1986). Although co-op and internship professional organizations have not established official codes of ethics for conducting research, the primary medium for disseminating research findings about co-op and internships, *Journal of Cooperative Education*, follows the guidelines of the American Psychological Association (APA). This organization has been a leader among professional organizations in formulating ethical principles and standards for researchers.

Ethical Principles in the Conduct of Research With Human Participants (APA, 1982) provides a comprehensive framework for ethical principles and standards for researchers. These standards and principles relate to researchers' competence, integrity, professional and scientific responsibilities, respect for participants' rights, concerns for others' welfare, and general social responsibility. This ethical framework is not intended to provide researchers ironclad rules about what is considered ethical or unethical, but instead, provides guidance to researchers as they address ethical issues.

In addition to the ethical standards provided by professional organizations, the federal government of the United States established regulations to protect the safety and rights of participants (Department of Health and Human Services, 1981). Under these regulations, every institution that receives funds from federal agencies must have an Institutional Review Board (IRB) that determines whether proposed research may be conducted. The IRB is composed of both scientists and nonscientists, members of the community, and legal specialists. The regulations categorized research according to the amount of potential risk of harm to those participating in a study in order to facilitate the ethical review of research. Consequently, research in which there is no risk is exempt from review. Examples of these no-risks research include anonymous questionnaires, surveys, educational tests, and naturalistic observation in public places when there is no threat to subject anonymity. Archival research in which the data being studied are publicly available or the participants are not identified is also exempt.

Another category for research is called *minimal risk*. As Cozby (1997) described, "Minimal risk means that the risks of harm to participants are no greater than risks encountered in daily life or in routine physical or psychological tests" (p. 44). When research is considered to be a minimal risk for participants, highly structured safeguards are less of a concern and approval by the IRB is routine. Any research procedure that places the participants at greater than minimal risk is subject to a thorough review by the IRB. In these studies, researchers are usually required to develop elaborate safeguards to protect participants and to gain complete informed consent.

CONCLUSION

Plummer (1983) identified two positions researchers take in sorting out ethics: the ethical absolutist and the situational relativist. The absolutist relies heavily on professional codes of ethics and establishes firm ethical principles in addressing ethical dilemmas in research. The situational relativist believes that ethical dilemmas are not only solved by absolute guidelines but instead need to be "produced creatively in the concrete situation at hand" (Plummer, 1983, p. 114). Plummer suggested finding a middle ground between these two positions by establishing broad ethical principles to guide researchers with the freedom for them to make personal ethical choices. Both professional codes and U.S. federal law, "assume the posture that researchers are in the best position to determine, within certain guidelines, what constitutes ethicality in ... research" (Lincoln, 1990, p. 290).

Ethical dilemmas are not easily resolved. Researchers are faced with difficult decisions about what constitutes "doing the right thing" throughout the research process. In this chapter, I address only some of the major ethical issues in research and argue that ethical concerns are paramount when planning, conducting, and evaluating research. The degree to which research is or is not ethical relies on the continuous efforts of researchers to protect participants' rights to privacy, dignity, and confidentiality, and to avoid subjecting them to harm. Ethical considerations should be at the forefront of our efforts to expand the scope of research on cooperative education and internships in order to further protect those we research.

Summary
- Researchers have an ethical obligation to protect participants' rights to privacy, dignity, and confidentiality, and to avoid subjecting them to harm. Researchers need to be mindful of ethical considerations in planning, conducting and evaluating research. Researchers are faced with difficult decisions about what constitutes "doing the right thing" throughout the entire research process.
- Researchers should be aware of the ethical codes developed by professional organizations and federal regulations and rely on these ethical principles in making decisions about what constitutes ethicality in research.
- Ethical considerations need to be at the forefront of our efforts to expand the scope of research on cooperative education and internships.

ANNOTATED BIBLIOGRAPHY

Mortensen, P., & Kirsch, G. (Eds.). (1996). *Ethics and representation in qualitative studies of literacy*. Urbana, IL: National Council of Teachers of English. The handbook provides a collection of studies on literacy and situates the research within discussions about various ethical dilemmas the researchers confronted during their research. The chapter authors addressed a wide range of topics about ethically approaching qualitative research and discuss the ethical considerations in representing informants' understandings and experiences. Because the book covers a variety of ethical issues in research and provides a discussion on how to approach ethical dilemmas using different methods in addressing ethical considerations, the book is a good resource for researchers who conduct experimental studies as well as qualitative researchers, the obvious intended audience.

Sales, B. D., & Folkman, S. (Eds.). (2000). *Ethics in research with human participants*. Washington, DC: APA. This book covers major ethical concerns within the research community and across the research process. The book also provides suggestions for methods for ethical decision making. At the end of the book, the United States federal regulations on the protection of human subjects and APA's ethical principles are provided as a resource for researchers. The chapter authors' thorough examination of the major ethical issues in planning, conducting, and evaluating research makes this a useful source for researchers as they think through and make decisions about ethical dilemmas. Although the book is written for psychologists the topics addressed are relevant to researchers across disciplines.

REFERENCES

American Psychological Association. (1982). *Ethical principles in the conduct of research with human participants*. Washington, DC: Author.

Burt, C. (1909). Experimental tests of general intelligence. *British Journal of Psychology, 3*, 94–177.

Burt, C. (1937). *The backward child*. New York: D. Appleton.

Burt, C. (1946). *Intelligence and fertility*. London: Eugenics Society.

Burt, C. (1955). The evidence for the concept of intelligence. *British Journal of Educational Psychology, 25*, 158–177.

Caswell, J. (1978). Risk and benefits to subjects of fieldwork. *American Sociologist, 13*, 134–143.

Cassell, J., & Jacobs, S. E. (1987). Introduction. In J. Cassell & S. E. Jacobs (Eds.), *Handbook on ethical issues in anthropology*, (pp. 1–3). Washington, DC: American Anthropological Association.

Chiseri-Strater, E. (1996). Turning in upon ourselves: Positionality, subjectivity, and reflexivity in case study and ethnographic research. In P. Mortensen & G. Kirsch (Eds.), *Ethics and representation in qualitative studies of literacy* (pp. 115–133). Urbana, IL: National Council of Teachers of English.

Cozby, P. C. (1997). *Methods in behavioral research* (6th ed.). Mountain View, CA: Mayfield.

Denzin, N. K., & Lincoln, Y. S. (Eds.). (1994). *Handbook of qualitative research*. Thousand Oaks, CA: Sage.

Department of Health and Human Services. (1981, January 26). Final regulations amending basic HHS policy for the protection of human research subjects. *Federal Register, 46*(16), 8366–8392.

Deyhle, D. L., Hess, G. A., & LeCompte, M. D. (1992). Approaching ethical issues in qualitative researchers in education. In M. D. LeCompte, W. Milroy, & J. Prissle (Eds.), *The handbook of qualitative research in education* (pp. 597–641). San Diego, CA: Academic Press.

Dill, C. A., Gilden, E. R., Hill, P. C., & Hanslka, L. L. (1982). Federal human subjects regulations: A methodological artifact? *Personality and Social Psychology Bulletin, 8,* 417–425.

Freedman, J. L. (1969). Role-playing: Psychology by consensus. *Journal of Personality and Social Psychology, 13,* 107–114.

Gould, S. J. (1996). *The mismeasure of man* (Rev. ed.). New York: W. W. Norton.

Heller, J. (1972, July 26). Syphilis victims in the U.S. study went untreated for 40 years. *New York Times,* pp. 1, 8.

Hopkins, M. (1993). Is anonymity possible? Writing about refugees in the United States. In C. B. Bretell (Ed.), *When they read what we write: The politics of ethnography* (pp. 119–129). Westport, CT: Bergin and Garvey.

Kamin, L. G. (1974). *The science and politics of IQ.* New York: Wiley.

Kelman, H. C. (1967). Human use of human subjects: The problem of deception in social psychological experiments. *Psychological Bulletin, 67,* 1–11.

Lincoln, Y. S. (1990). Toward a categorical imperative for qualitative research. In E. Esiner & A. Peshkin (Eds.), *Qualitative inquiry in education: The continuing debate* (pp. 277–295). New York: Teachers College Press.

Milgram, S. (1963). Behavioral study of obedience. *Journal of Abnormal and Social Psychology, 67,* 371–378.

Milgram, S. (1964). Group pressure and action against a person. *Journal of Abnormal and Social Psychology, 69,* 137–143.

Milgram, S. (1965). Some conditions of obedience and disobedience to authority. *Human Relations, 18,* 57–76.

Miller, A. G. (1986). *The obedience experiments: A case study of controversy in social science.* New York: Praeger.

Miller, A. G. (1972). Role-playing: An alternative to deception? *American Psychologist, 27,* 623–636.

Newkirk, T. (1996). Seduction and betrayal in qualitative research. In P. Mortensen & G. Kirsch (Eds.), *Ethics and representation in qualitative studies of literacy,* (pp. 3–16). Urbana, IL: National Council of Teachers of English.

Plummer, K. (1983). Documents of life: An introduction to the problems and literature of a humanistic method. London: George Allen & Unwin.

Punch, M. (1986). *The politics and ethics of fieldwork.* Beverly Hills, CA: Sage.

Rubin, Z. (1985). Deceiving ourselves about deception: Comment on Smith and Richardson's "Amelioration of deception and harm in psychological research." *Journal of Personality and Social Psychology, 11,* 233–260.

Smith, C. P. (1983). Ethical issues: Research on deception, informed consent, and debriefing. In L. Wheeler & P. Shaver (Eds.), *Review of personality and social psychology* (Vol. 4). Newbury Park, CA: Sage.

Smith, S. S., & Richardson, D. (1983). Amelioration of harm in psychological research: The important role of debriefing. *Journal of Personality and Social Psychology, 44,* 1075–1082.

Ulichny, P. (1996). Cultures in conflict. *Anthropology and Education Quarterly, 27*(3), 331–364.

Williams, C. (1996). Dealing with the data: Ethical issues in case study research. In P. Mortensen & G. Kirsch (Eds.), *Ethics and representation in qualitative studies of literacy,* (pp. 40–57). Urbana, IL: National Council of Teachers of English.

Appendix

Letter of Informed Consent

Title of Project: Examining the Perceptions of Academic Achievement
Investigators: Adam Howard, home phone number, work phone number
                      Robert Burroughs, work phone number

I understand that Adam Howard, a doctoral student at the University of Cincinnati, will be conducting a study in my child's English classroom to gather information about my child's understandings of their educational experiences. My child will be one of approximately fifty students to participate in this study.

I understand that Adam will audiotape and write notes about all the students as they participate in the classroom. He will talk with the students about what they are learning and interview them about the class. He will be observing two days a week during my child's English class. I understand that my child will continue with the daily activities during this time period if he/she does not participate in the research and Adam will not use audio tape, write notes about, or include my child in the research. The research will be conducted during the months of January through June.

I understand that my identity and the identity of my child will be protected at all times, that my child and I may ask questions about this project throughout these months, and my child may withdraw from this study at any time with no negative consequences.

I understand that upon completion of this project, Adam will write a paper about this research. I understand that the information Adam learns through this research study may be used in publications and presentations to help other researchers, teachers, and parents. If the material is no longer needed for the research proposed, the audio tapes and written data will be stored in a locked file cabinet that only Adam will have access to the contents. He may conduct secondary analysis of the data in the future.

Please sign and return the permission slip. Feel free to contact Adam if you have any questions, comments, or requests for additional information.

Permission Slip

I, the undersigned, have understood the above explanation, and give my consent for the voluntary participation of my child, _____ , in the study entitled "Examining the Perceptions of Academic Achievement."

_____   _____

Signature of Parent/Legal Guardian   Date

_____   _____

Signature of Primary Investigator   Date

VI

Implications for Research and Practice

21

Implications for Research and Practice

Patricia L. Linn
Eric Miller
Antioch College

Many of us have struggled through research methods texts that were both dull and dry. Research design theory can be difficult to apply in the absence of a question whose answer is of immediate concern to the reader. Potential researchers can also turn to research journals for guidance in research practice. However, after reading published studies we may not understand how the researcher worked through the dilemmas faced in the course of the project because choices made about study design elements are rarely explained: How to get started? How was the population chosen? Why was this question, and not another, the focus of the project? Research studies are written in a linear style that suggests all decisions were obvious and everything went as planned, yet we know from our own experience that is rarely the case. For educators or employers in cooperative education or internship programs, the gap between research theory and practice can seem insurmountable, although research holds promise in demonstrating the effectiveness of our programs or improving our practices to enhance student learning. Just as our students must overcome fear to enter a new workplace for the first time, the best approach may be to just dive in. Also as with our students, some guidance and support can make it possible to dive while avoiding some of the larger rocks that may lie below the surface.

With this volume we attempted to close the gap between research theory and research practice. We collected a set of research projects in cooperative education and internships that are examples of effective research. The projects were stimulated by different motives, employed different designs, varied in the sophistication of their designs and analyses, and described or tested features of different types of experiential learning programs. Beyond descriptions of the research projects as found in research journals, we've invited the reader *inside the heads* of the chapter authors to understand the research dilemmas they faced and how they solved those dilemmas. We asked each author to eliminate technical jargon and to make explicit how they made research design choices from the myriad options available. These authors also offer a more realistic view of the twists and turns every research project takes than is usually found in a published research article. As a practice, research involves trial and error. Surprises occur that can either derail us or lead us to new insights. By sharing our thinking, our triumphs and our disappointments we hope you are encouraged to start collecting information to answer your own questions about student learning in the workplace.

The chapters that comprise this book were selected from among those who responded to a Call for Chapters disseminated at a meeting of the Cooperative Education and Internship Association and on the Co-op and Placement Services Network (CAPSNET), a listserve used by many co-op, internship, and career development professionals. Because of the way the chapters were solicited, the book does not represent a comprehensive *review* per se of the current literature on cooperative education and internships. (A review of the literature might be called a Handbook *of* Research….)Therefore, we are limited in our ability to use the contents of this volume to draw conclusions about what is known (and not known) about these kinds of educational models. What we can do, however, is consider the implications of the offerings as compiled: studies from some of the top researchers internationally who study cooperative education and internships. We have divided our concluding remarks into implications for research and those for practice, although such a division is an artificial one because research and practice implications are interwoven.

IMPLICATIONS FOR RESEARCH

Although the projects in this volume represent a wide array of methods, institutions, and programs, these researchers did follow similar paths. Each started with some motivation for collecting information. Motives led to research questions. Resources were located. Questions led to choices about what to measure, of whom, and how. Data measured in certain ways plus questions led to choices of which variables to analyze and how to analyze those data. Results were interpreted and brought around full circle to ask if the original question was answered, the motive satisfied. Beyond these common steps, some questions and approaches have emerged that may be useful to consider in designing your project. The questions offered here are our choices; you will likely see others as you read through the chapters.

What Is the Context for Your Research?

Back up from your practice and problem-at-hand and ask this question. Our authors considered context in at least three ways: context in terms of research *purpose* and *stakeholders*, context in terms of the *standpoint* of the researcher, and context in terms of previously published *literature* in the practice domain. We would argue that all three questions are critical to consider in designing your research.

Purposes evident in these chapters include questions about program practice (Miller, chap. 17; Ricks, chap. 4; Mayo, chap. 13; Maynard, chap. 10, this volume), program assessment mandated by accreditation agencies (Lee-Thomas & Anderson, chap. 19; Cates & LeMaster, chap. 18, this volume), as well as personal motives like fulfilling graduate degree requirements (Eames, chap. 5; Gochenauer & Winter, chap. 8, this volume), or satisfying curiosity (Linn, chap. 6, this volume). Other common purposes are to demonstrate significant learning to "outsiders" (classroom faculty or administrators from your institution or those from other schools) and to encourage wider adoption of work-based learning programs in one's discipline (Tener, chap. 16; VanGyn, chap. 7; Baker, chap. 14, this volume). Howard and Haugsby (chap. 11, this volume) were struggling to help students reflect on class issues encountered on co-op but found a gap in the literature when they looked to published studies for advice. All are valid purposes for doing research that led to choices in study design.

A related question: Who are the *stakeholders* in your institutional context and how can you get them on board, either to help carry out your project or as an audience to consider when designing or disseminating your findings? Notice how Grosjean (chap. 3, this volume) found a way to encourage busy classroom teachers to let him survey their classes while he interviewed them. Lee-Thomas and Anderson (chap. 19) designed their presentation of results to suit the information-grasping styles of engineering faculty. Cates and LeMaster (chap. 18) were careful to include all local stakeholders in their design of learning modules. Although it is difficult to be inclusive if you practice in a large department, consider their use of the "relay race" as a metaphor for including everyone in some, but not all, aspects of the planning. Fogg and Putnam (chap. 12, this volume) knew that clear outcomes like postgraduate salaries would demonstrate the kind of added value that Northeastern administrators needed to market their programs. Tener (chap. 16) chose a theoretical approach because he suspected that construction engineers at Purdue and elsewhere would consider outcomes that matched predictions from learning theory to be "real learning," although that learning happened outside the classroom. Several authors (e.g., Cates & LeMaster, chap. 18; Lee-Thomas & Anderson, chap. 19; Mayo, chap. 13) realized that employers are key stakeholders and used information from them as part of their research, assessment or evaluation projects.

The *standpoint* of the researcher also provided a context that influenced the development of each project. Miller (chap. 17), Ricks (chap. 4), Maynard (chap. 10) and Howard and Haugsby (chap. 11) are all practitioners who sought to improve their practices by understanding how to help students cope with and reflect on co-op experiences. Their choices of action research and case studies fit with their applied and highly focused questions. Fogg and Putnam (chap. 12), self-described outsiders from co-op practice in their role as institutional researchers, were able to use their outsider standpoint to facilitate discussions between administrators (who are under certain pressures to demonstrate institutional effectiveness) and practitioners (who want to improve practice). They operationally defined (i.e., defined a variable in terms of how to measure it) what is a high-quality co-op and used that measure with a large sample of program graduates. They bridged the gap between stakeholders by collecting data that both informed local practices and demonstrated broader institutional objectives.

As a final note on context, almost every chapter offers a *review of the literature*. With co-op practice approaching its 100th year in 2006, many questions we might ask about student learning at work have been asked before. Once you have considered context in terms of your purpose and stakeholders, do a thorough review of the literature to understand where your project fits among other projects already attempted. It may be that your research question has already been answered! Grosjean (chap. 3) and Eames (chap. 5) both offer their thinking about how to narrow very broad areas of literature (like *learning*) into more manageable subcategories. Notice also how Miller (chap. 17) and Ricks (chap. 4) employ literature from fields (like African-American Studies and Philosophy) that might not normally be considered part of co-op practice. Find a balance between conducting a focused search while remaining open to theories or research from outside the boundaries of experiential learning. If you can find a *review article* or *meta-analysis*, these types of articles can be especially helpful. In the case of a review article, studies relevant to a certain topic have already been collected and reviewed; the reference list can be a gold mine of studies you can get through your library and use in the introduction to your research report. In the case of meta-analysis, many studies on one topic are analyzed together so conclusions about the general trend of effects can be drawn. Again, the results of a meta-analysis can be included in your thinking and your report's introduction.

Your literature review can give you ideas about measures to use (see the following), software programs that are available to help with analysis, and other educational programs and practitioners who may share your concerns and whom you can contact for consultation or information. In our experience authors of published studies are thrilled to hear from readers with questions and comments about their work. Some of these contacts we have made turned into very rewarding professional relationships; we encourage you to contact authors of published research reports whose work you find important.

Should I Collaborate? With Whom?

Many of the authors in this volume found that when they worked with other colleagues, especially those who came from different perspectives, disciplines, or standpoints, they found that "the whole was greater than the sum of the parts" in terms of collecting resources or settling on an effective design for their research project. Johnston and Angerelli (chap. 9, this volume) found a collaborator in a visiting research scientist to their university. Dr. Gajdamaschko was able to help identify and employ a methodology (Q sort) that fit their goals and their budget. Linn (chap. 6) found that a colleague trained in philosophy (Richard Meisler) brought to her project a phenomenological perspective that contrasted with and balanced her psychological one. A combined strategy resulted: finding fragments of interviews as examples of different kinds of learning while maintaining a life-history perspective that held each learning episode within the context of a student's life story. Ricks found that bringing together colleagues on her project on ethics in cooperative education allowed a sharing of human resources (time, energy) and financial resources (duplicating, postage, travel costs) that allowed the project to be completed without external funding. You do not have to bring a colleague into your project as a full collaborator to benefit from different perspectives on your project. Miller (chap. 17) used a variety of conferences, roundtables, and informal conversations with educators outside his department to test his ideas on others. By raising his ideas about atypical cross-cultural experiences in discussions on and away from his campus, Miller found that professionals in three diverse disciplines concurred with his interviews: cross-cultural educators, co-op educators, and scholars from African-American Studies. Testing his ideas publicly helped him to refine his analysis but also gave him the confidence to proceed with a project that ventured outside the boundaries of typical co-op theory and practice.

How Can I Make a Research Project Doable?

This was a question debated by almost every chapter author. Most co-op educators and some internship directors do not have faculty status or roles as institutional researchers with the accompanying expectations (and resources) for publishing. The previous section on collaboration discusses one strategy many authors used to accomplish more with less. When the work and costs are shared (see Ricks, chap. 4; Van Gyn, chap. 7), there are fewer demands on any one person and collaborators can encourage each other to stick with commitments and timelines. Undergraduate or graduate students who wanted research experience were brought into projects by Ricks, Linn, Tener, and others. This is a "win-win" situation because students can be trained to accomplish many research tasks to get the project going but they also benefit from working with a researcher or mentor and adding a research experience, publication, or presentation to their resumes. Students who have completed co-op or internship experiences can also offer ideas that might otherwise be overlooked. One of the principle findings reported by Linn (chap. 6) (that low performance on a co-op predicted later earning of a graduate degree) came from a suggestion from an undergraduate research assistant. This student was struggling to come to terms with a negative evaluation from a former employer, and recommended Linn take a closer look at those graduates with poor-performance ratings.

Another strategy to make research doable is to use (or modify slightly) information that is collected anyway in your program. Tener (chap. 16) added two open-ended questions at the end of the regularly used student internship evaluation form and found this "simple device" to be sufficient to answer his question about whether learning on construction engineering internships fit with Kolb's model of experiential education. Gochenauer and Winter (chap. 8) and Maynard (chap. 10) used information that was already collected for other purposes to understand features and outcomes of their internship programs. Baker (chap. 14) and Fogg and Putnam (chap. 12) used existing co-op evaluation questionnaires to define features of high-quality co-ops in order to learn what other variables were related to co-op quality.

There is a tension here between cost- and time-effectiveness that come with using extant measures and the dangers of collecting data that may not be suitable to answer your research questions. We recommend you review instruments already used by your department first before developing a new instrument, but make sure that the instruments you choose will produce data that can answer your questions and achieve your goals.

Finally, some research designs are more doable than others when there are limited time and resources. The major determiner of research design should be the question that one is asking (see measurement issues). Howard and Haugsby (chap. 11) argued that if understanding the way students construct the meaning of their experiences is the goal, a case study method can be doable with limited resources. They advise that data collection need not be complex but should be systematic. Eames (chap. 5) found that a longitudinal design worked well to answer his question about learning, but also because he was completing his degree while working and so had the time to wait for students to move through multiple co-op experiences.

Should I Use Theory to Guide My Work?

James Wilson (1988) and others have bemoaned the absence of theory-driven research in cooperative education. A good theory, Lewin said, can be a very practical thing. Theory can offer hypotheses to be tested, and so generate research. Although many theories apply to work-based learning (see Theory, chap. 2), Kolb's (1984) theory is most often invoked in this volume. Tener (chap. 16) used Kolb's theory of learning styles as a basis for his project about types of learning on construction engineering internships. Student responses to questions about what they had learned and how they had learned it fit well into Kolb's two continua of grasping information and processing it. Miller (chap. 17) had to look across disciplinary boundaries into cross-cultural learning theory and ethnic identity theory to help him understand his student's experiences. As the field of cooperative education matures, such theory broadening will likely occur at the edges of the discipline and will inform our process of development as a field.

When considering how and when to use theory, it is important to consider the strengths and limitations of both *deductive* and *inductive* approaches. For example, consider a *deductive* approach in which one draws hypotheses from a theory: *if* (theory x is true) *then* (learning should proceed in this way). Deductions drawn from a theory can guide you to select among all the possible variables you might measure. Using theory to guide the analysis of your data can also help you to avoid the pitfalls of analyzing every variable against every other variable. This data analysis strategy is sometimes called a "fishing expedition," a practice that is likely to lead to false positive findings. A better strategy is to analyze data to purposefully test hypotheses generated from theory.

Do you agree with Grosjean (chap. 3), Johnston and her colleagues (chap. 9), Linn (chaps. 2, 6), Eames (chap. 5), Howard and Haugsby (chap. 11) and others in this volume that it is important to consider the way students construct individual and personal meanings from their learning experiences? If so, then forcing student descriptions of their learning into pre-existing theories can limit what we discover; you may find only what you were looking for at the outset. Tener (chap. 16) avoided this pitfall of wearing theoretical blinders: He noticed student descriptions of their learning that fit with self-efficacy theory, although he was searching for matches to Kolb's categories.

Inductive approaches involve reading (and repeatedly rereading) transcripts of interviews, open-ended survey questions and other artifacts with an open mind to what one might find there. Inductive approaches suggest you do not start with theoretically derived categories, yet Wilson (1988) and others are concerned that research on cooperative education has suffered from being atheoretical. Both Eames (chap. 5) and Linn (chap. 6) claim to have used combinations of deductive and inductive analyses of their interviews. Johnston, Angerilli, and Gajdamaschko's (chap. 9) Q-sort is described as a middle ground between these approaches. Note, however, that Denzin and Lincoln (1984) and others would argue that a purely inductive approach (sometimes called *grounded theory*) will optimize learning from qualitative data.

What Are the Measurement Issues to Consider?

There are several issues about measurement that occur repeatedly across the chapters in this volume. Cates and LeMaster (chap. 18) offer a useful caution from Astin (2002) that value judgments are inherent in decisions about measuring learning outcomes. Note how both Cates and LeMaster and Van Gyn (chap. 7) spent considerable time and resources to decide (and test in pilot studies) what outcomes should be measured and how to measure them. Tener asked students what their most important learning was and how they learned it. Lee-Thomas and Anderson (chap.

19) used the outcomes specified by the accreditation agency for engineering programs; here again the dilemma of who should define learning outcomes (students or researchers) is evident in that almost 40% of their sample indicated that the ABET criteria were "not applicable" to their experiences! Measuring the outcomes of interest in at least three ways (*triangulation*) is an approach that will maximize understanding and the likelihood of finding some significant results in your study ("significant" both in a statistical sense and in terms of meaningfulness). Van Gyn's single measure of the ACT COMP test created difficulties when the standardized test version was changed to suit demographic changes in the U.S. population of students but not the demographics of her Western Canadian student population.

Self-report of learning versus using a *performance standard* is another important measurement issue. If, for example, one wants to determine if improvement of the "soft skill" of oral communication is an outcome of cooperative education or internships, there are different approaches to measuring that skill. You could ask a student to report on his or her oral communication abilities, ask an employer to report on the student's performance in communicating orally, or require the student to do an oral report that can be directly evaluated. Each successive approach is more performance based than the last. However, each of these measurement methods requires different amounts of time and resources; it may not be possible or practical to measure student performance directly in every case. Remember, however, that the *outcome* you want to measure is not necessarily identical to the *question* you should ask to measure that competency or skill. You must consider the individual who will be answering the question, what performance might reflect that skill, how to state the question in an understandable way, and how respondents' ideas of what is *excellent* or *poor* might differ if such categories are not tied clearly to performance criteria.

Another consideration evident in these research projects is how to measure *value-added* benefits of co-op jobs and internships when other factors may explain performance. For example, do factors like motivation or career awareness co-vary with choosing to enroll in a voluntary co-op program? When measuring performance at the end of a work experience, what classroom or other extracurricular learning experiences have co-occurred with the work experience that may explain performance? What about developmental maturation from one time to another? Cates and LeMaster (chap. 18) used a premeasurement and postmeasurement design to try to assess competence in understanding corporate culture before and after co-op. Similarly, Van Gyn (chap. 17) used the ACT COMP test at matriculation and before graduation. Lee-Thomas and Anderson (chap. 19) used a different approach to determine value-added by co-op: They asked students to indicate *where* they learned particular competencies, on co-op or elsewhere. Gochenauer and Winter (chap. 8) were surprised to find that a demographic variable (gender) predicted salary after graduation much more strongly than did internship experience. Their experience shows that it is important to be aware of variables that co-vary with the dependent variable you are studying so that you don't miss important determinants.

Measurement issues are different when *learning process* rather than *learning outcomes* are the subject of study. Researchers in this volume who focused on learning process used open-ended questions (Tener, chap. 16) on written surveys, student essays (Lee-Thomas & Anderson, chap. 19) and verbatim transcriptions of interviews (Eames, chap. 5; Linn, chap. 6; Miller, chap. 17) as their data: words rather than numbers. Analysis of verbal data can be time-consuming, but Tener found an interested graduate student who took the analysis on, and Linn and Eames both used computer software to aid in their qualitative analysis. Again, decisions about how to measure variables should be guided by the research questions that you are asking.

How Do These Various Approaches Relate to Each Other?

There are so many decisions to make when designing a research project that is easy to become overwhelmed by them. Are there some broad categories into which these various approaches can be placed that might help you decide on a general approach to use? We want to share with you one vision of how these research approaches relate to and differ from each other.

The research approaches taken by the chapter authors here might be considered to fall along two continua: one defined by the *motives* described for doing the research and another defined by the research *designs* employed. In Fig. 21.1 we offer our ideas of how these research projects might be located along these two continua.

The first continuum describes the *motives* or purposes that drive a researcher to begin a project. Among the chapters in this volume, *outcome-oriented* projects tend to ask *what* the outcomes were and what characteristics define the learners (*who?*). *Process-oriented* projects generally ask *how* learning happened or describe the contexts of that learning (*where?*). The process-oriented projects might be considered more *basic* research, just like a biological study of how a cell functions is considered basic versus the more *applied* question of what effects a particular disease has on that cell's functioning. Note, however, that the basic–applied dichotomy is not as clear as it might seem. Just as basic biological science can have immediate applications in medicine, chapters classified as basic here might have immediate practical applications. For example, Miller (chap. 17) studied how an African-American gay student experienced a cultural and work context in which his identities were, for the first time, majority identities. This project immediately informed Miller's practice: He credited that student as meeting the school's cross-cultural requirement policy.

The second continuum in Fig. 21.1 describes the general research methodology used by authors in this volume. Bryman (1984) offered a definition of methodology that encompasses both research techniques and epistemological[1] position. *Positivistic* refers to a scientific research tradition in the natural and social sciences

---

[1]Epistemology is the study of the origins of knowledge.

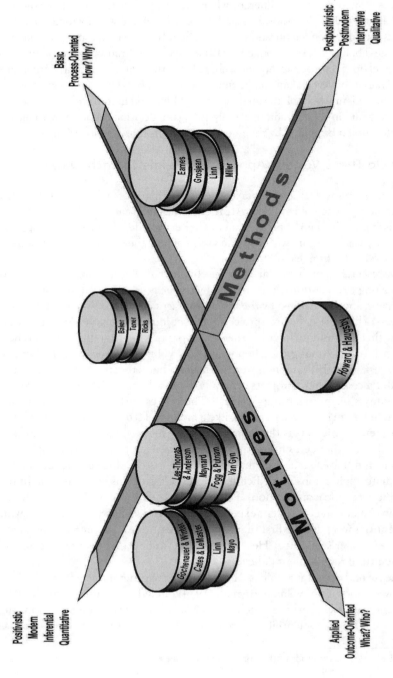

FIG. 21.1. One vision of chapter placement on two continua.

defined by the philosophical approach called logical positivism: If the rules of scientific methodology are adhered to, Truth can be discovered (Kuhn, 1970). This was the promise of *modern* science. The contrasting, *postpositivistic* view questions the very idea of Truth, rather claiming the *postmodern* belief that meanings are socially constructed: What is true depends on one's standpoint or perspective. Positivistic studies are usually experimental or quasiexperimental,[2] tend to be *quantitative* and use statistics to draw *inferences* about broad populations from which samples are drawn. Critics of positivism would ask whether experiments and numbered data can capture the complexity of human behavior or the degree to which humans construct different meanings from experiences that appear to be similar. Nonpositivistic studies are more likely to use *qualitative* data and use analytic strategies that are *interpretive* (i.e., have the goal of understanding an individual's experience rather than drawing inferences to a large population). Critics of nonpositivistic studies would ask what is really known if every respondent yields a different story. Neither perspective is right or wrong. They are different perspectives on how to do research that you should be aware of so that you can locate your own project and be forewarned of the criticisms that your choices might bring!

The end points of each continuum are described by terms that are grouped together here, but those descriptors of research motives and designs do not always co-vary. For example, the top end of the research motives continuum is labeled by terms *basic, process-oriented, how,* and *where,* but Lee-Thomas and Anderson (chap. 19) describe one measure in their outcome-oriented study that asked where learning happened.

Figure 21.1 shows the chapters falling into all four quadrants, although unevenly so. Most outcome-oriented studies fall toward the positivistic end of the design continuum. These studies are attempting to demonstrate learning outcomes from cooperative education or internships for co-op students in general, using quasiexperimental designs with either pretesting and posttesting or by using a comparison group of students who do not participate in these programs. These studies most often used numbered data and quantitative data analysis methods. The process-oriented studies are more likely to employ qualitative than quantitative methods, but the respondents' words are almost as likely to be categorized and counted (e.g., Baker, chap. 14; Ricks, chap. 4; Tener, chap. 16) as they are kept in context and interpreted (Miller, chap. 17; Grosjean, chap. 3; Eames, chap. 5). Projects that intentionally use both quantitative and qualitative measures are more difficult to classify. We found it more effective to split Linn's (chap. 6) study in two and describe each part separately rather than force it into the diagram as a unit. Johnston, Angerelli, and Gajdamaschko's (chap. 9) isn't included at all because the Q-sort methodology offers perhaps the only true example of a means of measuring both process and outcome that stands dead center on the diagram; their work isn't well described by any

---

[2]A true experiment would require the random assignment of students to co-op and non-co-op groups; quasiexperiments or natural experiments occur when some students opt into a co-op program and others do not.

one or two quadrants alone. Although respondents to a Q-sort are offered a limited universe of statements to rank (the *concourse*), they are allowed freedom in their rankings and the factor analysis of these rankings cluster segments of subjectivity in the data. Some of the statements in their concourse (chap. 9 Appendix) were process-oriented ("By watching other professionals, students can learn a lot as part of a project team.") whereas others are outcome-oriented ("With Co-op, a graduate has a better set of tools with which to sell themselves ...").

We argue that it is important for the field of experiential learning that research proceed in all four quadrants. Basic research can inform practice; qualitative case or interview studies generate hypotheses that can be tested with larger, quantitative studies. As researchers, our contexts, purposes and questions differ and our methodologies should reflect that diversity as well.

Please consider both the terms defining the continua and the placement of chapters in the quadrants to be idiosyncratic. We offer a postmodern explanation of the tentativeness of our placement of chapters on this diagram: From where you stand, the chapters might be organized very differently. The chapter authors themselves would likely create different continua or classify their projects differently than we have here.

IMPLICATIONS FOR PRACTICE

Co-op and internship faculty and practitioners, as professionals do in all endeavors, strive to improve their practice in whatever ways they can. We know from experience that co-op and internships are powerful sources of learning for our students, but we are still in the beginning stages of understanding how that learning happens and how we can enhance it through our own practice. So much of our practice seems to be the product of the accumulated wisdom gained through trial and error over the years, but perhaps now we are at a juncture where we can begin to base more of our practice on evidence that is produced quality research.

As stated, the implications for research and practice are interwoven and reciprocal. An essential element of good practice is research and assessment. All of the authors offer contributions to practice. Here we offer our perspective on how, taken together, they support and relate to each other. Following is our effort to present a brief summary of the findings of the research presented in this book. Many details and interpretations of the data by the authors have been omitted, so please read the chapters themselves for a more detailed view of what the authors actually recommended.

Is What We Do Worth Doing?

Let's begin at the beginning. What is the educational value of co-op and internships? How do people perceive their value? Can we demonstrate their value? As we read the contributions to this book, the value and the power of co-op and internships are what strike us most. From the largest empirical studies to the smallest qualitative case studies, all confirmed the dynamic quality of the learning that happens in these work situations. One of the most compelling findings is that, 50 years after the fact, 40% of the co-op alumni interviewed reported that co-op had the biggest impact on their undergraduate learning (Linn, chap. 6). This was the largest group and more than twice as many as the next largest groups, who reported classes and campus life as their biggest influences. Co-ops and internships can and do have life long effects.

Other authors (e.g. Eames, chap. 5; Fogg & Putnam, chap. 12; Tener, chap. 16; and Van Gyn, chap. 7) found an abundance of positive outcomes that are not readily attainable in academic settings. To briefly summarize, some of the findings are as follows: Through co-op, students are able to discover the complexities of practice, develop an understanding of what it is to be a practitioner, develop problem-solving skills and understanding of the social aspects of institutions, confirm or eliminate career choices before they are committed to them; develop belief in their own abilities; and increase their earning power at the beginning of their careers. Gochenauer and Winter (chap. 8) found that students who did not complete internships during their studies were significantly more likely to report being "Very Dissatisfied" with their jobs in the immediate months after graduation. Co-op and internships provide students with a wide range of practitioners from whom to draw examples, learning and knowledge (Eames, chap. 5). Cates and LeMaster (chap. 18) suggest that co-op can play a key role in the accrediting process by providing learning opportunities in areas in which accrediting agencies are beginning to require evidence of learning. Howard and Haugsby (chap. 11) point out that co-op places students in a vantage point from which they can examine difficult questions about culture and develop a critical awareness of their own class as well as other cultural realities.

On the other hand, many of the authors (e.g. Baker, chap. 14; Cates & LeMaster, chap. 18; Fogg & Putnam, chap. 12; Grosjean, chap. 3; Johnston, Angerilli, & Gajdamaschko, chap. 9; Mayo, chap. 13; and Rowe, chap. 15) point to the need for us to do a better job of informing the world about the value of co-op. In one of the most disturbing findings in this book, Johnston et al. found that none, of the eight different *worldviews* reflected among the students and practitioners in their study, perceived the activities for which co-op practitioners are responsible as any better than neutral in value to student learning. They suggest that this perception may be due to the need to either "improve the linkages" between the various elements present in the co-op model or improve our understanding and discourse on them. In the same study, however, they found among other things that students rated co-op as "the only real way to learn work skills."

Grosjean's (chap. 3) appraisal of learning in context elevates the importance of the workplace. He suggests that a new perspective would place academic activity in service to "learning *for* the workplace" whereas co-op and internships would continue to be "learning *in* the workplace." Baker (chap. 14) independently concurs and boldly suggests that we consider the notion of flipping the balance between academic and work-based learning. He asserts the radical idea that perhaps "most of students' learning" should be relocated "to real world practice and to clinical programs where students perform useful tasks under expert guidance." Although both Grosjean and Baker conclude that such a balance of work-based and classroom-based learning is unlikely to occur soon, it is important to note that these researchers independently interpret their data as evidence to make such a strong recommendation.

What Are the Recommendations for Specific Program Features?

The importance of quality in work-based experiences was a central focus of several of the studies. Fogg and Putnam (chap. 12) found a direct correlation between how students rated the quality of their final co-ops and the level of their earnings nine months after graduation. Those who had rated their co-ops as high quality were earning more than those who rated their experiences lower. They defined *high-quality* co-ops and internships as "those that provide opportunities for students to develop their base of knowledge, their skills and abilities." In their inquiry, Fogg and Putnam asked students to rate quality on the basis of the level of intellectual challenge, such as working independently or working as part of a team, and the variety and level of skills, such as writing, research and use of sophisticated technology, required in the job. They conclude that "it would be good to obtain high quality jobs for our students, because this would pay off in terms of higher postgraduation earnings."

Baker (chap. 14) found four significant factors that, if present, had a direct bearing on students ratings of the quality of the co-op:

- amount of time spent idle;
- difficulty receiving clarification;
- work assignment commensurate with skills; and
- supervisor honoring shared expectations.

It is interesting to note that the first two factors are negatives that improve the rating if they are not present. Baker offers several suggestions, such as: when in doubt give the student more work and we should advise students to take responsibility for their own learning by seeking clarification when they need it. The third factor seems to be one that is reliant on good advising from placement faculty or practitioners and experienced supervision by employers. The last factor seems deceptively simple—honoring agreements—but in the work setting, in co-op in particular, the employer's needs often come before the students'. This would seem to indicate the need for clarity, flexibility, and the setting of realistic expectations.

Mayo (chap. 13) described IBM's strategic plan for implementing a whole new set of program features aimed at improving the quality of students' experience and toward making them favorably disposed to considering permanent employment with IBM after graduation. Some of the features they instituted were:

- biweekly co-op e-newsletter;
- social events with a company-wide focus;
- improved options for student housing;
- increased financial support;
- provided meaningful activities and resources to students to enhance the quality of their overall experience;
- exposed to high quality resources; and
- expanded to recruit grad students.

They spent significant time and resources developing a program that enabled them to recruit high-quality students to high-quality high-profile projects. Among the steps they took was a greater attention to the process of matching students to mentors within the company. Many of these steps are striking in their attention to the comfort and happiness of the student—something that we think is probably common among employers but seldom recognized.

It occurs to us that we might consider a shift away from the old patterns of preparation sessions and workshops, job reports, and debriefing sessions, which were perceived as ineffective in supporting learning (Johnston et al., chap. 9), and focus on developing program features that support quality work-based experiences. More attention could be paid to job development and student-to-job matching to assure that the work was rewarding and challenging but not overwhelming (or *underwhelming*). Also, developing better employer understanding of the learning goals and process was recommended. Cates and LeMaster (chap. 18) found that when employers were explicitly involved in providing guidance for the students' learning objectives, students perceived that learning was enhanced.

Both Eames (chap. 5) and Linn (chap. 6) point out a feature of most co-op programs that we would do well to maintain, that is the practice of multiple placements. Linn found that this practice influenced directions and choices over the lifetimes of co-op alumni. Eames points out that multiple placements facilitate students' opportunities to experience the differences between practice and practitioner in different settings within a profession. Cates and LeMaster (chap. 18) found that students felt the majority of their learning about organizational culture came from their co-op experience and that this learning continued throughout all five co-ops.

What Specific Recommendations for Pedagogy Emerged From the Research?

The question of pedagogy takes on urgency, when we address the problem, raised by Johnston et al. (chap. 19), of making the role of the practitioner more relevant to learning. Cates and LeMaster (chap. 18) suggest that we should set up instructional goals and follow them up with specific pedagogy intended to facilitate the achievement of those goals. Ricks (chap. 4) and Howard and Haugsby (chap. 11) , speak directly to what we can do as educators. Ricks suggests that students encounter ethical issues often in the workplace and need training on how to address them. She proposes that students should be taught professional standards of good practice and skills to understand situations and make best choices. This type of knowledge and skill seems to relate to the two domains of learning—functioning in social situations and problem solving—in which Van Gyn (chap. 7) found that co-op did significantly better than non-co-op students. One can imagine teaching of other knowledge and skills that would help as well, for example creating, as Baker (chap. 14) suggests, virtual realities in the classroom to facilitate learning problem solving techniques.

Howard and Haugsby's (chap. 11) propose that we "ask students to consider class issues throughout their entire co-op process," and that we ask "difficult questions to establish an awareness of self and self in relation to others" (p. 223). This effort would also tie into and support learning in the area of understanding and functioning in social situations. It also indicates a Socratic approach to teaching and advising.

Co-op in liberal arts setting of Antioch College has fostered a focus on the 5-to-9 learning that can occur away from work while students are on co-op. Linn (chap. 6) and Miller (chap. 17) examine learning that happens in the communities outside of work where students become participants in ways that can be of equal significance to their participation at work. Howard and Haugsby's (chap. 11) use of the Socratic approach to surfacing learning is applicable with regard to 5-to-9 learning. In other words, we should ask about it. Often much of the material which would be considered the province of the liberal arts is found in what students are experiencing after work hours.

In the academic sphere, Grosjean (chap. 3) and Baker (chap. 14) both critiqued the current state of the use of simulations in classroom settings. Grosjean argues that they are inadequate and pale beside work-based learning. Baker accepts that they are going to be with us for a while still and need to be made more robust and less predictable.

Tener (chap. 16) addresses the question of learning style and has found that certain learning styles predominate in construction internships. What learning styles predominate in other types of work settings? Using teaching modalities in courses and at the work sites that are better suited to those styles would be indicated.

What Policies Are Recommended?

Grosjean (chap. 3) argues for a higher level of recognition for the learning that takes place on co-op and this should include the awarding of credit, evaluation of procedural knowledge and practical skills. Miller (chap. 17) suggests that a one-size-fits-all approach will under-serve some students and overlook some types of learning. He argues that students' ethnicity, sexual orientation, or other identity variables could influence how policies and requirements that make assumptions about identity or demographic status might result in entirely different sets of learning outcomes and implications for some students. Maynard has found that GPA requirements can be relaxed to GPAs of 2.7 and above with no decrease in employers' ratings of student performance.

What Other Practices Are Important to Maintain?

Publish or otherwise disseminate your work. Rowe (chap. 15) implores us to share our research so that all can benefit from our findings. Baker (chap. 14) advocates for the practice of purposeful and strategic publishing of your work and presumably your opinions as well. He engaged in an intentional barrage of target fora in an attempt to spur public debate and influence cooperative education and classroom practice. We would argue that one sign of a healthy discipline is a healthy debate.

We hope that you have found this handbook to be a useful resource in designing and carrying out your own research and informative of your practice. Research isn't easy, nor is it mysterious. We encourage you to share your research with various communities of practice through presenting at conferences and submitting articles for publication. This is essential to the continued growth and strength of our profession.

REFERENCES

Astin, A. (2002). *Assessment for excellence: The philosophy and practice of assessment and evaluation in higher education*. Westport, CT: Oryx Press.

Bryman, A. (1984). The debate about quantitative and qualitative research: A question of method of epistemology. *British Journal of Sociology, 35,* 75–92.

Denzin, N., & Lincoln, Y. S. (Eds.). (1994). *Handbook of qualitative research*. Thousand Oaks, CA: Sage.

Kolb, D. A. (1984). *Experiential learning: Experience as the source of learning and development*. Englewood Cliffs, NJ: Prentice Hall.

Kuhn, T. S. (1970). *The structure of scientific revolution* (2nd ed.). Chicago: University of Chicago Press.

Wilson, J. W. (1988). Research in cooperative education. *Journal of Cooperative Education, 24*(2–3), 77–89.

Author Index

A

Adler, P., 77, 88
Adler, P. A., 77, 88
Alexander, A., 283, 299
Alexander, J. P., 193, 206
Alm, C. T., 138, 153
American Bar Association Section of Legal
    Education and Admission to the
    Bar, 282, 293, 299
American Psychological Association, 303,
    308, 309, 414
Anastasi, A., 126, 135
Anderson, G., 54, 68
Anderson, V., 370, 381
Antioch College Center for Cooperative
    Education, 338, 343, 357, 361
Anyon, J., 212, 214, 225
Alvarado, M., 213, 225
Archambault, R. D., 25, 26, 27
Armon, C., 18, 27
Arnold, M. J., 140, 153, 154
Asante, M. K., 355, 359, 361
Astin, A., 366, 368, 369, 381, 427, 437
Atkinson, G., Jr., 322, 332
Austin, T. A., 160, 185
Ausubel, D. P., 35, 49

B

Baker, B., 280, 281, 286, 287, 288n6, 291,
    292, 293, 294, 295, 296, 297, 299
Baldick, T., 56, 68
Bandura, A., 15, 17, 27, 73, 86, 88, 89, 99,
    103, 107, 112, 329, 332, 339, 361
Banta, T., 364, 381
Bard, R., 192, 206
Barry, M., 282, 293, 299

Bartkus, K. R., 5, 10, 73, 77, 88, 89
Basow, R. R., 194, 206
Bauer, J., 282, 293, 300
Baxter Magolda, M. B., 20, 21, 27
Becher, T., 38, 49
Becker, G. S., 238, 249
Becker, L., 194, 206
Belenky, M. F., 19, 20, 27
Bell, J., 76, 88, 89
Bellack, A. S., 135
Biggs, J. B., 47, 49
Biklen, S. K., 7, 10
Billett, S., 44, 50
Bird, B. J., 104, 112
Birnbaum, R., 248
Blasi, G., 292, 299
Blaug, M., 248
Bloch, F., 282, 299
Blum, L., 56, 57, 68
Blum, L. A., 67
Bogdan, R., 7, 10
Bolman, L. G., 248
Bond, L. A., 126, 135
Boone, S., 6, 10
Bordieu, P., 212, 213, 220, 225
Boulmetis, J., 400, 401
Bourdieu, P., 24, 27
Bourland-Davis, P. G., 194, 206
Bowles, S., 24, 27
Boyd, T., 355, 361
Brantlinger, 213, 225
Branton, G., 5, 10, 73, 89, 121, 125, 129,
    135, 158, 159, 160, 186
Brougham, C. E., 139, 140, 154
Brown, J. S., 35, 50
Brown, L., 135
Brown, S., 34, 50
Brown, S. J., 160, 186

Brown, S. R., 163, 167n2, *186*
Bruner, J., 282, 291, *299*
Bruner, J. S., 18, *27*
Bryant, B. R., *135*
Bryman, A., 429, *437*
Bunn, D., 65, *68*
Burke, P. J., 351, 359, *361*
Burns, R., 41, *50*
Burt, C., 411, *414*
Burt, J. M., 359, *361*
Business-Higher Education Forum, 3, *10,* 35, *50*
Butterworth, G., 282, 291, *300*
Byrne, M. V., 194, *206*

C

Caffarella, R., 282, 291, *300*
Candy, P., 291, *299*
Cannon, J. A., 140, 153, *154*
Carrell, S. E., 99, *112*
Casella, D. A., 139, 140, *154*
Cassidy, J. R., 139, 153, *154*
Caswell, J., *414*
Cates, C., 5, *10,* 12, 14, 17, 18, *27,* 73, 74, 88, 89, 158, 161, *185, 186,* 370, *381*
Cates, M. L., 138, 140, *154*
Center for Multilingual/Multicultural Education in the Graduate School of Education at George Mason University, 388, *400, 401*
Center for Third World Organizing, 346, *361*
Chiseri-Strater, E., *414*
Ciofalo, A., 194, *206*
Clinchy, B. M., 19, 20, *27*
Cochran-Smith, M., 212, *225*
Cohen, A. J., 160, *186*
Cohen, L., 77, 78, 88, *89*
Coll, R. K., 79, *89*
Collins, A., 35, *50*
Commons, M. L., 18, *27*
Conoley, J. C., *135*
Co-op Employer's Forum, *271*
Cooperative education funding review advisory committee, 160, *186*
Costa, A. L., 21, 22, 23, *27*
Courtney, S., 282, 291, *299*
Cozby, P. C., *414*

Croissant, J., 99, *113*
Cronbach, L. J., 7, *10*
Cutt, J., 5, *10, 73,* 89, 90, 116, 121, 125, 129, *135, 136,* 158, 159, 160, *186*

D

D'Amico, C., *248*
Daugherty, E., 204, *206*
Davis, R., 184, *186*
Dawson, P., 73, *89*
Deal, T. E., *248*
DeFalco, A. A., 74, *89*
Delany, J. T., 56, *68*
Demarco, J., 56, *68*
Denzin, N., 99, *112,* 427, *437*
Denzin, N. K., *414*
Denzine, G. M., 163, *185, 186*
Department of Health and Human Services, *414*
Dewey, J., 25, *27,* 208, *225,* 291, *299,* 359, *361*
Deyhle, D. L., *415*
Dick, B., 54, *68*
Dill, C. A., *415*
Dippo, D., 80, *90*
Drenth, P., 65, *69*
Duckworth, E., 211, 224, *225*
Duguid, P., 35, *50*
Duncan-Robinson, J., 159, *186*
Dunn, M., 368, *381*
Dutwin, P., *400, 401*
Dyson, A., 209, 210, *225*

E

Eames, C. W., 79, 80, *89*
Eberlein, L., 56, *68*
Elliot, S. K., 192, *206*
Elsdon, I., 57, *68*
Emory University, 329, *332*
Engeström, Y., 34, 35, 44, 47, *48, 50*
Entwistle, H., 47, *50*
Entwistle, N., 35, *49, 51*
Entwistle, N. J., 47, *51*
ERIC database, *360*
Erickson, F., 209, 216, *225*
Erickson, R., 56, 57, *68*
Evers, F., 159, *186*
Eyler, J., 99, *112,* 138, 153, *154*

F

Faundez, A., 221, *225*
Ferguson, B., 213, *225*
Ferguson, J., 5, *10*, 101, *113*
Fields, C. D., 139, *154*
Filipczak, B., 138, *153*, *154*
Finn, K. L., 73, 89
Fitz-Gibbon, C. T., 126, *135*
Fletcher, J., 15, *27*, 99, *111*, *112*
Fletcher, J. K., 33, *50*, 73, *89*, 160, *186*
Flood, J., *224*
Fogg, N. P., 238, 242, *249*
Foggin, J. H., 3, *10*
Folkman, S., *414*
Foucault, M., 46, *50*
Fowler, H. W., 303, *308*, *309*
Freedman, J. L., *415*
Freire, P., 54, *68*, 208, 221, *225*
Fulmer, H. W., 194, *206*

G

Ganley, D., 20, *28*
Gardner, H., 17, *27*, 74, *89*, 282, 295, *299*
Gardner, P. D., 3, *10*, 21, 23, *27*, 99, *112*,
    139, 140, 141, *153*, *154*
Garfat, T., 56, 57, 65, *68*, *69*
Garmston, R. J., 21, 22, 23, *27*
Garth, B., 285, 285n1, 285n3, 286, 286n5,
    298, *299*
Gawthrop, J. C., 56, *68*
Geertz, C., 209, 210, 216, *225*, 340, *361*
Gilden, E. R., *415*
Gillespie, D., 282, 291, *298*, *299*
Gintis, H., 24, *27*
Givelber, D., 282, *300*
Givelber, J., 281, 286, 291, 292, 293, 294,
    295, *299*
Glaser, B. G., 74, *89*, 99, *113*
Goldberger, N. R., 19, 20, *27*
Goldman, B. A., *134*, *135*
Goleman, D., 3, *10*
Gore, G., 99, *113*
Gould, S., 209, *225*
Gould, S. J., *415*
Graham, B. L., 194, *206*
Grantz, R., 99, *113*
Granum, R., 56, 57, *68*
Greene, M., 211, *225*

Gregory, V., 285, 286, 289, *300*
Griffin, S., 65, 66, *69*
Gronlund, N. E., 124, *135*
Grosjean, G., 35, 44, 47, *50*
Gross, L. S., 193, *206*
Guadino, J. L., 194, *206*
Guba, E. G., 77, *89*

H

Habermas, J., 54, *68*
Hackett, E. J., 99, *113*
Hall, D. T., 21, 23, *27*
Halpin, G., 359, *361*
Hammill, D. D., *135*
Hamadeh, S., 192, *206*
Handelsman, M. M., 56, *68*
Hanesian, H., 35, *49*
Hanslka, L. L., *415*
Harrington, P., 231, 242, *249*
Harrington, P. E., 238, *249*
Harris, E. L., 340, *361*
Harrisberger, L., 319, *332*
Hart, M., 291, *299*
Heath, S. B., *224*
Heinemann, H. N., 74, *89*
Heller, F., 65, *69*
Heller, J., *415*
Herr, K., 54, *68*
Hersen, M., *135*
Hess, G. A., *415*
Heydinger, R., 319, *332*
Hill, P. C., *415*
Hill, R. L. M., *271*
Hoffman, P., 282, 293, *299*
Hoffman, R., 292, *298*, *299*
Holter, I. M., *69* not in text
hooks, b., 212, *224*, *225*
Hopkins, M., *415*
Hopkins, R., 323, 324, *332*
Hounsell, D., 35, *49*, *51*
Howard, G., 6, *10*
Howard, G. S., 57, *69*
Huberman, A. M., 82, *89*, 99, 107, *112*,
    113
Hughes, C., 73, *90*
Human resources development Canada,
    program evaluations branch,
    159, *186*
Hutchinson, J. F., 348, 359, *361*

I

Ignelzi, M., 17, 19, 21, *27*
Imel, S., 139, 140, *154*
Impara, J. C., *135*
Iran-Nejad, A., 297, *299*

J

Jacobs, S. E., *414*
Jarrell, D., 21, *27* , 99, *113*
Jarvis, P., 291, *299*
Johnson, A. G., *360*
Johnson, M., 194, *206*
Johnston, N., 159, 160, 161, *185, 186*
Jones, P., 5, *10*, 12, 14, 17, 18, *27*, 73, 74, 88, *89*, 158, 161, *185, 186*, 370, *381*
Jones, R. S., 353, *361*
Jones, Y. V., 350, *361*
Journal of Career Planning and Employment, 140, *154*
Judy, R. W., *248*

K

Kamin, L. G., *415*
Karenga, M., 359, *361*
Katz, L. F., 230, *249*
Kegan, R., 19, 20, 21, *28*
Kelle, U., 39n1, *50*
Kelly, G., *134, 135*
Kelman, H. C., *415*
Kemmis, S., 54, *69*
Keenan, K., 194, *206*
Keyser, D. J., *134, 135*
Kidder, R., 56, 60, 66, *69*
Kidder, R. M., *67*
Kirsch, G., *414*
Knowles, A., xi, *xiv*
Kolb, D., 159, *186*
Kolb, D. A., 14, 15, *28*, 74, *89*, 99, *113*, 214, *225*, 321, 322, 323, *332*, 426, *437*
Kooperman, P., 65, *69*
Kotkin, M., 282, *299*
Kreiling, K., 282, 293, *299*
Krapels, R. H., 138, 139, *154*
Krmpotic, J., 159, *186*
Kuhn, T. S., 431, *437*

L

Laing, D. A., 73, *89*
Lambert, S. E., 139, 140, 141, *153, 154*
Lantz, G., 56, *69*
Lapp, D., *224*
Laser, G., 282, *300*
Lave, J., 22, 23, *27, 28*, 35, 46, 50, 74, *89*, 100, 110, *112, 113, 186*, 282, 291, *298, 300*
LeCompte, M. D., 39, *50, 415*
Lee-Thomas, G., *400, 401*
Lewis, M., 3, *10*
Light, P., 282, 291, *300*
Lincoln, Y. S., 77, *89*, 99, *112, 414, 415*, 427, *437*
Lindenmeyer, R. S., 117, *135*
Lindheim, E., 126, *135*
Linn, P., 5, *10*
Linn, P. L., 20, *28*, 101, 109, *113*, 159, 160, 161, *186*
Linn, R. L., 124, *135*
Lips, H., 152, *154*
Loken, M., 5, *10*, **73**, *89*, 90, 116, 121, 125, 129, *135, 136*, 158, 159, 160, *186*
Lyons, E., 117, *136*
Lyons, E. H., 12, *28*, 160, *187*, 306, *309*
Lytle, S. L., 212, *225*

M

Maher, S., 282, *300*
Manion, L., 77, 78, 88, *89*
Mannell, R. C., *49, 51*
Marable, M., 341, 344, 347, *360, 361*
Martin, P., 285, 285n1, 285n3, 286, 286n5, 287, *298, 299*
Marton, F., 35, *49, 51*
Marx, K., 24, *28*
Maslow, A., 291, *300*
Matson, L. C., 35, *51*
Matson, R., 35, *51*
McBride, J. L., Jr., 139, *154*
McDevitt, J., 281, 286, 287, 291, 292, 293, 294, 295, *299*
McGin, C., *68*
McGovem, T., 56, *69*
McIntyre, J., 159, *186*
McLaren, P., 221, *225*
McLeod, J., 24, *28*
McMillan, J. H., 120, 121, 124, *135*

McTaggart, R., 54, 69
Meeske, M. D., 193, 194, *206*
Meisler, R., 109, *113*
Meltsner, M., 282, *300*
Merriam, S., 282, 291, *300*
Merriam, S. B., 39, *51*, 209, *225*
Michelson, E., 99, *113*
Middaugh, M. F., 233, *249*
Miles, M. B., 39n1, *51*, 82, 89, 99, 105, 107, 112, *113*
Milgram, S., *415*
Miliano, R., 281, 286, 287, 291, 292, 293, 294, 295, 299
Miller, A. G., *415*
Mincer, J., 238, *249*
Mintzberg, H., 65, 69
Mitchell, D. F., *134, 135*
Moreno, J., 54, 69
Morgan, A. E., 99, 100, *113*
Morris, L. L., 126, *135*
Morrison, J., 56, 69
Morrison, K., 77, 78, 88, 89
Mortensen, P., *414*
Morton, L. L., 73, 89
Mosbacker, W. B., 77, 89
Motley, J., 282, *300*
Mueller, S. L., 99, *113*
Muffo, J. A., 139, *154*
Muller, H. J., 3, *10*
Murphy, K. M., 230, *249*
Murrell, P. H., 322, *332*

N

Naipaul, V. S., 340, 356, *361*
Newkirk, T., *415*
Ney, T., 73, *89*, 121, 125, *135*, 159, 160, 186
Nihlen, A., 54, 68
Novak, J. S., 35, *49*
NSEE Foundations Document Committee, 26, 28

O

Oglivy, J., 293, *300*
Oldham, M., 192, *206*
Oreovicz, F. S., 321, 323, 324, *332, 333*

P

Paige, R. M., 342, 348, 351, 354, 356, *361*

Palomba, C., 364, *381*
Papillo, J., 282, 293, *300*
Paterson, L., 212, *225*
Patton, M., 214, *225*
Patton, M. Q., 39, *51*, 55, 69, 77, 89, 99, *113*
Pea, R. D., 75, 89
Pennsylvania State Data Center, 344, 345, *361*
Perkins, D. N., 75, 90
Perry, W. G., Jr., 18, 19, 20, *28*
Peshkin, A., 76, 89
Peterson, M. W., 233, *249*
Petrysack, N., 33, *51*, 159, 160, *186*
Pettit, D. E., 4, *10*
Piaget, J., 18, 20, *28*
Pittenger, K., 33, *51*
Plummer, K., *415*
Porter, J. L., 3, *10*
Porter, M. E., 159, *186*
Preissle, J., 39, *50*
Pumphrey, G., 34, *51*
Punch, M., *415*
Purpel, D., 207, *225*

Q

QSR Nudi*st Vivo, 105, *113*

R

Raisisnghanim, D., 65, 69
Ramsden, P., 47, *51*
Ransby, B., 355, *361*
Rashotte, C. A., 15, *28*, 33, 34, *51*, 73, 90, 133, *136*
Reason, P., 54, 69
Redeker, L. L., 194, *206*
Rehder, R. R., 3, *10*
Report of the Committee on the Future of the In-House Clinic, 282, 293, *300*
Rhodes, M., 56, 69
Richards, F. A., 18, *27*
Richardson, D., *415*
Ricks, F., 5, *10*, 56, 57, 58, 65, 66, 68, 69, 73, 89, 90, 116, 121, 125, 129, *135, 136*, 158, 159, 160, *186*
Rogers, G., 387, 400, *401*

Rogoff, B., 35, 49, 51, 74, 85, 88, 89, 282, 288n6, 292, 295, 298, 300
Rorty, R., 56, 69
Rosaldo, R., 8, 10
Rosch, E., 282, 300
Rose, H., 282, 300
Rowan, J., 282, 300
Rowe, P. M., 33, 49, 51, 99, 112, 160, 186
Rowland, M., 206
Rubin, I., 159, 186
Rubin, Z., 415
Rudner, L. M., 126, 135
Rus, V., 65, 69
Rush, J., 159, 186
Ryan, C., 138, 139, 154
Ryan, G., 73, 90
Ryan, M., 139, 153, 154
Ryder, K. G., 306, 309

S

Sales, B. D., 414
Säljö, R., 35, 51
Salomon, G., 75, 90
Sando, J., 387, 400, 401
Saupe, J. L., 233, 249
Schenke, A., 80, 90
Schneider, B., 99, 113
Schön, D., 6, 10, 186, 282, 300
Schön, D. A., 57, 66, 69
Schwartz-Barcott, D., 69 not in text
Scott, M. E., 271
Scribner, S., 44, 51
Seeley, J., 319, 332
Seidenberg, J. M., 99, 113
Senge, P., 53, 55, 69
Shalleck, A., 282, 293, 300
Shannon, P., 212, 225
Sharma, L. A., 33, 49, 51
Shim-Li, C., 6, 10
Siedenberg, J. M., 129, 135
Simon, H., 65, 69
Simon, R. I., 80, 90
Smaglik, E. J., 325, 326, 327, 332, 333
Smith, C. P., 415
Smith, H., 117, 135
Smith, J., 283, 299
Smith, S. S., 415
Socell, D., 56, 68
Somers, G., 33, 51
Stake, R. E., 39, 51

Standards for Educational and Psychological Testing, 123, 134, 135
Stanton, M., 138, 154
Stark, J., 282, 293, 300
Stark, J. S., 112
Steele, J. M., 125, 126, 130, 132, 135
Stephenson, W., 162, 165, 185, 187
Sternberg, R., 133, 136
Sternberg, R. J., 15, 28, 33, 34, 51, 73, 90, 100, 103, 113, 133, 135, 136
Stickgold, M., 282, 300
Storti, C., 342, 355, 361
Strauss, A. L., 74, 89
Stringer, E., 54, 55, 68, 69
Strunk, W., Jr., 303, 308, 309
Stull, W. A., 5, 10, 73, 77, 88, 89
Sum, A., 231, 249
Svensson, L., 35, 51
Sweetland, R. C., 134, 135

T

Talburtt, M., 319, 332
Tarr, N., 282, 300
Tarule, J. M., 19, 20, 27
Tener, R. K., 318, 327, 332, 333
Teta, D., 56, 69
Thanos, M., 99, 113
Theoret, A., 65, 69
Thompson, E., 282, 300
Thorndike, R. M., 123, 135
Tinsley, E., 6, 10
Tinsley, H., 6, 10
Toby, A., 33, 51, 159, 160, 186
Toma, J. D., 112
Toohey, S., 73, 90
Tooley, J. A., 194, 206
Tulgan, B., 3, 10
Tymchuk, A. J., 65, 69

U

Ulichny, P., 415
U.S. Bureau of the Census, 237
US News and World Report College Rankings, 385, 401

V

Van Gyn, G., 5, 10, 73, 89, 90, 121, 125, 135, 158, 159, 160, 186

Van Gyn, G. H., 6, *10*, 116, 129, *135, 136*
van Manen, M., 221, 223, *225, 226*, 341, *361*
Varela, F., 282, *300*
Vygotsky, L. S., 74, *90*

W

Wagner, R. K., 15, *28*, 33, 34, *51*, 73, *90*, 100, 103, *113*, 133, *135, 136*
Walvoord, B., 370, *381*
Wankat, P. C., 321, 323, 324, 328, *332, 333*
Warwick, D. P., 56, 69
Weaver, K. A., 5, *10*
Weber, S., 317, *333*
Wegner, E., 22, 23, *28*, 100, 110, *112, 113*
Weinstein, D. S., 160, *187*
Weitzman, E., 105, *113*
Weitzman, E. A., 39n1, *51*
Wenger, E., 35, 46, 49, 50, *51*, 186, 282, 291, *300*
Wessels, W., 33, *51*
West, C., 349, 350, 359, *361*
Weston, W., 99, *113*
Weston, W. D., 73, *90*

White, C. L., 351, 359, *361*
White, E. B., 303, *308, 309*
Williams, C., *415*
Williams, W. M., 15, *28*, 33, 34, *51*, 73, *90*, 133, *136*
Wilson, J., 117, *136*
Wilson, J. W., 5, *10*, 12, *28*, 34, *51*, 73, *90*, 160, *187*, 306, *309*, 426, 427, *437*
Wilson, R. L., 73, *90*
Winstead, M. S., 327, *333*
Winstead, M. T., 321, *333*
Wolcott, H. F., 99, *112, 113*, 340, 341, 343, *361*

Y

Yin, R. K., 39, *51*
Young, R., 213, *226*

Z

Zaruba, K. E., *112*
Zillman, D., 285, 286, 288, *300*

Subject Index

5-to-9 learning, 107, 108, 436

A

Abstract, 304
Abstract conceptualization, 14, 214, 322,
    325–326, 327, 328, 330, 335–336
Academic context, 34, 49
    cooperative education and, 171, 178–179
    learning in, 47–48, 83–84
Academic support center, 18–19
Accommodation, 20–21
Accommodative learning style, 328, 330
Accreditation Board for Engineering and
    Technology (ABET), 317
    Education Criterion (EC2000), 384,
    391–392, 399
Accreditation Council of Cooperative Edu-
    cation, 271
Accreditation process, 5, 433
Accrediting Council for Education in Jour-
    nalism and Mass Communica-
    tion, 194–195
Action research, 54–67, 68, 78, 203n6,
    207, 211–212, 213
    community partners in, 54, 55, 57, 67
    methodology, 57–59
    selecting subjects, 215
Action science, 54
Active experimentation, 14, 214, 323, 325,
    326, 328, 330, 336
ACT process, 256–267
Adaptability, 23
Administrators, research needs of, 230,
    231–233
Adolescence, intellectual change in late,
    20–21
Affective knowledge, 122

African-American culture, 340, 345, 346,
    347–349, 350, 354–355
    diversity in, 358–360
African-American identity, 359
African-American studies, 337, 343–344,
    346, 347
Africanity, vs. Afrocentricity, 354–355
Allied health professions, teaching ethics
    in, 56–57
American Assembly of Collegiate Schools
    of Business (AACSB), 138
American Bar Association, 293
American College Testing Program
    (ACT), 125–127
American Psychological Association
    (APA), 303
    ethical guidelines, 412
    publication guidelines, 303, 304, 308
American Society of Engineering Educa-
    tors, 384
Am I Black Enough for You?, 355
Analysis. *See* Data analysis
Analysis of Variance (ANOVA), 392
Analytical thinking, 66
Anonymity, research participation and,
    408–409
Anonymous works, citation of, 310
Anti-cooperative education, 169, 172,
    176, 182
Antioch College, 216
    cross-cultural experience requirement,
    337, 338, 357–358
    liberal arts co-op education program,
    97–98, 100–101, 105–107,
    109–110
Apparatus, 304
Applied ethics, 67
Applied methodology, 430

Apprenticeships, 23
Archival research, 412
Area of Darkness, An, 356
Article
    descriptive, 306
    format, 303
    parts of, 303–305
    research, 306
Assessment, 364, 369
    ABET criterion, 384n3
    authentic, 400
    basics, 387–388
    diagnostic, 400
    instruments, 389–392
    plan, 387–388, 400
    prognostic, 400
    of soft skills, 386, 394–398
    strategy, 387–388
    tools, 134
Assimilative learning style, 328
Association of American Law Schools, 293
Atlas.ti software, 39
Audience, for dissemination of research,
    281, 292–293
Authentic assessment, 400
Authentic involvement, 319–320
Authority, obedience to, 403–405
Author note, 305
Authors
    name, 304
    text citations, 310–311
Authorship, 303

B

Bad news, reporting, 409
Base group, 240, 243
Basic research motives, 431
Best practices, 63–64
Bias, 124–125, 127, 132
    controlling, 196, 198
    informed consent and, 407
Bivariate correlation, 199n4
Body language, 354–355
Book
    reference listing, 312
    text citation, 310–311
Boundedness, of case study, 210
Buy-in
    for cooperative education, 32
    faculty, 41–42
    for research study, 37–38, 41

C

Canadian Nursing Code of Ethics, 56
Canadian Psychological Association Code
    of Ethics, 56
Career development, impact of coopera-
    tive education on, 33
Career identity, cooperative education
    and, 73
Career services, 388, 389
Case studies, 78, 81
    constructing, 208, 210–211, 216,
        223–224
    cross-cultural experiences, 337,
        345–360
    methodology, 209–211
    narrative, 211
    nested, 39, 40
    peer review and, 215–216
    samples, 82–88, 216–219
    selecting subjects, 215
    single, 340–341
Categorical data, 144, 145, 198–199, 205,
    211, 214
Ceiling effect, 129, 130
Census, 197
Center for Multilingual and Multicultural
    Education, 388
Center for Science and Technology Educa-
    tion Research, 77
Center for Third World Organizing
    (CTWO), 346
Chapter, reference listing, 312
Chi square, 102n2, 103n3, 144, 145, 146,
    392
Cincinnati Plan, The, 368
Classical works, citation of, 311
Classroom context, 34, 49. *See also* Aca-
    demic context
Clinical Law Review, 293
Closed-universe syndrome, 295, 297
Closing the loop, 388
Coding, 107, 109
Cognitive contextualism, 291
Cognitive skills, 122
Cognitive stage theory, 18–22
Cohort, 236
Collaboration, 107, 216, 424–425
College labor market occupations,
    242–243

College Outcomes Measures Program test (COMP), 125–133
Communication internships, 194
Communication skills, 3, 386, 394, 396, 397. *See also* Social skills
Communities of practice, 22–23, 45, 49
Community development, 54
Community partners, 54, 55, 57, 67
Comparative data analysis, 234, 236
Comparative means, 201, 202
Computer-aided qualitative data analysis, 99, 105
Conceptual outcomes, 366
Concourse, 165–166, 184, 188–190, 432
Concrete-abstract continuum, 322
Concrete experience, 14, 214, 322, 325, 326, 328, 330, 334–335
Conferences, disseminating research findings via, 302
Confidentiality, 9, 81, 408–409
Confounding factor, 122
Conscientization, 208
Consciousness, 68
Construction engineering internships, 315–332
    experiential learning theory and, 321–323, 325–329
    interns' written reports, 324–325
    self-efficacy and, 329
Content analysis, 81
Content knowledge, 22
Content validity, 17
Context
    defined, 34–35
    literature review, 34–36
    for research, 423–424
    See also Academic context; Workplace context
Contextualism, 291–292
Contextualist cognitive science, 282
Contextualized learning, 31–32, 35, 43–48
    in academic context, 47–48
    literature review on, 34–36
    research participants, 37–39
    research setting, 36–37
    research study design, 39–42
    survey results, 42–48
    in workplace, 44–46
Control group, 196, 201, 389
Convergent learning style, 328

Co-op and Placement Services Network (CAPSNET), 422
Co-op data, 234
Co-op effect, 44, 48
Cooperative education, 318
    academic context and, 171, 178–179
    analysis of teaching opportunities for, 62–66
    assessing engineering soft skills in, 386–387, 389–398
    creating concourse on, 165–166
    educational value of, 432–433
    employability outcomes of, 170, 176–177
    employment preparation and, 171, 179–180
    ethics in, 55–67
    higher education and, 5, 364
    history of, 4–5
    implications of research for, 432–437
    importance of workplace in, 433–434
    levels of analysis of, 13–14
    literature review, 33–34, 159–161
    making meaning from, 32, 33–35
    measuring, 158, 429
    need for research on, 5–6
    organizational behavior learning and, 377–378
    policy recommendations for, 436–437
    practitioner views on, 169–180
    program recommendations for, 434–345
    recruiting and, 252, 255, 260–261, 266–267
    research design for, 233–236
    research questions, 158, 159, 161–162
    situated learning theory and, 23
    skill transfer and, 177–178
    socioeconomic class and, 207–209, 212–214
    technical skills and, 169, 172, 173, 174–175
    See also Contextualized learning; Cross-cultural experiential learning; Internships; Learning outcomes
Cooperative Education and Internship Association, 422
Cooperative Education Association, 341, 374
Cooperative jobs

impact on post-graduation earnings, 229–248
job quality, 240, 261–262, 273–274, 434–435
   student employee development plan, 275
   tracking employees, 255, 264, 266
Cooperative legal education program, 281, 283–284
   clinical model, 294
   literature review, 282
   ranking as learning experience, 286–290
   reform recommendations, 294–298
   research questions, 284–287
Coordinator role, 180, 181
Corporate employee resource information system (CERIS), 254–255
Correlation, 15n1
Correlation analysis, 78, 191, 199–203
Correlation coefficient, 124
Correlations, research design and, 98
Cost, Q-methodology, 184
Cost-effectiveness, of research, 427
Criterion-based selection, 39
Criterion-referenced test, 126
Critical awareness, 221
Critical thinking, 66
Cross-cultural credit, 342–343
Cross-cultural experiential learning, 337–360, 425
   African-American cultural diversity, 358–360
   Antioch goals for, 357–358
   case study, 339–344
   co-op setting, 345–346
   cultural origins and, 344–345
   expectations for, 347–349
   language and, 354–355
   perceived cultural difference and, 355–356
   status and, 356–357
   Type I adjustments and, 349–350
   Type II adjustments and, 351–354
   visibility-invisibility and, 351–354
Cross-cultural learning theory, 339, 427–428
Cross-disciplinary research, 424–425
Cross-sectional study, 117–118, 234, 236
Cultural adjustments, 342, 349–354
Cultural capital, 24
Cultural difference, 355–356

Cultural identity, 38
Cultural influences, research and, 409–410
Cultural origins, 344–345
Culture, test bias and, 125, 132
Curriculum, improving cooperative education, 368

D

Data
   case study, 211
   categorical, 144, 145, 198–199, 205, 211, 214
   descriptive, 343
   simplifying, 145
   subsets, 379
   See also Qualitative data; Quantitative data
Data analysis, 387–388, 392–393
   action research, 214–215
   comparative, 234, 236
   descriptive data, 343
   methods, 234, 235–236
   posttest, 130–133
   pretest, 128–133
   qualitative, 8, 39
   selecting research instrument and, 120
   statistics and, 144–153
   survey, 143–145
   textual, 81
Data collection
   action research, 211–212, 213
   Q-methodology and, 164–165
   self-reporting and, 197–198
Debriefing, 406
Deception, 406–407
Deductive approach, 98, 428
Deep-level learning, 47
Democracy, educational outcomes and, 21–22
Dependent variable, 119, 121, 144
Description, 343
Descriptive article, 306
Descriptive data, 343
Development, stages of cognitive, 18–22
Developmental context of learning theory, 13
Developmental psychology, 97
Dewey's philosophy, 25–26
Diagnostic assessment, 400

Dichotomous responses, 392
Disciplines, 38
    cooperative education and, 101–104
    knowledge attributed to co-op and
            classroom and, 379–380
    See also Major
Discourse, 181
Discussion, 305
Dispatches from the Ebony Tower, 344
Dispositions, 22
Dissemination of assessment findings, 398
Dissemination of research findings, 213,
            231, 246–247, 437
    forums for, 8-9
    identifying audience, 281, 292–293
    representation and, 409
    writing research reports, 9, 301–312
    See also Publication
Distribution of instrument, 375
Divergent learning style, 328
Divergent thinking, 66
Diversity, educating students in, 3
Dummy variables, 240

E

Earnings. *See* Salary
Earnings regression (earnings function),
            238–239
Ecological learning, 279–281
    implications for clinicians' practice, 296
    research questions, 284–287
    theory of, 291–292
Economic dimension of social class,
            219–220
Economy, impact of education on, 248
Educational outcomes, 21–22, 98
    College Outcomes Measures Program
            test, 125–128
    of cooperative education, 73
    defining, 121–122
    researching, 116–128
    See also Learning outcomes
Educational Resources Information Center
            (ERIC), 360
Educational Strategic Plan, 365–367
Educational tests, 412
Effective Grading, 370
Effectiveness, self-efficacy and, 15
Employability outcomes, 170, 176–177
Employers

cooperative education evaluation form,
            390, 392
    evaluation of student job performance,
            98, 100, 101
    role in learning and assessment, 370,
            372–373, 376, 378–380
Employment
    cooperative education and preparation
            for, 3–5, 171, 179–180
    effect of internships on postgraduate,
            145–148, 194
Enactive mastery, 17, 103, 107
Engineering cooperative education, assess-
            ing soft skills in, 386–387,
            389–392, 393–398. *See also*
            Construction engineering
Epistemology, 18, 430n1
Error, 124, 134
    acceptable, 100n1
    sampling, 142
Essays, 306
Estimated coefficients, 238–239
Ethical absolutist, 413
Ethical dilemmas, 9, 60, 61, 65, 66, 413
    defined, 57
Ethical issues in research, 403–414
Ethical issues in workplace, 436
*Ethical Principles in the Conduct of Research
            with Human Participants,* 412
Ethical reasoning, 65–66
Ethical responsibility, 386, 394, 395, 396
Ethics
    codes of, 56, 412–413
    in cooperative education, 55–67
    publication and, 302–303
    research, 81, 412–413
    teaching, 3, 56–57
Ethnicity, 240
Ethnocentrism, 342
Ethnography, 78
Experiential learning theory, 35, 99, 159,
            214, 291–292, 332
    construction internships and, 320–329
    learning cycle, 14–15, 17, 74, 282, 291
Experimental design, 98
Experimental research, ethical issues,
            403–414
Experimentation, 78
Experiments, types of, 431n2
Expertise, 291–292, 298, 359
Explanation, correlations and, 98

Ex post facto research, 119

F

Factor analysis, 164, 167
Factor loading, 167–171
Factors, 162, 163, 167
Faculty
    assessment of student learning out-
        comes, 373–374, 378, 380
    obtaining buy-in from, 41–42, 366
    role in co-op program, 384, 399
Feedback
    developmental, 273–274
    student intern, 276–278
Figures, 305
Fishing-to-learn metaphor, 279–281
Flexibility, 23
Focused learning outcomes, 368, 369
Focus groups, 134
Forced sorting format, 183–184
Foundation Coalition, 400
Fraud, research, 411
Frequencies, 392
F test, 129n1
Funding for research, 53–54, 58, 119–120,
    167, 321

G

Gangsta culture, 355
Gender, effect on starting salary, 149, 152
Generalizability, 123
Generative knowing, 20–21
George Mason University, Center for Mul-
    tilingual and Multicultural Edu-
    cation, 388
Globalization, educating students for, 3
Goal, 387
Going home experience, 338, 339–340, 358
Government research regulations, 412
Grade point average (GPA)
    cooperative education eligibility and,
        47, 119
    correlation with internship grade,
        199–200, 202, 203, 204
    internship eligibility and, 141, 191–205
    as measure of educational outcome, 117
Grades
    assessment of cooperative education us-
        ing, 47–48

for internships, 195–196, 203
as learning tool, 370, 374
transposing to numbers, 198–199
using to predict success, 193
Great Accommodation, 20–21
Grounded theory, 428
Grumman and Wang Labs, 192
Guided participation, 291

H

Habitus, 220–221
Hermeneutic theories, 12
Higher education
    challenges facing, 3–5
    cooperative education and, 5, 364
    history of, 230–231
    organizational dynamics of, 248
Higher Education Act (1965), Title VIII,
    4
Homophobia, 351–354, 357–358
Human capital, 238
Hypotheses, 36
Hypothesis testing, 389

I

IBM (International Business Machines)
        cooperative education and in-
        ternship program, 253–271,
        434–435
    ACT process, 256–267
    background, 251–252
    cooperative job quality, 261–263
    enculturating cooperative education
        program, 256–257
    Extreme Blue summer internships,
        267–268
    student feedback on, 276–278
Identifier, 235
Identity, self-esteem and Afri-
    can-American, 359
Identity theory, 339
Independent impact of the variable, 239
Independent variable, 119, 144, 149, 162
In-depth interview, 39, 134
Individual internship project, 195–196
Inductive approach, 98, 428
Inductive review, 216
Inferential research, 426, 431

Inferential statistics, 236
Informed consent, 81, 406, 407–408
    sample letter, 416
Institutional affiliation, 304, 305
Institutional researchers, 233, 247–248
Institutional Review Board (IRB), 412–413
Instructional goals, 365, 368, 369
Integrative thinking, 66
Intelligence
    practical, 15, 17
    studies, 411
Intercultural experiential learning theory,
    339
Intercultural learning experience, 341–343.
        See also Cross-cultural experien-
        tial learning
International co-ops, 338
Internship Bible, 138
Internships, 137–138
    business, 141–142
    in construction engineering, 315–332
    defined, 318–319
    educational value of, 432–433
    effects on postgraduate employment,
        145–148, 194
    grade point average and eligibility for,
        191–205
    grade point average and internship
        grade, 199–200, 202, 203, 204
    grading, 195–196, 320
    IBM, 253–254, 260–271
    implications of research for, 432–437
    importance of quality, 434–435
    literature review, 138–141
    need for research on, 5–6
    program recommendations, 434–435
    reports, 320, 324, 325
    situated learning theory and, 23
    See also Cooperative education
Interpersonal skills
    cooperative education and, 73
    learning in workplace context and, 46
    professional standard issues and, 64
Interpretation of descriptive data, 343
Interpretive methodology, 216, 426, 431
Interpretive research, 426, 431
Interval level, 106
Intervention, 196
Interviews, 121
    in-depth, 39, 134
    protocol, 91–94, 341

schedule of, 81
semistructured, 77–78
student, 43–48
using questionnaire data as starting
    point, 104–105
Introduction, article, 304
Inventories, 120–121
Inventory of abilities, 390
Ipsative approach, 184

J

Job placement, 175, 177
    expectations for, 139–140
Job satisfaction, 139
    effects of internships on, 145, 152
Journal for Curriculum Theorizing, 343
Journalism internships, 194
Journal of Career Planning and Employment,
    140
Journal of Cooperative Education, 72, 302,
    303, 306, 307, 412
Journal of Legal Education, 293
Journals, disseminating research findings
    via, 302. *See also* Publication
Judgment, 86

K

Knowledge
    affective, 122
    content, 22
    as educational outcome, 122
    generative, 22
    learning and, 322
    procedural, 122
    tacit, 34, 133

L

Labor market, 230–231, 249
Language, culture and, 354–355
Learning
    academic context for, 47–48, 83–84
    context and, 31–32, 43–48
    creating concourse on, 165–166
    deep-level, 47
    defined, 34, 322
    ecological, 279–281, 284–287, 291,
        292, 296

experiential, 35, 74, 99, 159, 214, 282,
        291–292, 332
life-long, 386, 394, 395, 396, 397
literature review, 34–36
meaningful, 35
measuring, 121–122, 158
school-based, 285
situated, 74
sociocultural view of, 74–75
sources of, 287, 288, 289
surface, 47
vicarious, 17
work-based, 285
workplace context for, 44–46, 83–84, 87
See also Contextualized learning;
        Cross-cultural experiential
        learning; Ecological learning
Learning cycle, 14–15, 17, 74. See also Ex-
        periential learning
Learning module, 369–374
    Organizational Culture Learning,
        374–377
Learning-organization theory, 55
Learning outcomes, 98
    assessment planning, 365–371
    cooperative education and, 112, 160
    documenting, 5
    focused, 368, 369–370
    of initial cooperative education experi-
        ences, 377–378, 379
    literature review, 99, 138
    measuring, 429–430
    See also Educational outcomes
Learning processes, 99, 430
Learning strategies, 35
Learning Style Inventory, 15
Learning styles, 328, 330, 331, 427, 436
Learning theories, 73–75, 99–100, 158–159
    analysis of work experience and, 17
    cognitive, 18–22
    experiential. See Experiential learning
        theory
    focus on particular work experience
        and, 13, 14–17
    multiple intelligence, 74
    practical intelligence, 15, 17
    reasons to study, 11–12
    schooling in general and, 22–25
    selection of, 12–13
    self-efficacy, 15, 17, 73–74

situated learning, 22–24, 35, 74, 100,
        110–112, 178, 282, 298
social learning, 49, 73–74, 298
social reproduction theories, 24–25
traditional, 22
See also Theory
Legitimate peripheral participation, 23
Liberal arts co-op education program,
        97–98, 100–101, 105–107,
        109–110, 111
Life-long learning, 386, 394, 395, 396, 397
Likert scale, 370, 374, 390, 392
Limitations
    of grade point average research, 203
    of business internship research,
        150–151
Linear regression, 144
Literature review, 423, 424
    choosing literature, 33
    clinical legal education, 282
    cooperative education, 33–34
    cooperative learning, 159–161
    internships, 138–141
    job placement expectations, 139–140
    job satisfaction, 139
    learning and context, 34–36
    learning outcomes, 138
    starting salary, 139
    undertaking, 72–73
Longitudinal study, 78, 80–81, 117–118,
        234, 236

M

Major
    effect on post-graduate earnings, 239,
        241, 242, 245
    importance of internships and, 146,
        148
    See also Disciplines
Manuscript preparation, 306
Marginal effects, 244
Marginal impact of the variable, 239
Materials, 304
Mean comparisons, 392
Meaningful learning, 35
Meaning-making, 19–20
Mean percentages, 144
Measurable outcomes, 387
Measurement
    of cooperative learning, 158

instrument, 196
issues of, 115, 428–430
of learning, 121–122
of programmatic success, 254–255
Mediated action, 74
Mental skills, cooperative job quality and, 244
Meta-analysis, 424
Metacognition, 22, 109
Metacognitive skills, 66, 122
Metaphors, 279–280
Metaskills, 21
Method, article section, 304
Methodology. *See* Research methodology
Milgram experiments, 403–405, 406
Minimal risk, 412–413
Möbius strip, 32
Moral dimension of social class, 220
Moral reasoning, 65–66
Moral theory, 67
Motives for research, 430
Multiple assessments, 365
Multiple author works, 310
Multiple intelligence, 74
Multiple placements, 435
Multiple regression analysis, 144, 289, 392
Multivariate analysis, 289n7

N

National Society for Experiential Education conference, 216
Natural experiment, 196, 205, 431n2
Naturalistic inquiry, 77
Naturalistic observation, 412
Nested case study, 39, 40
Networking, 273
New York Times, 405
Newcomers, 22–23, 74, 75
Nominal level, 106
Norfolk Southern, 192
Norm-referenced test, 126–127
Northeastern University, 283–284
Novices, experts and, 291–292, 298, 359
NUDIST, 81
Numbers, range of, 143

O

Objective, 387
Observation, 121

Office of Institutional Research, 233
Old timers, 22–23, 74, 75, 85, 87
Operant subjectivity, 161, 163
Opportunity books, 192
Organizational behavior, 377–378, 379
Organizational Culture Learning Module, 374–377
Outcome, 429. *See also* Educational outcomes; Learning outcomes
Outcome measures, 366
Outcome-oriented methodology, 426, 430

P

Participant observation, 39, 77–78
Participants, 304
selection criteria, 38, 40–41
Participatory appropriation, 74–75
Participatory research, 55
Pattern analyses, 103
PCQ Method software, 167, 168, 184
Pedagogy
instructional goals and, 368
opportunities in cooperative education, 62–66
recommended reforms, 295–297, 435–436
Peer review, 215–216, 307
Penicillin, discovery of, 377
Percentages, 392–393
Perceptual shifts, cooperative education and, 108
Performance, self-efficacy and, 15
Performance criteria, 387
Performance standard, 429
Periodical, reference listing, 312
Permission slip, 417
Personal communication, citation of, 311
Personality assessment measures, 120
Phenomenography, 49
Phenomenology, 107
Physical harm, research and, 405
Pilot study, learning outcome assessment, 374–377
Planning, research findings and, 247
Policy recommendations, 247, 436–437
Politics, dissemination of research findings and, 246
Positivistic methodology, 426, 430–431
Postmodern methodology, 426, 431
Postpositivistic methodology, 426, 431

Posttest data analysis, 130–133
Posttesting, 117, 124, 370–371, 431
Practical intelligence, 15, 17, 73, 100
Practice
    issues in, 58, 60, 61, 63, 66
    research vs., 421–422
    research implications for, 432–437
Practitioners
    facilitating reflective practice, 222–223
    making research doable, 425, 427
    research needs of, 230, 231–233
    researcher role and, 410–411, 423–424
    views on cooperative education,
        169–182
Predicting Learning Advancement through
    Cooperative Education (PLACE),
    161
Prediction, correlations and, 98
Pretest data analysis, 128–133
Pretesting, 117, 124, 370–371, 431
Primary Trait Analysis (PTA), 370, 374
Privacy, research and, 9, 408–409
Probability, 144
Problem finding, 107
Problem solving, 126, 398, 436
Problem-solving methodology, 256–260
Procedural knowledge, 122
Procedure, 304
Processes (skills), 22, 99
Process-oriented methodology, 112, 426,
    430, 431
Productivity, human capital and, 238
Profession, enculturation into, 45–46,
    85–87
Professional codes, 412, 413
Professional Practice Instruction, 368
Professional programs, 364
Professional standards, 63–65, 66
Prognostic assessment, 400
Program changes, assessment and, 388
Program evaluation, 232–233, 251–278. See
    also Assessment
Programmatic relevance, of research, 247
Program outcomes, ABET criterion, 384n3
P sample, 166–167
Psychological harm/stress, research and,
    405
Publication
    ethical considerations in, 302–303
    process of, 306–308
    selecting a journal, 292–294, 305–306

*Publication Manual of the American Psycho-
    logical Association,* 303, 304, 308
Purdue University Construction Engi-
    neering and Management In-
    ternship Program, 317–332
    experiential learning theory and,
        321–323, 325–329
    interns' written reports, 324–325
    self-efficacy and, 329
Purpose, 423
Purposeful sampling, 39, 41, 100

Q

Q-methodology, 162–166
    for cooperative research and practice,
        183–184
Q-sample, 166
Q-sort, 163, 184, 428, 431–432
QSR Nud*ist Vivo, 105
Qualitative data, 97, 384n2
    analysis of, 39, 99, 105–111, 112
    descriptive, 343
    Q-methodology and, 163
    vs. quantitative, 123
    summarizing as numbers, 106
Qualitative methods, 8, 9, 36, 104–105,
    426, 431
    case study, 341
    ethical issues, 405–414
QUANAL, 168
Quantitative data, 97, 101–104, 384n1
    analysis of, 101–104
    vs. qualitative, 123
Quantitative methods, 8, 36, 76, 426, 431
Quasiexperiment, 431n2
Questionnaire, 123, 412

R

Race, 240
Race Matters, 349
Random sampling, 100
Rankings, 392, 432
Rank ordering, 163, 164
Reality, construction of, 18–22
Recruiting, cooperative education and,
        252, 255, 260–261, 266–267,
        269–270
Reference group, 127, 240
References, 305

reference list, 312
text citations, 310–311
Reflective-active continuum, 322
Reflective observation, 14, 214, 322–323, 325, 326, 327, 328, 330, 335
Reflective practice, 221–223
Reflective practicums, 282
Regression analysis, 144, 149, 150, 236, 240–246, 289
Regression towards the mean, 130–131
Reliability, 124, 134
Repertory Grid, 134
Representation, 409–410
Research
    action. *See* Action research
    approaches to, 426, 430–432
    archival, 412
    assessing quality of, 302
    collaboration, 216, 424–425
    conducting, 6–10
    context for research, 423–424
    dissemination of findings, 8–9, 246–247
    ethical considerations, 81, 403–414
    ethical principles, 412–413
    ex post facto, 119
    funding, 53–54, 58, 67, 119–120, 321
    levels of focus, 13–14
    literature review, 33, 72–73
    making doable, 425–427
    measurement issues, 428–430
    obtaining administrator buy-in, 37
    vs. practice, 421–422
    selection criteria, 38, 40–41
    setting, 36–37, 78–79
    using theory to guide, 427–428
Research agenda, 230, 231–233
Research article. *See* Research report
Research design, 7–8, 80–82, 98, 233–236, 430
    contextualized learning, 39–42
    cross-sectional, 117–118
    longitudinal, 117–118
    natural experiment, 196
    pretest and posttest, 117, 124
    selecting, 427
Researcher-practitioner model, 6
Researcher's roles, 410–411
Researcher standpoint, 423–424
Research findings. *See* Dissemination of research findings
Research instruments

assessment, 389–392
bias and, 124–125, 127
characteristics of, 115
College Outcomes Measures Program test (COMP), 125–133
developing, 125
reliability, 124
selecting, 120–121
validity, 123–124
See also Survey instrument
Research methodology, 6, 7–8, 76–78
    action research, 57–59
    case study, 209–211
    interpretive, 216, 426, 431
    outcome-oriented, 426, 430
    positivistic, 426, 430, 431
    process-oriented, 112, 426, 430, 431
    problem-solving, 256–260
    Q-methodology, 162–166, 183–184
    R-methodology, 162, 167
    selecting, 162
Research motives, 431
Research practice, case study, 83–88
Research practitioner inquiry, 54
Research question, 389
    case studies and, 211
    construction engineering learning, 320–321
    cooperative learning, 158–159, 161–162
    ecological learning, 284–287
    formulating, 7, 36, 75–76
    learning outcomes, 116–117
    relation to outcome, 429
Research report, 9, 301–308, 310–312
    article format, 303
    assessing research quality, 302
    ethical considerations, 302–303
    manuscript preparation, 306
    parts of article, 303–305
    publication process, 306–308
    selecting publication, 305–306
    writing style, 303
Research strategy, 320–321
Resource allocation, research findings and, 247
Resources for research, 7, 67. *See also* Funding for research
Response rate, 375–376
Results, 304–305
Resumix tracking system, 254–255

Return rate, 142, 152
Review article, 424
Review of Post Secondary Cooperative Educa-
    tion Funding in the Province of Brit-
    ish Columbia, A, 160
Review outcomes, 307
R-methodology, 162, 167
Role-playing, 406–407
Rose-Hulman Institute of Technology,
    385–386

S

Salary
    educational attainment and, 236–237
    effect of internships on starting, 139,
        141, 143, 149–150, 152
    impact of co-op job quality and,
        236–248
Sample, 304
    p sample, 166–167
    Q-sample, 166, 167
    single case study as, 340–341
Sample size, 197, 389
Sampling, 375
    errors in, 142
    purposeful, 39, 41, 100
    Q-methodology and, 164, 183
    random, 100
    strategy, 39, 80
School-based learning, 285. *See also* Aca-
        demic context
Schooling, socioeconomic class and, 24
School success, socioeconomic class and,
        24
Self-analysis, 390, 392, 393–394
Self-authoring, 21, 22
Self-awareness, 66
Self-confidence, 15, 17
Self-development, work-based learning
        and, 25–26
Self-directed learning, 291
Self-efficacy, 15, 17, 73–74, 86, 99, 107
    construction internships and, 329, 336
    cross-cultural experiences and, 339
Self-employment types, 103–104
Self-esteem, African-American identity
        and, 359
Self-referenced test, 134
Self-reporting, 121, 150, 197–198, 240,
        390, 392, 429

Service learning, 23
Sexual orientation, cross-cultural experi-
        ence and, 351–354
Shippensburg University, 141
Silence, 19
Simon Fraser University, 158
Simple-device inquiry, 324, 327, 334
Simulation, 284, 406–407, 436
Single author work, 310
Site visits, 169, 175, 177, 180, 181
Situated learning theory (SLT), 22–24, 35,
        74, 100, 110–112, 178, 282, 298
Situational relativist, 413
Skill, 22
Skill competence, 160
Skill development, 273
Skill transfer, 177–178
Social context of learning theory, 13
Social injustice, 108
Social learning theory, 49, 73–74, 298
Social participation, learning and, 22–24
Social reproduction theories, 24–25
Social skills, 126, 436. *See also* Communi-
        cation skills
Socioeconomic class, 207–209, 212–214
    contextualized learning and, 43
    crossing class boundaries in coopera-
            tive education, 219–221
    defined, 214–215
    facilitating analysis of, 222–223
    moral dimension of, 220
    schooling and, 24
    test bias and, 125
Socratic approach, 436
Soft skills, 386, 394–398, 429
Software, Q-methodology, 167, 168
Spot check, 198
Staffing, cooperative education programs
        and, 252, 255–256, 260–261,
        266–267, 269–270
Stakeholders, 230, 423
    cooperative learning and, 181–182
    dissemination of research findings to,
            246–247
    See also Administrators; Practitioners;
            Students
Standard deviation, 199n3, 201
Standards of practice, 56
States of mind, 22
Statistical analysis, 101–107, 144–150
Statistical methods, 144, 392

Statistical Package for Social Sciences
    (SPSS), 168, 199
Statistical significance, 143–144, 145, 146
Statistics, 8
    chi square, 144
    data analysis with, 144–153
    inferential, 236
Status, cross-cultural experience and,
    356–357
Storylines, 109–110
Student essays, 390, 392, 395, 397–398
Student evaluation, 389–390
Student project, 365, 369, 371–374
    student attitude towards, 378–379
Student records, 234–235
Student report, 334–336, 390, 392, 395,
    397–398
Students
    implications of ecological learning
        theory for, 297
    obtaining buy-in from, 41
    ranking co-ops as learning experiences,
        286–290
    as research assistants, 425
    selecting as case studies, 215
    views on cooperative education,
        169–182
Style, writing, 303, 308–309
Subjectivity, 20
    Q-methodology and, 163, 164, 183
Supervision in cooperative education,
    283–284, 288, 289, 294
Surface learning, 47
Survey instrument, 234, 235, 304, 412
    business internships, 142–143
    co-op quality, 282, 284, 286–288
    designing, 123
    questions, 80
    sample, 155–156
    selecting, 142
    student feedback, 276–278
    student satisfaction, 255–256, 268–272
    work history, 101–105
Systematic, 212

T

Tables, 305
Tacit knowledge, 34, 73, 133
Taco Bell, 192
Target group, 201

Teachers, role as researchers, 224. *See also*
    Practitioners
Teaching. *See* Pedagogy
Teaching Engineering, 321
Teaching to Transgress, 212
Teams
    job quality and, 273
    skills for, 3, 386, 394, 396, 397
Technical skills, cooperative education
    and, 169, 172, 173, 174–175
Test group, 196
Tests, 120–121
    norm-referenced vs. criterion-
        referenced, 126–127
Text analysis, 81, 105–107
Text citations, 310–311
Thematic understanding, 221–222
Theory, 6, 13–25, 75
    finding metaphors for, 279–280
    grounded, 428
    research and, 427–428
    See also Learning theories
Theory of Multiple Intelligences, 74
Theory proliferation, 12
Title, 303–304
Title page, 303–304
Trend analysis, 234, 235–236
Triangulation, 78, 388, 392, 399, 429
True experiment, 431n2
t-statistics, 238–239
t-test, 100n1, 392
Tuskegee Experiment, 405
Type I adjustment, 342, 349–350,
    355–356, 359
Type II adjustment, 342, 351–354, 359

U

Unanticipated results, 149
Universal truth, belief in, 20
University of Cincinnati (UC)
    assessment program, 363–364,
        374–377
    Educational Strategic Plan, 365–367
    Project to Improve and Reward
        Teaching, 364, 365
University of Victoria, 116

V

Validity, 123–124, 134, 203, 205, 243
Value-added benefits, 429

Value judgments, measuring learning and, 428

Values
educational outcomes and, 122
ethical dilemmas and, 57, 58, 60, 65, 67

Variables
dependent, 119, 121, 144
independent, 119, 144, 149, 162
independent impact of, 239
reducing number of, 288–289
selecting, 192

Vault Reports, 138

Vicarious learning, 17

Virtual Q sorting, 164

Virtual realities in classroom, 295, 297

Visibility-invisibility, 351–354

W

WebQ, 165

Web site, IBM cooperative education, 255, 267

Why Blacks are Committed to Blackness, 353

Women's Ways of Knowing, 19

Work, attitudes toward, 220–221

Work-based learning, 159–161, 285. See also Cooperative education; Internships

Work experience
cognitive stage theory and, 18–22
focus on particular, 13, 14–17
learning theory and schooling in general and, 22–25
salary and, 238

Work force, challenges facing, 3–5

Work history questionnaire, 101–105

Workplace context, 34
ethical dilemmas in, 60–62
importance in cooperative education, 433–434
learning in, 44–46, 83–84

Work report, 177, 181

Work-term, 160

World views, Q-methodology and, 167, 168, 172, 181

Writing style, 303, 308–309

Z

Zone of proximal development, 288n6